THE MUSE OF HISTORY

THE MUSE *of* HISTORY

The Ancient Greeks from the Enlightenment to the Present

OSWYN MURRAY

The Belknap Press of Harvard University Press
Cambridge, Massachusetts
2024

Printed in the United States of America

Original edition first published by Allen Lane, an imprint of Penguin Books,
a division of Penguin Random House UK, 2024

First Harvard University Press edition, 2024

Set in 10.2/13.87pt Sabon LT Std

Typeset by Jouve (UK), Milton Keynes

Library of Congress Cataloging-in-Publication Data

Names: Murray, Oswyn, author.
Title: The muse of history : the ancient Greeks from the Enlightenment to the present / Oswyn Murray.
Other titles: Ancient Greeks from the Enlightenment to the present
Description: First Harvard University Press edition. | Cambridge, Massachusetts : The Belknap Press of Harvard University Press, 2024. | Includes bibliographical references and index. | Summary: "Oswyn Murray charts the shifting uses of the ancient past, showing how three centuries of scholars interpreted Ancient Greece in the light of contemporary political interests. Rich in stories and portraits of influential thinkers, *The Muse of History* is a powerful reminder that the meaning of the past is always made in and for the present."—Provided by publisher.
Identifiers: LCCN 2024003412 (print) | LCCN 2024003413 (ebook) | ISBN 9780674297456 (hardback) | ISBN 9780674298088 (pdf) | ISBN 9780674298095 (epub)
Subjects: LCSH: Historians--Europe--Attitudes--History. | Historiography--Europe--History. | Historiography--Study and teaching--Europe--History. | Civilization, Classical--Historiography. | History--Methodology. | Greece--Historiography. | Rome--Historiography.
Classification: LCC DE8 .M87 2024 (print) | LCC DE8 (ebook) | DDC 938--dc23/eng/20240216
LC record available at https://lccn.loc.gov/2024003412
LC ebook record available at https://lccn.loc.gov/2024003413

Ogni vera storia è storia contemporanea.
Benedetto Croce

Dis Manibus

Contents

PART ONE
The Muse of History

PART TWO
The Angel of History

PART ONE

The Muse of History

Introduction: Past and Present

She's dressed in blue, head turned to the painter's gaze,
blue-glaucus leaves of laurel in her hair. She's carrying
a book. Thucydides. Her eyes are closed, but her name, Clio,
comes from glory, from telling the things men do.
Women too, sometimes. There's a death-mask

on the table for she deals in what is past. She holds,
as if she doesn't know what to do with it, might prefer
a lute, a seventeenth-century trumpet
into the light from an unseen window, white
as interstellar dust on a galactic nebula,

say, the Pillars of Creation. She's posed in the studio
beneath an unlit chandelier, by a map whose North is torn
from South, the West on top, any thought of East
is lost. On the easel, he's only got as far
as Greek laurel. The real painting, the prize

picture Vermeer never sold, even at his poorest,
is himself with his back to us, painting History.
Historein: to find out what went on.
The West, the East. The wars, the rifted peace.
Take her hand, step her down

past all the embroidery, out of the frame.
Dress her in jeans and a tee shirt. Open her eyes.
She is not a professor collating the sources

though she cares about him (it is usually him
even now) and will help if he is balanced and fair.

She is not a journalist, looking for the hot
story, twisting words to make scandal and sell.
Though with these, too, she is on their side
when they mean well. She will look for the thing itself
and will often despair. She is all we have got.

Ruth Padel, 'The Muse of History' (2009)[1]

Ruth Padel here describes Jan Vermeer's most famous painting which was also his favourite, the one that he refused to sell throughout his life: among art historians it is usually given the misleading title *The Art of Painting*.[2] It depicts the artist, dressed in his best clothes, seated in his studio before an easel and engaged in painting a young female model wearing stylish blue who is standing by a window. The highest form of painting was historical painting, and so the subject that the artist is painting is 'Clio or The Muse of History', as described in Cesare Ripa's standard work *Iconologia*:

> Let us represent Clio as a girl with a laurel wreath, holding a trumpet in her right hand and in her left a book on whose cover is written THUCYDIDES.
>
> This muse is named Clio from the Greek word κλεα which means praise, or from the other word κλεος meaning glory, which the poets possess among learned men as Cornutus says, as also from glory which those men receive who are celebrated by the poets.
>
> She is represented with the book of Thucydides because attributing history to this muse, Virgil says in his book *de Musis*:
>
> Clio gesta canens transacti tempora reddit
> (Clio singing the deeds of past times brings them alive)
>
> It is appropriate to demonstrate this by the work of the famous historian Thucydides.
>
> The laurel wreath signifies that as the laurel is evergreen and keeps fresh for a long time so the work of history keeps times past fresh as if they were still present.[3]

Or again more explicitly in a later edition of Ripa published in Venice in 1645:

> You should depict a woman turning her head back over her shoulder, and on the ground where she gazes there are some half-obliterated bundles of writing. She holds a pen in her hand and should be clothed in azure, the dress being all bedecked with that foliage which is called evergreen; and elsewhere one should depict a winding stream, like that called the Meander in Phrygia, which turned back on itself.[4]

Vermeer in 1666 probably used the Dutch translation of Ripa (Amsterdam 1644). His most obvious additions are two: firstly himself in back view, dressed in inappropriately elegant clothes, and secondly in the background a map of the seventeen United Provinces of the Spanish Netherlands (in fact no longer united), which was first published in 1636 by Claus Jansz Visscher. Vermeer has clearly thought long and hard about the symbolism of the image, and wishes to render explicit the relation of the Muse to the history of his own native country: like the Meander, his Muse turns back on herself and her creator.

The importance of Thucydides for the interpretation of contemporary events in the seventeenth century is the subject of many learned studies, starting from the significance of Thomas Hobbes's famous translation of Thucydides, whom he called 'the most politick historiographer that ever writ'; he represents the importance of ancient history for the understanding of the modern world. But Vermeer's depiction of himself creating the Muse of History also invites us to consider the relation between the work of the historian and the reflection of his own experiences onto the world that he studies. In the background of every historian's work is his own contemporary world: it is that world which provides the questions that he deems it relevant to study, and the shape of the solutions to the questions that he asks. All history is contemporary history, as Benedetto Croce said; and it follows that all history must be rewritten in every generation. In that sense historical narrative is not false, but doomed to be superseded in each generation; for none of us can understand the past except through our own contemporary distorting mirror. But in that sense too ancient history, as the seventeenth century saw, is modern history.

In an essay on Virgil of 1944 T.S. Eliot said:

> In our age when men seem more than ever prone to confuse wisdom with knowledge and knowledge with information, and to try to solve problems of life in terms of engineering, there is coming into existence a new form of provincialism which perhaps deserves a new name. It is a provincialism, not of space, but of time; one for which history is merely the chronicle of human devices which have served their term and been scrapped, one for which the world is the property solely of the living, a property in which the dead hold no shares. The menace of this kind of provincialism is that we can all, all the peoples on the globe, be provincials together; and those who are not content to be provincials, can only become hermits.[5]

In an effort to escape from these predicaments, I have always felt it to be important to understand the past interpretations of the discipline that I have practised all my life, to reflect on how earlier historians have approached the past, and to attempt to liberate myself from my own preconceptions by seeing the world that I perceive through the eyes of successive earlier students of the past. Otherwise we are imprisoned by our ignorance in a form of sterile presentism, forgetting our own transience. The past is a rich and varied tapestry that may never be completely understood and must always be renewed, yet to approach our predecessors with due humility creates a richer interpretation than we can achieve on our own.

It is also true that history without theory is an antiquarian study, a sterile collection of 'facts', which are often confused with events: facts are not themselves events, but statements about events – namely that which happens. Wittgenstein said, 'the world is the totality of facts, not of things' – 'Die Welt ist die Gesamtheit der Tatsachen nicht der Dinge':[6] that is, we can only know statements by observers, not the events themselves – there is an inevitable veil between ourselves and the past; and without theory these 'facts' are even more fatally contaminated by our inability to perceive our own hidden prejudices according to which we arrange them into allegedly meaningful patterns. So without theory we simply see ourselves in the mirror of history, as if we look only at the map on Vermeer's wall and ignore the interplay between the observer/creator and his Muse.

I was appointed a lecturer in Ancient History at Oxford University in the revolutionary year of 1968; with the arrogance of youth, I plotted to throw a great party to celebrate the centenary of the current Oxford syllabus of Ancient History, which had remained unchanged since 1872.[7] But my courage failed me when I reflected on the verdict that the greatest of all Oxford historians, Sir Ronald Syme, would pass on this hubristic act of presumption. Instead over the next forty years I worked less conspicuously to introduce some sort of progress. I became one of the group that instigated the introduction of classical literary studies into the Final Examination of 'Literae Humaniores' (Philosophy and Ancient History) at Oxford (and earned my reward when I found myself chairman of examiners in its first year – in which because both old and new systems were simultaneously in operation I presided over an examination where the number of papers to be set was actually greater than the number of candidates). Bert Smith, Professor of Classical Archaeology, and I introduced in 2001 a new course, Classical Archaeology and Ancient History, which enabled students to study archaeology for the first time in the final examination, healing a sore that had festered in Oxford since 1887. But my most significant reform, abetted by one of my most conservative colleagues, George Cawkwell (1919–2019), was the creation of a joint School of Ancient and Modern History; in the forty years since the introduction of the degree in 1979 many of the best historians of the ancient world have graduated from this combined discipline.

My book is therefore a reflection on this relationship. Its underlying argument is that, until the dominance of nationalism in the late nineteenth century, Ancient Greek and Roman History was by far the most advanced form of historical study in terms of techniques and interpretations, and it was where all the new approaches to history were pioneered. It was pan-European, and led by France and Germany. Only with the rise of nationalism in the second half of the nineteenth century did the study of Modern History break free and dissolve itself into a series of feuding myths for the newly invented nation states. And yet even through two European 'World Wars' the old unity of the Republic of Letters has struggled to survive in the study of Ancient History.

My aim in this book is to raise for all students of history, not just for historians of the ancient world, the questions of the relativity of historical narrative and its relation to the possibility of a theory of human society. These may be questions that we cannot answer, but unless we consider them seriously we are condemned to being mere technicians of the trivial fact. At one level my book is a history of the study of Greek History from its modern origins in the eighteenth century to the present day, offering a largely new interpretation of this branch of historical studies. However, many of the historians discussed are not 'ancient' but 'modern' historians, and some of them are even heroes or victims in the actual world of events, who have themselves been creators of history in their own generation; so at a deeper level this book is a study of Modern History and how it is conditioned by the past as much as the present. It is based on original research published over the last twenty years in obscure places; but I have tried to present my thought as a whole, as a book intended to be read from cover to cover.

The European tradition of Ancient History was dominated by French philosophical interpretations of history in the eighteenth century and by systematic German scholarship in the nineteenth century. Compared with these two approaches the Anglo-Saxon tradition has lacked any theoretical or conceptual basis, with the exceptions of Utilitarian and Marxist historiography. All the main ideas in the study of Ancient History in Britain and the anglophone diaspora have been derived from the European continent, from the historians John Gast and Edward Gibbon onwards. In contrast, British empiricism or positivism is based on the belief that only facts exist (whatever they may be), and that history can always be interpreted on the basis of an unreflective search for an illusory certainty contained in an explanatory system which is held to be constantly changing, yet universal in human history.

The book thus shows through the example of Greek Ancient History the problematic nature of this Anglo-Saxon positivist tradition and its dependence on techniques and ideas from the continent of Europe. But it also demonstrates the impossibility of understanding the past or the present outside our common European heritage, and our debt to this heritage in the past and in the future; and it shows the centrality of the study of the ancient world for the understanding of both English and continental literature and thought throughout these three centuries, a period when the study of Greece and Rome was fundamental to the creation of European culture. I trace the shifting patterns of these preoccupations over the last three centuries, in which each generation has reinterpreted the Greeks in the light of their contemporary world, through times of revolution, conflicting ideologies and warfare. And through the study of different historians, many of them unjustly forgotten, I demonstrate the ambiguities of democracy, and the impossibility of understanding the past or the present outside our common European heritage. In the twentieth century I acknowledge the continuing spiritual importance of the ancient Greeks for European culture under totalitarian and capitalist persecutions, and I end by offering suggestions for the future of the study of the Greeks in the context of world history. The mirror of the Greeks is the way in which we view ourselves, now and in the future.

The Republic of Letters

1

The Western Traditions of Ancient History

Time present and time past
Are both perhaps present in time future,
And time future contained in time past.
If all time is eternally present
All time is unredeemable.
T.S. Eliot, *Four Quartets: Burnt Norton* (1944)

The study of classical historiography is not only part of the 'classical tradition': the purpose of the study of the past of ancient history is to influence its future, and to clarify the methods and principles that may determine the activity of writing history. All history is and has always been written in and for the present, and is valid only as a myth for the present or as a step towards the future. Unless we are aware of the constraints of tradition on this picture, future histories will continue to be determined by the past: in order to liberate ourselves from tradition and prevent the preoccupations of the present and its past from distorting the future of history, we must investigate the roots of our current concerns.

The study of 'ancient history' in Western Europe has always been connected with the influence of Greece and Rome on the formation of European culture. The critical and comparative study of this tradition with other ancient civilizations such as Israel, Egypt, the Near East, India, China, and Japan to create an 'ancient world history', arrived late and has remained peripheral to the study of the origins of Western culture. My purpose in this chapter is to explore the consequences of this fact.

The Western outlook on 'Ancient History' is limited, and has since the eighteenth century centred around two distinct concepts: imperialism and liberty. The first interest, imperialism, explains the fundamental importance of Roman history with its exemplification of the fate of empires, to rise, decline, and fall. It began with the discussion provoked by the famous French author Montesquieu in his work *Considérations sur la grandeur et décadence des Romains*, published in Holland in 1734. In this short essay Montesquieu traced the growth of the Roman Empire in the second century BC and attributed it to the *vertu* of the Romans, their moral and political character. He showed how moral and political corruption followed, until the traditional liberty of the Romans was extinguished in a monarchic form of government, and their moral character was corrupted by the luxury consequent on empire. This analysis was part of a general movement in the early eighteenth century to contrast the declining power of the French monarchy under its greatest ruler, Louis XIV, in the face of the rise of the English version of constitutional monarchy, in a country essentially governed by the merchant classes after the Glorious Revolution of 1688. The success in war of the English armies under the Duke of Marlborough and the creation of an English naval empire around the world were making it clear that absolute monarchy and territorial conquest were incompatible with the modern expansion of overseas trade based on government by the landed aristocracy and the merchants of the City of London. The message of Montesquieu was accepted by all the thinkers of the Enlightenment and became the basis of the new critical historiography that reached its zenith in the famous work of Edward Gibbon, in which the whole history of Europe from antiquity to the Renaissance was incorporated into a *History of the Decline and Fall of the Roman Empire* (1776–88).

This perception has dictated the shape of Roman history ever since. The fundamental questions remain the same today as they were formulated in the eighteenth century: how did Rome become an imperial power, on the basis of what political structures was her success achieved, how was her political, social and economic development affected by the consequent advent of luxury and wealth, and why did the system end by only finding stability under a form of absolute monarchy that was incompatible with political liberty? It was the advent of a new religion, Christianity, and the impact of nomadic barbarian invasions that introduced a new dynamic to history; but this required a break with the past that was only partially resolved in the Renaissance. From this perspective of ancient history as Roman history, it is empire, its rise and fall, that provides the questions to which we still seek answers. And much of the justification of Western imperialism in the modern age has been based on the model of the Roman example, from Edmund Burke's eighteenth-century analysis of the faults and virtues of English imperialism in Ireland, North America, and India, to the systematic education of administrators for the British Indian Empire on principles that were directly derived from Roman provincial administration. The French and German empires were no different: throughout Europe the virtues and vices and indeed the methods of imperialism have always been conceived in terms of the ancient Roman example.

The second interest, the history of liberty, includes the history of political liberty and democratic forms of government, together with personal liberty and the rise of the concept of the individual: this is seen in terms of a continuing process of development from antiquity to the present, and as especially exemplified in the history of ancient Greece. It explains the obsession of historians of ancient Greece with Athens and the principles of democratic government. We still idealize Athenian democracy as the best form of government, and discuss modern governmental systems in relation to this ancient example. We are still obsessed with the idea of liberty, both political and personal; and as a consequence we judge all forms of government, whatever their historical traditions, in relation to standards that are regarded as absolute. This strand in the history of the ancient world is often seen as consequent on the Hegelian view of history as the history of liberty, and on the concern of the Romantic period with the idea of the creativity of the individual artistic genius, standing outside tradition in a free society. And it is believed that the nineteenth-century philosophical movement known as Utilitarianism established the apotheosis of democracy and liberty in the *History of Greece* (1846–56) composed by the Utilitarian radical politician and city banker, George Grote.

But in fact this concern with liberty and democracy is also a product of the eighteenth century, and of much the same impulse that inspired Montesquieu. The catalyst was the presentation by the Frenchman Nicolas Boileau in 1674 of an obscure ancient work of literary criticism known as *Longinus, On the Sublime*. In the last chapter of the work the author mentions an ancient theory that relates artistic creativity to political liberty. This work with its emphasis on the importance of the sublime was fundamental to literary theory in the eighteenth century, and its conclusion was interpreted as an explanation of and a vindication for the renewed literary activity in contemporary Britain after the Glorious Revolution of 1688. The literature of ancient Greece and especially Athens was interpreted as being a consequence, not of aristocratic patronage (as in the contemporary world), but of political liberty and Athenian democracy. This view of the benefits of democracy became widespread in the eighteenth century, and it lies behind the change from an almost universal dismissal of democratic forms of government as dangerous, unjust, and anarchic to an increasing idealization of democratic institutions. This in turn led to a close identification of ancient Athens with modern Britain and subsequently modern America. The difference between ancient and modern democracy was rightly seen as a difference between direct and representative democracy: the most important innovation in eighteenth-century political theory, due largely to Montesquieu again, was the realization that representation could be harnessed to the idea of democracy. Despite this obvious difference it was believed that ancient and modern democracy shared common characteristics. The consequent rise of the principle of democratic representative government justified the historical movement away from aristocratic forms of government to a new 'democratic', capitalist, oligarchic control of government by the bourgeoisie.

These two strands, imperialism and democracy, have in our generation come together in the new democratic imperialism of the United States of America. This seeks to promote the principles of democracy and capitalism under an American imperial hegemony held to be self-evidently the teaching of human history, for in Hegelian terms the triumph of the individual and of liberty is the lesson of history.

Yet each of these theoretical approaches is problematic in a number of respects, and concentration on them to the exclusion of all others represents an impoverishment of the varieties of human experience. Let us consider each concept in turn.

Imperialism is not synonymous with exploitation and expropriation; it requires an ideology to persuade the master race to conquer and even more to maintain control over other societies: you must believe in your mission or the rulers will lose the will to rule. The Romans came to believe that their version of Graeco-Roman civilization was a gift that would benefit all who came under their domination; in this they were helped by a conception of citizenship that (with certain conditions) was perhaps the most inclusive that the world has experienced. The result was that in the end all subjects of the empire became Roman citizens, and were eligible for the benefits of empire; these benefits changed over time, but always remained real enough, and could and did include the possibility of even becoming the emperor himself. The later Western model built on this conception of the benefits of civilization, and added to it the principle of conversion to Christianity as the true faith. But it was always recognized that in essence, if in the distant future the subject peoples should embrace these principles of Western government and Western religion, such empires would dissolve themselves into some unspecified relationship, whether of universal citizenship or of independence. Moreover, whereas the Roman conception of empire had been of an eternal empire (*Roma aeterna*), there was built into its successor, the eighteenth-century conception of empire, the notion of decline and fall; there was therefore always a 'dying fall', a sense of a future ending embodied in Western imperialism: the end of empire is envisaged in its beginning. Of course, the events of history falsified or usurped these dreams in a variety of ways. But the pure conception of imperialism as exploitation never existed in the West (with the possible exception of the Belgian Congo); and while the analysis of imperialism in terms of its economic benefit to the ruler may help, it is not sufficient to explain all the human motivation involved.

The ideas of democracy and freedom are equally problematic. Direct and representative democracy have been recognized to be wholly different forms of government since the eighteenth century. Direct democracy is only suitable for small-scale institutions in which the members of a homogeneous group can meet and make decisions in a form of assembly that contains only those who will execute those decisions. It is today seldom practised even in groups small enough to qualify, and the right to decide or even influence decisions has become simply a residual right confined to occasional, almost ritual events. No one believes in direct ancient democracy as practised by the ancient Athenians, and few people would wish to see its return as a viable form of government. In the nineteenth century it was agreed to be dependent on a form of political education that was essentially unattainable, and the twentieth century added the even less democratic idea of the need for expertise in government. These criticisms of democracy go back at least to Plato's *Protagoras*.

They have been incorporated into the theory of representative government, which allows an elite to rule with the consent of the majority. The problem that results is that of all forms of government in all periods: the creation of a divide between the rulers and the ruled. In ancient Greek terms all modern forms of government are not democracies, but either tyrannies or oligarchies, depending on whether they obey the rule of law or not.

At least since the time of Benjamin Constant's famous essay, 'On the liberty of the ancients compared to the liberty of the moderns' (1819), it has been recognized that this difference between ancient and modern democracy is the determining factor behind the difference between ancient and modern conceptions of liberty:[1]

> [Ancient] liberty consisted in exercising collectively but directly most aspects of ancient sovereignty, deliberating in the public square about war and peace, concluding with foreigners treaties of alliance, voting on laws, pronouncing legal judgements, examining the accounts and the decrees and the decisions of magistrates, making them appear before the assembled people, putting them on trial, condemning or acquitting them. But at the same time that this was what the ancients called liberty, they admitted as compatible with their collective liberty the total subjection of the individual to the authority of the community.

Modern ideas of liberty, in contrast, privilege the freedom of the individual from interference by a system controlled by the ruling classes. Far from deriving from ancient world conceptions of liberty it is a consequence of centuries of conflict between the various sects of the Christian religion, which resulted in the assertion of the freedom of the individual conscience in religious matters. In the modern age this has become extended beyond the sphere of religion to all aspects of the private life of the individual.

Modern writers have wrestled with these differences between ancient and modern democracy and ancient and modern liberty; Isaiah Berlin, for instance, tried to distinguish between a positive '*freedom to*' (act), which was more akin to ancient political freedom, and a negative '*freedom from*' (interference), which seemed to him to be exemplified in the modern concept of the freedom of the individual. The most recent attempts to relate ancient and modern ideas of freedom and democracy tend to emphasize the importance of duties or responsibilities in the ancient ideas of community life leading to a constraining of the freedom of the individual, in contrast to the absolute selfishness and the anarchic consequences of modern liberty. In that sense the modern Western conceptions of democracy and liberty might well indeed learn the limitations of these ideas from studying the ancient world view.

My reflection is however intended to contrast these two conceptions of history derived from ancient Western ideas, with the historical traditions that are found elsewhere. It is clearly not true that these two sets of problems exhaust all the historical possibilities that the long history of human society exemplifies. If we reflect on other historical traditions, we can see that this Western conception has many faults. It does not consider the necessity of order or decorum in the construction of civilizations, nor the significance of continuity and tradition, as exemplified for instance in the Chinese tradition.

Even within Western culture this dual tradition also almost completely ignores one of the most powerful forces in historical formation, the importance of religion and the way that beliefs about the divine world permeate and structure almost all social systems: after the collapse of the grand nineteenth-century theories of universal religion, it was not until J.-P. Vernant offered a social and psychological interpretation of ancient religion that it escaped from the sterile grip of myth and ritual antiquarianism. Ancient Western history has indeed been inclined until very recently to regard ancient religion as unimportant and irrelevant, no doubt partly due to the bias against all forms of polytheism as primitive and faulty representations of a divine world that was only revealed by God through the true religion of Christianity: so, while apparently ignoring religion, ancient Western history has also been profoundly conditioned by a response to the advent of Christianity.

But it is not only Christianity that appears to be marginalized by the dominant Western conception of ancient history. Another Western religion has claims to be far older than Christianity, and possesses a complex historical tradition at least as old as the Chinese – Judaism. The question of how Jewish history might be incorporated into ancient history also began as early as the eighteenth century, as part of the enlightenment revival of the study of history. This, in turn, built upon a much-neglected aspect of the work of the sole surviving Jewish historian in the ancient classical tradition, Josephus. For it was really Josephus who, in his *Jewish Antiquities*, even more than in his account of the Jewish War, set out to normalize the Jewish historical tradition in terms of classical historiography: he was indeed himself an ancient historian, and shared with them many of the political and rational attitudes that made his account compatible with the canons of ancient history. Independently of the holy texts of Judaism and Christianity, it was he who made it possible for later generations to compare and contrast the Jewish historical tradition with that of Greece and Rome. In terms of later generations he therefore bridged the gap between sacred and secular history, and may be regarded as perhaps the most important of all ancient historians for the future of historical writing.

Already in antiquity Josephus was performing this function for the early Christian Church. This explains their interest in preserving his works, and even in improving them at a very early date, by interpolating the notorious references to Jesus Christ, his brother James, and John the Baptist; by this means Josephus could be made to offer historical support not just to the Old Testament, but also to the Gospel narrative. Josephus has indeed always been more highly regarded in the Christian tradition than in Judaism itself, which has often tended to consider him a renegade and a traitor.[2]

Translations of Josephus into the modern European languages were very popular, and especially in Protestant England. At first they were simple translations. The earliest was by Thomas Lodge, the contemporary of Shakespeare in 1602, 'faithfully translated out of the Latin and French'.[3] This was arranged as a continuous historical narrative, from the Antiquities to the Life, the Jewish Wars, Against Apion, and the martyrdom of the Maccabees. Exactly a century later, in 1702, Sir Roger L'Estrange offered a new translation, following almost the same order, but with the Life coming after the Jewish Wars and Philo's Legation added to extend the historical account. He added two 'discourses' and several 'remarks' on the veracity and chronology of Josephus.[4] This edition was reprinted in Dundee in 1766.[5] But in the meantime the most popular of all the translations of Josephus, that by William Whiston, had been published in 1737. This became the most widely read and most widely owned book after the Bible in the English-speaking world for the next two centuries.[6]

Whiston had been the successor of Isaac Newton as Professor of Mathematics at Cambridge, and like Newton he combined an interest in ancient chronology with scriptural scholarship.[7] To him Josephus appeared to present a narrative of Jewish history directly comparable to that found in classical ancient historians, and like his predecessors he arranged his translation of the various works to provide a chronological narrative. But in many later editions of his translation an interesting transformation occurred: the narrative of Josephus was combined with a section usually entitled something like 'Sequel to the history of the Jews; continued to the present time'.

The first person to realize the possibility of recording a continuous history of Judaism in this manner was the Huguenot antiquary and friend of the sceptical encyclopedist Pierre Bayle, Jacques Basnage, Sieur de Beauval (1653–1723), who published in 1706–7 in the Netherlands a work that was immediately translated into English with the author's approval.[8] The English title page reads:

> The History of the Jews from Jesus Christ to the Present Time: Containing their Antiquities, their Religion, their Rites. The Dispersion of the Ten Tribes in the East, and the Persecutions this Nation has suffered in the West. Being a Supplement and Continuation of the History of Josephus. Written in French by Mr Basnage. Translated into English by Tho. Taylor, A.M. London 1708.

Despite its claim to be a supplement to Josephus, Basnage's work did not include the text of Josephus itself. The earliest edition of Josephus to have combined the two elements in a single volume appears to have been the lavishly illustrated folio of George Henry Maynard, which claims to be a new translation prepared under the royal licence of George III, and contains, after the usual works of Josephus and Philo and an appendix defending the authenticity of Josephus's references to Christianity, 'a Continuation of the History of the Jews from Josephus down to the present Time Including a Period of more than One thousand seven hundred Years'.[9] The 'Translator's Address to the Reader' ends with the statement:

> To compleat the work, we have annexed a Supplement, collected from authentic Manuscripts, bringing down the Jewish History to the present times, which, being an attempt entirely new, we flatter ourselves, will stamp an additional value upon our undertaking, and make it in every respect worthy the patronage of a judicious and candid public.

The importance of this book is suggested by the existence of a second similarly undated but contemporary illustrated edition in quarto (rather than folio) by 'Thomas Bradshaw D.D. Late of Emmanuel College Cambridge, Lecturer of Painswick, near Gloucester; Master of the Grammar School of Painswick; Chaplain of Pentonville-Chapel and Afternoon-Preacher of Allhallows-Barking, published by Royal Authority and Act of Parliament.' This similarly claims 'The whole Newly Translated from the Original in the Greek and Hebrew Languages, and Diligently Revised, Corrected, and Compared with other Translations . . . to which is added a Continuation of the History of the Jews from the Death of Josephus to the Present Time, including a period of more than 1700 Years.'[10] Bradshaw's preface makes it clear that his is a cheaper version of Josephus:

> By means of Types of peculiar construction, and other Oeconomical measures, [it] will be comprised on the most Cheap and Moderate Scale, in order that the Readers may have the Whole at about Half the usual Price, and not be deprived of any part of the genuine History.[11]

Both these continuations of Josephus, though differing from each other in length and competence, are marked by strong Christian bias and sentiments hostile to the Jews.

The tradition of updating Josephus to provide a complete history of Judaism continued. In the (again undated) nineteenth-century family edition of Whiston's *Josephus* that I inherited from my grandfather, I find a long sequel of 222 pages that terminates with a full account of the debate inside and outside the British Parliament on the Jewish Emancipation Bill of 1847, which was provoked by the election of Lionel de Rothschild as MP for the City of London and his inability to take up his seat because he would not swear the normal religious oath required of Members of Parliament. The debate was indeed the high point for the articulation of English philosemitism; speakers included Lord John Russell the Prime Minister, Gladstone, Disraeli, Sir Robert Peel, and Lord Ashley the evangelical Zionist (who surprisingly spoke against the Bill). The Bill passed in the Commons by a majority of 73 (277 votes to 204) but was rejected by the House of Lords, and Rothschild did not take up his post until another election success in 1858.[12] In contrast to the earlier sequels this whole account is favourable to Judaism and to the emancipation of the Jews. Martin Goodman has suggested that it was in fact compiled from the notes of the antiquarian Isaac D'Israeli by his daughter and amanuensis Sarah shortly after her father's death in 1848, with the help of her brother, the politician Benjamin Disraeli. The change in tone of this sequel and its emphasis on the debate in 1847–8, which saw the most memorable and thoughtful speeches, together with the fact that it does not mention either the rejection of the Bill by the House of Lords or the final triumph of Rothschild, suggests that this may explain its learned but somewhat incoherent approach. It would indeed be an interesting study to follow the successive stages of this conception of the continuity of Jewish history under the protection of Josephus.[13]

The first modern Jewish history in English was not therefore as revolutionary as it might have seemed, for it built on this tradition. H.H. Milman's three-volume work *The History of the Jews* of 1829 began, like Josephus, with Moses, and in its earlier stages was essentially a rationalistic account of his narrative and the Old Testament.[14] For the later period, Milman disparaged Basnage and preferred the German Jewish historian Isaac Jost.[15] Milman's work was published contemporaneously with the earliest English translations of the new German scientific histories of the ancient classical world by August Boeckh (1828), Barthold Georg Niebuhr (1828–32), and Karl Otfried Müller (1830).[16] Milman was a close friend of many of the translators who were responsible for these works, and his book is (as his first reviewers saw) an early product of the new interest in German critical history and theology that came to be known as the Higher Criticism. Although his *History* was generally welcomed in orthodox Jewish circles, it caused an immense scandal in both High and Low Church circles because it applied rational historical principles to the narrative of a sacred text: the ideas that Abraham was a simple 'nomad Sheik' and that the Jews were an oriental people, 'more or less barbarians', fighting for their existence among hostile neighbours were simply too much to accept; this 'was the first decisive inroad of German theology into England: the first palpable indication that the Bible could be studied like another book; that the characters and events of the sacred history could be treated at once critically and reverently.' The book was withdrawn soon after publication, and the series in which it was published collapsed.[17] As a later writer put it, 'In this work came a further evolution of the truths and methods suggested by Bentley, Wolf and Niebuhr, and their application to sacred history was made strikingly evident.'[18] Milman himself remained theologically suspect for the rest of his distinguished career: a liberal churchman, who compounded doubts about his orthodoxy when he edited the standard nineteenth-century edition of Gibbon, despite his literary talents he never rose beyond the position of Dean of Canterbury. Ultimately Milman's *History*, revised to take account of later German scholarship, became the standard narrative history of the Jews in English, and remained in print for most of the twentieth century.

Milman defended his approach in the introduction to the third volume of the first edition, and again towards the end of his life in the preface to the edition of 1863:[19]

> What should be the treatment by a Christian writer, a writer to whom truth is the one paramount object, of the only documents on which rests the earlier history of the Jews, the Scriptures of the Old Testament? Are they, like other historical documents, to be submitted to calm but searching criticism as to their age, their authenticity, their authorship; above all, their historical sense and historical interpretation? . . .
>
> Lawgivers, prophets, apostles, were in all other respects men of like passions (take the word in its vulgar sense) with their fellow-men; they were men of their age and country, who, as they spoke the language, so they thought the thoughts of their nation and their time, clothed those thoughts in the imagery, and illustrated them from the circumstances of their daily life. They had no special knowledge on any subject but moral and religious truth to distinguish them from other men; were as fallible as others on all questions of science, and even of history, extraneous to their religious teaching . . .
>
> This seems throughout to have been the course of providential government: lawgivers, prophets, apostles, were advanced in religious knowledge alone. In all other respects society, civilization, developed itself according to its usual laws, The Hebrew in the wilderness, excepting as far as the Law modified his manners and habits, was an Arab of the Desert. Abraham, excepting in his worship and intercourse with the One True God, was a nomad Sheik. The simple and natural tenor of these lives is one of the most impressive guarantees of the truth of the record.

But problems always remained. While allowing for the insertion of Jewish history into the prevailing conceptions of the progress of civilization, and for the possibility of comparisons such as Moses with Solon, it was not entirely possible to reconcile the principles of Jewish history with those adopted in the new scientific history of ancient Greece and

Rome. Even discarding miracles and the direct intervention of God in history in favour of a rational approach, there remained two fundamental problems. Throughout the long tradition of Sacred History the Jews had been regarded as the Chosen People, and their history was the history of the fulfilment of God's covenant to grant them the Promised Land. These were in turn justified in Christian terms by their divine role in producing the Messiah. Christian writers could escape from these aspects of the Jewish tradition by claiming that the failure of the Jews to recognize the Messiah had caused them to pass on their special status as chosen people to the Christian community, and they had thereby forfeited their right to a Promised Land. But it nevertheless made it extremely difficult to produce a historical account that would enable Judaism to be directly compared with Greece and Rome. And Milman himself believed in the divine dispensation of human history; he ends with the declaration:[20]

> History, which is the record of the Past, has now discharged its office: it presumes not to raise the mysterious veil which the Almighty has spread over the Future. The destinies of this wonderful people, as of all mankind, are in the hands of the All-Wise Ruler of the Universe; his decrees will be accomplished, his truth, his goodness, and his wisdom vindicated.

Milman did his best to create a modern scientific version of history from the biblical tradition, explaining the interventions of God on rationalistic principles and even playing down the historical significance of the Crucifixion to the same extent as the (interpolated) narrative of Josephus:[21]

> We leave to the Christian historian the description of this event, and all its consequences – inestimable in their importance to mankind, but which produced hardly any *immediate* effect on the affairs of the Jewish nation. Yet our history will have shown that the state of the public mind in Judaea, as well as the character of Pilate, the chief agent in the transaction, harmonize in the most remarkable manner with the narrative of the Evangelists.

The crucifixion, despite the earthquake and unnatural solar darkness that accompanied it according to the Gospel narratives, created no more perturbation than the fall of Icarus in Brueghel's famous painting.

Milman had many fewer problems to contend with than either his predecessors or his twentieth-century successors. He could leave behind the notion that the sufferings of the Jews in the Diaspora were a consequence of their refusal to recognize Christ, and admire the Jewish community for its tenacity and its ability to overcome persecution; he could welcome the new era of mutual tolerance and even assimilation of nineteenth-century Western Europe. The future, fortunately for him, as he says was 'in the hands of the All-Wise Ruler of the Universe'. To him classical history and Jewish history were indeed flowing together, and comparison was simply a question of selection from tradition. But how does Milman's problem seem now? What sort of Jewish history do we want to write today in the shadow of the Holocaust, and how far will it be compatible with the dominant conception of a secular Graeco-Roman history? These are the problems with which my teacher Arnaldo Momigliano wrestled throughout his life.

Before we consider this question we need also to recall a quite different tradition of the writing of Jewish history, that which arose out of the needs of the Jewish community to understand its own past. In his early editions Milman had already recognized the importance, if only as a source, of the work of Isaac Jost, and he refers in the preface to the edition of 1863[22] to other recent works of Jewish scholars. But he was scarcely aware of the profound reinterpretation of Jewish history that emerged in the age of Romanticism amid the struggles between the various traditions of German Judaism. In 1846 the young Heinrich Graetz published his famous manifesto 'Die Construction der jüdischen Geschichte'[23] and in 1853 began his multi-volume *History of the Jews* in the middle, with volume 4 on the period AD 70–500: 'Another history of the Jews!' said Leopold Zunz, the eminent rabbinic scholar – 'But this time a Jewish history!' Graetz replied.[24]

In starting his enterprise from the destruction of the Temple by the Roman authorities, Graetz indicated a new interpretation of Jewish history based on the concept of the Diaspora, which made it fundamentally different from the standard histories of other peoples. His narrative was to combine the political story of the persecutions of the Jews with the history of their inner life, which in the spirit of Maimonides revolved around their moral or divine mission to uphold the true principle of monotheism against their Christian persecutors:

> The Christian conception of history, as is well-known, fully denies to Judaism any history, in the higher sense of the word, since the loss of its national independence, an event which coincided with another of great importance to the Christian world.[25]

In contrast, Graetz proclaimed the idea of history as the story of a cultural or spiritual mission:

> There is scarcely a science, an art, an intellectual province in which Jews have not taken a part, for which Jews have not manifested an equal aptitude. To think was as much a characteristic feature of the Jews as to suffer.[26]

> History still has not produced another case of a nation which has laid aside its weapons of war to devote itself entirely to the peaceful pursuits of study and poetry, which has freed itself from the bonds of narrow self-interest and let its thoughts soar to fathom its own nature and its mysterious relationship to the universe and God.[27]

And on the completion of his *History* in 1874 he reflected on the twin legacy of Western history in Hellenism and Hebraism:

> The classical Greeks are dead, and toward the deceased posterity behaves properly. Envy and hatred are silent at the grave of the dead; their contributions are, in fact, usually exaggerated. It is quite different with that other creative nation, the Hebrews. Precisely because they're still alive their contributions to culture are not generally acknowledged; they are criticized, or given another name to partially conceal their authorship or to dislodge them entirely. Even if the fair-minded concede that they introduced the monotheistic idea and a higher morality into the life of nations, very few appreciate the great significance of these admissions. They fail to consider why one creative nation with its rich talents perished, whereas the other, so often on the brink of death, still wanders over the earth having rejuvenated itself several times.[28]

Graetz concludes by characterizing the Jewish tradition:

> The history of the Israelite nation manifests, therefore, at the beginning a thoroughly irregular pattern. Two factors determine its rise and fall, a physical and spiritual one, or a political and a religious-ethical one.[29]

Thus Graetz's *History* has a dual structure, as a celebration of Jewish philosophy and learning, but also a history of a religious culture surviving persecution. Despite the romantic language of its formulation and the somewhat unsatisfactory nature of his essentially biographical narrative, this alternative vision of the meaning of ancient history surely deserves more attention than it is given today as a future direction for the study of world ancient history. At the start of the fateful age of the creation of national histories as national myths, Jewish history liberated itself; in this respect it stands alongside the earlier Enlightenment traditions of Greek and Roman ancient history, but it transcends them in offering a new sort of history based on the cultural life of the spirit. No wonder this escape from the political history so dominant in the second half of the nineteenth century earned in 1879 the wrath of the most extreme of the German nationalist historians, Heinrich Treitschke.[30]

What is revealed by reflecting on the presuppositions of the Western traditions of ancient history is the extent to which the modern Western world has continually developed a myth of the past in order to justify contemporary preoccupations. This is true of all history that is not pure antiquarianism, but it is important to know why we think in this particular way in order to understand that it is not the only way in which world history can be structured. And when we Westerners criticize other historical political traditions for their inability to translate, or understand or even to see as important, concepts such as liberty and democracy, we should remember that these are not transcendental human values. The Western traditions of ancient world history rest on the eighteenth-century foundations established by the Enlightenment, which combined imperialism with democracy and the free-market economy of Adam Smith to create a Western interpretation of history; to this it married a Judaeo-Christian tradition of a religion capable of being translated into rational history because it was ultimately based on historical narrative rather than myth. But the example of Graetz suggests that this dominant Western view is not the only way to structure ancient history. Perhaps the twenty-first century will enable us to construct a new vision of ancient world history that is inclusive of other cultures like China, India, and the Near East, and is not based solely on traditional Western European values.

Eight bookes of the Peloponnesian warre. Interpreted by T. Hobbes.
1629 London for H. Seile: title page

2

Enlightenment Greece: Sparta versus Athens

Thomas Hobbes had introduced the importance of the contrast between Sparta and Athens for the study of political events in his famous translation of Thucydides, initially published in 1629; this was the first scholarly translation into English from the Greek (rather than from the Latin translation of Valla).[1] Its title page demonstrates what was for Hobbes the central message of the book: at the top, the map of Greece that Hobbes himself had constructed out of references in ancient sources; on the left, successive images of the village-like city of Sparta, the figure of King Archidamus in warlike guise and the elders denominated *hoi aristoi* in conclave; on the right, the spectacular city of Athens with its acropolis, the defiant figure of Pericles and the people, *hoi polloi* of Athens, being addressed by an orator; between them the image of Thucydides holding a scroll on which is written *ktema es aei* ('a possession for all time'). On the lowest register the massed army of the Spartans opposes the fleet of the Athenians.

Hobbes himself had no doubt that Thucydides preferred *hoi aristoi* (the best) over *hoi polloi* (the many), but that his ultimate ideal lay in the monarchical leadership of Pericles:[2]

> For his opinion touching the government of the state, it is manifest that he least of all liked the democracy ... Nor doth it appear that he magnifieth anywhere the authority of the *few*: amongst whom, he saith, everyone desireth to be the chief; and they that are undervalued, bear it with less patience than in a democracy; whereupon sedition followeth, and dissolution of the government. He praiseth the government of Athens, when it was mixed of *the few* and *the many*; but more he commendeth it, both when Peisistratus reigned, (saving that it was an usurped power), and when in the beginning of this war it was democratical in name, but

> in effect monarchical under Pericles. So that it seemeth, that as he was of regal descent, so he best approved of the regal government.

Perhaps the greatest translation of Thucydides, nothing could be more appropriate to the generation that saw the beginning of the English Civil War: it became a seminal reference point in the struggles between King and Commons.

The systematic study of Greek history began in the eighteenth century.[3] The political message of all the Enlightenment works was centred on a comparison between Sparta and Athens, each of which was described from the contrasting accounts in Plutarch's lives of the founders of their constitutions, Lycurgus and Solon. In the case of Athens, Plutarch's *Life of Solon* offers both the false view (though it was prevalent in antiquity) that the democratic constitution of Athens was created by Solon, and the political judgement that all subsequent events were perversions of the original ideal state. A more accurate perception of Athenian democracy was only possible with the discovery on papyrus of the Aristotelian *Athenian Constitution* in the 1890s – and then only with difficulty. Before that, it took a great deal of radical faith to discover, let alone approve of, fifth-century Athenian democracy, as the resistance throughout the nineteenth century to George Grote's idealized Athens by Georg Schömann and other Germans show.[4] In contrast, Plutarch's *Life of Lycurgus* offers an almost perfect model for the eighteenth-century antiquarian approach.

TEMPLE STANYAN

The first substantial narrative history of Greece was written by the minor diplomat Temple Stanyan, the first volume of whose *The Grecian History from the Origins of Greece to the End of the Peloponnesian War* (1707) was republished in London with a second volume, *From the End of the Peloponnesian War to the death of Philip of Macedon*, in 1739; its importance was immediately recognized across Europe through the French translation of Diderot (Paris 1743, 3 vols). It set the tone for all subsequent Greek narrative histories throughout Europe, and went through several editions; it is later described as 'a compilation that held the field for educational purposes until the appearance of the much larger history by William Mitford the younger'.[5]

Chapter III of volume I, book I, of Stanyan's work, entitled 'The kingdom and commonwealth of Lacedaemon', offered a long account of Spartan history, in which Lycurgus is central: the description is taken directly from Plutarch in relation to both biography and institutions. Thus Lycurgus' reforms continued the principle of two kings but reduced their power through a senate of elders, and the Spartan assemblies were a mere matter of form. He divided the land into 30,000 equal plots, 9,000 for the city of Sparta; he abolished the use of gold and silver. His next ordinance was levelled against private luxury, and decreed that the men should not eat at home with their families, but in one common hall, without distinction of dignity or fortune. Stanyan gave a long account of Spartan education and its effect in forming the 'laconick stile'. The women engaged in sport naked, and adultery was permitted. Sparta had no walls; and the institution of the 'cryptia' (the ritual hunting of helots by adolescent Spartans) was described:

> Such was the Form of the Commonwealth instituted by Lycurgus . . . Nor is it less surprising, that a Pagan, who was indeed too indulgent to Adultery, Theft, and, in some cases, to Murder itself, should in the rest approach so near to Christian Morality, as sometimes to overtake it . . .[6]

But Stanyan did not approve of this model state, created by one man:

> Her constitution however was not without its faults. I have mention'd some notorious ones as to the moral part: And the Government in general carry'd such an Air of Horror with it, that it was rather admir'd, than imitated. Their strict discipline was harden'd into a Moroseness of Temper; so that they knew not how to abate of their Rigour upon occasion, but extended the same harsh Severity to their Allies, which they used towards one another. Besides, there was no Peace, nor Truce observ'd in a Commonwealth devoted to Arms, and whose very Constitution was War. This by degrees made their government distasteful; and favour'd the Ambition of the *Athenians* their Rivals, and indeed their Reverse: Who had liv'd a great while without any thoughts of command; but at last exerted themselves . . . and drew both their own, and their Neighbours Necks out of the Collar.[7]

Whereas Stanyan gave Lycurgus the status of a founding figure, Solon was treated at a later stage (ch. VI) as part of the history of Athens, rather than as the creator of a new constitution; and Stanyan was more interested in his reform of the law code and political position.

> Thus he finish'd his new Settlement, wherein his chief Aim was to poise one part of the State with the other: So that what the Commons wanted in Wealth and Honour, was sufficiently made up to them in their Share of the Government. This was reducing things, as near as he could, to an exact Equality: And indeed it was no easy Task to find out a Cure for such a Complication of Distempers, where the Weakness of those he had to do with, would hardly permit him to make use of suitable Remedies. And therefore when one ask'd him, if he had prescrib'd good Laws to the *Athenians*, *Yes*, says he, *as good as they are capable of receiving*. Since therefore they would admit of no Government but a *Democracy*, he form'd his Laws according to that Model. It did not indeed come up to that of *Sparta* laid down by *Lycurgus*; and the Difference is easily accounted for, from the Temper of the *Athenians*, which was too delicate and capricious to be brought to those grave and regular Austerities; and without considering the great Sway the People bore in the Execution of the Laws, the Laws themselves were more numerous and confus'd, and could not therefore be so religiously observ'd, as they were at *Sparta*. Yet such this Establishment was, as restor'd the Love of Labour and Husbandry, made way for Commerce, put the *Athenians* into a condition of being rich at home, and powerful abroad, and with the Rules of Justice, Order, and Discipline, serv'd to tame and polish a People bred up in Liberty, and persuaded that Force and Violence were the only Preservatives against Oppression.[8]

Stanyan was well aware of the political use to which the two constitutions could be put in modern controversies. He discusses this in the preface to volume II:

> And in some respects they have copied after them, particularly in their Forms of Government, which have serv'd as Models to several considerable States in this Part of the World, but with such Variations and Improvements, as the Wisdom of the later Ages has found necessary. For though the general Plan of Government in *Greece* was founded upon Principles of Liberty, there were great Errors and Defects in it, which I have cursorily taken notice of, in relating the Tumults and Disorders that

> have been occasion'd by them. Some of these Imperfections are still retain'd in the Republics which are now subsisting in Europe, and others have been added, by refining too much, and aiming at more Perfection than that sort of Government is capable of.

Stanyan proceeded to criticize Sparta and Athens in detail, before concluding:

> I have made a farther Digression from my Subject than I intended: But in speaking of the *Grecian* Governments, and of those which have been grafted upon them, I could not, as an Englishman, resist the Temptation of saying something in Preference of our own, which is certainly the nearest to Perfection, and is attended with very few Evils, but such as are of our own making.

CHARLES ROLLIN

In England over the eighteenth century, Stanyan's views were complemented by Charles Rollin's prolix and encyclopedic *Histoire ancienne* (1730–38), covering all the ancient civilizations; this was itself intended for schools; and, although it was too long to have much success here, it nevertheless became the standard reference work for educated readers across Europe. It began to be translated as early as 1734 as (finally) Charles Rollin, *The Ancient History of the Egyptians, Carthaginians, Assyrians, Babylonians, Medes and Persians, Macedonians, and Grecians*. Rollin offered two consecutive chapters on 'The Spartan government. Laws established by Lycurgus', and 'The government of Athens. The laws of Solon'.

The section on Sparta offered a full account of the information given in Plutarch, and concluded with 'reflections upon the government of Sparta and upon the Laws of Lycurgus', divided between 'Things commendable' and 'Things blameable'. The five things commendable are: the nature of the Spartan government; equal division of the land, gold and silver banished from Sparta; the excellent education of their youth; obedience; respect towards the aged. The seven things blameable are: the choice made of the children that were to be brought up or exposed; their care confined only to the body; their barbarous cruelty towards their children; the mother's inhumanity; their excessive leisure;

their cruelty towards the helots; modesty and decency entirely neglected. The Spartan laws therefore fall far short of the laws of Moses and those of the Gospel. The comparison suggests the seriousness with which Sparta was taken.[9]

In contrast, Solon was seen as creating a compromise:

> Solon, who was an able and prudent man, was very sensible of the inconveniencies that attend a democracy, or popular government: But, having thoroughly studied, and being perfectly well acquainted with the character and disposition of the Athenians, he knew it would be a vain attempt to take the sovereignty out of the people's hands; and that if they parted with it at one time, they would soon resume it at another by force and violence.[10]

Stanyan's preface already claimed that he composed his works 'before Rollin appear'd in the World . . . but it has been of service to me in the Revisal of them', and he distinguished his own work from Rollin, who 'cull'd out the Flowers of the Grecian Story, and interspers'd them in the Accounts, which he has given of the other ancient Kingdoms and Commonwealths'.

OLIVER GOLDSMITH

The drive towards the rediscovery of ancient history represented a revolution in the educational aims of a new generation: no longer was the study of the classics confined to the construing and explication of ancient texts in the service of philology. The classical past was expected to explain and provide models for the gentry and the bourgeoisie of an ever-widening ruling class, in commerce, manufacture, and trade, as well as agriculture. This movement can be seen throughout Europe in schools and universities, and it brought a response from authors and their publishers. From 1764 Oliver Goldsmith earned his livelihood composing histories of England, Greece, and Rome, intended for use in schools: these were continually being produced in successive editions well into the nineteenth century. His *The Grecian History from the earliest state to the death of Alexander the Great* was first published in 1774 posthumously, and reprinted almost annually until around 1842, and even occasionally in updated format

('Whittaker's Pinnock's Goldsmith') as late as 1862; it was translated into most European languages, including Russian, Greek, and Ottoman Turkish. Goldsmith's work was essentially a brief narrative history; two consecutive chapters, 'Of the Government of Sparta, and the Laws of Lycurgus' and 'Of the Government of Athens, the Laws of Solon, and the history of the Republic from the time of Solon to the commencement of the Persian War', once again perhaps reflected in their arrangement the practice of comparing the two cities; but there was no actual comparison offered, simply a retelling of the Plutarchean story as a straightforward narrative.

Thus in general in the English tradition, apart from Stanyan's forthright preference for the British constitution, and in contrast with their significance in France both before and after the Revolution,[11] there was little serious discussion of the importance of the roles of Sparta or Athens as political systems.

ADAM FERGUSON AND THE SCOTTISH ENLIGHTENMENT

More interesting views are to be found in the works of the Scottish Enlightenment. The political message of these works was again centred on a comparison between Sparta and Athens, described on the basis of Plutarch's lives of the founders of the constitutions, Lycurgus and Solon. In almost every respect the Spartan system was considered to be the better. The most influential political thinker of the Scottish Enlightenment, Adam Ferguson, in his work *An Essay on the History of Civil Society* (1767), describes the virtues of Sparta:[12]

> Every institution of this singular people gave a lesson of obedience, of fortitude, and of zeal for the public: but it is remarkable that they chose to obtain, by their virtues alone, what other nations are fain to buy with their treasure; and it is well known, that, in the course of their history, they came to regard their discipline merely on account of its moral effects. They had experienced the happiness of a mind courageous, disinterested, and devoted to its best affections; and they studied to preserve this character in themselves, by resigning the interests of ambition, and the hopes of military glory, even by sacrificing the numbers of their people.

In contrast, Ferguson's picture of democratic Athens was dark and uncomprehending:

> The Athenians retained their popular government under all these defects. The mechanic was obliged, under a penalty, to appear in the public market-place, and to hear debates on the subjects of war, and of peace. He was tempted by pecuniary rewards, to attend on the trial of civil and criminal causes. But notwithstanding an exercise tending so much to cultivate their talents, the indigent came always with minds intent upon profit, or with the habits of an illiberal calling. Sunk under the sense of their personal disparity and weakness, they were ready to resign themselves entirely to the influence of some popular leader, who flattered their passions, and wrought on their fears; or, actuated by envy, they were ready to banish from the state whomsoever was respectable and eminent in the superior order of citizens: and whether from the neglect of the public at one time, or their maladministration at another, the sovereignty was every moment ready to drop from their hands.

WILLIAM ROBERTSON

This philosophical view entered the school tradition. The 'other' William Robertson (1740–1803), namesake and contemporary of the great historian rival of David Hume and Edward Gibbon, published *The History of Ancient Greece* in Edinburgh in 1768.[13] In his youth Robertson had been secretary to a Scottish laird, in which capacity he is recorded as having in 1773 offered Dr Johnson boiled haddock for breakfast, and a walk through the park. Johnson refused both, the first out of disgust, the second because he had come to Scotland to see noble mountains, not civilized parkland. Later Robertson became Deputy Keeper of the Records of Scotland, and a great expert on the Scottish peerage and Scottish charters. In origin his *History* was a plagiarism of a popular French educational work by Pons-Augustin Alletz;[14] but it had a wide influence in Scottish education, and was republished at least twice.

As in Plutarch's account, after his marital problems Lycurgus travelled to Crete, Asia (where he collected the works of Homer), and Egypt:

> The result of all these painful researches, was the famous Spartan legislation, which has been the wonder of succeeding ages; and to us, in these latter times, would appear to be altogether chimerical and impracticable, were it not attested past all possibility of doubt by every ancient author who speaks of it, many of whom, such as Plato, Aristotle, Xenophon, and Plutarch, were eye-witnesses of what they deliver. It is, besides, an undoubted fact, that this system subsisted during a space of more than 700 years. We cannot, however, sufficiently admire how it was possible for one man to succeed in establishing a form of government, so violently repugnant in several particulars to the most powerful passions of the human soul.[15]

Robertson set out to give in a systematic Appendix (part 1) an account *Of the Spartan and Athenian governments*. The Spartan is divided under two headings, the public government of the State, and the private lives of the citizens. The constitution is described on the scheme of the ancient historian Polybius as a mixture of monarchy, aristocracy, and democracy. In it the Senate was most important, and the people had limited powers. This constitution lasted for 150 years until the ephors were introduced, as tribunes of the people, five in number.

The private institutions began from the equal distribution of lands, and the prohibition on the use of gold and silver in favour of iron money: all this was designed to prevent luxury. Lycurgus instituted common tables of fifteen persons, each providing a bushel of flour, 8 gallons of wine, 5 pounds of cheese and 2½ pounds of figs. In the consequent insurrection, Lycurgus had one of his eyes knocked out; nevertheless, he founded schools of temperance. The education of children is described, and that of young women. Robertson seems even to recommend to his young readers the marriage principles of Lycurgus:

> His sagacity was no less conspicuous in contriving things so, that their marriages were all clandestine, and rather a rape than a formal conjunction. By these means the interviews between the new-married couple were few, difficult, and short. Hence temperance in their pleasures.

This was doubtless a very Scottish and Presbyterian presentation of the married state!

'To several eminent writers some of the customs and institutions have appeared reprehensible.' Lycurgus' treatment of young women was indelicate, the freedom allowed to married women immoral. But Robertson defended these as showing 'the corruption of the manners of those who account it such'. He remarks on 'the diversion of filial affection to the state as common father: a circumstance which distinguishes the Spartan polity from that of every other nation, so far as we know, which ever appeared on earth.' Sparta was more the subject of reproach for its cruelty, especially its savage barbarity to the helots and 'the horrid amusement of the Cryptia'. 'Most of the ancient philosophers were of the opinion, that the government of Sparta approached the nearest of any to perfection, as comprehending all the advantages, and excluding all the disadvantages, of the other forms of government.'

This was a full, and philosophically interesting, if derivative account of Spartan society, obviously intended to be part of a contrast with Athens; but unfortunately Robertson's comparison is weak: and he has not much of interest to say about Athens, all of whose institutions are similarly derived from one man, Solon.

GEORGE DUNBAR

The Scottish Enlightenment tradition continued until at least 1813. In that year a new edition was published in Edinburgh of Archbishop Potter's well-known antiquarian handbook *Archaeologia Graeca*, first published in 1697: John Potter, *Archaeologia Graeca or the Antiquities of Greece, to which is added an Appendix containing a concise history of the Grecian states by G. Dunbar, F.R.S.E. and Professor of Greek in the University of Edinburgh.*[16] This appendix in volume II, separately numerated, is in fact a full history of Greece, which has been ignored in previous modern accounts.

George Dunbar (1774–1851) was the child of humble parents. He was apprenticed as a gardener but injured himself falling from a tree; he attracted the notice of a neighbouring proprietor, who helped him acquire a classical education. He studied at Edinburgh around 1800, and while tutor in the family of the Lord Provost, was selected to act as assistant to the Professor of Greek, Andrew Dalzell; on Dalzell's death in 1806, Dunbar became Professor of Greek, until his own death in 1851 (though in later years a substitute fulfilled his duties). He was not a historian; he wrote books on grammar, language, dictionaries, and textbooks. 'As a classical scholar Dunbar did not leave behind him a very enduring reputation, and the bulk of his work has little permanent value. His industry however was very great. His best work was the compilation of lexicons.'[17]

Despite this rather low estimation of his merits, Dunbar's history is perhaps the most philosophical of those produced within the Scottish tradition; it is explicitly based on the principles of Adam Ferguson, especially in the section devoted to Lycurgus. Two long sections follow one another, *Of the Spartan Constitution and Government* (14–42), and *A few Observations on the Athenian Constitution and Government* (42–55).

In the first the laws of Minos were the model for Lycurgus, whose legislation was based on two principles: 'that all free men were equal, and that slaves were necessary to relieve them from every servile employment'. But for the first time in the Scottish historical tradition, under Ferguson's influence, Dunbar confronted directly the question of how one man could impose such an ideal state on his fellow citizens. Before Lycurgus the Spartans were pirates and warriors:

> It is at least probable that the government of Sparta took its rise in a great measure from the situation and genius of the people; for no legislator in a free country could, all at once, efface the memory of old institutions, root up inveterate habits, and give a totally new temper and tone to the spirits of the people . . . An eloquent philosopher (Dr. A. Ferguson) has with truth asserted, 'that the founders of nations only acted a superior part among numbers who were disposed to the same institutions, and that they left to posterity a renown, pointing them out as the inventors of many practices which had been already in use, and which helped to form their own manners and genius as well as those of their countrymen.'[18]

Dunbar followed the Plutarchean legend of Lycurgus on his exile and travels, especially to Crete, whence he imported the poet 'Thales' (Thaletas). 'Lycurgus calculated that in Greece with its warring states . . . that state which combined the best military institution with the strictest form of civil polity, would most likely survive and triumph over all the rest':

> The minds of the Spartans were not yet accustomed to those severe privations, to those laborious exercises and habits of temperance which their descendants bore without repining, as they never experienced a milder discipline from their infancy. They felt the rough hand of their legislator

> imposing intolerable burdens, and were disposed to shrink from their pressure; but his calmness, authority and address in soothing the enraged multitude, and converting his enemies into steadfast friends, enabled him to try the effect of his measures, and gradually overcome the repugnance of the people.[19]

'In all democratical states, unequal distribution of property, and the accumulation of wealth in the hands of a few individuals, have uniformly been the sources of discord between the higher and the lower orders.' Lycurgus therefore instituted equal division of property, into 39,000 shares. 'A regulation of this kind was not in favour of commerce or the cultivation of the arts; and Lycurgus wished to banish them effectually by prohibiting the use of gold and silver.' For that reason he instituted iron currency. His principal aim was to render the Spartans warlike, and his intention was to form one great family, under the superintendence and discipline of the laws. All servile occupations and selfish passions were excluded, along with luxury and private property:

> By these singular institutions of their legislator, they were shut out as it were from all the world, and left alone to practise the severest virtues, and the most rigorous self-denial, without any of those innocent gratifications and elegant amusements with which other nations were accustomed to unbend and exhilarate their minds.[20]

Youth was given over to training, but women were left a great share of natural liberty. In government everything natural and factitious was turned to the purposes of war. As to stealing and the hunting of helots, it 'seems hardly consistent with the consummate prudence of Lycurgus to sanction such a measure'.[21] Helots were actually well looked after: they outnumbered the Spartan citizens seven to one at Plataea; the claim of Thucydides that 9,000 were done away with is probably mistaken, deriving more from hearsay than good authority.

The power of the kings was abridged by the Senate: in contrast, the system of government that Solon established at Athens left too much power in the hands of the multitude. Lycurgus' system was better, as Polybius says in his sixth book. The council of twenty-eight above sixty years of age made for caution. Whether Lycurgus or Theopompus instituted the ephors is disputed; the most important part of their duty was to inspect the education of the Spartan youth. No poetry was permitted except that of Homer and Tyrtaeus. It was the rigidity of the Spartan system that caused its fall; but Dunbar ends by quoting Adam Ferguson in praise of the continuity of Sparta. 'Sparta under every supposed error of its form, prospered for ages, by the integrity of its manners, and by the character of its citizens . . . the last community of Greece that became a village in the empire of Rome.'[22]

In Athens in contrast, according to Dunbar, Solon:

> . . . left the multitude in the enjoyment of too much liberty, which enabled them to undo all his other wise regulations, and to make the other parts of the government only a name. Were the people of this country, with the privileges they possess, allowed to elect their representatives annually for the great council of the nation, what would likely be the consequence? Among themselves riots and disorders, inflamed by designing men, who, knowing the proneness of the people to suspicion, and their constant habit of judging actions by their results, take every occasion to awaken their suspicion, to excite their discontent, by directing their attention to unfortunate events, without once examining the causes that produced them, and to set themselves off by profession of devotedness to their interest, while their sole aim would be to aggrandise themselves . . . Such was a picture of the Athenian government occasioned through the excess of liberty, and such would be the practice in our own, were we, with some inconsiderate or ill designing men, to adopt the errors and defects of the most renowned republican constitution in all antiquity.[23]

Athens nevertheless possessed many virtues. 'That lively, ingenious people bestowed honours on men of abilities, in a way most effectual to excite emulation.' The arts were encouraged:

> The Athenian government possessed this advantage above all others, that it gave free access to every man, however mean his birth or moderate his fortune, to rise by the force of his talents to the highest situations in the state. Genius and abilities were not rebuked by the frowns of power, or kept down by the insolence of high birth and rank . . . If a nation is virtuous and rising to distinction, the human mind receives an impulse and enlargement of its powers, which it scarcely ever experiences in a state of higher promise. One great action becomes the prelude to another. The

> place of one illustrious member of the community is supplied by thousands. The same spirit that animates the soldier or the sailor in the day of battle, pervades the peaceful abodes of philosophy and the arts. There too emulation is kindled, and there men appear illuminating the world by their discoveries and the efforts of their genius, and transmitting to posterity a reputation, better intitled to the veneration of mankind, than that of those desolating conquerors who attempt to subjugate nations to gratify their ambition and avarice.[24]

The decline and fall of Athens was due to her licentiousness, frivolity, anarchy and disorder:

> The philosophic enquirer, from a knowledge of their laws and government, and from the character of the people, might have predicted the nature, and almost the period of its termination . . . [W]hen Pericles introduced a new kind of policy into the state, a policy by which the attention of the people was turned to amusements, shows, speculations and pleasures, to objects in which wealth, not honour and glory, formed the principal features, the republic soon betrayed symptoms of decay.

In comparison with earlier writers, this is excellent philosophical history, based on the ideas of the Scottish Enlightenment; but by the time that it was published in 1813, it was also rather old fashioned, given the arrival of the new history of William Mitford (see ch. 5).

The picture of the importance of the Spartan model and the weakness of a democratic Athens was therefore the dominant theme throughout the eighteenth century during the Enlightenment, in which the idea of history was enshrined in the concept of history as instruction for the present, *historia magistra vitae*, and in the acceptance of the biographies of Plutarch as models of political behaviour.[25] The predilection of Scottish writers for Sparta perhaps reflects the view of the Scots of themselves as a highland, disciplined, austere, and moral people, compared with other nations. In contrast, the English might regard themselves as more civilized and democratic, but they therefore had a greater incentive to differentiate themselves from the Athenians and assert the superiority of their own modern constitution over ancient examples. Most modern writers have concluded that there was a general preference in the Enlightenment for the Spartan oligarchic model over the Athenian democratic one: only a few radical writers like Tom Paine and Voltaire[26] are thought to have opposed this tendency.[27] But in fact there existed a countervailing tradition more sympathetic to Athens.

J.-J. BARTHÉLEMY, *VOYAGE DU JEUNE ANACHARSIS EN GRÈCE* (1788)

Meanwhile during the late Enlightenment in France new ways of understanding the Greeks were being explored. The immensely popular *Voyage du jeune Anacharsis en Grèce* by J.-J. Barthélemy (1788) was a long (indeed almost interminable) description in seven volumes of the adventures of an imaginary young Scythian traveller in fourth-century Athens. Although now almost forgotten, it was an international success, translated into most European languages, and became an important text in promoting European philhellenism:[28] the demotic Greek translation (1797) was made in part by the famous revolutionary Rigas Feraios (1757–1798), and was apparently intended as a call to arms; a year later Feraios and his companions were captured on their way to link up with the French revolutionary army of Napoleon in Venice, and strangled by the Ottomans in a castle on the Danube.

Barthélemy (1716–1798) was a famous antiquary, exemplary keeper of the royal *Cabinet des médailles*, Fellow of the Royal Society of London (1755), and a member of the *Académie Française*, the first modern to decipher ancient scripts (Palmyrene and Phoenician); later he was recognized by J.-F. Champollion as an important precursor of himself in his decipherment of Egyptian hieroglyphics. Barthélemy was the friend and confidant of the popular Duc de Choiseul, Minister for Foreign Affairs (1759–70), and reformer of the French army under Mme de Pompadour and Louis XV. Barthélemy had earlier accompanied Choiseul when the latter was appointed ambassador to Italy in 1753, where Barthélemy met the pioneer of the modern study of Greek art, J.J. Winckelmann. When Choiseul was finally dismissed by Louis XV, Barthélemy went to live with him on his country estate and survived the French Revolution: briefly imprisoned, he was rescued by his patroness, 'Citoyenne Choiseul'; he was even restored to his former post at the *Cabinet des médailles*. His autobiography, written in his final years, laments his former glory under the *ancien régime*.[29]

On his return from Italy in 1757, Barthélemy had begun to write the *Anacharsis*, which took thirty years to complete. It was a serious response to the call of Voltaire's *Essai sur les moeurs* (1756), which had asserted that custom was the true basis for a study of the past, and therefore allowed the researches of the *érudits* (antiquaries) to be given equal prominence with those of the *philosophes* in the explication of political and military history. The impact of this controversy throughout Europe on the development of historical writing is shown by the first publication of the twenty-four-year-old Edward Gibbon, his *Essai sur l'étude de la littérature.*[30]

Because it is couched in terms of the memoirs of a fictional character, Barthélemy's work has been regarded by modern historians as lacking in seriousness as either history or scholarship.[31] In fact it is deeply serious, learned, and accurate. The form of epistolary narrative and fictitious memoirs by a foreigner had been popular since Montesquieu's *Lettres Persanes* (1721, 1758), partly as a means of avoiding censorship.[32] Barthélemy's polished and elegant narrative was accompanied by footnotes giving the sources for every piece of antiquarian information, and each volume was provided with additional notes on controversial points. The attached volume of maps and plans was prepared by the geographer Barbie du Bocage, and represented a major advance in historical mapmaking.[33]

The protagonist Anacharsis is a young Scythian who travels to Athens in the year 363 BC, visiting Greek cities and islands on the way; he remains in Greece recording events and his travels in a journal and letters until the victory of Philip II of Macedon at Chaeronea (338 BC). The work begins with a long introduction of some 470 pages of orthodox narrative history (containing only one reference to the alleged narrator), giving a detailed history of Greece to the point of Anacharsis' arrival; although verbose, this was much superior to earlier histories. Because it was centred on Athens, it abounded with the achievements of Solon, which take up some seventy pages:[34]

> In adopting this form [of popular government] he so tempered it, as to give the idea of an oligarchy in the body of the Areopagites; of an aristocracy in the mode of electing magistrates; and of a pure democracy in the liberty granted the lower citizens to have a seat at the tribunals of justice.

Any faults in Athenian democracy were attributed to its perversion under Pericles:

> . . . the most dangerous of those leaders who paid court to the multitude, disgusted them with business, and their little remaining virtue, by largesses which exhausted the public treasury, and amongst other advantages, facilitated their access to the public spectacles.

Barthélemy started his account of the Persian Wars (Section II: the Age of Themistocles and Aristides) with a somewhat surprising comment for the protégé of the Duc de Choiseul, architect of the wars of Louis XV:

> It is with pain that I prevail upon myself to describe campaigns and battles; it should suffice to know, that wars originate in the ambition of princes, and terminate in the misery of nations: but the example of a people preferring death to servitude is too sublime, and too instructive, to be passed over in silence.

Again, at the end of the Peloponnesian Wars (called 'the age of Pericles', and regarded as primarily notable for the introduction of courtesans), 'At present let us turn our eyes from these afflicting scenes, and fix them on more agreeable and more interesting objects.'

At the end of the first volume, Barthélemy begins the actual travels of Anacharsis. He passes from Panticapaeum (Kerch in the eastern Crimea) to Athens, recounting the history of the various cities and islands on the way. In Thebes he manages to meet Epaminondas and the future Philip of Macedon as a young hostage. At last Anacharsis arrives at Athens where he. attends a meeting of the Academy, and meets Plato, Aristotle, Demosthenes and other Attic orators, and even Diogenes the Cynic. He goes to the Lyceum, where on the way he studies Hymettan beekeeping, and meets the aged Isocrates, who is about to dine with Ephorus and Theopompus (later discussed at length in chapter LXV on the historians); he studies the gymnasium and the palaestra and takes part in an Attic funeral. Interspersed with the narrative text is a series of disquisitions on the library of his Athenian protector Apollodorus, which enables Anacharsis to introduce the intellectual achievements of the Greeks in literature, history, poetry, philosophy, and the physical sciences. There is a whole chapter on Socrates, which attempts to combine

Xenophon, Plato and all the anecdotes about him, and portray him as a true believer in divine inspiration.

It is not until chapter XLI in volume III that Anacharsis travels to Laconia and begins an account of the history and antiquities of Sparta, which although treated fully over several chapters is thus isolated and given a subsidiary role in Greek history. By chapter LIX he is back in Attica discussing Athenian agriculture, and visiting Brauron, Thorikos and the silver mines, and Sunium.

One of the more striking aspects of Barthélemy's narrative sections is the vividness that allegedly eyewitness testimony added to the usual historical descriptions, especially by enabling him to insert into their historical context the personal anecdotes that can be found in later tradition.[35] An excellent example of this is his account of Philip's destruction of the city of Olynthus in ch. LXI; basing it on Demosthenes' Olynthiac speeches, he manages to involve his readers in the tragic and sudden fall of the city and the sale of its inhabitants into slavery; today the ruins of the city remain both a monument to the ruthlessness of Greek warfare, and the best physical evidence for a classical city-state in the age of Aristotle.

At the cost of enormous length Barthélemy succeeded in covering the entire history and antiquities of Greece as they were known at the time: it was an ingenious attempt to solve the problems of Enlightenment historical writing. Contemporaries appreciated the learning and elegance of the work, but recognized immediately that he was more often describing the manners and customs of his own France than those of ancient Greece: although he had succeeded in uniting erudition with history, he had not solved the underlying problem that according to a later generation was only finally achieved by Walter Scott (see ch. 6) – the inclusion of *l'histoire des moeurs* was not sufficient to lift his account out of his own generation into a true *histoire des sentiments*.[36]

CORNELIUS DE PAUW

The Enlightenment historical orthodoxy was finally challenged by the Abbé Cornelius de Pauw of Xanten (1739–1799), the most interesting of all the eighteenth-century authors in the great conflict between Athens and Sparta as model societies. Now largely forgotten in the annals of Enlightenment or Republican history, in his day he was famous: under the *ancien régime* he was briefly 'Private Reader to Frederick II King of Prussia' but decided he did not like court life;[37] and he subsequently appears as a contributor to the supplement of the *Encyclopédie*.[38] After the Revolution he was listed among those foreigners given honorary French citizenship of the new Republic in August 1792.[39] When Napoleon visited Xanten in 1802 he remembered the learned author and, displeased with his simple gravestone, ordered a small Egyptian obelisk to be erected in his honour, which still stands in the town.

There is very little biographical information about de Pauw. I have not investigated the cathedral or civic archives at Xanten, but unless there are papers preserved there, the only surviving contemporary references to him seem to be a pair of letters addressed to him that form a chapter of *La République Universelle* (Paris 1792) by his nephew, the notorious revolutionary Anacharsis Cloots.[40] De Pauw was clearly an important inspiration for Cloots (whom he is said to have educated); Cloots was a wealthy Prussian baron, the advocate of a world parliament, and one of the most extreme of the revolutionaries, who was guillotined by the Committee of Public Safety in 1799 at the instigation of Robespierre on a trumped-up charge of being an Hébertiste.

De Pauw appears to have been well known among Enlightenment authors as a radical thinker; his works are listed in the comprehensive library of Edward Gibbon,[41] and Carlyle knew of him:[42]

> But of all strangers, far the notablest for us is Baron Jean Baptiste de Clootz; or, dropping baptisms and feudalisms, World-Citizen Anacharsis Clootz, from Cleves. Him mark, judicious Reader. Thou hast known his Uncle, sharp-sighted thoroughgoing Cornelius de Pauw, who mercilessly cuts down cherished illusions; and of the finest antique Spartans, will make mere modern cutthroat Mainots. (De Pauw, Recherches sur les Grecs, &c.) The like stuff is in Anacharsis: hot metal; full of scoriae, which should and could have been smelted out, but which will not.

He had earlier been the author of two works of *Recherches philosophiques*.[43] The first was on the native Americans (1768), which aroused great controversy at the time, but is now chiefly recalled for his eccentric views, in believing (without ever having visited it) that the New World bred stunted natives and plants, and even caused the deterioration of the

European settlers.[44] Olivier Contensou has shown that this is a polemical work designed to discredit Rousseau's theory of the Noble Savage. De Pauw's second work, 'sur les Égyptiens et les Chinois' (Berlin 1773), was similarly intended to combat the ideas of Voltaire and his acolytes on the origins of Chinese civilization in a migration from ancient Egypt and its superiority over European culture.

On the eve of the Revolution de Pauw turned his attention to the ancient Greeks in his last work, *Recherches philosophiques sur les Grecs*, in two volumes, which was published simultaneously in Berlin and Paris (1787–8) and collected in his *Oeuvres Philosophiques* as vols VI–VII in year III of the Revolution. His nephew Anacharsis Cloots welcomed the book:[45]

> I congratulate you on the prodigious success of your Greeks. This profound and luminous work will mark an epoch in the Republic of Letters. Despite the great number of your admirers, the yelping voice of three or four critics is only to be expected. But if the most famous of the Greeks has found a Zoilus, is it not natural that the author of the Researches on the Greeks should meet with a Fréron? It is the inevitable fate of the most distinguished writers to be praised by some and blamed by others.

And he described his uncle as:

> A philosopher whose writings have contributed to the destruction of all aristocracies, sacred and profane. The French place your name on the list of the great workers for civil and religious liberty. Voltaire, Rousseau, Pauw etc., are our true liberators.

After the fall of the French monarchy the work was swiftly translated anonymously into English as *Philosophical Dissertations on the Greeks* (published by Robert Faulder, London 1793), which received at least two reviews, one by Tobias Smollett: 'The picture of Greece is by no means flattering, but a faithful likeness, and the author sees often with clearness through the splendid rays, with which antiquarian superstition has illuminated the history of Greece.' It does not seem to have otherwise attracted much attention.[46]

This anonymous translation was by a Captain J. Thomson, who later translated and acknowledged his translation of the work on the

Egyptians and Chinese; and it is connected through complex copyright negotiations with one of the wealthiest and most successful radical publishers of the eighteenth century, George Robinson. A section of Robinson's accounts preserved in Manchester Public Library lists a payment to the translator, who is named; it is not clear whether Thomson was a professional employed by Robinson or a fellow radical. Robinson himself is now almost equally obscure, but is described by a contemporary as the 'King of booksellers'. From the surviving section of his accounts it emerges that he was also the publisher of the famous anarchist and radical William Godwin (1756–1836), husband of Mary Wollstonecraft and father of Mary Shelley. Robinson was known as a convivial and generous man: he supported Godwin with subventions over many years and throughout the gestation of his most famous work, *Political Justice*, for which he paid over a thousand guineas. It too, like the translation of de Pauw, was published in 1793, and only escaped being prosecuted for seditious libel because according to William Pitt the Younger its price of three guineas put it out of the reach of working men; however, in the same year Robinson's firm was fined £250 for publishing Tom Paine's *Rights of Man*. This connection at least demonstrates the radical credentials during the Reign of Terror of the translation of Cornelius de Pauw; and I have gladly used it for my quotations.

After its brief appearance on the radical stage in Britain the work was almost forgotten: in 1894 the author was merely described as 'one of the first to apply the wand of scepticism to Greek history. He questioned the existence of Lycurgus, and depicted the early Greeks as barbarians and pirates.'[47] Subsequently it was noticed briefly by Pierre Vidal-Naquet in 1990, and has since been the subject of three excellent articles by Claude Mossé.[48]

At the start of his work on the Greeks de Pauw places it in the succession of his *Recherches philosophiques*:

> Having published successively some observations on the degraded state of the savage Americans; and afterwards on those nations condemned to eternal mediocrity, like the Chinese and Egyptians: we will now complete this long train of discussions, relative to the natural history of man, by some investigations respecting the Greeks. From the perfection attained by this people in the arts and sciences, we look back with fondness to that point of the globe, which was for us the source of light.[49]

Described as a 'savant écrivain et philosophe paradoxale',[50] de Pauw was in fact a true revolutionary, hostile to the aristocratic world he inhabited and the religion he professed; he was also a very gifted polemicist. The title *Recherches philosophiques* distinguishes his works from narrative history and aligns them rather with contemporary versions of anthropology. Nevertheless, he began his study of the Greeks from the standard eighteenth-century contrast between Athenians and Spartans, but immediately and emphatically declared himself against the Spartans, 'barbarians through obstinacy and pride':

> The Lacedaemonians, in the first place, so far from ever contributing to the progress of science, or the perfection of any one art, conceived glory to consist solely in amassing spoils amidst devastation and carnage. Declared enemies to the repose of Greece, they counted peace in the number of public calamities, and only terminated one war to commence another; until at length they were consumed by the very flames they themselves had kindled . . .[51]

> While the different studies [of philosophy] flourished in this manner at Athens, as completely were they neglected at Sparta; and it is reasonable to suppose, that the observations concerning the Lacedaemonians, contained in the fourth part of this work, will cause some revolution in the opinions of those who have admired that nation with a degree of enthusiasm bordering on blindness. Such erroneous judgements were evidently adopted, from not having examined the constitution of their military government, by the rules of true criticism. Even a very moderate share of penetration will enable us to conceive, that a society composed entirely of soldiers who, as Aristotle observed, languished in peace, and revived but in war, must have proved a dreadful scourge to all the adjoining states. In reality Lacedaemon can be regarded no otherwise than as the focus of civil discord, until, by dint of slaughter and depredation, it had amassed all the treasures of exhausted Greece.[52]

Three-quarters of de Pauw's book was therefore devoted to discussing the Athenians. Behind his interpretation lay a new principle of research. He rejected the importance of the surviving ancient historical narratives of warfare and politics as simply a trivial record of the activities of uncivilized 'brigands'. Even famous battles were dismissed: of Thermopylae he wrote, 'In fact, the whole of that affair was nothing more than the massacre of some men, whose lives were thrown away without any utility either to their own state, or the rest of Greece.'[53]

The great historians of antiquity were also dismissed:

> More occupied with the shocks of discord than the arts of peace, they have confined their observations to the wars of the Greeks, and reserved their encomiums for the lawless actions of robbers. Yet philosophers ceased not to blame, and must always condemn that manner of writing, which occasions so many useless efforts of the imagination, without tending in the least to improve the understanding.[54]

Modern historians were even worse:

> By these details it may be judged, how far the moderns have succeeded, in writing the history of ancient Greece. No new light has ever been thrown by them on this important subject, and they seem to have contented themselves with copying each other ... Doctor Gillies, in publishing a voluminous work on ancient Greece, has not failed to repeat all the common prejudices with regard to the Amphictyons. Men of his class discover a wonderful sagacity in disputing not only on trifling things, but on such as are altogether fabulous.[55] They collect the most insignificant circumstances of the siege of Troy, and the expedition of Jason, even to the number of oars employed by the Argonauts, and doctor Gillies knows exactly the value of the golden fleece in pounds sterling.[56]

De Pauw was no respecter either of earlier *philosophes*: Montesquieu, Voltaire, Adam Smith, and David Hume were all dismissed; he described Rousseau as 'the most inconsistent of all reasoners, [who] has asserted, that the gods alone are capable of living in a pure democracy; but when asked to define the nature of his divinities, he knew not what to answer. When a man puts himself in a situation of being silenced by a single question, his opinions in all such matters should go for nothing.'[57]

He had an equal disdain for learned *érudits*; he described his Dutch predecessor Johannes Meursius (1579–1639) as 'the greatest of compilers and the worst of critics'.[58] Mr Mably was 'the author of some very superficial works on the Greeks'.[59] De Pauw had already attacked the accounts of contemporary travellers in the Americas and China; now he regarded the accounts of modern travellers in Greek lands as deeply flawed, especially the opinions of 'Guys of Marseille' who believed that ancient and contemporary Greek institutions and culture were identical;[60] but even more respectable travellers like Jacob Spon and George Wheler were almost as unreliable. Instead, de Pauw's researches were based on the close reading of references in extant ancient orators, especially the non-political speeches of Demosthenes, and on fragments of lost writers preserved in the late antique lexicographers such as Hesychius and Suidas; few people have ever read these compilations with equal diligence. From these sources he constructed a picture of the Athenians that is startlingly modern in its approach. What interested him were social and cultural questions: the attitude of the Athenians to their countryside; the difference between private meanness and public splendour in architecture; the disposition of Athenians and other Greeks towards melancholy;[61] 'nympholepsy'; the effect of slavery on the economy; the differences between the status of married women and 'courtesans'; the origins of the gymnasium culture,[62] and of nudity; the vice of horse-racing;[63] the strength of Greek wine[64] and its effects on social behaviour; the symposium; the importance of swimming and diving in a system of education that he imagined was devised for a naval community fighting in low-slung ancient warships (hence the justified condemnation of the generals at the battle of Arginusae for neglecting to rescue the drowning rowers: otherwise the Athenians would never have been able to recruit citizens into their fleet).[65] His explanations are not always well-founded, and sometimes frankly bizarre, as for instance his account of 'the causes of what is commonly called depravity of instinct among the Greeks'.[66] But de Pauw consistently asked questions that still resonate with modern historians, even if his answers are often ill-judged and bereft of the evidence that archaeology can now produce.

De Pauw introduced a long section on the Athenian economy with a discussion of the question of '*le luxe*', the luxury of the Greeks,[67] the impulse that, according to Adam Smith and others in the eighteenth century, was being given by conspicuous consumption to the growth of civilization in a world of free trade and commercial enterprise.[68] 'Athens, abounding in manufactures, and peopled almost entirely with artists, was in reality the workshop of luxury, but not its habitation.'[69] Ancient luxury had been much exaggerated: he discussed false views of the excessive luxury of Sybaris,[70] and the effect of female clothing on Athenian consumption. In relation to Athenian luxury he laid special emphasis on the public games, the institution of clubs ('*eranes*'[71]) and symposia, religious festivals and funerals; he concluded that luxury among the Athenians was 'the offspring of religion'. On slavery he made an attempt to calculate the numbers, origins and prices of slaves, and was able to determine the number of domestic slaves in Athens by using what still remains the only firm evidence: the records of manumission in the wills of philosophers given in Diogenes Laertius.[72]

From this de Pauw turned (section V) to the 'Commerce and Finances of the Athenians':

> Great Britain is now generally allowed to excel in manufactures, and the Dutch are considered as the greatest dealers in Europe; but the Athenians anciently united both qualities; and the exports of their celebrated productions would have been incomparably more lucrative than those of the Tyrians or Carthaginians, had they not been constrained to expend enormous sums in purchasing grain at foreign markets.[73]

The chief of these markets was the Tauric Chersonesus, 'now called the Crimea', which he described at length. He also made extensive use of the maritime speeches of the orators, discussing ancient bills of exchange,[74] laws respecting trade, the importance of fairs and the distant travels of merchants as far as China and the Baltic.[75] Athenian shipowners were experts in maritime insurance frauds (loading cargoes of worthless goods in ships that then sank),[76] such as only the Dutch know how to control. There were Athenian farmers in the Crimea, which had a lucrative trade in grain, salt fish, leather, and wool; Amphipolis was an important trading post for timber and silver.[77] For the money of Athens, 'the figure of a screech-owl was generally chosen for such purposes, as if it had been intended to select the least graceful of animated forms, like those barbarous and gothic hieroglyphics, called arms by the nobility of Europe'. Their standard was their native silver not gold; bankers could expect as much as 30 per cent on loans, but more usually 12 per cent.[78] The revenues of the Republic of Athens are listed and compared with those of France, as computed by M. Necker in his book, who records a mere 3 per cent land revenues for France, while the Thriasian plain was taxed at 8 per cent.[79] De Pauw deplored the hoarding of precious metal by Pericles in temples, but noted that the Athenians had no national debt except under the

Spartan regime of the Thirty Tyrants. This is the most insightful analysis of the Athenian economy until at least the work of August Boeckh a generation later (see ch. 8).

> Some nations, like the Poles and Sclavonians in general, seem to have an innate propensity for anarchy; but the Athenians, on the contrary, were no less naturally inclined towards order and legislation.[80]

De Pauw's description of Athenian law and law courts was startlingly original, and was combined with a panegyric of Solon's activities as a lawgiver, though as a political reformer he had failed, and his work had to be completed by Cleisthenes – the first mention of the role of Cleisthenes in the creation of the democracy.[81] He approved of arbitration as the first step in law; ostracism was an excellent institution[82] and Solon's legal reforms in relation to the economy were praised for their encouragement of manufacture and trade. Again, de Pauw used the orators to give a good account of such complex institutions as the use of mortgage stones to record debt on property. Because of the size of their juries and their selection by lot, the Athenian law courts were greatly superior to modern European ones, which were 'worthy of cannibals'[83] and allowed no appeals; he added advice for his own age:

> General maxim: in a well-governed country all criminal courts belonging to lords of manors must be abolished; because they are neither properly constituted, nor composed of enlightened men[84]

Like the British, the Athenians encouraged piracy to disrupt the trade of others;[85] they had excellent measures to prevent illegal exploitation of the silver mines, and to curb the control of the aristocratic council of the Areopagus. De Pauw highlighted the importance of the reform of the Solonian law code by Nicomachus at the end of the fifth century,[86] and discussed the law on impiety.[87] Torture was not allowed in investigations, and sentences of death were mitigated by the invitation to both prosecution and defence to propose penalties;[88] even the use of hemlock was softened by the addition of opium. He praised the institution of Scythian police, the practice of funeral eulogies, and the care for the orphans of those killed in battle. He concluded:

> Englishmen complain that they are destined to suffer two great evils, the influence of their kings in parliament, and that of robbers on the highway. The Athenians, who enjoyed more liberty, reasoned better, and did not consider themselves predestinated to any such calamities.[89]

There followed a long section VII on the fine arts, sculpture, music, and tragedy, the philosophical sects, the grammarians and the growth of theology in late antiquity. The decline of Greece in the Roman period was related to these 'violent debates on incomprehensible points of theology':

> It was in this manner that theological quarrels, which are the true symptoms of an ignorant age, were fatal to the Greeks; and every nation, absurd enough to follow their example, must experience a similar destiny.[90]

De Pauw's ideas were conceived in the last years of the *ancien régime*, and his true revolutionary colours were revealed in his account of the government of the Athenians. In contrast to the republic of Venice, whose institutions were produced by chance:

> The republic of Athens, on the contrary, was formed with reflection; for whenever any thing appeared defective, it failed not to be corrected; and even that law was changed, by which Solon had excluded the lowest class of citizens from the magistracy.
>
> Aristotle is deceived when he pretends, in his political works, that this legislator established a perfect democracy at Athens. Modern authors have repeated the same error, without perceiving that Solon had formed in reality a mixed constitution, where the popular interest was strongly chained down by aristocracy.
>
> Whenever a man of probity, acknowledged as a citizen, can be excluded from the magistracy under pretence of indigency, we may be assured that democracy is there very imperfect: and dreadful inconveniences must result from such principles. Athens would have suffered greatly by being deprived of the abilities of many illustrious citizens, had poverty removed them from the government. There, as in other places, the rich possessed less sagacity than the poor, whose necessities served to sharpen a weapon, which soon grows blunt in the bosom of abundance . . .

> Many suppose that a degeneracy has since succeeded gradually in the moral character of most European nations, until reduced to the condition of Asiatics, they are now no longer capable of supporting the weight of a republican government . . .
>
> Independent of this change in the moral characters of men, enervated by luxury, and accustomed for many ages to the yoke of an individual, it is easy to observe, that the whole of Europe has been conquered by German nations, who were notoriously averse to republican government. Each horde had a king; some had even more than one; and every conquered state became a monarchy.[91]

The institutions of the classical Athenian democracy were described in remarkably accurate detail. There were nine archons chosen by lot whose position was purely honorific and did not extend to the command of the army:

> Never was Montesquieu more unfortunate than when he undertook to speak of the Greeks; unacquainted with their language, he depended on faithless interpreters, and proceeded without having any notion whatever of the republic of Athens.[92]

The Senate was also appointed by lot, and likewise had no power of executing anything, unless it had been examined and approved by the nation. It was composed of 500 men, fifty from each of the ten tribes, who were called 'Prytanes' and partook of a dinner every day; 'Whenever an Athenian had distinguished himself by his patriotism, either in war, or peace, he was entitled ever afterwards to a place at the table of the senators.'[93]

By the year 1793 such an account of Athenian democracy was extremely controversial, and de Pauw's English translator had to apologize for it in his preface, asserting that ancient slavery was introduced by the rich in order to subvert democracy, and to ensure that the free population remained stable at 20,000; this might help to reassure English readers imbued with the standard conservative prejudice against Athenian democracy. He also pointed to de Pauw's distinction between 'fits of *Laocracy*, the great disease of popular constitutions', and representative democracy.[94]

As for the religion of the Athenians, de Pauw had no respect for 'the immense chaos of Grecian paganism',[95] 'a fantastical edifice, which had neither root in heaven, nor foundation on earth'.[96] He despised oracles:

> Impostors have never been wanting in either savage or civilized nations, to appropriate to themselves alone the power of interpreting pretended mysteries; and such was the origin of the oracle of Delphi.[97]

The Mysteries of Eleusis were designed for the profit of the State and the 'hierophantes':

> The dames of Athens, in open cars, superbly ornamented, led the way in these orgies; and their amorous adventures, says Aristophanes, commenced long before they reached the place of their destination ... Le Poussin has chosen these ambulatory Bacchanalia to decorate several of his paintings, and they appear likewise on some ancient bas-reliefs, found at Eleusis.[98]
>
> It was therefore altogether natural, that the women of Athens should discover the greatest predilection for Eleusis, where luxury, love, intrigue, libertinism, gaming, and commerce, were so closely connected.[99]

Callias was 'the great torch bearer of Ceres, and consequently one of the principal actors in these holy frauds, called mysteries':

> This man was regarded as the model of bad citizens; and never did Athens produce any person with a more depraved heart, or more fatal genius. He had publicly an incestuous connexion with a mother and her daughter; and after having dissipated the large fortune of his father Hipponicus, he lived afterwards entirely by exactions, calumnies and intrigues. Greece never produced a greater villain, or more despicable wretch; and Iphicrates treated him as an imposter before all the Athenians.[100]

Turning to Sparta in the last section of the book, de Pauw described the character of their conquests:

> This depredation, carried on for many centuries by such insatiable robbers, forms the most gloomy picture in Grecian history. Perfidy is constantly seen there substituted for open force; and all notions of justice, however sacred, were always sacrificed to the smallest allurements of sordid interest.[101]

De Pauw attacked the dissertation of M. de Gourcy ignorantly crowned by the Academy of Inscriptions: he was 'an extravagant enthusiast, who betrays a total ignorance of ancient history'.[102] As for the non-existent 'Laws of Lycurgus':

> From all these whimsical arrangements, in which Lycurgus had no part, resulted at length a form of government so irregular, that it could not be defined by any Greek politician; and no nation ever attempted to adopt it as a model.[103]

The chief vice of the Spartans was their national avarice; de Pauw expanded on their covetousness and consequent wealth, the corruption of the Ephoroi by the rich, their military incompetence, even their armour (the short pike was no match for the Macedonian *sarissa*). As for the women of Sparta:

> Among military nations, the morals of the women must necessarily be very corrupt; and this cause, more than any other, accelerates the ruin of all societies founded on force, and maintained by violence. In considering the miserable debasement of those women who now follow armies, we perceive what terrible chastisement nature has destined for a profession so contrary to its view, as well as to all notions of reason . . . It is equally surprising and true, that the women of military states are exceedingly fearful, and more cowardly than those of pacific nations.[104]

On the famous Spartan education he said:

> As it is a great error in agriculture to overlabor the ground, it was equally injudicious in the Lacedaemonians to harass their troops too much with military exercises . . . It has been the constant care of all polished nations to restrain the quarrelsome propensity of male children: but at Sparta, on the contrary, it was encouraged . . . As the song of War among the savages of America, without having any influence on the courage of warriors, augments the spirit of vengeance, which is terrible among barbarians; in the same manner, the verses of Sophron, Spendon, and Tyrtaeus inflamed the vindictive spirit of the Lacedaemonians . . . It is easy to judge from such facts to what a pitch the human mind can be degraded, from a total

> neglect of laws, arts, sciences, and all the civil institutions which alone render man superior to the wild beasts . . . It is sufficient to reflect on the plan of this education, which combined wrestling, boxing, running, hunting, music, dancing, tactics, robbery, and assassination, to be convinced that it affected the bodily functions alone, and smothered the culture of the mind.[105]

Of their conquest of Messenia, de Pauw stated:

> Without excepting even the Tartars, Moguls, Turks, and Mandhuis of China, it is impossible to cite any conquerors, who ever imposed such an infamous yoke on any subjugated country of Europe, or Asia.[106]

The basis of the Spartan military organization was fear of the Messenians; it explained their melancholy, and their taciturnity.[107] Of their famous kings, on Agesilaus 'Xenophon wrote a very pompous eulogy of that pretended hero, who in reality was nothing more than a notorious robber';[108] Cleombrotus, 'who commanded the army of his country at the battle of Leuctra, had got drunk with all the other generals of his council. During this fit of intoxication they determined to attack the Thebans, and in consequence of this they lost Messenia, and brought destruction on the state.'[109]

The town of Lacedaemon itself had initially been ornamented in Eastern style with extravagant pomp and profusion. (Thucydides' description refers only to the city after the earthquake of 460 BC.) Equality of fortune was a chimerical project attributed to Lycurgus: in fact, the Spartans were extremely unequal:

> These inconveniences cannot be remedied by the introduction of the right of primogeniture, because its very essence is destructive of all equality, and tends to reduce all the younger branches to beggary. Since equality of fortune must therefore be considered among the number of projects, morally and physically impossible, it follows, that men who pretended to be philosophers, like Rousseau, or historians like Plutarch, have attributed views to Lycurgus, the absurdity of which is evident even to children.[110]
>
> The nature of political governments is judged, with more certainty from the effects they produce in the country where they are established. Wherever towns are seen successively falling into ruins, it may be

> considered with safety, that the government is oppressive, and consequently unjust. Of this Laconia has furnished a striking example; for, so far from having flourished more under the domination of the Doric Spartans than under the ancient Achaeans, it exhibited nothing more than a depopulated country, stained with blood, and covered with the ruins of its towns.
>
> Such will ever be the fate of all governments purely military: they rise by making conquests, and fall suddenly by losing them. This happened to Lacedaemon from a long train of events, the investigation of which will be sufficient to dispel many ancient and modern illusions.[111]

De Pauw proceeded to describe 'The Causes of the Grandeur and Decadence of the Lacedaemonians':[112]

> The general error of those who have written the history of Greece, consists in a false perception of causes and effects. They always believed that the power of the Lacedaemonians resulted only from the nature of their civil institutions and military exercises; while, on the contrary, they owed every thing to the augmentation of their forces from the conquest of Messenia. No sooner had Epaminondas, after the battle of Leuctra, deprived them of that country, than they were absolutely incapable of making any effectual resistance; and their annals, since that event, form one continual chain of terrible defeats and calamities.[113]

As for their political constitution, 'The government of the real Lacedaemonians of the Doric race, who composed the ruling nation, was an imperfect democracy, kept in chains by two hereditary captain-generals, called kings.' In fact, they were ruled by the Ephors and 'a senate of twenty-eight old men, none of whom could be admitted under the age of sixty, when they began to want vigor and energy';[114] 'these decayed senators' gradually lost their importance in 'that whimsical constitution, formed, as we have observed, by a concurrence of unforeseen causes and political errors'.[115]

Of their colonies (Tarentum, Byzantium, Cyrene and Heraclea), de Pauw said:

> The origin of the Tarentines is not obscure, for they owed their existence to the incredible debauches of the Lacedaemonian virgins. They afterwards embarked for Grecia Magna, which was then, what America is in our days;

> and adventurers, who had not a house in their native country, went thither to build a city.[116]

A brief description of the fate of Sparta in the Hellenistic period followed:

> It is sufficient to reflect on the series of events, exposed here with so much rapidity, to conceive that such must have been the destiny of a constitution purely military. Erected at first by conquests, and plunged afterwards in luxury, it expired at last amid robberies, anarchy, perversity, and corruption.[117]

De Gourcy had praised the descendants of the Spartans, the 'Mainots' who had so successfully defended themselves against the Turks; de Pauw ended with a highly coloured account of the 'history and manners of the Mainots' who finally fled to Corfou and Corsica, where they live as brigands to this day.

It is evident that de Pauw was a true revolutionary, despising not only the learning of the *ancien régime*, indeed, but also its political institutions, its monarchy, its religion, and its economy. His interpretation of Greek civilization was idiosyncratic and unique; his praise of democracy together with his undoubtedly arrogant dismissal of so many other scholars[118] led to his being ignored by the generation that took up again the study of ancient Greece after the Revolution and continued for the most part to praise the model of Sparta, especially in France. But he remains the most spirited and original of all the Enlightenment writers on the Greeks and, even if we may sometimes find his answers superficial or unsatisfactory, perhaps the only one to continue to offer the modern student of ancient Greece serious questions worthy of study.[119]

The frontispiece to the 1793 edition of Gast's History of Greece. *The engraver Henry Brocas (1766–1837) was a prominent Dublin artist, chiefly known for his portraits and caricatures of public figures in late eighteenth-century Dublin. He often worked for the publisher John Exshaw.*[1]

3
Ireland Invents Greek History: The Lost Historian John Gast

The growing interest in historical studies observable throughout much of western Europe in the eighteenth century is apparent in Ireland also.

J.C. Beckett[2]

This discovery, indeed, is almost of that kind which I call Serendipity, a very expressive word, which, as I have nothing better to tell you, I shall endeavour to explain to you: you will understand it better by the derivation than by the definition. I once read a silly fairy tale, called the three Princes of Serendip: as their Highnesses travelled, they were always making discoveries, by accidents and sagacity, of things which they were not in quest of: for instance, one of them discovered that a mule blind of the right eye had travelled the same road lately, because the grass was eaten only on the left side, where it was worse than on the right – now do you understand Serendipity?

Horace Walpole[3]

It was in Ireland that, even before the French Revolution, the search for a radical history of Greece began. One of my more innocent occupations in retirement was a fortnightly duty as a room steward in the decayed National Trust property of Chastleton House. It was built just after 1600 by Walter Jones, an immensely wealthy lawyer in the Star Chamber, the Court of High Treason, under Queen Elizabeth and James I, who had managed (by whatever means) to obtain the estate of Robert Catesby shortly before he was executed for his part in Guy Fawkes's

Gunpowder Plot. Jones built a uniquely ostentatious house with craftsmen diverted from the Oxford colleges, which is today the most unchanged Jacobean house in England. The reason is that the family of Walter Jones completely failed to match up to their grand house: for four hundred years they simply vegetated in indigent obscurity, often on the verge of bankruptcy. They neither acquired nor married title or fortune; the name of Jones does not resound through British history; scarcely a single member of the family pursued a respectable or rewarding profession; there are no successful lawyers after Walter, nor members of the armed forces, no clergymen, and few of them seem even to have gone to university. Their diaries are full of the price of turnips and the number of crows shot.[4] They claimed to have lost their money in 'the war', by which they meant the Civil War (one of them had fought at the battle of Worcester); and they excused their idleness by saying that as Stuart royalists they were excluded from the benefits of Hanoverian patronage. In the nineteenth century they showed their level of occupation by inventing the rules of croquet, and several card games. They slowly lost whatever land they had; but they loved the house, their only claim to gentility, and they kept it in repair as best they could. Finally in 1991, after nearly 400 years, the last owner departed with her twenty-four cats, and the National Heritage Fund presented the house and its contents to the National Trust. After undertaking essential repairs to the property, the National Trust opened it to the public in 1996.

It is a numinous place, full of dust and neglect. The grandest room of all, the Long Gallery in the attic, is still unfinished. The contents (apart from some wonderful early tapestries) are of little value, and so the task of a steward is a peaceful one, to sit in a different room on each occasion, chatting to visitors and reflecting on the minute changes wrought over four hundred years of uneventful history.

The library (apart from housing the Bible that was reputedly used by Charles I on the scaffold, donated by the family of Archbishop Juxon of Little Compton, just down the road), is a relatively modern creation and quite unremarkable; it represents the quiet silting-up of the pastimes of unbookish generations, whose chief reading was the *Gentleman's Magazine*, the novels of Walter Scott, or works on estate management and local antiquities. I had spent many happy afternoons staring at the spines of the books (which are protected from being inspected by piano wire) – before slowly one of them began to impinge on my consciousness: it was labelled

'Gast's History of Greece', in an obviously eighteenth-century binding. This was a book I had never heard of: what could it possibly contain?[5]

This nagging question drove me finally in March 2008 to investigate John Gast on the web. There was no information available in any current biographical dictionary (another eighteenth-century John Gast, the first trade unionist in the dockyards, captures all the attention). I turned to the ultimate source for all serious bibliomaniacs, the website AbeBooks, which offers a comprehensive list of those books for sale in the English-speaking world and most of the continent of Europe. To my delight there were several copies of Gast's *History* for sale, with various dates and different titles, and with different publishers, all from the eighteenth century. I ordered the cheapest – obviously, I thought, a pirated edition, being printed in Dublin, that notorious centre of book pirates, and published later than all but one of the others, in 1793.

I was wrong. It arrived as two unbound volumes, and the title page revealed that the work was written by John Gast D.D., Archdeacon of Glandelagh and vicar of Newcastle, a tiny hamlet just within the Pale near Dublin. This two-volume edition had been seen through the press by his friend and former pupil Joseph Stock after Gast's death in 1788, and it was published by John Exshaw, a very respectable publisher and bookseller, twice Lord Mayor of Dublin.[6] Most valuable of all, the editor had included a personal memoir of the author as a preface, which contained a description of how the work had been created in its various versions, to arrive at its final form as a grand narrative of more than twelve hundred pages.

But there was an earlier version of the work, which was entitled *The rudiments of the Grecian history, from the first establishment of the states of Greece to the overthrow of their liberties in the days of Philip the Macedonian. In thirteen dialogues.* It was published in Dublin by private subscription in 1753,[7] a generation earlier than any other known critical history of Greece, and the year before the publication of the first volume of David Hume's *History of England*, ultimately a far more popular subject, which however at the start Hume claimed 'after the first ebullitions of ... fury ... seemed to sink into oblivion', only forty-five copies being sold in a twelvemonth. In the summer of 2009 a copy of this first version that had once belonged to Erasmus Darwin appeared on the antiquarian market, and I was unable to resist the temptation to buy it: it is autographed 'Dr. Darwin' and contains a number of manuscript notes.[8] This book covers the history of Greece from the mythical period to the death of Philip of Macedon in approximately 650 pages – already a substantial work compared to anything before the early nineteenth century.

This first version was apparently occasioned by Gast's work as a teacher (he ran 'a school of great reputation' in Fishamble Street alongside his clerical duties),[9] and is written in dialogue form. There are three characters, 'a master, a scholar who has made some progress in ancient history, and a novice'. The catechismal style of teaching goes back in Irish education as far as Saint Patrick and early Anglo-Latin; it was fascinating to find it still in use in Dublin as late as the eighteenth century. As a result of this publication the University of Dublin conferred on the author the degree of D.D. 'without any expence'. But later his friends persuaded Gast that in the age of David Hume the dialogue form was too antiquated for the modern world, and he undertook to turn the text into a straightforward narrative.

JOHN GAST AND JOHN MURRAY

Before doing so, however, he wished to continue his history from the age of Alexander 'to the present day'. This took Gast many years; finally in the early 1780s John Murray, the famous London publisher, in contact with Joseph Stock, who was editing for him the works of Bishop Berkeley, got wind of other histories of Greece being prepared, those of John Gillies in Edinburgh and of William Mitford in England.[10] Murray urged Gast through Stock to publish at least this second part of the work separately to forestall competition, and the book *The History of Greece, from the Accession of Alexander of Macedon, till its final subjection by the Roman Power* was finally issued by John Murray in London in 1782. This book is available in the Bodleian Library in a fine quarto volume, in the same format as the original edition of Gibbon's *Decline and Fall* (whose first volume was published by Thomas Cadell in 1776, and the remainder between 1781 and 1788); and, as I later verified, this is the volume in the library at Chastleton. On a visit to Dublin I was able to inspect the copy presented by the author himself to Archbishop Marsh's Library of St Patrick's Cathedral.

The Chastleton copy shows little sign of having been opened, but it does contain the autograph on the flyleaf of 'J.H. Whitmore'. John Henry Whitmore (1795/6–1853) was the great-grandson of Sir William Whitmore, whose sister had married the fourth owner of Chastleton; and he inherited the house in 1828 on the demise of the direct line of Joneses, taking the name Whitmore-Jones; he came with money and ideas: he was responsible for buying much of the antique 'Jacobean' furniture in the house, and for rearranging its internal layout, creating for instance the first dining room, installing a modern range in the kitchen, and probably reducing most of the fireplaces in order to take coal, now available in the Banbury region with the opening of the Birmingham–Oxford canal. To judge from the way John Henry Whitmore signs his name (still unhyphenated), this book, like many in the library, came with him from his own family. In view of the relationship between Gibbon and Gast discussed below, it is interesting that the Chastleton library contains a set of Gibbon with 'Gibbon Decline Fall Roman Empire' on the spine, the first volume in the third edition of 1777, the last five volumes in the first editions of 1781 and 1788; and it also contains the separately published first volume in the first edition of 1776, with 'Gibbon's Roman Empire' on the spine. None of these books gives the impression of having been opened, and none contains an autograph.

Joseph Stock's introduction of 1793 includes a number of letters about the competition for primacy between Gast, Gillies, and Mitford; and in the autumn of 2008 I visited the John Murray Archive, recently deposited in the National Library of Scotland, Edinburgh.[11] This contains a series of manuscript books into which all letters written by John Murray were copied in longhand, as a record of the publisher's dealings with his authors. These letters reveal in great detail the entire publishing history of the volume of 1782; they offer indeed one of the most complete records of the publication of any book before the modern age.[12]

In fact, from the John Murray Archive, it appears that the connection with Gibbon was far more than accidental. John Murray had been impressed by the huge success of the first volume of Gibbon's *Decline and Fall* (which ended with the controversial chapters XV and XVI on the role of Christianity in the decline and fall), published in 1776 by one of his main competitors in publishing, Thomas Cadell; and he was searching for a response. From the correspondence it emerges that John Murray had heard through Joseph Stock (one of his authors) about his friend John Gast's work, and the idea of a rival history of Greece greatly attracted him. Gast replied that the entire work would consist of three volumes in quarto, but he was not yet ready to publish, and not worried about forestalling other writers, notably John Gillies. He did, however, suggest the possibility of publishing separately as 'a thick quarto' ten of his 'books' that were already finished, 'from the beginning of Alexander's reign to the final subjection of the Grecian people to the Roman power'. The rest could follow later. This idea of a 'decline and fall of Greece' was even more attractive to John Murray, who wrote with suitable advice on how to approach such a theme:

> I have observed that all our successful historical writers, particularly Hume, Gibbon and Robertson, have reduced their works to the level of the understanding of common readers. They interrupt not their narratives either with deep learning or with profound criticism. They preserve the thread of their story from interruptions of all kinds; they heighten its interest, and carry their readers to the conclusion impatient to unwind the chain of events, and to enjoy the catastrophe . . . I do not mean that references to Authorities should not be given; these we find in the authors I have mentioned and should be given in a similar manner. I only contend that an historian should render his work as interesting to the reader as truth will permit. Affect the heart properly, and the business is accomplished.

But when the first sections of Gast's manuscript arrived, Murray began to have doubts: he wrote confidentially to Stock, 'If the performance is deficient in anything it is in elegance and correctness of style.' This work was clearly never going to compete with the great triumvirate of historians. Nevertheless, Murray was impressed with the subject matter and the way that 'Mr Gast writes more from the heart than any of the Historians.' He proceeded to enlist the help of half a dozen literary friends to rewrite Gast in more elegant English. Then he got cold feet at this tampering with the manuscript, and decided to send Gast twenty-two sheets printed up, for him to agree to the corrections, made by 'a few learned Friends who approved of the intrinsic Merit of the performance, but recommended, as indispensibly necessary, a little more polish to be made in the Style in order to accommodate the Work to the Taste of the Times'. Unfortunately, he sent the package through William Hallhead, a publisher in Dublin, who went bankrupt and never delivered it. When Murray received no reply, he became very anxious; and when the next batch of proofs was ready, he persuaded his brother-in-law, Mr John Ormston of Dublin, to deliver them personally to Gast's house. Only then was the reason for Gast's silence revealed, and the package was retrieved from the bankrupt publisher. But the damage had been done: Gast now had over 400 printed pages of his corrected text, and it was far too late to object.

Gast was a dilatory author, and the last sections arrived very slowly. Murray had heard that Gillies's as yet unpublished volume 'enlarged a good deal upon the manners, customs, weapons, literature, philosophy etc of the Ancient Greeks . . . It may be advanced that you mean to perform what I require in the first part of your History, which is to follow the present publication – it may be answered that it is necessary to do it in both, the Age of Miltiades and Aristides etc being very different from the successors of Alexander down to the final reduction of Greece to the Roman yoke.' So Murray asked for a preface and an introduction giving 'some account of manners, Customs etc etc of the periods of people whose history you record'. On 14 January 1782 he asked plaintively if the work was to finish with Book VIII, since Gast had indicated more sections, but had not sent them. Finally on 26 February he gave up, and decided to publish what he had, rewriting the preface and leaving the introduction, an index, and the fragments of books IX–X that Gast had finally released, to a possible future edition.

Murray tried to mollify Gast, who (he imagined) would naturally object to his treatment of the text:

> Now that the business is thus far advanced, I have to assure you that if my nearest relation had been the author of the work I could not have attended to it more diligently, or taken more pains to introduce it with reputation into the world. Some errors it is impossible but you should discern, but I flatter myself that these are but few compared with the improvements (and these without altering intentionally a single idea of the authors) which have been made. But were the errors derived from my management to be much more numerous than at present I can conceive them to be, you have this consolation that 500 copies only are printed, and that if the book is in request you will soon have an opportunity of removing all errors in a new edition.

In April, Murray was busy pushing the book: he sent sixty copies to Gast in Dublin, to be sold for his benefit and in an attempt to forestall a pirated edition from Dublin publishers; he asked Stock to contact his important friends in Ireland, and himself proposed delivering copies to the two most famous Irishmen in London, Edmund Burke and Edmund Malone. There is no record of any response from Burke; but Malone, a friend of Johnson and Boswell, the first scholarly editor of Shakespeare, and schoolfellow of Gibbon's great patron Lord Sheffield, was complimentary.[13] Murray arranged for a review in the new *European Magazine* for May, which remarked on the previous lack of any serious history of Greece and the fact that 'the learned author of this work, belongs to a country which is now rising to eminence in every path of national glory', and compared Gast favourably with Gibbon:

> Dr Gast is equally a friend to religion, and to the liberties of mankind; and, unlike to the historian of the Roman empire (Gibbon) the zeal of our historian is uniformly directed to promote the best interests of human society.

One suspects indeed that Murray had a hand in the actual writing of the review; for he had asked Gast or Stock to supply some biographical information for the section of 'Anecdotes of the Author', which (despite their apparent failure to comply) duly appeared in the June issue of the magazine, clearly invented by the publisher.[14]

There was also a long review of the work in *The Monthly Review* for 1782; the review is anonymous, but was in fact written by William Enfield, a prolific reviewer with no special expertise in antiquity.[15] He begins by commenting on the originality of Gast's subject:

> It is somewhat surprising, that, although there is no portion of history which seems to invite the labours of the historian with fairer promise of success, than that of ancient Greece, this undertaking has never yet been executed in the English language, in a manner which has commanded any high degree of attention or applause. From the valuable materials for such a work, preserved in records which always lie open to the examination of the learned, it was natural to expect that some able and industrious writer, for the reputation of his country, and for his own, would, long before this time, have produced a history of Greece, which might have appeared with credit on the same shelf with our modern histories of Rome, England, and Scotland.

> This, we presume, is the undertaking which, with respect to a part of the Grecian History, Dr. Gast has here attempted. For what reason he has chosen to write the history of the Decline and Fall of the Greek States, rather than that of their Rise and Progress, we are uninformed. In the latter, he would certainly have found a greater variety of interesting facts, and a richer collection of excellent models: and there seems no ground to apprehend that the execution would have been attended with greater difficulty, or that the work would have been less acceptable to the Public. That part of the Grecian history of which Dr. Gast has chosen to treat, is, however, sufficiently splendid and instructive to merit the labour he has bestowed upon it.

These comments show the reviewer's independence from John Murray's promotional efforts, and the originality of Gast's theme of Greek history, as well as the evident oddity of starting with the 'Decline and Fall'. The reviewer continues with a brief account of the contents of the work, before passing judgement on it:

> Such, in a general view, is the field of history which Dr. Gast has gone over. The materials (except perhaps that, in some cases, he leans towards the side of credulity, particularly in retailing so much at large the marvellous tales of Quintus Curtius respecting Alexander) are judiciously selected; and the arrangement is clear and perspicuous. If the Author discovers no peculiar depth of penetration in his reflections, he neither offends his reader with novelties, nor dazzles him with subtleties. In this respect, a pretty close resemblance may be observed between his manner and that of the popular *Rollin*. His style, if not highly ornamented, is, in common, correct and perspicuous.

After several pages of quotation, the review concludes:

> On the whole, we are so well satisfied with the execution of this History, that we recommend it to our Readers, without scruple, as a work of real merit and utility. – A judicious Index would have been a valuable addition to so large a work.

A similar judgement was pronounced by the *Critical Review* for 1782;[16] after a long synopsis of the work, with excerpts from Gast's descriptions of Alexander the Great and Julian the Apostate, the author concludes:

> It now remains, that we offer a definitive opinion of the merits of our historian. – His judgement is greater than his genius; and his learning is more considerable than his discernment. Among the second class of historians he is entitled to a place. His research is laborious; and he has been enabled to make the proper use of his industry, by an intimate acquaintance with the Greek learning. The authorities upon which he builds are the best and the most authentic; and his subject, at least in the English language, has the charm of novelty; for the Grecian story, though rich in events, has been unaccountably neglected by British writers. In his manner our author is modest and unassuming; and though his knowledge does not allure by its brilliancy, nor strike with its force, it is flowing and perspicuous.

Despite these somewhat lukewarm receptions, the publication was by no means a failure; but equally it was not a great success, as Murray's final letter to Gast reveals. In 1784 Gast asked for £100 in royalties, and offered a further volume of the *History* to be prepared in return. Murray was not willing to meet his demands:

> I attend to what you mention of the first part of the Grecian History that you have nearly ready, and which you have been induced to proceed in from 'the flattering reception given to the part already published, and at the earnest solicitations of several perhaps too flattering friends'. It will not be supposed that I have an Interest in opposing your Book, for next to the Author I believe I possess the greatest Affection for it, but this affection were it even greater would not permit me to shut my Eyes to facts. – The flattering reception a book meets with is ascertained according to the Ideas of a Bookseller by its sale. The Sale is the <u>touchstone</u> of its reception. Your book has not been reprinted at Dublin, now sixty in all were sent there, are those sold – if they were, it would be no very flattering reception for the Kingdom of Ireland to purchase Sixty copies of any one Book but if they are not sold believe not too much in the flattering reception your Book has met with.

Nevertheless, Murray was willing to accept further volumes on the same conditions as before, to split all profits fifty-fifty. But he was frank about the problems that he had experienced with Gast's style:

> The little Omissions and alterations in the Volume published which you complain of I admit may have happened, but in no great degree. – You was at too great a distance to consult in every Emergency, and it is to be hoped that the correction given to the Style much more than Compensates for these. The truth is that in the dress you sent it your MS. could not have been printed with the remotest Prospect of success. This was not particularly my own Opinion, but that of every Gentleman of learning and taste to whom it was submitted. In this situation what was to be done the reputation of the author as well as the Sale of the Book were concerned and I must either have returned your Work, or venture on the step I took, – the first must have mortified you exceedingly, and the second was dangerous, as few Authors chuse to have their MSS. corrected even to their advantage. I ventured however on the last at the expense of 50 guineas which it cost me and this money which I paid will convince you how essentially necessary I thought the Improvement. Nor perhaps will your Pride suffer upon the Occasion when I tell you that Dr Stuart Author of the History of Queen Mary, Mr Richardson Author of a dissertation on the Manners and Literature of Eastern Nations as well as of a Persian and English Dictionary Mr Liston whom I expect in Town from Madrid as he is now superseded at that Court by Lord Chesterfield and some other Gentlemen of Taste and Learning are the persons to whom your history is obliged for the alterations and I hope Improvements made in its Language. If ever your facts and sentiments were altered it must have been done inadvertently as they studied always to preserve these religiously. After this narrative let me not conceal one thing – the last Book was by far the best written and stood in need of the least Correction and I hope the Improvement Exhibited in it will be continued in that portion of the work which you are now finishing – you should however be active for a history of Greece by Dr Gillies which I formerly mentioned is not abandoned. The Author is expected in Town from Lausanne about this time, if he is not already arrived and his Work I should think will be published early in the next Winter.

After this verdict it cannot have surprised the author that the accounts presented up to 6 April 1784 revealed that although 350 copies had been sold out of 500 printed, there remained a loss of £6 15s 2d on an expenditure of £286 15s 2d.[17] Of that cost a huge £52 was attributed 'To Paid Sundries Correcting and Improving the Language'. Nor can it have surprised the publisher that the author continued to fail to produce the promised new volume.

The volume of 1782 had a respectable afterlife on the continent of Europe. It was reprinted by the notorious book pirate J.J. Tourneisen of Basel in 1797 and was simultaneously translated into German by L.T. Kosegarten as *Geschichte von Griechenland seit Alexanders des Macedoniers Thronbesteigung bis zur endlichen Unterjochung durch die Römer* (Weidmann, Leipzig 1796 and 1798).[18] In 1812 it was used for an *Histoire de la Grèce* that combined Oliver Goldsmith for the early history with Gast for the later, translated by the Duchesse de Villeroy and published in Paris.[19] Thereafter the book fell into obscurity; although I fear that it may well have given John Gillies of Edinburgh the idea of continuing his own very boring *History of Greece* (1786) with a further pedestrian volume in 1807 entitled *The History of the World from the reign of Alexander to that of Augustus*.[20] In Britain the last reference I have been able to find is its use as a source in the twelfth edition (1837) of the standard schoolbook of the late eighteenth and early nineteenth century mentioned in the last chapter, Oliver Goldsmith's *History of Greece*.[21]

THE RUDIMENTS OF THE GRECIAN HISTORY OF 1753

In the preface to his later works[22] Gast divides Greek history into five periods. The first is 'from the earliest accounts to the expulsion of the Pisistratidae'; the second is the 'age of glory' from the Pisistratidae to the death of Cimon; the third the decline from the death of Cimon to that of Philip of Macedon; the fourth 'from the succession of Alexander the Great to the first interference of the Romans in the affairs of Greece'; and finally 'the period which closes the melancholy prospect of the Grecian decline, comprehends the several plans of avowed hostility and of disguised perfidiousness, which the Romans employed in order to subject and accustom this illustrious people to the yoke of servitude'. This stage has lasted until the present age and 'the condition in which the abject race, who now bear the name of Greeks, are to be found at this day, under the cruel and humiliating scourge of despotism'.

The volume of 1753 is devoted to the first three of these periods; and despite its curious dialogue form it is a work of very considerable originality.[23] Indeed, it is the pedagogical device of the dialogue itself that enabled Gast to write the first truly critical account of Greek history in terms both of scholarship and of personal and political opinions. For the pupils are made to repeat and defend the conventional narrative as it appears from a careful but literal study of the ancient sources, while their Master continually explains to them that there is another reality behind the texts that they have misunderstood. Not all Gast's rationalizing interpretations would command widespread assent today, but there is no doubt that they represent critical attempts to discover the truth behind the ancient sources. Thus the view of the 'Second Trojan War' as a trade dispute is nowadays held only by a few dim archaeologists; and only modern producers of Hollywood epics believe that Achilles was treacherously murdered while attempting to change sides, tricked by the offer of the hand in marriage of Priam's daughter – even if Gast can produce a footnote referring this information to two apparently reputable ancient sources, Dictys Cretensis and Hyginus.[24] Nevertheless, the Master in these dialogues is attempting to introduce modern French rational standards of historical criticism to his rather conventional and text-ridden students, in the style that, according to Joseph Stock, Gast himself practised on his own pupils: we are indeed privileged with a view directly into the eighteenth-century Irish classroom.[25]

In the 1753 version the first four dialogues are taken up with the historical treatment of Greek myth, based on French and English antiquarian scholarship of the early eighteenth century. One example of Gast's method, the account of the myth of Saturn and his children, will illustrate how he approaches his task:

> The Poets have feigned, that his Father *Saturn* attempted to devour all his male Children; but that three of them, *Jupiter*, *Neptune*, and *Pluto*, being saved by the Artifice of their Mother *Rhea*, made War on their Father, dethroned him, and banished him to the remotest and most dreary Regions of the Earth. The Universe was afterwards divided among the three Brothers; *Jupiter* had the Heavens for his Portion, *Neptune* the Sea, and *Pluto* the Dominion of the Infernal World – What is the Key to this monstrous Tale, the Learned have not yet agreed. Some will have it, that the whole Account is allegorical, and that these Gods are only the Parts and Powers of Nature represented under sensible forms. Others will tell you, that it is the History of *Noah* and his Children. And others as

> strenuously insist, that it contains nothing but the Revolutions of the Royal Family of *Crete*, which now appear covered with so much Obscurity, through the Ignorance and Love of Fiction of the first Ages. I should be tempted to say, that the greatest Mistake is, to seek the Interpretation of all the Parts of the Fable either in History or Allegory: some, it is likely, belong to the one, and some to the other. The main Parts of the History of the *Grecian Jupiter* may be true, that he reigned in *Crete*, that he was a victorious and happy Prince, and that, after his Death. his grateful Subjects advanced him to divine Honours. But as for his father *Saturn*, his devouring his Children, and his being cast from his Throne, *&c.* it may be conjectured, that here the Allegory comes in: perhaps by this the Wise Men of old meant to say, that the Beauty and Order of Things owe their Rise to the eternal *Jupiter*, and that the Misrule and Confusion of jarring Principles, which had prevailed before, were expelled by his Almighty Will.[26]

Gast continues 'But . . . it is the History of *Greece*, which we are to consider, and I am leading you into the Fairy-Land of Allegory.' Gast was clearly a learned author: the footnotes to this section refer to Vossius, Samuel Bochart, Pierre Daniel Huet, Edward Stillingfleet, Antoine Banier, Richard Pocock's *Travels*, and Cicero's *De Natura Deorum*; elsewhere he cites regularly Newton's *Chronology*, Robert Potter, Henry Dodwell, John Selden, Samuel Prideaux and Bishop Ussher among the English, and André Dacier among the French.

In this account perhaps the most important source is the famous work of the Abbé Antoine Banier, whose work *Explication Historique des Fables* is cited by Gast from the second French edition, although there already existed an English translation of the longer third French edition.[27] It is surely significant that this second edition of Banier had been written in dialogue form as twenty-five 'entretiens': this was probably the literary model that Gast chose for his own work, with its three interlocutors:[28]

> Finally, to render less tedious the reading of a book that treats of so dry a matter, I have preferred the dialogue form to that of dissertations. The discussion takes place in the country house of Eliante; the learned abbé Theophile is the main speaker in the dialogue, his friend Alcidon adds his conjectures to those of the Abbé, and Eliante contributes a few reflections such as an educated lady might provide. (Preface)

But Gast's interpretations are a good deal more imaginative than Banier's rather pedestrian versions of 'mythistory'.

In this section Gast's abiding religious preoccupation is how the Greeks, having descended from the Descendants of Japhet, 'fell from the Knowledge of One Supreme Being, Creator of the World, into Idolatry and Ignorance'.[29] The answer for him lies in the confusion brought into Greece by early migrations, especially the Egyptian migration that came with its own priesthood and rituals, and its allegorical forms of explanation, and in the Greek habit of divinizing great historical figures:

> Their Fables are a Mixture, not only of antient Religious Truths, of Natural Philosophy, and Metaphysical Learning, but also of *Egyptian*, *Phoenician*, *Grecian*, and I may add, *Jewish*, History: so that really it is extremely difficult to arrive at any certain well-grounded Solution concerning any of them. And let me tell you, they, who are most earnest in this kind of Enquiry, oftentimes, after all their Labour, find that they have been pursuing a Phantom, and their whole Reward is to embrace a Shadow. Let us therefore take our Leave of these dim Regions: if I am ever obliged to bring you back to them, it shall only be, when it is easy to find out the Event, disguised under the fictitious Story.[30]

The fourth Dialogue ends with a long essay on 'the several Causes of that Love of Fable, which the *Grecians* were possessed with'.[31]

Gast (we shall see) was a member of an enterprising Irish Huguenot community, and he was very interested in the development of civilization through migration. The Egyptians introduced agriculture and the Eleusinian Mysteries; it was Phoenician settlers who brought 'Commerce, which naturally enlarges the Mind, and opens more extensive Views'; they also introduced 'the Use of Letters' as opposed to Egyptian hieroglyphics, which 'were not Letters of a determinate Signification, but Symbols and Enigmatical Representations, and, as a very ingenious Modern calls them, *a System of Natural Similes*,[32] extremely obscure, and which might be employed to signify different Things'. It was from these immigrants that the Greeks learned 'Commerce, Navigation, and several other valuable Sciences' such as bronze and iron working; only the skills of carpentry, statuary, and architecture, invented by the Athenian Daedalus, are allowed to be indigenous:

> Those Strangers, *especially*, were in Truth all adding to the Strength of *Greece*; they formed her Manners, they encreased her Wealth, and by Degrees made her Mistress of the Improvements of other wise and cultivated Nations. And also, happily for her, they soon forgat their Native Home, they incorporated into one People, and shewed themselves as sollicitous for her Prosperity, as if this had been their original Country ... And possibly to this Mixture it was owing, that she ever attained to that extraordinary Proficiency in Arts and Sciences, and that her Institutions are to this Day the Subject of Admiration.[33]

After this long discussion of the mythical period, Dialogue the Fifth[34] offers a somewhat stilted account of the geography of Greece. The section on Greek history 'proper' begins with 'Dialogue the Sixth'[35] and presents what was to become a typical Enlightenment view: there is of course no conception of an archaic period, which had to wait for its discovery until a century and a half later with Jacob Burckhardt.[36] The references given are mainly to the ancient sources, although Dialogue the Sixth begins with a discussion of Sir Isaac Newton's views on Attic and Spartan chronology,[37] and quotes Rollin,[38] before offering a long account of Lycurgus derived largely from Plutarch's *Life of Lycurgus*. This ends with a discussion of his 'Institutions', some of which may be 'censured without Injustice':

> I have, in the first Place, a Difficulty about the *Spartans* becoming *merely* a *Military* Nation. – Was not Liberty to be purchased, but at the Expence of the Liberal Sciences, and of all the gentler Ornaments of the Mind? Is it not possible, that a People should be *brave*, *virtuous*, *happy*; and be also a *Literate*, *Polite*, *Accomplished* People?[39]

Dialogue the Seventh[40] presents a history of Sparta from the Messenian to the Persian wars, with the customary emphasis on the romance of Aristomenes drawn from Pausanias; it includes a learned discussion of the date of Pheidon of Argos (omitted in the 1793 edition) and an account of Cleomenes and Cleisthenes of Athens. Chronology, it is clear, is an abiding interest of Gast, as it had been of the great chronographers from Joseph Scaliger and Johannes Kepler to Newton and beyond.[41]

Dialogue the Eighth[42] is concerned with Athens. There is a full account of Solon and his constitution, derived mostly from Plutarch, but with a detailed account of the Athenian constitution drawn from earlier French and English antiquarians. Again the importance of trade is emphasized: 'The Advancement of Industry and Virtue was likewise consulted by many excellent and well devised Laws. – Trade and every kind of industrious Occupation was declared honourable'.[43]

Dialogue the Ninth[44] records 'one of the most memorable Periods of Antient History, *the Age of Glory of the Athenian People*', from Harmodius and Aristogeiton to the death of Cimon when 'The *Lawrel-Crown* and the *Ivy-Wreath* were both theirs. And those Men, who yielded to none in the Day of Battle, were also foremost in every refined Improvement'.[45] The explanation for this development is their 'unshaken Resolution in the defence of the noblest Cause, the Cause of *LIBERTY* and the *PUBLIC WEAL*'.

More surprising is Gast's extended praise of Athenian democracy and especially of the Athenian assembly:

> There was also the Great Assembly, in which every Citizen, not declared Infamous, had a Suffrage. – So that in *Athens* the poorest Member of the Commonwealth was immediately interested in the Public Fortune. In Despotic States, it matters not, at least to the meaner Ranks of Men, who has the Power; and Revolutions of Government only bring on a Change of Masters. But here, the lowest *Athenian* had a Country, in the properest sense, to fight for; he was one of the Lords of the Commonwealth; he had real Rights and Privileges; and could not give up the Constitution without being a Traitor to himself.[46]
>
> *Liberty* . . . was also the principal Cause of this; for Science and Arts are always the Attendants of *Liberty. Genius* is, as it were, licentious; it loves to sport itself after its own wanton manner, neither exposed to the Jealousies of Tyrants, nor to the Threats of Laws. It is then only, that the Mind becomes capable of the *wide-expatiating* View, and the *bold-towering* Thought. – Thus it was at *Athens*. There, *Imagination* knew no bounds; and all the Excess of Liberty was fully indulged, except when the Religion of the Superstitious People happened to be wounded.[47]
>
> Another Cause, that contributed to the Advancement of Literature at *Athens*, was *the Form of Polity*. All Matters were referred to the great Assembly of the People; and, as I have told you, neither Domestic Regulations, nor Foreign Alliances, neither Peace, nor War, could be ultimately determined on, till their Consent had given ratification. On these accounts,

> *Persuasion* was among the principal Instruments of the *Athenian* Government; and the lowest Citizens were accustomed to be addressed by Persons, exercised in all the Arts of Speech. Now, this not only made Oratory necessary for those, who were desirous of appearing to advantage in the Public Councils; but also by these means the People themselves were rendered *nice* and *critical Hearers*.[48]

This is the earliest favourable account of Athenian democratic institutions known to me within a standard historical narrative, and is a forerunner of the later radical emphasis on the importance of Athens for the modern history of liberty, from Bulwer-Lytton to George Grote.

In Dialogue the Tenth[49] the story of Xerxes' expedition is told with dramatic and heightened colour. In Dialogue the Eleventh[50] 'Culture and Peace now succeeded to the horrors and desolation, which had afflicted *Greece*; and *Athens* began to rise from her Ruins in far greater Splendor, than even before her Destruction.'[51] The divide between zenith and decline comes with the age of Cimon, the last great Athenian; with Ephialtes and Pericles, Athens entered a period of luxury and decline: of Pericles he says, 'What a Patriot, what a Blessing might this Man have been! but Ambition is a treacherous guide':[52]

> Thus affairs went on, till at length the growing vanity, the haughtiness, and ambition of the *Athenians*, on the one hand, and the envy and various resentments of the *Grecian* States, on the other, brought on a war, which tried the strength of this specious *Fabric*, and has left to succeeding Ages this instructive lesson, that *there is not any Empire can be lasting, but what is founded in Moderation, Justice, and Virtue*.[53]

In the last two Dialogues[54] Gast resorts for the most part to following the narrative of Thucydides and other ancient historians; the twelfth covers the Peloponnesian War, the thirteenth the whole period from its end to the death of Philip of Macedon. There are few notes apart from source references, and those there are concern mostly problems of chronology discussed by Newton and Dodwell. On the other hand the narrative is lively and full of moral judgements, on Pericles and his successors; Epaminondas for instance receives a footnote quoting the eulogy of Le Chevalier de Folard.[55]

The one significant departure in this section from straightforward narrative is Gast's long account of the trial and death of Socrates,[56] whom he portrays as a believer in a '*GOD, One, Supreme, Arbiter of Events, of a Spiritual Nature, Infinite, Eternal, sole Source of Being and Happiness to all, possessing in himself every thing, that is Lovely, Great, and Good*':[57]

> Thus died, says *Plato*, the best, the wisest, the most just of Men, and safely may we say, the Greatest of the *Pagan* World, a Man, who far exceeded all the Heathen, that went before him, and whom none of those, that followed, ever equalled, even with the advantage of that train of light he left behind him. In whom it seemeth as if Providence meant to shew, what the mere strength of Reason could avail towards rescuing Human Nature from its depraved state, and restoring the Empire of Truth and Virtue.[58]

As Gast draws to a close his moral stance becomes ever clearer; referring to Alexander the Great he says 'So has History falsely called him; as if Martial Fury, and the wanton Invasion of Nations, were the excellence of Princes.'[59] And he concludes his *History* with the following sentiment:

> Such are the Effects of *Upright* and of *Degenerate* Manners; the latter always ending in *Weakness* and *Servitude*; the former productive of *Liberty*, *Wealth* and *Empire*. Never, my *Eudoxus*, never my *Cleanthes*, may ye forget the instructive Lesson: *The Ways of Virtue are the Ways of Happiness*. Have it in rememberance. Make the trial. And certainly shall ye find the one, if ye sincerely pursue the other.[60]

Apart from its mild Christian colouring, Gast's account is remarkable for its liveliness and free judgements, and for its liberal sentiments. The approval of Athenian democratic institutions and the criticism of many aspects of Sparta distinguishes his story from other eighteenth-century histories of Greece. The independence of judgement and narrative skill are superior to any other Greek history of the period; the emphasis on the importance of trade and migration reflects the preoccupations of the age of the Scottish Enlightenment, and the moral attitude towards the duties of empire is characteristic of the age of Edmund Burke.[61] Gast is not indeed seeking to change the world in his portrayal of Greek history, but rather to understand those constants that are for him reflected in all periods of history.

This new departure in the study of Greek history was noticed in one review. Matthieu Maty's *Journal britannique* was founded in 1750 to inform French readers of new books in English and ran for six years until 1755. Maty (1718–1776) was himself (as we shall discover) from the same background as Gast; he was the son of a Huguenot exile in Holland who wrote a thesis at Leiden University, published as *Essai sur l'Usage* (on Custom), and was much influenced by Montesquieu. Maty moved to London as a physician, where he promoted vaccination for smallpox and became secretary of the Royal Society and ultimately principal librarian of the British Museum. Maty's periodical is mentioned admiringly by Edward Gibbon in his *Memoirs*, who sent Maty a draft of his first work, the *Essai sur l'étude de la littérature*. Gast's *Rudiments* was given an extensive review in the *Journal* for July–August 1754.[62] After a description of the contents and approval of the dialogue form the reviewer comments in detail on two novel aspects, Gast's treatment of Greek religion, and his emphasis on 'l'amour de la liberté' of the Athenians and 'le part que l'on accorda au Peuple dans le Gouvernement de la République', which were responsible for the florescence of their culture. The article is signed by 'J de C', presumably Jean de la Chapelle (1655–1723) to whom Maty's father had addressed his most controversial work.

THE *HISTORY OF GREECE* OF 1782

To the modern reader the most original and most interesting part of Gast's *History* is his account of the last two periods of Grecian history, which constitute the independent work of 1782 and the second volume of the edition of 1793, and which covers Greek history from Alexander the Great to the Roman conquest, or alternatively the present day. In his article in the *Monthly Review* William Enfield had compared this volume of Gast's with that of Charles Rollin's account of the period, published in 1738;[63] but whereas Rollin merely provides a simple narrative, accompanied by the superficial moral judgements much criticized by his contemporaries, Gast's account offers much more. At first sight it seems indeed an excellent full-length narrative of the political history of

Hellenistic Greece, based on a careful comparison of Arrian, Curtius, Diodorus, Polybius, Livy, and Plutarch, with few references to earlier modern authorities (which scarcely existed for this period). At least this shows how much could be extracted from the ancient literary sources, and Gast's judgement in discussing and choosing between alternative accounts of events is impeccable: for instance, on Alexander the Great he has a very low opinion of Quintus Curtius' account, and always prefers Arrian. It contains some excellent biographical summaries of the character, defects, and achievements of Alexander, his successors down to Demetrius Poliorcetes, Aratus, Philopoemen, Philip V, Cleomenes, and Nabis of Sparta, and Flamininus, Perseus of Macedon, Mummius, and Sulla. But as you read on a deeper argument emerges. Gast is interested (like Gibbon) in the theme of decline and fall. He attributes that of mainland Greece to two main causes, on which he expatiates throughout the narrative. The first is the inability of the Greeks to unite, and their constant appeals to Macedon, the Egyptian Ptolemies, and the Romans to intervene: again and again he takes a particular historical moment and discusses what Aratus or Philopoemen should have done, or why the activities of the Aetolian League were so detrimental to the Greeks. The second theme is the insidious imperialism of the Romans, who emerge as the real villains. Gast is especially opposed to Flamininus, whom he accuses of deliberately fostering disunity among the Greeks in order to provide future opportunities for Roman intervention; but all other Romans are also attacked. In contrast, the figure of Philip V emerges in a highly sympathetic portrayal, as condemned by Roman intransigence to lose his kingdom and his family. This perception of Roman imperialism is opposed to that given in our sources, who take the view that the Romans always acted from the best of motives, and actively promoted the freedom of the Greeks; it is also opposed to the modern orthodoxy that tries to see Roman imperialism as an accidental by-product of a series of random interventions. I confess that I find Gast's view infinitely more persuasive than either alternative as a long-term analysis of Roman intentions. The real villain in the end turns out to be the Roman Senate, whose active pursuit of the interests of their ruling military class created an empire that destroyed the freedom of all peoples elsewhere, and ultimately their own. The final conclusion is therefore that, despite all the mistakes and inadequacies of the Greeks, the fall of free Greece to the Romans was a deliberate consequence of an aggressive imperialism on the part of the Romans. On the death of Philip, 'Rome exulted in her success: she beheld with joy all his bold and well-concerted projects at an end, and in the future vassalage of Macedon, contemplated one more prostrate kingdom groaning under Roman domination.'[64]

It is history presented as tragedy, and it contains such magnificent scenes as the final end of Perseus, the last king of Macedon in 168 BC, who, despite his superior power, having lost the war with incompetent Roman commanders because of his cowardice and meanness with his wealth, is finally left by the Cretan captain who had promised to save him, weeping for his lost gold cups as the night fades, alone on a deserted beach in Samothrace.[65]

The verdict is a powerful condemnation of Rome: finally, the great kingdom of Macedon comes to an end:

> A more severe humiliation can hardly have been devised: indeed, a more complete debasement almost baffles imagination. Must we not then turn with disgust and indignation from those writers, who, after the narration of such facts, wish to convey the idea, that the Roman conquest bestowed liberty on Macedon?[66]

Or a little later:

> In this manner did Rome establish her dominion on the ruins of every national constitution. At first her yoke was for the most part laid on with an affectation of gentleness; but afterwards, repeated arbitrary and oppressive proceedings having provoked resistance, every manly effort against them became an excuse for additional exertion of power; until the system was by degrees completed, and appeared in all the stern severity of despotism.[67]

No Roman ever acts with anything but cruelty and slaughter, massacring whole populations and sending women and children into slavery. The sole redeeming feature of the brutal and philistine Mummius is that he recognized the corrupting dangers of culture when he ordered the sack of Corinth: 'To save Rome he burned Corinth.'[68]

The decline of Greece is attributed to five causes (we may note the keenness on the number five – five periods of history and five causes):

competition between small states; endless jealousies; perpetual revolutions and competing constitutional forms; the natural corruptions of 'the democratical form' in the absence of '*virtue*'; and finally, the 'fatal prevalence of atheistical tenets' spread by Epicureanism.[69]

THE FINAL EDITION OF GAST'S *HISTORY OF GREECE* (DUBLIN 1793)

By the time of the final composite publication in 1793, both the author and John Murray the publisher were dead; John Gast had died of gout in 1788 aged seventy-two without ever finishing the revision of his dialogue volume of 1753. That was done by Joseph Stock, with the final publication of the combined work in two volumes; and it is this version of the text that I had originally bought. According to Stock's preface the dialogue of 1753 had been revised by Gast as far as the second book, when he changed his plan in favour of a more discursive treatment of myth; but after Gast's death Stock returned to the original text, and was himself responsible for the editorial work of creating a narrative out of the dialogue. This version of the first part of Gast's work is in fact less interesting than the original published dialogue; for it has been reduced to a plain narrative that omits the digressions and the learned footnotes that in the text of 1753 often take up all but three lines of the page, and are so important and so curious a feature of the original. But the volume of 1782 appears faithfully transcribed in the new edition. Stock's edition does not seem to have been well received in at least one contemporary review, where it was criticized for its lack of an index or chronological charts, and for the absence of ancient citations.[70] Some of these faults are due to Stock's editing, and others to the failure of the author to carry his project through to completion; but by the end of the century many of the views that Gast had espoused forty years earlier were indeed superseded. It is perhaps symptomatic that my own copy, purchased by someone who is not listed among the 427 subscribers, had never been bound, but is still in its original boards.

GAST, FRANCE AND IRELAND

Despite his dilatoriness and alleged insufficiencies as a writer the virtually complete disappearance of Gast from the historical record is a gross injustice.[71] In his 1952 inaugural lecture at University College London, Arnaldo Momigliano, the greatest expert on the history of ancient history, had begun from the famous words quoted below (p. 107). But Greek history was invented in Ireland thirty years before either John Gillies of Edinburgh or William Mitford of England had published a word. Moreover, although Mitford's work is still of great interest, not least for provoking the early nineteenth-century radicals into writing their own histories of Greece, as a work of critical history Gast's work is superior to both Gillies and Mitford. And above all it was Gast who was the first to write a serious history of the Hellenistic age, eighty years before the German J.G. Droysen (between 1833 and 1843), whose account, while more enthusiastic, offers little historical advance on Gast, as far as the history of Greece 'properly so called' is concerned (though Droysen's work also covers Syria and Egypt);[72] for Droysen was blinded by his Prussian nationalism to the dangers of Roman aggression.

Gast's volumes are a learned and passionate account of Greek history: what are they doing in mid-eighteenth-century Dublin? How could they be so far in advance of any of his contemporaries in both Greek and Roman history? Gast's only significant predecessor had been Temple Stanyan, who remained largely oblivious of antiquarian scholarship.[73] John Gast (1715–1788) belongs rather to the dawn of the new age of critical and engaged narrative history: Hume began publishing his *History of England* in 1754; William Robertson began his great series of histories of Scotland, Charles V, and America from 1759; and Gibbon (1737–1794) was a younger contemporary of Gast. Yet the early beginning of Gast's works and his choice of the history of Greece mark him out in this generation.

The idea of a *History of Greece* was indeed in the air: in 1759, six years after the publication of Gast's initial work, David Hume wrote two letters to William Robertson after the publication of his *History of Scotland*, suggesting to him that he might try his hand at 'the ancient history, particularly that of Greece', and discussing the problems that he might encounter in seeking to improve on Rollin's brief and superficial account:[74]

> The antient Greek History has several recommendations, particularly the good Authors from which it must be drawn: But this same Circumstance becomes an Objection, when more narrowly considered: For what can you do with these Authors but transcribe & translate them? No Letters or State Papers from which you could correct their Errors, or authenticate their Narration, or supply their Defects. Besides Rollin is so well wrote with respect to Style, that with superficial People it passes for sufficient.[75]

One at least of his English contemporaries was known to Gast; in his account of Greece under the Roman Empire he mentions chapter VI of Gibbon's *Decline and Fall* in a footnote:

> With particular pleasure I take the opportunity of acknowledging my obligations to the elegant work, from which the above quotation is borrowed. I have had frequent recourse to it in this part of my history. If I have attempted to place some matters in a different light from that in which this ingenious writer seems to have considered them, I shall hope, from the liberality of sentiment which his writings assure me he possesses, that he will not disapprove of a freedom of enquiry, always serviceable to the cause of truth.[76]

And there are scattered references to Gibbon thereafter. But all these references are to volume I, published in 1776; Gast hardly had time to take account of the next two volumes published in 1781, which end with Gibbon's famous 'General Observations on the Fall of the Roman Empire in the West'.[77]

In Ireland this was the age of the Protestant Ascendancy (1691–1801), also known as the 'long peace'. Dublin was at the height of its prosperity; it was a largely tolerant society concerned with social justice: during the 1770s and 1780s the penal laws were gradually relaxed and Henry Grattan's reforms of 1782 won major concessions for Catholics, until in the 1790s Wolfe Tone's United Irishmen brought Nonconformists, Catholics, and patriots together in a great agitation for reform, which resulted in the disastrous Irish Rebellion of 1798, the Act of Union of 1801, and the end of Irish parliamentary independence.

The most famous Irishman of the day was Edmund Burke, champion of the American Revolution, opponent of the French Revolution, prosecutor of Warren Hastings for his corruption in India, and founder of the theory of empire as a trust, as more generally of modern English conservative political thought. Gast's evident political enthusiasms sit easily in this age: he composed various pamphlets addressed to the Catholic majority in his parish, writing in a conciliatory vein; and after his death his parishioners composed a fine memorial to his good work as a pastor; it is clear that he was instinctively more comfortable with toleration and non-confessional philanthropy than many earlier Huguenots had been. But that scarcely explains his interest in Greek history and the rise and decline of liberty.

I think there is more to be gathered from Gast's ancestry. For he is an outstanding example of cultural transference. According to Joseph Stock's memoir, his parents were Huguenot refugees who came to Dublin after the renewed persecution surrounding the revocation of the Edict of Nantes in 1685; at this time Huguenots were settled in large numbers in Ireland: the Duke of Ormond, who had been himself an exile in France during the English Civil War, was especially active as Lord Deputy in promoting immigration (1662), and many came over with the army of William of Orange.[78] Gast's father, Daniel Gast, had left Saintonge in Guyenne in 1684 to escape persecution, and served as an officer under Queen Anne; he was a doctor by training, and settled in Dublin, where John Gast was born in 1715. Gast was bilingual in French and English, and his clerical career began as chaplain to the important Huguenot military colony at Portarlington, founded by Henri de Massue, Marquis de Ruvigny, a prominent Huguenot courtier in the court of Louis XIV, who had become a supporter of William III, and was created Earl of Galway. In the early eighteenth century Portarlington was a largely French-speaking town composed of veterans divided between Calvinism and the established Church; it possessed a French church and school.[79] Most importantly of all for our present purposes, John Gast's mother, Elizabeth Grenoilleau, is described as a close relative of the Baron de Montesquieu, and later in life Gast received a large inheritance from his French relatives.

In the period before the French Revolution all the English historians of the ancient world acquired their learning from France. Gibbon was a trivial and careless student at Oxford: everything he learned came from his sojourn in Lausanne, and his purchase of the twenty volumes of the *Académie des Inscriptions*:

> I cannot forget the joy with which I exchanged a bank-note of twenty pounds for the twenty volumes of the Memoirs of the Academy of Inscriptions; nor would it have been easy by any other expenditure of the same sum to have procured so large and lasting a fund of rational amusement.[80]

Gibbon's first publication, the *Essai sur l'étude de la littérature*, was written in French. His fellow officer in the Hampshire militia, William Mitford (who had similarly failed to acquire any learning at Oxford), discovered his vocation for history on an extended stay in France in 1776.[81] It is plain from his footnotes that the origins of John Gast's intellectual and historical power lie in France. It was France and Ireland that together made him a serious historian. I have spent many years in tracing the fortunes of the translation of scholarship between the various European languages: the main traffic is between France and England in the *ancien régime*, and outwards from Germany in the nineteenth century. But translation is only a small part of the phenomenon of cultural transference (*transferts culturels* as Michel Espagne calls them).[82] Emigration, personal contact, and bilingualism are equally important, as the example of John Gast shows.

It was France and Ireland that together created the new Irish school of ancient history. Thomas Leland of Trinity College Dublin, translator of Demosthenes and author of the first full-length biography of a figure from the ancient world, the *History of the Life and Reign of Philip of Macedon* (1758), had begun his historical career with a long introduction to his translation of Demosthenes' speeches, following the example of Jacques de Tourreil (1701).[83] For his biography of Philip of Macedon he borrowed the entire structure and much of his material from a French author, Claude-Mathieu Olivier, *Histoire de Philippe* 1736 (Paris 1740); every division of the narrative in Leland is identical to those in Olivier's book, and only the brief comparison between Philip and Alexander at the end of Olivier is missing, with an explicit refusal to follow this practice.[84]

It is plain from his footnotes that the learning in Gast's earlier volume rested largely on French antiquarian scholarship. His philosophical ideas also derive from Montesquieu, who was indeed a dominant influence in eighteenth-century Ireland.[85] For Gast's second volume the grand historical theme of decline and fall had first been adumbrated by Montesquieu in his *Considérations sur les causes de la grandeur des Romains et de leur décadence* (1734), a book that was published simultaneously in French and in English translation, and was the most immediately popular of all his works.[86] Thus in focusing on the idea of decadence Gast and Gibbon have no relationship of interdependence: they rather shared a common model in Gast's relative, the Baron de Montesquieu; both applied antiquarian scholarship to a philosophical model derived from him. Montesquieu also provided the moral dimension for Gast's view of Greek history; this is evident from the one direct quotation of Montesquieu in the work: 'The vital principle of democracy, as a celebrated writer justly observes, is *virtue*.'[87] It comes therefore as no surprise to discover that the entire theoretical structure of Gast's picture of Hellenistic Greece is derived from chapter VI of Montesquieu's *Considérations*, 'De la conduite que les Romains tinrent pour soumettre tous les peuples': it was Montesquieu who attributed the growth of Rome's power overseas to the perfidy and double-dealing of its leaders in the interests of the Roman state. Even Gast's apparently idiosyncratic connection of the decline and fall of Greece with the influence of Epicureanism is to be found at the start of Montesquieu's chapter X in relation to Roman decline, 'De la corruption des Romains': 'Je crois que la secte d'Épicure, qui s'introduisit à Rome sur la fin de la république, contribua beaucoup à gâter le coeur et l'esprit des Romains.'

Long before Gibbon's or his own version of the theme of decline and fall, Gast had already adopted this view of Montesquieu. In his 1753 account of Thessaly he describes 'the *Pharsalian* Plain':

> That fatal Plain, where *Caesar* triumphed over the Liberties of *Rome*. Long ere this happened, had the *Romans* imposed the Yoke on *Greece*: and now *Greece* saw the Day, when *Rome* herself lost her Freedom, and felt the Scourge of Tyrants. Such, *Cleanthes*, is the Fate of the Kingdoms of the Earth. Liberty and Empire are obtained, and lost again, as Nations rise to Virtue, or sink into Dissoluteness. When once *Greece* was enervated thro' Luxury and Vice, she fell an easy Prey to the Power of *Rome*; and when *Rome*, venal and corrupted, was no longer able to preserve her Liberties, *Caesar* stepped in, and inslaved her, as she had inslaved the World before.[88]

Reinhart Koselleck has shown how the end of the eighteenth century is the bridge or *Sattelzeit* between the static conception of *historia magistra vitae* and the conception of history as a dynamic living process in human society. John Gast stands at the start of the older tradition of the eighteenth century: for him the truths of history are eternal and unchanging; and yet the conception of a decline and fall, the potential corruption or destruction of apparently stable human societies is (as for Gibbon) the underside of the age of Enlightenment, the morbid fear of and preparation for the revolution that was indeed to destroy their world. Gast had experienced the intolerance as well as the benefits of the *ancien régime*, and he lived in an Irish society poised between urban prosperity and rural poverty: as many as 400,000 may have died in the first Great Irish Famine of 1740–41, while the 1780s saw an unprecedented economic boom in Dublin.[89] The classical parklands created by the Irish aristocracy, which were celebrated in the paintings of one of Ireland's greatest artists, Thomas Roberts (1748–1777),[90] involved extensive enclosures and 'improvements', with consequent dispossession for the Irish peasantry, as Oliver Goldsmith revealed in his moving lament for a vanished world, *The Deserted Village* (1770):[91]

> Ill fares the land, to hast'ning ills a prey,
> Where wealth accumulates and men decay.
> Princes and lords may flourish, or may fade;
> A breath can make them, as a breath has made.
> But a bold peasantry, their country's pride,
> When once destroyed, can never be supplied.
>
> (lines 51–6)

A reflective spirit might indeed detect something unhealthy in the great age of Irish classicism; and the Huguenot refugee John Gast, however much he was a member of the Ascendancy ministering to the education of the elite of his day, was in a position to understand well the insecurities of human society. His final sentences read:

> Of how uncertain a tenure are even the advantages of human genius! Greece, famed for arts and arms, from whose horizon beamed forth those rays of science, which have gradually illumined our European world, now stands in need of the instruction she was wont to give. From those nations, whom she held most in contempt, she is at this day to learn what Greece once was. And were it not for the learned researches of those very

> barbarians, whom in her age of glory she had deemed it a reproach to have numbered among her denizens, the fierce German, the unlettered Caledonian, the barbarous Briton, the rude Gaul, many of her most highly valued marble records had remained unread, and some of her noblest memorials had been buried in oblivion.[92]

He adds a footnote recording the glory of Britain, the Society of Dilettanti, and Chandler's *Travels* (1776) and the *Ionian Antiquities* (1769) that it produced. But in what category I wonder does Gast include himself – is he the barbarous Briton or the rude Gaul?

The complex story of the fortunes of John Gast's historical works requires us to rethink the origins of the modern historiography of the ancient world. It is not just a personal story: his heritage in Irish and French culture exemplifies the importance of migration and of the Huguenot refugees in the creation of a unified European culture. Many strands in his historical thinking lead back to that fusion of the older seventeenth-century *érudit* tradition with the French *philosophes*, of the combination of antiquarianism and philosophical history that Gibbon celebrated in his early *Essai sur l'étude de la littérature*, and that Momigliano showed still stands as the basis of all modern historical study.[93] In his earlier volume Gast offers an excellent example of the fusion of religious and secular antiquarianism with its special interest in chronology, in the service of history.[94] The typically eighteenth-century theme of decline and fall is seen to derive from the earliest and most influential of the Enlightenment figures, Montesquieu himself. The importance of history as narrative seems indeed to have been invented or rediscovered in the British Isles; but the combination of narrative and antiquarianism to create the idea of a critical history demanded authors like Gast and Gibbon who had immediate access to the whole range of continental scholarship. This was the solution to Hume's problem of how to create a modern narrative from ancient texts whose authority could not directly be questioned.

Publishers were well aware of these new trends. With their plans for multi-volume critical histories men like Thomas Cadell, William Strachan, and John Murray were feeding a new audience of the educated gentry. Gast had the misfortune to be continually revised by those who objected to his style if not his content or his scholarship; but despite this, he deserves a place alongside the great eighteenth-century triumvirate of Hume, Robertson, and Gibbon.

The political message of such works is muted, but clear. Behind the development of modern historiography on the ancient world lies the cultural context of an age of free trade, manufacture, and commerce, steeped in Montesquieu, and which accepted Burke's views of the morality of empire based on the concepts of the reward for civic virtue and a duty towards the subjects: Gast's Greeks belong to a world of Huguenot enterprise and free trade that lay at the foundation of eighteenth-century mercantilism. Overt political stances are of minor importance in these eighteenth-century histories, which reflect the opinions of the age rather than seeking to transform it through the reinterpretation of the past. It was not until the nineteenth century that a truly politically engaged history emerged, inspired by the American and French Revolutions; and Greek history became directly partisan with the works of William Mitford, Bulwer-Lytton, and George Grote.

William Page (1794–1872) View of the Plain of Marathon *(1818)*

William Page visited Greece in the company of William Campbell and Lady Ruthven, cousins of Lady Elgin, just before the outbreak of the Greek War of Independence in 1821.

4
The Philhellenes and Marathon

In pursuit of the origins of the rise of Athens as a modern ideal let us follow the resonance of the battle of Marathon for the modern history of Greece, as it developed from the eighteenth century through the age of John Stuart Mill and beyond. In 1846 Mill had begun his review of the first two volumes of his friend George Grote's *History of Greece* with the words:

> The battle of Marathon, even as an event in English history, is more important than the battle of Hastings. If the issue of that day had been different, the Britons and the Saxons might still have been wandering in the woods.[1]

This was not the first time that Mill had reflected on the significance of Marathon, for earlier in the *Westminster Review* of 1832,[2] in a discussion of the conspiracy of Catiline apparently written by him together with Jeremy Bentham and Sir John Bowring, there appears the following rather irrelevant quotation from Byron:

> Man does not feel a fullness of the heart on the plain of Marathon because so many Athenians beat so many Persians there, but because a Greek standing there might say –
>
> 'The mountains look on Marathon,
> And Marathon looks on the sea,
> And musing there an hour alone,
> I dream'd that Greece might still be free;
> For standing on the Persian's grave,
> I could not deem myself a slave.'

The worship of the soil of Marathon was clearly an established part of the idealization of ancient Greece and the vision of Utilitarian philosophy that Mill had inherited from his father and Jeremy Bentham. But in the knowledge that the Utilitarians were always ready to assert the originality of their own opinions and forget earlier views, I have been led to cast my net a little wider and ask when in the English consciousness this idealization of the battlefield of Marathon began.

The comparison between Marathon and early British history certainly goes back at least as far as Samuel Johnson, who asserts in his early work, *A Journey to the Western Isles* (1775):[3]

> That man is little to be envied, whose patriotism would not gain force upon the plain of Marathon, or whose piety would not grow warmer among the ruins of Iona.

So Byron's musings on his visit to Marathon in 1809 have an ancestry; and that ancestry seems to be revealed in his poem *Childe Harold's Pilgrimage* (1812–18):[4]

> Where'er we tread 'tis haunted, holy ground;
> No earth of thine is lost in vulgar mould,
> But one vast realm of Wonder spreads around,
> And all the Muse's tales seem truly told,
> Till the sense aches with gazing to behold
> The scenes our earliest dreams have dwelt upon;
> Each hill and dale, each deepening glen and wold
> Defies the power which crushed thy temples gone:
> Age shakes Athena's tower, but spares gray Marathon.
>
> The Sun, the soil – but not the slave, the same;
> Unchanged in all except its foreign Lord –
> Preserves alike its bounds and boundless fame
> The Battle-field, where Persia's victim horde
> First bowed beneath the brunt of Hellas' sword,
> As on the morn to distant Glory dear,
> When Marathon became a magic word;
> Which uttered, to the hearer's eye appear
> The camp, the host, the fight, the Conqueror's career.

The flying Mede, his shaftless broken bow –
The fiery Greek, his red pursuing spear;
Mountains above – Earth's, Ocean's plain below –
Death in the front, Destruction in the rear!
Such was the scene – what now remaineth here?
What sacred trophy marks the hallowed ground,
Recording Freedom's smile, and Asia's tear?
The rifled urn, the violated mound,
The dust thy courser's hoof, rude stranger! spurns around.

And so on, as Byron reflects on his hero's misspent life of revelling. But the source of his experience is revealed in that line, 'The scenes our earliest dreams have dwelt upon'. Although travellers since at least the start of the nineteenth century (as William Page's sketch reveals) had visited Marathon,[5] the origin of Byron's ecstatic vision lies not in geographical description or his actual visit, but in his childhood and the classical education that he had received.[6]

The first praise of Marathon that I have been able to discover is that in John Gast's *Rudiments of the Grecian History* of 1753, discussed in the previous chapter, which was originally conceived as a school textbook in dialogue form.[7] When he comes to the Persian Wars and 'one of the most memorable Periods of Antient History, *the Age of Glory of the Athenian People*', when 'The *Lawrel-Crown* and the *Ivy-Wreath* were both theirs. And those Men, who yielded to none in the Day of Battle, were also foremost in every refined Improvement', we sense a new enthusiasm.[8] Of Marathon he says:[9]

> Every *Athenian* fought for himself on this occasion; every *Athenian* was *personally* concerned in the Fortune of this important Day – he fought for the Temples of his Gods, for the Sepulchres of his Fathers, for all, that the ties of Domestic Life can render dear – he fought for Laws and Liberties, such as no Change of Government could restore to him; and, if he did not conquer, Death, or Slavery worse than Death, lay before him. Accordingly, Historians tell us, that though the Disposition and Conduct of the Battle was owing to *Miltiades*, yet was it difficult to say, to which of the *Athenians* the first Praise was due, for Intrepidity of Courage, and bold Atchievements. It was an Army of Heroes, and they all wrought wonderous things.

This exaltation of the Athenian achievement at Marathon relates to a number of different phenomena that have been overlooked in most modern accounts of this period. It was not so much a result of learned discussion as of the trend in school textbooks, and therefore in the wider culture of the educated public. As we have seen, eighteenth-century attitudes established a contrast between the constitutional models of Athens and Sparta, as exemplified in descriptions derived from Plutarch's *Lives* of Lycurgus and Solon; and modern historians have emphasized the number of philosophers and historians who preferred Sparta to Athens.[10] But in fact already before the French Revolution the general opinion was beginning to move against Sparta, which was seen as irrelevant to the needs of the contemporary mercantile world, and in favour of Athens. The crucial turning point was exemplified by the battle of Marathon, at which the Spartans had not been present, rather than Thermopylae and Plataea: this established the close connection between military success, liberty, and democratic government. Earlier writers and earlier travellers exploring the antiquities of Greece had in fact reflected the 'Spartan version' of Greek history in concentrating on the battle of Thermopylae, which was the supreme example of Spartan virtue.[11]

Herodotus had already pointed out the change in Athens' military fortunes in his description of the consequences of the expulsion of the tyrants in Book 5:[12]

> Thus Athens went from strength to strength, and proved, if proof were needed, how noble a thing freedom is, not in one respect only, but in all; for while they were oppressed under a despotic government, they had no better success in war than any of their neighbours, yet, once the yoke was flung off, they proved the finest fighters in the world. This clearly shows that, so long as they were held down by authority, they deliberately shirked their duty in the field, as slaves shirk working for their masters; but when freedom was won, then every man amongst them longed to distinguish himself.

What was it that made Marathon so resonant in the British teaching of Greek history in the eighteenth century? The history of antiquity had always been central to the school curriculum, but this was the period in which attention began to focus as much on Greece as on Rome. Montesquieu in the age of French imperialism had discussed the phenomenon of decline and fall in relation to the Roman Republic and its subsequent empire; the British example of a maritime imperial republic of free enterprise made the example of Classical Greece, and especially Athens, more relevant and more comforting – at least until the revolutions in America and France swung the pendulum against liberal thought, and back towards a Rome that could provide examples for the British government of the Indian Empire.[13]

Liberty had been at the centre of British Whig political thought since at least the Glorious Revolution of 1688. Tyranny or absolute monarchy was defined as slavery and subservience; liberty meant freedom and courage, and as emphasis shifted from Sparta to Athens the battle of Marathon became the supreme ancient example of this relationship. This connection continued (and still continues) throughout the subsequent study of Greek history. In the words of the radical historian Bulwer-Lytton:[14]

> And still, throughout the civilized world (civilized how much by the arts and lore of Athens!) men of every clime, of every political persuasion, feel as Greeks at the name of Marathon. Later fields have presented the spectacle of an equal valour, and almost the same disparities of slaughter; but never in the annals of earth, were united so closely in our applause, admiration for the heroism of the victors, and sympathy for the holiness of their cause. It was the first great victory of OPINION! and its fruits were reaped, not by Athens alone, but by all Greece then, as by all time thereafter, in a mighty and imperishable harvest, – the invisible not less than the actual force of despotism was broken ... One successful battle for liberty quickens and exalts that proud and emulous spirit from which are called forth the civilization and the arts that liberty should produce, more rapidly than centuries of repose. To Athens the victory of Marathon was a second Solon.

After the battle of Waterloo, Marathon indeed became inextricably bound up with the idea of creating a monument to the new heroes of the defeat of Napoleon.[15] It is, then, not entirely due to Byron and not at all surprising that Marathon has continued to have a resonance in English poetry. Elizabeth Barrett (Browning)'s earliest published poem was an epic in rhyming couplets entitled *The Battle of Marathon* (1820): I refrain from quoting from it out of respect for her subsequent poetic reputation, but it responds to the same theme. Her future husband Robert Browning achieved greater success fifty years later with his poem *Pheidippides* (1876), which finally fused in the modern consciousness the two stories of the Marathon runner, that in Herodotus of Pheidippides' run from Athens to Sparta asking for help before the battle, and that of the run from Marathon to Athens to report the Athenian victory, not mentioned in Herodotus but given in different versions by Plutarch and Lucian, together with the runner's death as he gasped the words 'Hail! we have won' (*chairete, nikōmen*).[16] Even in antiquity the legend had been growing, and the differences between Plutarch and Lucian are significant in this development: Plutarch gives evidence of a learned dispute about the name of the messenger, which is either Thersippos or Eucles, while Lucian clearly combined the Herodotean Spartan runner with the Marathon runner and gave his name as Philippides, a well-attested (and possibly correct) manuscript variant of Pheidippides in Herodotus.

It is often said to have been Browning's poem that inspired the Baron de Coubertin to create the modern Marathon run;[17] and it was certainly Browning above all who emphasized the Athenian nature of the victory and the refusal of the Spartans to help the Athenians; Pheidippides tells the story of his reception at Sparta:

> Athens, shall Athens sink,
> Drop into dust and die – the flower of Hellas utterly die,
> Die, with the wide world spitting at Sparta, the stupid, the stander-by?
>
> . . . Did Sparta respond?
> Every face of her leered in a furrow of envy, mistrust,
> Malice – each eye of her gave me its glitter of gratified hate!
> Gravely they turned to take counsel, to cast for excuses.

However, this view of Browning's influence seems to ignore the fact that the theme of the dying Marathon runner was already well known in the eighteenth century and appears to have originated in France. The death of the Athenian soldier at the moment of announcing the victory in Athens is mentioned in Rollin's *Histoire ancienne* (1730–38), the source of most standard school texts of the period, although he does not name him or relate the Herodotean story of Pheidippides' run to Sparta.[18] Similarly Oliver Goldsmith, who is mostly derivative of Rollin, gives the runner's name as Eucles, found in Plutarch, and mentions only the appeal, not the run to Sparta.[19]

The theme was standard in both British and French art. B.R. Haydon's *The Death of Eucles* was exhibited in London in 1830.[20] A marble sculpture of 'Le soldat de Marathon annonçant la victoire', created for Louis-Philippe by Jean-Pierre Cortot, is still displayed in the Louvre; it is dated 1834, but the original plaster maquette is of 1822.[21] The young Luc-Olivier Merson used the theme of *Le soldat de Marathon* in 1869 for his prize entry for the *Grand prix de Rome de peinture d'histoire*.[22] It seems, therefore, that the Plutarchean version of the story was the standard one in both England and France, but that it was not attached to the name of Pheidippides before Browning's poem.

The myth has continued to grow. Even in the twentieth century, the resonance of Marathon inspired generations of British soldiers, as Robert Graves's ironic counter-use of it to pillory the failures of the military high command of the First World War attests. His poem 'The Persian Version' portrays the battle as if it were a staff report on the disaster of Gallipoli:

> Truth-loving Persians do not dwell upon
> The trivial skirmish fought near Marathon.
> As for the Greek theatrical tradition
> Which represents that summer's expedition
> Not as a mere reconnaissance in force
> By three brigades of foot and one of horse
> (Their left flank covered by some obsolete
> Light craft detached from the main Persian fleet)
> But as a grandiose, ill-starred attempt
> To conquer Greece – they treat it with contempt;
> And only incidentally refute
> Major Greek claims, by stressing what repute
> The Persian monarch and the Persian nation
> Won by this salutary demonstration:
> Despite a strong defence and adverse weather
> All arms combined magnificently together.

Throughout the nineteenth century, Marathon was an essential point of reference in the Greek version of the Grand Tour. The traumatic moment of truth came in April 1870, when Lord and Lady Muncaster and their friend Frederick Vyner, together with two junior but well-connected diplomats (Edward Herbert and Count Alberto de Boÿl) from the British and Italian Legations decided, like many others before them, to visit the battlefield. Although careful arrangements were made with the police to ensure the safety of the party, on their way back a band of brigands kidnapped them at Pikermi. Demands were made to the Minister of War for a ransom from the Greek government totalling £25,000. The case became an international incident, and the foreign press was loud in its demands for action. Negotiations with the government convinced the brigands that the authorities were not acting in good faith, and soldiers were sent to hunt the brigands down. When the fugitives were spotted near Dilessi, the brigands, anxious to escape, massacred their hostages with cutlasses and muskets.[23]

The incident caused an international outcry, and had a serious effect on the credibility of the Greek government, which was held responsible for the failure to deal with the episode effectively. It was particularly problematic for Anglo-Greek relations, precisely because it exposed the difference between the ancient heroic world and the contemporary state of the countryside of Attica around Marathon. There was a long debate in the House of Commons on 20 May 1870, in which an amendment was proposed censuring the Greek government for its conduct of the incident. The proposer of this amendment was the brother of Bulwer-Lytton, Sir Henry Lytton Bulwer, who was not only a personal friend of Edward Herbert, the British diplomat killed in the incident, but also a prominent philhellene who (as we shall see) as a young man nearly fifty years earlier, in 1824, had been the emissary from the London Greek Committee instrumental in transferring £130,000 in gold sovereigns for the conduct of the War of Independence to the provisional Greek government in Nauplion. He was answered in Parliament by another famous philhellene, William Gladstone, who, while deploring the episode, defended his government's more conciliatory approach, and persuaded Lytton Bulwer to withdraw his amendment.[24] Nevertheless, by July the Greek government of Zaimis had fallen as a direct result of the murders.

It was this episode above all that served to demystify the legend of Marathon, and to allow a more realistic approach on the part of English philhellenes to the emerging Greek nation. Seven years later, the traveller and scholar J.P. Mahaffy upbraided Byron for being 'carried away by his enthusiasm to fancy a great future possible for the country . . . He paints the Greek brigand or pirate as many others have painted the "noble savage", with the omission of all his meaner vices.' And Mahaffy proceeded to denigrate the significance of the battle:[25]

> But Byron may well be excused his raving about the liberty of the Greeks, for truly their old conflict at Marathon, where a few thousand ill-disciplined men repulsed a larger number of still worse disciplined Orientals, without any recondite tactics – perhaps even without any very extraordinary heroism – how is it that this conflict has maintained a celebrity which has not been equaled by any of the great battles of the world, from that day down to our own?

But even Mahaffy was forced to conclude:

> Yet what signifies all this criticism? In spite of all scepticism, in spite of all contempt, the battle of Marathon, whether badly or well fought, and the troops of Marathon, whether well or ill trained, will ever be more famous than any other battle or army, however important or gigantic its dimensions . . . Marathon was fought by Athenians; the Athenians eclipsed the other Greeks as far as the other Greeks eclipsed the rest of the world, in literary power. This battle became the literary property of the city, hymned by poet, cited by orator, told by aged nurse, lisped by stammering infant; and so it has taken its position, above all criticism, as one of the great decisive battles which assured the liberty of the West against Oriental despotism.

So, for good or ill, the battle of Marathon remained for the British nation symbolic of the meaning of Greek history, and John Stuart Mill was right to regard it as the most important battle in English history.

Radical History

Wm Mitford.
Engraved by E. Scriven from an Original Drawing
BY H. EDRIDGE.
Published July 20. 1835 by T. Cadell, Strand, London.

William Mitford 1744–1827

5
The Contested Reign of Mitford

> May I remind you that it is uncertain whether Greek history was invented in England or in Scotland? The two claimants are the Englishman William Mitford, who published the first volume of his *History of Greece* in 1784 but did not finish his work until 1810, and the Royal Historiographer of Scotland John Gillies who in 1786 published a complete Greek history in two volumes in quarto and by 1778 had already published a discourse 'on the history, manners, and character of the Greeks from the conclusion of the Peloponnesian War to the battle of Chaeronea'.

This was the starting point of the inaugural lecture of Arnaldo Momigliano as Professor of Ancient History at University College London in 1952.[1] As we have seen, his account of the development of Greek history ignored John Gast, and privileged large-scale modern narrative histories over the earlier tradition of more or less systematic accounts of antiquities; but it is true that both Gillies and Mitford were acutely conscious of the new demands of continuous narrative history consequent on the works of the famous triumvirate of eighteenth-century historians, David Hume, William Robertson, and Edward Gibbon.

JOHN GILLIES

John Gillies was an enthusiast of modest means educated at Glasgow University, who found patronage from the aristocratic Hope family.[2] He was a disciple of William Robertson, Historiographer Royal of Scotland; and succeeded to Robertson's official position in 1793. He is described as '"a man of good intentions, a passable scholar, an indefatigable reader, and a most respectable character", but there was no touch of genius in his writings', which were 'written in a readable but somewhat pompous style'.[3] His *The History of Ancient Greece its colonies and conquests from the earliest accounts till the division of the Macedonian empire in the east* (1786) was popular enough in its day, achieving many further editions until 1841 and partial or complete translations into French and German;[4] but it is in fact a rather disappointing production in relation to other works of the Scottish Enlightenment, and does not live up to the grandiose political claims in its dedication to King George III:

> Sir,
> The History of Greece exposes the dangerous turbulence of Democracy, and arraigns the despotism of tyrants. By describing the incurable evils inherent in every form of Republican policy, it evinces the inestimable benefits, resulting to Liberty itself, from the lawful dominion of hereditary Kings, and the steady operation of well-regulated Monarchy. That your Majesty may long reign the illustrious Guardian of public freedom, and the unrivalled Patron of useful learning, is the fervent prayer of Your Majesty's Most dutiful Subject and Servant, John Gillies. London Feb. 10, 1786.

This royalist sentiment looks forward to royal patronage, and of course back to the American War of Independence; but its message was almost immediately dramatically reinforced by the French Revolution and the collapse of the *ancien régime*, the most important event in changing the historical consciousness of modern Europe. Gillies claims, however, that 'the principal part had been written many years ago. During that long interval, different portions of Grecian history have been ably treated in English, as well as in foreign languages (Among the foreign works, I distinguish with pleasure those of Mr. Meiners of Gottingen).'[5]

Gillies' main contribution was the integration of literature and history: in his preface he says:

> In the view which I have taken of my subject, the fluctuation of public affairs, and the vicissitudes of war and fortune, appear scarcely the most splendid, and surely not the most interesting, portion of Grecian history. By genius and fancy, not less than by patriotism and prowess, the Greeks are honourably distinguished among the nations of the earth. By the Greeks, and by them alone, Literature, Philosophy, and the Fine Arts, were treated as important concerns of state, and employed as powerful

> engines of policy. From their literary glory not only their civil, but even their military transactions, derive their chief importance and dignity. To complete, therefore, my present undertaking, it seemed necessary to unite the history of arts with that of empire, and to combine with the external revolutions of war and government, the intellectual improvements of men, and the ever-varying picture of human opinions and manners.

Politically, however, Gillies offered an extreme example of pro-Spartan sentiment. The whole of the first volume of his *History of Greece* treated Greek history as if it were indeed the history of Sparta and of her dominion over the Greek world. Chapter III contains a section on 'The Spartan Laws'. Despite his claim that 'in the Work throughout, I have ventured to think for myself; and my opinions, whether well or ill founded, are, at least, my own', his narrative was actually rather conventional. He has the usual story of problematic relations in the royal family and Lycurgus' exile to Crete and Egypt, with his collection of the poems of Homer in Ionia:

> The sagacity of Lycurgus thus contemplating the relation and interests of his country and his family, regarded martial spirit and political liberty as the great ends of his legislation. These important objects had been attained by the primitive institutions, so faithfully described by Homer. Lycurgus determined to imitate the simple beauty of that illustrious model; and, to the end that the Spartan constitution might enjoy a degree of permanence, and stability that the *heroic policies* had not possessed, he resolved to avoid the rocks on which *they* had shipwrecked, to extinguish the ambition of distant or extensive conquest, to level the inequality of fortune, to crush the baneful effects of wealth and luxury; in one word, to arrest the progress of what is called the refinement, but what seemed to the manly discernment of this legislator, the corruption, of human society.

With the help of 'Thales' and the Delphic oracle:

> Fortified by this authority, Lycurgus proceeded with a daring yet skilful hand, first, to new-model the government; secondly, to regulate wealth and possessions; thirdly to reform education and manners; judiciously pursuing this natural order of legislation, because men are less jealous of power than tenacious of property, and less tenacious of property itself, than of their ancient usages and customs.

The account of the constitution was equally conventional, running through kings, council, ephors (a footnote seeks to prove this is a Lycurgan invention), greater and lesser assemblies, the equal division of property in land, the absence of movable wealth, gold and silver; the prohibition of strangers, helot agriculture, the military organization. Lycurgus restored the natural rights of women (Gillies ignores the problematic aspects of adultery and nudity); his account of education includes both theft and respect for elders. His final conclusion was, however, extremely positive:

> Such were the celebrated institutions of Lycurgus, which are eminently distinguished by the simplicity of their design, the exact adaptation of their parts, and the uniform consistence of the whole, from the political establishments of other countries, which are commonly the irregular and motley production of time and accident ... if the whole be attentively considered, we shall perceive that they contain nothing so original or so singular as is generally believed. From the innumerable coincidences that have been remarked between the heroic and the Spartan discipline, there seems sufficient ground to conclude that the one was borrowed from the other; and if we accurately contemplate the genius of both, we may discern that they tended not (as has often been said) to stop and interrupt, but only to divert, the natural current of human propensities and passions. The desire of wealth and of power, of effeminate ease, of frivolous amusements, and of all the artificial distinctions and enjoyments of society, are only so many ramifications of the love of action and of pleasure; passions which it would be impossible to eradicate without destroying the whole vigour of the mind. Yet these propensities, which it is often the vain boast of philosophy to subdue, policy may direct to new and more exalted objects. For the sordid occupations of interest, may be substituted the manly pursuits of honour; the love of virtuous praise may control the desire of vicious indulgence; and the impressions of early institution, confirmed by example and habit, may render the great duties of life its principal employment and pleasure. Such a condition of society seems the utmost elevation and grandeur to which human nature can aspire.

Sparta's decline was only gradual. In contrast, Gillies postponed 'treating fully of the Athenian government and laws, until the establishment of what was called the Athenian empire'. And even then his section on the internal state of Athens (in ch. XIII) is brief; it is clear where his sympathies lie. Gillies's *History* is in fact, as de Pauw saw, merely a rather conventional version of earlier eighteenth-century accounts.

WILLIAM MITFORD

William Mitford's major *History of Greece* was a product of the new historiography of the late eighteenth century.[6] His model was Edward Gibbon, his fellow officer in the Hampshire militia, with whom he shared the doubtful privilege of having failed to acquire an education at Oxford from 1761 (where he belonged to the same breakfast club as Jeremy Bentham, who thought 'his conversation commonplace').[7] Like Gibbon, Mitford's formative experience had been his encounter with the French *érudit* tradition: the death of his wife and a serious illness led to a trip to France in 1776 where he met M. de Meusnier, M. de Villoison, and the Baron de Sainte-Croix,[8] and spent time with the latter at Mormoiron near Avignon; Mitford records that when he urged Sainte-Croix to undertake a history of Greece, he replied, 'adverting to the restrictions upon the press in France, and the advantage which familiar acquaintance with a free constitution, through association in its energies, offered in England, "Only an Englishman could write a history of Greece."'[9] Mitford returned to live the life of a country gentleman on his family estate of Exbury in Hampshire, and joined the Hampshire Militia, as captain, serving for a year under Major Edward Gibbon. According to his brother, 'Their conversations, in those hours of leisure which the militia service afforded, frequently turned on ancient history; and Mr. Gibbon, finding the eagerness of his friend in the pursuit of Grecian literature, urged him to undertake the History of Greece.'[10]

Mitford's *History of Greece* was originally published in successive volumes between 1784 and 1810, and was highly idiosyncratic in a number of ways. His style was ridiculed by contemporaries such as Lord Byron,[11] being based on principles of grammar and orthography invented by himself out of his study of the 'saxon language'. But in fact he was an original historian in terms both of historical method and of his approach to the usefulness of parallels between ancient and modern history; whatever its political views, Mitford's work was based on considerable study of the ancient texts, and a refreshing ability (like his friend and model Gibbon) to use comparative studies of other societies, derived from wide reading and serious reflection on the history of his own country. His *History of Greece* was generally regarded as superior to that of Gillies; after the death of Gibbon, in 1790 he found himself in competition with Gillies for the sinecure of Professor of Ancient History at the Royal Academy: the vote was split, and had to be abandoned when it was alleged (somewhat implausibly) that Gillies was a radical. Mitford was not finally appointed until 1818.

Mitford's early volumes are the most imaginative. His 'mythical period' of Greek history was based on comparative evidence of primitive societies, citing Leland and Robertson on Germanic tribes. His defence of Homer as a historical source for the Trojan War compared the rape of Helen with the twelfth-century AD story of the rape of Dervorghal by Dermot of Leinster and Henry II's subsequent conquest of Ireland.[12] The origins of Greek polytheism are connected with the beginning of civil society, and there is an excellent attempt to relate Greek literacy with Eastern systems of writing.[13] Mitford discussed the origins of navigation, social manners, the absence of clans in contrast to Scottish Highlanders,[14] the importance of hospitality, the early freedom of women, and the lack of homosexuality, 'that unnatural sensuality which afterward so disgraced Grecian and not less Roman manners'. And in his discussion of social movements and his ability to empathize with the ordinary citizen, even while he disapproved of these developments, Mitford often hit on a sympathetic interpretation of events, as for instance in his description of the conflict between Sybaris and Croton, and the history of Poseidonia and Paestum.[15] He was always sensitive to the role of slaves in Greek society;[16] he noted, for instance, how their status improved after the Peloponnesian War.[17] There is a learned appendix to ch. VIII, 'Of the Ancient Ships of War', comparing ancient triremes with the *bouanga* of the Pacific islands observed by a French naval officer circumnavigating the world in 1757.

But as Mitford entered the classical period of the fifth century BC, despite its fluent and commonsensical narrative, his work became indeed highly and increasingly political under the stress of the French Revolution. On the period of the Persian Wars he dismissed 'the zealous partisans of democratical rule'[18] and portrayed the wars, not as glorious victories, but as riven by faction and by inter-state rivalries; his account emphasized throughout the disunity of the Greeks and the feuds after the Persian retreat over the celebration of victory. The consequence for Athens of the

Greek victory was the growth of a spirit of democracy in 'the party of the lower people' that even their leader Themistocles could not control.[19] Like previous writers he ignored the reforms of Cleisthenes, who appears only as an Alcmaeonid faction leader, and he portrayed the Athenian constitution as late as Ephialtes as simply the product of Solon's reforms.[20] Cimon was the last great leader of Athens; it was under him that Athens became the centre of art and science.[21] But the reforms of Ephialtes created 'that union of all the powers of government, legislative, executive, financial, and judicial, in the same hands, which, according to the sage Montesquieu, constitutes the essence of despotism; and hence the word tyrant, was even in that age, applied to the assembled Athenian people'.[22]

Although Mitford gave full credit to the patronage of Pericles over the art and philosophy of the classical age, he highlighted the declining status of women in classical Athens due to democracy.[23] And the rise of Pericles 'was ultimately the most pernicious to the commonwealth, and involved incalculable evils for all Greece':[24] all his merits did not outweigh 'the concurrence, at least, which is imputed to him, in depraving the Athenian constitution, to favour that popular power by which he ruled, and the revival and confirmation of that pernicious hostility between the democratical and aristocratical interests, first in Athens, and then, by the Peloponnesian War, throughout the nation'.[25] Even the creation under Pericles of a reserve fund of money and ships at the start of the war 'strongly marks the inherent weakness and the indelible barbarism of democratical government'.[26] The Peloponnesian War itself is described as a civil war[27] and the corrupt nature of the democratical system was revealed in Mitford's final verdict at its end:[28]

> It is observed by Aristotle, that democracy and tyranny are, of all governments, most hostile to each other, as, according to Hesiod's proverb, two of a trade never agree: for, he adds, absolute DEMOCRACY is TYRANNY.

Despite this hostile view of Athens, Mitford's account was critical of the previous tradition. 'Historians have ... found it convenient ... to select two commonwealths, Athens and Lacedaemon, as main channels in which their narratives should run.'[29] But Mitford took a new view of this opposition, although he was still bound by his general acceptance of literary Greek traditions whether in Plutarch or elsewhere:

> It has been the fancy of some modern authors, that the institutions of Lycurgus were but the revived usages of the heroic ages; and of others, that they were those of the rude Dorian highlanders, improved and systematised. All antiquity contradicts both opinions, and particularly the writers of highest autherity [*sic*] . . . On the other hand again it is urged, that to change at once the manners and ancient usages of a people by any effort of legislation is impossible. In a great nation we may grant it so; but in a small commonwealth not: and certainly so the ancient legislators thought. We find it universally their great object to legislate for the manners; and hence all the political theories of the Greek philosophers are calculated for limited and narrow societies.

His final assessment of Lycurgus was as a great statesman:

> Other states which have flourished by the wisdom of their laws, and the goodness of their constitution, have risen by slow degrees to that excellence which has led them to power and celebrity; and fortunate circumstances have often done more for them than their wisest legislators, who have indeed seldom dared to attempt all that themselves thought best. But for Lycurgus nothing was too difficult, nothing too dangerous: he changed everything at once; new-modelled government, manners, morals, in a manner new-made the people: and yet with all these violent alterations, those experiments in politics hazardous to such extreme, no one consequence seems to have escaped his penetrating genius; no one of his daring ideas failed in practice; he foresaw, and he provided for every thing.

On the other hand Mitford did not seek to establish the Spartan constitution as an ideal. Lycurgus was treated as a real person who redivided the land of the nobility, abolished the use of gold and silver, and instituted the practice of living away from home; in so doing he created a nation of philosophers and soldiers. Mitford describes the rearing of children, marriage and women, the selection and education of the youth. Lycurgus prescribed sobriety – 'probably all legislators would prescribe sobriety, if they could hope to make the law effectual' – restraint in mirth, laconic speech, respect for age, and modesty. The greatest fault in his system was the necessity of slavery to maintain the equality of every citizen as 'in the strictest sense of the modern term, a gentleman, without business', and the status of the helots, who were habitually humiliated and often also murdered: 'never was human nature degraded by system to such a degree as in the miserable Helots'.[30] The threat of a helot uprising required a standing army whose main function was their intimidation and control, not external conquest. Few historians have expressed so clearly the paradoxical relation between oppression and egalitarianism.

The account of Solonian Athens begins:

> Barbarous ages are most favourable for legislation. History affords few instances of great improvement in the constitution of polished states . . . The English constitution stands singular in the circumstance of its gradual improvement.

As with Sparta, in discussing the Athenian constitution it is important, Mitford claimed, to consider the composition of the city. The total adult male population rose from 14,040 to 21,000 over the classical period, whereas the total of slaves, male, female, and children, was 400,000.[31] 'This proportion of slaves to freemen, in a commonwealth so boastful of liberty as its darling passion, astonishes.'[32] On this observation, and on the debilitating and degrading nature of manual labour in the fields (which justifies modern colonial slavery, in the absence of hired labour), Mitford proceeded to build a picture of the absolute difference between ancient and modern constitutions:

> From this point of view of things then it appears that DEMOCRACY was a mode of government not so absolutely absurd and impracticable among the Greeks as it would be where no slavery is. For tho in democracies the supreme power was nominally vested in all the people, yet those called the people, who exclusively shared that power, were scarcely a tenth part of the men of the state. The people, moreover, were almost all in circumstances to have received some education, and to subsist by easier means than those which, through constant labor of the body, disable the mind for liberal exertion.

For this reason slavery was 'absolutely necessary' to ancient democracy.

Mitford's argument for the essential connection between Athenian democracy and slavery has indeed often since been both asserted and denied; but outside the Marxist tradition it has not been taken very seriously. It is not enough to counter it by pointing out that his figures are derived from a much-disputed passage in Athenaeus reporting 'Ctesikles'. It is true that the slave number of 400,000 had already been dismissed by David Hume,[33] but modern assessments suggest a relationship in Athens between slave and free population of 4 to 1 (adult males), which is still enough to make Mitford's argument plausible, despite its general neglect by historians, who since Grote have been favourable to Athenian democracy. Of course in Mitford's day the proportion of electors in England before 1832 was considerably less, but then he did not consider his England to be a democracy; according to him the House of Commons represents 'properly the Aristocratical part of the constitution'.[34] On the occasion of the trial of the generals after the battle of Arginusae, he pauses to compare the British and the French political experience. His panegyric of the British constitution concludes with the statement 'A Grecian history, and indeed any history perfectly written . . . but especially a Grecian history perfectly written, should be a political institute for all nations.'[35]

Mitford came into his own again when discussing the early fourth century, during the period of the 'Lacedaemonian empire'. This was partly because the story was told from the Spartan point of view out of his empathy with the historian Xenophon, whose military narrative he respected, although he recognized his silences and his bias towards the Spartan king Agesilaus; and partly because he understood the underlying conflict between aristocratic and democratic factions in the Greek world. 'The republicans of Greece, like some in modern times, we find were liable to be strangely deceived by the names of liberty and sovereignty.'[36] He also had a realistic conception of the nature of ancient warfare, despite never having actually commanded troops in battle or visited Greece. His narrative was indeed far more concrete (though less accurate) than that of his critic Grote, and still highlights the inability of modern historians to discover any principle of coherence in the endless wars of the fourth century before the rise of Macedon.

Mitford's was the standard history of Greece as the Age of Reform arrived. In this new climate he was attacked for his political views. But these attacks were not wholly fair; in the preface to the posthumous edition of Mitford's history, Lord Redesdale (himself a most reactionary figure on the Irish bench) tried to defend his brother's views. According to him it was not that Mitford had sought to distort Greek history in order to provide examples for modern history. Quite the opposite: he opposed all such attempts, and believed firmly that the experience of all Greek states was 'not suited to the extensive territory and the free condition of the British islands'. In Greece, 'true freedom, the freedom of all, such as he conceived British freedom long to have been, never existed'; in contemporary Britain, unlike ancient Greece, there was security of person and property, and absence of slavery. Mitford in fact belonged to the generation formed by the experiences of the American and French Revolutions, and held the traditional opinions of the landed gentry; he was against the subversive utopian principles of the French and other enlightenments. According to his brother, he rejected the views of 'some distinguished persons of the freedom enjoyed by all in the Grecian republics, whose institutions were represented as tending more to the happiness of man than those which had prevailed in this country'; he 'attempted to show the evils that had arisen from institutions adopted by the most distinguished Grecian states, [and] he . . . sought to impress on the minds of his countrymen that such institutions, even if suited to the condition of those states, were not suited to the condition of his own country; [and] to warn them against the influence of that seduction which the splendid display of talent in the Grecian character might produce'.

To Mitford the question of the freedom of the individual was crucial. The British 'were therefore never objects of that oppression which, in other countries, where slavery has existed to a great extent, has been produced by fear; as in Greece, and especially in Sparta, where a systematic tyranny, of the most atrocious kind, was practised, to prevent the danger, more than once seriously felt, and which at all times was dreaded, from the number of those in bondage, giving them physical power superior to the physical power of the freemen, the sole possessors of political power'. Similarly Athens: the Athenian constitution was not really a democracy because of slavery.[37] Mitford could therefore idealize neither Sparta nor Athens, because for him the only free society was that which had been created through the historical development of English institutions; and there was nothing comparable in the ancient world. The accusation that Mitford was excessively favourable to monarchic regimes such as those of Philip and Alexander, and opposed to 'republican' states, is part of this same picture of the importance of monarchy in the British constitution. Mitford was therefore a 'resolute friend of Philip' against Demosthenes. Nevertheless, the work 'remained popular and had the merit of supplying a laborious English work on a neglected subject' for two generations, going through six further editions down to 1835.[38]

THE OPPOSITION TO MITFORD

Mitford's robust but parochial view was anathema to those who wished to idealize antiquity, and his reception by reviewers shows the difficulty of writing on so sensitive a topic during the French Revolution. His first volume (published in 1784) was criticized even by conservatives as being exceptionally reactionary, although his comparison of British and Homeric monarchy was applauded; by 1797, later volumes were being commended for their denunciation of radical views, their praise of Sparta and of Xenophon, and of those traditionally regarded as tyrants such as Dionysius of Syracuse and Philip of Macedon. In contrast, reviewers in the *Edinburgh Review* had from the start attacked his strong bias against democratic Athens.[39]

In this next generation it was especially this portrayal of Athens to which they objected, because it was especially Athens that they wanted to appropriate as a model of radical democracy. Mitford's consistent use of modern parallels made it easy to accuse him of writing with a modern bias. The young Macaulay attacked Mitford as early as 1824;[40] but the most famous attack on him came from George Grote in a long article, which was ostensibly a review of Clinton's *Fasti Hellenici*, in the *Westminster Review* of 1826:[41]

> The qualities desirable in an historian may be divided into two classes; those which qualify him to trace out and report the facts of the period which he selects; and those which qualify him to embody the facts into results, to survey the general characteristics of society among the people of whom he treats, and to ascertain the comparative degree of civilization which their habits and institutions evince them to have reached.
>
> To appreciate the success of Mr. Mitford as an historian, we must examine in what degree he possesses the great mental qualities above described.
>
> And first with regard to the higher philosophising powers: a mere inspection of the titles of his chapters, almost without perusing the body of his work, would suffice to show, that so far from having employed them, he is insensible even to the necessity of employing them in order to elicit the genuine and valuable results of history. He has hardly attempted any analysis of the great social and political characteristics of Greece. His account of the political institutions of Lycurgus is the nearest approximation to such

an undertaking, and evinces a greater freedom from his usual prejudices than is to be found any where else throughout his work. If even that, however, falls very short of what it ought to be and might be, the sketch which he has professed to give of the Athenian constitution is still more lamentably defective. We can hardly wonder that this sketch should be very incomplete and meagre, even as a description, since the author confesses himself to have borrowed it entirely from Potter's Antiquities,[42] and has attempted no collation of the authorities for himself: and, when we compare this avowal of Mr. Mitford with the new lights which Niebuhr's ingenious and original researches have thrown upon the constitution of Rome, we are made painfully sensible of the difference between the real knowledge of the ancient world possessed or inquired for by a German public, and the appearance of knowledge which suffices here. Nor has Mr. Mitford accompanied his imperfect sketch with any philosophical exposition of the tendency of Athenian institutions; of the extent to which they failed in providing securities for good government; and of the reasons which occasioned their failure . . .

There is a strong tendency in the human mind to the worship of power: a principle which has been explained by Adam Smith, with as much philosophy as eloquence, in his Theory of Moral Sentiments. Every thing in an English education tends to nourish, to strengthen, and to perpetuate this tendency; and in the mind of Mr. Mitford, a mind priding itself on adherence to every thing English, it has become absolute idolatry. The whole of his favourable affections are turned towards the man of power. He is devoted to kingly government, and to kings, not only with preference, but even with passion and bigotry; the average kingly character is in his eye a compound of perfections, from which indeed there may be, in individual cases, a few rare and unaccountable deviations; but the worst king that ever existed appears to him better, than the best system possible with no king at all . . .

But the bias of Mr. Mitford exhibits itself still more copiously on the side of his hatred than on the side of his love; partly because the language of blame is so much more poignant than that of praise, partly because Grecian history deals so much more with republics than with monarchs. The number of images and epithets, indicating hatred and contempt, which he has heaped upon the democratical communities, in one part or another of his history, is truly surprising. He is not even solicitous to preserve these images in consistency one with the other, provided each will

> separately conduce towards his object. Sometimes he describes the sovereign assembly at Athens as composed of fullers, shoemakers, braziers, &c. at other times he tells us that 'a sovereign people would not work'; sometimes he reproaches them as inspired with a restless thirst of conquest, at other times he arraigns their self-indulgence and luxury, because they will not serve on expeditions for conquest; in one place he talks awfully of the irresistible might of the sovereign assembly, in another he exhibits to us the 'inherent impotence' of the most renowned ancient democracies. He exclaims loudly against the extortions of the Athenian commanders in the Aegean, and terms them (generally, we believe, with justice) 'the greatest of pirates.' But this is only so long as they are acting in the name of the democracy, and while the democracy can be charged with the guilt of their acts; for when any of these commanders return home, and are brought to trial for the very peculations which he has described as habitually practised, Mr. Mitford's tone instantly changes, and he depicts them as innocent sufferers under the scourge of democratical jealousy and ingratitude. If they are tried and acquitted, this he urges as a proof of the uncommon licence of false accusation; if they are found guilty, it is a proof of that still, but it is besides a proof of the greediness and malevolence of a democratical tribunal.

Grote's long article impugned Mitford's accuracy as a historian and his ignorance of German scholarship as well as his political bias, and marked a turning point in the study of ancient Greece. It was essentially a defence of ancient democracy against its ancient and modern critics, and was part of a widespread movement in the British re-evaluation of Sparta and Athens: Grote was in fact denying the right of Mitford to declare the autonomy of ancient history, and asserting the claim of the radical tradition to appropriate Athens for the modern world; the change from the idealization of Sparta to that of Athens is usually thought to have begun with his article, and to have been consummated in his *History of Greece* (1846–56), whose influence has been dominant on Anglo-Saxon attitudes to classical Greece for more than a century, and that remains the only serious full-scale history of Greece written in English.[43] But the rediscovery of Bulwer-Lytton's *Athens* (ch. 6, below) has revealed details of a different picture.

However justified, Grote's attack showed the characteristic arrogance of the Utilitarians in thinking that everyone ought to hold the same views as themselves, and in their complete failure to understand the generation influenced by the American and French Revolutions, or the difference between the mercantile culture of the nineteenth century and the still largely agrarian culture of the eighteenth century. Nevertheless, it was true that by the time of its final publication Mitford's scholarship was out of date, and that his work lacked even the philosophical background of the Scottish Enlightenment that had been provided by writers such as Adam Ferguson. It survives as the best example of the anti-democratical tendency in Greek history and for its independent evaluation of political events in the struggle between Athens and Macedon.

And as we enter the twenty-first century, which is surely destined to be seen historically as the Age of Oligarchy, as the twentieth was that of (pseudo-)Democracy, maybe we should follow the example of Jacques Rancière in *La Haine de la démocratie* and of Jules Isaac in his revered work *Les Oligarques* and pay more attention to oligarchy, and not just as the Iron Law of History. For the apotheosis of Greek democracy in the modern world has led us to forget the historical variety of oligarchies and their extraordinary record for stability. As Aristotle and Thomas Hobbes saw, stability of government must be the ultimate aim of all constitutions, and the variety of oligarchies has surely been the source of their strength. Whatever the official terminology, effective oligarchies may be based on a traditional aristocracy of birth and landholding, on the prerogatives of a founding elite (such as Greek colonies, Israel and Hispanic South America), on the power of wealth (in plutocracies such as the USA and Britain),[44] on an intellectual elite (Plato's Republic and modern France), on military power (Myanmar and Pakistan), on theocracy (the Islamic states and early Christian Europe), on tribal supremacy (modern Africa), on control of the media (Italy), or on systemically organized corruption (Sicily and Calabria, Columbia, Russia and the Ukraine) – and of course on a mixture of any or all of these elements. The stability of oligarchies and their ability to resist social change is one of their most important characteristics; and ultimately Mitford may well be right: of all the varied oligarchic forms of the consolidation of power, perhaps the most benign may be the '*patrios politeia*', 'the mixed constitution' based on historical tradition, in the vision that unites Solon, Mitford and Polybius with Montesquieu and the Founding Fathers of the essentially undemocratic American constitution.

Edward Bulwer-Lytton, 1803–1873.

6
Romantic History in Britain and Europe

Consider History with the beginnings of it stretching dimly into the remote Time; emerging darkly out of the mysterious Eternity: the ends of it enveloping us *at this hour, whereof we at this hour, both as actors and relators, form part! . . . In essence and significance it has been called 'the true Epic Poem, and universal Divine Scripture,* whose *"plenary inspiration" no man, out of Bedlam or in it, shall bring in question.'*

Thomas Carlyle[1]

The notion of a philosophy of history expresses the reasonable idea that history has a meaning and is not just a contingent set of random events without connection or explanation. Traditionally that meaning has been sought in the belief that the narration of history itself will reveal a general pattern or purpose in human events, rather than in the attempt to formulate explicitly general laws of history. After the decline of a Christian view of history as the realization of God's purpose in the human sphere, the Enlightenment believed in the existence of eternal truths of reason, which the philosophical mind could elucidate; and it developed the optimistic idea that history was part of a constant universe and could therefore provide standards or models in a world of rational progress, whether that progress might be seen as the will of God or as the gradual triumph of human reason.

In contrast, the premise of nineteenth-century historiography was developmental, based on a conception of laws of history that privileged cause and effect, and that saw the whole of human existence as a development in terms of spiritual or material progress towards a goal or *telos* embodied in the modern age. History replaced Philosophy as the most important of the human sciences, because it interpreted the present in terms of its derivation from the past, and the future in terms of the Laws of History. Thus the nineteenth century began the Age of History in which society was embedded in a nexus of causation stretching back into the distant past. History ceased to be a series of moral exemplars; the old view of *historia magistra vitae* gave way to the belated discovery of the ideas of the *Scienza Nuova* of Giambattista Vico, of history as a science of progress, the study of the inexorable and mysterious changes in human society, which each society exemplified in its development, until it culminated in a Darwinian Origin of Species, where the ends of each nation state could be discerned in its origins. The sources of this revolution in consciousness are manifold and can be traced in every aspect of European civilization.

The catalyst was of course the French Revolution, which revealed the inadequacies of earlier attempts to understand the forces that shaped events. The history of antiquity had expressed the idea of a unified past, in which Greek history could come to exemplify liberty and progress, against Roman history which embodied the stability and order of the *ancien régime*. This vision of the *République des Lettres* had been dominated by France; now that the old world had disintegrated in revolution, Germany emerged to lead the new order. This coincided with Romanticism and the apotheosis of liberty, both personal and national, and led ultimately to the growth of the idea of national destinies and therefore separate histories.

ROMANTIC HISTORY AND THE NOVEL

> Sir Walter Scott . . . has used those fragments of truth which historians have scornfully thrown behind them in a manner which may well excite their envy. He has constructed out of their gleanings works which, even considered as histories, are scarcely less valuable than theirs. But a truly great historian would reclaim those materials which the novelist has appropriated.
>
> Lord Macaulay[2]

The historical novels of Sir Walter Scott began to be published from 1814 onwards; their immense influence on European culture can be traced through the rise of the novel in Germany and Russia,[3] through the history of opera,[4] and not least through the writing of history. It was Scott who showed how the old antiquarian and moralizing history of the previous century could be transformed through the novelist's imagination into a narrative of passion and vigour to inspire the new Romantic age:

> These Historical Novels have taught all men this truth, which looks like a truism, and yet was as good as unknown to writers of history and others, till so taught: that the bygone ages of the world were actually filled by living men, not by protocols, state-papers, controversies and abstractions of men. Not abstractions were they, not diagrams and theorems; but men, in buff or other coats and breeches, with colour in their cheeks, with passions in their stomach, and the idioms, features and vitalities of very men. It is a little word this; inclusive of great meaning! History will henceforth have to take thought of it.
>
> Thomas Carlyle[5]

The Romantic use of the narrative of history for political ends emphasized the importance of the individual and the freedom of the human spirit as much as Hegel was to do in his theory of the philosophy of history (see ch. 8 below). Ultimately the difference between Hegel and this new Romantic history was not as great as Hegel imagined; for both were true expressions of the Hegelian spirit of the age. Romantic history was not just painted in vivid colours; it was about the struggle for freedom and the role of individuals in that struggle. It is this vision that unites the great historians of the age of historicism – Augustin Thierry, François Guizot, Jules Michelet, and Victor Cousin in France,[6] Barthold Georg Niebuhr, Karl Otfried Müller, and the young Theodor Mommsen in Germany,[7] Jean Charles Léonard de Sismondi in Geneva,[8] Thomas Carlyle and Lord Macaulay in Britain,[9] were representatives of a new school of historiography that swept Europe under the influence of Scott.

But the new style of history had a basic weakness. Because of the difficulty of recreating the human feelings of the past, it identified the trivial and mundane facts of daily life as the means of creating a historical vividness: it substituted *l'histoire des moeurs* for *l'histoire des sentiments*. This was the problem that had defeated Voltaire in his *Essai sur les Moeurs*, and lay behind Barthélemy's attempt to recreate Voltaire's programme in an epistolary form. Carlyle indeed sought to present an illusion of reality in his *History of the French Revolution* through a combination of detailed observation and creative imagination. But it was ultimately Balzac who pointed out the fallacy of confusing the vividness of the mundane with the portrayal of human emotions in the *Avant-propos* (1842) to his monumental programme for a collection of his novels entitled *La Condition Humaine*, which was to be centred on the portrayal of human emotions in their historical context, a programme that could only be achieved through the novel, and not through history:[10]

> In the first place, these actors, whose existence becomes more prolonged and more authentic than that of the generations which saw their birth, almost always live solely on condition of their being a vast reflection of the present. Conceived in the womb of their own period, the whole heart of humanity stirs within their frame, which often covers a complete system of philosophy. Thus Walter Scott raised to the dignity of the philosophy of History the literature which, from age to age, sets perennial gems in the poetic crown of every nation where letters are cultivated. He vivified it with the spirit of the past; he combined drama, dialogue, portrait, scenery, and description; he fused the marvellous with truth – the two elements of the times; and he brought poetry into close contact with the familiarity of the humblest speech . . . Though dazzled, so to speak, by Walter Scott's amazing fertility, always himself and always original, I did not despair, for I found the source of his genius in the infinite variety of human nature. Chance is the greatest romancer in the world; we have only to study it. French society would be the real author; I should only be the secretary. By drawing up an inventory of vices and virtues, by collecting the chief facts of the passions, by depicting characters, by choosing the principal incidents of social life, by composing types out of a combination of homogeneous characteristics, I might perhaps succeed in writing the history which so many historians have neglected: that of Manners.

For Balzac the answer lay not in history but in the freedom of the historical novel; and the spell of Sir Walter Scott over the writing of history was broken. But not before one novelist had escaped. Bulwer-Lytton, the author of the first Byronic history of the freedom of Greece, disciple of Sir Walter Scott, and like Scott a novelist who understood the power of words, belongs to this European school of Romantic history.

BULWER-LYTTON AND ANCIENT GREECE

> It was a dark and stormy night; the rain fell in torrents – except at occasional intervals, when it was checked by a violent gust of wind which swept up the streets (for it is in London that our scene lies), rattling along the housetops, and fiercely agitating the scanty flame of the lamps that struggled against the darkness.
>
> Bulwer-Lytton, *Paul Clifford*[11]

Early in the summer of 2002, I was idly perusing a Dutch book catalogue on the internet when my eye was caught by a strange entry:

> BULWER-LYTTON, E., Athens; its Rise and Fall. With Views of the Literature, Philosophy, and Social Life of the Athenian People. Galignani, Paris, 1837. XII, 469p. Bound. Bit rust stained. Ex libris. € 29.50

Bulwer-Lytton was known to me as the author of *The Last Days of Pompeii* and other novels, the Knebworth edition of which I had once bought for £2 in a leather-bound set, in my *fin-de-siècle* days, to decorate my study at school, and in one of which I had carefully hollowed out a secret container to hide my cigarettes from a prowling housemaster. But I did not recall ever having come across any reference to a work of history with such a grandiose title by this prolific novelist of whom I had not then read a word, and the entry intrigued me. What was he writing in 1837, and why was his work published by an Italian living in Paris in that very street, the Rue Vivienne, where the much-revered ancient Bibliothèque Nationale was once housed? So after some hesitation, having carefully considered the price I ordered the book.

This adventure of the rediscovery of Bulwer-Lytton's forgotten work was one of the most exciting episodes in my academic life. As a pupil of Arnaldo Momigliano sixty years ago, I had learned that there seemed no book in any library of the world whose existence was not recorded in duplicate in the little cash books that filled the pockets of his dark and shapeless suits: it was quite impossible to present him with a work that he did not know, and whose contents he could usually recall with astonishing exactitude. Given that Momigliano was at the point of retirement I felt like a naughty schoolboy who has caught out his teacher: I had discovered a book that he had not read! Moreover, it was a book that sheds radical new light on the history of Greek historiography, the specialism that he founded. And at every stage of this amazing exploration I have been the recipient of new information in ways that I could never have foreseen, many of them involving modern means of discovery unknown to my teacher.[12]

Another serendipitous event: at a very boring board meeting in Oxford University I sat next to a professor of mathematics, and told him of my current obsession. 'Bulwer-Lytton,' he said, 'is my ancestor, and I was brought up in his country house: you should contact my cousin who has all the papers, but especially our ninety-year-old grandmother, his great-great-granddaughter Lady Hermione.' So it was that in May 2003 I eventually found myself at the Bulwer-Lytton bicentenary birthday celebrations in the baronial hall of Knebworth.

Then in February 2004, when I arrived in Princeton to talk on Bulwer-Lytton, I was told that the Princeton Library actually contained the largest collection of Bulwer-Lytton manuscripts outside Britain. I spent three days working through more than 300 of these manuscripts, and my most important discovery concerns the publication of this very book *Athens* by Galignani in Paris, apparently simultaneously with its publication in Britain.[13]

THE DANDY

> I am perhaps less ignorant than I affect to be: it is *now* my object to be a dandy; hereafter I may aspire to be an orator – a wit, a scholar, or a Vincent. You will see then that there have been many odd quarters of an hour in my life less unprofitably wasted than you imagine.
>
> Bulwer-Lytton, *Pelham*[14]

Bulwer-Lytton (or Lytton Bulwer, as he is correctly described on the title page of *Athens*, for he had not yet changed the ordering of his name so as to lay claim to an Elizabethan heritage) was born in 1803. Having antagonized his mother by making an unsuitable marriage, his allowance was cut off; he decided, like Sir Walter Scott and many a later Member of Parliament, to save himself from bankruptcy by writing popular novels, and then buy himself a seat in the House of Commons. Within a decade (1828–37), after twelve novels, two long poems, two works of historical analysis, a play, a political pamphlet, and a heap of essays, he had recouped his fortunes; he was a reforming MP, first for the rotten borough of St Ives (1831), and then, after supporting the Great Reform Bill, for Lincoln (1832–41). He became a prominent member of the group of philosophical radicals who supported the secret ballot, a friend of the Utilitarian philosophers around James Mill (father of John Stuart), and a colleague in Parliament of the future historian of Greece, George Grote, then a banker and MP for the City of London from 1832 to 1841. In 1838 Bulwer-Lytton made his most famous speech, advocating the abolition of the last vestiges of slavery – a speech so brilliant that it silenced all opposition.

Bulwer-Lytton also had family connections with the Philhellenes; for in 1824 his older brother Henry ('a silly supercilious young man') had volunteered to oversee the transfer of £130,000 in gold sovereigns to the provisional Greek government in Nauplion from the London Greek Committee, in order to finance the War of Independence (1821–32): this 'loan' rapidly disappeared into the hands of brigand leaders, and was to poison Anglo-Greek relations for half a century.[15]

Bulwer-Lytton himself was a figure of some social style: at sixteen he had fallen passionately in love with the daughter of a confidence trickster; as a young man he had run away with a gipsy, and had been a lover of Byron's former flame, Lady Caroline Lamb; with his youthful looks and 'glitteringly golden hair that, worn in ringlets, played about his shoulders',[16] he had cut a swathe through the salons of Paris. His first successful novel, *Pelham, or the adventures of a gentleman* (1828), was a fashionable social satire, belonging to the 'silver-fork order of fiction', which destroyed the image of the Byronic hero and established the male vogue for black evening dress.[17] The hero was modelled on himself as that newly discovered figure, the dandy:

> A fop, a philosopher, a voluptuary and a moralist – a trifler in appearance but rather one to whom trifles are instinctive, than one to whom trifles are natural – an Aristippus on a limited scale, accustomed to draw sage conclusions from the follies he adopts, and while professing himself a votary of pleasure, desirous in reality to become a disciple of wisdom.[18]

In the fashionable world Bulwer-Lytton prospered: he was reconciled to his mother, who left him her family's Elizabethan ancestral seat of Knebworth, which he decorated with oriental cupolas, lions, and griffins.[19] But his marriage to a penniless Irish beauty never recovered from a decade of neglect while he was writing his novels; their relations became one of the scandals of the age: they separated, and began a feud that lasted until her death; she continued to appear at his political meetings with such effect that on one occasion he leaped from the podium into a flower bed to make his escape. In 1852 he had returned to Parliament as a very Tory MP for Hertfordshire, and in 1858 was made Secretary of State for the Colonies; his wife appeared at his election meeting dressed entirely in lemon yellow silk, with a yellow parasol, rouged face, and yellow dyed hair (the colours of the opposition party), mounted the platform and shouted out, 'Fiend, villain, monster, cowardly wretch, outcast. I am told (she hissed) you have been sent to the colonies. If they knew as much about you as I do they would have sent you there long ago.' Bulwer-Lytton (who had not set eyes on her for twenty-two years) fainted clean away. As a result of this episode he tried to have his wife incarcerated as a lunatic, and succeeded in creating a public outcry in favour of the 'Tigress of Taunton'.[20] In 1858 she wrote to Queen Victoria accusing her husband of sodomy with his friend Disraeli.[21] It was in fact Bulwer-Lytton who (having read his views on Homer) sent Gladstone into exile as governor of the Ionian Islands in 1858, thus being responsible indirectly for introducing cricket and the umbrella to Corfu. In 1862 on the abdication of King Otto of Bavaria, Bulwer-Lytton was even offered the throne of Greece, which (along with many other more sensible people) he declined.

In his day Bulwer-Lytton, 'Poet, Essayist, Orator, Statesman, Dramatist, Scholar, Novelist' (*The Times*, 1873) was described as 'not only the foremost novelist, but the most eminent living writer in English literature' (*Quarterly Review*, 1873); the novelist Plumer Ward called him 'the most accomplished writer of the most accomplished era in English letters, practising all classes and styles of composition, novelist, dramatist, poet, historian, moral philosopher, essayist, critic, political pamphleteer – in each superior to all others, and only rivalled by himself'.[22] In early life he was both a friend of and literary model for Disraeli; and later he was a close and much-admired friend of Charles Dickens. Bulwer-Lytton was buried in Westminster Abbey, with a sermon by Benjamin Jowett on 'one of England's greatest writers and one of the most distinguished men of our time'. Now he is remembered (if at all) as the author of two of the most famous phrases in the English language, 'Poverty makes for strange bedfellows' and 'The pen is mightier than the sword'.[23]

RADICAL HISTORY

Why is *Athens: Its Rise and Fall*, this unknown work of history by Bulwer-Lytton, so obscure that it has escaped the attention of the greatest scholars of nineteenth-century historical writing, from Arnaldo Momigliano to Richard Jenkyns and Frank Turner, the respective authors of the two standard works on the period?[24] It does not even appear in the ferociously learned work of Martin Bernal, *Black Athena* (London 1987), despite its central importance for his theme.[25]

The answer is given in part in the preface to the later reprint, the Knebworth edition of Bulwer-Lytton's *Miscellaneous Works* (1874):

> No more than half the author's original design was ever realised. The Rise of Athens alone, it will be seen, is herein described: the Fall is only dimly foreshadowed. When the manuscript of the present unfinished work was already in the hands of its publishers, the appearance of Mr Thirlwall's 'History of Greece' induced the author of 'Athens' to suspend his labours; and he finally abandoned them in consequence of Mr Grote's great work upon the same subject. In his Preface to that work, Mr Grote himself had frankly declared, 'If my early friend Dr Thirlwall's "History of Greece," had appeared a few years sooner, I should probably never have conceived the design of the present work at all; I should certainly not have been prompted to the task by any deficiencies such as those which I felt and regretted in Mitford.' But it was from a strong sense of those deficiencies that Lord Lytton had commenced his narrative of Athenian history; and, therefore, he had no motive to continue it when the historical method he had employed was being exhaustively applied by Mr Grote to the same field of historical research.

So the book, being incomplete and apparently superseded, was almost entirely forgotten, and has disappeared from all accounts of the development of historical writing in the nineteenth century. That is a pity, for it is the first serious radical history of Greece in modern Europe, and the most important work from that most important period of what Bernal has described as the transition from the ancient model to the Aryan model of Greek history. It is also the earliest and most significant work of the English Romantic school of history, hitherto exemplified by Carlyle and Macaulay, and constitutes the most original English contribution to the continental movement that began the great age of history.

Moreover, the book is not as incomplete as it may seem. For, following up a clue in one of the biographies of Bulwer-Lytton, I was led to the Hertfordshire Archives, where, in the autumn of 2002, I opened a dusty brown paper parcel – to discover not only the original manuscript of the first two volumes, but also a manuscript of several hundred pages containing the draft of volume III, on the 'Fall of Athens'. Much of this manuscript is a simple retelling of the narrative of Thucydides. But I was able to transcribe and publish in 2004 enough to prove that Bulwer-Lytton had anticipated by decades most of the radical views on Athenian history hitherto attributed to George Grote. For example, Cleon is for the first time recognized as a talented and truly democratic politician. There is a full account of the Pylos affair, in which Cleon 'the able demagogue' is recast as the hero of the story long before Grote attempted the same:

> Thro' his whole course on this occasion one cannot but suspect that he was in secret correspondence with Demosthenes and acted by his intelligence and advice. We have seen before the little unison that existed between Demosthenes and the Commanders of the Fleet Eurymedon and Sophocles. It is highly probable, that among the reasons which deterred Demosthenes from assault on Sphacteria, was the non co-operation of the two commanders. From what follows Cleon evidently had been acquainted with the plan formed by Demosthenes – he names him as his Colleague in the Expedition. What more likely than that Demosthenes really stood in need of Cleon's influence with the popular Assembly to force the rival commanders to the measures he meditated? If Thucydides is not clear in this somewhat obscure business we must remember that he was in opposition to Cleon and that the most penetrating investigator cannot discover all the true springs of conduct in the Party he opposes.

The Pylos episode clearly fascinated Bulwer-Lytton. Reading the forgotten manuscript of *Athens* in the County Archive, a letter fell out from between the pages: it was a reply to a request by Bulwer-Lytton for information about the bay of Pylos. The writer signed himself Edward Codrington; the name was vaguely familiar. Then I suddenly remembered – this was Sir Edward Codrington, the British admiral at the battle of Navarino, who had destroyed the Turkish fleet in 1826, and so guaranteed the freedom of the Greeks.[26]

The introduction to the unpublished 'volume III' reveals in fact most clearly the ultimate purpose of this fundamental rewriting of Greek history:

> We have traced the rise of the Athenian Commonwealth – we have now before us its meridian and decline. In the Peloponnesian War we approach events not more memorable in the Annals of the Ancient World, than instructive to the Societies of the Modern. For as it has been justly said, 'there is an ancient and a modern period in the History of every People, the ancient differing, and the modern in many essential points agreeing with that in which we live'.[27] In Greece then, as through Europe now, a great Popular spirit was at work. To the earlier times, when Aristocracy protects freedom from the single tyrant, to the later era of civilization when wealth becomes the innovating principle and enfeebles by extending the privileges of Nobility and Birth, now succeeded the graver struggle between Property and Numbers – that struggle which has produced the greatest calamities in the Past, and with which unreasoning Fanaticism and Speculative Philosophy have alike threatened the Futures of existing Nations. Whatever our several opinions and predilections, we can only profit by the lessons which the history of this struggle in the most brilliant period of Grecian civilization should bestow, by preserving the disproportionate judgement which distinguishes the guide who bequeathed to Mankind the narrative of the Peloponnesian War – κτῆμα ἐς αἰεί – 'an everlasting possession,' not to subserve the aims of malignant partizans, but to enrich the experience of every statesman and warn the factions of every Land.

As was already apparent from the published volume, Bulwer-Lytton's work belongs to his reforming days as a Radical and a Utilitarian. His aim was to make Greek history live and serve the radical cause. While he was well acquainted with the latest German scholarship, he also sought to create a history that would stir his contemporaries: as one of his biographers says, 'His Athens sensibly promoted the English interest in Greek civilization, history, art, and letters first excited by Byron. In politics there was no question of the times about which, on the Whig or Radical side, he had not written or spoken with destructiveness and effect.'[28] Bulwer-Lytton's *Athens* is in fact the earliest and most forthright of those histories of Greece that set out to destroy the reputation of William Mitford; in his novel *Pelham* (1828) he had actually inserted a footnote in describing one of his characters:

> His knowledge of the liberty of Greece was not drawn from the ignorant historian of her Republics;* nor did he find in the contemplative and gentle philosophy of the ancients, nothing but a sanction for modern bigotry and existing abuses.
>
> *It is really a disgrace to our University, that any of its colleges should accept as a reference, or even tolerate as an author, the presumptuous bigot who has bequeathed to us, in his 'History of Greece', the masterpiece of a declaimer without energy, and of a pedant without learning.[29]

And of the twenty-six references to Mitford in Bulwer-Lytton's *Athens*, all but one are critical.

The unfinished book was immensely popular at home and abroad throughout the nineteenth century: Escott wrote in 1910 that 'some thirty years ago . . . Northumbrian miners and Midland artisans I then found to be well-acquainted with, not only Bulwer-Lytton's fictions, but the serious historical sketches contained in his essays and his Athens'.[30] The book was translated into German apparently three times in 1837 (Bulwer-Lytton is one of the major British influences on the German novel);[31] it was issued in a popular Tauchnitz (Leipzig) edition for railway travellers (1843), and twice pirated in his collected works.[32] In the United States copies can be found in a variety of American editions in many libraries (I have reports of editions of 1837, 1847, 1852, 1860, and 1874). There is an Italian translation of 1838, of which three copies still exist, in the public libraries of Milan and Bergamo, and in the archbishop's library in Turin.[33] The Royal Library in Copenhagen records a Danish translation of 1856 in three volumes, as part of the collected works of Bulwer-Lytton, which ran to sixty-nine volumes in all.[34] The edition that I had purchased is indeed evidence of this popularity, for it was printed by the man whom Byron affectionately called 'the old pirate Galignani', an Italian publisher in Paris who from 1800 to 1852, before the copyright agreement between Britain and France, made a speciality of reprinting, within a month and at one-fifth of the price, the works of the most famous English authors of the Romantic age, such as Byron, Shelley, Coleridge, and even a very scholarly first collected edition of Keats.[35]

The relationship between Bulwer-Lytton and Galignani reveals the underside of publishing in this period. In the Princeton collection of Bulwer-Lytton's manuscripts I found a letter concerning the publication of *Athens* by Galignani, apparently simultaneously with its publication in Britain. This was no accident, but was provoked by Bulwer-Lytton himself, who sent the following letter in his own handwriting to Galignani: it is undated but clearly written a few months before the publication of the work in 1837:

> Monsr [?] Galignani / Editeur. Libraire / Rue Vivienne / Paris
>
> Sir,
>
> I know not if you are desirous of entering into any negotiations with me for the proofs of my future works, & I have received an offer else where – But our former transactions, give you at least, the right of an option – I wish to know what you would give for the proofs of 'Athens, its Rise & fall' – 2 large volumes containing more matter than 3 volumes of a Novel – On my side, in this work, I engage that it will be 3 months passing thro' the press. That you will receive it in parcels containing 6 or 7 sheets at a time – & that the Last parcel will be forwarded to you 10 days before publication in this country.
>
> On your side I require a sacred promise that the proofs I have not serve the purpose of any french translation – but be kept rigidly [?] for your own English edition – & that the money agreed on shall be punctually [?] paid [?] – half on receipt of the first proofs – half on receipt of the last.
>
> I desire also to know what you would give for a volume selling here for £10 which I am about to give to press – containing 2 tragedies in 5 Acts each one called The Duchess de la Valliere – the other Cromwell. – on the same conditions. This volume will be about 6 weeks going thro' the press – & will be sent in the same regular manner as the History. Requiring me . . . [*illegible*] answer at your leisure[??]. ELB.[36]

In other words, Bulwer-Lytton was regularly engaged in surreptitiously sending the proofs of the English edition of his own books to Galignani in Paris, so that Galignani could publish a cheap edition (approximately one-third of the price) simultaneously with the expensive London edition – Bulwer-Lytton was cheating his own English publisher.[37] No wonder I also found in Princeton a letter from Bulwer-Lytton's publisher George Routledge about a different matter, warning his correspondent not to trust Bulwer-Lytton, who was 'a sly fox'.

Athens is important because of the author's recognition that he stood at the turning point of the writing of Greek history, and because his aim was to present to a popular audience the current state of modern controversy. He offered for instance the most reasoned view that I have yet discovered for what Martin Bernal has called 'the ancient model' of the origins of Greek culture, the view that it resulted from Egyptian colonization.[38] Bulwer-Lytton argued explicitly and persuasively for the ancient view that Cecrops was Egyptian, and for the proposition that many high cultures have derived from colonization by a more civilized power. But his second chapter was devoted to 'the unimportant Consequences to be deduced from the Admission that Cecrops might be Egyptian'. He stood therefore exactly at that turning point between the 'ancient' and the 'Aryan' model of Greek history which Bernal had hypothesized without being able to find the evidence. This age of transition certainly existed; one of Bulwer-Lytton's reviewers noticed it explicitly:[39]

> With regard to one species of foreign influence – that exerted by Egypt – Mr Bulwer properly characterises it as 'faint and evanescent.' Yet the early intrusion of Egyptian settlers on the Attic soil must, we think, be admitted as a fact – not upon the direct testimony of Greek writers, but upon the much stronger, though more oblique evidence of some remarkable traces in Athenian religion, policy, and art. On this head we agree with Frederick Thiersch, Dr Arnold, and Mr Bulwer himself, rather than with Mr Keightley, Mr Thirlwall, and the Germans whom they follow.

In 1842, J.A. St John, in a dedication to his son, rather poignantly claimed to have lost his eyesight in pursuing the Egyptian origins of Greek civilization:[40]

> Whithersoever we have travelled, the wrecks of Grecian literature have accompanied us, and the studies to which these pages owe their existence have been pursued under the influence of almost every climate in Europe. Nay if I pushed my researches still further and visited the portion of Africa commonly supposed to have been the cradle of Hellenic civilization, it was solely in the hope of qualifying myself to speak with some degree of confidence on the subject of those arts which represent to the Modern World so much of the grandeur and genius of Greece. Here, probably, the action of pestilential winds, and of the sands and burning glare of the desert commenced that dimming of the 'visual ray', which, in all likelihood, will wrap me gradually in complete darkness, and veil forever from my sight those forms of the beautiful which have been incarnated, if I may so speak, in marble. This is a language which neither you nor your sister can read to me.

In like fashion Bulwer-Lytton had read and rejected the opinions of the recently translated Karl Otfried Müller (see below, ch. 8) on the Dorian race; he considered German views of the origins of Greek religion, only to reject them in favour of a rationalizing interpretation along French lines. He had read the first two volumes of Bishop Connop Thirlwall, but dedicated his work to the last (and maddest) representative of the English tradition of pseudo-exact scholarship, Henry Fynes Clinton, author of the once famous *Fasti Hellenici* (1824–7), a treatise on chronology that Bulwer-Lytton compared later to Bayle's *Dictionary* or Gibbon's *History*, 'a book to which thousands of books had contributed, only to make the originality of the single mind more bold and clear'.[41]

ATHENS AGAINST SPARTA AGAIN

As we have seen, it was traditional in French and English (and even more in Scottish) works on Greek history of the eighteenth century to present a contrast between Sparta and Athens, based respectively on the accounts in Plutarch's *Lives* of Lycurgus and Solon: Sparta usually won by a large margin. What is most interesting about Bulwer-Lytton's book is his use of this contrast. It is expressed with the rhetorical force of a professional politician skilled in persuading; and it sought to create a chorus of public opinion that should lead to action; his work was designed 'not for colleges and cloisters, but for the general and miscellaneous public'. His views therefore represented and also sought to influence the public opinion of contemporary British society; they are politically of far greater importance than those of professional historians. It seems indeed to have been partly the difficulty of combining scholarship with political views, and his sense of the increasing dominance of professionalism in historical studies, especially the prospect of competition with the scholarship of Thirlwall, that caused Bulwer-Lytton to abandon his projected history after the first two volumes, which carry the story down to the death of Pericles, and an appreciation of Sophocles. For he had intended originally to continue the work down to 'the period when the annals of the world are merged into the chronicle of the Roman Empire'.[42]

Bulwer-Lytton's aim was clearly presented in his title: he saw the history of Greece both conceptually, and in its relation to the modern age, as a history of the rise and fall of Athens, on which the histories of all other Greek cities were dependent. By his very denial of the charge, his preface already admitted that his interpretation was likely to be regarded as politically motivated:

> As the history of the Greek Republics has been too often corruptly pressed into the service of heated political partisans, may I be pardoned the precaution of observing, that whatever my own political code, as applied to England, I have nowhere sought knowingly to pervert the lessons of the past to fugitive interests and party purposes. Whether led sometimes to censure, or more often to vindicate, the Athenian People, I am not conscious of any other desire than that of strict, faithful, impartial justice.

Bulwer-Lytton's description of Sparta is traditional in its approach, although he is aware of the views of Müller; for instance, on the legend of the Return of Heraclidae, Bulwer-Lytton rejects Müller's opinion: 'The true nature of this revolution has only been rendered more obscure by modern ingenuity; which has abandoned the popular accounts for suppositions still more improbable and romantic.'[43] But under the influence of Müller he abandons the view that Lycurgus was responsible for the Spartan constitution:[44]

> I enter not into the discussion whether he framed an entirely new constitution, or whether he restored the spirit of one common to his race and

> not unfamiliar to Sparta. Common sense seems to me sufficient to assure us of the latter. Let those who please believe that one man, without the intervention of arms – not as a conqueror but a friend – could succeed in establishing a constitution, resting not upon laws, but manners – not upon force, but usage – utterly hostile to all the tastes, desires, and affections of human nature: . . . For my part, I know that all history furnishes no other such example; and I believe that no man was ever so miraculously endowed with the power to conquer nature.

Lycurgus' aim was to restore not create; Crete already had Dorian customs, and the regulations of Lycurgus must be regarded as not 'peculiar to Sparta but as the most perfect development of the Dorian constitutions, as we learn from Pindar'.[45]

But rather than follow the principles proposed by the racial typology of Müller, in Book I, chapter VI, section VI, Bulwer-Lytton gave 'a brief, but I trust a sufficient outline, of the Spartan constitution, social and political', of a traditional type, until he arrived at 'the most active and efficient part of the government, viz. the Institution of the Ephors':

> It is clear that the later authority of the ephors was never designed by Lycurgus, or the earlier legislators. It is entirely at variance with the confined aristocracy which was the aim of the Spartan, and of nearly every genuine Doric constitution. It made a democracy as it were by stealth. This powerful body consisted of five persons, chosen annually by the people. In fact, they may be called the representatives of the popular will . . . Its influence was the result of the vicious constitution of the gerusia, or council. Had that assembly been properly constituted, there would have been no occasion for the ephors . . . Of two assemblies – the ephors and the gerusia – we see the one elected annually, the other for life – the one responsible to the people, the other not – the one composed of men, busy, stirring, ambitious, in the vigour of life – the other of veterans, past the ordinary stimulus of exertion, and regarding the dignity of office rather as the reward of a life, than the opening to ambition. Of two such assemblies, it is easy to foretell which would lose, and which would augment, authority . . . The ephoralty was the focus of popular power. Like an American Congress, or an English House of Commons, it prevented the action of the people, by acting in behalf of the people. To representatives annually chosen the multitude cheerfully left the management of

> their interests. Thus it was true that the ephors prevented the encroachments of the popular assembly; – but how? by encroaching themselves, and in the name of the people! . . . The ephors gradually destroyed the constitution of Sparta; but, without the ephors, it may be reasonably doubted whether the constitution would have survived half as long . . . Had the other part of the Spartan constitution (absurdly panegyrized) been so formed as to harmonize with, even in checking, the power of the ephors; and, above all, had it not been for the lamentable error of a social system, which, by seeking to exclude the desire of gain, created a terrible re-action, and made the Spartan magistrature the most venal and corrupt in Greece – the ephors might have sufficed to develop all the best principles of government. For they went nearly to recognize the soundest philosophy of the representative system, being the smallest number of representatives chosen, without restriction, from the greatest number of electors, for short periods, and under strong responsibilities.

The distinction between ancient direct democracy and modern representative democracy was later to become a central theme in Utilitarian political thought: it is here clearly enunciated.

Bulwer-Lytton's view of the social system was equally negative:[46]

> If we consider the situation of the Spartans at the time of Lycurgus, and during a long subsequent period, we see at once that to enable them to live at all, they must be accustomed to the life of a camp; – they were a little colony of soldiers, supporting themselves, hand and foot, in a hostile country, over a population that detested them . . . to be brave, temperate, and hardy, were the only means by which to escape the sword of the Messenian, and to master the hatred of the Helot . . . Accordingly the child was reared, from the earliest age, to a life of hardship, discipline, and privation; he was starved into abstinence; – he was beaten into fortitude; – he was punished without offence, that he might be trained to bear without a groan; – the older he grew, till he reached manhood, the severer the discipline he underwent. The intellectual education was little attended to . . . The youth . . . was stimulated to condense his thoughts, and to be ready in reply; to say little, and to the point. An aphorism bounded his philosophy . . . The absorbing love for his native Sparta rendered the citizen singularly selfish towards other states, even kindred to that which he belonged to. Fearless as a Spartan, – when Sparta was unmenaced he was lukewarm as a Greek.

Again he does not believe that there was equality of property in Sparta:

> It is said that Lycurgus forbade the use of gold and silver, and ordained an iron coinage; but gold and silver were at that time unknown as coins in Sparta, and iron was a common medium of exchange throughout Greece. The interdiction of the precious metals was therefore of later origin . . . A more pernicious regulation it is impossible to conceive. While it effectually served to cramp the effects of emulation – to stint the arts – to limit industry and enterprise – it produced the direct object it was intended to prevent; – it infected the whole state with the desire of gold – it forbade wealth to be spent, in order that wealth might be hoarded; every man seems to have desired gold precisely because he could make very little use of it! From the king to the Helot, the spirit of covetousness spread like a disease. No state in Greece was so open to bribery – no magistracy so corrupt as the ephors. Sparta became a nation of misers precisely because it could not become a nation of spendthrifts. Such are the results which man produces when his legislation deposes nature! . . .[47]

> The whole fabric of the Spartan character rested upon slavery . . . The motives that render power most intolerant combined in the Spartan in his relations to the Helot – viz. first, necessity for his services, lost perhaps if the curb were ever relaxed – second, consummate contempt for the individual he debased . . . Revolt and massacre were perpetually before a Spartan's eyes; and what man will be gentle and unsuspecting to those who wait only the moment to murder him?[48]

> Such are the general outlines of the state and constitution of Sparta – the firmest aristocracy that perhaps ever existed, for it was an aristocracy on the widest base . . . Although the ephors made the government really and latently democratic, yet the concentration of its action made it seemingly oligarchic; and in its secrecy, caution, vigilance and energy, it exhibited the best of the oligarchic features . . . It was a state of political freedom, but of social despotism.[49]

'With this, I close my introductory chapters and proceed from Dissertation into History'[50] – unlike the origins of Sparta, Solon and Athens belong to history; and Bulwer-Lytton's long and favourable account of the life and activities of Solon ended with a panegyric[51] of that traditionally most suspect of Athenian institutions, the democratic assembly:

> We cannot but allow the main theory of the system to have been precisely that most favourable to the prodigal exuberance of energy, of intellect, and of genius. Summoned to consultation upon all matters, from the greatest to the least, the most venerable to the most trite – today deciding on the number of their warships, tomorrow on that of a tragic chorus; now examining with jealous forethoughts the new barriers to oligarchical ambition; – now appointing, with nice distinction, to various service the various combinations of music; – now welcoming in their forum-senate the sober ambassadors of Lacedaemon or the jewelled heralds of Persia, now voting their sanction to new temples or the reverent reform of worship; compelled to a lively and unceasing interest in all that arouses the mind, or elevates the passions, or refines the taste; – supreme arbiters of the art of the sculptor, as the science of the lawgiver, – judges and rewarders of the limner and the poet, as of the successful negotiator or the prosperous soldier; – we see at once the all-accomplished, all-versatile genius of the nation, and we behold in the same glance the effect and the cause: – every thing being referred to the people, the people learned of every thing to judge. Their genius was artificially forced, and in each of its capacities. They had no need of formal education. Their whole life was one school . . . All that can inspire the thought or delight the leisure were for the people. Theirs were the portico and the school – theirs the theatre, the gardens, and the baths; they were not, as in Sparta, the tools of the state – they *were* the state! Lycurgus made machines and Solon men. In Sparta the machine was to be wound up by the tyranny of the fixed principle; it could not dine as it pleased – it could not walk as it pleased – it was not permitted to seek its she machine save by stealth and in the dark; its children were not its own – even itself had no property in self. Sparta incorporated under the name of freedom, the worst complexities, the most grievous and the most frivolous vexations, of slavery. And therefore it was that Lacedaemon flourished and decayed, bequeathing to fame men only noted for hardy valour, fanatical patriotism, and profound but dishonourable craft – attracting indeed the wonder of the world, but advancing no claim to its gratitude, and contributing no single addition to its intellectual stores. But in Athens the true blessing of freedom was rightly placed – in the opinions and the soul. Thought was the common

> heritage which every man might cultivate at his will. This unshackled liberty had its convulsions and its excesses, but producing unceasing emulation and unbounded competition, an incentive to every effort, a tribunal to every claim, it broke into philosophy with the one – into poetry with the other – into the energy and splendour of unexampled intelligence with all. Looking round us at this hour, more than four-and-twenty centuries after the establishment of the constitution we have just surveyed, – in the labours of the student – in the dreams of the poet – in the aspirations of the artist – in the philosophy of the legislator – we yet behold the imperishable blessings we derive from the liberties of Athens and the institutions of Solon. The life of Athens became extinct, but her soul transfused itself, immortal and immortalizing, through the world.

Bulwer-Lytton, writing in the age of philhellenism, expressed the values already formulated by the Irishman John Gast and now increasingly accepted by the British ruling class. The admiration of Sparta that they had learned from their reading of Plutarch, and from traditional history books written under the influence of French and Scottish models, had disappeared; it had been replaced by a devotion to Athenian democracy, once held only by the most desperate of radicals such as Tom Paine and de Pauw, but now diffused through the entire liberal intelligentsia in the age of the Great Reform Bill, which itself was perceived as making Britain for the first time a true democracy. And most surprisingly of all, the focus of this admiration for the Greek past lay in the newly discovered cultural and educational consequences of that democratic assembly, which in antiquity had been almost universally held in contempt by authors such as Thucydides and Aristophanes, Plato and Aristotle, and had been presented as a centre of corruption in the Athenian democratic system even by the young George Grote in 1826. This was in political terms the decisive moment in the move from the eighteenth-century idealization of Sparta to the nineteenth-century love affair with Athens. It is no wonder that, despite the central role played by Maniote leaders (so often compared to ancient Spartans), in October 1834 the tiny frontier village of Athens, with no public buildings or hospital or school, rather than Sparta (or Nauplion, Aegina, or Syra), was chosen as the capital of the new Greek state: as Bulwer-Lytton's reviewer in the *Edinburgh Review* for 1837 put it:[52]

> Century after century rolls on in merited obscurity. Athens is insulted by the name, without the substance of freedom, until her conquest by Omar. She is an appendage of the harem, and 'a pander and eunuch governs her governor', until the Greeks of our own time show something of their fathers' spirit. Then – 'Last scene of all / That ends this strange eventful history' – A Bavarian prince builds his palace in the city of Theseus – his subjects address him in a jargon which mingles Turkish, French, Italian, and German with remnants of the lowest Hellenic dialect – and the traveller, who has been landed by a steam-boat at the mole of the Piraeus, returns from a day's shooting in Boeotia to an English Hotel in Athens, kept by a native of Wapping!

Athens' rival, Sparta, was rewarded with a neoclassical town plan by the Bavarian architect Friedrich Stauffert on its vacant site, a plan that it still possesses, organized on rational principles with the main square containing the town hall, palace of justice, and post office, while religion and crime – the orthodox cathedral and the prison – were relegated to separate quarters in the wings.[53]

Bulwer-Lytton's *Athens* should indeed be compared with a far more famous work, published in the same year of 1837 – Thomas Carlyle's bizarre and compulsively unreadable *French Revolution*, whose relentless addresses to the Reader required him to partake of every event and every emotion, and whose reliance on the minutiae of history to create a sense of vividness exactly followed Macaulay's conception of the significance of Walter Scott's techniques of historical *bricolage*. Bulwer-Lytton relied in contrast on the more traditional methods of dialogue and vivid narration, and succeeded in being more effective precisely because he was less outlandish.

The power of Bulwer-Lytton's style was that of the professional orator and novelist. Its sources can be found in his long final account of the poet Sophocles. To the modern reader perhaps that analysis reads oddly, although it is wholly in place in the German Romantic tradition that Bulwer-Lytton knew well. The centre of Sophocles' art lies in two supreme strengths, those of plot and pathos. His own writing could not be better characterized: slightly later, Thirlwall saw history as the validation of the Niebuhrian method of research, Grote saw it as the unending demonstration of the rightness of Utilitarian principles; Bulwer-Lytton's aim was that of the true Romantic novelist, to make the story immensely vivid, to engage the reader in the action, and to make him suffer with the pathos of successive victories and defeats. Plot and pathos, narrative virtues unknown to Thirlwall and Grote, make Bulwer-Lytton's work as vivid as that of any of his contemporaries in Britain or on the continent.

On its first publication, the importance of Bulwer-Lytton's work was recognized in both Radical and Tory circles. Everyone remarked in almost identical words on the surprising fact that a fashionable novelist and a dandy should turn to philosophical history: the Radical journals, the *Edinburgh Review* and the *British and Foreign Review*, published long and appreciative essays;[54] even the Tory press was respectful[55] – except for the High Tory satirical journal, *Fraser's Magazine* (patron of Bulwer-Lytton's estranged wife), which made fun of the book:

> With that restless ambition of authorship, which the love of glory or of gold can alone keep at fever heat, the honourable member for Lincoln has chosen to appear this season in the character of a learned doctor from the Academy of Athens; having matriculated, we presume, at Pompeii, and taken his A.M. degree at the University of Stinkomalee.

The author went on to attack the 'philosophical cutthroat' of the French Revolution who had made a cult of Athens, and to praise the partisan 'zeal' of Mitford in his demonstration that 'a mob in the agora could act the tiger as well as the autocrat on his throne'.

More respectfully the High Tory historian and reactionary Sir Archibald Allison[56] began his review with the trenchant declaration:

> It is a remarkable fact, that so numerous and pregnant are the proofs afforded by history in all ages, of the universal and irremediable evils of democratic ascendency, that there is hardly an historical writer of any note, in any country or period of the world, who has not concurred in condemning it as the most dangerous form of government, and the most fatal enemy of that freedom which it professes to support.

Bulwer-Lytton knew the dangers: in June 2003 I acquired a letter advertised for sale on the web by Roy Davids, and written in Bulwer-Lytton's characteristic style. The letter is addressed, 'London June fourth 1837, Col. D'aguilar Dublin Ireland'. George Charles D'Aguilar (1784–1855) was a close friend of Bulwer-Lytton, who dedicated the essays collected in *The*

Student (1836) to him; D'Aguilar was some twenty years older, and a professional soldier from a military family. He had fought in India and in the Mediterranean during the Napoleonic Wars, and later commanded the British troops in China. In 1813–15 he had served as a major in the regiment of Greek Light Infantry raised in the Ionian Islands by one of the future liberators of Greece, Sir Richard Church, and had moved in the circle of the friends of Byron. By 1837 D'Aguilar was Deputy Adjutant General of the Dublin garrison; he was the author of a standard work on courts martial, and translated the military maxims of Napoleon, as well as Schiller's *Fiesko*; he had a great love of the theatre, and it was in D'Aguilar's Dublin house that Bulwer-Lytton met the actor William Macready for the first time. He was just the man to appreciate the new history of Greece:[57]

8 Charles St
Berkeley Sq
June 4
My dear d'Aguilar

I am delighted at your kind & spontaneous criticism on Athens. – I suppose it must be a work of time to secure the public attention to a dry work of that kind. Meanwhile your praise feeds hope. You ask about His Majesty From all I can hear – his illness appears mortal. Water in the Chest. – His state is one cause that keeps the Govt. together as he does not wish the tumult of change at such a time – If Victoria follow the policy of the Duchess the Whigs will keep a long sway – if not – the Moderate Tories will repossess themselves. The loyal feeling for the Princess is astonishing and will probably, with any popular leaning on her side – retard for years the Movement.

Mrs B. favoured me with a copy of severe verses the other day. This is all I know of her. – . . . What weather one glimpse of sunshine today. I am going to adopt Wordsworth's advice 'Up – up my friends & leave your Books' & dine at Putney! – so my letter like my time must be short. – I think you will be pleased with a Novel I am printing which will be out in 6 weeks The Hero is a literary cove! Time Modern – Style sentimental o – reflective, o Germanico!

You will find me ensconced in Charles St with a spare bed for you when you come to town.

Yrs Ever
EL Bulwer

The work of time for a dry work! It was finally on the bicentenary of Bulwer-Lytton's birth, 2003, that we celebrated at his ancestral seat of Knebworth the republication of the (at last almost complete) *Athens: Its Rise and Fall*, and offered readings from his revolutionary book at the venue that has been graced by so many rock idols.

George Grote (1794–1871)

7
Utilitarian History: Mill and Grote

WAITING FOR GROTE

The Utilitarian engagement with Athenian democracy seems to go back at least to James Mill, the self-educated Scotsman who had attended Edinburgh University as a young man. The fascination with Athens of his son John Stuart began in childhood – he started learning Greek with his father at the age of three and had read all of Thucydides by the time he was twelve; his particular passion was ancient history. In John Stuart's description of his austere education at the hands of his father, he describes James's enthusiasm for Greek history, and his antipathy to Mitford:[1]

> History continued to be my strongest predilection and most of all ancient history. Mitford's Greece I read continually; my father had put me on my guard against the Tory prejudices of this writer, and his perversions of facts for the whitewashing of despots, and blackening of popular institutions. These points he discoursed on, exemplifying them from the Greek orators and historians, with such effect that in reading Mitford my sympathies were always on the contrary side to those of the author, and I could, to some extent, have argued the point against him: yet this did not diminish the ever new pleasure with which I read the book.

Again it was his father who drew John Stuart's attention to the insight that Demosthenes 'afforded into Athenian institutions, and the principles of legislation and government which they often illustrated'. For James Mill the study of the Greek language that he imposed on his son was essentially a preliminary to understanding the virtues of Athenian democracy. As a young man John Stuart Mill had dreamed of becoming a historian and emulating his father's achievement in writing a *History of British India* (1817); in the 1830s he contemplated a history of the French Revolution, and collected much material, which he handed on to Thomas Carlyle, in the production of whose great work he participated in a variety of ways – not least by inadvertently burning the only manuscript of the first volume in a traumatic episode not entirely free of Freudian overtones.[2]

The young banker George Grote's adherence to Utilitarianism stemmed from his friendship with James Mill, his neighbour in Threadneedle Street, to whom he was introduced in 1819 when he was twenty-five, and through whom he also met David Ricardo and Jeremy Bentham. Grote became a committed disciple in their inner group; in 1821 he had taken the manuscript arguments of Bentham in favour of atheism and turned them into a book that he published under the pseudonym of Philip Beauchamp as *An Analysis of the Influence of Natural Religion* (London 1822). Grote was also a leading protagonist in the struggle for the Great Reform Bill, writing theoretical works and organizing the City of London banking community in favour of the reforms. He was a Member of Parliament for the City of London in the reformed Parliament from 1832 to 1841 and was widely expected to be leader of the Philosophical Radicals as they pressed for further reforms. But he proved to be a disappointment; despite their lifelong friendships with Grote, James Mill and his son were especially disillusioned, as the early draft of Mill's autobiography reveals:[3]

> Nobody disappointed my father & me more than Grote because no-one else had so much in his power. We had long known him fainthearted, ever despairing of success, thinking all obstacles gigantic; but the Reform Bill excitement seemed for a time to make a new man of him: he had grown hopeful, & seemed as if he could almost become energetic. When brought face to face however with an audience opposed to his opinions, when called on to beat up against the stream, he was found wanting. The years which he withdrew from his History & spent in the House of Commons were almost wasted. Except an annual motion for the ballot (to which he continued to stick after the change of times had made it no longer desirable) and an honourable stand made now & then against a bad measure, such as the Irish & Canada Coercion Bills, Mr. Grote was almost an inactive member of parliament.

The reference to the annual motion for the ballot reveals a fundamental difference between the political views of Mill and Grote, for Grote was an ardent supporter of the secret ballot in elections, whereas Mill long insisted that they should be held with an open ballot. There are perhaps signs in these views of Mill of a fatal weakness and a depressive personality in Grote. Even to close friends like Richard Cobden, he appeared a singularly unsuccessful politician who insisted on behaving as if he were in Plato's Republic.[4] Certainly Grote's wife Harriet was a far more forceful character, who dominated her husband throughout their lives and protected his legacy after his death.[5]

It is clear, however, that Grote's interest in writing a history of Greece began early in his relationship with the Utilitarians. Harriet Grote claimed that it was she who had proposed to her husband the writing of a history of Greece as early as 1822, although the draft of Mill's autobiography suggests otherwise; talking of the *Westminster Review* he says:[6]

> Grote also was a contributor only once [1826], all the time he could spare being already taken up by his *History of Greece*, which he had commenced at my father's instigation. The article he wrote was on his own subject, & was a very complete exposure & castigation of Mitford.

And Grote's fragmentary essay 'Of the Athenian Government' is dated April 1821 (see below), two years after he first met James Mill.[7] There seems no difficulty in supposing that it was indeed the elder Mill's influence that turned Grote towards Greek history. It is often thought that his long delay in producing his *History* was due to Grote's preoccupation with parliamentary business as a Radical MP; but whatever the reason it is clear that, in the years that he spent working (or not working) on his *History of Greece*, even as late as 1837, few were aware of its future contents.

Meanwhile the only Radical history of Greece was that of Bulwer-Lytton. The relationship between Bulwer-Lytton's *Athens* and Utilitarian views on Greek history is clear. His book shows that the political ideas later expressed by Grote were already widespread in radical circles for a generation before Grote began publishing, and reveals how much had changed and become common knowledge in the period between the death of Lord Byron in 1824 and the start of the reign of Grote – precisely in the age marked within Britain by the Great Reform Bill of

1832, and externally by the activity of the British Philhellenes in the Greek War of Independence.

Grote, the Mills, and Bulwer-Lytton were closely connected in the exciting period before the Reform Bill. But although the younger Mill's views on Athens were very similar to those of Bulwer-Lytton and the later Grote, he seems to have arrived at them independently: there is at least no sign in Mill's correspondence of any discussion or close involvement between the three men. The early morning meetings organized by John Stuart Mill in Grote's house, where he lent a room, were indeed attended by Bulwer-Lytton; but according to Mill the discussions concerned his father James Mill's writings, political economy, logic (Grote joined them for this), and analytical psychology – not Greek history. In the late 1820s up to 1829 James Mill ran a debating society that included both the Greek historian Connop Thirlwall and 'Edward and Henry Lytton Bulwer';[8] but again, although there was plenty of opportunity for exchanges, there is no evidence that any of this activity concerned ancient history. And although John Stuart Mill belonged to the same reforming circle as Bulwer-Lytton, one imagines that their different personalities would not have mixed well: Bulwer-Lytton's problems concerned his mother and his wife, while John Stuart's desire to escape from the influence of his father resulted in a fixation on Carlyle as a metaphysical mentor;[9] and Carlyle detested all that Bulwer-Lytton stood for – the dandy posings and the social and literary success that for so long eluded the self-made, cantankerous, hirsute Scottish guru.

Nevertheless, the Utilitarians were a close-knit tribe; they were fully aware of the importance of Bulwer-Lytton's venture. In the 1830s the younger Mill and Bulwer-Lytton were engaged in writing for each other's Radical journals, and Mill (wittingly or unwittingly) contributed an appendix on Jeremy Bentham to Bulwer-Lytton's British version of de Tocqueville, *England and the English* (1833); Mill persuaded Carlyle to read this book despite his opinion of Bulwer-Lytton as 'a poor fribble'.[10] But in October 1835 Mill joked with Carlyle when he heard Bulwer-Lytton was writing a Greek history: 'Perhaps, bye the bye, you did not see, before you went away, the announcement that Bulwer-Lytton is to publish a History of Athens – what will the world come to! but I much wonder what it will be like.'[11] A year later Mill wrote to Bulwer-Lytton, eagerly anticipating its publication.[12] In May or June 1837 he wrote again to Bulwer-Lytton, 'I had not time the other evening to tell you how much I am delighted with "Athens" – the book is so good, that very few people will see how good.'[13]

Although Bulwer-Lytton and Grote held similar political views in the reformed Parliament of 1832, in the nine years that they shared together (1832–41) they were not easy bedfellows: in 1838 Grote dismissed Bulwer-Lytton in a speech as 'a literary Whig',[14] and Bulwer-Lytton's view of Grote is perhaps already exemplified in his portrait of 'Snap, the academical philosopherling':[15]

> If our philosopherling enters the House of Commons, he sets up for a *man of business*; he begs to be put upon the dullest committees; he would not lose an hour of twaddle for the world; he affects to despise eloquence, but he never speaks without having learnt every sentence by heart. And oh! such sentences, and such delivery! for the Snaps have no enthusiasm! It is the nature of the material philosophy to forbid that beautiful prodigality of heart; he unites in his agreeable style, the pomp of apathy with the solemnity of dulness. Nine times out of ten our philosopherling is the son of a merchant, his very pulse seems to enter its account in the ledger-book. Ah Plato! Ah Milton! did you mean the lute of philosophy for hands like these!

When Grote's magisterial *History of Greece* finally emerged a generation later, in the second Victorian age of reform, it had far less relevance, and Grote seems to have forgotten his predecessor. In his explanations of his failure to complete his *Athens*, Bulwer-Lytton had deferred to his rivals Thirlwall and Grote; and the original manuscript suggests indeed that he only finally abandoned his project soon after 1846, when Grote's first volumes were published.[16] But his account hides a more serious situation. Consider the chronology. Grote did not begin to publish until 1846,[17] nine years after Bulwer-Lytton's work; the main political section of his history was not completed until 1856, more than a decade after Bulwer-Lytton's unpublished thoughts on radical Athens. Connop Thirlwall's first volumes were indeed published in 1835, in time to be used by Bulwer-Lytton; but its publication too extends to 1844. For most of its course Bulwer-Lytton's book was indeed the earliest of a group of works that represented the reaction to Mitford, in the light of the new enthusiasm for Greece aroused by Byron and the Philhellenes. But in his great work a decade and more later, although he often cited Thirlwall, George

Grote nowhere mentioned the work of Bulwer-Lytton, despite the fact that it anticipated his approach in many essential respects: it too is, in the words of Eduard Meyer, 'not a history but an apologia for Athens';[18] it too mounts a sustained attack on Mitford; it too uses German sources consistently, both those in translation and those in the original (Bulwer-Lytton met Benjamin Jowett in Germany in 1844, when both were pursuing their interest in German culture); like Grote, Bulwer-Lytton sees the reason for Athenian pre-eminence in the sphere of culture as due to the spirit of 'unceasing emulation and unbounded competition'. Bulwer-Lytton had presented the first full panegyric of democratic Athens in Britain; Grote's description of the effects of the reformed *ekklesia* of Kleisthenes is very close to that of Bulwer-Lytton on the Athenian assembly quoted above (pp. 142–3):

> Men were thus trained to the duty both of speakers and hearers, and each man, while he felt that he exercised his share of influence on the decision, identified his own safety and happiness with the vote of the majority, and became familiarized with the notion of a sovereign authority which he neither could nor ought to resist.[19]

Bulwer-Lytton was indeed the first to accept the view later made famous by John Stuart Mill, that the Athenian people were 'the true hero of the epopee of Greek history, the most gifted community of human beings which the world has yet seen';[20] and, in its previously unpublished section, a decade before George Grote, he had offered the first defence of Cleon as a radical politician, and the first sustained attack on the character of his conservative rival, Nicias. In short, Bulwer-Lytton presents a view of Greek and especially Athenian history in all essential respects remarkably similar to that of Grote.[21] When Grote came to describing Sparta he again echoed almost verbally the views of Bulwer-Lytton (above p. 140).[22] The Spartan citizen:

> . . . lived habitually in public, always either himself under drill, gymnastic and military, or a critic and spectator of others – always under the fetters and observances of a rule partly military, partly monastic – estranged from the independence of a separate home – seeing his wife, during the first years after marriage, only by stealth, and maintaining little peculiar relation with his children. The supervision not only of his fellow-citizens, but also

> of authorized censors or captains nominated by the state, was perpetually acting upon him: his day was passed in public exercises and meals, his night in the public barrack to which he belonged.

But perhaps it is not surprising that both Grote and John Stuart Mill in the 1850s should forget the earlier contribution of their former friend and colleague, who had after all deserted the Radicals to become a successful Tory MP (1852–66) and a close adherent of Disraeli. And the fact is that George Grote, and even more his wife Harriet (in her somewhat tendentious biography), became intent on portraying Grote alone as the founder of the modern study of Greek history: it was he (and of course his wife, who had inspired and encouraged the great work) who had single-handedly or together rediscovered the truth about the glorious past of Greece.

Grote published his history a generation too late: its political views, which so clearly belong to the age of Reform, were not made public until the high Victorian age, when that type of reform was no longer on the agenda. We can begin to see, in the contrast with Bulwer-Lytton, how a work ostensibly begun in the 1820s and taking thirty years for its gestation, had missed its original purpose, to give a classical Greek underpinning to the movement for reform. That explains the curious combination in Grote's work, of academic quality and depth, with a political message belonging to an earlier generation, and a fatal lack of urgency. The great success of Bulwer-Lytton's *Athens*, written with speed and panache and published at the right time, must have irritated beyond belief the dilatory and pedestrian Grote. The passionate history of the man who had once been his friend and colleague was deliberately written out of history by the cold and cautious Grote. Nor is it perhaps surprising that John Stuart Mill chose to stick by his father's old friend, however melancholy he might be, rather than praise the disreputable radical turncoat and Tory popular novelist.

GEORGE GROTE'S *HISTORY OF GREECE*

When Grote's *History* finally began its stately publication, it was recognized across Europe as a major work. The first two volumes that appeared in 1846 were revolutionary in their historical method. They treated of

'Legendary Greece' in critical Niebuhrian terms, not as all previous accounts had done, as a source from which to extract a hypothetical past, or as attempts to analyse the gods in terms of primitive explanations of natural forces. Instead, in his masterly concluding chapter XVI Grote argued that mythical thought was created by 'the primitive poet or story-teller' in an age 'full of religious faith', and denied the possibility of using myth to reconstruct either the history of the distant past or the philosophical ideas of earlier centuries; 'Grecian mythes' [sic] should be regarded 'as understood, felt, and interpreted by the Greeks themselves': 'the mythopoeic faculty is *creative*', he insisted;[23] '[Myths] are creations of the productive minds in the community, deduced from the supposed attributes of the gods and heroes.'[24] Despite their traditional nature, the myths we possess are essentially an expression of the world view and the beliefs of the author who recounts them or the period in which they are formulated; they are neither more nor less historical than the stories told about the distant past in Herodotus or Thucydides. So myths were seen as products of the Greek imagination in the various periods in which they were first recorded, 'a past which never was present – a region essentially mythical, neither approachable by the critic nor measurable by the chronologer'. Grote proceeded to analyse the succession of mythical interpretations by Greek poets and philosophers in a section that foreshadows his treatment of the whole development of intellectual thought among the Greeks. Each successive generation reinterpreted the existing body of myths in relation to its own preoccupations and interests, progressing from naïve belief to rational and then to allegorical interpretation: the interplay between this and 'the mythopoeic faculty is creative', constituting 'the universal mental stock of the Hellenic world'. This insistence on analysing myth by period rather than place or origin, and interpreting myth within the development of Greek historical and philosophical thought in a chronological context as evidence for contemporary beliefs rather than 'semi-historical' traditions, is a pragmatic and ultra-rational approach that has, I think, no parallel on the continent, and was too radical and dismissive to find much following even in England; although again it has close analogies with modern 'post-Marxist' interpretations by J.-P. Vernant and others of myth as expressions of the contemporary archaic and classical psychology of the Greeks.[25]

Grote's chapters on myth and religion were welcomed by Mill in a long essay in the *Edinburgh Review*;[26] they rest on firm Utilitarian and indeed atheist principles: religion has no transcendental source, but is the product of the collective imagination that invents its supporting myth. It was unfortunate that a generation later the historical basis of the Homeric age was apparently established by the discoveries of Heinrich Schliemann at Troy, Mycenae, Troezen and other sites from 1870 onwards: the evidence that Grote was denying appeared to many to be provided by excavation. But in fact the question of the historical existence of a 'Mycenean age' does not invalidate the theoretical approach of these two volumes; and the precise historical relation of the Bronze Age civilizations of Greece to the Minoan trading outposts of the contemporary Near East has still to be determined.[27]

ATHENIAN DEMOCRACY

In his first unpublished essay into Athenian history of 1821, Grote had somewhat surprisingly described the classical Athenian state of the age of Demosthenes in the fourth century as an aristocracy; but by the time of his denunciation of Mitford in the article of 1826 he had changed his mind; and when he began to write the historical portion of his history Grote was seeking to present the government of Athens as an ideal version of direct democracy, and to offer an account of Athenian history that refuted all the accusations of unjust or unwise political decisions made by earlier writers. This was the most systematic version of the democratic thesis that had yet been offered, and was intended to demonstrate the suitability of Athens as a model for the present age. It is often characterized as an attempt to dress Athenian politics in the clothes of the Victorian age, but that is to misunderstand its purpose.

All their lives both Grote and Mill wrestled with the problems of democratic government. They recognized fully the distinction between ancient direct and modern representative democracy, but still worried about the lack of political judgement in the non-political classes, and their tendency to follow demagogues or populist leaders, which seemed to belong to both versions of democracy, and were exemplified in the contemporary United States of America. Mill thought optimistically that education might one day provide an electorate capable of following rational leaders; Grote as a practising man of politics attempted to use the example of Athens to argue for the importance of an institutional framework to limit the dangers of democracy.

Grote's picture of Athens began from its success as a political system: in contrast to the earlier belief in the virtues of Sparta, Athens had proved the most stable and successful ancient city-state during the three centuries from the age of Solon to its disruption by the rise of Macedon. This involved him in the detailed justification of the various episodes used by earlier writers to show the degeneracy and incompetence of the Athenian government; but it also and more importantly led him to analyse the character and achievements of alleged demagogues such as Kleon, in order to show that they were neither the product of nor a threat to the democratic system.

His detailed account of ancient democracy began with chapter XLVI on the reforms of Ephialtes and Pericles. These according to Grote had created the system of jury courts at Athens, which resulted in the Athenian reputation for love of litigation so much attacked by Aristophanes, Thucydides, and Plato. The Athenian legal systems were compared not unfavourably with the later European jury courts. Grote's positive description of the predominance of Pericles was of course based on Thucydides and did not admit any criticism of his hero. In his account of politics after the death of Pericles a new class of politician emerged in which Kleon the tanner was favourably compared with his rivals, Nikias the slave contractor for the silver mines and the vainglorious Alcibiades, who between them brought about the downfall of Athens (ch. L). Kleon's actions over the capture of the Spartans at Sphakteria were defended, although Grote did not go as far as Bulwer-Lytton in postulating collusion between Kleon and Demosthenes. The enslavement of the Melians with its famous dialogue in Thucydides justifying the right of power against conventional justice was compared with the notorious British bombardment of Copenhagen in 1807; and Grote offered a detailed account of the events around the trial of the victorious generals after the battle of Arginusae, designed to explain if not justify the decision of the Athenians to condemn them. For each of these controversial episodes he offered accounts that exonerated or at least explained the actions of the Athenian assembly. The later volumes continued the demolition of Mitford begun in his article of 1826; the Athenian record of a relatively successful conduct of affairs in the fourth century was defended, as was the activity of Demosthenes during the conflict with Philip of Macedon.

Grote's most significant contribution to the history of Greek thought came in chapter LXVII, where he mounted a passionate defence of the sophists (of whom he asserted that Socrates was one) against the claim of both Plato and his modern German disciples that they had corrupted Athenian society.[28] The foundations of his later three-volume work on Plato were laid here. Grote concluded: 'If then we survey the eighty-seven years of Athenian history between the battle of Marathon and the renovation of the democracy after the Thirty, we shall see no ground for the assertion, so often made, of increased and increasing moral and political corruption. It is my belief that the people had become both morally and politically better, and that their democracy had worked to their improvement.'

In the next chapter Grote described the ideas of Socrates and the reasons behind his trial and condemnation by the Athenian people, which (as we shall see in ch. 11) was for earlier writers perhaps the greatest crime attributable to Athenian democracy. He described Socrates as 'a religious missionary doing the work of philosophy', seeking to create a new field of ethics through public discourse. The inevitable unpopularity of his self-imposed mission was intensified by his relations with Kritias and Alcibiades. Socrates showed by the very tone of his defence that he scarcely wished to be acquitted; even so he was only found guilty by a majority of five or six in a jury of perhaps 500. He then refused to accept the conventions of the Athenian legal system that after conviction prosecutors and defence should each offer suitable penalties, and instead proposed for himself the greatest public honour available to the Athenians, of free meals for life at the prytaneum. In so doing he deliberately brought about his own death – by drinking the poisonous hemlock – as the fitting end to his mission.

KLEISTHENES

The power and originality of Grote's analysis are perhaps best demonstrated in an earlier chapter on the 'Revolution of Kleisthenes and Establishment of Democracy at Athens'.[29] For Grote the historical period had begun in 776 BC, a view almost universally accepted ever since. His account of the earliest period of Athenian history ended with the foundation of Athenian democracy, not by Solon (as the ancient world had always claimed),[30] but by Kleisthenes. All previous British histories of Greece (with one possible exception)[31] had followed the ancient biographical tradition in making Solon the founder of democracy, ignoring Kleisthenes or portraying him as little more than a political schemer. Grote, however, saw him as the true originator of the Athenian democratic system, and demonstrated how his detailed reforms of the tribal system from four to ten tribes, composed of local demes or villages geographically separated from each other, rather than hereditary kinship groups, destroyed the power base of the aristocracy, and gave through the new Council of the 500 selected by lot absolute and effective sovereignty to the Assembly of all male citizens. He reconstructed a detailed account of the Kleisthenic constitution with its popular law courts, its generals elected one from each of the ten tribes, its civil calendar, and the organization of the Council by tribal prytaneis selected by lot. He explained how the institution of ostracism (hitherto much attacked as an unjust and arbitrary measure) was an essential element in a coherent attempt to destroy the influence of the aristocracy, and that the reforms had indeed permanently fragmented their power.

In his earlier attempt at understanding the reforms Grote had paid no great attention to Kleisthenes, seeing him like others simply as another potential tyrant and an aristocratic protagonist seeking to undermine the power base of his rivals.[32] His new analysis built on the work of G.F. Schömann on the Athenian tribal system, who however had failed to understand their political significance.[33] There is no doubt that Grote's new political interpretation derived directly from his personal experiences as a Radical Member of Parliament, where he had been a great protagonist of the reform of local government, and had understood at first hand the power of Tory patronage. Even sympathetic contemporaries like Mill ridiculed his obsession with attempting to introduce the secret ballot into parliamentary elections, but Grote was convinced that the lack of success of the Radicals was due to the continued influence of the Tories in controlling parliamentary and local elections: thus he saw the secret ballot as the necessary basis for true reform. (The secret ballot was finally introduced only after Grote had despaired of it and had left politics.)

Central to his analysis of the importance of Kleisthenes lay the traditional problem of political thought identified by Machiavelli and Montesquieu, of how to define political *virtù* or in French *vertu*, that element in public life that is essential to the working of any political system: beyond theoretical arguments for the justice or efficiency of a system lay the need in any society to accept a form of public morality that ensured the success of its system of government, 'the indispensable condition of a government at once free and peaceable'.[34] This Grote defined in Athens as 'constitutional morality' or 'democratical sentiment', the acceptance by the community of a complex nexus of the rights and obligations of citizenship as a set of values shared by all. By weakening the various forms of aristocratic control operating through social ties of religion, kinship, and locality, Kleisthenes had created a unified conception of citizenship based on the working of the democratic assembly, and hence ensured its stability and success over subsequent generations. This seemed to Grote a model for the reform of British politics; and it was this achievement that was to elude both him and his fellow Radicals, as it would elude all subsequent radical reformers. Nevertheless, as Alexander Bain wrote, 'The historian's concluding reflections on the reforms of Cleisthenes stir the heart like the sound of a trumpet. Never weary of the theme of human liberty, he retouches it on each occasion with fresh and glowing colours. What Herodotus puts in the front rank of the advantages of democracy – "its most splendid name and promise" – is no mere rhetoric, but a real power, the source of all the exploits that have conferred immortal renown on the Athenian name.'[35]

One crucial development eluded Grote. In the preface to the *History* he had deplored the loss of Aristotle's detailed studies of 150 'town constitutions'. The discovery on papyrus and publication of a virtually complete copy of Aristotle's 'Constitution of the Athenians' in 1891 would surely have completed his picture.[36] The failure of subsequent historians to take account of the importance of this discovery, from Gustav Gilbert (1895) to Charles Hignett (1952), is one of the most shameful episodes in the modern study of Greek history.[37] And it was not until the researches of the Danish scholar Mogens Herman Hansen in the late twentieth century that a third democratic constitutional reform was revealed in the changes made on the restoration of democracy in the years 404–403 BC, which modified the hitherto customary conventions of democratic procedure, and created a firm distinction between constitutional law (*nomos*) and Assembly decisions (*psephismata*).[38]

Grote's interpretation of the Kleisthenic reforms was finally vindicated in the mid-twentieth century by the researches of David Lewis and the detailed epigraphic work of John Traill,[39] which demonstrated that they had indeed effectively split the pre-existing village structures of Attica from each other, and that Kleisthenes's basic local reorganization of the Athenian tribes had persisted throughout the history of the Athenian democracy. This in turn has justified the late twentieth-century obsession with the '2,500th anniversary of the origins of democracy', which is the most recent development in the legacy of Grote, derived from the propaganda conflicts of the Cold War and the influence of American ideology.[40] Thus Grote sought to establish in historical terms the practical viability of democracy (direct and perhaps representative) on the basis of a shared 'constitutional morality' and the existence of institutions to safeguard its operations against the abuse of populism or demagoguery. These are problems that we still face in the aftermath of the tyrannies of the twentieth century.

Despite the many new interpretations and modern discoveries in archaeology, Grote's *History* remains the fundamental full-scale account of ancient Greece in any language. But it has a number of weaknesses, most of which were already recognized at the time of its publication. Even friends of Grote, like his disciple Alexander Bain and his friend Mill, were curiously defensive against attacks on literary grounds:[41] compared to earlier accounts the details of Grote's controversial opinions had resulted in a work that was too long and whose style was verbose and pedantic. Carlyle was privately scathing: 'a fetid quagmire, with nothing spiritual about it';[42] and Ruskin's cruel public jibe has not been forgotten: 'Grote's History of Greece ... There is probably no commercial establishment between Charing Cross and the Bank, whose head clerk could not write a better one, if he had the vanity to waste his time on it.'[43] In the end Grote probably had more effect on German readers, who had the advantage of reading the work in translation.

More important were the criticisms that Mill levied in his second main review, on the completion of the work in 1853.[44] From the Utilitarian standpoint Grote's idealization of Athenian democracy had caused him to ignore two fundamental defects in Athenian society, the recognition of which had ironically been two of the main strengths of William Mitford's account[45] – its dependence on the institution of slavery, and the subordination and exclusion of women. Although ancient slavery is mentioned briefly at various points, it is never connected to Athens; 'slaves' and 'women' each appear only once in the index to the work, for very trivial aspects. These were the main criticisms contained in Mill's review, and they caused him to wonder whether this impugned the right of Athens to be considered a true democracy. But he eventually decided that such criticism was historically unjustified, since it had not deterred de Tocqueville in the modern world from analysing the United States of America as a democracy, despite the fact that slavery and the subjection of women both existed there.[46]

JOHN STUART MILL AND GROTE

Grote and Mill had been friends since being introduced by Mill's father in 1819; during the 1830s, as we have seen, they were fellow workers on reform, and Mill reviewed favourably in the *Edinburgh Review* or *Spectator* each volume of Grote's history as it appeared.[47] But their friendship cooled (along with many others of Mill's friendships) when Mill began his unorthodox association with the married woman Harriet Taylor from the early 1830s onwards. This was interpreted on Mill's side as conventional disapproval of the new relationship, particularly on the part of the wives of his married friends, who were deemed unwilling to invite the couple to their houses. Recent reflection, however, supports the view expressed in an early review of Mill's autobiography by one of his childhood friends,[48] that the problem lay more in Harriet Taylor and in the solipsistic character of their relationship, which was incompatible with Mill's former intimacies with other women; certainly women like Harriet Grote and Sarah Austin were not unused to disregarding public conventions. From the late 1830s Mill did not visit Grote's house, although Alexander Bain, the Scottish philosopher and biographer of Mill father and son, recorded London walks with Grote and Mill from about 1845. But there does not seem to have been any close discussion between the two men during the writing of Grote's history; and Mill rebuffed an attempt by Mrs Grote to thank him for his review of 1853.[49] The friendship of the two men remained formal even after the marriage of the Mills in 1851 (after the death of Harriet's husband in 1849), until the death of Harriet in 1858, when Grote and Mill exchanged letters of condolence and renewed their friendship. Mill had fully accepted Grote's picture of the sophists and Socrates in the *History*, and the two men engaged in active correspondence during the writing of Grote's major later work on *Plato and his Contemporaries*.

The extent of Mill's relation with Grote and his *History* is not just revealed in his published reviews. The residue of his library surviving in England (much must have been disposed of in Avignon, where he died in 1873) was presented to Somerville College, Oxford, in 1905 by Mary Taylor, acting under power of attorney for her aunt Helen Taylor, Mill's stepdaughter and companion after her mother's death, on the suggestion of John Morley, who had opened the new Library building the previous year. It included books even from James Mill's library, but was given without condition, to be used as the nucleus of a working library for students, and was treated as such, only being reassembled as a separate collection in a designated Mill Room in 1969 – by which time it is probable that some volumes had been lost, some disposed of, some annotated or otherwise disfigured by undergraduate use. In 2018 I was alerted by Professor Frank Prochaska to the existence in this collection of a first edition of Grote's *History* with successive inscriptions to John Stuart Mill from the author. These volumes had from their dilapidated condition been used, especially for the fifth and fourth centuries BC, by generations of undergraduate readers; but they were also copiously annotated in the margins by Mill himself, showing how carefully he had read them. I made a preliminary collation of these for the college, and they have subsequently been fully analysed by Professor Albert Pionke of Alabama University.[50] There are over a thousand marginal comments spread across all volumes; perhaps the most frequent occur in the chapters on the sophists and Socrates. Many are the pedantic notes of a careful reader, many concern the correctness of Grote's translations of Thucydides; there are occasional comments on historical points or parallels with other periods of history. But disappointingly there are no significant remarks on Athenian democracy. By far the largest number of comments are geographical, and based on personal observation of the terrain of Sicily and Greece; they show that Mill had visited all the major battlefields and had a sharp eye for topography. There is the occasional addition of recent material, for instance information from the decipherment of the Behistun inscription of the Persian king Darius, the German excavations on the Acropolis, or remarks like that on the sacred grove at Kolonos: 'There is now no grove there, but the tomb of Otfried Müller on the summit.' Perhaps the most idiosyncratic comment is Mill's addition in the margin of a further fourteen names to Grote's list of seven famous women of the heroic age.[51] Pionke has determined that the marginalia relate to at least two readings of the work. The first was naturally in relation to Mill's various reviews over the period 1849 to 1856.

Grote himself never visited Greece, although in 1862 Mill and his stepdaughter Helen had invited him to accompany them on their adventurous camping tour, which he declined on grounds of poor health. The expedition was a great success: the Mills were present in Athens during the uprising of the garrison at Nauplion, which heralded the deposition of King Otto of Bavaria, and travelled widely in the countryside. On his return Mill sent Grote a brief account of their experiences during the events that led to the deposition of the king, and reported on the new excavations of the German archaeologist Ernst Curtius on the Acropolis.[52] Mill had also previously visited Italy, Sicily, and Greece alone during his wife's lifetime in 1855, and sent her a detailed travelogue of this long trip (April–June 1855) in a series of letters.[53] The geographical annotations in his copy of Grote's *History* highlight the fact that Grote never visited Greece (just as James Mill never visited India); and they clearly relate to this earlier visit, the year after the completion of Grote's work, which he must have reread on his return from Greece. Pionke has analysed the later editions of Grote's *History* down to 1862, and shown that a number of Mill's comments seem to be reflected in later revisions. This implies that Mill was communicating some of his thoughts to Grote during the publication of the work, despite the absence of any reference in his correspondence.

These marginalia show the depth of their mutual regard and intellectual friendship over the decade of publication, and their shared attitude to the significance of the history of Greece. When Grote died in 1871, Mill could write that Grote had been his oldest and closest friend, although he only reluctantly attended the pomp of Grote's funeral in Westminster Abbey, in the third carriage: 'In no very long time I shall be laid in the ground with a very different ceremonial from that.'[54] Mill's claim of lifelong friendship was therefore only a slight exaggeration; Grote's *History* belonged to Utilitarianism, and was based on views that he had learned from the Mills; and John Stuart Mill's long essay on the publication of the final volumes shows how much he shared of Grote's analysis, particularly of Athenian democracy.

Grote may have been provoked to write his history in part by a desire to refute the Tory interpretation of Mitford, and that is certainly how many readers have seen his radical bias. But in fact his purpose was far deeper, to establish the place of Greek history in the Utilitarian canon, and to provide a model for the future reform of any constitution aiming at democracy. Now that few read Hume's *History of England* or James Mill's *History of British India*, Grote's *History of Greece* remains the chief and most distinguished history yet provided by any philosophical school.

The Triumph of Germany

B.G. Niebuhr (1776–1831)

8
Hegel, Niebuhr, and Critical History

TRANSLATION

Looking back at the progress of learning in 1819, Arthur Schopenhauer deplored the breakdown of a universal language:

> The fact that Latin has ceased to be the language of all scientific investigation has the disadvantage that there is no longer an immediately common scientific literature for the whole of Europe, but rather national literatures; thereby, every scholar is in the first instance limited to a much smaller public, and also to one that is steeped in nationally biased opinions and prejudices. And so now he must learn the four principal European languages, besides the two ancient languages.[1]

The unity of European learned culture had already begun to break down early in the eighteenth century, as Latin ceased to be the universal language of academic discourse for both published and unpublished communication; it was replaced as the language of learning by French. An industry of translation from the French had emerged in the eighteenth century as part of the interchange between the aristocracies of learning in France and the receiving cultures of Britain and Germany. The disappearance of the French aristocracy coincided with the rise in Germany of a new historiography, and the age of the German *Handbuch* gave way to the dominance of German historical works that inspired a new generation throughout Europe, and the rise of the great universities of Göttingen and Berlin. At the same time national traditions in scholarship were appearing, which meant that the types of scholarship practised in different countries no longer rested on a common set of assumptions, but began to show pronounced national characteristics. The subsequent establishment of separate national academic traditions was one of the results of the growth of national cultures and vernacular scholarship within the context of these different reformed university systems during the nineteenth century.

Throughout the century for a variety of reasons it was felt necessary to gain access to the knowledge published in other languages. German scholarship was dominant in many spheres (classical studies, philosophy, theology, law, and medieval and modern history, to mention the most obvious); a number of English works were translated into German; French scholarship remained important in archaeology and theology. Around the end of the century eastern European cultures felt the need to relate their national traditions to the scientific culture of the day: there was widespread translation of academic works into Russian, modern Greek, and Hungarian for instance. The importance of the phenomenon of translation for the transmission and preservation of a common European culture is clear in general terms: even when individual scholars were able to read works in other languages, the diffusion of ideas in the wider literary culture and especially among university students was dependent on the existence of translations. In England this translation activity was dominated by women, often from Unitarian or less conventional backgrounds, who had received equal education with their brothers, but were denied access to universities or the world of learning. The importance of these women in the history of scholarship is only beginning to be recognized; but many, such as Mary Ann Evans (George Eliot), Sarah Austin, Susanna Winkworth and her sister Catherine set new standards in the transmission of learning.[2]

THE RISE OF GERMANY

The compilation of antiquarian handbooks of information without any theoretical interest was already well established as a typically German academic activity by the late eighteenth century. But it was in the early nineteenth century that the critical study of history emerged as an academic discipline in Germany, and the systematic exploration of the past was developed.[3] Three schools of thought within this new discipline of critical history can be discerned. The first was the realization that all historical narrative was built out of a succession of earlier accounts showing biases and preconceptions which needed to be discounted, before it was possible to arrive at a narration of the 'true facts'; this approach was primarily associated with the work of the classical historian Barthold Georg Niebuhr (1776–1831). This approach continued to be important throughout the nineteenth century; it resulted in an obsession with *Quellenforschung* (source criticism), the unfolding of the successive layers of distortion that enabled a return to the original 'facts'. Implicit in this attitude was the assumption that all history (including that of the present day) was inherently liable to distortion through especially political bias; it therefore included in its claim to be interested in the truth and the methods of establishing the truth a contradictory admission that the activity of historians was itself affected by contemporary politics.

The second area of scientific history might seem at first sight more neutral. The discovery of the importance of archives and documentary evidence associated with the name of Leopold von Ranke (1795–1886) laid claim to producing an account of history 'as it really was'. Much of the organization of nineteenth-century historical scholarship was oriented around the collection and publication of archives in an apparently value-neutral way – private papers, official documents and reports, inscriptions, charters, medieval texts, coins, historical dictionaries of European languages. But this activity, though it could correct the bias of memoirs and past historians, was not in fact free of all bias; it failed to recognize, first that the choice of materials to collect was subject to the bias of the historical researcher, and second that the archives themselves had been created for a purpose, usually determined by earlier governments: they gave an official view of history, but not necessarily a true view. Nevertheless, the school of Ranke established a permanent link between archival research and the writing of history.

The final important area of empirical research was the study of legal history. Lawyers had their archives ready-made, and the legal approach is a powerful combination of the historical with the philosophical. The study of the historical origins of Germanic law in Roman law and ancient customs was closely connected with the attempt to create a new legal system based on historical principles, in opposition to the theoretical principles of the Napoleonic Code. The many political reforms of continental states were based on a conception of constitutional law and its relation to politics that made constitutional history one of the most important branches of historical research. From the great founders of

German legal studies, K.F. Eichhorn and F.C. von Savigny, to Theodor Mommsen's studies of Roman public and private law at the end of the nineteenth century, the importance of law as 'the expression of the life of the people' was recognized. But it is obvious that such approaches to history are bound up with the process of self-definition of the nation state, and provide another example of the close relationship between historical research and contemporary political concerns.

HEGEL AND THE NEW HISTORY

In his posthumously published 'Lectures on the Philosophy of World History', delivered in Berlin on five occasions between 1822 and 1831, Hegel had formulated a theory of history as a universal process involving the gradual realization of the idea of spirit through a succession of phases of world history.[4] The dialectic of the spirit of nations had resulted in a gradual unfolding of the human spirit until (as Nietzsche wickedly put it) 'for Hegel the apex and culmination of the world process coincided with his own existence in Berlin'.[5]

For Hegel the history of the world had also a geographical orientation, for it travels from East to West, in conformity with the course of the sun of self-consciousness. The East knows that *One* is free, the Greek and Roman world that *Some* are free, while the German world knows that *All* are free. History is therefore essentially the history of the development of the freedom of the human spirit. As a theory this corresponds to that held by many self-styled liberal historians today, especially in the United States, even if it is no longer expressed in such metaphysical terms. It is clearly intrinsically attractive; the problem lay in its detailed working out as a historical narrative by Hegel. His lectures traced the course of human affairs from the ancient Near East through antiquity and the Middle Ages to the Reformation and the present day. Hegel was not a professional historian, and his exposition was both schematic and subordinated to the needs of his theory.

As the creators of the new historical science the founders of the German historical tradition possessed a self-conscious perception of its role, and a transcendental conception of the meaning of 'world history'. The figure of Hegel dominated the philosophy of history throughout the first half of the nineteenth century; it lies at the basis of Marxism, which finally replaced it as the most successful philosophical explanation of the meaning of historical events. Even for those historians who tried to see history as an empirical investigation in which general theories must be determined by the shape of the factual evidence, the belief that history had a spiritual meaning retained a continuing fascination. The early drafts of Hegel's lectures on the philosophy of history in 1822 and 1828 (not published until after his death) capture the complexity of this new importance of history in the nineteenth century, as he sought to reunite philosophy and history within the Hegelian system in order to create a philosophy of world history. At the start of his lectures Hegel distinguished three different modes of historical writing – original history, reflective history, and philosophical history. Original history consisted of the relatively straightforward accounts written by protagonists at or near the time; and philosophical history was the new history of the story of the human spirit in its progress towards freedom, which would be written as a result of the acceptance of the Hegelian philosophy of the spirit.

For my present purpose, it is his 'reflective history' that offers most interest, for it is a critical account of history as it is written now, in the 1820s at the start of the historical age. For Hegel the underlying problem with this sort of history, the history of the past written by the present, is that 'the writer approaches it in his own spirit, which is different from the spirit of the object itself'.[6] In general the French and the English are better than the Germans at writing this sort of history; 'every German writer begins with an individual theory as to how history should be written . . . we are still in the position of struggling to find out how to write history'. Such historical surveys often try to present the past as it was experienced by contemporaries; but that is not possible: 'when the historian tries to depict the spirit of bygone times, it is usually his own spirit which makes itself heard'. As well as modern German historians, Hegel uses the example of Livy contrasted with Polybius:[7]

> This is an attempt to transport us completely into the past as something immediate and alive, – [which] we [can] no more achieve than can the writer himself; the writer is one of us, he is part of his own world with all its needs and interests, and he honours the same things which it esteems. For example, whatever [the age] we live in, we can [immerse ourselves] as fully as we like in the life of Ancient Greece . . . yet we will never

> be able to sympathise with the Greeks and to share their feelings in the most important issues of all . . . Just as [we] cannot share the sensations of a dog, [even if we] have a clear impression of a particular dog, know it well, and can predict its mannerisms, attachments and idiosyncrasies.

While the inability of the historian to escape from the spirit of his age and recreate the spirit of another age was particularly problematic within Hegel's philosophy of history, he was clearly here reflecting a general concern among historians, who had responded to the challenge in a variety of ways:

> But there are other ways in which historians have tried to bring the past closer to us, not by writing in a tone designed to enlist our sympathy, but at least by eliciting intuitive and lively emotional responses, responses as lively as those of immediate experience, entering into all the details of the events – location – mode of perception – distinct presentation.

In seeking to escape from the dry narration of facts, 'certain historians attempt to attain at least an intuitive or representational liveliness, if not an emotional liveliness, by depicting each individual trait in a faithful and lifelike manner'. They aim not at a personal interpretation of past ages, but:

> . . . to create a faithful and accurate portrait of them. [They] gather the materials for this from every conceivable source (Ranke).[8] A motley assortment of details, petty interests, actions of soldiers, private affairs, which have no influence on political interests, – they are incapable [of recognising] a whole, a general design.

This, says Hegel, results in:

> [A] series of individual characteristics – as in one of Walter Scott's novels – collected from every quarter, painstakingly and laboriously assembled. . . . [They ought to] leave this sort of thing to Walter Scott's novels, this detailed portraiture incorporating all the minutiae of the age, in which the deeds and fortunes of a single individual constitute the work's sole futile interest and wholly particular matters are all put forward as equally important.

Hegel contrasted with this type of immediate or emotional reflective history what he called pragmatic history, which seeks to establish the meaning of institutions and their importance by using the experience of the historian's age. This type of history takes the history of states, great individuals or institutions as its theme, and regards them externally from the viewpoint of the present. It too has its vices: the worst types of pragmatic historian are the psychologist who looks for subjective motives, and the moralizer 'who sporadically awakens from his weary ramblings to utter edifying Christian reflections, attacking events and individuals in the flank with his moral onslaughts, and throwing in an edifying thought, a word of exhortation, a moral doctrine, or the like'. Pragmatic history seems to produce general laws, and lessons or examples; but we should not be misled by these: 'there is nothing so insipid as the constant appeals to Greek and Roman precedents we hear so often, as for example during the French Revolution'. Only someone like Montesquieu could endow such reflections with truth and interest.

The third variety of reflective history is critical history, the dominant new historical method in Hegel's Germany: 'It does not constitute history as such, but rather the history of history; it evaluates historical narratives and examines their authenticity and credibility.' Niebuhr's *Roman History* is the great example of a method, originally practised by the French in critical treatises rather than histories. Hegel dismisses this 'so-called "higher criticism"', which:[9]

> has been the pretext for introducing all the un-historical monstrosities a vain imagination could suggest. It too is a method of bringing the present into the past, namely by substituting subjective fancies for historical data – fancies which are considered the more excellent the bolder they are, that is, the less they have to substantiate them, the scantier the details on which they are based, and the more widely they diverge from the best established facts of history.

Finally, Hegel considers a fourth variety of reflective history, 'specialized history' based on a single general perspective on national life, such as the history of art, law, religion or the constitution; because of their theoretical basis, these are an excellent transition to the discussion of what he regards as the true sort of history, the philosophical history of the world.

Hegel's ideas were not available to contemporaries outside his lecture audience in Berlin, but they express well the general European view of the writing of history. The new critical history of Niebuhr and his school was already seen as problematic: it was based on the study of historians not history, and its conclusions were fanciful and arbitrary – even if sometimes seductive, as when Niebuhr's theory of the ballad sources of early Roman history inspired Macaulay to recreate the lost poems behind the narrative of Livy in his *Lays of Ancient Rome* (see p. 187). Ultimately, we may perhaps see that it was Hegel's 'pragmatic history' that combined with 'specialized history' to create the anti-Hegelian school of positivism which became dominant in professional university circles; but in the Romantic age, as we have seen, it was the problem of recreating the immediacy of the past in the manner of Walter Scott that dominated the writing of history throughout Europe.

The apparently empirical and positivist historical research proclaimed by the opponents of Hegel was therefore deeply affected by a conceptual framework that enabled historical studies to appear as the basis for the understanding of modern societies: history in the nineteenth-century age of historicism played the same role as sociology and anthropology today. It was therefore inconceivable that history should lack a meaning; in the age of historicism, history provides the explanation, but history itself is in need of an explanation. Thus Hegel could be and was combined with the new 'science' of history, and this combination helps to explain the dominance of historical studies in Germany in the age of historicism; for history replaced philosophy as the fundamental science of human nature and the explanation of all human society. The objections from historians to the Hegelian view of history were not therefore on philosophical grounds, but on grounds of the facts and the methods of their discipline. It was not until Nietzsche that the premises of historicism were fundamentally challenged; and Nietzsche's attack was itself inspired, or perhaps rather provoked, by the lectures of Jacob Burckhardt.

During the long gestation of Grote's *History*, from around 1830 the influence of the new German historical scholarship was beginning to be felt, with the British discovery of the new German Romantic *Wissenschaft* of Barthold Georg Niebuhr, August Boeckh, and Karl Otfried Müller. In the study of Greek history the most significant translation was that of Müller's *History of the Doric Race*, by two future radical politicians, Henry Tufnell and George Cornewall Lewis (1830, second edition 1839), who were contemporaries at what was then the leading intellectual institution in England, Christ Church, Oxford. Cornewall Lewis was the first and most important of the translators from the German; while still a student at Oxford he had translated August Boeckh's *Public Economy of Athens* (1828, 1842),[10] and published it anonymously with a long critique of its economic doctrines along Utilitarian lines; in 1830 he attended the lectures of John Austin, the Utilitarian Professor of Law at University College London. He also translated Müller's *History of Greek Literature* (1840–42), and later wrote a critique of Niebuhr's theories on early Roman history (see below, p. 182). He was a leading Radical politician, from 1833 commissioner on a wide range of government reports, author of one of the best critiques of the British Empire (*Essay on the Government of Dependencies* [1841, 1891]), Liberal MP from 1855, editor of the *Edinburgh Review*, and finally Chancellor of the Exchequer under Lord Palmerston. Cornewall Lewis died in 1863, aged fifty-six; otherwise he might well have succeeded Gladstone as leader of his party. His philosophy of life is summed up in his remark, 'Life would be tolerable but for its amusements.'

The first thing the new German science of Müller required was that we should forget Lycurgus the founder of Sparta: 'If now we apply the method above stated to the history of Lycurgus, we shall find that we have absolutely no account of him as an *individual person*' (*History of the Doric Race*, Book I, ch. 7, sec. 6). The second lesson to be learned was based on Friedrich Schlegel's theories of the superiority of the Doric race over the Ionian: the Spartan constitution was not specific to Sparta, but simply the most perfect example of a common Dorian way of life:[11]

> In the genuine Doric form of government there were certain predominant ideas, which were peculiar to that race, and were also expressed in the worship of Apollo, viz., those of *harmony* and *order* (τὸ εὔκοσμον), of *self-control* and *moderation* (σωφροσύνη), and of *manly virtue* (ἀρετή). Accordingly, the constitution was formed for the education as well of the old as of the young, and in a Doric state education was upon the whole a subject of greater importance than government. And for this reason all attempts to explain the legislation of Lycurgus, from partial views and considerations, have necessarily failed.

This exposition of a new German version of an idealized Sparta, quite different from the pre-existing French and Scottish philosophical approaches, caused much discussion in Britain: even the translators felt obliged to dissociate themselves from some of Müller's views in their preface; and the racial element in his theories was discussed without ever really gaining acceptance. However, the relegation of Lycurgus to the status of myth, and the question of the relation between the Spartan social system and those of other Dorian states, became central. Müller's views were also partly responsible for the British rejection of Sparta in favour of Athens: his Prussian racially defined Dorians lacked any appeal to the British urban elite of the age of reform, who were choosing rather to identify themselves with democracy and Athens.

NIEBUHR IN BRITAIN

In a letter of 1817 Barthold Georg Niebuhr, at that time Prussian ambassador to the Holy See (1816–23), describes his new apartment in the Palazzo Orsini, which is built on top of the remains of the Teatro di Marcello:[12]

> Nicolovius will remember the theatre of Marcellus, in which the Savelli family built a palace. My house is the half of it ... The apartments in which we shall live, are those over the colonnade of Ionic pillars forming the third story of the ancient theatre ... these enclose a little quadrangular garden, which is indeed very small, only about eighty or ninety feet long, and scarcely so broad, but so delightful! It contains three fountains – an abundance of flowers; there are orange trees on the walls between the windows, jessamine under the windows. We mean to plant a vine besides.

It so happened that a former pupil of mine was holding a position similar to that of Niebuhr, as Irish ambassador to the Vatican; and because of restoration work at his official residence in the Villa Spada by the Porta San Pancrazio on the Gianicolo (once Garibaldi's headquarters during the siege of Rome in 1849), he was compelled to take refuge in the same apartment that Niebuhr had rented in the Teatro di Marcello, which then belonged to the daughters of the famous author and society beauty, Iris Origo.[13] So in the spring of 2005 I was able for the first time to visit, indeed to reside in, the garden and the apartments that had so entranced Niebuhr two hundred years earlier. A delightful formal orange grove lies in the former *cavea* of the theatre at first-floor level, the three fountains are still there, and some of the trees may go back almost to the time of Niebuhr (the palazzo was extensively renovated soon after his stay there). Here it was that the modern study of ancient and especially Roman history was born.

During the first half of the nineteenth century Niebuhr was the most famous and most widely translated classical scholar in Europe; he is indeed the most important international figure in classical studies in the century that runs from Winckelmann to Mommsen. In Britain he became the centre around which the new school of critical history was developed and the most important influence on the formation of British classical education in the early nineteenth century.

Niebuhr was born in the then Danish province of Holstein in 1776, the son of Carsten Niebuhr, the orientalist and explorer of Arabia; in his childhood he became acquainted with Johann Heinrich Voss, the German translator of Homer. Niebuhr studied at Kiel University (1794–6) and entered the Danish public service; after six years as private secretary to the Danish Minister of Finance, in 1806 he was invited to Prussia, where for four years he was a member of the circle around Baron von Stein, the great reformer and architect of modern Germany, struggling to rebuild the finances of a state crippled by Napoleon at Jena. In 1810 he resigned in dispute with the financial policy of Karl August von Hardenberg, and at the age of thirty-four accepted the post of historiographer in the new university of Berlin. From 1810 to 1813, 'in the evil time of Prussia's humiliation', Niebuhr delivered famous lectures on Roman history. In 1813 he published the first edition of his *History of Rome* before returning to public life to take part in the negotiation of the treaties consequent on Napoleon's retreat from Moscow and the liberation of Prussia. From 1816 to 1823 he was Prussian ambassador in Rome, and from 1825 to his death in 1831 he returned to academic life as a professor at the University of Bonn.

As a young man Niebuhr had visited Britain from June 1798 to November 1799; his experiences are recorded in his *Life* from his journal and letters written to his betrothed; unfortunately, his letters to his parents, which 'contained many details of general interest respecting English political and civil institutions, the character of the nation and remarkable individuals', were later burned, and only nine letters survive. The twenty-two-year-old graduate of Kiel University was at the time primarily interested in a career in the public service. In London, apart from visiting Alexander Pope's famous garden and grotto at Twickenham, meeting Captain Bligh of the *Bounty*, and visiting the theatre, where he saw Mrs Siddons as Lady Macbeth, he spent much of his time reading about India in Sir Joseph Banks's library. Niebuhr acquired a lifelong admiration of the English constitution and the 'superior, almost universal cultivation of the burgher class' (who however were little interested in politics or philosophy); but he met only friends of his father in the Royal Society and the British Museum: 'I positively shrink from associating myself with the young men on account of their unbounded dissoluteness.' Indeed, since he was in London only from June to October, when most people were out of town, he cannot have expected to meet many interesting people. It is, however, characteristic of the culture of that age that it never occurred to Niebuhr to visit either Oxford or Cambridge, where the moribund state of classical studies (and indeed of university life in general) was notorious throughout Europe. 'Of the English scholars . . . I have a very mean opinion: I keep to my assertion, that they are without originality; also that England can boast of no true poets at the present time.'[14]

Instead, Niebuhr went north to the real intellectual capital of the British Isles, Edinburgh, a city then at its height as the centre of the Scottish Enlightenment; on the way he was very interested in the agrarian aspects of his journey, the miserable villages of Bedfordshire, and the prosperity of Lincolnshire and Nottinghamshire. At Edinburgh he enrolled for a year as a student of science – physics, mathematics, anatomy, but also natural history, botany, and agriculture. Apart from the universal drunkenness of both lowland and highland Scots and the fact that 'beauty is extremely rare in Scotland', he was much impressed by the academic life of Edinburgh, where the philosophy of Kant was already well known; though he seems not to have heard the Professor of Moral Philosophy since 1785, the famous Dugald Stewart. Niebuhr also spent time studying the estates and practices of his Scottish acquaintances. In November 1799 he returned to Copenhagen, to take up a post as Assessor at the Board of Trade for the East India Department and Head Clerk of the Standing Commission of the Affairs of Barbary (in charge of the consulates in Africa) – and to be married.

Niebuhr regarded his year in Edinburgh as the foundation of his career in politics and finance. But at this time 'philological and historical studies he only prosecuted by himself, and by way of recreation. In these departments he regarded the learned men there as incomparably inferior to the Germans.' The most important strands in Niebuhr's new conception of history are perhaps his interest in agrarian matters, and his invention of the principles of source criticism; and Scottish lowland agriculture undoubtedly had a significant effect on his views of the peasant society of early Rome. But the young Danish scholar found nothing to interest him in the historical studies of the city of David Hume (died 1776) and William Robertson (died 1793), let alone in an England that Gibbon had left in 1783, to return in 1793, but only to die within a year.

It is curious that among Niebuhr's Scottish acquaintances one name is missing, that of Walter Scott. This is perhaps one of the most surprising missed opportunities of the Romantic age; for Scott was then a young lawyer only five years older than Niebuhr, just married to a French refugee, and already at the centre of Edinburgh social and intellectual life; he was busy translating from the German, and collecting and composing his first border ballads.[15] As we have seen, Scott was the other main influence besides Niebuhr on the transformation of European historiography, by his demonstration of the power of the historical novel to create a new form of history. It was also Scott who, by collecting and reviving the border ballad tradition in British poetry, offers the closest analogy to Niebuhr's well-known ballad theory of the origins of Roman history. When a generation later Macaulay recreated Niebuhr's lost ballads in his *Lays of Ancient Rome* (1842), he was at the same time continuing the literary ballad tradition of Scott. But, as far as I have been able to discover, the historical theories of Niebuhr were evolved independently of the poetry or ideas of Scott, and the two young men never met. During their later years of fame, they were undoubtedly aware of each other's existence, for it is recorded that in May 1832, four months before his death, Scott visited Niebuhr's disciple, secretary, and successor as Prussian ambassador in Rome, Chevalier (later Baron) Bunsen; knowing Scott's interest in popular poetry, Bunsen arranged for his children to sing to him German ballads of the war of liberation of 1813.[16]

One consequence of Niebuhr's visit to Britain was that he became a recognized expert among the Anglophiles in the circle of Baron von

Stein; when Stein's lifelong friend and fellow liberal politician, Ludwig von Vincke, published his account of the English administrative system in 1815, *Darstellung der innern Verwaltung Grossbritanniens*, it was edited by Niebuhr, who notes that the author did not have the opportunity to study Scottish institutions.[17]

The first edition of Niebuhr's *Römische Geschichte* (1811–12) was a product of 'a time full of hope, when the university of Berlin was opened'; from 1810 to 1813 he lectured on Roman history during the French occupation and invasion of Russia: 'to have enjoyed this, and to have lived in 1813, this of itself is enough to make a man's life, notwithstanding much sad experience, a happy one'.[18] The second edition was written after his period as ambassador in Rome, when he was a professor at Bonn, and was published in 1827–30, with a third posthumous volume in 1832. Although the two editions differ in important ways,[19] they were marked from the start by the application of Niebuhr's new method of source criticism to the history of Rome, which was conceived as a Vico-style conflict between patricians and plebeians, ending in the struggle of the orders and the Twelve Tables; according to Niebuhr, this reality could be dimly detected in the narrative of Livy, which was itself based ultimately on the survival of popular plebeian ballads.

By the time of the second edition Niebuhr was already famous throughout Europe; within a year two young historians at Cambridge, Julius Hare and Connop Thirlwall, began publishing a translation of it (1828–32), to which in 1842 two other important figures in our story, Leonhard Schmitz and William Smith, added the final posthumous volume. The translation provoked immediate controversy in Britain since it rejected the evidence of the only surviving ancient source, Livy, in favour of the author's modern theories.[20] Throughout its subsequent long life as a standard history it continued to be controversial, and was often attacked even by allies such as George Cornewall Lewis, in his work entitled *On the Credibility of Early Roman History*.[21]

Niebuhr's influence was not confined to the study of antiquity: he came to symbolize the ability of the modern scholar to think for himself, subordinating the ancient evidence to his own theories. It was indeed Niebuhr who was the catalyst behind the emergence of modern historical studies in Britain, for he liberated historians from the tyranny of the ancient text as the paradigm of truth: for the first time, historians could use their imagination and their critical skills to portray the past 'as it really was'. The dangers to religious orthodoxy of this new historical approach were recognized from the start. Niebuhr's historical method, which involved the dethronement of the 'sacred text', was often regarded as a dangerous form of unorthodoxy connected with the criticism of the foundations of Christianity espoused by German theologians.

In the universities the translation of Niebuhr's *History* began a new epoch in historical studies; modern history and indeed historical theology were not then taught to students, and instead they came to the new critical history directly through Niebuhr and the study of the classical world, both Greek and Roman. In the course of its long life the *History of Rome* had an enormous influence in Britain; according to Niebuhr's disciple and champion Bunsen, 'a much larger number of copies of the English translation . . . have been sold than of the German original'.[22] Even before its translation Thomas Arnold, the great reforming headmaster of Rugby (later briefly Professor of Modern History at Oxford), had been persuaded by Hare to learn German in order to read the first German edition; he reviewed it in an article on early Roman history for the *Quarterly Review* in 1825: 'In our literary intercourse with Germany, we have hitherto been as passive traders as the Chinese: we have suffered our own productions to be exported, without any desire to import those of our neighbours in return; or if we have purchased any of their commodities, we have trafficked like savages, bartering things of real value for the mere glass beads, toys and tawdry finery of those with whom we have traded.' According to Arnold, the works of Niebuhr, Georg Friedrich Creuzer, and Wilhelm Gottfried Wachsmuth on early Rome were different; he commends Niebuhr especially for his approach to source criticism, his collection of the fragmentary evidence, and his use of Roman law to uncover the origins of Roman social history.[23]

In 1827 Arnold met Bunsen in Rome and in 1830 he made a visit to Niebuhr himself in Bonn.[24] It was the 'essay on the social progress of states' published in Arnold's 1830 edition of Thucydides (appendix 1) that introduced Giambattista Vico to the English world and linked him with Niebuhr in the creation of a theory of the origins and decline of aristocracies.[25] Arnold's own *History of Rome* was the first work in Britain explicitly to follow not just Niebuhr's subject matter but also the Niebuhrian method of historical research: in his preface he describes it as an attempt 'to practise [Niebuhr's] master art of doubting rightly and believing rightly'. This work was begun in 1838 and was intended to extend 'to the revival of the western empire, in the year 800 of the Christian era by the coronation of Charlemagne at Rome'; but at Arnold's death in 1842 it had only reached the third volume and the Second Punic War.

Similarly in Cambridge, Niebuhr's translators Thirlwall and Hare were inspired to create a short-lived classical journal, *The Philological Museum* (1831–3), in emulation of the master's *Rheinisches Museum*; and Thirlwall began to follow Niebuhr's methods in a major new *History of Greece* that was published in eight volumes (1835–44). This contained a fascinating attempt to analyse Lycurgan Sparta and Solonian Athens – an amalgamation of the new science with older views, which lacked the fervour but had many analogies with his exact contemporary Bulwer-Lytton. Thirlwall's *History of Greece* was however, as he himself recognized, destined for oblivion at the hands of his friend and former schoolfellow George Grote, for his work displays a fatal combination of stylistic turgidity with a Niebuhrian obsession for emphasizing the uncertainty of the historical record.[26]

Cambridge, rather than Oxford, would indeed have been the centre of the new school of ancient history in Britain, if Niebuhr's two translators had received more encouragement. But Hare left to become a country clergyman, and Thirlwall was deprived of his teaching post for publicly suggesting that compulsory daily attendance at chapel for students should be abandoned.[27] Their departure (Thirlwall to exile in a Welsh bishopric, Hare to a family living in southern England) saw the disappearance of Cambridge from the intellectual map of ancient history for a full century, until Moses Finley arrived as an exile from the United States in 1955.[28]

In Oxford, the other English university, the study of ancient history had been from 1800 a compulsory part of the BA for all students, and the influence of Niebuhr on university teaching was profound: his views and methods dominated the subject for forty years, from 1830 to 1872.[29] During this period the main text for Roman history was the early legendary books of Livy, studied under the influence of Niebuhr. Travers Twiss (later Professor of Law, architect of the ruthless Constitution of the Belgian Congo, and victim of a famous libel case which ruined his career)[30] wrote a four-volume Niebuhrian commentary on

Livy (1840–41) and a 360-page *Epitome of Niebuhr's History of Rome* designed for students (1836). They certainly needed it: Mark Pattison describes the life of a student in the 1830s:[31]

> Then the text of Livy alone did not quite fit one out for answering their questions on the early history of Rome. One was expected at that time to know something of Niebuhr's views; I set out to discover these for myself, not in an epitome, as I ought to have done – there were such things – but by reading for myself the two volumes of Thirlwall's translation. A ploughed field was nothing to this. It was a quagmire, a Serbonic gulf, in which I was swallowed up.

A contemporary student parody of the new practice of written examinations offers this examination question:[32]

> Niebuhr, from observing that caps have tassels, and that the streets of Oxford are not macadamized, comes to the conclusion that the University of Oxford was originally inhabited by Pelasgi, which he further confirms by observing that the inhabitants of it depart and return periodically, according to the vacations, in which we see the migratory habits of the Pelasgi exemplified. State the force of the argument.

In truth the reading of Niebuhr was always a thankless task for those who believed in history as narrative. 'One imagines oneself at the bottom of a mine, with the murky light of a lamp, close to a miner scratching laboriously at the hard rock,' wrote Hippolyte Taine.[33] In the Oxford debate on reforms of 1850, Benjamin Jowett complained of the triviality of studying the endless and meaningless succession of Volscian wars.[34] Nevertheless, this was the education of all British intellectuals in Victorian England; as late as 1861 a student handbook still declared 'that incomparable historical genius left little for others to do in this department'.[35] It was only finally in 1872 that the new view of Roman history of Theodor Mommsen was accepted: Polybius replaced Livy as the primary text for study, and Roman history was declared to have begun with the Punic Wars. Since that time until almost the present day, Livy has not been seriously studied by historians in Britain: I well remember the incredulity among my elders that greeted the first signs of a renewed interest in Livy, with the article of Arnaldo Momigliano, 'An Interim Report on the Origins of Rome', in the *Journal of Roman Studies* for 1963, and Robert Ogilvie's *Commentary on Livy 1–5*.

Outside the ancient universities, London was an even greater centre of the influence of Niebuhr. Leonhard Schmitz had studied under Niebuhr at the University of Bonn, and had been a private tutor there to the future Prince Albert; a native of Alsace he married an Englishwoman, and moved to Britain where he proceeded to spread the new historical gospel. In contact with Thirlwall and Chevalier Bunsen, he published in 1844, in English and for the first time, his notes from the lectures of Niebuhr on Roman History that he had heard in the 1820s: for this he received a gold medal from the King of Prussia. This text was actually translated back into German, and provoked the publication in Germany of a complete official set of Niebuhr's lectures. These in turn were successively translated into English by Schmitz, beginning with a version of the *Lectures on the History of Rome* improving yet further on the German edition,[36] *Lectures on Ancient History*, and *Lectures on Ancient Ethnography and Geography*. In each case Schmitz claimed to be able to improve on the German editions by consulting his own notes taken as a student of Niebuhr. By now, at the height of the Germanophilia created by Queen Victoria's marriage to Prince Albert, Schmitz was a figure of great importance, as Rector of Edinburgh High School and private tutor to the Prince of Wales and the Duke of Edinburgh. From 1843 to 1850 he founded and edited the first serious classical journal in Britain, the *Classical Museum*; it was subtitled 'a Journal of Philology, and of Ancient History and Literature' and was once again modelled on Niebuhr's *Rheinisches Museum für Philologie, Geschichte und griechische Philosophie*. His collaborator in many of these enterprises was his fellow translator of the third volume of Niebuhr's *History*, another great Victorian figure: William Smith was one of the first graduates of University College London, who studied law before coming to Latin and Greek, became a master at University College School, and produced a series of reference works and dictionaries, together with an edition of Gibbon. He ended as editor of the *Quarterly Review* (1867–93), and received an honorary degree from Oxford (1870) and a knighthood from the Queen (1892): now long forgotten, his obituarist could once claim, 'his name will always be associated with a revival of classical teaching in this country'.[37]

Behind this translating activity stood the indefatigable Christian Bunsen (1791–1860), who had lived for twenty-two years in Rome first as Niebuhr's secretary and later his successor as Prussian ambassador (1831–8); in 1836 he founded the great classical library of Rome, the library of the Istituto Germanico (the *Deutsches Archäologisches Institut*). Like Schmitz, Bunsen had also married an Englishwoman, and came to London as Prussian ambassador from 1842 to 1854: in Rome and London his acquaintance included almost every literary, political, and religious figure of the day.[38] When he sought a translator for the *Life and Letters of Niebuhr* he approached first Sarah Austin, the wife of the Utilitarian legal philosopher John Austin, Professor of Jurisprudence at University College London,[39] but apparently she was not available; he then turned to Susanna Winkworth of Bristol, like Sarah another educated woman brought up in Unitarian circles who turned to translation as a means of using her talents; she later became his literary secretary and translator. She produced the excellent *Life and Letters of B.G. Niebuhr and Selections of his Minor Writings* in three volumes (1852), which established Niebuhr in Britain as the model of a modern historian, statesman, and public servant.[40]

Thus his friends and admirers kept the memory of Niebuhr alive in Britain through translation and adaptation; it may be said that for more than a generation after his death in 1831, he was a far more important figure in Britain than in Germany. But his influence runs deeper still, into the literature of the period. His ballad theory of early Roman history influenced the Romantic view of epic deeply, and caused Macaulay to reinvent the lost ballads in the most popular poetic work after Byron of the nineteenth century, *Lays of Ancient Rome* (1842). Generations of late Victorians were taught to compose ballads in the style of Scott and Macaulay, and their children were brought up learning these poems by heart. Through Macaulay, Niebuhr may be said indeed to have had a powerful effect on the education of the administrators of the British Empire:

> Lars Porsenna of Clusium
> By the nine gods he swore
> That the great house of Tarquin
> Should suffer wrong no more . . .

'Oh Tiber! father Tiber!
    To whom the Romans pray,
A Roman's life, a Roman's arms,
    Take thou in charge this day!'
So he spake, and speaking sheathed
    The good sword by his side,
And with his harness on his back
    Plunged headlong in the tide.

No sound of joy or sorrow
    Was heard from either bank,
But friends and foes in dumb surprise,
    With parted lips and straining eyes,
Stood gazing where he sank;
    And when above the surges
They saw his crest appear,
    All Rome sent forth a rapturous cry,
And even the ranks of Tuscany
    Could scarce forbear to cheer.

Macaulay goes on to describe how this ballad is sung on winter nights by the fire, 'When the oldest cask is opened, And the largest lamp is lit.' It is a scene straight from Niebuhr's imagination.

But greater poets than Macaulay were influenced by Niebuhr. He is closely associated with the history of the word 'palimpsest'; in 1816, as he was proceeding south to take up his post in Rome, news of Angelo Mai's discovery in the Vatican library of palimpsests of classical texts hidden in manuscripts reused for Christian writings was reaching the European world. In 1814 Mai had found lost speeches of Cicero, in 1815 manuscripts of Plautus, the unknown letters of Fronto and, most dramatically of all, in 1819 he found large sections of Cicero's lost work *De republica*, previously known only from its use by Saint Augustine as a major inspiration in his *City of God*. Passing through Verona in 1816, Niebuhr himself discovered the long-lost *Institutes* of Gaius, which was immediately recognized as the missing foundation text of Roman law; on his arrival in Rome he located in the Vatican library further fragments of Cicero speeches and of Seneca and Hyginus (which were published in 1820). Niebuhr found himself competing and collaborating with Mai in work on this new material.

Suddenly through Mai and Niebuhr the concept of the palimpsest entered the Romantic consciousness. Giacomo Leopardi used Mai's discoveries to characterize the rebirth of the Italian nation in one of the most famous of all his poems, *Il Palimpsesto*, addressed to Angelo Mai in 1820:

E come or vieni
Sì forte a nostr'orecchi e sì frequente,
Voce antica de' nostri,
Muta sì lunga etade? e perchè tanti
Risorgimenti?

(And how do you sound so strong in our ears and so insistent, ancient voice of our fathers, silent for so long an age? and why such renewals?)

This ballad of the Risorgimento inspired the revolutionaries of the age to such effect that it was suppressed by the Austrian authorities.[41]

For Leopardi the palimpsest was inscribed in the soul of the Italian people; for the English Romantics it presented an image of the individual soul. The origin of this important Romantic metaphor in the new discoveries is clear. The first recorded modern usage of the word 'palimpsest' in English occurs in a reference in the *Gentleman's Magazine* for 1825 to 'Monsignore Angelo Mayo . . . celebrated for his discoveries in the 'Palimpsestes'.[42] In 1838 Arnold's *History of Rome* mentions Niebuhr's discovery: 'The Institutes of Gaius . . . was first discovered . . . in a palimpsest, or rewritten manuscript of . . . works of S. Jerome, in the Chapter Library at Verona.'[43] It was Samuel Taylor Coleridge in 1829 who first used the word metaphorically of the human mind:[44] in the second edition of his 'collected poems' he writes:

I have in vain tried to recover the lines from the palimpsest tablet of my memory: and I can only offer the introductory stanza, which had been committed to writing for the purpose of procuring a friend's judgment of the metre, as a specimen.[45]

Thereafter for the Romantics the palimpsest became the metaphor for what since Freud we have learned to call the subconscious, that multiple layering of consciousness from childhood onwards, from which lost early memories may suddenly emerge: 'What else than a natural and mighty palimpsest is the human brain?' wrote Coleridge's disciple, Thomas De Quincey, in *Suspiria* (1845).[46] One of De Quincey's most famous essays is indeed entitled 'The Palimpsest': in this he plays the mock instructor of the ignorant female mind:

> You know perhaps, masculine reader, better than I can tell you, what is a Palimpsest. Possibly you have one in your own library. But yet, for the sake of others who may not know, or may have forgotten, suffer me to explain it here: lest any female reader, who honours these papers with her notice, should tax me with explaining it once too seldom; which would be worse to bear than a simultaneous complaint from twelve proud men, that I had explained it twelve times too often. You therefore, fair reader, understand that for your accommodation exclusively, I explain the meaning of this word. It is Greek; and our sex enjoys the office and privilege of standing counsel to yours, in all questions of Greek. We are, under favour, perpetual and hereditary dragomans to you. So that if, by accident, you know the meaning of a Greek word, yet by courtesy to us, your counsel learned in that matter, you will always seem not to know it.
>
> A palimpsest, then, is a membrane or roll cleansed of its manuscript by reiterated successions.[47]

In *Aurora Leigh* (1856), Elizabeth Barrett Browning uses the same image in a curiously complex inversion of the historical realities, in which it is God's text that is overwritten with a pagan romance:

> Let who says
> 'The soul's a clean white paper' rather say,
> A palimpsest, a prophet's holograph
> Defiled, erased and covered by a monk's, –
> The apocalypse, by a Longus! Poring on
> Which obscene text, we may discern perhaps
> Some fair, fine trace of what was written once,
> Some upstroke of an alpha and omega
> Expressing the old scripture[48]

In the second half of the nineteenth century the influence of Niebuhr on ancient history in Britain declined; this period increasingly belonged to George Grote and Theodor Mommsen. With these two authors classical history came of age. Nevertheless, the influence of Niebuhr on Britain was both deeper and significantly different from the impact that he had in his native German language, and went far beyond the creation of a professional school of history.[49] The translation of academic texts is part of a complex activity of cultural transference that affects the consciousness of an age both scientifically and at all levels of its spiritual life; and it is not possible to understand the nature of British intellectual culture in the first half of the nineteenth century without taking account of the multiple effects of the phenomenon of Niebuhr.[50]

Jacob Burckhardt 1818–1897

9
Burckhardt and Cultural History

The lifetime of Jacob Burckhardt (1818–1897) spans the great age of nineteenth-century historical writing. As a young man he had been taught in Berlin by the generation of scholars who rebelled against the Hegelian conception of history to create historical positivism; his teachers were the Greek historians August Boeckh and J.G. Droysen, and the great founder of modern historical studies and archival research, Leopold von Ranke (whose chair in Berlin he was subsequently offered in 1872). Burckhardt was a contemporary of Charles Darwin, Karl Marx, and Theodor Mommsen; he belonged (though as a Swiss in a characteristically oblique way) to the revolutionary 'generation of 1848', and the great watershed of nineteenth-century Europe. Among philosophers he admired most Schopenhauer, and was a friend and colleague of the young Nietzsche; other colleagues in Basel whom he admired included the anthropologist J.J. Bachofen, the philologist Otto Ribbeck, his pupil and successor the art historian Heinrich Wölfflin, and the philosophical historian Wilhelm Dilthey.[1] Burckhardt was (as we shall see) less happy with the scholars of a younger generation like Ulrich von Wilamowitz-Moellendorff, who tried to create a science of philology and elevate it above the history of the human spirit. It is symptomatic that Wilamowitz's first work was a violent attack on Nietzsche's 'philology of the future' (1872), which was defended by the young Erwin Rohde equally intemperately, while at the height of his powers after Burckhardt's death Wilamowitz could damn Burckhardt's lectures on *Greek Cultural History* with the magisterial comment mentioned below (p. 214). Yet it is this work that now appears to be the foundation of modern approaches to the Greek world; the mature Wilamowitz misunderstood Burckhardt just as the young Wilamowitz had misunderstood Nietzsche's *Birth of Tragedy*.

In conformity with the dominant nineteenth-century view of historical development the nation state was not an artificial modern post-Metternich invention, but the expression of the *Volksgeist* of a primitive tribal past; states were natural entities, racially homogeneous, but each differing in their institutions, which derived from individual legal and social traditions; and all must therefore of biological necessity hate their neighbours. By such means the Age of History defended and justified the emergence of nationalism from tribalism, and bequeathed a terrifying legacy to the twentieth century. This initially Hegelian view of a teleological history was reinforced and revalidated by the emergence of scientific and especially biological models in the course of the century: Darwin's *On the Origin of Species* (1859) fundamentally justified a view of history as the story of origins, in which change was explained by the conception of the survival of the fittest. In such a view we may commiserate with the victims of history, but must still recognize that history reflects a form of beneficent social evolution.

Burckhardt's conception of *Kulturgeschicht*, as the investigation of the complex interplay of universal forces within a chronological frame, stands against this dominant view.[2] Burckhardt had no interest in origins, no concern for any genetic input; to him systems interrelated, and each historical period was a discrete entity composed of interlocking phenomena, different from whatever came before or after – and equally (one is left to imagine) different from ourselves who are encapsulated in Burckhardt's conception of 'the contemplative historian'. That is why Nietzsche found Burckhardt's wisdom so fascinating, and his views so antipathetic.

LIFE

Jacob Burckhardt was born in 1818 into a family that was a minor branch of one of the great burgher clans of Basel: the name of Burckhardt had been prominent in the city since the fifteenth century.[3] His father was a Protestant minister who had been much influenced by Friedrich Schleiermacher's theology. Basel was a patrician city, conservative and increasingly prosperous, at the same time as being detached from the turbulence of European political events; Burckhardt belonged to its intelligentsia. He completed a degree in theology at Basel, but ceased to be religious, having become convinced by his youthful studies that the life of Christ was a myth. In 1839 he went to Berlin to study history under the reigning positivists; but his closest friend and greatest influence was Franz Kugler, the bohemian professor in the new subject of art history. In another friend, Gottfried Kinkel, he found one of the last of the great Romantics; he moved into the circle of Kinkel's mistress, the divorced Johanna Matthieux, and of Bettina von Arnim, who had once loved Goethe and who lived in Berlin with her sister, the widow of the great legal historian F.C. von Savigny. Burckhardt was Kinkel's best man at his wedding with Johanna in 1844; but he distanced himself from him during Kinkel's subsequent career as a revolutionary. Kinkel was condemned to death in 1848 and escaped with his wife's help to exile in London, where Johanna finally committed suicide.

Burckhardt was safely back in Basel in 1844, where he served for eighteen months as editor of the main conservative newspaper, the *Basler Zeitung*. He was already lecturing at the university on the history of painting, where he caused offence in religious circles by criticizing the dominant Nazarene School, a group of German religious painters in Rome who served as a model for the later Pre-Raphaelites. In 1852 he resigned from the university and left for Italy, where he wrote the immensely popular *Cicerone* (1854), 'a guide to the enjoyment of art in Italy', which remained the standard guidebook to Renaissance Italian architecture, sculpture, and art for three generations and went through seven editions during his lifetime. On the basis of this he was given a post at the Zurich Polytechnic. In 1858 he was appointed Professor of History at Basel, where he was required to lecture both at the university and at the high school; from 1874 he was also Professor of the History of Art. The first post he held until 1885, and the second until 1893. He was a conscientious and assiduous lecturer in both history and history of art, who taught as much as ten hours weekly, and also gave many lectures for the general public.

Burckhardt never married (although as a young man he was in love and wrote poetry to a girl whose parents disapproved); his youthful German friends drifted away, and in his thirties he confessed to being lonely beyond all expectations. He had a few close friends with whom he corresponded, and lived a regular and uneventful life in two rooms above a baker's shop, devoting himself to his lectures, his books, and his travels.

Politically Burckhardt was a natural conservative, who disliked and despised the new industrialization and the development of the nation state: he foresaw in the course of his own lifetime the coming of an age of '*terribles simplificateurs*' and demagogues, who would control the masses and bring ruin to Europe. This pessimistic conservatism is characteristic of a reflective historian, who cultivated irony and distance from the enthusiasms of contemporary nationalist historians. In so far as he foresaw the development of industrial society towards the totalitarian popular regimes of National Socialism and Marxism, he was a prophet out of his time, standing against the tide of history. But he was not a political thinker; and these prejudices, however clear-sighted, are merely the regrets of a marginal observer over the decline of the patrician order to which his own family so clearly belonged. Hence his attack on the vice of reading newspapers and concerning oneself with the agitations of the present in the introduction to the lectures on *Greek Cultural History*.[4] It is not Burckhardt's political views or his pessimism in regard to the future that matter, but his conception of historical method; as he wrote already in 1846:[5]

> But my dear friend, Freedom and the State have lost nothing in me. States are not built with men like me; though as long as I live I mean to be kind and sympathetic to my neighbour; I mean to be a good private individual, an affectionate friend, a good spirit; I have some talent in that direction and mean to develop it. I can do nothing more with society as a whole; my attitude towards it is willy-nilly ironical; the details are my affair . . . we may all perish, but at least I want to discover the interest for which I am to perish, namely the ancient culture of Europe.

So he developed the mask of a dilettante, immersed in his work and his few friends, and devoted to the study of European culture, by which he meant the artistic, literary, and spiritual achievements of the past, placed in their context and explained as the result of the forces of history. History was the contemplation of the past: 'leisure, the mother of contemplation and of the inspiration that springs from it' (writing from London): 'Listen to the secret of things. The contemplative mood.' 'How is the collector of inscriptions to find time for contemplative work? Why, they don't even know their Thucydides! Don't bother about others.'[6]

EARLY WORKS

In the 1840s, while still a student, Burckhardt rebelled against the prevailing conception of history, 'the one-sidedness of the present that only wants to have a biased history (*Tendenz-Geschichte*), just as it has a biased poetry and a biased art'.[7] 'For me the background is the chief consideration, and that is provided by cultural history, to which I intend to dedicate myself,' Burckhardt wrote in 1842.[8] From the start his conception of history was concerned, not with actions and events or the great men who appeared to have caused them, but with the cultural context in which such events occurred, a context that might explain the changes far more satisfactorily than by ascribing them to the actions of individuals or the workings of chance. How had Constantine converted the Roman Empire to Christianity, and what did that mean to contemporaries? This was the subject of Burckhardt's first book (1852), which was translated into English as *The Age of Constantine the Great* a century later (1949),[9] and had an enormous effect on my generation of historians, who were in the process of discovering, for the first time in the Anglo-Saxon world since Gibbon, the inexhaustible fascination of late antiquity; for Burckhardt taught us how to see the age as a cultural phenomenon, rather than in terms of its politics and power structures, or its governmental organization, as more recent historians had interpreted it.

In *The Age of Constantine the Great* the analysis was already arranged around three thematic centres – politics, religion, and culture. Politics in this period was a necessary evil, a defence against barbarian invasion and internal anarchy. Culture was in decline: literature was reduced to dependence on power (in panegyric) or religion; art was an adjunct of religion: 'the relevant myths were represented as symbolic husks of general ideas, and the separation between kernel and shell could in the long run only be injurious to art'.[10] Philosophy was a solitary pursuit, even if as Themistius said, 'the value of a philosopher's discourse is not diminished if it is delivered under a solitary plane tree with none but cicadas to hear'.[11] The Christian Church was already a powerful corporation. In this picture Constantine was simply a man of his age, almost irrelevant to the revolution in consciousness that he brought about; he belonged firmly in a world of mixed pagan and Christian beliefs, and his conversion simply ratified a formal division of equality between two cultures that already existed. The core of the argument lay in Burckhardt's portrayal of the dominance of religious modes of thought. Late antique paganism was an immensely complex set of rituals and beliefs trying to make sense of the spiritual world:[12]

> Christianity was bound to conquer in the end because it provided answers which were incomparably simpler, and which were articulated in an impressive and convincing whole, to all the questions for which that period of ferment was so deeply concerned to find solutions.

Burckhardt's most famous book, on which his reputation still rests, was *The Civilization of the Renaissance in Italy* (1860). Lord Acton, the founder of modern historical studies in Cambridge, described it as 'the most penetrating and subtle treatise on the history of civilization that exists in literature'.[13] It is indeed this book that still shapes and challenges all subsequent attempts to explain the central phenomenon in European history. Burckhardt set out to present an analysis of the new forces at work in the period, and how they interrelated. The first part treated of politics and warfare under the provocative heading, 'The State as a Work of Art'. That is to say, political life was no longer determined by traditional forms of government or by underlying forces revealed by the modern historian, but by the conscious knowledge of protagonists that there existed a science or art of government, which could be discovered either by experiment or by reflection. The catalogue of murder, treachery, and tyranny that ensues showed the consequences of believing in the power of reason rather than tradition: it is a view of the history of events that placed the new political science of Machiavelli at its centre; yet whatever its consequences in terms of anarchy and suffering, Burckhardt showed how politics had never before or since been conducted at such a high intellectual level by leaders with such practical and theoretical talents.

The second part described 'The Development of the Individual'. This was a constant preoccupation of nineteenth-century post-Hegelian thought: how the modern idea of the individual had arisen from the tribal and religious stages of history. Burckhardt did not explain – he simply described the forces that separated individuals from their communities, the creation of the ideal of the 'universal man' and the modern conception of fame, together with its antithesis, the modern idea of wit and satire:[14]

> Man was conscious of himself only as a member of a race, people, party, family or corporation – only through some general category. In Italy this veil first melted into air; an *objective* treatment and consideration of the

> state and of all the things of this world became possible. The *subjective* side at the same time asserted itself with corresponding emphasis; man became a spiritual *individual,* and recognized himself as such.

So Burckhardt established that 'it was not the revival of antiquity alone, but its union with the genius of the Italian people, which achieved the conquest of the western world'.[15] His third section concerned 'The Revival of Antiquity' and the education of this new man through contact with ancient literature and culture. The discovery of the New World was treated in a section which relates it to the inner exploration of the psyche, to the development of poetry and biography, and to descriptions of the external world, in 'The Discovery of the World and of Man'.

Under 'Society and Festivals', Burckhardt treated of how men and women actually lived in this new world, the principles of courtesy, good manners and outward refinement, styles of language and conversation, lovemaking, physical exercise and music, the equality of men and women within a masculine ideal of the courtier, and the development of a style of official popular festival, which was modelled on conceptions of ancient triumphs and bacchanals. Finally, 'Morality and Religion' sought to relate this new age to the medieval religious forces that it never wholly superseded, so that the last chapter concerns the mixture of ancient and modern superstition that led towards the inevitable disintegration of belief.

It is this work that marked the definitive establishment of a new form of history, which has come to be known in German as *Kulturgeschichte,* 'cultural history'.[16] Each theme was seen from an entirely new viewpoint, which is on the one hand descriptive and concerned with the details, and on the other corresponds to an underlying view of the basic elements that through their interrelation make up the idea of a culture. In this book Burckhardt was able to discard the determinism inherent in the philosophical problem of the meaning of history for the development of the human spirit, as Hegel had formulated it, while using contemporary philosophical concepts such as the State, Religion, and the Individual to structure his description of reality. At the same time, he avoided the trap of historical positivism, which consists in believing that the meaning of history is contained in a chain of cause and effect, and in the certification of the truth or falsehood of alleged events or facts. For Burckhardt the explanation of events lies not in their causes but in the interrelations between them, of which the idea of cause is only a partial and pseudo-scientific two-dimensional reflection. Societies are not linear series of events, but highly complex and interconnected systems, where a change in any element may provoke multiple effects elsewhere. Moreover, what people believe and how they behave are far more important than whether their beliefs are true or useful: it is not the event that matters, but the perception of that event as a 'fact', which is neither true nor false, but simply believed.

It is a valid criticism of Burckhardt's view of culture that he concerned himself essentially with high culture, with the expression of values contained in the activities and beliefs of an educated elite. His concept of cultural history is therefore fundamentally different from that prevalent in modern universities, where 'cultural studies' means the investigation of popular culture and especially minority cultures. Even so the appropriation of the nineteenth-century term by this new modern discipline points to the fact that the tradition begun by Burckhardt opened the way to the study of gestures, customs, and behaviour patterns, festivals, and other forms of popular expression. Even if Burckhardt might not have relished it, he was in a sense also the father of this discipline, derived from a multicultural and egalitarian conception of society. But it is important to realize that the techniques, concepts, and archival materials necessary to make this leap into the future were not available in Burckhardt's day; and that the great strength of his own reliance on the elite culture was that it was this culture that was self-conscious and fully realized, recorded in the literature and art of the period.

At one time the *Constantine* and the *Renaissance* had been intended to be the beginning and end of a great study of the development of European culture from antiquity to the start of the modern age.[17] But *The Civilization of the Renaissance* was the last book published by Burckhardt during his lifetime. Burckhardt came to believe that teaching was far more important: 'in my experience learned authorship is one of the most unhealthy, and mere teaching (however troublesome it may be and however detailed the studies and preparations need to be) one of the healthiest activities in the world'.[18] Behind this ironic withdrawal from the duty to publish, and his refusal to accept that teaching and writing are part of a continuous process of communicating ideas, lay a deeper distaste for the activities of his academic contemporaries, with their unreadable multiple volumes, their obsession with detail and facts, and the pompous arrogance of 'the *viri eruditissimi* in their professorial chairs'[19] whom he refused to join in 1872, when he turned down the offer of Ranke's chair in Berlin. Heinrich von Sybel had proclaimed the programme for the first number of the new historical journal *Historische Zeitschrift* in 1859: it was to be devoted to the true method of historical research, which was to be combined with a special place for modern history rather than older history and German history rather than the history of other peoples.[20] Increasingly Burckhardt could accept neither the political purpose nor the conceptual method of this new history. He no longer believed in the way positivist historicism was going, and could not bring himself to betray his vision of history as contemplation. The lecture hall in Basel was the one place where it was still possible for a professor to meditate on history rather than making political propaganda or writing boring books designed to kill the interest in his subject. As he said in conversation with his successor Heinrich Wölfflin:[21]

> A teacher cannot hope to give much. But in the first place he can keep alive belief in the value of spiritual things. And secondly he can awaken the conviction that there is real happiness to be found in such things.

LECTURES ON THE STUDY OF HISTORY

Three times between 1868 and 1873 Burckhardt gave a course of lectures 'On the Study of History'. The notes for these lectures (which Nietzsche heard in 1870) were edited as a literary text and published in 1905 by Burckhardt's nephew, Jacob Oeri. More recently, in 1982, my friend Peter Ganz published a scholarly edition of the original drafts, from which it is clear how carefully Oeri worked to create a composite original, incorporating Burckhardt's ideas into the creation of a single written text on the basis of the spoken versions. But Oeri made one significant change in the title: he called the work *Weltgeschichtliche Betrachtungen*; and this grand reference to 'World History' with its deep Hegelian connotations has distorted discussion of the text ever since (the English translation is called *Reflections on History*, which though strictly inaccurate reflects better the title that Burckhardt himself gave the lectures).[22]

Burckhardt as a young man knew of the Hegelian view of history,[23] but he arrived in Berlin at the time of the first historical reaction against the philosophy of history. He always claimed to be lacking in all philosophical interest, and it does indeed seem that he had never made a deep study of Hegel; as Ganz has shown, he did not possess a copy of Hegel's *Lectures on History*, and did not even borrow one from the university library until a mere three weeks before his first set of lectures on the subject in 1868;[24] even then his references in his notes suggest that he never got beyond the first hundred pages. In his own lectures Burckhardt insisted correctly that he is not concerned with any Hegelian philosophy of history:[25]

> The philosophy of history is a centaur, a contradiction in terms, for history coordinates, and hence is unphilosophical, while philosophy subordinates, and hence is unhistorical.

His interest is different and his method less systematic:[26]

> All the same, we are deeply indebted to the centaur, and it is a pleasure to come across him now and then on the fringe of the forest of historical study. Whatever his principles may have been, he has hewn vast vistas through the forest and lent spice to history . . .
>
> For that matter every method is open to criticism, and none is universally valid. Every individual approaches the huge theme of contemplation in his own way, which may be his spiritual way through life: he may then shape his method as that way leads him.

Burckhardt's approach to the theory of history was clearly based on his earlier studies of Constantine and the Renaissance. It proposed three great 'powers' in historical human societies, which were not laws of history so much as principles around which historians may group their attempts at historical explanation. These are once again the State, Religion, and Culture. Each is essentially independent of the others; the first two, 'the expressions of political and metaphysical need, may claim authority over their particular peoples at any rate, and indeed over the world'. They were therefore constants. But Culture is 'something essentially different':[27]

> Culture is the sum of all that has *spontaneously* arisen for the advancement of material life and as an expression of spiritual and moral life – all social intercourse, technologies, arts, literatures and sciences. It is the realm of the variable, free, not necessarily universal, of all that cannot lay claim to compulsive authority.

The formation of historical societies was a process of interaction between these three powers. Societies can be analysed in terms of six combinations, as each power is discussed in relation to the other two. Thus history cannot be reduced to a single explanation such as the political, but results from the complex interplay of competing powers. We might today perhaps quarrel with Burckhardt's choice of powers: for instance, a modern theory would presumably wish to include 'the Economy'. But there is no doubt that Burckhardt's theory of history is, with Marxism, one of the two most important modern attempts to understand the historical process.

The theory owed nothing to Hegel; the first formulation of the idea of the three powers is found in Kierkegaard's notes of lectures on the method of academic study given by F.W.J. Schelling in Berlin in 1841, which Burckhardt may have attended.[28] But if the origin of the idea lay in his student years in Berlin, its detailed elaboration is original, and based on his own appreciation of the problems of writing cultural history, which takes as its focus the interplay between different spheres of human activity. For that reason the most important part of the theory is not the discussion of the individual powers in the first part of the lecture course, but the sections where Burckhardt discussed the six types of reciprocal action between the three powers – Culture determined by the State and Religion, the State determined by Religion and Culture, and Religion determined by the State and Culture.

The weakness of such a theory of history is the weakness of all attempts to study history synchronically, rather than diachronically: if society is viewed as a unity composed of interdependent forces, this makes it difficult to understand the idea of change that is the focus of the traditional history of events, based on cause and effect and arranged as a chronological progression. Burckhardt addressed this problem in his final lectures. The first of these dealt with 'the crises of history' – that is to say change was viewed in terms of catastrophe or revolution, rather than development. The second group of lectures was entitled 'Individuals and the Community' or (on one occasion) 'the Great Men of History': here Burckhardt seems to suggest that the power of the individual great man can break through the static forces which hold cultures together: 'for great men are necessary to our life in order that the movement of history may periodically wrest itself free from antiquated forms of life and empty argument'.[29] It was of course these lectures that particularly attracted Nietzsche.

From these attempts it is clear that Burckhardt understood only too well the problem that his theory was faced with; but he was, I think, ultimately unable to find a satisfactory solution. Although 'the essence of history is change', Burckhardt's view of the process scarcely went beyond a combination of external forces and internal degeneration:[30]

> In nature, annihilation only comes about by the action of external causes, catastrophes of nature or climate, the overrunning of weaker species by bolder, of nobler by baser. In history, the way of annihilation is invariably prepared by inward degeneration, by decrease of life. Only then can a shock from outside put an end to the whole.

Still, since the whole theoretical structure was seen as simply one especially productive way of approaching the 'contemplation' or writing of history, 'a mere device to enable us to cover the ground',[31] Burckhardt might well think that his analysis was adequate: it was Nietzsche, determined to use history for action, who would feel most clearly the unsatisfactory nature of these answers in relation to his own purposes.

BURCKHARDT AND NIETZSCHE

Friedrich Nietzsche was appointed Professor of Classical Philology at the University of Basel in 1869, at the astonishingly early age of twenty-four. Burckhardt was fifty, and had been teaching at the university since 1844, the year Nietzsche was born; Burckhardt had been Professor of History since 1858.[32] From the start Nietzsche admired his colleague enormously; in 1870 he wrote to a friend:[33]

> Yesterday evening I had the pleasure which I would have liked you above all people to have shared, hearing Jacob Burckhardt lecture. He gave a lecture without notes on Historical Greatness which lay entirely within the orbit of our thoughts and feelings. This very unusual middle-aged man does not, indeed, tend to falsify the truth, but to concealments, though on our confidential walks and talks he calls Schopenhauer 'Our Philosopher'. I am attending his weekly lectures at the University on the study of history, and believe I am the only one of his sixty hearers who understands his profound train of thought with all its strange

circumlocutions and its abrupt breaks wherever the subject fringes on the problematical. For the first time in my life I have enjoyed a lecture: and what is more, it is the sort of lecture I shall be able to give when I am older.

In turn Burckhardt attended lectures of Nietzsche in 1872:

> He is still indebted to us for the last, from which we awaited some solutions to the questions and lamentations that he threw out in such a grand and bold style . . . He was quite delightful in places, and then again one heard a note of profound sadness, and I still don't see how the *auditores humanissimi* are to derive comfort or explanations from it. One thing was clear: a man of great gifts who possesses everything at first hand and passes it on.[34]

They had in common their love of Schopenhauer: 'The Philosopher's credit has risen again these last weeks. Living here is one of his faithful, with whom I converse from time to time, as far as I can express myself in his language,' wrote Burckhardt about Nietzsche to a friend in 1870.[35]

On the personal level, Nietzsche always maintained his admiration for Burckhardt, 'our great teacher': even after he left Basel in 1879, and as late as 1887, he continued to send him copies of his books from *Untimely Essays* (1873–6) to *Human, All-too-Human* (1879), *The Gay Science* (1882), *Thus Spake Zarathustra* (1883), *Beyond Good and Evil* (1886), and *The Genealogy of Morals* (1887). But Burckhardt's letters of thanks reveal his increasing distance from Nietzsche's philosophy.[36] Nietzsche was oblivious of this change in the feelings of 'my honoured friend Jacob Burckhardt of Basel' to whom 'above all Basel owes its pre-eminence in the humanities', as he describes him in *Twilight of the Idols* in 1889.[37] Indeed, Burckhardt was one of the recipients of Nietzsche's strange messages from Turin, written in late 1888 as he descended into insanity:

> To my most honoured Jacob Burckhardt.
>
> That was only a little joke, on account of which I overlook the tedium of having created a world. Now you are – thou art – our greatest teacher; for I, together with Ariadne, have only to be the golden balance of all things, we have in every part those who are above us . . .
>
> Dionysus

His last letter to Burckhardt began:

> Dear Professor,
> In the end I would rather be a professor at Basel than God; but I did not dare to press my private egoism so far as to abstain from the creation of the world.

It was this letter, arriving in early January 1889, which caused Burckhardt to consult Nietzsche's friend Franz Overbeck. He had the final responsibility of bringing Nietzsche back to Basel and committing him to medical care.

In old age Burckhardt liked to distance himself from the 'publicity stunt' that Nietzsche had become; in 1896 at the age of seventy-eight he wrote:[38]

> Moreover, since the philosophical vein is entirely wanting in me, I recognized from the time of his appointment here that my relations with him could not be of any help to him in this sense, and so they remained infrequent, though serious and friendly discussions. I never had any dealings with him in respect of *Gewaltmenschen,* the power maniacs, and do not even know whether he clung to this idea at the time when I still saw him fairly often; from the time when his illnesses began I only saw him very rarely.

But there is no doubt that in the early 1870s the two men were very close. Both of them refer to the delight they experienced in finding someone who shared the same veneration for 'the Philosopher' as they both called Schopenhauer; each was profoundly affected by the same distaste for the growth of Prussian power and the cultural consequences of the triumph of Germany over France in 1870–71. And intellectually each influenced the other in a variety of ways.

At first impression it is the differences between the two that are most striking, to the extent that it becomes clear that each reacted against the other, and essentially found the other useful in the process of clarifying his own ideas. Nietzsche's belief in Burckhardt's agreement with him was unverifiable since the latter's views were expressed only in lectures, whereas his own were published. Thus he could claim that Burckhardt had accepted his great contrast between the Apollonian and Dionysian aspects of Greek culture:[39]

> Whoever has investigated the Greeks, such as that profoundest student of their culture now living, Jacob Burckhardt of Basel, realizes at once the value of this line of approach: Burckhardt inserted a special section on the said phenomenon into his *Culture of the Greeks*.

He wrote this in *Twilight of the Idols*. But in fact, whatever may have led Nietzsche to believe it, there is little reference to Nietzsche's theories in the surviving manuscripts of Burckhardt's lectures on Greek culture, either in relation to Greek religion and Greek morals, or in relation to tragedy.[40] And indeed the whole argument of *The Birth of Tragedy*, with its attempt to relate ancient tragedy to the modern music of Wagner, can scarcely ever have appealed to Burckhardt, whose musical interests lay rather with Mozart and Verdi, and whose silence about Wagner hides a profound distaste for him.

Nietzsche had claimed that he was the only hearer to understand Burckhardt's lectures on the philosophy of history. In the 1870s Nietzsche was indeed struggling to free himself from the historical vision of his age. But his famous essay 'On the Use and Abuse of History for Life', published independently in 1874 and two years later in *Untimely Essays*, was essentially a statement of rejection of all that Burckhardt had stood for in those lectures, even if at one point he referred to Burckhardt's description of the Italian Renaissance with approval.[41] The modern age was viewed as suffering from a surfeit of history, produced for entertainment, which led to self-irony and cynicism; like the Roman from the imperial age, the modern human being:

> ... continually has his historical artists prepare for him the festival of a world's fair. He has become a spectator who strolls about enjoying himself, and he has been reduced to a condition in which even great wars and great revolutions can scarcely change anything, even for a moment ...
>
> Or is it necessary to have a race of eunuchs to stand guard over the great historical world-harem? Certainly pure objectivity is quite becoming in eunuchs. It almost seems as if the task is to watch over history so that nothing will ever come of it but stories – but certainly no events![42]

Although Burckhardt might have approved of Nietzsche's dismissal of objectivity, the main criticisms surely relate to Burckhardt's pose of the connoisseur and dilettante, writing and lecturing for the general public:

> Now picture to yourself the present-day historical virtuoso: is he the most just man of his age? It is true, he has cultivated in himself a sensibility so tender and sensitive that absolutely nothing human is alien to him: his lyre can echo in kindred tones the sounds of the most diverse ages and persons; he has become an echoing passivity whose resonance, in turn, has a resounding effect on other passivities of the same sort, until ultimately the air of an age is filled with the buzzing counterpoint of such tender and kindred echoes. Yet it seems to me that only the harmonics, as it were, of that original historical note remain audible: the harshness and power of the original can no longer be divined in the thin and shrill sound of the lyre strings. Moreover the original tone usually wakened deeds, difficulties, and terrors, whereas this pure tone just lulls us to sleep and turns us into gentle epicures. It is as though the *Eroica* symphony had been arranged for two flutes and were intended for the benefit of dreaming opium smokers.[43]

Burckhardt well understood that this was a criticism of himself, and replied to the gift of the book with a characteristic defence of 'amateurism':[44]

> In the first place my poor head has never been capable of reflecting, even at a distance, as you are able to do, upon final causes, the aims and the desirability of history. As teacher and professor I can, however, maintain that I have never taught history for the sake of what goes under the pompous title of World History, but essentially as a propaedeutic study: my task has been to put people in possession of the scaffolding which is indispensable if their further studies of whatever kind were not to be aimless. I have done everything I possibly could to lead them on to personal possession of the past – in whatever shape or form – and at least not to sicken them of it; I wanted them to be capable of picking the fruits for themselves; I never dreamt of training scholars and disciples in the narrower sense, but only wanted to make every member of my audience feel and know that everyone may and must appropriate those aspects of the past which appeal to him personally, and that there might be happiness in so doing. I know perfectly well that such an aim may be criticized as fostering amateurism, but that does not trouble me overmuch.

Indeed, for Burckhardt amateurism was part of his historical ideal:[45]

> The word 'amateur' owes its evil reputation to the arts. An artist must be a master or nothing, and must dedicate his life to his art, for the arts, of their very nature, demand perfection.
>
> In scholarship, on the other hand, a man can only be a master in one particular field, namely as a specialist, and in some field he *should* be a specialist. But if he is not to forfeit his capacity for taking a general view, or even his respect for general views, he should be an amateur at as many points as possible, privately at any rate, for the increase of his own knowledge and the enrichment of his possible standpoints. Otherwise he will remain ignorant in any field lying outside his own speciality, and perhaps, as a man, a barbarian.

Nietzsche in fact had refused to accept the central conception of Burckhardt's lectures on history, though he borrowed a tripartite division: his own theory of history saw it as divided into three types, monumental (great men), antiquarian (facts), and critical (moral judgements). These categories are very crude and offer no great insight, except that his excessive emphasis on the first, which is concerned with history as the record of the actions of great men, showed that he already viewed history primarily as the arena for a display of the power of the *Übermensch* or the free spirit. Although Burckhardt had indeed tackled the problem of the Great Man in history, he saw history as concerned, not with individuals or facts or moral judgements, but with the three fundamental forces whose interaction shaped the development of civilizations. Nietzsche's own theory was concerned with the uses of history for his philosophy of revolutionary change in society; Burckhardt might set him thinking, but, from Nietzsche's point of view, he belonged in the historicist culture that must be destroyed.

What united them most was their common rejection of certain fundamental principles of historicism. They both dismissed the attitudes of the so-called professional scholars: while Nietzsche was provoking his colleagues and calling for a new philology related to the needs of a new vision of the world, Burckhardt was finding himself more and more at odds with the historical perception of the '*viri eruditissimi*' in their professorial chairs. Burckhardt must have approved of Nietzsche's dismissal of objectivity and historical neutrality as historical ideals. And behind this lay a common rejection of the importance of facts and events in history. As Nietzsche wrote, 'The fact is always stupid and has at all times looked more like a calf than a god.'[46] At precisely the same time, Burckhardt was writing to a friend during the preparation of his lectures on Greek culture, and in relation to current political events:[47]

> To me, as a teacher of history, a very curious phenomenon has become clear: the sudden devaluation of all mere 'events' in the past. From now on in my lectures, I shall only emphasize cultural history, and retain nothing but the quite indispensable external scaffolding.

At much the same time he wrote to a young historian:[48]

> I further advise you simply to omit the refuse of mere facts – not from your labour – but certainly from the presentation. One really only needs to use such facts as are characteristic of an idea, or a vivid mark of a time. Our nervous strength and our eyesight are too precious to waste on the study of external facts of the past, unless we are archivists, county historians or something of the sort.

This rejection of the tyranny of factual history was elevated by Burckhardt into one of the most powerful methodological challenges that positivist historiography has faced. In the lectures on Greek culture Burckhardt developed a formal rejection of the cult of the event:[49]

> One great advantage of studying cultural history is the certainty of the more important facts compared with those of history in the ordinary sense of narrated events – these are frequently uncertain, controversial, coloured, or, given the Greek talent for lying, entirely the invention of imagination or of self-interest. Cultural history by contrast possesses a primary degree of certainty, as it consists for the most part of material conveyed in an unintentional, disinterested or even involuntary way by sources and monuments; they betray their secrets unconsciously and even, paradoxically, through fictitious elaborations, quite apart from the material details they may set out to record and glorify, and are thus doubly instructive for the cultural historian.

Cultural history deals with phenomena that are '*recurrent, constant, typical*'.[50] It does not matter whether the stories that it uses are true, as long as they are believed to be true. And even a forgery is an important piece of evidence for the period that perpetrated it, since it reveals more clearly than a genuine article the conceptions and beliefs about the past of the age that created it. This principle of unconscious revelation through representation derives ultimately from Schopenhauer's conception of the world as representation; and it is one of the most powerful tools in the modern historian's study of mentalities. As Burckhardt saw very clearly, it offers a solution to the sterile disputes of positivism as to whether a fact is true or false, and how such a proposition can be established: cultural history is primarily interested in beliefs and attitudes, rather than events – and falsehoods are therefore often more valuable than truths:

> Even where a reported act did not really occur, or not in the way it is said to have occurred, the attitude that assumes it to have occurred, and in that manner, retains its value by virtue of the typicality of the statement.

It is this common attitude to the unimportance of events compared to the significance of beliefs or statements about events that seems to me to unite Burckhardt and Nietzsche as the forerunners of relativist and 'postmodern' historiography.

Apart from the creative enthusiasm that resulted from their meetings, undoubtedly the most significant specific idea about the Greek world that Burckhardt and Nietzsche shared was the belief in the importance of the 'agonal' aspect of Greek and (in Nietzsche's case) modern culture. The realization that individual contest and the desire to be supreme lay at the centre of early Greek attitudes to the world is their joint discovery (see ch. 10 below). Nietzsche seems to have realized the importance of the *agon* or contest, even before he arrived in Basel; but Burckhardt had already formulated it independently, and was busy working out in detail the consequences of this discovery for the understanding of every aspect of Greek culture.[51] This is indeed the most important of all Burckhardt's insights into the Greek mentality, and has proved continually fruitful in Greek history to the present day, where Greek ethical values are often seen as a conflict between competitive and cooperative virtues.[52] It can also be said that the unorthodoxy of each contributed to liberating the thought of the other about the Greeks in this great creative period for both of them. Thus Nietzsche's very critical approach to Socrates mirrors Burckhardt's equally critical but ironic version of the standard myth (see ch. 11 below). And both men shared in very different ways a hatred of the Greek city-state and of Athenian democracy as destructive forces.

LECTURES ON GREEK CULTURAL HISTORY

It was in this climate that Burckhardt began the preparation of a new series of lectures on the history of Greek culture, which he was to call his *Lieblingskolleg* (favourite set of lectures).[53] Although (like Winckelmann, the great eighteenth-century creator of neo-classicism) Burckhardt had never visited Greece, he had been interested in the Greeks since his student days: while it is true that his Greece was a place of the mind, he did not idealize it; and he had studied the displays of Greek antiquities in the Vatican and London, as well as in many smaller museums.

The earliest clear reference to the idea of such a series of lectures is in a letter to the philologist Otto Ribbeck in July 1864:[54]

> Now or never I am going to read through Aristotle's *Politics* with my pen in my hand, besides on the heath stuffing Catullus together with your paper in my knapsack. I am still somewhat obsessed with that idea we talked about over a beer in the pub opposite the Baden station: somehow to roam through the Greeks in my strange and wayward fashion and see what emerges, not of course for a book, but only for a course of university lectures 'on the Greek spirit'. I imagine myself like La Fontaine's milkmaid, lecturing first very timidly one hour a week, then after more study for two hours and three hours to a small but serious audience. There seems to be much comparative eastern material from the Old Testament and the Zend-Avesta ... But you must not betray me, otherwise I shall feel embarrassed.

What had started as 'an idea *inter pocula*' (in his cups)[55] slowly took on reality. The formal decision was taken in February 1869, the preliminary plan was established in January 1870. It was based on a systematic reading and rereading of the ancient sources; on Burckhardt's summer holidays in 1870 he was reading Pindar:[56]

> Here and there, and despite all my admiration, the most disrespectful thoughts occur to me, and from time to time I catch sight of a lot of philistines, and Pindar with all his great pathos in pursuit. Pindar obviously had to deal from time to time with real thugs.

In December 1871 he could say:[57]

> My consolation is that I have gradually wrung a goodly portion of independent knowledge of antiquity directly from the sources, and that I shall be able to present by far the greater part of all I have to say as my own.

By January 1872 the sketch of the final section was established. The lectures were given first in the winter semester of 1872, to an audience of fifty-three people; they were repeated in 1874, 1878, and 1885.

At one point Burckhardt had considered turning the lectures into a book; he revised what are now the first two volumes (essentially on politics and religion), but the second half was left in lecture form. In 1880 he was even approached by a publisher. But when asked later, he denied that he had ever intended to write a book: 'the mistaken belief that I was to publish a history of Greek culture derives from the work of the unfortunate Professor Nietzsche, who now lives in a lunatic asylum. He mistook a lecture course that I used often to give for a book.'[58] To a close friend he explained:[59]

> No, my friend, such a miserable stranger who stands outside the guild fraternity, would not dare to do it; I am a heretic and an ignoramus, and my dubious views would be severely handled by the *viri eruditissimi*. Oh yes, believe me, *je connais ces gens*. In my old age I need peace.

In his will Burckhardt made provision for the destruction of his lectures:[60]

> Since modern booksellers have the presumption to advertise in their catalogues the lecture-notes of dead professors, whereby immature and provisional drafts of opinions reach the public, the following notebooks shall be unconditionally destroyed:
>
> [these include lectures on ancient history]
>
> On the other hand there may be preserved as the personal property of Jacob Oeri of the history of Greek culture both the detailed plan of the

> whole and also the developed working out of the first half (pages in folio), on condition that no part of it is published.

Burckhardt was right; when contrary to his wishes the lectures began finally to be published, the master of the guild, Ulrich von Wilamowitz-Moellendorff, thundered in 1899:[61]

> I would hold it cowardice if I did not here assert that the *Griechische Kulturgeschichte* of Jacob Burckhardt ... does not exist for scholarship ... that this book is incapable of saying anything either of Greek religion or of the Greek state which deserves a hearing, simply because it ignores what the scholarship of the last fifty years has achieved in relation to sources, facts, methods and approaches. The Greece of Burckhardt no more exists than that of the classical aesthetes, which he could rightly have attacked fifty years ago.

Others followed suit: 'a book by a clever dilettante for dilettantes,' wrote Julius Beloch; 'these Greeks never existed,' said Theodor Mommsen. But with the general reader it was an immediate success; Freud, on the threshold of the Oedipus complex, wrote to his colleague Wilhelm Fliess in January 1899, it 'is providing me with unexpected parallels'.[62]

The experts were in a sense justified; even when the lectures had first been given, they were based on Burckhardt's private reading of texts, and on the handbooks of his youth; they did not indeed take account of recent discoveries, notably of inscriptions and papyri. 'He built his knowledge of the Greeks on what they had written, not on what German professors had written about them in the last forty years.'[63] Twenty years later this product of the age of Nietzsche seemed doubly antiquated. How then has it emerged as the greatest work of nineteenth-century cultural history, and the most convincing portrait of the Greeks in the modern age? The answer to these questions lies on the one hand in its importance as an exemplification of the principles of Burckhardt's new methodology for cultural history, and on the other hand in the personal insights that the contemplative Burckhardt possessed into the nature of Greek culture.

The lectures on Greek cultural history are firmly based on the principles established in the lectures on the study of history. The material is organized around a structure of nine sections, the first eight of which are divided between the three powers of politics, religion, and culture.

Thus volume I concerns the State (1. The Greeks and their myth, 2. State and nation); volume II, Religion (3. Religion and cult, 4. The enquiry into the future, 5. The general characteristics of Greek life); volume III describes Culture (6. The fine arts, 7. Poetry and music, 8. Philosophy, science, and rhetoric). To these is added volume IV (9. Greek man in his historical development).

Thus the modern division in the three first volumes corresponds roughly to Burckhardt's standard grouping of sections in relation to the three powers. The first section in volume I tackles the traditional problem of the historical value and meaning of Greek myth, with a refreshing combination of common sense and disregard for the wild theories that abounded (and still abound) in their study. The second section on politics deals with the nature of the *polis* and its development in history through kingship, aristocracy, and tyranny, culminating in discussions of the two fully developed Greek cities, Sparta and democratic Athens. As in *The Civilization of the Renaissance in Italy*, the portrayal of the political sphere is of the State as a systematic 'work of art', essentially hostile to the other powers and to the development of the individual; Burckhardt finishes with a discussion of the origins of Greek political thought and political philosophy, and the conception of Greek unity and superiority over the world of the barbarians. The whole picture of the *polis* is both negative and ironic, expressing Burckhardt's dislike and fear of political power and his recognition of the excessive importance that the Greeks attributed to political life. 'Power is of its nature evil, whoever wields it';[64] the *polis* is an all-powerful instrument of compulsion, idealized as religion and as law, a presence from which there was no possibility of escape, a *città dolente* (Dante, *Inferno* II,1) or city of suffering. Even culture could not set the individual free:[65]

> Culture was to a high degree determined and dominated by the State, both in the positive and in the negative sense, since it demanded first and foremost of every man that he should be a citizen. Every individual felt that the *polis* lived in him. This supremacy of the *polis*, however, is fundamentally different from the supreme power of the modern State, which seeks only to keep its material hold on every individual, while the *polis* required of every man that he should serve it, and hence intervened in many concerns which are now left to individual and private judgement.

That attitude makes his picture of Athenian democracy in particular essentially unsympathetic: the ability of the demagogues to manipulate the masses becomes the most dangerous and most tyrannical form of political power that can be imagined. The prevalence of malicious and arbitrary prosecution by individual sycophants in a system where the law was the expression of the will of the people led to a permanent situation, like that which had existed temporarily during the reign of terror in the French Revolution, where the power to impose confiscation of property, dishonour, removal of citizen rights, exile, and death was absolute, and the individual had no rights at all against the will of the *demos*.

In this portrayal of Greek political life two points should be emphasized. The first is that it was Burckhardt who invented the modern conception of the *polis* as a specifically Greek form of social organization, and who set out to determine in what ways it was different from other types of 'city-state' organization.[66] Earlier discussions had either assumed comparability with other small-scale political systems, or failed to establish any difference at all between the ancient and the modern world. Burckhardt therefore stands at the beginning of all attempts to understand the individuality of Greek political life, whether or not we agree with his portrayal. A second clear break with previous historians is the way that Burckhardt ignored the problem of the importance of the great man. Pericles, Demosthenes, Philip, Alexander the Great are simply representatives of their age: in Burckhardt the great man disappears from history, to be replaced by the unseen movements of a culture as a whole. So despite his hostile attitude to the importance of politics in Greece, it was Burckhardt who first revealed the central importance of the political in Greek life, and who laid the foundation for modern attitudes to the study of Greek politics and political institutions.

In the second volume, on religion, he begins with the phenomenon of metamorphosis as grounded in the sense that all of the natural world is full of the divine, before discussing the Greek conception of their gods as a polytheistic system, and the special Greek phenomena of hero cult and oracle cult. Here his account, although interesting, lacks true insight: it is too much based on literary texts, rather than ritual, and is insufficiently concerned with the depth of real religious experiences as they were later described by Nietzsche's friend Erwin Rohde in his work *Psyche* of 1894, to mention only the book towards which Burckhardt would have been most sympathetic. But not without reason Burckhardt believed that 'the world of the Greeks and Romans was entirely secular', and Greek religion was subordinate to the other powers:[67]

> The religions of that world were mainly determined by the State and Culture. They were State and Culture religions, the gods were State and Culture gods, while the State was not a theocracy; hence the absence of a priesthood in these religions.

Personally indeed, Burckhardt's irony and his lack of religious involvement created a distance between himself and the object of study, which is only occasionally relieved by flashes of real insight.

He ends the discussion of religion in section 5, with a fascinating and highly original account of 'the general characteristics of Greek life', which contradicts the traditional picture of the Hellenic ideal with a deliberately negative image of the Greeks, as a people for whom lying, treachery, cruelty and vengeance are essential aspects of a moral code which is divorced from religion and opposed to the basic beliefs of Christianity, and which is in no way compatible with modern views of morality in private or public life:[68]

> Among the Greeks ... morality was practically independent of religion and in all probability more closely connected with the ideal of the State.

There is here a close relationship with Nietzsche's view of the Greeks in *The Birth of Tragedy* and elsewhere; but whereas Nietzsche wanted to see the Greeks as models for a new cult of the amoral, Burckhardt seeks merely to establish that the Greek moral code was fundamentally different from ours, and that we should not therefore idealize the Greeks.

The section concludes with a description of the nature of Greek pessimism, the terrible burden of being Greek, their despair of life and their fascination with suicide. Here too there is a connection with Nietzsche's portrayal of the Greeks in *The Birth of Tragedy.* Both authors in fact took their starting point from Schopenhauer's conception of pessimism as a creative force in human culture, which in itself is a development of the Renaissance idea of melancholy and the melancholic man as genius.[69] But Schopenhauer believed that it was Christianity, with its asceticism and doctrine of the meritorious nature of celibacy, which had asserted the denial of the will-to-live, and that it therefore lay at the origin of modern pessimism: earlier peoples (even the Jews, despite the temporary aberration of the doctrine of the Fall of Man) had been endowed with an incurable optimism.[70] This created a problem especially in relation to the development of Greek tragedy: was tragedy an expression of a pessimistic view of the world, and of the powerlessness of humanity in the face of the divine will, which was in itself unconcerned with human morality and human suffering – or could Greek tragedy be viewed as an optimistic vision of the human predicament, a form of higher 'cheerfulness'? It is the second view that is argued by Nietzsche in *The Birth of Tragedy*; for him Greek 'cheerfulness' is a fact, which resides in the Dionysian power of emotion to fuse with the Apollonian or rational aspect of tragedy, and asserts life in the face of human disaster. It is primarily this paradox which has made Nietzsche's view that tragedy is a triumph of the human will so influential in the modern world.[71]

Burckhardt took the other way forward, by presenting the Greeks as the creators and the sufferers in relation to Schopenhauer's vision of hopeless pessimism. As a view of tragedy this perhaps lacks the depths that the Nietzschean tradition has been able to achieve through the idea of tragedy as a form of reconciliation of opposites; but he grounded it, not in one literary genre, but in the whole Greek perception of the transitory nature of human happiness and of life itself. He saw that the real problem and the real achievement of the Greeks lay in their refusal to accept the existence of an afterlife of any significance, which made the pleasures and pains of this life so powerful and so intolerably sweet even in suffering. He refers to:

> The religion of the Greeks, who, with their clear insight into humanity and the limits of the individual, presupposed only a colourless world to come and spent little thought on it, leaving eschatology as a physical problem to the philosophers.[72]

It is easy to endure life if one regards it as simply a preparation for a future existence; the true tragedy lies in the realization that there is no future but the continuation of the present beyond individual sensation. So Christianity ceases to be the cause of pessimism, and the tragedy of the human predicament lies in the necessity of accepting the absoluteness of the here-and-now. For all the power of religion in the Greek world, Burckhardt's Greeks were the first to understand what it is to be human in the modern sense, and to live in the present without hope for the future. It is in this sense that the Greeks still provide us with a model of how to live, beyond morality and beyond hope. In this analysis Burckhardt developed the ideas of Schopenhauer into an explanation of the continuing power of Greek culture; for in his account of Greek morals he revealed what is the basis of the difference between ourselves and the Greeks, and in his account of Greek pessimism he showed why the Greeks nevertheless express the fundamental predicament of humanity in Western culture.

In volume III on the arts in Greek culture, Burckhardt is at his most conventional: here if anywhere he is old-fashioned, unwilling to rethink the categories of the philological handbooks and the idealistic lectures of his youth, or to accept either new discoveries or the insights of Nietzsche into the relationship between ancient and modern art forms. The vision of *The Birth of Tragedy* is strangely absent, and Burckhardt remains bound in an aestheticizing appreciation of Greek literature and Greek art as timeless models, unrelated to the society that produced them. Despite the intelligence of his survey of Greek art, literature, and science, it offers no permanent new insight, and makes us remember that one aim of his lecture course was simply 'to put people in possession of the scaffolding which is indispensable if their further studies of whatever kind were not to be aimless'.[73]

It is the fourth and longest volume, comprising a single section on 'Greek man in his historical development', which presents a major new departure in Burckhardt's method. It corresponds on the conceptual level to the problems he had tried to face in the second half of his lectures on the study of history – how to combine the three powers into a picture of the culture of a society as a whole, which would also be capable of explaining how such cultural units might change and develop over time. Burckhardt presents a series of portraits of 'Greek man' (or 'the Greek' – the concept *Mensch* in German has no specific connotation of gender, and Burckhardt devotes a great deal of space to the changing role of women in Greek culture). Five historically successive phases of Greek culture are identified: the heroic, the colonial and agonal (as we might say, the archaic; see below, ch. 10), the fifth century, the fourth century, and the Hellenistic. This series of portraits is a sustained and successful attempt to exemplify in detailed analysis those complex processes of interrelationship between the three powers that are described in the central sections of the lectures on the study of history.

The final problem of the lectures on the study of history had been how to explain the process of development from one period to another; in the lectures on Greek culture this is not addressed directly. Instead, each separate portrait contains the elements that point forward to the next, as if to indicate the natural process of movement from one period to another. Perhaps the most important question that is raised by Burckhardt's presentation of his theory in action in relation to a historical society is how far this device in fact succeeds in solving the problem that his theory had identified. But in contrast to the various attempts that Burckhardt had explored in his earlier lectures, as in his other historical books he seems determined to avoid easy solutions: it is once again noticeable how he refused to rely on the dynamic of the great man in order to move the historical process forward: for Burckhardt, Pericles, and Alexander the Great explain nothing:[74]

> When knowledge flows more freely, it is supremely desirable that the great man should be shown in conscious relationship to the culture of his time; that an Alexander should have had an Aristotle as his tutor.

Burckhardt's lectures on Greek culture are therefore important for two reasons. First, in them Burckhardt used and exemplified the theoretical categories that he had developed for the study of cultural history. They constitute in fact the final expression of his attempt to found a new historical method, based on contemplation and understanding of the way in which cultural and social systems are composed. In an age in which the importance of cultural history has finally come to be recognized, in the study of the history of mentalities and the new trends in historical scholarship since Foucault, it is important to return to the work of the half-forgotten founder of this type of historical investigation, and consider what he has to teach us. For it was Burckhardt who overthrew positivism in history, and established the insignificance of the history of events in the face of the relativity of historical facts.

Second, in the process of elaborating a new picture of Greek culture based on the insights that he had won in other periods of history, Burckhardt inevitably rethought the conventional categories of classical scholarship, just as Nietzsche did. And that, combined with his ironical and detached view of the 'glory that was Greece', enabled him to identify those leading aspects of Greek culture that remain at the centre of all modern studies of the Greeks. These are the primacy of the political 'power' in Greek life, which imposed a form of political rationality on Greek society such as has not existed in any other culture: Burckhardt did not invent the *polis*, but he uncovered its significance, and brought it to the centre of the discussion.[75] He also saw the fundamental importance of the agonal, competitive aspect of Greek life especially in the archaic age, but continuing through the whole of Greek moral and social history. He identified the specific nature of Greek pessimism and its relation to the intensity of the Greek experience of life. And continually in detail he surprises us with the sharpness of insight into specific aspects: it was for instance only after some years of working on the significance of Greek drinking customs that I recalled a series of brief paragraphs in this work, which together constitute the first serious analysis of the phenomenon of the *symposion*. In this and in so many other ways, Burckhardt will continue to surprise us: his work remains the first and the best modern account of Greek culture.[76]

Jacob Burckhardt crossing the Münsterplatz, Basel on his way to lecture.

10
The Archaic Age

Burckhardt had organized the final section of his lectures on Greek Culture around the idea of different historical periods with different characteristics. Most of these divisions were conventional, but one was not; for although the idea of a classical age and of a Hellenistic age[1] had long existed, he was the first to distinguish an earlier period between the heroic and the classical worlds as the 'colonial and agonal age'. This claim has had a lasting impact on the study of Greek history in defining an 'archaic age'.

There are two elements in the formulation of the idea of a specific archaic age. The first is less important, and suggests that the invention of such a period is relatively recent. It concerns the history of the use of the word 'archaic' in relation to the periodization of Greek history in the various European languages. This aspect has been studied for the German tradition by Glenn Most; and I believe that his conclusion could be substantiated for other languages. Like many of the words used to describe historical periods, 'archaic' in this sense was first used as the designation of an artistic style by professional historians of art. Glenn Most links the establishment of an archaic period in art to Heinrich Brunn, Professor of Archaeology at Munich from 1865; his earliest published use of the word was in a work of 1897.[2] Similarly in English the earliest recorded use (1833) refers to 'a later specimen of the archaic period of bas-relief', in relation to the Parthenon marbles; it appears to be first used of a historical period by historians of Egypt.[3] A search of nineteenth-century English historical texts on ancient Greece has not revealed any use of the term to describe a historical period, and it does not occur in this sense in the first edition of the *Oxford English Dictionary* (1888). Most's article places the high point of German interest in the archaic in Germany of the 1920s, 'the decade of the archaic', when the concept permeated ideas on Greek philosophy and Greek literature. Historians seem to have been more resistant to the idea of an archaic age, finding difficulties in establishing the beginning and ending of such a period and worrying over the anachronistic use of Pindar to define it. But in 1931 Helmut Berve devoted an otherwise rather conventional section of his *Griechische Geschichte* to 'die archaische Zeit'; and in M.P. Nilsson's classic *Geschichte der griechischen Religion*, first published in 1940, his fourth section is called 'die archaische Zeit' and begins with this declaration:[4]

> The period that extends from the beginning of the historical age of Greece to the decisive turning-point in the life of the people, the Persian Wars, and the subsequent flowering of Greek culture, is often called the archaic age; sometimes it is referred to as the Middle Ages or the aristocratic age of Greece.

Nilsson continues by explaining that these last two terms have misleading connotations. His discussion suggests to me that the designation 'the archaic age' still required explanation at this date. By 1946 the ideas of neo-humanism had returned to fashion, and Bruno Snell could devote the second issue of the new journal *Antike und Abendland* to:

> . . . archaic Greece, the period in which the creative vigour of Greece blossomed and laid the foundations of all aspects of European culture. Today, when the future of Europe is so uncertain, it seems especially important to turn one's attention back to this age.[5]

In England the phrase does not seem to have been widely used before the 1970s, with Moses Finley's *Early Greece: The Bronze and Archaic Ages* (1970)[6] and L.H. Jeffery's *Archaic Greece* (1976); by 1980 it was well established, being used in that year for the title of A.M. Snodgrass's *Archaic Greece*, and simultaneously being described as 'universally recognized' in chapter 12 of my *Early Greece.*[7] In Italy the introduction of the term is, I believe, due to Santo Mazzarino, who in 1947 gave his fundamental study of the period, *Fra oriente e occidente*, the subtitle *Ricerche di storia greca arcaica*. Mazzarino had studied in Munich before the war, and much of his work is focused on a discussion with his teacher Berve, who (despite his stature as a historian) was rightly held by Mazzarino to be committed to a racial interpretation of history which laid great emphasis on the contrast between *Ionertum* and *Doriertum*: much of Mazzarino's book reflects his attempt to contest and escape from the influence of his former teacher. But (to anticipate) at this period of his life Mazzarino does not appear to have reflected deeply on Burckhardt himself, whom he quotes only tangentially: his characterization of the period is filtered through his German teachers, and his own belief in the importance of *habrosyne* (sophisticated luxury) as a defining characteristic of archaic Greek culture.[8]

The second question is more important: the invention of the idea of a specific cultural period and the definition of its characteristics. It is in this respect that I believe Burckhardt to have been the inventor of the concept of an archaic or 'agonal' age. No historian before Burckhardt seems to have had the faintest idea that the period before the Persian Wars was intrinsically different from the classical age: they treated it simply as a succession of political events, less well attested but essentially similar to later periods and even to the modern age.

The originality of Burckhardt's conception of this period can be seen clearly in his relationship with the professional ancient historian whom he most admired. Ernst Curtius was the first German to write a substantial *Griechische Geschichte*, and the first modern historian to do so with a long experience of the physical landscape and the modern culture of contemporary Greece. He was a highly original and imaginative historian, so much so that his 'idealistisch-ästhetisierende Auffassung des Griechentums' (idealizing aestheticizing conception of Greece) was dismissed by later generations, who regarded his fantasies as deleterious to the study of the real political power relations of serious Greek history.[9]

Burckhardt and Curtius admired each other.[10] It was Curtius who was responsible for the invitation to Burckhardt in 1872 to take Ranke's chair at the University of Berlin, the most prestigious chair in the German-speaking world. Burckhardt never ceased to praise the work of Curtius to his students in his lectures,[11] and Jacob Oeri in the preface to volume IV of the *Griechische Kulturgeschichte* points out that the only recent work on Greek history cited by Burckhardt in his lectures was Curtius's *Griechische Geschichte*, which had indeed been published between 1857 and 1867: this was still the most recent history of Greece in any language when Burckhardt began composing his lectures in 1870. The lectures reveal the traces of his reading of Curtius at a number of points: on the one hand, for instance, he praises Curtius's description of the Greek language as the first and highest achievement of the Greek artistic sensibility;[12] on the other hand, it was in reaction to Curtius's uncritical elevation of Delphi as a pan-Hellenic centre that Burckhardt composed his definition of Delphi, with its great buildings donated by victors from the booty of their wars, as 'above all the monumental museum of Greek hatred for Greeks, of mutually inflicted suffering immortalized in the loftiest works of art'.[13]

However, there is nothing in Curtius's history to suggest the existence of an archaic age. His first volume was remarkable for the vividness with which it evoked the Greek landscape, and was structured around two basic explanatory concepts. The first was the concept of migrations, which according to Curtius in some earlier period had swept back and forth across the eastern Mediterranean, mixing Greeks with Phoenicians in multiple displacements that could be dimly traced in myth. The second was the importance of amphictyonies or religious leagues: here it is clear that the future excavator of Olympia was already convinced of the primacy of religious centres over the Greek *polis*. The first volume extends, it is true, to the Persian Wars, but the articulation is geographical and conventional, with two main chapters devoted to Sparta and Athens, and their respective Dorian and Ionian backgrounds.

In one respect it may be that Curtius influenced Burckhardt; at least he shows the background from which Burckhardt's characterization of the archaic age springs. Although it is not reflected in the *Griechische Geschichte*, in 1856 Curtius had delivered a *Festrede* at the University of Göttingen with the title 'Der Wettkampf'. In this he emphasized the importance of 'the contest' for the understanding of Greek life: 'The whole of Greek poetry became great through the contest. In the palaces of the nobility, at the grave mounds of the heroes, before the temples of the gods, in the crowded marketplaces of the towns, the rhapsodes competed.' Music, drama, and religion were all organized around the contest: 'If I were to choose one word as characteristic of Greek life and distinguishing it from the life of all other peoples, I would say it is the [victor's] crown.'[14]

Although the ideas expressed here bear some similarity to Burckhardt's characterization of the *agon*, there are crucial differences: for Curtius the contest is universal in Greek culture, for Burckhardt the *agon* distinguishes a period; for Curtius it is an idealized and wholly beneficial force, which continues to motivate the competition between modern German universities in the education of youth – the university is a 'Kampfplatz . . . in Erweckung der Jugend' (an arena in which to stimulate our youth); for Burckhardt the *agon* is a dark and demonic power, as dangerous as it is creative. The comparison of their views serves only to emphasize the gap between Curtius's naïve idealism and Burckhardt's pessimistic conception of the forces of history. Similarly, when Curtius talks of 'griechische Cultur' he refers to an unchanging and wholly beneficent feature of Greek civilization, 'a new rationality – ein neue Rationalität)', that descends through Christianity to modern Germany.[15] Burckhardt's conception of cultural history was quite different and was conceived in direct opposition to the dominant *Ereignisgeschichte* (history of events) of Curtius and his contemporaries.

Burckhardt presents the 'colonial and agonal age' as the whole period from the end of the Dorian invasion to the Persian Wars, thus defining that period which we still broadly distinguish today as the archaic age.[16] This 'Middle Ages' of Greek history is characterized by two pairs of conflicting principles – the alternating dominance of aristocracy and monocratic tyranny, and the conflict between the aristocratic ideal of *kalokagathia* and the banausic skills carried on for profit (agriculture, crafts, trade, as well as more intellectual activities such as poetry, prophecy, the arts and architecture). In fact, Burckhardt has relatively little to say about the first, political phenomenon: whereas a modern historian might seem obsessed (like Aristotle) with the question of how the Greek aristocracy lost power and what sort of regime the subsequent tyrannies actually were, once again Burckhardt was little concerned with the movement of historical forces. His interest is essentially focused on the second conflict.

Burckhardt subdivided his period into two ages, the 'colonial' and the 'agonal'; at first sight this might seem merely a chronological distinction, but in fact it has a far deeper significance. The colonial age is the period of the definition of the Greek people, from the last of the *nostoi* (returns of the heroes), the Dorian invasion, through the Ionian migration to Asia Minor, to the great period of colonization, which spread Greek culture throughout the Mediterranean and Black Sea coastlines. This created a unity of culture that continued as a dominant force through Greek history until at least the Hellenistic age: it created the division between Greek and barbarian, together with the forces of what we now call 'acculturation' that led such barbarian peoples to seek out and adopt what they regarded as the superior Greek culture. But Burckhardt also had another end in view: his whole picture of Greek colonization is presented as a comparison with the countervailing force of Carthaginian or Phoenician colonization. The Carthaginians led the way, but their settlements were created for trade, and always remained dependent on the mother city of Carthage. In contrast (with the partial exception of the Corinthian colonies), Greek colonies were always independent and sovereign communities, and were often in advance of their mother city both politically and in terms of rational urban planning. The purposes of Greek colonies were varied, in terms of trade, exile, and political freedom, over-population, plague, earthquakes and other natural disasters, and the comparative sterility and fertility of the land; to this exemplary list of reasons for migration, even the modern world can add only the new horrors of religious conflict and ethnic cleansing. Burckhardt's analysis, firmly based on the ancient conception of the causes of exile, is a supreme example of his imaginative use of evidence to produce a picture that is more perceptive and more finely nuanced than most modern accounts, despite over a century of accumulated archaeological evidence.[17]

The chief purpose of this characterization of the colonial age lies in the contrast between Carthage and Greece, which serves to introduce the main theme of Burckhardt's account of the agonal age, the conflict between wealth and culture. The Carthaginians chose the banausic way, the Greeks chose the way of variety and freedom. I would not wish to discuss the validity of this basic analysis, which has indeed seen a revival, at least in its recognition that the Greek experience was partially dependent on the previous example of the Phoenicians. Rather I will simply emphasize its consequences for Burckhardt's analysis of the agonal age.

Archaic Greek society was conceived of as centred on an aristocracy, described as neither a *Landjunkertum*, a scattered rural squirearchy, nor a *Reichsrittertum*, a military caste. Burckhardt saw the aristocracy rather in terms of the patriciate of the medieval Italian cities, 'a large urban aristocracy living chiefly on income from property, whose aim in life, and ideal, was combat – not so much in the military sense as in that of equals pitted against each other',[18] 'a social group living together in the city and taking an energetic part in its administration, while at the same time constituting its society; the ethos of the *agon* would have sufficed to unite such a group even in the absence of other factors.'[19] In this period only Pythagoras sought to present an alternative communistic version of the political community.

As Burckhardt himself indicated, in one sense the source and structure of his portrayal of the agonal age were based on his conception of Renaissance Florence, in particular Part Five of the *Civilization of the Renaissance* entitled 'Society and Festivals':

> Every period of civilization which forms a complete and consistent whole manifests itself not only in political life, in religion, art and science, but also sets its characteristic stamp on social life.

In this comparison with the Renaissance, Burckhardt captured the essential quality of archaic art, poetry, and life – its sense of the freshness of the world, the festive splendour of the moment, and the transience of the human spirit. In the words of Lorenzo de' Medici:

> Quanto è bella giovinezza,
> Che si fugge tuttavia!
> Chi vuol essere lieto, sia:
> Di doman non c'è certezza.

Or as Robert Herrick in 1648 expressed it:

> Gather ye Rose-buds while ye may,
> Old Time is still a-flying
> And this same flower that smiles to day,
> To morrow will be dying.

The Renaissance Masque of Bacchus and Ariadne recreates the true spirit of archaic lyric.[20] Although Burckhardt could not in any way see the archaic age as a *rebirth* (because for him the Mycenaean Age did not yet exist), he would have been delighted to discover that the modern version of the origins of his age regards it as the renewal of culture under the influence of Homer and the rediscovery of the heroic age: the first sign of this view came in the work of the archaeologists, A.M. Snodgrass and N. Coldstream during the 1970s.[21]

To return to Burckhardt's agonal age, the *agon* is the contest as an end in itself. Already present in the Homeric age with its well-developed ethos of games, it became the centre of aristocratic life: 'Competitive games were instituted everywhere, even in the smallest communities; the full development of the individual depended on his constantly measuring himself against others in exercises devoid of any practical utility.' Moreover, the agonistic spirit penetrated every aspect of aristocratic life, both its public institutions such as the gymnasium and the festival, and their intellectual expression in music, poetry, philosophy, and education. This portrayal of an aristocratic lifestyle embodied in competitive activity that is in itself a useless form of display (and therefore marked off from economic activity) has had many subsequent followers, most notably Thorstein Veblen in his *Theory of the Leisure Class* (1899) and Johan Huizinga in *Homo Ludens* (1938).[22] It is a brilliant and essentially correct insight into the nature of Greek aristocratic culture, and ranks alongside Burckhardt's definition of the *polis* as a uniquely Greek phenomenon, as one of his two main contributions to the understanding of Greek culture.

It is in this central insight that Burckhardt and Nietzsche seem most closely related, for Nietzsche's conception of the competitive ethos of Greek morality from the *Birth of Tragedy* onwards is remarkably similar to that of Burckhardt. Many of us have wondered about the extent to which the two Basel colleagues may have influenced each other in the 1870s (see above, chapter 9). But a comparison of their views does not suggest an easy or simple relationship.

In the first place I would point out the inappropriateness of attempting to establish any relationship of dependence between the two thinkers. It is not a question of who influenced whom; indeed to view the problem in this way is to fall into the very trap that Burckhardt himself sought to free us from, with his denial of the significance of the genetic model of cause and effect in cultural history and the history of ideas: it is the use made of concepts within the thought-world of each individual that matters, not where he may have derived his ideas from. This is especially important in the case of Burckhardt and Nietzsche, each of whom used the central insight of the *agon* in wholly different ways. Burckhardt saw the *agon* much as de Pauw had viewed it a century earlier, as the unifying historical factor that explained all the phenomena of archaic Greek society, from its interest in the useless physical activity of sport to the *symposion*, including such different elements as the importance of nudity and the art of statuary, the attitude to women, and the dominance of homosexuality: the *agon* was a historical phenomenon existing in a particular age, which distinguished that age from all others before or since. Nietzsche's view was more comparable to that of Curtius in its emphasis on eternal human values, although Nietzsche recognized that the competitive spirit of the Greeks differentiated them from Christian cultural ideals, and made them especially important models for his philosophy of the future; his aim was not historical but to incorporate the Greeks as models into the new philosophy.

It is I think for this reason that, however close their views might become, neither Burckhardt nor Nietzsche can be said ever to have significantly influenced one another. The relationship is intrinsically one of 'use and abuse', as Stefan Bauer and I have both pointed out in our discussions of *Vom Nützen und Nachteil der Historie für das Leben.*[23] The very different forms of irony that characterize both men, which one might contrast as the irony of detachment for Burckhardt and the irony of engagement for Nietzsche, meant that as soon as they understood each other they found themselves in opposition, as Nietzsche expresses it clearly in his Basel writings, notably the early version of the *Birth of Tragedy* and his essay on the use and abuse of history. The consequence is that whatever each may have understood from the other was expressed not as *use* but as *abuse*, both (as far as Nietzsche was concerned) in its polemical sense and in its sense of deliberate misuse or alteration. No attempt to relate the ideas of Burckhardt and Nietzsche will ever make sense for these reasons.

I think it is more important to point to the obvious sources for Burckhardt's conception of the *agon* as an independent discovery, probably made before his serious contact with Nietzsche. The entire narrative of this section on the agonistic age is based on remarkably slim evidence, most of which (as Burckhardt himself recognizes) derives from later periods. As always in nineteenth-century perceptions of the past, the essential evidence was literary, in the reading of texts interpreted through a conceptual framework related to contemporary life. Burckhardt's view of archaic culture is clearly based on his reading of Pindar in the summer of 1870 (see above, pp. 212–13). Pindar is in fact the single most important source for Burckhardt's picture of archaic Greece. We might indeed most accurately compare and contrast the views of Burckhardt and Nietzsche by saying that Burckhardt's view of the *agon* is derived from a reading of Pindar, whereas Nietzsche's is derived from a reading of Theognis, the poet on whom he wrote his first serious exercise in philology as a schoolboy in Pforta, his *Dissertatio de Theognidi Megarensi* of 1864.[24] Burckhardt and Nietzsche arrived at similar conceptions through the reading of two different poets.

Again the conceptual framework employed by Burckhardt is clearly his own invention. The primary conflict is that between the aristocratic *agon*, with its ideal of *kalokagathia*, and the economic life of the Greek city, which (as he says) must have existed, but which is systematically disguised in our sources. The world of specialized *banausia*, of the trader, the craftsman, the artist, even the agricultural labourer, is ignored by our literary evidence in favour of the ideals of the aristocracy:[25]

> It may sound very grand when the Greeks are praised as the people among whom, as far as possible, everyone cultivated his gifts, and lived in the pursuit of wholeness, and not for one thing only; but we in posterity are bound to feel we owe more to some of their one-sided specialists than to those who hardly knew what to do with themselves for sheer harmonious *kalokagathia*.

Burckhardt compares the Greeks to the modern age, where 'even today there are certain limits on the activities a so-called cultivated person is prepared to envisage'; and he refers to 'the kind of "Bildung" (culture) in the modern German world which roughly corresponds to the *kalokagathia* of the ancients'.[26]

Yet not even Burckhardt could escape from the influence of the present. Here surely is revealed the origin in the contemporary world of Burckhardt's framework for understanding the archaic age. His agonal age, with its conflict between a *rentier* aristocracy of competitive leisure and the despised world of the craftsman and trader (both more admirable and more essential to the prosperity of the city), is his native Basel: once again, as Lionel Gossman has so definitively established, we find the source of Burckhardt's profound originality in his perception of the workings of history within his own city.[27] For this reason alone we do not need, and will never be able, to find the models for Burckhardt's thought outside its native context in his own mind. His originality as a historian depends upon Burckhardt's origins in Basel. And we may well believe that he was right to see that the closest modern comparison to the ancient Greek *polis* lay in the free cantons of the Swiss federation.[28]

One of Burckhardt's most delightful works is his last, prepared before his death, and left with instructions for posthumous publication. It is an essay on his favourite artist, Rubens, whom Burckhardt rightly saw as a supremely happy genius, who had lived a prosperous and successful life based on his ability to give pleasure to his contemporaries, and who had not mistaken worldly success for the secret of happiness, but had placed his family and his love for his wife above all public honours. Although Burckhardt never married, he was a private man, who was happiest with his small circle of relatives and friends and in his work as a teacher. He might understand the pessimism of the Greeks; but he too possessed the love of beauty, the wisdom, and the happiness of his artistic hero. His *Rubens* is a work of old age and contentment; Burckhardt remained the ironical contemplative historian to the end, one of those who:

> . . . attain an Archimedean point outside events, and are able to 'overcome in the spirit'. Nor is the satisfaction of those who do so, perhaps, very great. They can hardly restrain a rueful feeling as they look back on all the rest, whom they have had to leave in bondage.[29]

And so, at the end of my account of Jacob Burckhardt in these two chapters, I take leave of a lifelong friend and teacher, and hope that even a century after his death I have fulfilled in part the words of Burckhardt himself in his last letter to an old friend, written during his final illness:[30]

> And now, goodbye, and continue to be well disposed to your old 'Cicerone'; our lives having crossed and recrossed so often and in such a friendly fashion; and after my death, take me just a little (not too much) under your care; it is said to be a meritorious work!

Socrates (Hellenistic statuette)

11
The Problem of Socrates

The problem of Socrates (and to a lesser extent that of Diogenes the Cynic) is one of the unsolved problems in the history of ancient philosophy. Gregory Vlastos turned to this problem at the end of his long life, and revealed that it had been preoccupying him since he began the study of ancient philosophy. In his brilliant and sympathetic book, *Socrates, Ironist and Moral Philosopher*, based on lectures given in Cambridge in 1983 and at Cornell in 1986, Vlastos revealed that the problem of Socrates remains the same problem that has preoccupied Western thought since the eighteenth century, and that, however skilled we are at clarifying it, we still do not have any answers. His revival of the Socratic question led to a lively discussion that still continues among professional philosophers, and which has been transformed into a fundamental problem of Western philosophy by Alexander Nehamas in his amazing work, *The Art of Living: Socratic Reflections from Plato to Foucault.*

Let me briefly expound this problem as it was first formulated by such different investigators as Friedrich Schelling, Johann Gottlieb Fichte, and Georg Ast in the generation of Hegel. The issue is composed of a number of different but interlocking strands. Firstly, who was the historical Socrates? It is quite clear that the picture drawn by Plato in his dialogues as a whole is incompatible with the evidence of Aristophanes and Xenophon, to say nothing of the later tradition stretching from Aristotle to Diogenes Laertius. Indeed, already in antiquity there were as many portraits of Socrates as there were observers: Plato makes Alcibiades say as much in his praise of Socrates in the *Symposium*, when he compares Socrates to one of those Silenus figures that open up like Russian dolls, to reveal images of the gods (215a–b). Paradoxically, it is easier to know what Socrates looked like than who he was, as Paul Zanker showed in his book, *The Mask of Socrates*. Perhaps the basic problem is that it is especially clear that the description of the 'tirelessly didactic, monotonously earnest, Socrates'[1] described in the 'shallow and stunted observations' of Xenophon with his 'lack of ear for rejoinder' and his 'gadding observation wandering about in the polygon of empiricism',[2] cannot be a description of the same charismatic intellectual figure as Plato imagined; nor does it much help if we argue (as most people have done) that Plato portrays two Socrateses, a 'Socratic' Socrates in the early dialogues and a 'Platonic' Socrates in the middle and later dialogues. So there exists a problem as old as Aristophanes and Alcibiades: who was Socrates?

Secondly, however, that problem is part of a wider problem: what is the thought of Socrates? What did he actually believe in and what did he believe the method of philosophy to be? We may perhaps dismiss the Aristophanic Socrates in his comedy *The Clouds*, which combined two previously existing stereotypes, the earlier 'pre-Socratic' philosopher interested in the physical nature of the universe and the contemporary sophist running an educational establishment or *phrontisterion*. But that still leaves three basic possible Socrateses: Socrates the late fifth-century sophist; Socrates the sceptic who attempts to prove simply that no one is wise because no one knows anything (perhaps because nothing can be known); and Socrates the proto-Platonist, whose apparently destructive arguments are intended to clear the way for the constructions of a systematic Plato.

Thirdly, there is a question that has preoccupied philosophers at least since Hegel: what is the significance of Socrates for the history of philosophy? Does he represent a major change in the development of philosophical thought, or (to put it in a more Romantic way) does he embody or did he create a shift in human consciousness?

And behind these questions, which might at one level be thought to be at least capable of resolution, there is another question that inevitably throws the whole enterprise into doubt: what is the nature of that 'Socratic irony' which (following the German Romantics), as Kierkegaard and Vlastos have shown, lies at the heart of so many of those situations where we see the Platonic Socrates at least in action? Perhaps strictly we should refer to Platonic irony, since (with a few exceptions) this irony is not visible in Xenophon. That may be a fault in Xenophon, who perhaps (as Kierkegaard thought) could not understand irony; but again it may point to a characteristic that belongs to the Platonic rather than the historical figure of Socrates. At least the presence of irony (whatever the word may mean) precludes us from being certain about the seriousness of most of the evidence we may wish to draw upon. The use of the dialogue form by Plato is perhaps simply a special case of the ironic ambiguity of so much of this evidence; for in the dialogue irony can work on a number of levels: Does the speaker believe what he says, or is he simply trying to disturb the belief of the other? Who is the dialogue intended to persuade, and how far is it a genuine representation either of real conversations or of the Socratic method of argument? What is the purpose of this style of argument? Does it represent the correct method of philosophical discourse, or is it intended to substitute persuasion for rational argument?

All these elements of the Socratic question are still debated; and all were already in place before Hegel. But I shall start with Hegel, because he set the agenda for the whole nineteenth-century discussion of the nature of Socrates. However, in proceeding chronologically I do not wish to suggest that the discussion of the last two centuries has been a story of development, in which we find ourselves gradually approaching a better understanding of Socrates. In her book *Socrates: Fictions of a Philosopher*, Sarah Kofman was surely right to believe that, until we can make up our own minds what we think, there is no point in arranging our past witnesses in an order that might suggest a gradual progression towards a truer perception of the Socratic question. I shall argue that she is only perhaps wrong in characterizing these different images of Socrates as 'Socratic novels' rather than 'Socratic autobiographies'.

Hegel described Socrates in the biographical mode as the ideal citizen, a little given to cataleptic states perhaps, but a brave soldier who rescues his friends from danger and is awarded decorations by the State, a citizen active in politics, and in general a civilized and cultivated man of 'Attic urbanity', possessing all the social virtues.[3] This long and rather surprising characterization of his hero was intended to place Socrates in a social context and to indicate his allegiance to traditional values. The only problem in his relation to society was his uncompromising pursuit of philosophy, which however did not initially lead to any overt break with traditional values. It is, however, the contrast between Socrates the perfect citizen and Socrates the great thinker that Hegel wished to emphasize.

For Hegel, 'Socrates constitutes a great historic turning point'[4] in both the history of philosophy and the history of the human spirit, which is conceived of as a progression towards freedom through self-consciousness. Earlier philosophers had not challenged the norms by which society regulated the life of its members, through religion, law, and custom; they may occasionally have questioned specific beliefs about the gods, or about the decision-making process of consulting oracles; they may occasionally have criticized specific practices, or pointed to the relativity of human customs. But they had not sought to destroy the certainties of traditional values by systematic questioning of the meaning of the inherited language of moral discourse. For Hegel, the picture drawn by Plato of Socrates' dialectical questioning of moral terms, in which he forced the imagined respondent to admit his ignorance and confusion, was a representation of the actual method of questioning used by the historical Socrates. It was not the beliefs that Socrates held, but his persistent questioning of the beliefs held by Athenian citizens, that constituted a destruction of the values which were essential to the operation of Athenian society: the Athenians were therefore right to accuse Socrates of corrupting the youth of their city. But Socrates had received a perhaps rather traditional directive from the Delphic oracle: although he did not possess foresight into the Platonic answer that might restore certainty to moral discourse, he knew firstly that the internal *daimon* of the individual must be the basis of moral behaviour, and secondly that no one, not even himself, was wise in his understanding of moral values. The mission to convince others of their mutual ignorance was a categorical imperative that could not be avoided. This was the true tragedy of Socrates, in a situation where both he and the Athenians were right.

The culmination of the tragedy occurred when at his trial Socrates had been declared guilty; at that point he is caught in an insoluble dilemma. As a member of the Athenian community he must obey the laws, but he cannot accept that his mission is not divinely inspired. He therefore insists that he will continue to behave exactly as he has in the past, even if he is killed – for (as Kierkegaard emphasized later in a brilliantly ironical passage) Socrates announces his intention of continuing to question the dead. Moreover, he cannot accept that he is guilty;

and therefore he cannot collude with the laws in proposing an acceptable fine or penalty. As a consequence he forces the Athenian people to vote for his death, although neither wish it.

In a certain sense (Hegel claims) Socrates is to blame; for he has placed himself in the same position as Antigone: he has claimed a higher right than the will of the people, embodied in the State. But whereas the right of Antigone is the divine law, the right of Socrates is a new philosophical principle, and therefore a true turning point – the universality of the idea and 'the emergence of self-consciousness, subjectivity, interiority'.[5] The State cannot permit this claim, firstly because individuals are very seldom right when they choose to defy the community, and the community cannot continue to exist if it permits that right. Secondly, Socrates is not simply asserting freedom of conscience: he has sought to disrupt the basic beliefs of the community, and cannot therefore continue to live as a member of it. However, he is also morally blameless, because his perception of morality is the true one: he replaces 'public morality' with 'reflective morality',[6] and in so doing he becomes the embodiment of a future stage in the progress of the world spirit; the fact that Socrates is right presages the disappearance of Athenian and of Greek civilization. When after his suicide the Athenians repent and punish his accusers, this demonstrates that they themselves have come to recognize the impending end of their own society.

This view of Socrates is not fictional; indeed, it is surely a largely correct interpretation of the historical situation of the biographical Socrates. Moreover, it is surely also a largely correct understanding of the philosophical points at issue: it does not say (as so many more superficial later writers have done) that Socrates was betraying Athenian democracy or teaching oligarchy: that is a banal political interpretation, which is clearly false. Rather, Socrates was far more dangerous, for he was threatening the historically grounded phenomenon of Greek civilization. But in terms of the development of human thought, the history of the world, Socrates did indeed represent a turning point.

My point is that this interpretation is not false in terms of Socrates' biography or (probably) in terms of his philosophical beliefs. It is not fiction. Nor is it an interpretation based solely on the biography or beliefs of its inventor: Nietzsche's comment (see p. 172) is unfair. We do not have to believe in the whole of Hegel's theory or in its detailed working out to be able to accept that on his terms he has correctly characterized a turning point in world history. Hegel's portrayal of Socrates is simply a genuine attempt to understand accurately, but of course with hindsight, the significance of his contribution to Western culture.

Kierkegaard offered what is at first sight a wholly different interpretation of the figure of Socrates. *The Concept of Irony with Continual Reference to Socrates* was submitted in 1841 as his thesis for the degree of Master of Arts; it was his first substantial work of philosophy, written in opposition to the prevailing Danish Hegelian orthodoxy. Having been deterred from taking Faust as his heroic model of 'personified doubt', because a contemporary, Johannes Martensen, had anticipated his intended argument, Kierkegaard turned from the idea of Faustian doubt to the concept of irony as embodied in the figure of Socrates.

For Hegel, Socratic irony was 'a particular mode of carrying on intercourse between one person and another ... Socrates taught those with whom he associated to know that they knew nothing; indeed what is more he himself said that he knew nothing, and therefore taught nothing.' Irony in this sense is 'infinite absolute negativity', and simply expresses the 'opposition of subjective reflection to morality as it exists'.[7] But for Kierkegaard irony is not 'only a subjective form of dialectic', as Hegel put it, but a fundamental dynamic and psychological principle of argument. The invention of irony is itself a philosophical turning point and 'the concept of irony makes its entry into the world through Socrates'[8] (compare his Thesis X: 'Socrates primus ironiam introduxit'); again 'irony constituted the substance of [Socrates'] existence'[9]. This irony is 'infinite absolute negativity':

> If we turn back to the foregoing general description of irony as infinite absolute negativity, it is adequately suggested therein that irony is no longer directed against this or that particular phenomenon, against a particular existing thing, but that the whole of existence has become alien to the ironic subject and the ironic subject in turn alien to existence, that as actuality has lost its validity for the ironic subject, he himself has to a certain degree become no longer actual.[10]

Thus Kierkegaard can criticize Hegel for trying to establish the figure of Socrates in a particular historical framework. Rather, Socrates becomes a metaphor for the activity of the systematic ironist:

> One may ask a question with the intention of receiving an answer containing the desired fullness, and hence the more one asks, the deeper and more significant becomes the answer; or one can ask without any interest in the answer except to suck out the apparent content by means of the question and thereby to leave an emptiness behind. The first method presupposes, of course, that there is a content, the second that there is an emptiness; the first is the speculative method, the second the ironic. Socrates in particular practised the latter method.[11]

'Socrates gets at the nut not by peeling off the shell but by hollowing out the kernel.'[12] Kierkegaard's metaphors are vivid: 'the ironist is the vampire who has sucked the blood out of her lover and fanned him with coolness, lulled him to sleep and tormented him with turbulent dreams'.[13] In the *Protagoras*, 'at the end of the dialogue Socrates and the Sophist are left – as the Frenchman actually says of only one person, *vis-à-vis au rien*. They stand face-to-face like the two bald men who, after a long, drawn-out quarrel, finally found a comb.'[14]

The purpose of Socratic irony in argument is to humiliate and infuriate the victim into recognition of his blindness, so that he achieves true insight into the absence of knowledge: 'Every philosophy that begins with a presupposition naturally ends with the same presupposition, and just as Socrates' philosophy began with the presupposition that he knew nothing, so it ended with the presupposition that human beings know nothing at all.'[15] In this sense Socrates provoked his own death by deliberately acting as the gadfly to the Athenian consciousness. Similarly, Kierkegaard's own argument was intended to infuriate and provoke through its deliberate irony, to such an extent that his original examiners were unsure of the status of his thesis as a work of scholarship. It was not indeed until the rediscovery of Kierkegaard in the twentieth-century 'Frankfurt School' that this thesis was taken seriously as an important work of philosophical insight.

Reading the thesis in the light of these modern interpretations, it is clear that it was through his reinterpretation of Socratic irony that Kierkegaard found his own *persona* as a philosopher, and that he was using the figure of Socrates to create a new mode of thinking. The brilliance of his analysis of the Platonic dialogues lies in his ability to take seriously the playfulness and provocations of the Platonic Socrates. For him, Xenophon by contrast is incapable of understanding this irony, except on rare occasions: Xenophon's Socrates deserves to die simply for being so boring.

But in the end Kierkegaard's interpretation of Socrates is merely a variant on that of Hegel, universalizing the negative aspect of Socratic irony as a method of instilling doubt, and thereby dividing Socrates off from Plato. The result is a metaphor for the life of the ironist, who takes up a stance of systematic scepticism, who practises the suspension of belief, and can therefore be accused by society of '*apragmosyne* or indifferentism'.[16] Kierkegaard has simply identified Hegel's attribution to Socrates of self-consciousness and the discovery of the subjective with the concept of irony; but unlike Hegel he has proceeded to declare this to be the aim of philosophy rather than a stage in its development. Nevertheless, Kierkegaard's debt to Hegel is so strong that later he came to disparage this early work and to exclude it from his major writings.

By the time that Kierkegaard's thesis was presented, the reaction to Hegel had already begun. Eduard Zeller's *Philosophie der Griechen*, published in its first edition between 1844 and 1852, became the standard scholarly work on Greek philosophy for the rest of the nineteenth century: it was republished in four editions down to 1876, and was also translated into many European languages.[17] Zeller represents in the history of philosophy the same reaction as occurred in historical studies to the attempts of Hegel to make all history appear an instantiation of his philosophical system. The new positivist and empirical approach to historical studies rested on the collection and analysis of the surviving evidence, in accordance with the principles of source criticism. But in the history of philosophy this proved to be more problematic than for the history of events and institutions. Although Zeller was much indebted to other German and also French interpretations of Socrates, the general frame of his account of Socrates is clearly modelled on Hegel's presentation of the evidence, and the questions Zeller addresses are much the same. But Zeller sought to solve the problem of the historical Socrates by setting him firmly within a Platonic and Aristotelian idealizing tradition. For him there was no essential conflict between Socrates and Plato: although Socrates had no general theory, he saw clearly that the domain of philosophy was the study of conceptions and our knowledge of them, not of the physical world: 'this connection of knowledge and conceptions is the common peculiarity of the Socratic, the Platonic, and the Aristotelian philosophy'.[18] It was

Socrates' belief in the importance of the problem of knowledge that led him to the study of morals, for one of the few positive doctrines that can be attributed to him is the belief that 'all virtue is knowledge'.[19] While recognizing that Socrates constituted a turning point, for Zeller his importance lay in the development of Platonic idealism rather than in the Hegelian idea of self-consciousness and its accompanying potential for irony; and the idea of irony as a suspension of belief was replaced by its role in the attempt to discover conceptual truths. Knowledge of one's own ignorance, achieved through Eros (a combination of philosophy and friendship) and irony, and by means of the dialogue, was simply a stage in the search for true knowledge:[20] in a certain sense Zeller's Socrates disappears, to be replaced simply by a Platonic *prosopon* or mask. But Socrates as a biographical subject is still treated in much the same way as Hegel had treated him, as a man caught in the conflict between feeling and intellect, or between external agencies and his *daimonion*, 'the time when the power of origination is felt solely to belong to ourselves'. And Zeller, like Hegel, admitted that Socrates represented 'an irreparable breach in the artistic unity of Greek life',[21] although his long chapter on the death of Socrates regarded it, not so much as an inevitable tragedy, but rather as an unfortunate accident of history.[22] Once again Socrates had been fitted into a system, but this time into a system that saw the history of philosophy as a progression to a form of idealism, rather than to the development of the human consciousness towards freedom; as a result it is somewhat surprising to find that Zeller believes Xenophon's Socrates to be a truer representation than Plato's.[23] It seems perhaps only too obvious to us now that Zeller's picture also is simply a response to the problem of placing Socrates in a conceptual context, and that the change of perspective derives from the observer's viewpoint, rather than (despite the enormous learning brought to bear by Zeller) from a genuine progress in the understanding of a historical Socrates.

It seems that Jacob Burckhardt had never read Kierkegaard, and that his direct knowledge of Hegel's work was slight; yet he had read Zeller, if only as a useful systematic handbook in his youth, and a source of material later. Despite his self-proclaimed incapacity to understand philosophy, he was of course aware of the Hegelian tradition, and of the fact that his own approach to history was a rejection of the philosophy of history as 'a centaur, a contradiction in terms'. Moreover, Burckhardt's general theory of cultural history gave little space to the importance of the great man in history, and did not allow him to see Socrates or any other individual as a significant turning point. For him, therefore, Socrates is merely one example among many of 'the free personality', of the philosopher who used his power of thought to escape from the conventions of Greek culture and the tyranny of the *polis*. In this Burckhardt was assisted by his lack of interest in the philosophical problems that the Socratic method poses. For Burckhardt the *polis* of Athens was a state that ignored or opposed the pursuit of knowledge in its own golden age, and Socrates was a supreme example of the independence of the power of Culture from the other two fundamental powers in history, the State and Religion. The philosophers of the Greek *polis* existed as small cells, comprising master and pupils, teaching their own opinions without regard to religion or political life. They had developed one particular skill (and here Burckhardt is surely mocking the busy public professors, the *viri eruditissimi*, of his own day), the ability to be poor, and a lack of concern for public opinion.

The historian who understood the importance of the development of the individual in the origins of the Renaissance could at least value one aspect of the Hegelian view of Socrates. But it is transformed into a historical observation: for Burckhardt, Socrates was the best-known Greek, apart from the mythical Odysseus – Socrates is the first person from antiquity whom we can truly know as an individual. While living as a model of piety, discipline, selflessness, and strength of character (up to this point we sense the Hegelian emphasis on the external normality of Socrates as an Athenian), he nevertheless turned his back on the State. His celebrated ignorance was an ironical comment on the claims of his fellow sophists to possess useful knowledge. Rather than pursue their aim of useful education, Socrates set out to persuade the ordinary people of Athens to live a life of true virtue, a 'sophist in the service of the good'. Naturally such activity was not popular: 'no one who talks incessantly, not even Socrates, can always be talking wisely, and he bored his hearers with his eternal comparisons . . . They reviled Socrates, and in the end put him to death; apparently no one possessed sufficient irony simply to leave him alone; his own irony was enough to baffle anyone.'[24]

The Socrates of Burckhardt therefore represents the fate of a man who seeks to stand against the tyranny of the *polis*. The absolute demands of the *polis* on its members preclude the acceptance of any form of thought that will endanger the community. Socrates with his irony and his search for truth through the questioning of other citizens represents precisely the unacceptable aspect of the education offered by the sophists: that is the reason why their views were identified with his in Aristophanes' portrait of him, and in the accusations of Socrates' prosecutors, which merely express public opinion on this matter. Socrates was a natural victim in a society where intellectuals were often persecuted for unpopular opinions.

The freedom of Socrates' personality lies in his rejection of the values of the ordinary Athenian, and therefore of the rules of the *polis*. From this point of view there is no significant difference between Socrates, who questioned his fellow citizens about their beliefs, and Diogenes the Cynic, who rejected those beliefs and sought to live completely outside the rules of the *polis*: the free personality is the man who lives outside the *polis* as a 'cheerful pessimist'. But the price to be paid is high: it is either death or ridicule: Socrates suffered both.[25]

How far is this picture 'autobiographical'? Not in the direct sense: Burckhardt did not see himself directly as a free personality (that would be truer of Nietzsche), nor did he feel himself persecuted by the city of Basel, of which he felt himself so profoundly to be a citizen.[26] But in a more abstract sense it is surely true that he saw himself as the detached observer, both of his own small world and of the whole European civilization of which he was the master historian. It is in his irony that Burckhardt felt most at one with Socrates, even if we can see that the irony of the historian has little to do with the irony of the philosopher. It is this irony of Socrates that most appealed to Burckhardt, as he shows when he suggests that we will understand Socrates better if we transpose him to our own age. He would, says Burckhardt, be hated by all responsible citizens who earn their living; the masses would admire him only in so far as he shook the complacency of the bourgeoisie; the powerful and influential would mock him; men of religion would attack him for his superficial conception of guilt and repentance, while criminals would be quite unable to understand his enlightened doctrines about the impossibility of being an intentional criminal. He might appeal to a tiny minority, but even they would be unable to stand his self-satisfaction, as revealed in Xenophon's *Apology* and *Symposium*. Here Socrates is firmly put in his contemporary place: the picture pays back Socrates with his own irony. But does it not also represent mockery by Burckhardt of himself as the detached outsider, an ironical warning to himself not to take himself too seriously?

In February 1870, Nietzsche delivered a lecture in Basel entitled 'Sokrates und die [griechische] Tragödie', and that seems to have been the title of an early draft of *The Birth of Tragedy* at a time when the work concluded with section 15.[27] In this version of the work it was the fusion of the Apollonian and Dionysian that made Greek tragedy the ultimate expression of the Greek genius; and the portrait of Socrates was already fully worked out.[28] Socrates was 'the second spectator' alongside Euripides; they had together broken this fusion, for both of them sought to establish a wholly Apollonian conception of the Greek spirit. For Nietzsche, it is Socrates with his *daimonion*, derived from the oracle of Apollo, who asserts the primacy of the intellect over instinct: he is 'the typical non-mystic, in whom, through a hypertrophy, the logical nature is developed as excessively as instinctive wisdom is in the mystic'. Together Socrates and Euripides manage to kill off the union of the two forces that constitute Greek tragedy; and Socrates creates from it the Platonic dialogue, which 'was as it were the barge on which the shipwrecked ancient poetry saved herself with all her children: crowded into a narrow space and timidly submitting to the single pilot, Socrates, they now sailed into a new world, which never tired of looking at the fantastic spectacle of this procession.' Ultimately from the Platonic dialogue arose the art form of the novel.

Nietzsche's interpretation reflects the traditional philosophical view in that he continued to see Socrates as a turning point. For Socrates, 'to be beautiful everything must be conscious'; and yet at the point of death in prison he 'occasionally had the feeling of a gap, a void, half a reproach, a possibly neglected duty': a dream apparition urged him, 'Socrates practise music', and in this moment he recognizes that 'what is not intelligible to me is not necessarily unintelligent'.[29]

Despite this final insight into his predicament, Socrates bequeathed to posterity the type of the 'theoretical man', and transformed the Greeks into 'this presumptuous little people', against whom Nietzsche must rage. The death of Socrates was reinterpreted by later generations, not as a moment of doubt, but as an image of the man 'whom knowledge and reason have liberated from the fear of death'.[30] He becomes the theoretical optimist dedicated to *sophrosyne*. This later Socrates figure is a teacher, teaching an 'altogether new form of Greek cheerfulness' that spreads in ever-widening circles and embraces the whole world of appearances. Nietzsche at the gates of the present and the future searches in vain for the Socrates who practises music:

> Concerned but not disconsolate, we stand aside a little while, contemplative men to whom it has been granted to be witnesses of these tremendous struggles and transitions. Alas it is the magic of these struggles that those who behold them must also take part in the fight.

It has often been pointed out that Nietzsche's Socrates is a psychological self-portrait of the superego from whom he is trying to escape.[31] Alexander Nehamas has emphasized the fundamental ambivalence of Nietzsche towards Socrates throughout his life: 'his constant problem, forever gnawing at him, was that he could never be sure that Socrates' ugly face was not after all a reflection of his own'.[32] But in the moving passage that ends the first draft of what later became *The Birth of Tragedy*, do we not see a fascination with the figure of an older man with a different set of values, expressing that struggle within Nietzsche's own psyche? In Nietzsche's picture, it is Jacob Burckhardt who is Socrates; and that final sentence surely expresses the point at which Nietzsche recognizes that his mentor and his *alter ego* have deserted him, and he is alone. Nietzsche was right; his 'greatest teacher', both model and ultimately enemy, had escaped from him: Burckhardt was not prepared to 'take part and fight' – he had been saved by his version of Socratic irony.

The whole story of Socrates in nineteenth-century Germany can be interpreted both as an attempt to find a replacement for the Christ figure in a secularized society, and in terms of a series of intellectual biographies: each individual's picture of Socrates reveals him as embodying an essential aspect of the writer's own conception of the world. But that does not mean that each of these thinkers misunderstood Socrates in their use of him: each observer sees a different Socrates, because he views him from a different angle. Rather it means, as Burckhardt again saw clearly, that Socrates is the first Greek whom it is possible to know as a real person, in all his diversity and complexity; and so Socrates is the first (indeed the only) Greek about whom it is possible to write a biography.

Max Müller (1823–1900)

12
In Search of the Key to All Mythologies

In one of the most famous novels of the nineteenth century, George Eliot's *Middlemarch* (1871–2), the central character Dorothea falls in love with the idea of scholarship, and marries an old bachelor clergyman, Mr Casaubon, whose life's work is an enormous and encyclopedic enterprise entitled 'The Key to All Mythologies'. Dorothea imagines acting as his amanuensis in his library, reading learned treatises for him, and eventually herself becoming a scholar. The story of the relationship is based on a notorious misalliance of the century, when Mark Pattison, the most learned scholar in England (who was working on his famous biography of Isaac Casaubon, which was finally published in 1875), was in 1861 elected Rector of Lincoln College, Oxford, and was therefore, according to the statutes, allowed to marry without resigning his fellowship (only professors and heads of colleges at Oxford could be married at this time): in the same year he married a young and beautiful bluestocking aged twenty-one, nearly thirty years his junior. The subsequent disastrous relationship continued in mutual hatred for twenty-three years, until Pattison finally died; as he lay on his deathbed, he called for books to be piled on his bed: 'These are my only friends', were his last words.[1]

In *Middlemarch* the first doubts about Casaubon's pretensions to scholarship are revealed to his young wife by her husband's estranged relative, Will Ladislaw; Casaubon's life's work is worthless:

> '. . . it is a pity that it should be thrown away, as so much English scholarship is, for want of knowing what is being done by the rest of the world. If Mr Casaubon read German he would save himself a great deal of trouble.'

> 'I do not understand you,' said Dorothea, startled and anxious.
>
> 'I merely mean,' said Will, in an offhand way, 'that the Germans have taken the lead in historical inquiries, and they laugh at results which are got by groping about in the woods with a pocket-compass while they have made good roads. When I was with Mr Casaubon I saw that he deafened himself in that direction: it was almost against his will that he read a Latin treatise written by a German. I was very sorry.'[2]

George Eliot knew what she was talking about; for she had begun her literary career in 1846 as the anonymous translator of the most notorious of all these German works, David Friedrich Strauss's *Life of Jesus Critically Examined* (originally published in 1835; the English translation is of the fourth edition of 1840).[3] It was this work above all that established the reputation of German scholarship for theological unorthodoxy in the English-speaking world. Indeed Strauss himself was *persona non grata* even in Germany; the scandal of his book prevented him from obtaining an academic post in any department of theology in the German university system; and when finally, at the third attempt, in 1839 he was offered a professorship in Zurich, the offer had to be withdrawn after a public outcry, and a referendum of the citizens had voted by forty to one against his appointment. He spent the rest of his life as a private scholar, seeking to defend or modify his views against almost universal criticism.

The basis of Strauss's argument was the attempt to apply scientific principles of the study of mythology to the Gospel narrative: of the three types of myth currently identified according to him, the historical, the philosophical, and the poetic, the life of Jesus was to be regarded as a philosophical myth; it could not be interpreted as history, although that did not (he argued) impugn the validity of Christianity as a religion, since the foundation stories of most institutions were myths, which embodied spiritual or philosophical truths within a narrative structure. The important point was to recognize that the study of Christianity was no different from the study of any ancient belief system: all of them began in myth.

The idea that all cultures reflected a universal set of human characteristics that could be reduced to a system was an essential part of the Enlightenment world view, which came in a variety of formulations. Pagan mythology had long been held to provide evidence for a primitive stage in the general history of humanity. For Giambattista Vico in 1725 humanity had once lived in an age of poetic wisdom: myth was the expression of this early age of man, the dim record of giant *bestioni* who developed into heroes, and then into men: only the Jews were exempted from the historical process by the benefit of divine revelation. There were many other more or less half-baked universalist theories, involving phallus-worship, pan-Egyptianism, and the primacy of the worship of Isis.[4] The main characteristics of these theories were the beliefs that myth was a secret language disguising a universal earlier stage of humanity, that poetry was the chief literary vehicle for primitive societies, and that ancient art as well as the written record could be used as evidence in the decipherment of this encoded text of a universal lost past.

It was Christian Gottlob Heyne who first sought to present a more rational view of the role of mythology. Since he wrote in Latin not German he did not need to be translated into English, and he was well known in Britain because the University of Göttingen was considered to be a British university, for it belonged to the electors of Hanover who were also kings of England: an essay by Thomas Carlyle of 1828 praises 'the labours and merits of Heyne' as 'better known, and more justly appreciated in England than those of almost any other German, whether scholar, poet or philosopher'.[5] It was Heyne who first used the word *mythus* to distinguish a particular type of story. These stories began as concrete representations of the needs of human beings in pre-historic times and in the childhood of mankind; their meanings should be explained by their double origins in the desire to explain natural phenomena or to praise great deeds. Since the childhood of man was universal, in order to understand myth it should be compared across cultures; on the other hand, since both natural environments and historical events differed between nations, each nation would have its own variety of mythical stories. This view therefore encapsulates three disparate tendencies – universalism, comparativism, and myth – as defining different societies.[6]

Nineteenth-century ideas on the continent of Europe oscillated between these different attitudes to myth. The Romantic age was by no means exempt from the drive to explore mythology as the record of a universal past. The most controversial of such theories was that of Friedrich Creuzer in his *Symbolik und Mythologie*, first published in 1819 and given a French edition in 1825–31, occasionally referred to in English writers but never translated into English. For Creuzer the explanation of Greek myth lay in its origins as a symbolic language used by Indian priests about a universal religion in order to communicate with proto-Greek savages, who misunderstood its meaning: myth was grounded in symbolism and should be explained in these terms. Despite its controversial nature (from Christian A. Lobeck's *Aglaophamus* of 1829 onwards) and the implausible account of the relation between Indian and Greek mythology, Creuzer's attitude to the symbolic connection between visual and literary evidence was to have a long future on the continent, but scarcely affected Britain until it was introduced by Jane Harrison at the beginning of the twentieth century.

In Britain the first important development came with the realization that there was no justification for Vico's theologically prudent separation of pagan from Judaeo-Christian beliefs. Already in 1829, Dean Milman had asserted that the Old Testament was a factual rather than a divinely inspired account of the history of the Jews, which necessarily involved interpreting many episodes as mythic expressions of historical events.[7] But for English readers it was indeed Strauss in George Eliot's translation who broke the barriers between classical myth and Christianity by asserting that the New Testament was a mythical account of the origins of Christianity. Judaism and Christianity no longer held a privileged position within the sphere of myth: comparativism and universalism were all the rage, and involved both pagan and Christian myths, which were regarded as equally founded in religious beliefs.

Two types of opposition to such universalist views of myth emerged, each related to a particular aspect of Heyne's interpretation. Karl Otfried Müller's *History of the Doric Race* (see above, chapter 8) was much discussed in the 1830s; one of his most controversial claims was developed from the ideas of Schlegel that the myths of Dorian Sparta were centred on Apollo, and were fundamentally different from those of the Ionian world: they served to define the nature of Dorian society. Later in 1844, Müller's *Introduction to a Scientific System of Mythology* (*Prolegomena zu einer wissenschaftlichen Mythologie*, Göttingen 1825) was also translated, though it does not seem to have had the same impact as the book on the Dorians.[8] For Müller, Greek myths were Greek, and expressions of racial differences between different tribes such as Dorians and Ionians; this was an extreme version of Heyne's and Herder's conceptions of myth as reflecting essential differences between national or racial groups. 'The ascertainment of this *where*, the *localization* of the mythus' and the '*by whom* was the mythus originally formed' are essential steps in understanding its meaning; for each tribe has its own deity, and myth is the particular expression of a general religious feeling: 'the tendency to individualize, and the endeavour to comprehend the universality of deity, stand at antagonism with each other'.[9] This whole emphasis on the origin of myth in the differences between ethnic groups has had a bad press, because of its reflection in arguments about racial superiority; but it has recently come back into favour with the emphasis on ethnicity and ethnic conflict as an explanatory force in Greek history.[10] The other main opposition to a universalist approach (contemporary with the translation of Müller's *Introduction*) is of course the rational and historical approach of the first two volumes of Grote's *History of Greece* discussed above and published in 1846.[11]

Despite these alternatives, universalist theories were reinforced by the development of Indo-European studies, which were popularized in England not through translation, but by a different form of transmission – migration. The German scholar, Max Müller, came to Britain in 1846 to study the manuscripts in the library of the East India Company, and settled in Oxford. He became Professor of Comparative Philology in 1854, and subsequently (having failed to become Professor of Sanskrit because of his suspected religious unorthodoxy) ended paradoxically as Professor of Comparative Theology (1868). In an essay of 1856, Max Müller combined Sanskrit and Indo-European philology with Indian and Greek mythology to construct a view of mythology as an early form of speculation about natural phenomena:[12]

> But if we cut into it and analyse it, the blood that runs through all the ancient poetry is the same blood; it is the ancient mythical speech. The atmosphere in which the early poetry of the Aryans grew up was mythological, it was impregnated with something that could not be resisted by those who breathed in it.

Max Müller postulated a common stratum to all Indo-European or Aryan religions centred on the worship of a sky god, Jupiter, Zeus, Dyaus Pita, and a mythology based on the dawn and sunset of the sun god. In principle this could have led to a distinction between the Graeco-Indian religious tradition and the Judaeo-Christian tradition as a product of the Semitic language group, which would have allowed the sort of independence of Christianity from pagan mythology that Vico had postulated. But in fact Max Müller was keen to stress the parallelisms between Eastern religions and Christianity, and the very influential fifty-volume collection of *Sacred Books of the East* edited by him sought to emphasize the common elements in all religions and all mythologies. It was therefore his influence which in Britain fostered the widely held belief that all myths and a considerable amount of history were in some sense 'nature-myths': the historian G.B. Grundy describes the history lectures he attended as a student at Oxford in 1888 thus:[13]

> The Minotaur tradition was a solar myth – whatever that might be: the Trojan War was legendary, and so forth. Nearly all this destructive criticism has been proved to be false; but at that time it was regarded as showing great mental acumen on the part of the critics.

The most important influence on the study of mythology in the second half of the nineteenth century was common to all the human sciences, and had a far greater effect in England than elsewhere. The eighteenth-century view of successive stages in the civilization of man was held to have been scientifically justified by the ideas of Charles Darwin's *On the Origin of Species* (1859), which were themselves a biological expression of the Victorian belief in progress. A century before the ideas of Richard Dawkins became fashionable, every aspect of social theory was contaminated with this 'Whig interpretation of history' as a series of developments in social systems, in which each level represented a stage in progress to the present day. Almost all the social theories of the second half of the nineteenth century, from those of Henry Maine (the development of law from contract, 1861), Fustel de Coulanges (the development of the early city from Indo-European family religion, 1864), and E.B. Tylor (modern survivals of primitive beliefs, 1865, 1871), to those of the American L.H. Morgan (1877) on human social progress and Friedrich Engels (1884) on 'the origin of the family, private property and the state', made use of the Darwinian scientific model to construct theories of the origin and development of human systems, from primitive religion or custom to modern law and human society. Despite the criticisms of Herbert Butterfield, this 'Whig interpretation of history' remains today an unexplored assumption on the part of many historians.[14] Such are the comfortable if unspoken assumptions of an Anglo-Saxon world chiefly concerned with empirical and antiquarian investigations.

Alongside the belief in this type of theory ran an acceptance that modern primitive societies were no different from the earliest cultures, and that even within more sophisticated societies there were primitive survivals. Tylor was especially important for his claim that primitive culture could be investigated through its 'survivals' in the folklore of modern European peasants or primitive peoples: 'there seems no human thought so primitive as to have lost its bearing on our own thought, nor so ancient as to have broken its connection with our own life'.[15] On this view, which represents the ultimate form of historicism, the present was always to be explained by the past, and was always there to explain the past. The folklorist and popularizer of fairy tales Andrew Lang went even further in claiming that behind the Aryan religions of sun worship there lay a common ancestry of all religions in fetishism, which could still be detected in modern folktales.[16]

This search for supportive material in modern survivals was combined with the developmental model in an increasingly wide-ranging and systematic investigation into the origins of human society. Every mythological tradition was studied; classical, Indo-European and northern mythologies from the pseudo-poem of Ossian onwards were combined with more or less fanciful Celtic, Irish, Scottish, Welsh, and Romany traditions by writers such as the fantasist George Borrow (1803–1881) to create the new comparative science of mythology. This was to include the materials gathered by folklore collectors and antiquarians, most of whom were home-grown,[17] although they were able to look back to the earlier and more international Romantic age of Sir Walter Scott and the Grimm brothers in Germany.[18]

This tradition was combined with the material from European folklore. But above all the evidence collected by the explorers, administrators, and missionaries of the British Empire from Africa to Polynesia and the North Americas, created a world view of primitive man based on the indigenous peoples of the European empires. This muddy stream flowed into the new science of anthropology to produce the most famous work of all, Sir James Frazer's *The Golden Bough: A Study in Magic and Religion* (1st edition, 1890; 3rd edition in 12 vols, 1915). Here the entire mythological and ritual tradition of the world was systematically categorized as a progression from magic to religion to science, with every item placed in its appropriate stratum as survival or part of a recorded culture. With the simultaneous appearance of Robertson Smith's *Lectures on the Religion of the Semites* (1889), which asserted the primacy of ritual over myth, the Myth and Ritual School of biblical and anthropological research now reigned supreme, until it was dethroned between the two world wars by Bronisław Malinowski's functionalist theory of culture and emphasis on field research.

Throughout the nineteenth century in Britain it had not been doubted that there existed a key to all mythologies, which would explain also all rituals and all religions, from magic to fetishism, totemism and tabus, nature worship, the higher polytheisms, monotheisms, and finally science itself. This was the mythology created for the British Empire, for the progress it implied was the gift of that empire to humanity. For such reasons mythology became a mainstream science in nineteenth-century Britain, and the subject of immense popular attention: throughout the Victorian age books on the mythology of all periods were produced and sold in enormous quantities. The search for a key to all mythologies was even more alive at the end of the century than it had been in the days of Mr Casaubon.

Reflecting on this development of the 'science' of mythology in Britain throughout the nineteenth century, we can see the importance of German scholarship for its origins and the variety of channels through which German influence flowed, but nevertheless the subordination of this influence to the needs and attitudes of British culture: it is an excellent case-study in the complexity and limitations of cultural transference (*transferts culturels*) as it is defined by the French scholar Michel Espagne, that is, the manner in which one culture is transferred to another, the modes of transference, and the effects on the receiving culture, the uses to which the import is put and the ways in which it is adapted to the needs of its new home. In the view of Espagne there is no such thing as simple transference, appropriation, or borrowing: every exchange involves change and adaptation. While normally the donor is not affected by this export, the receiving culture will always adapt and modify the material it accepts, incorporating it into existing ways of thinking.[19]

Beyond that we might also reflect that at no time has the study of mythology been a truly independent science. As Arnaldo Momigliano pointed out in discussing Karl Otfried Müller's *Prolegomena*, Müller was unable satisfactorily to define the notion of myth, and like all other researchers he ignored the problematic origin of the word in Greek. The Greeks regarded 'myth' as an unstable and essentially negative concept: for them 'myth, as a well-defined concept, exists only in the context of a controversy conducted by certain poets, historians and above all philosophers against received notions'.[20] Myths are indeed traditional stories with a wide variety of functions; they are significant if at all by virtue of being repeated in a way that suggests they are central to society. Myths may exist: it is less certain that 'Mythology' does.

For every theory proposed has been determined not so much by the evidence as by the needs of the contemporary world to validate its own beliefs. The nineteenth century sought to create a mythology for its own age through the interpretation of ancient mythology: ancient myth re-enacted itself as modern myth. But is our world any different? Does the modern age offer a foundation any more stable for a science of mythology than that of the Victorians? The study of myth from Freud and Jung to Lévi-Strauss, Derrida, and beyond is not a scientific study, but the story of the continuing contemporary search for our own mythic origins. We are condemned to the fate of Mr Casaubon.[21]

PART TWO

The Angel of History

Mein Flügel ist zum Schwung bereit,
ich kehrte gern zurück,
denn blieb ich auch lebendige Zeit,
und hätte wenig Glück

Gerhard Scholem, *Gruss vom Angelus*

(My wing is ready for flight, I would like to turn back, yet if I waited a whole lifetime I would have little chance.)

A Klee painting named 'Angelus Novus' shows an angel looking as though he is about to move away from something he is fixedly contemplating. His eyes are staring, his mouth is open, his wings are spread. This is how one pictures the angel of history. His face is turned toward the past. Where we perceive a chain of events, he sees one single catastrophe which keeps piling wreckage upon wreckage and hurls it in front of his feet. The angel would like to stay, awaken the dead, and make whole what has been smashed. But a storm is blowing from Paradise; it has got caught in his wings with such violence that the angel can no longer close them. The storm irresistibly propels him into the future to which his back is turned, while the pile of debris before him grows skyward. This storm is what we call progress.

Walter Benjamin,
'Theses on the Philosophy of History', IX (1940)[1]

The Crisis of the Republic of Letters

Gilbert Murray at Rest *and* James Murray at Work *(photograph taken by his youngest son, Jowett Murray, with a new box camera that he had just received for his thirteenth birthday).*

13
The Repentance of Gilbert Murray

The *République des Lettres* (*respublica litterarum*) is in continual need of renewal because it suffers from periodic crises.[2] The earliest of these crises was caused by the wars of religion and the persecution and flight of the Huguenots to Protestant countries. The renewal in the Enlightenment was disrupted by the French Revolution and the shift of intellectual power from France and Britain to Germany. In our own times we have witnessed a new crisis of the Republic of Letters in the great Renaissance caused by the Jewish diaspora of 1933–34, which transformed the world of learning in Britain and the United States; more recently the collapse of the Iron Curtain and the intellectual flight from Communism have opened up new tensions. But no transformation has been more sudden and dramatic than that which was caused by the outbreak of the First World War.

During the long rule of the bourgeoisie that characterized the nineteenth century Germany reigned supreme in international scholarship. All developments in the humanities throughout Europe and the United States were judged according to standards set by their new historical, philosophical, and philological principles of idealism and positivism: the highest honour a foreign scholar could aspire to was to enter into correspondence with one of the great German professors. When France sought to discover the reasons for the debacle of 1870, a scientific mission was despatched to Germany to investigate the Prussian educational system. In England the great debate on the purpose of a university was viewed as a choice between the traditional education for gentlemen and clergymen, and the new German emphasis on research under the control of professors, as can be seen in the conflict at Oxford University between Benjamin Jowett and Mark Pattison.[3]

Gilbert Murray belonged to this English tradition.[4] He began his academic career teaching the standard classical disciplines, based on translation and composition in Greek and Latin prose and verse; but he added an Edwardian emphasis on literary criticism and the new discipline of anthropology. In 1889 at the age of twenty-four he was appointed to the prestigious chair of Greek at Glasgow University which he held for ten years. After a spell as a private scholar, in 1908 he was appointed to the most important post in Britain as Regius Professor of Greek at Oxford University, a position that he held until his retirement in 1936, when in a notorious episode of patronage he was actually responsible for choosing his successor.[5] He was the most famous classical scholar of his age in Britain, the author of popular books on the Greeks and Greek literature and of texts of the Greek tragedians. But he was also before the First World War a playwright, whose translations of Euripides dominated the London stage; he was a friend of actresses such as Mrs Patrick Campbell, and of all the leading contemporary authors, poets and playwrights. In 1905, George Bernard Shaw cast Murray, his wife, and mother-in-law as the central characters in his comedy *Major Barbara* with cruel and revealing accuracy.[6] He describes his character thus:

> Cusins is a spectacled student, slight, thin haired, and sweet voiced ... His sense of humor is intellectual and subtle, and is complicated by an appalling temper. The lifelong struggle of a benevolent temperament and a high conscience against impulses of inhuman ridicule and fierce impatience has set up a chronic strain which has visibly wrecked his constitution. He is a most implacable, determined, tenacious, intolerant person who by mere force of character presents himself as – and indeed actually is – considerate, gentle, explanatory, even mild and apologetic, capable possibly of murder, but not of cruelty or coarseness.

He is also a professor of Greek who quotes Murray's own translation of the *Bacchae*, and Granville Barker, the original actor of the part, took great care to study Murray's personal characteristics. In the play Cusins is seduced by the arguments of Undershaft, an arms manufacturer whose daughter Cusins loves, into accepting management of the arms factory as a form of higher morality:[7]

> Plato says, my friend, that society cannot be saved until either the Professors of Greek take to making gunpowder, or else the makers of gunpowder become Professors of Greek.

Bernard Shaw's play was prophetic. Murray's marriage in 1889 to Lady Mary Howard, daughter of the Earl of Carlisle, began his political career. The Carlisles belonged to the coterie of aristocratic liberals who ruled Britain in the period before the First World War: they were radicals, teetotallers, and devoted to reform. Murray gladly accepted his role of intellectual adviser to the dominant clan of British politics, and from time to time even stood as a candidate for election to Parliament, though never successfully.

It was this background that led him to take a prominent position in the destruction of the Republic of Letters that began the First World War. Intellectuals in every combatant country rushed to support their governments' national aims in the war, and to denounce their former colleagues on the opposite side. Murray was responsible for the first and most devastating of these moves to dismantle European scholarship; he was the originator of a formal letter known as 'The Writers' Manifesto' published in *The Times* on 18 September 1914, headed:

BRITAIN'S DESTINY AND DUTY
DECLARATION BY AUTHORS
A RIGHTEOUS WAR

The letter denounced the German invasion of Belgium, and accepted in full the justification for war put forward by Britain and France. It continued by laying the blame on German academics specifically:

> We observe that various German apologists, official and semi-official, admit that their country has been false to its pledged word, and dwell almost with pride on the 'frightfulness' of the examples by which it has sought to spread terror in Belgium, but they excuse all these proceedings by a strange and novel plea. German culture and civilisation are so superior to those of other nations that all steps taken to assert them are more than justified; and the destiny of Germany to be the dominating force in Europe and the world is so manifest that ordinary rules of morality do not hold in her case, but actions are good or bad simply as they help or hinder the accomplishment of that destiny.
>
> These views, inculcated upon the present generation of Germans by many celebrated historians and teachers, seem to us both dangerous and insane. Many of us have dear friends in Germany, many of us regard German

> culture with the highest respect and gratitude; but we cannot admit that any nation has the right by brute force to impose its culture upon other nations, nor that the iron military bureaucracy of Prussia represents a higher form of human society than the free constitutions of Western Europe.

The letter was signed by fifty-two of Britain's leading writers including the scholars Jane Harrison and G.M. Trevelyan, the poets Robert Bridges and John Masefield, and the novelists G.K. Chesterton, John Galsworthy, Rider Haggard, Thomas Hardy, Jerome K. Jerome, Rudyard Kipling and Mrs Humphrey Ward.

Murray's initiative provoked a formal disruption of European culture across the combatant nations. Similar actions were taken in Russia, France, and Italy: honorary degrees and memberships of academies were rescinded and eternal enmity against 'the Huns' was declared. In France in the session of 8 August 1914 the President of the *Académie des Sciences morales et politiques*, Henri Bergson, had already gone even further:[8]

> The struggle we are engaged in against Germany is the very struggle of civilization against barbarism. The whole world feels it, but our Academy has perhaps a particular authority to declare it. Devoted in great part to the study of psychological, moral and social problems, it is fulfilling a simple scientific duty in declaring that the brutality and cynicism of Germany in its contempt for all justice and all truth is a regression to a state of savagery.

Many individual writers like Maurice Maeterlinck, Romain Rolland, and Anatole France joined in denouncing the barbarism of the Germans – the cry went up 'the Hun is at the gate!'

In Germany the popular author Ludwig Fulda replied to the provocation in *The Times* with a notorious open letter, published on 4 October 1914, *An die Kulturwelt!* signed by ninety-three famous German professors, directors of museums and theatres, and directors of music; among the signatories were such names as Adolf von Harnack, Eduard Meyer, Max Planck, Max Reinhardt, Siegfried Wagner, and Ulrich von Wilamowitz-Moellendorff (who later took to defiantly listing among his honours that of being a deposed member of the *Académie des Inscriptions et Belles-Lettres*, 'plerumque in hoc orbe academiarum socius, e Parisina honoris causa eiectus').[9] The letter specifically denied the allegation of atrocities in the invasion of Belgium and defended

German 'militarism' as essential to German culture. This only confirmed the opinions of the other side: an English translation of the letter was later published in the United States and circulated widely with a reply denouncing its contents.[10]

Meanwhile the British responded in *The Times* of 21 October with a 'Reply to German Professors. Reasoned Statement by British Scholars', signed by 118 eminent academics from all the universities of Britain, including its protagonist Gilbert Murray.

It is less easy to discover the names of those few honourable individuals who refused to take part in this despicable propaganda war, but they include some of the greatest names of the twentieth century – in Berlin, Georg Friedrich Nicolai, Professor of Medicine, and his friend Albert Einstein, Professor of Physics (who together created a counter-organization for peace), and in Göttingen, David Hilbert, Professor of Mathematics; the author Hermann Hesse denounced 'those who make war in the safety of their studies'. In Italy, musicians like Puccini, Leoncavallo, and Mascagni (for whatever reason) refused to join. It would be interesting to know whether any Frenchmen stood against the dominant trend.[11] In Britain, those who refused to sign included the poet W.B. Yeats, the playwright George Bernard Shaw, and the philosopher Bertrand Russell. Indeed, a full list of those who stood up for the Republic of Letters deserves to be inscribed in a public Roll of Honour.

It is for me a source of family pride that my great-grandfather Sir James Murray (no relation to Gilbert Murray), the editor of the *Oxford English Dictionary*, was one of this number, giving as his reason for refusal that philology was more important than patriotism, and that when the war was over he would need to collaborate with his German colleagues. In his son's unpublished biography there appears the following passage:

> In 1914 he applauded the decision to join in the War, and, though he refused to sign the manifesto of Oxford Professors in the autumn of the year lest his doing so should be inimical to the interests of the Dictionary, he wrote to friends in South Africa in grateful recognition of what the Dominions were doing in aid of the mother country.[12]

I have not yet discovered Sir James's original letter which must be in the voluminous papers of Gilbert Murray. But in 2015, in preparation for a talk on the centenary of his death, among the unsorted papers of Sir

James Murray (Bodleian Library) in the box relating to 1914, under the rubric 'undated', I discovered the following letter:

> 82 Woodstock Road Oct 15th [of course 1914]
>
> Dear Sir James Thank you for your letter. I fully understand your position and think you are quite right not to sign. After all there will be peace some day & we must not imperil the Dictionary.
>
> Yours very sincerely
> Gilbert Murray

My ancestor's friendship and respect for the world of scholarship were reciprocated by some of his colleagues on the opposite side. He had been a Corresponding Member of the Vienna Royal Academy since 1905; in 1916 it published an obituary of him by Karl Luick, which ends with these warm words:[13]

> In his conversation there rang energy and perseverance, but also good will. Like Furnivall he was always ready to recognize German collaboration in research. How many of its bearers have spent stimulating hours in his 'Scriptorium' and his welcoming house in Oxford!

Ulrich von Wilamowitz-Moellendorff wrote in sadness to Gilbert Murray in 1915, 'It is unfortunately true that we shall not meet again in our lifetime, and that memories such as I cherish of my stay in Oxford . . . will for years seem to the younger generation like something from a lost paradise . . . I do not know if greetings from me will still be welcome to my former friends at Oxford, but if so please pass them on.' In his memoirs published after the war in 1929, Wilamowitz wrote of the post-war coolness between himself and Murray, although they did finally exchange friendly letters before Wilamowitz's death in the same year. As he had recognized in his memoirs, this was the definitive end to four hundred years of the international Republic of Letters: it poisoned relations between European intellectuals on both sides of the conflict until at least 1928, when for the first time in fourteen years German delegates were admitted to an international scientific conference, that of mathematics at Bologna; they were only readmitted to meetings of the Corpus Vasorum

Antiquorum (CVA) in 1930, and it was not until 1935 that Austria and Germany were finally admitted to the Union Académique Internationale. Germany had of course not been admitted to membership of the League of Nations until 1926, and she withdrew in 1933. It was not in fact until the diaspora of Jewish intellectuals expelled by Hitler that the wounds were healed, or at least superseded in a new crisis.

As the war went on doubts began to emerge even among those who had initially signed the various public declarations. Gilbert Murray himself remained a passionate defender of the war as long as his friends Asquith and Sir Edward Grey were in power: he took it upon himself to defend Grey's record against the very serious accusations that, without consulting Parliament or informing the English people, he had entered into those secret treaties that had forced Britain into war.

Murray's friendship with Bertrand Russell and other pacifists was compromised by his actions. But the introduction of universal male conscription in January 1916 revealed an important group of conscientious objectors, whether on grounds of religion or moral conviction, who refused to enlist, and were initially sent to prison; it was alleged that some had even been forcibly enlisted and immediately drafted to France, where they could be shot without trial as deserters. Many of Gilbert Murray's intellectual friends belonged to this group, including members of the 'Bloomsbury set', a number of prominent Quakers such as the pacifist Stephen Hobhouse, communists and others. Those who were unconvinced by the arguments for the justice of this particular war were perhaps in the first place most at risk, since they could not shelter behind religious conviction or the absolute demands of moral pacificism. Bertrand Russell was dismissed from his Cambridge Lectureship, and finally imprisoned in 1918 for organizing the 'No-Conscription Fellowship'.[14] Although Murray still supported the war and was never himself a pacifist, he began campaigning for the rights of these individuals and for the proper working of independent tribunals to hear their cases. This was the point at which his liberal principles first came into conflict with the policy of the government, which was under pressure from public opinion to make life as difficult as possible for those cowards who refused to fight for 'King and Country'.

In December 1916, David Lloyd George (whom Murray detested) became Prime Minister, and Murray began to have deeper doubts about the whole conduct of the war. He argued publicly for a negotiated peace, and in 1918 he and the conservative politician Lord Robert Cecil became the prime movers in Britain of the League of Nations Union. Murray was a vice-president from 1919 to 1923; between 1923 and 1938 he was chairman, and from 1938 to 1957 co-president of what subsequently after the Second World War became the United Nations Union.[15] For almost forty years Murray built up and led a popular movement which had at its peak over 600,000 members, a far larger number than any British political party or any protest movement (such as Bertrand Russell's Campaign for Nuclear Disarmament in the 1950s) ever achieved; during this period he was a major influence on public policy in favour of peace and international co-operation across the world. The League of Nations itself was formally founded in 1920; in 1921, Murray was appointed by General Smuts as an official delegate for South Africa, and thereafter until 1924 as a British delegate he took part in the detailed negotiations for the League's foundation.

Murray was also the founder of the Committee for International Co-operation in 1922, along with Henri Bergson, Marie Curie, and Albert Einstein, and its chairman from 1928 to 1931; he established a set of principles governing broadcasting, literature, and the arts, and the development of international scientific collaboration. This activity was the origin of the present UNESCO, the most successful of all modern international institutions. Here perhaps is the ending of the personal odyssey of repentance for Murray's activities in 1914. For it was largely the work of the Committee for International Co-operation that began the formal reconciliation between German and other scholars.

Murray's international work was not always appreciated by his academic colleagues. In 1923 the Vice-Chancellor of Oxford wrote to him formally suggesting that he might like to resign as Professor of Greek since he was spending so much time on international affairs. Murray refused, but offered to give up half his salary for five years to fund a new post in Greek studies. A later generation has indeed accepted the view that Murray's best work in Greek literature was done before 1914, but he continued as a popularizer and an inspiration to Greek studies throughout this period. As a liberal in international politics Murray has been unfairly judged by later generations because of the ultimate failure of the League to maintain world peace. The modern consensus in the study of international relations is dominated by the 'realist' views of E.H. Carr on the uselessness of the League; but these were formulated only in 1939, after it had been destroyed by the Japanese invasion of Manchuria, and the aggressions of Mussolini, Hitler, and Franco; and it ignores the fact that Carr himself had supported Mussolini, Hitler, Franco, and appeasement, and ended as a dogmatic apologist for Stalin's Soviet Union in fourteen turgid volumes.

Murray's ultimate mistake was to underestimate the crisis for the ancestral liberal leadership caused by the massacre of the working classes during the First World War: the peoples of Europe rebelled against the old regime and handed power to demagogues and tyrants for the next seventy years. Like the rest of his contemporaries Murray could not fully understand this tectonic shift; but he did create the most successful popular peace movement of the twentieth century, and so saved England from the contemporary European cult of strong men. And throughout his life, although he did not live to see the false dawning of a new age with the dismantling of the Soviet bloc, he continued to keep faith with the Gladstonian politics of his youth.

In 1933 Murray was the earliest and one of the most active supporters of Lord Beveridge's initiative described in the next chapter; he was its chief agent in Oxford in soliciting funds and finding for the refugee professors places to live and work. He also offered accommodation in his own house and hospitality to his refugee colleagues: there is a charming letter from the classical scholar Eduard Fraenkel to Murray, written in Latin because he felt his English was not good enough, thanking him for his friendship and help.

The repentance of Gilbert Murray was long and complex, and never acknowledged explicitly; he would indeed have seen his life as a unity devoted to liberal principles and Greek rationalism. In 1900 he had written to his mother-in-law, Lady Carlisle, 'Greece has a profound and permanent message to mankind, a message quite untouched by "supernaturalness" and revealed religion: it is humane and rational and progressive, and affects not Art only but the whole of life . . . I have got a faith and a message . . . and I want to speak them out . . . Greek literature contains the germs of almost everything, so you can treat of almost all tendencies in treating of it.'[16] It was this faith that unified his life in all its later aspects, and informed all his activities. Still in my own welfare-state generation, it made Murray a hero for his belief in the importance of translation and in the spreading of Greek ideas to the whole of society through education and popularization.

Gilbert Murray's BBC broadcasts ran almost from the start of the BBC National Service in 1922 to 1956, less than a year before his death aged ninety-one. These reveal his humanity and his continued importance as a revered public figure. His first broadcast was on 13 May 1926, the day after the collapse of the General Strike; he had been chosen by Lord Reith to offer a hope of reconciliation, and began by praising the leaders of the Trades Union Congress for their courage in calling off the strike. Thirty years later his last broadcast was on 8 October 1956, a plea on behalf of the voiceless refugees of Europe, who had once again flooded in as a result of the Soviet invasion of Hungary.[17] It ends with an anecdote: 'I once had a talk with Ribbentrop, who said he was puzzled about the real feeling of England on political things. I said: "There is one thing for certain – that England will not persecute, nor tolerate those who do persecute."' Gilbert Murray was indeed one of the greatest Europeans of the twentieth century; we should not wonder that the rationalist Murray was given a public funeral in Westminster Abbey with a reading from Ecclesiasticus (44:1–8):

> Let us now praise famous men, and our fathers that begat us.
> The Lord hath wrought great glory by them through his great power from the beginning. Such as did bear rule in their kingdoms, men renowned for their power, giving counsel by their understanding, and declaring prophecies: Leaders of the people by their counsels, and by their knowledge of learning meet for the people, wise and eloquent are their instructions: Such as found out musical tunes, and recited verses in writing: Rich men furnished with ability, living peaceably in their habitations: All these were honoured in their generations, and were the glory of their times. There be of them, that have left a name behind them, that their praises might be reported.

Tess Simpson (1903–96)
Secretary of the Society for the Protection of Science and Learning (1933–1978)

14
Saving Civilization: The Warburg Institute and the SPSL

THE WARBURG INSTITUTE

The foundation of the Warburg Library is shrouded in myth. It began in 1879, when the two eldest sons of the Jewish banking family of Warburg in Hamburg were children: the eldest Aby (1866–1929), aged thirteen, said to his twelve-year-old brother Max, 'you can have the bank, provided you buy me all the books I want for the rest of my life'. Max later said it was the only blank cheque he ever signed.[1] When his family later objected to this frivolous expense, Aby is said to have replied, 'Andere Banquiers halten sich einen Rennstall und werden von ihren Jockeys betrogen. Ihr habt eine Bibliothek mit einem Herrenreiter, und der bin ich.' (Other bankers have racing stables, and are fleeced by their jockeys. You have a library with a head jockey, and that is me.)[2] He went on to amass an enormous private library and in 1926 to found the *Kulturwissenschaftliche Bibliothek Warburg* (KBW) devoted to the *Nachleben der Antike*, the ways in which the ancient Greek and Roman world had influenced the Renaissance and European culture, in literature, thought, and art. Aby Warburg himself had become an important historian and theoretician of Renaissance art and of the relation between reason and imagination within the classical tradition. Traumatized by the fact that Germany and Italy had fought on opposite sides in the Great War he suffered a long period of mental illness for six years until 1924, during which time his librarian Fritz Saxl (appointed in 1919) developed his ideas:[3]

> From the chrysalis of a private library – in an unexpected metamorphosis, after years of secret evolution – there emerged a scholarly institution that still subsists to this day, though not on its original site. The founder's

researches, deeply personal though their motivation had been, were now to be subsumed – having been supported, expanded, and modified by Saxl – within an Institute of 'Cultural Studies'.

By the time Aby Warburg died in 1929, the library was attached to the new university of Hamburg (founded in 1919) through its first professor of philosophy, Ernst Cassirer (1874–1945), who was also Rektor of the University from 1929 until his resignation as a result of the Nazi election victory in 1933 – a century after the death of Goethe. Although still technically a private institution under the direction of Warburg and later Saxl, the KBW had established a programme of lectures and publications, and through its research grants had brought together the most distinguished group in the world of researchers into 'Kulturgeschichte' and the relation between art and thought in Western civilization, attracted both by its library and by the philosophical ideas of Cassirer.

The library was and remains unique. As Cassirer said when he first visited it, 'This library is dangerous. I shall either have to avoid it altogether or imprison myself here for years.'[4] It is still organized without regard to different traditional areas of research or chronology according to categories developed by Warburg himself, with four main sections devoted to 'Orientation' (philosophy, religion, magic, science), 'Image' (art history, archaeology), 'Word' (literature), and 'Action' (history, society, festivals, theatre, technology).[5] It has also developed the practice of selecting important articles to be bound in card and placed on the bookshelves next to the books on the theme they illustrate, under Warburg's 'Law of the Good Neighbour'. All decisions were and are made by the library staff, who must be trained scholars (since they need to read the works in order to determine their placement), more than professional librarians. It was and is the most powerful institute for the history of ideas and of art in its cultural context, encouraging cross-disciplinary research and intertemporal approaches. Its second great innovation was in art history, the creation of a photographic archive arranged according to iconographic principles, in order to investigate the continuing meaning (or iconology as Erwin Panofsky expressed it) of each representation.[6]

Almost all the staff and the scholars working in the library were classified as 'non-Aryan' under the Nazi law of the *Gesetz für Wiederherstellung des Berufsbeamtentum* (*Berufsbeamtengesetz* or 'law for the reconstitution of public services', 7 April 1933; later reinforced in 1935), and were therefore dismissed from whatever official posts they held. Two young scholars were instrumental in saving the library. Raymond Klibansky, researching on medieval Platonism, had already been appointed at the age of twenty-six as *Privatdozent* in the University of Heidelberg, and saw what was happening in his own university; he had himself refused to complete the required statement of 'race', instead sending a letter in which he proudly declared to the authorities that his ancestors since the Middle Ages had professed the Jewish faith. He was dismissed in August 1933 and hastened to Hamburg convinced that the Institute must leave Germany immediately; he suggested founding a centre abroad for 'trying to preserve an Anglo-German school of history and philosophy of civilization'.[7] Saxl recognized the urgency, and asked Klibansky to prepare a memorandum for Max Warburg, the head of the bank, who was responsible for providing much of the funding of the Institute. The memorandum does not seem to have survived (it was doubtless too sensitive to have been kept), but Max was convinced by it, and discussions began on possible destinations: Leiden and Jerusalem were ruled out for various reasons; it was decided that neither Italy nor France was safe, and the United States was not suitable for an institution devoted to European culture. England was the only possible choice, and negotiations were begun with London University.

The role of Edgar Wind in the actual transfer of the library is ignored in the official accounts because of the subsequent quarrel between him and Saxl over the directorship of the Institute (described below); but Wind was the central figure.[8] He was born in Berlin in 1900 of Argentinian and Russian parents, and educated in Germany and the USA. After studies at Berlin, Freiburg, and Vienna he came to Hamburg to work under Erwin Panofsky and Cassirer, where Wind completed a dissertation on the methodology of art history in 1922. From 1924 to 1927 he was in New York and North Carolina (where he came to appreciate the philosophy of C.S. Peirce), and married his first wife Ruth (they were married from 1926 to 1928).

In May 1926 the KBW had moved to a new specially designed building separate from the private residence of Aby Warburg. Wind met Warburg for the first time in the summer of 1927; from then until Warburg's death in 1929 he acted as Warburg's private assistant, especially in relation to the USA, in which Warburg had been interested since his visit to study the Pueblo Indian dance rituals: there is extensive correspondence in the archive of the Warburg Institute conducted by Wind for him in the period 1928–29. Wind formally joined the staff of the Institute in 1928, and a year later was appointed *Privatdozent* at Hamburg University.

During 1931–32 Wind made three visits to England to study eighteenth-century heroic portraiture in relation to the philosophy of David Hume.[9] While in New York, he had stayed with an older cousin, whose stepdaughter had been married to the son of the Honourable Mrs Henrietta Franklin (1866–1964), the daughter of Lord Swaythling of the Montagu banking family. In May 1933 on his own initiative Wind visited London and stayed with her. Mrs Franklin was a hostess with a wooden leg whose luncheon parties were famous: she had wide contacts with the wealthy Jewish community in Britain. She introduced Wind to Sir Philip Hartog and through him to C.S. Gibson, Professor of Chemistry at Guy's Hospital, who was subsequently the first honorary secretary of the Academic Assistance Council (see below). There is no doubt of the importance of Mrs Franklin's connections: Wind referred to the indefatigable efforts of 'die Matriarchin' in letters to Saxl and Gertrud Bing in Hamburg. With her help and his perfect command of English, he was the ideal intermediary in negotiations between London University and the Warburg Institute.

It was at one of Mrs Franklin's lunches that Wind met the dancer Agnes de Mille, niece of Cecil B. DeMille (and later famous choreographer of *Oklahoma!* and other musicals), and began a passionate relationship with her. Agnes records her first impression: 'I spoke to a charming young German girl at the table, asking her by way of conversation if she intended to stay long in this country. "I think so," she said smiling sadly at the young Jew beside her, an impressive, large, black-haired person, Professor Edgar Wind. "I think we'll all be here quite some time," he said. He is transferring the Warburg Institute (art history) intact from Hamburg to London. Permanently.'[10]

Mrs Franklin wrote a letter of introduction to Sir William Beveridge and his newly formed Academic Assistance Council on 25 May 1933. From June of that year Wind led these negotiations with Lord Lee of Fareham, who a year earlier had organized the creation of the Courtauld Institute, W.G. Constable, first director of the Courtauld, and Edwin Deller, Principal of the University reporting to the Vice-Chancellor; at their request Wind drew up a seven-page confidential report approved by Saxl on the purpose and function of the Warburg in a London context. Its urgency is revealed in the first draft, which survives in the

Jan Vermeer, *The Art of Painting, or the Muse of History* (1665–8)
(See Introduction)

Nicholas Poussin, *The Triumph of Pan* (1638)

A vision of a festival of Greek women painted for the Cabinet du Roi in the Chateau of Cardinal de Richelieu (See Chapter 2)

The *ancien régime* (ca. 1775)

Jacques Wilbaut, the antiquary J-J. Barthélémy with the Duc de Choiseul and the famous beauty Mme de Brionne, royal favourite, examining a medal from the Cabinet des Médailles (See Chapter 2)

Napoleon's memorial for Cornelius De Pauw, Xanten

The inscription reads: *Içi repose Corneille De Pauw né à Amsterdam le 12 aout 1739 auteur des recherches sur les Egyptiens les Chinois les Grecs les Americains mort à Xanten le 5 juillet 1799. Ce simple monument a été erigé aux frais de la ville de Xanten An MDCCCXI. VIII année du règne de Napoléon le Grand.* Note the bullet marks from the battle for Xanten in the Second World War (See Chapter 2)

The announcement of the victory at Marathon

Luc-Olivier Merson, *Le soldat de Marathon* (Grand prix de Rome de peinture d'histoire 1869) (See Chapter 4)

Hablot Knight Browne ('Phiz')
The successful novelist and his creations accompanied by his loot.
A caricature of Edward Bulwer-Lytton (See Chapter 6)

The historian's search

Paolo Uccello, *The Night Hunt in the Forest* (c.1465–70) cover illustration of Pierre Vidal-Naquet, *The Black Hunter* (See Chapter 18)

Paul Klee, *Angelus Novus*, monoprint 1920,
Israel Museum, Jerusalem

Vice-Chancellor's archive of the University of London. It was a brief but comprehensive document with seven heads:[11]

1. The Purpose of the Warburg Institute
2. The Equipment of the Warburg Institute
3. The Activities of the Warburg Institute
4. The Reasons for Removing the Warburg Institute from Hamburg
5. The Reasons for Removing the Institute to England and to London in particular
6. The Organisation in London
7. The Cost of Maintenance

Wind wired Saxl in Leiden from London advising him to come to London for the first meeting of the executive committee of the Academic Assistance Council. At this meeting on 14 June 1933 the transfer of the Warburg to London was discussed with Wind; and Gibson and Constable together with Sir Edward Denniston Ross, director of the School of Oriental and African Studies, were deputed to visit Hamburg. Since the library was a private institution and had a rule that books could be lent abroad, it was agreed that the entire library should be loaned to London for three years. The local Hamburg authorities were invited not to intervene with a promise of no adverse publicity and an affidavit from the American consul that the foundation was largely American owned; they were persuaded that Goebbels' central ministry did not need to authorize the transfer. They made only one condition: 2,000 books of Warburg's collection on the First World War were demanded as a 'Faustpfand'; in my own day as a Research Fellow of the Warburg (1967–68) the shelf entitled 'Prophecy and World War' still remained symbolically almost empty.[12]

The main problem was funding, both for the transfer and in the longer term. London University had no money, but it was agreed to seek external funding for four staff and the librarian and running costs estimated at £7,000, while the Warburg family would provide a similar amount for the transfer. As the banker behind the Hamburg shipping industry, Max Warburg was able to supply two small steamers, into which 531 boxes containing 60,000 books and 25,000 images were loaded, together with all the furniture and four members of staff. They arrived at London docks in December 1933. Other donors covered the tiny costs of transport from the docks to London (£50) and temporary storage (£32 a week) until the Institute could be housed in Thames House, and subsequently in the Imperial Institute Buildings, South Kensington (1938–58), and (after the librarian's death in an air raid) in a country house at Denham (Uxbridge). The Institute was finally incorporated into the University of London in 1944, after a census had been held of the books in the library which revealed that approximately 30 per cent of them were not in the British Museum library.

In London, Wind became Deputy Director (1934), and his influence was clearly central in settling the new, very German institute into its London environment. He effectively organized the public face of the Warburg; he created the first sets of lectures and programmes, which were outstanding in their range, including speakers such as the Danish physicist Niels Bohr; and Wind was the founding editor of the Journal of the Warburg (later and Courtauld) Institute. In 1939 he went to America on leave, and when war broke out was advised by Saxl not to return, in order to strengthen connections with the American branch of the Warburg bank. After the fall of France in 1940, Wind was indeed asked to investigate a possible transfer of the Institute to the USA, and remained there as an unofficial representative, until in 1945 Saxl came to try and persuade him to return to the Warburg as his successor as Director. Meanwhile Wind had married Margaret in 1942 and was now settled in the States. There were tense negotiations over questions of status, staffing, and the purpose of the Institute, which centred on Wind's disapproval of a new Saxl plan to create a 'Pauly-Wissowa', an encyclopedia of the Middle Ages and Renaissance. This led to a final breakdown of relations between the two men, and the suppression of Wind's role in the transfer to England.

THE ACADEMIC ASSISTANCE COUNCIL

The rescue of the Warburg Institute can only be compared with the arrival in Italy of the future Cardinal Bessarion in 1439, fleeing the impending destruction of Byzantium and laden with ancient Greek manuscripts to become the catalyst for the Italian Renaissance.[13] But it was part of a far wider initiative as a result of the new threat to the Republic of Letters, which had begun with the dismissal from government posts of all those German citizens who could not certify their Aryan descent for two generations: those of Jewish descent were the main intended victims, but non-Germans and those of illegitimate birth or obscure nationality were included. The resulting exodus between 1933 and 1939 has been often recorded in the individual memoirs of the survivors of the Nazi Holocaust and in the story of the *Kindertransporten*. One aspect of this mass expulsion concerns the large number of mainly 'Jewish' academics dismissed from their posts in 1933 and 1935 by the Nazi race laws, and from 1938 also in Italy. In response to this emergency, Sir William Beveridge, Principal of the London School of Economics (subsequently Lord Beveridge, author of the Beveridge Report which created the post-war British Welfare State), established the Academic Assistance Council, which was renamed the Society for the Protection of Science and Learning[14] in 1935 when it became clear that this was a permanent problem. This society, now called the Council for At-Risk Academics (CARA), is still devoted to rescuing academics at risk from persecution, and enabling them to find equivalent research posts in the free world; in 2008 it celebrated seventy-five years of activity with a conference at the British Academy.[15] Its foundation was the greatest act of generosity ever undertaken within the Republic of Letters, for it was funded initially by voluntary contributions from the salaries of British academics, as well as by many charities and academic institutions; a major appeal was launched, addressed by Albert Einstein in the Royal Albert Hall on 3 October 1933 to a packed audience; and between 1933 and 1939 the Society was responsible for saving the lives of some 2,600 mainly Jewish academics and their families, and providing them with grants to continue research in Britain until they could find positions either during or after the war. Those assisted include many of the intellectual leaders of the past generation – the doctor Ludwig Guttmann; the scientists Albert Einstein, Max Perutz, Max Born, Hans Krebs, Klaus Fuchs (no fewer than sixteen Nobel laureates in the sciences), the philosophers Ernst Cassirer, Karl Popper, Leo Strauss, Theodor Adorno, and Richard Walzer; the sociologists Karl Mannheim and Norbert Elias; the classical scholars Eduard Fraenkel, Rudolf Pfeiffer, Gunter Zuntz, Charles Brink, Otto Skutsch, Victor Ehrenberg, and Arnaldo Momigliano; the art historians Nikolaus Pevsner, Erwin Panofsky, Edgar Wind, Raymond Klibansky, and Ernst Gombrich; the Roman lawyers Fritz Schulz and David Daube, and many others: these were the personal friends and intellectual models of my youth. In the Anglo-Saxon world it led to the creation of modern art history and the revival of classical scholarship, as well as being of direct benefit to victory in the war by the creation of the atomic bomb.

The archive of the Society for the Protection of Science and Learning (SPSL) exists in the Bodleian Library in Oxford, and reveals in detail the great care and humanity offered to the families of the refugees under the care of its secretary, the Quaker Tess Simpson, who devoted her life to them.[16] From May 1940, as a result of a vicious smear campaign by the *Daily Mail*, the government was forced to intern them in makeshift concentration camps, and finally on the Isle of Man. In this period, Tess Simpson did everything in her power to help the families of those interned.[17] A concerted campaign by the SPSL and British academics such as Gilbert Murray led to questions in Parliament, and the academics were eventually released. But throughout the war years the position of these refugees was precarious: no regular employment was available for most of them. After the Blitz the offices of the Society moved from London to Cambridge; in Oxford a committee, composed of Hugh Last (Professor of Roman History), W.D. Ross (Provost of Oriel College), and Gilbert Murray dispensed funds provided by the SPSL, and the University of Oxford and its colleges were particularly generous in the early years: it was therefore natural for Oxford to become a centre for academic refugees. Kenneth Sisam, Secretary to the Delegates of the Clarendon Press of Oxford University, was also secretary of the Oxford committee, and in fact was its chief fundraiser: later, although the United States were always reluctant to admit any but the most eminent and useful Jewish refugees, the Rockefeller Foundation supplied funds to Oxford University Press to enable the Press to enter into book contracts with the refugees in order to provide them with financial support.

The refugees survived, but they were not rich; the standard SPSL grant for single scholars was £150 a year, for a family £250, from which were deducted any other earnings. They found whatever employment they could, and in Oxford lived in rooms or small houses often on the outskirts of the town. Stefan Weinstock, for instance, had a couple of rooms in the house of a college servant on the edge of the city, where he lived with his amazing collection of books.[18] I got to know this collection many years later, when Weinstock had bought Felix Jacoby's house in north Oxford; by then it contained many books from the libraries of Cumont and Kroll, and was the largest collection I had ever seen in private hands (it was bequeathed to the British School at Rome).

I select from the files of the SPSL almost at random the stories of four different members of this great exodus.

RAYMOND KLIBANSKY (1905–2005)

I came to know Raymond Klibansky in his eighty-second year through one of my pupils at Wolfson College, and my wife invited him as the only surviving author of the famous work *Saturn and Melancholy* to be the keynote speaker in a conference entitled 'Genius: The History of an Idea' held on 23–24 April 1987 at the new European Humanities Research Centre of Warwick University. Klibansky spoke informally on the theme of '*Saturn and Melancholy* revisited': 'Could a happy man have written Hamlet?' he asked.[19] I was deputed to drive him from Oxford to Warwick and back; and during these long car rides he told me the story of the rescue of the Warburg Institute from Hamburg to

Raymond Klibansky (1905–2005)

London in 1933. I could scarcely believe his account, but I have since verified it from documents in the archives of the SPSL and the Warburg Institute.

Klibansky's list of academic references in 1933 for the SPSL began with Einstein; the Director, Fritz Saxl, wrote a long six-page testimonial letter, which is preserved in Klibansky's file.[20] It begins:

> October 5th 1933
> To the Academic Assistance Council
> Dear Sirs
>
> I am requested to give my opinion of Dr. Klibansky which I hereby do with the greatest pleasure. I have known him for many years and saw him develop into the brilliant young scholar he has become. In showing the general fertility of his ideas I wish to state here a few details only with regard to the Warburg Library.
>
> The idea of moving the Warburg Library from Hamburg to another intellectual centre, in which it could continue as a living source of scientific research and provide for a group of scholars a centre of culture and learning, emanates from Dr. Klibansky. This plan immediately appealed to both the Warburg family and myself, especially as it conforms with the aims hitherto pursued by the Library.
>
> From the very beginning we were convinced that to bring this scheme to fruition, Dr. Klibansky's co-operation was indispensable, his work in the history of philosophy being essential to the scientific aims of the Library.

Klibansky came to Britain in 1934, and managed to bring over his mother and sister; his work on the Platonism of Meister Eckhardt and Nicolas of Cusa was sabotaged by Nazi scholars, and in response he began work on the *Plato Latinus* project on behalf of the Warburg. His name is scattered through the dossiers in the files of the SPSL, so many are the people he recommended to the organization. During the Second World War he was head of the German and Italian intelligence sections of the Political Warfare Executive; after it he became Professor of Philosophy at McGill University in Canada, and he founded and was President of the International Institute of Philosophy, dedicated to maintaining connections between philosophers on either side of the Iron Curtain, and throughout the world. His memoirs show that he had significant influence in most of the major events of his lifetime.[21]

FELIX JACOBY (1876–1959)

'Perhaps the most distinguished Greek historian now living' (E.R. Dodds), Felix Jacoby was officially 'retired' in 1934; although baptized in the Evangelical Church, he was still classified as 'non-Aryan'. He had spent his life from 1909 onwards collecting and publishing *Die Fragmente der Griechischen Historiker* (*The Fragments of the Greek Historians*),[22] the most important work of the modern age for the study of Greek history; he arrived in Britain in 1939. He was given a grant of £180; Christ Church, Oxford, offered him a refuge and raised his grant to £250; other Oxford charities contributed. At the end of the war the SPSL archives contain a moving enquiry of 1945 from his relative Georg Jacoby, just released from Theresienstadt concentration camp, appealing for news of him.

In 1958 he reported to the SPSL:

> The invitation by a famous Oxford college and the generous help given by this college and Oxford University through more than twelve years, apart from probably saving my life, enabled me to go on with what may be called the work of my life and now to hand it over (in my 83rd year) to a friend and colleague of Harvard University (Professor Herbert Bloch).

In thanks for British help Jacoby wrote the two volumes of his commentary on the fragments of the Athenian historians (1954) in English, together with his book on them (*Atthis*, Oxford 1949). For seventeen years his house in Oxford had remained a haven of German culture, until 1956, when his wife became ill and he returned to the care of relatives in Berlin.

MARTIN BRAUN

At the other end of the academic spectrum, the young Martin Braun was born in 1904 and received his doctorate from Heidelberg in 1930; after a period as German Lektor in Milan he arrived in Britain on 13 March 1934. He took a second doctorate at Cambridge (1934–36) and found a Senior Research Fellowship at the poorest of the Oxford colleges, Manchester. His book was published by a great patron of the refugees, Sir

Basil Blackwell, and is dedicated to Manchester College 'by an exile'. It is in fact a version of his Heidelberg dissertation, called *History and Romance in Graeco-Oriental Literature* (Blackwell 1938).[23] It concerns a fundamental problem still unsolved today, the origins in Hellenistic Jewish literature of the Christian Gospel narratives. Despite its preface by Arnold Toynbee and a reference from the leading historian of Greek religion A.D. Nock, Braun failed to find an academic post; in 1939 he was offered a temporary lectureship at Cardiff, but only if the SPSL would pay his salary. In 1940 he wrote from Peveril Internment Camp:

> I was interned on 4th July while doing farm work under the Oxford University Harvest Scheme. The first four weeks I spent at Warble Mill of ill fame. Now I am living under somewhat better conditions on the Isle of Man. But for all of us the question of release continues to be in the foreground of our thoughts.

He was released thanks to the Principal of Manchester College and subsisted on a tiny grant of £2 a week, until he found employment from 1941 in the BBC German service as an announcer and translator, a post he still held in 1947. The last record in his SPSL file is a letter to *The Times* in 1946 denouncing the philosopher Martin Heidegger as a prominent Nazi.[24]

VICTOR EHRENBERG (1891–1976)

Victor Ehrenberg was a late arrival: born in 1891 he had served with distinction in the First World War. In 1929 he became Professor of Ancient History at the German University in Prague. Under the threat of the German occupation of Czechoslovakia, expecting to be dismissed, in November 1938 he contacted the SPSL He was awarded a grant of £250 to enable him and his wife to obtain visas; the problem was that their two sons aged seventeen and fifteen were not eligible to come without an invitation. His wife described how they hung on to the last minute, until finally through one of her friends, contact was made with a chance acquaintance met on a train, who contacted the Methodist headmaster of Rydal School, Colwyn Bay, who offered them school places at the ridiculously reduced rate of £5 a term (plus extras which

Victor Ehrenberg (1891–1976) and Eva

came to more than as much again).[25] Visas arrived and they departed on almost the last train from Prague, escaping through Germany.

The problem was that, although Ehrenberg benefited from the English sympathy with the Czech refugees over their own appeasement government's betrayal of Czechoslovakia, nevertheless arriving so late and at the same time as the Italian refugees, he could not be found academic hospitality and became dependent on the SPSL. His sponsors were lukewarm; from Oxford, Hugh Last wrote, 'Prof Ehrenberg is, in my judgment, not of the same class as Prof Momigliano, but he is nevertheless an honest, industrious and competent worker who would thoroughly deserve an opportunity to continue his studies in ancient history.'[26] And M.P. Charlesworth in Cambridge echoed this view: 'I can't say that he is a Rostovtzeff, but he is a sound and able scholar, and certainly deserves (as well as needs) support.' Professor Max Cary of London was more generous and offered Ehrenberg hospitality in his house; Sir Basil Blackwell befriended Ehrenberg, published his first English book on Alexander, and offered him an advance of £150 for two further books, on Aristophanes and another on Alexander in 1940 and 1941.[27] Grants from the SPSL were extended until December 1940. Ehrenberg found a post as classics teacher at Carlisle Grammar School in 1941, and then as a temporary lecturer at King's College, Newcastle, in 1943. When the war ended in 1945 he was appointed classics teacher at the Quaker Bootham School, York, and his wife became a house tutor at St Mary's School,

Durham. Finally in 1946 he was appointed a lecturer at Bedford College, London, from which he eventually retired as a Reader. Of his two sons, the elder, Sir Geoffrey Elton, saw action in Italy during the war, and eventually became the dominant historian of Tudor England and Regius Professor of History at Cambridge University; the younger son was a distinguished mathematician, engineer, and educationalist.

Despite his many books Ehrenberg never received the respect of the Oxbridge establishment. Yet his historical imagination was responsible for three major breakthroughs. The first came in a brief chapter in the first English book, translated from the German, *Alexander and the Greeks* (Blackwell 1938), entitled '*Pothos*'. He traced this concept back to Alexander's own insight into his *pothos*, his continual longing to explore the unknown, to go beyond the limits of human experience. The ancient portrayal of Alexander in sculpture presents him as turning his head to the right and gazing upwards, and it has since been suggested that this was the artistic expression of the same *pothos*, and showed the ancient recognition of the uniqueness of his genius; it is an insight that has remained basic to the study of Alexander ever since. Ehrenberg's book *The People of Aristophanes* (Blackwell 1943) was written during the uncertainties of his wartime life, and is the first and still the most vivid sociological account of the ordinary people of democratic Athens.[28] His third insight was his highly imaginative analysis of the relations between two leading Athenian generals, the statesman Pericles and the tragedian Sophocles: he dared to suggest that these two heroic figures were psychologically in opposition to each other, and that the causes of their conflict could be analysed from Sophocles' famous plays, the *Antigone* and the *Oedipus Tyrannus*. This trespass across the boundaries of literature and history infuriated the conventional English classical establishment, who never forgave him.[29]

These few examples show that the German diaspora not only had a profound effect on the study of the Greeks in the Anglo-Saxon world, establishing it for the first time as a systematic and professional discipline; but it also demonstrates the strength of the faith in academic scholarship that sustained the exiles in their suffering.

Arnaldo Momigliano and family arrive in Oxford, 1939.

15
Momigliano on Peace and Liberty[1]

Criticism of history consists in recognizing whether an historical narrative is full or empty, that is, whether or no it has at its heart a motive which links it up with the seriousness of life as it is lived, and in discerning how far in it the intellectual element is united with the intuitive; that is to say, how far there is an exercise of the historical judgment and how far this is shirked.

Benedetto Croce, *History as the Story of Liberty*[2]

On 2 September 1938, in pursuit of his aim of a closer alliance with Hitler, Mussolini issued his notorious racial decree dismissing from public office all those of Jewish descent. There had been little earlier sign of any danger to Italian Jews, who were indeed as completely assimilated as the Jews of England. They had played an important part in the foundation of the modern Italian state, and had thereafter been active in all areas of Italian life, both cultural and political. From its beginnings the Fascist Party itself had many Jewish supporters, who included the parents of Arnaldo Momigliano, and there was no discrimination against Jews in Italy.

Like all young scholars who sought appointment to university or other public posts in the Fascist period, Momigliano was required to be a nominal member of the party; but his chief intellectual contacts who supported him throughout their lives were two famous figures from an older generation who were resolutely opposed to Fascism, his teacher Gaetano De Sanctis and the great liberal philosopher Benedetto Croce. The attitude of the younger generation was later described in the candid confession of the only pupil of De Sanctis to be involved in Fascism, Mario Attilio Levi; as he wrote in 1989, in relation to Momigliano:[3]

> These political oppositions found no echo in the university life of the second decade of the century, even if De Sanctis and all his pupils, with the exception of myself, had taken up positions hostile to Fascism in a generally inactive fashion, while L. Pareti had adhered to Fascism from the beginning.

Italian cultural life at the time lacked clear oppositions, except for those who were politically on the extreme left and associated directly with the Communist Party, or hereditary socialists like Piero Treves.[4] De Sanctis was a Catholic recusant who believed that ultimate authority lay with the Pope; Croce was politically an old-fashioned liberal. The most prominent Fascist intellectual, Giovanni Gentile, was himself an old friend and colleague of Croce; before the war he organized the great Italian encyclopedia, the *Enciclopedia Italiana*, for which he was happy to employ all the young scholars of talent (including Momigliano), whatever their political or religious affiliations: indeed, the section of the *Enciclopedia* devoted to the ancient world was under the general editorship of De Sanctis, and became famous as a refuge and a source of patronage for all those having problems with the regime.[5] Gentile himself had been Mussolini's Minister for Education from 1923, reforming Italian education in many useful ways, and remained loyal to him to the end, until in 1944 he was assassinated by communist partisans.[6]

In 1938, Momigliano was still very young, aged only twenty-nine; his contacts with overseas scholars were largely confined to those whom he had met in Rome at their respective archaeological schools, for example, the great Romanian scholar, D.M. Pippidi, who was a young researcher at the Romanian Academy from 1931 to 1933,[7] and Mason Hammond (1903–2002), the Harvard historian of ancient Rome, whom he met while Hammond was director of classical studies at the American Academy between 1937 and 1939.[8] Momigliano himself had never travelled in Europe, lacking the money to do so, and his contacts with Britain were confined to Oxford and Cambridge. In Cambridge he had corresponded with (but had never met) two of the editors of the great British project of the interwar period, the *Cambridge Ancient History* (*CAH*). Frank E. Adcock (1886–1968), one of its original editors and from 1927 the chief editor, was Professor of Ancient

History at Cambridge from 1925 to 1951. M.P. Charlesworth (1895–1950), Fellow of Jesus College from 1921 and Reader in Ancient History from 1931, President of St John's College from 1937, had been an editor of the *CAH* from volume VII onwards. Both of them must have corresponded with Momigliano over the two chapters that he contributed to volume X, on Herod of Judaea and on Nero, and a third long section of a chapter on the provincial rebellions, covering the Jewish rebellion of AD 66–70. These contributions were published in 1934, and had been translated into English by Charlesworth. It was Hugh Last (1894–1957) in Oxford who had originally brought Momigliano to the attention of the editors of the *CAH*. He had recognized the brilliance of Momigliano's first substantial book, written while he was still a graduate student, *L'opera dell'imperatore Claudio* (1932) in a review in the *Journal of Roman Studies* for 1932, and had arranged its publication in English translation.[9] Adcock, Charlesworth, and Last dominated the study of Ancient History in Britain between the wars; all were competent but largely unproductive scholars in a period that produced little true scholarship before the influx of German academic refugee scholars from 1933 onwards. They were, however, all men of affairs with a wide knowledge of continental scholarship: in his youth Adcock had studied in Berlin under Wilamowitz and in Munich under Eduard Meyer; while Last was a great traveller in Italy. It was presumably this fact (for Last had surely met Momigliano in Italy, and knew his teacher De Sanctis well) that caused Momigliano to approach Last rather than either of the other two.

At this point Momigliano was then known in England as an outstanding young scholar from the school of Gaetano De Sanctis: he had contributed to the *Cambridge Ancient History*, and English scholars were aware of him as a historian of late Hellenistic and imperial Judaism (his first book had been *Prime Linee di storia della tradizione Maccabaica*, 1930) and as an expert on the Julio-Claudian period; but it does not seem that any British Greek historian had paid attention to his equally important work on Philip of Macedon (*Filippo il Macedone*, 1934).

Two days after the proclamation of the decree of dismissal, Arnaldo Momigliano wrote in Italian to Hugh Last on 4 September 1938 (I give the letter in Last's translation made for the SPSL):[10]

Turin 4.ix.1938
via Cibrario 36 bis

Dear Professor Last,

In consequence of the decree of 21 September I have been deprived, as a Jew, of my chair at the University of Turin. I am completely without private means, and I have a wife and daughter and other dependent relatives. I know that England is full of foreign Jews; yet I think it my duty to ask you if an arrangement of any sort, even the most humble, would be possible there – not so much as a teacher of ancient history (in which capacity there is certainly no need of me) as in the role of a reader of Italian or a clerk in a library (where I should be able to combine technical competence in antiquity with my pretty intimate knowledge of everything Italian). Naturally I should be available for a post in a private business like Blackwell's or something similar.

There has also occurred to me the possibility that the British School at Rome might be able to make use of an Italian librarian who was also an expert in ancient history. Before applying directly I should be glad of your opinion and, ultimately, of your support.

My knowledge of English is at present slight. In that I see an additional difficulty. Still obviously I should do everything possible to make good this defect, though I do not pick up languages easily.

I should be grateful to you if you could acknowledge this by return. And I should be grateful too if you would convey the contents of this letter to my Cambridge friends Charlesworth and Professor Adcock.

Yours very sincerely,
Arnaldo Momigliano

My cursus is – born 5.ix.1908; graduated magna cum laude 25.vi.1929 at the University of Turin under G. De Sanctis. I was his assistant at the University of Rome in 1930 and 1931. From December 1931 'Privatdozent' in Ancient History. From November 1932 to 1936 official teacher of Greek History in the University of Rome. From 1936 Professor of Roman History (appointed from a field of 10) and official teacher of Greek History at Turin.

What Momigliano presumably did not realize, when he made his personal appeal, was that Hugh Last was deeply involved in the organization set up in 1933 by William Beveridge. Experience with the refugees from Nazi Germany had taught the Society of the importance of speed in rescuing their colleagues. The day that Last received Momigliano's letter he wrote urgently to Walter Adams, the first secretary of the society; within less than a week a reply came from the new secretary, David Cleghorn Thomson, who in the meantime had already written to the three names that Last had mentioned – Adcock, Charlesworth, and Gaetano De Sanctis in Rome. On 14 September, Last partially filled out the standard form required by the Society for those it was asked to help, and by the end of September letters in support of Momigliano had arrived from all three of the referees that the Society had contacted. Thus within three weeks of his first appeal a preliminary dossier of references and forms for an application to the Society for the Protection of Science and Learning had been collected; and it had in principle been decided to help Momigliano.

The young and dynamic Raymond Klibansky seems to have been active in promoting the cause of Momigliano. It was probably Klibansky who in early 1939 brought the formal dossier compiled by Momigliano from Italy to the Society,[11] which was received on 19 February 1939: this contained the standard form (bilingual in English and German) which Momigliano had clearly been sent, a list of his publications recording 108 items plus his articles for the *Enciclopedia Italiana*, and testimonials held by Momigliano from Giovanni Gentile, Direttore of the *Enciclopedia*, Augusto Rostagni, Professor of Latin Literature in Turin, Benedetto Croce, Senator of the Kingdom of Italy and Doctor *honoris causa* of Oxford University, and G.Q. Giglioli, organizer of the great exhibition in Rome, the *Mostra Augustea della Romanità*; only the last of these (as befitted a convinced Fascist)[12] might seem to have been written in slightly cold and formal terms. Momigliano also included the official report on the *concorso* for his election to the chair of Roman History in Turin in 1937.

But by the time this dossier was received, the Society's committee had already met and decided on 28 January to award Momigliano the standard grant of £250 for a year from the date of his arrival in England to carry on historical work; Momigliano replied on 31 January. By 20 March the details of his stay in England were decided: he was invited to Oxford under the protection of Hugh Last. A note of 31 March in the archive records a telephone call from Professor Last, that Momigliano had arrived the previous night. By July his wife and daughter were also safely in Oxford. The speed with which the Society had acted and the absence of formal protocol are truly remarkable. Momigliano never forgot the debt that he owed to Hugh Last, nor the fact that it was his personal intervention that had saved the lives of both himself and his immediate family.

When Momigliano arrived in Oxford on 30 March 1939 he was still only thirty, a brilliant and exceptionally learned pupil of the best masters of the Italian school. Officially he was the pupil of De Sanctis, but he himself recognized that Julius Beloch and Plinio Fraccaro had been far more influential in forming his thought; Momigliano's time in Rome on the staff of the *Enciclopedia Italiana* had introduced him to German culture; for the Istituto Germanico was a favourite meeting place then as now. At that point the relationship with Croce did not perhaps seem as important as it would later. Personally they were close: for in December 1938 Croce had written a testimonial on Momigliano's behalf for his migration to Oxford. But intellectually it was not until after the war, when Momigliano was invited to be the head of Croce's new Istituto Storico at Naples, that he began to renew his student enthusiasms.[13] From all accounts, in 1939 he regarded history primarily as a professional discipline rather than as an aspect of philosophy or culture; he therefore found himself in sympathy with the mainstream of English historical writing, exemplified in the Mommsenian tradition of figures such as Hugh Last and Isobel Henderson. Momigliano recognized the relationship between the remaining outposts of this approach in his essay of 1960 in memory of Fraccaro:

> Fraccaro therefore found himself almost alone on the continent of Europe in maintaining alive the problems and methods of Mommsen, at least for the constitutional and political history of the Republic. Since the other place where these problems remained alive was Oxford, it is natural that already before the war the name of Fraccaro was held in particular honour among English scholars. Relations strengthened after the war. The leading Roman historian of Oxford, H. M. Last, and Fraccaro became close friends – a friendship which brought light to both men in their last years. Oxford conferred an honorary degree on Fraccaro, and (even rarer distinction) he was elected honorary member of the Society for the Promotion of Roman Studies. A number of young Oxford scholars went to complete their studies at Pavia.[14]

By contrast, the new realism of Ronald Syme, inspired by the work of Friedrich Münzer and Matthias Gelzer, had little appeal. Historical accident and personal relations combined with intellectual convictions. Younger scholars like Syme, Russell Meiggs, A.H.M. Jones, and A.N. Sherwin-White, were absent on war service. It was Hugh Last who had personally arranged all the details of Momigliano's invitation to England, and who was his protector and friend in the next decade.

The Oxford society in which Momigliano lived from 1939 to 1947 was not in fact an English society. It was the greatest gathering of the humanist scholarship of Europe since the Council of Florence in 1439. The library of the Ashmolean Museum was in these years the centre of intellectual life; it provided space, warmth, and companionship, while the rest of England was engaged in war. Those English university teachers remaining in Oxford were employed in government service, and were mostly preoccupied with preserving a semblance of the Oxford college life; they regarded the refugees with awe and amusement, if not outright xenophobia. They christened the group centred on the Ashmolean 'the Bund', in ironical reference to the famous Russian Jewish Marxist faction; Hugh Last was once heard to describe Fritz Pringsheim as 'one of the less distinguished members of the Bund'. That judgement is not unduly harsh, for the Bund was indeed distinguished: it included Pfeiffer, Maas, Fraenkel, Jacobsthal, Jacoby, and Weinstock; Fritz Schulz worked more often in the Codrington Law Library in All Souls; the distinguished Arabist, Richard Walzer, was also in Oxford. Some of these scholars became integrated into university life. Fraenkel was Professor of Latin in Oxford from 1935, and Jacobsthal and Jacoby were members of Christ Church, but others became teachers in the university either very late or never.

Momigliano was the only Italian connected with this group (with the possible exception of Lorenzo Minio-Paluello);[15] he was also very much younger than the others, and less well established. It is not easy to find in the work of the German refugee scholars any sign of this wartime experience; their research continued on lines already established in the context of German philology. But on Momigliano the impact was profound. It is surely this experience of daily contact with the greatest scholarship of Europe in a context of pure research, which turned him from the learned but orthodox Italian ancient historian into the European polymath, who took the whole classical tradition as his domain.

And it was perhaps that ideal of scholarly discourse which he carried with him through the rest of his life. As he wrote in 1945 in his very perceptive essay on 'La storia antica in Inghilterra':[16]

> One must add the influx of exiles from many lands, to whom Great Britain has generously offered hospitality, and to whom Oxford in particular has given the possibility of continuing scientific work without distractions. Some of the greatest classical philologists of our age, like F. Jacoby, E. Fraenkel, P. Maas, R. Pfeiffer and the Roman lawyer F. Schulz, are today at Oxford. A displacement of this nature, which will not be permanent for all the exiles, can only be evaluated in its spiritual significance after decades have passed.

In Cambridge in 1940, Ernest Barker had determined to contribute to the funds of the SPSL by persuading the History Faculty to pay for a series of lectures by eminent refugee professors: each of four named professors was to be paid £50. Momigliano was the only historian of the ancient world included in the list: it was appropriate that the invitation should come from the Faculty of History, not Classics, simply because ancient history in Cambridge was by tradition organized as part of modern history, rather than falling under Classics, although options for study were available to students for degrees in both Classics and History; this 'sidelining' of ancient history from Classics is indeed the chief reason for the academic weakness of ancient history in Cambridge until the 1950s with the arrival of another exile, this time an American Marxist (exiled by the Committee for Un-American Activities under Senator Joseph McCarthy) Moses Finley (see below, chapter 19); for comparatively few students took ancient history as an option, and there were correspondingly few teachers in the university.

Sir Ernest Barker (1874–1960) himself had a varied career as a teacher of political philosophy in Oxford, as Principal of King's College London (1920–27), and finally as Professor of Political Science at Cambridge (1927–38), where for the last three years before his retirement he served as chairman of the History Faculty. Throughout the 1930s he had been an outspoken liberal opponent of Nazism, Fascism, and Soviet dictatorship, and a committed European. The device of lectures that he persuaded the History Faculty to adopt was primarily a means of distributing its money to a deserving cause: there was no especial desire to hear the lectures, or indeed to honour the persons chosen. By the time the lectures were actually given, Barker himself had retired, and was director of studies (1939–41) in charge of a course in military and political studies run at Cambridge by the War Office for selected officers. Indeed by this time, apart from the medically unfit, women, and officers on specific courses, there were very few students in Cambridge, and most of the Faculty except for the elderly were already involved in war work; so the audiences for any wartime lectures were bound to be small. Whether or not Momigliano realized the background to this request, he agreed to give a series of eight lectures and seminars in the History Faculty at Cambridge in the spring of 1940 in return for the honorarium offered.

It must be said that his lectures were scarcely a success. The audience was minuscule: the absence of male students in wartime added to the unappealing prospect of listening to an unknown foreign professor talking off the syllabus, and any women students would have been equally reluctant. Momigliano wrote to his friend Carlo Dionisotti about his 'audience faithful unto death', which consisted in fact of seven (presumably senior) members.[17] Some of the local names can be guessed – Barker, Charlesworth, Adcock, and G.T. Griffith (who is mentioned in a personal fashion in Lecture III by Momigliano for his views on *koine eirene*).[18] 'A barely repressed air of the ridiculous marked the occasion. The modern historians had omitted to mobilize their classical colleagues. No students came. Introduced by Ernest Barker, who evidently knew nothing of his work, Momigliano faced a thin row of refugee professors. Yet the discussion was worthwhile, enlivened by "a youngish-looking lady, who could have been a star girl student" – none other than Jocelyn Toynbee, the distinguished archaeologist.'[19]

Despite this minuscule audience, Momigliano had taken great trouble to prepare and write out the English text of his lectures in longhand; the preparation was done with the help of friends in Oxford – certainly his friend and mentor Isobel Henderson, Fellow of Somerville College, and perhaps his student and admirer, Iris Murdoch.[20] The stress accents of English words and the need for pauses between sentences were marked in the text to help the lecturer: the sentences themselves were kept short and clearly separated in a way that suggests Momigliano had not yet mastered the art of the subordinate clause in English. The linguistic effort that had gone into preparing the lectures is evident in their stilted style and occasional mistakes.[21]

Momigliano's audience was not accustomed to lectures by foreigners, which were very rare in that period. Even today the written text is idiosyncratic and not always easy to follow; and to the end of his life Momigliano's heavy Piedmontese accent was often found difficult by those who were not familiar with it: in these early days it must be doubtful how well the lecturer's English could be understood by the original audience. Moreover, the content of the lectures was so different from anything on offer in British scholarship at the time as to compound the incomprehension; of his identifiable audience only Ernest Barker could be said to have been concerned with the history of ideas: with his ever-increasing interest in European culture he was perhaps the only listener on the same wavelength, and potentially able to understand the profound message of the lectures. Barker's later and unusual interest in ancient political thought from the Hellenistic age to Byzantium may indeed owe something to these lectures;[22] but apart from this, I can find no trace of any intellectual discussion or reflection of Momigliano's ideas in the writing of others, and one wonders what the seminars (which must have involved some discussion) were actually like. Yet despite all this, in the surviving written text there emerges already a mastery of irony and sophistication, a clarity and a passionate belief in his subject which was to make Momigliano, like so many other refugees (Karl Popper, Ernst Gombrich, Erwin Panofsky, Raymond Klibansky), one of the great masters of English academic prose, better by far than any native contemporary except for Ronald Syme. Moreover, the message of Momigliano is in my opinion the most profound interpretation of the meaning of ancient history that survives from the twentieth century – something that can still inspire us all to understand today the true meaning of history.

The lectures were delivered in that brief period known as 'the phoney war'. Immediately afterwards the atmosphere changed. Winston Churchill replaced Neville Chamberlain as Prime Minister on 10 May 1940, the British troops were evacuated from Dunkirk and French resistance disintegrated. On 10 June, Italy declared war on Britain and France; and Momigliano and his family became 'enemy aliens'; in mid-July the Battle of Britain began. Amid these alarms all male German and Italian refugees were ordered to report for internment: it is alleged that when Momigliano presented himself at Oxford Police Station, he was asked to empty his pockets, and extracted John Stuart Mill's essay *On*

Liberty. The months of internment in Cornwall and subsequently on the Isle of Man are recorded in the letters between Momigliano, his wife, and Tess Simpson of the SPSL. They were anxious months for all refugees; the flavour of those months and the suffering of the refugees are well brought out in the mostly unpublished memoirs of the German refugees, describing life in the German camp.[23] Later Momigliano himself could look back on it as a time of new intellectual friendships and the reading of Plato and Aristotle.[24] The contrast between the two internment camps for Germans and Italians is captured in a story told by Momigliano about this time of his 'Choice of Hercules'. The commandant of the Italian camp took pity on the three professors in his charge – Piero Sraffa, Minio-Paluello, and Momigliano – and offered them a transfer to the German camp, where they might find more intellectual companionship. The others were keen to go, on the grounds that it would improve their German; but Momigliano persuaded them to stay where they were, insisting that it was better to be three professors in a camp full of waiters and restaurant proprietors than three waiters in a camp full of German professors.

Momigliano arrived back in Oxford on 17 November; it had been an anxious five months; but he settled down to a life in Oxford centred on the Ashmolean Library, which provided warmth and companionship in a time of austerity, when central heating in private houses was unknown. For the rest of the war and for some years subsequently, until he moved to London, Momigliano's home remained in Oxford, in rented accommodation usually sharing a kitchen, at 38 Lonsdale Road and 47 Beechcroft Road. There were various efforts to find him a post in the United States in Wisconsin-Madison University or Chicago; these all fell through, not least because Momigliano's spoken English was not good. That was, for instance, given as one reason why he could not be invited to give the British Academy Italian lecture for 1940.

PEACE AND LIBERTY

The theme of the lectures of 1940 on 'Peace and Liberty in the Ancient World' is profound, and based on the unity of Greek and Roman history as an expression of the fundamental truths of Western society. The Greeks understood and indeed created the Western ideal of liberty, but could not reconcile it with the idea of peace; the Romans, who inherited something of the Greek idea of liberty, lost it in the pursuit of peace. These two great ideals of Western civilization were in perpetual conflict until they were reconciled by Christianity: only in Christianity could peace – the peace of God – be reconciled with the idea of the freedom of the individual. For anyone brought up in the empirical tradition of English historical research, this was a completely new way of looking at ancient history as the interplay between great concepts, rather than as the history of events and the political and military power struggles of a long-dead civilization.[25]

The general conception of a history based on great ideas reflects the idealist tradition in Italian scholarship.[26] Elsewhere in nineteenth-century Europe the fundamental meaning of history had been seen in the development of nationhood; as I have argued, this nationalist tradition had broken the old eighteenth-century set of universal humanistic values and replaced them with a view of history as a myth useful towards the creation of the nation state, under the guise of establishing a form of scientific history based on archival research: this (as Momigliano's later work showed) is the paradox beneath the development of a positivist empirical methodology which proclaimed the importance of the single truth in history and the search for the facts that supported it. Few historians escaped this form of sophisticated tribalism, which was to lead directly to the struggles of European nation states in two world wars and the collapse of European civilization. In Italy itself the concept of a national history, derived from the Risorgimento and the unification of Italy, was deeply embedded in society and lay at the foundation of the Fascist ideology. In particular in the 1930s the foundation of the Roman Empire was promoted as a national celebration of the forerunner of Fascist Italy, with the bimillenia of the births of Virgil (1930) and Augustus (1937), the creation of the great exhibition of the Roman Empire, the *Mostra Augustea della Romanità* (1937), to which Momigliano contributed before his exile,[27] as well as the creation of the triumphal *Via dei Fori Imperiali* (1931–33) and the archaeological excavations that accompanied it.

It was Benedetto Croce and his disciples in southern Italy, notably Guido De Ruggiero, the philosopher and historian of liberty, and Adolfo Omodeo, historian of Christianity, who created a specifically Italian approach to the philosophy of history that offered an alternative liberal conception of history opposed to the nationalist tradition.[28] Croce's idealist philosophy went back to Hegel in viewing history not as a random set of events, but as the actualization of Reason in the world: as with Hegel, history was the history of the development of liberty; but whereas for Hegel history had reached its culmination in the freedom of the individual, for Croce history must continue as the story of the struggles for liberty; 'All history [has] the character of "contemporary history" because, however remote in time events there recounted may seem to be, the history in reality refers to present needs and present situations wherein these events vibrate.'[29] All history must be understood in its relation to the present, and its meaning is not independent of the present. Such a view predisposed Croce and his followers towards liberalism rather than nationalism as the political expression of progress in history, at the same time as validating the idea that history had no intrinsic meaning apart from its function in the present: for such reasons the break with Giovanni Gentile in 1921 marked a fundamental split in Italian culture between the idea of history as an expression of those present forces of national progress that were embodied in Fascism, and the traditions of secular liberalism and its political expression, espoused by Croce, with its contested relationship to the Catholic tradition – which for Momigliano was embodied in the figure of his teacher De Sanctis. As Momigliano later saw, the resulting conception of history, which had influenced him so deeply in his youth, needed to be carefully distinguished from the postmodern view of history as a branch of rhetoric lacking in absolute truth, a story told simply as a myth for the present.[30]

The idealism of Momigliano was tempered by the professional teaching of De Sanctis, which belonged to the strictly philological and positivist tradition inherited by Italian scholarship from the German nineteenth century; this tradition saw history as a science, emphasized the importance of methodical research and the exercise of a rational scepticism in the discovery of true facts; its chief weakness was that only too often this rational scepticism operated on the assumption that the past could be reconstructed on the basis of the prejudices of the historian's own day. De Sanctis had been a close pupil of Julius Beloch (1854–1929), who for reasons of health had migrated to Italy in his youth, and was educated at Palermo, Rome, and Heidelberg before becoming a professor at Rome University from 1879 to 1929.[31] Beloch was one of the most rigorous representatives of this style of rational scepticism, which he applied especially to political history and the quantification of ancient and modern populations.[32] De Sanctis's own contribution was to broaden this approach by modifying its scepticism in relation to the ancient evidence, and applying it to cover all periods of the ancient classical world and all aspects of ancient societies; he was held in very high regard for his rigour and acumen by the corresponding Anglo-Saxon positivist tradition. Momigliano himself never questioned this basic methodology, which he indeed found increasingly compatible with the traditions of exact Jewish scholarship, and which he practised throughout his life. As a young man his aim seems therefore to have been to use this methodology in order to illuminate those problems suggested to him by the idealist tradition, and so to provide a solid historical basis for the study of conceptual questions: 'what has no value, has no history. Yet the values of history are not a matter for polemics, but for plain knowledge.'[33]

The importance of liberty for Momigliano lies initially in its role within a Crocean view of history, but he approached it from a scientific point of view learned from De Sanctis; and in the last year of his life (1985) Momigliano claimed that liberty was an especial preoccupation of this school. In the Cambridge lectures he was building on his previous incomplete researches, which had been inhibited by the difficulty of speaking about liberty under Fascism. The move to Britain enabled him for the first time to think and speak freely: 'The true evil created by Fascism in the study of ancient history lies not in the stupidity of what was said but in the thoughts that were no longer thought. Many of the best, if they said nothing that should not have been said, refrained from saying everything that they could have said.'[34]

So in these lectures Momigliano was a true disciple of Croce, who saw the purpose of history as a lesson for the present. Even more than earlier, in 1940, Momigliano saw that the stupendous conflict in which European civilization was involved was a conflict between liberty and a false peace, between liberalism and the sterility created by the unity of a national purpose. That is of course the choice that still confronts Western culture today, and it is (as Croce argued) why history has no end: we must always continue to care about history and its interpretation. It is indeed this moral function that makes the difference between idealist and postmodernist views of history, because in postmodernism the truth does not matter, whereas in idealism it is a moral imperative related to the future of humanity.

On the other hand, Momigliano avoided the confusion common among both pre-war and post-war twentieth-century historians: he did not confuse the history of ideas with the history of ideologies, which he particularly identified with certain right-wing tendencies in history, although it was not entirely confined to these.[35] His verdict was forthright:

> Only in the very last years has an interest in the political reality developed. Unfortunately, political reality has a worse, more subtle enemy than juridical abstraction: it has to cope with political ideology, with the promises which nobody gave seriously and which, very often, nobody took seriously. Even some very good books of these last years are marred by confusion of ideology and reality, for instance the French volume of Professor Carcopino about Caesar[36] and the Italian volumes of Professor Levi about *Ottaviano capoparte*,[37] leader of party. Such a confusion appears especially strong in some German books. I quote only one: *Princeps* of Professor Weber, a sort of commentary of the *Monumentum Ancyranum*, learned and, in the end, useful, but amusingly naive.
>
> If we ignore ideology and look at reality or, better, if we give to ideology its own place, which is in hell and not in paradise, among the destructive and not among the constructive elements of history, we are left with two recent books, apart from the *Cambridge History*: the big memoir of the late Professor von Premerstein, *Vom Wesen des römischen Prinzipats*,[38] on the essence of the Roman Principate, and above all, the recent very important book of Mr. Syme, *The Roman Revolution*.[39]

In this brief dismissal of ideological historians, Momigliano focuses on one prominent Nazi historian (Wilhelm Weber), his own fellow pupil of De Sanctis and Fascist rival for the chair at Turin (M.A. Levi), and (with considerable prescience) the eminent French historian and wartime collaborator Jérôme Carcopino, who was shortly afterwards to become Minister of National Education and Youth under the German occupation.[40] Similarly in Lecture 3 Momigliano dismisses the views of the Nazi historian Helmut Berve on Alexander the Great.[41]

The first important event that had happened on Momigliano's arrival in Britain was not the outbreak of war, but earlier than that (in the summer of 1939), the publication of the most significant book on Roman history since the beginning of the century, Ronald Syme's *Roman Revolution*. He read Syme's book 'in a copy given to me by the author when war had just been declared and the nights grew ever longer in an Oxford plunged into darkness'.[42] Momigliano confronted the book head-on from the start. He recognized its fundamental dismissal of all forms of intellectual history in favour of a forthrightly Machiavellian view of human nature based on self-interest and family power not ideals. Brought up in the tradition of Croce and the importance of history as the story of liberty, he was profoundly shocked; this was the source of a continuing conflict, however muted, between Syme and Momigliano that lasted for the rest of their long lives. As pupils of both scholars, we used to think that this conflict began after the war, when Syme (it was said) asked Momigliano to write in support of his candidacy for the Oxford Camden chair of Roman History, in a deliberate attempt to prevent him from putting his own name forward.[43] However true or *ben trovato* that story was, Momigliano's sympathies were always against Syme in the quarrels between him and Hugh Last, Syme's predecessor (and now Principal of his college), and the protector who had (as we have seen) saved Momigliano's life. Momigliano's great affection for Last continued until the latter's death, when in a letter to Isobel Henderson he commented on the fact that he had long suspected the truth then revealed, that Last had Jewish ancestry.[44]

But we can now see that this conflict between the two most distinguished ancient historians of their generation goes back to an intellectual incompatibility which Momigliano recognized from the beginning of his time in Britain. From the start he understood the power of Syme's vision, and saw Syme both as a master historian – the greatest English historian of the ancient world since Gibbon – and as the representative in ancient history of an Anglo-Saxon historical tradition that Momigliano as a newcomer from continental idealism had to confront. Later (much to Syme's annoyance, who claimed not to have been influenced by Namier at all) he connected Syme's chosen method with the relatively new arrival in Britain of the historical study of prosopography, which had been pioneered by Lewis Namier in his work *The Structure of Politics at the Accession of George III* (1929). But at this stage he regarded Syme's use of prosopography as deriving from the work of

Matthias Gelzer, *Die Nobilität der römischen Republik* (1912) and Friedrich Münzer, *Römische Adelsparteien und Adelsfamilien* (Stuttgart 1920), together with the latter's articles on the Roman *gentes* in the encyclopedic reference work, Pauly-Wissowa; under their influence from 1933 onwards the great biographical dictionary of the Roman imperial aristocracy, the *Prosopographia Imperii Romani* first compiled by Hermann Dessau in the nineteenth century, was being renewed by E. Groag and A. Stein.[45]

The first two of Momigliano's lectures begin from the shock of this first encounter with Syme. That is the reason why the story of peace and liberty starts unexpectedly from an analysis of the modern historiography on Republican and Augustan Rome since Mommsen, and presents Augustan Rome as the turning point in the history of the ancient world. The first lecture is on modern research on the Roman Empire, and the causes of the weakness of earlier attempts to understand the phenomenon. It refers to claims of the medieval Church in relation to the Roman Empire, the juristic tradition, European writers and especially Edward Gibbon; later histories since Mommsen lead on to Tenney Frank and the recent completion of the *Cambridge Ancient History*. This was ground already for the most part covered in Momigliano's work for his great article on the Roman Empire published in the *Enciclopedia Italiana*.[46] But the lecture ends with the challenge presented by two recent works, each in a very different style, A. von Premerstein's posthumous *Vom Werden und Wesen des Prinzipats* (1937)[47] and 'Mr Syme':

> The problem is clear. Is the passage from the Republic to the Empire a simple crisis inside the Roman-Italian leading class or is it a crisis of the whole Mediterranean world? The *Cambridge History* inclines to the second point of view, but not very clearly; Prof. v. Premerstein indirectly, Syme directly support the first interpretation. The choice is relevant to our immediate purpose. It amounts to establishing whether the Empire represented the mere replacement of six hundred lords – the Roman senators – by one lord – the Emperor – or whether it was a new form of human society. We must choose, we will choose.[48]

The second lecture addresses the problem, what is the crisis of the Roman Republic? It begins with discussion of the prosopographical approach and its limitations:

> Prosopographical research has the great virtue of dealing as much as possible with individuals or small groups, but does not explain their material or spiritual needs: it simply presupposes them. History is the history of problems, not of individuals or groups. If the tacit assumption of many prosopographical researches is that people are moved by personal or family ambitions, the assumption is not merely one-sided: it exchanges generic trends for concrete situations. Each ambition is possible only in *one* historical situation. The personal or family interests of every man depend directly or indirectly on the situation of thousands of other men. This argument, trivial as it is, is sufficient to show how absurd it is to think that in the last centuries of the Republic the history of Rome might be in the hands of some hundreds of leading men. Political power was in their hands, but not history, which is another matter. Furthermore, it is fair to admit that men have better and worse impulses than the defence of their personal and family position.[49]

He concludes with the magnificently epigrammatic statement, 'The Principate was to be a product not of men, about whom it is possible to write articles in Pauly-Wissowa, but of the obscure people, whose name is legion.'[50]

Momigliano then proceeds to discuss the meaning of clientship, and to show that the clients of the late Republic were intrinsically different from earlier forms of clientship, and possessed serious political aims and grievances. This is true of Caesar's control of the Po valley, and the Pompeian control of Spain and later of Sicily. His final verdict is:

> The old Romans – the Romans of the aristocracy, the Romans of the *comitia* – lost their freedom because they had not shared it. The triumph of clientship completely confirms the fact that people who have not sufficient rights become the prey of the political agitator. Clientship is the manifestation of an immense movement of people, who to the freedom of the others preferred a government, which immediately gave them fair prospects of a career, and promised peace with tolerable justice. The monarch was, inevitably, monarch for everybody. If one considers the Augustan State as the simple result of a triumph of a party, one will never understand that for twelve or thirteen centuries, if not more, that State was the only conceivable State.[51]

This is to anticipate the views of an entire post-war generation of Roman historians, from Ernst Badian in *Foreign Clientelae* (1958) to Peter Brunt in *Social Conflicts in the Roman Republic* (1971).

> The circular process is clear: the non-political man makes the non-political soldier; the non-political soldier reinforces the non-political man. The career of the soldier is a step to the honours of civil life. The army, therefore, has no special interest in conquests. Emperors may be adventurous, but not the soldiers, not even, as a rule, the generals. The ideal of the Empire remains the ideal of the classes, which helped to found the Principate: *pax augusta*. As a result of the Augustan revolution, any future revolution of the Empire, depending on the army, will be without a political programme. The only aim will be to choose a better or better-paying master. Constantine is probably the first emperor after Augustus, the choice of whom really implies a revolutionary programme. For this reason he begins a new age. The non-political State has found an insidious enemy, the Church. With Constantine the peace assumes a new significance. It is firstly, the religious peace.[52]

The third and fourth lectures are concerned with the concept of peace as it developed in the ancient world. In the third lecture Momigliano begins from the relations between the peace of the Roman Empire and the earlier Greek conceptions of peace. One of the crucial turning points in the analysis of the ancient concept of peace is for him the derivation of the *pax augusta*, the political peace of the Roman Empire, from the Greek ideal of a 'common peace', *koine eirene* – the conception of peace that became prominent in Greece from the fourth century onwards. The phrase *koine eirene* appeared as a political aspiration of the Greeks soon after the end of the Peloponnesian War, which had demonstrated the appalling cost of a generation of internecine warfare in search of an impossible hegemony, and had split the city-states of the Greek world under the leadership of Athens and Sparta. Autonomy seemed only possible for the smaller states with the acceptance by all cities of the overriding necessity of a common peace. First appearing in a speech of Andocides of 390 BC, it came to be viewed as an ideal. But it was only when that ideal was proclaimed as a concrete reality in 387/6 BC that the price of such a common peace was recognized. In the absence of any general forum for enforcing an inter-city agreement, it was inevitable that a common peace could only be imposed and maintained by an external political force: so the 'King's Peace', presented as a command to the Greek world from the king of Persia, with Persian silver as backing and the Spartan state acting as its enforcer, set the conditions for a 'common peace'. The proclaimed ideal covered a brutal reality, the compulsory disbandment of all forms of federation or treaty in the interests of a spurious autonomy, to be policed by Sparta, one of the two powers that had been most active in infringing the autonomy of cities in the previous century.

This development in Greek international relations fascinated the generation that was struggling to establish through the League of Nations a suitable post-war international order that would enshrine the credentials of a war to end all wars, and to prevent the renewed destruction of European civilization through nationalist rivalries. Not surprisingly, historians of the ancient world saw the struggles of the fourth century BC in terms of the growth of strong powers under non-democratic regimes and the ultimate triumph of Macedonian monarchy over Greek liberty. The phrase *koine eirene* came to reflect the hopes and failures of modern politics; scholars took sides in a debate about the value and importance of an idea that seemed so close to the preoccupations of the contemporary world: was it simply a propaganda phrase designed to disguise the realities of the power struggle, or was it a genuine aspiration that many Greeks desired, however often it was betrayed in the event?

Momigliano had taken a leading role in this characteristic debate of the inter-war period: 'The struggle to organize a *koine eirene*, that is a permanent system of peace between the Greek cities guaranteed by sanctions, emerges ever more clearly as one of the most important goals in Greek history starting with the fourth century BC.'[53] The idea of a *koine eirene* was used to justify first the Persian and then the Macedonian hegemony over Greece; and finally it provided the ethical basis for Roman control of the Greek cities. As he wrote in 1935, 'I never understood so clearly the meaning of *pax romana* until I recognized the *koine eirene* as an ethical and juridical concept of fourth century Greece.'[54]

So in the lectures of 1940 he sees the continuity between Greek and Roman ideas:

> The new [Augustan] peace absorbs the Greek aspirations; it is peace among the States and within the States. It has, furthermore, a clear touch of Messianic hope. Influenced by Greek and Oriental ideas, it can

> influence especially Greek and Oriental people. Yet the *pax romana*, the *pax augusta* remains a political idea and sometimes has a rather hard sound even in the most humane of the poets, *parcere subiectis*, but *debellare superbos*.[55]

The articles on *koine eirene* date from 1933–36; they are not (as so much writing on the subject was) idealistic. Momigliano recognized that an important and limiting factor in the idea of a common peace was always the presence of an external guaranteeing force; in that sense peace was incompatible with political liberty. This limitation on the concept of peace was one that could not be directly emphasized in the political climate of Fascist Italy. So the demonstration of the ambivalent relationship between peace and liberty was left obscure in Momigliano's major writings of this period, his Turin inaugural lecture of 1936, and the long article on the Roman Empire for the *Enciclopedia Italiana*.

Nevertheless, from his first encounters in 1931 with the ideas of Benedetto Croce and Benjamin Constant, the problem of liberty in the ancient world was central to Momigliano's thinking.[56] It was for this reason that throughout his life he laid especial emphasis on the essay of 1819 by Benjamin Constant, *De la liberté des anciens comparée à celle des modernes*. The political liberty of the classical Greek world had given way to the personal liberty of conscience independent of the city-state, which was established as an ideal by Cynics and Stoics and fought for by Jews in their various wars of resistance, and by Christians in the age of persecutions. Only with the conquest of the Roman state by religion could this conception of liberty be restored.

Momigliano thus came to see religion as the key to understanding the relation between peace and liberty in the ancient world: world peace had created the conditions for a universal religion which had in turn contributed a new conception of liberty that transcended the old idea of political liberty. This was also the reason why in the 1930s Momigliano became preoccupied with the conception of 'Hellenism', first formulated by J.G. Droysen a century earlier.[57] Droysen had sought to understand the history of the post-Alexander age as the development of a universal Greek culture viewed as a preparation for the coming of Christianity; according to Momigliano, no subsequent historian had been able to replace this conception: 'it may be humiliating for us to confess that nothing really new has subsequently been found for the general interpretation of Greek history'.[58] Momigliano had to admit that his interpretation of Droysen attributed especial importance to the original separate publication of the life of Alexander with its highly Christian message, rather than to Droysen's later political narrative of the successor kingdoms, volumes which were incomplete as a history of the Hellenistic world, and which were written by an author steeped in Prussian nationalism, who ignored such questions of cultural history.

Momigliano's involvement with Judaism and Christianity as historical forces was central to his understanding of history in this period. This is most clearly revealed in some of the forty-nine surviving letters between Momigliano and De Sanctis; they run from 1930 to the death of De Sanctis in 1957. The openness and independence with which the young Momigliano expresses his feelings and the extraordinary warmth of the austere De Sanctis' response to his favourite and most loyal disciple are manifest; more surprising is the basis of their friendship in a mutual fascination for the relations between Judaism and Christianity in human history: 'Our age will perhaps have an essential value in human history because it is anxiously seeking to give a deep sense to human activity, to create a meaning for history without recourse to a distant God who no longer suffices for us,' wrote the twenty-two-year-old Momigliano on 12 October 1930:

> But if it is true, as indeed it is, that you are more Jewish than me because Christianity validates Judaism, then I am more Christian than you because modern thought validates Christianity. In sum I do not believe in the actuality of Judaism as an established religion: from this point of view I am outside Judaism without a doubt and with good reason. But I believe that the Jews can today have a useful function in our culture, if they remain faithful to certain experiences of their history and certain demands of their mentality: super-nationalism (which is not internationalism) and the hard experience of persecutions should bring them, and often do bring them if in utopian ways, to seek the brotherhood of man; the need for justice, the profound sense of the sanctity of life, which is permeated with ethical values, can equally act as leaven for good, and are maintained by contact with the Hebrew tradition, and especially with the Bible. So I view with sympathy every Jewish cultural initiative. But I repeat, I believe that Jews can make something useful only if they intermingle, with the

state of mind that comes to them from long tradition, the demands of our immanentistic and historicist way of thinking.[59]

Such sentiments reveal the thinking behind Momigliano's publicly expressed opposition to Italian Zionism in 1937,[60] and the sense in which he could say in 1939 in response to the standard question posed in the form of the Society for the Protection of Science and Learning:

Write 'Yes' against the name of religion to which you belong/Schreiben Sie 'Ja' neben den Namen der Religion, der Sie angehören

Jewish Orthodox/Orthodox jüdisch

I am a Jew by birth. I profess no confessional religion

They also explain the pride in the tradition of Jewish scholarship and its contribution to Italian culture that is expressed in his letter of resignation to the Faculty of Turin University, which was read out to the Council of the Faculty by its President on 20 October 1938 (but not recorded in the official minutes):

Dear President,

Now that I am compelled to leave this University, which was my alma mater before I became a teacher here, my thoughts reach out in gratitude towards you and the other teachers of the Faculty. From you I learned as a student to search disinterestedly for the truth in fulfilment of my primary duty towards my fatherland; and by you I was welcomed and fostered with renewed benevolence on my return. I consider myself able to state that in the eight years during which I had the privilege of numbering myself among the teachers of the Universities of Rome and Turin, I have proved myself not unworthy of you. I have loved deeply this school as the natural locus for the search of one's self, and this love has been reciprocated by my students, a living demonstration that differences of religion and any differences of race disappear in the communion of duty. I also consider myself able to state that I have always worked in accordance with the strictest Italian tradition, that which numbers among its most revered names those of Alessandro D'Ancona and Graziadio Ascoli,

> and has been hallowed by the learning of men such as Giacomo Venezian. Whatever the future, now without hope, holds in store for me, my wish is that I might be able to continue to devote to Italy all my efforts. The memory of you all, teachers and students in this our Faculty, will be my constant companion.[61]

In 1985 at the end of his life, talking about Italian scholarship during the 1930s, Momigliano said:

> Two facts are beyond question. The most important discussion on ancient history which developed in Italy in the Thirties was about Greek liberty. Though inspired by Benedetto Croce, it remained almost entirely a discussion internal to the school of De Sanctis, involving De Sanctis himself, Aldo Ferrabino, Piero Treves and myself. Its meaning was inescapable. The History of the Greeks by De Sanctis (1939) came out of it. The other fact is that the discussion of the Empire in relation to the Church got into new, not exactly orthodox, depths: here I must claim some special credit.[62]

The fourth lecture explores this last personal contribution of the 'new, not exactly orthodox, depths'. At this point it is important to understand the meaning of *pax christiana* for Momigliano in his own words; the peace of Christianity is different from that offered by either Greeks or Romans:

> Even in this highest formulation, it is however apparent that peace derives from faith, but is not of the very same substance with faith. God gives peace, but faith is not itself peace. Moreover the conception of universal peace was a rare moment in Judaism. Christendom affirms that peace not only is proper to men of good will, but is the very condition of the life in God. The *Epistle to the Romans* is particularly definite: 'Therefore being justified by faith, we have peace with God through our Lord Jesus Christ' (5), 'for to be carnally minded is death, but to be spiritually minded is life and peace' (8). So much is sufficiently clear, even if the sentence *pax in terra hominibus bonae voluntatis* involves very difficult question [*sic*], as the corresponding Greek text – ἐπὶ γῆς εἰρήνη ἐν ἀνθρώποις εὐδοκίας[63] – is of obscure interpretation. Grace and Peace, *charis* and *eirene*, go together through the *Epistles* of St. Paul. Peace is Salvation. 'The peace of God, which passeth all understanding shall keep your hearts and minds through

Christ Jesus.' These are words of the *Epistle to the Philippians.*[64] The quotations might be multiplied. Of course, in the end, this peace is the restfulness of a will surrendered to God. Here, better than St. Paul, speaks Dante: 'E la sua voluntade è nostra pace.'[65]

Two points must be stressed. First, Christian peace was not passive, like Stoic peace. Christian religion was active, it was a *militia*: *militia Christi.* The blessing of God is to the peace-makers, who shall be called the children of God. Christ himself is the peace-maker, the *eirenopoios* 'through the blood of his Cross', as we read in the *Epistle to the Colossians.*[66] In the Old Testament the Messiah had been called more than once the peace-maker (cf. for instance *Zachariah*, 9, 9). Secondly, Christianity was not only an individual condition like the peace of the Stoics, it was the communion of men, who had received Grace, 'endeavouring to keep the unity of the Spirit in the bond of peace', as the *Epistle to the Ephesians* (4) says.

In these two points, the *pax christiana*, distant as it is from Stoicism, may be compared to the *pax romana*. In a very different order of ideas, the *pax romana* was an active ideal, and was not individual, but social. We just now saw the importance given to the peace-makers, the *eirenopoioi*. In the Roman Empire the Emperor is supposed to be the peace-maker . . .

It is now evident that the Christian idea of Peace, although born from Judaism, became more and more a reaction against the dry spiritual life of the Empire. It gave a new content to the daily life of men. They had to work not for the Empire, as the Empire required, but for another higher Lord. It declared the Empire insufficient, but it did not substitute another type of State. It superimposed a religious on a political idea of life. We must appreciate the significance of this fact if we want to understand the history of the Empire. As a rule, when people are not satisfied with a form of government, they try to replace it with another government. Political discontent ends up in a political crisis. Moments are very rare in the history of Mankind in which a political crisis turns into a change of religion. This is the case of the Roman Empire. Great as was the popularity of the idea of Rome in the provinces, the subjects of the Empire were less and less impressed by the government. People admired Rome and looked to it for political advantages, but had to find elsewhere a more profound interest for their life. The voice of the government was boisterous in propaganda, harsh in giving orders. It could impress, but not satisfy. In the third century AD weariness became widespread. Difficulties provoked not a greater concord but rebellions. Hearts failed. On the whole, the rebellions of the

> third century do not raise any political programme. It is now admitted by everybody that even the so-called Gallic Empire of Postumus has nothing to do with a national movement of Gaul. From a political point of view the rebellions were senseless. But they ended with the adoption of a new religion by Constantine. The crisis of the third century has its explanation in its achievement. People apparently fought about economic difficulties, about the Senate, about rivalries of unworthy or worthy men and about Barbarian enemies – and they discovered a new religion. The Principate began with the triumph of the non-political man, it ended with the triumph of the religious man.[67]

The last four lectures turn to the history of liberty, and complete a project that had been in Momigliano's mind since his first encounters with Croce and Constant, but which he had largely been unable to express before he came to Britain: 'For many years I studied the problem of freedom and peace in the Ancient World as two different problems. Only slowly, the accurate analysis of the two terms compelled me to recognize that the problem I was studying was one; and one, too, the spiritual interest, which moved me in the research.'[68] Momigliano begins from the idea of liberty, as it was conceived within the liberal idealist tradition of Croce and his disciples:

> Liberty is the eternal force of human activity. Where we find moral life, we may safely presuppose liberty. But liberty has historical manifestations of widely different character. The task of the historian is to recognize without any polemical deformation the historical forms of the problem of freedom during the centuries. Historians see with desperation or with satisfaction – in conformity with their personal outlook – centuries of history running without an apparent sign of freedom. Such are the centuries of the Roman Empire. These historians do not ask whether liberty assumed forms which are different from political freedom, whether human dignity, which was expelled from the field of political life, did not take refuge in the more inaccessible fields of spiritual life.[69]

This overarching explanation of the meaning of liberty begins from a study of the differences between ancient and modern liberty, as they were expressed by Benjamin Constant and Croce. The theme of ancient liberty as political, as opposed to modern liberty as personal, foreshadows the later and simpler distinction of Isaiah Berlin between two concepts of liberty, one positive ('freedom to') and one negative ('freedom from').[70] Berlin seems indeed to have been only partially aware of the long discussion that had preceded his inaugural lecture of 1958. What distinguishes Momigliano's approach is not just his knowledge of preceding ideas from Lord Acton and Georg Jellinek to Croce, but his insistence on the importance of the contribution of Christianity to the development of personal liberty, which he recognized as a significant aspect of Acton's views.

The sixth lecture traces the history of *eleutheria* among the Greeks, from its original conception as the right to take part in political life, 'to rule and be ruled in turn' as Aristotle put it, to the rejection of political life by the Cynics and their conception of freedom as independence from civic ties. In the seventh lecture Momigliano turns to Rome, and the fusion of a deeply held belief in political *libertas* that characterized the senatorial aristocracy with a personal view derived from Stoicism, that provided the individual with the possibility of being independent of fortune, while maintaining the belief in the primacy of political liberty: the tyrant could not impinge on the freedom of the politically active individual, for neither torture nor death had any power to overturn the beliefs of a true Stoic wise man. The result was a willingness to accept a form of political martyrdom and suicide that gave to the examples of Brutus and Cato a heroic status previously only accorded to Socrates in ancient thought. Even Augustus was forced to accept the essential primacy of Roman *libertas* in formulating the rules of his autocratic regime; and the Stoic opposition to the emperors continued as a form of senatorial resistance to imperial autocracy throughout the first century AD.

In his last lecture Momigliano explores the relationship between the Christian freedom provided by a belief in God, and the spiritual freedom of the human spirit independent of any god which was offered by the Cynics and Stoics;[71] both represent a turning away from the present world of the Roman Empire and an acceptance that true freedom lies in the spiritual life of the individual, which combines both liberty and peace.

So the autonomy of religious belief becomes a guarantee of the continuity of the eternal force of liberty; and Christianity is its bearer through the centuries. The liberties of the Greek free city-states and the Roman Republic which began as political ideals were transformed through Stoicism into a spiritual internalized form of liberty, the freedom of conscience regardless of the constraints of the external world. A long comparison between Cynic and Christian ethical conceptions of liberty leads to the conclusion that the loss of liberty in the Roman world was essentially the cause of the triumph of Christianity and the transformation of the ancient world into the medieval world of Christendom.

Gibbon had seen the decline and fall of the Roman Empire as caused by the triumph of Christianity. Momigliano broadened the canvas. What was at stake was the decline and fall of the ancient world in all its varied manifestations, Greek, Roman, and Jewish: 'He who does not know the legacy of Greek and Jewish history may well renounce the study of Roman History.'[72] The hidden message of his earlier *Enciclopedia* article on '*Impero Romano*' is revealed with this new emphasis on liberty as an eternal force in human nature; there he had pointed out the inadequacy of the currently fashionable economic explanations of history offered by Michael Rostovtzeff and others – theories that could themselves be seen as the result of reflections on the contemporary Great Depression. Gibbon was right to connect the theme of decline and fall with the rise of Christianity, but he had been unable to explain that rise: for Momigliano it was the failure of the ancient world in its search to combine peace and liberty that had caused the victory of a new religion. When liberty is suppressed in one sphere it must emerge in another.

Momigliano was not alone in his generation in placing a fundamental value on the transition from political to spiritual freedom in the Roman Empire. His views were shared by contemporaries: his mentor Croce in 1946 used the example of the Stoic opposition to the Roman emperors to explain his own political opposition under Fascism.[73] And Momigliano's concern for the shift in consciousness from philosophy to religion in the High Empire was later independently explored by E.R. Dodds in a famous study, *Pagan and Christian in an Age of Anxiety* (Cambridge 1965). But to a modern audience there is one obvious omission in this account, as Franco Basso pointed out to me when I presented these lectures to a group of Cambridge graduate students in theology and classics in October 2006: there is no discussion of the phenomenon of Greek democracy. This absence itself reflects the distance between ourselves brought up with the ideas of the Cold War and the interwar generation. The central importance of the concept of democracy in political and historical thought is surprisingly recent: although many of the new states created at the end of the First World War were explicitly founded on democratic principles, within a few years the idea of democracy was almost universally despised;[74] and it regained significance only after the Second World War in the period of the Cold War, when both the Soviet Union and the USA sought to proclaim their faith in democracy, despite the fact that neither Soviet nor capitalist democracy was or is in fact a democracy in any ancient sense. It is now too often forgotten that between the two world wars both Italy and Germany had become totalitarian states largely through the free votes of their respective peoples: liberalism and the popular will were often in opposition to each other; and freedom, both individual and political, was often threatened by democracy, as it is indeed today. So swiftly does the significance of apparently stable political concepts change – and who is to say that our present perceptions are any more true than those of a previous generation?

Momigliano revealed an extraordinarily powerful view of history. It is not surprising to find him writing to his closest friend still in Italy, Carlo Dionisotti, immediately after giving these lectures, 'all in all I do not seem to escape from the conclusion that here is my way forward, whether I succeed or fail' (*qui è la mia via, del fare o fallire*).[75]

We should not ask how it came about that someone brought up in an orthodox Jewish household within a dominant Catholic culture was able to transcend the rigidities of his environment and produce a theory of history that is superior to any other offered in his generation or earlier. This was an age of grand theories – I think of Marx, Toynbee, Spengler, and a number of Catholic historians. It was also an age of belief in the power of the human spirit rather than organized religion to rebuild a world of peace and liberty: here one may compare the influence of Croce in Italy between the wars with that of Gilbert Murray in Britain and Werner Jaeger in Germany. Rather we should ask what led Momigliano subsequently to abandon (at least explicitly) this approach to history.[76]

There was a turning point sometime in the 1950s. Perhaps Momigliano made a passing reference to it, when he said later in jest, 'I have now lost faith in my own theories, but I have not yet acquired faith in the theories of my colleagues.' But why did he lose faith in the power of religion to carry forward the history of liberty, if that is what happened; and does this make his lectures merely an episode in his intellectual biography? I have no real answer to these questions. In a certain sense

Momigliano's intellectual history presents a continuity from his earliest writings to the end of his life. While remaining constantly open to new discoveries and new ideas, he never really abandoned his view about any subject on which he had written; and his attitude to method and to the underlying ideas of history remained the same. Themes from earlier research keep recurring.

It may be that after the war Momigliano came to feel that, in turning to religion in order to protect his conception of liberty, he had too easily followed the example of those Romans in the Empire who had turned to Christianity in similar circumstances; when after the war it was possible once again to hope in a future which might preserve political liberty, religion was no longer needed to face a present deprived of it: 'minds were open again to hope'.[77] Again, if he abandoned his project through a loss of faith, it was perhaps not so much in his own ideas as in a view of Western civilization as being essentially based on Christianity. In early 1940 few had real knowledge of the atrocities being perpetrated by Nazism against a harmless minority; by 1945, Momigliano understood that the Christian civilization in which he had once put his trust was responsible for the murder of his own aged parents and the systematic destruction of the entire culture in which he had been brought up. It was no longer possible to believe that Christianity could protect the liberty of the individual against the forces of modern tyranny. For many Zionism became a necessity; but not for Momigliano, however much he recognized the historical inevitability of the state of Israel. Despite his claim to belong to no religion, Momigliano had believed in the power of religion for too long. Religion was not the answer. Rather, as the great German historian Friedrich Meinecke saw, the historian had a more mundane and more human task, the duty to rebuild Western culture (and especially for Meinecke, German culture) from its ruins.[78] For Momigliano that could only be done by seeking to understand the methods by which one might create a true picture of the past as a model for the future: historiography, not as a trivial antiquarian pursuit but as the study of historical method, the study of how historical knowledge is attained, was the new task that he set himself.

Momigliano never abandoned the essential attitudes of his Crocean youth, the intense spiritual commitment to the task of the historian, and a belief in the unity of history, together with the rejection of the trivial view that history is the simple collection of facts or solving of problems.

History was for Momigliano always a set of questions rather than of answers; the methods remained the same that he had learned in his youth, but the answers belonged to the individual historian. In the modern age, when all ideas are out of fashion and history is seen as the province of the dilettante and the technician, or worse of the propagandist for a return to a national past, we can learn from these lectures of Momigliano the lessons of the spiritual claims and the seriousness of history. In after-dinner mode in 1977 he asserted, 'The historian can explain everything, but he cannot explain why it is that he has become a historian.'[79] A century after his birth, an understanding of the complexity of human society and the pursuit of liberty remain the two best reasons for being a historian; and these lectures of 1940 can serve as an inspiration for a new generation.

Arnaldo Momigliano (1908–1987)

16
Momigliano in England

Every year the ancient historians of all the universities of the British Isles used to gather for a curious ritual in the small market town of Wellingborough in Northamptonshire. The ritual was known as 'a visit to the zoo', because once there had been a small and rather seedy zoo in the town, whose animals were held by the more irreverent younger members to resemble their senior colleagues; the zoo had long since disappeared.[1]

The occasion originated in the 1920s when the first triumvirate, Hugh Last, Norman Baynes, and Frank Adcock, controllers of the *Cambridge Ancient History*, decided to hold an annual meeting at a place equidistant from their respective universities of Oxford, London, and Cambridge; here the triumvirs would hold court, and dispense their patronage: each young initiate would have to undergo the terrifying experience of being taken aside by one of his elders, and questioned closely on the subject of his research. Originally, the event had been held in Tring in Hertfordshire, but an unfortunate incident induced by alcohol had caused a change of venue. Bedford had then been chosen; this had to be abandoned when the management introduced music in the bar, which was incompatible with learned conversation.

When I first visited the zoo in Wellingborough, only Adcock was still living in the late 1960s; but the ritual was firmly fixed, and so well established that it was agreed no change was possible until his death. Two rules gave the occasion its special character. No woman, however eminent, was ever permitted to attend (does this explain the absence of women from the first *Cambridge Ancient History*?); and no formal business of any sort, such as lectures or discussion sessions, was allowed. By then the railway system of England had been dismantled, so carloads of ancient historians would make their way laboriously across the country to an old coaching inn, arriving in time for an English tea, followed by a visit to the bar, where the local regulars would be astounded to be invaded by thirty or forty professors, discussing the persecution of the Christians or Caesar's Gallic command over pints of beer. There followed a formal dinner of mediocre quality and appalling service, and a descent once again to the bar, where we remained until closing time. We stayed overnight in the hotel, and departed silently the next day after an English breakfast.

My generation grew up with the 'second triumvirate' of Syme, Momigliano, and Hugo (A.H.M.) Jones (and later Moses Finley); their approaches to history were so very different that the occasion at Wellingborough actually served a useful purpose, as a neutral meeting ground to resolve tensions and renew allegiances in the innocent pleasures of the English country pub. Arnaldo was by far the most assiduous of the professors in his attendance,[2] and I often wondered how he viewed the occasion, so different from his post-war seminar at the Scuola Normale in Pisa; for me, his annual visit to the zoo has become the symbol of his relationship to English culture.

He did not himself drink alcohol, and in the later stages of the evening he retained a clarity of thought that made it quite difficult for others to understand what he was saying. The high point of his visit was the period between tea and the opening of the bar at six o'clock according to the local rules. It was then that we took a traditional walk, through a churchyard and a trading estate to a canal on the outskirts of the town, where we would watch a cricket match, played by boys from an English boarding school. On the boundary a group of earnest historians discussing the *Historia Augusta* with European gestures and pockets full of proofs and patent medicines; in the distance the gilded youth of England immaculate in white flannels. It seemed in some curious way to evoke the ordered richness of English culture in that period.

Most other meetings with Momigliano took place in his London haunts, the British Museum, the Warburg Institute, between piles of books in his room, but especially in the canteens and corridors of University College, or its magnificent coffee room. Here too he moved surrounded always by a group in conversation, making no concessions, yet completely at ease in a society whose attitudes and presuppositions were very diverse and quite different from his own. Only in monolithic Oxford did he seem out of place, unable to sympathize with its minute obsession with the individual student in tutorials and its elevation of teaching above research. In one sense it is true that Momigliano always remained outside English culture; yet in another sense he himself represented one important strand in the culture of a particular period.

To those who returned from the war to pick up old threads, Momigliano no longer seemed an ancient historian: a striking figure daily in the Ashmolean with his green eyeshade, he had become a polymath, whose direction was still uncertain but lay outside the established confines of the subject. Ancient history in England at that time consisted indeed of a series of periods to which one was expected to belong, a set of problems suitable for students and teachers alike, and a limitation to the history supplied by texts, literary or epigraphic, which was mainly political or military history; only the Marxist historians and the archaeologists offered an alternative approach. It is the achievement of Momigliano and of Moses Finley to have broken down these barriers in their very different ways.

The Bund (see above, p. 297) gradually dissolved. Two stages marked the departure of its members. The first was the award of compensation from Germany, which made some of them richer than any Oxford professor could hope to be. They bought houses in north Oxford, and their dependence on the Ashmolean Library for working space and companionship diminished. Then they were offered reinstatement. The decision to return was less difficult for Catholics than for Jews; to some the New World also offered economic security, and better conditions for work than post-war Britain. Those who remained slowly became assimilated into the English academic system. So they went their different ways.

Momigliano's old position was not available, but he was reinstated to a professorship at Turin in 1946, and returned there briefly. He was offered the directorship of Croce's Istituto Storico at Naples, but declined. Other possibilities came to nothing; and in the meantime one of the first English posts to be offered in ancient history since the start of the war was advertised at Bristol, in the department run by the traditional English Hellenist, H.D.F. Kitto, and William Beare, a Latinist, both of them at the time primarily interested in the theatre. They were astonished to receive Momigliano's application, and he was appointed to a lectureship in preference to the young English scholars returned from the war; very soon he was promoted to Reader. While at Bristol he continued to live mainly in Oxford, returning there on weekends and during holidays.

I have the impression that in this period at Oxford and Bristol personal friendships were more important than institutions. The influence of Last waned as he moved from the Professorship of Roman History to become Principal of Brasenose College in 1948; younger teachers and a new professor were less interested in 'antiquarian' learning. Momigliano's closest friend of this period was perhaps Isobel Henderson, the daughter of a famous Oxford figure, J.A.R. Munro, Rector of Lincoln College from 1919 to 1944. Intellectually, she was a disciple of Last; she could appreciate Momigliano's learning and his culture, and introduce him to her colleagues and to the inner circle of Oxford life. Another lifelong Oxford friend was Beryl Smalley, the medieval historian. He always sought the stimulus of younger scholars and students. Dan Davin was an undergraduate when he met Momigliano first before the war as a young New Zealander studying classics at Balliol College, and remembered Momigliano's delight in discussion with even such a beginner. Peter Fraser of All Souls recalled his graduate time, the atmosphere of the Ashmolean after the war, and the days of work and discussion together with Momigliano. Iris Murdoch remembered Momigliano's rooms in Saint Margaret's Road, the green eyeshade, and the vast reading lists that accompanied their mutual explorations of European and English culture. His Bristol friends, the refugees, the philosopher Stephan Körner, the classicist David Eichholz, and the English scholar Henry Gifford, were similarly struck by the combination of directness and warmth with enormous learning and intellectual enthusiasm in his personal relations.

For Momigliano himself the development of his thought can perhaps best be charted in his relations with the Oxford University Press. His first contract with the Press had been for a book on the history of liberty and peace in the ancient world discussed above. It is a theme that illustrates well the enlightened patronage exercised by Kenneth Sisam – topical and relevant in the world of the 1940s, but also suited to the talents of a scholar trained in the Italian tradition, and aware of the work of Croce. Momigliano himself in his last writing, the brief preface to the reprint of his *Filippo il Macedone* of 15 August 1987, recalls the importance that the theme of liberty had for him in the early 1930s, and how it related to discussions begun in the liberal circles of De Sanctis and Croce. This theme was identical with the Cambridge lectures of 1940, the manuscript of which was only discovered after his death; and many traces of this research recur throughout the later work of Momigliano. But no manuscript of the promised book ever existed; some of his subsequent distance from Oxford may perhaps reflect a latent unease at this unfulfilled obligation. Instead, towards the end of the war a second project was being discussed, a history of the influence of Seneca. In the late 1940s a preliminary draft was shown to Dan Davin, then Sisam's assistant at the Press. But the main fruit of that was a fascinating study of Seneca and Christianity, and, more importantly perhaps, the beginnings of Momigliano's serious interest in Late Antiquity.[3]

Dan Davin, the New Zealand novelist and later chief executive of Oxford University Press, had as a student taken tutorials with Momigliano in Oxford before enlisting as a soldier to fight at Monte Cassino – 'the bravest man I ever knew', said Sir Edgar Williams, Montgomery's chief of staff. Davin described to me a fraught meeting shortly after the war when Momigliano announced to him as editor at OUP that he had finally decided to abandon his book on 'Peace and Liberty', and study instead the unknown (and unpublishable) subject of the historiography of ancient history. The first clear sign of this new direction was the article published in 1946 on 'Friedrich Creuzer and Greek Historiography'. The place of publication, the *Journal of the Warburg and Courtauld Institutes*, is significant.[4]

This was the crucial turning point. Historiography was utterly alien to the English tradition of historical writing; it was also generally despised, regarded as a waste of time. Collingwood's *The Idea of History* was in England merely thought to indicate the extent to which he had been corrupted by Croce, and another sign that as a historian he was not to be taken seriously. More recently, those academics who have engaged in self-criticism (mostly of the Cambridge Modern History school) have done so merely in order to reinforce the parochialism of their own tradition; the devoutly Christian Methodist historian, Herbert Butterfield, was perhaps the only contemporary English historian to combine original research with an understanding of the theoretical issues. But Momigliano's interest was very different; it lay in the effect of history on the individual historian, and of the individual historian on the study of history, and so in the development of the critical approach.

Its origins lay in a variety of influences, none of them decisive. His Italian training had taught him the importance of mastering the bibliography as a first stage in research (whereas the English tradition was and is to master the texts). His English friends were exceptionally learned and antiquarian in their approach to history. But perhaps most of all the Bund had opened his eyes to the richness and diversity of European culture. And on a deeper level (which Croce surely recognized in his offer of the Naples *Istituto*) he was engaged, like so many of the best minds during and after the war from Lord Beveridge to Friedrich Meinecke and Ernst Robert Curtius, in the renewal of a European culture whose potentiality for evil, demonstrated so clearly on the personal and the public level, had called into question its very right to exist. That is what Momigliano meant when he once acidly observed that the natives of Europe were civilized in the nineteenth century.

The move to University College London in 1951, to one of the three great chairs in ancient history, one which moreover was situated in a Department of History rather than of Classics, brought responsibility and authority. It also enabled Momigliano to recreate the intellectual atmosphere of Oxford in the war years; for in London the émigré culture remained until almost the present day. It was in this context that he became a colleague of the Renaissance scholar Roberto Weiss (1906–1969), Professor of Italian at University College and one of the pioneers of the classical origins of the Renaissance in England. He also joined his lifelong friend Carlo Dionisotti (1908–1998), whom he had persuaded to become Professor of Italian at Bedford College in 1949, and whose memoir recalls this period and their Italian youth.[5] Throughout his life he also had many friends in the Department of Hebrew.

Apart from University College, Momigliano forged close links with the Warburg Institute. He was first introduced to the Warburg during the war by Fritz Saxl. As he wrote in 1972, 'When I arrived in Oxford in 1939, it was enough to mention the word "idea" to be given the address of the Warburg Institute.'[6] In 1939, Saxl suggested Momigliano for the British Academy Italian lecture; but the idea was not pursued: 'In any case Momigliano's English is far too weak for him to be a suitable lecturer in the circumstances,' wrote David Cleghorn Thomson, general secretary of the SPSL. Momigliano's first article in the *Journal* of the Warburg Institute was published in 1942; subsequently he was drawn into ever closer contact with the Warburg by two friends: Gertrud Bing, who was Saxl's devoted adjutor, and perhaps most responsible for the successful preservation of the 'Warburg spirit' in its new London home, and who was Director from 1955 to 1959; and Anne Marie Meyer,

Secretary of the Institute, who retired in 1984 after forty-seven years in its service, and whose selfless work as Arnaldo's literary executor has placed us all in her debt.

Momigliano's most important initiatives, especially in the early years of his tenure of the chair at University College, before his connections with Pisa and later with Chicago became well established, took place in the context of the Warburg Institute. His most famous papers of the period were often given in the context of lecture series at the Warburg: the paper on 'Ancient History and the Antiquarian' was delivered there in 1949;[7] in 1951 he spoke in a series on 'Heresies'; the paper 'An Unsolved Problem of Historical Forgery: The *Scriptores Historia Augustae*' was part of a series on forgeries;[8] and in 1958–59 he was invited to edit the lectures that were published as *The Conflict between Paganism and Christianity in the Fourth Century* (1963) as the first volume in the new Oxford-Warburg series. Also in 1963 he delivered the essay on 'Time in Ancient Historiography' in a series on 'Time and Eternity',[9] and in 1964 'Roman "bestioni" and Roman "eroi" in Vico's *Scienza Nuova*' was part of a series on 'Myth and History'.[10]

In 1962, at the age of fifty-four, Momigliano delivered the Sather Classical Lectures at the University of California, Berkeley, on 'The Classical Foundations of Modern Historiography'; the text of these lectures was once again only finally published after his death, with a foreword by Riccardo Di Donato.[11] This is a crucial event for the understanding of his intellectual development; for his evident struggles and ultimate failure to prepare the book for publication can now be seen to relate to the completion of a stage in his intellectual biography.

Three grand themes had matured in his mind during this middle period in England, and two of them were to have a great impact on English classical scholarship. These themes were the history of late antiquity, the history of historiography, and the origins of Rome.

It was Momigliano who opened up for English scholarship the study of late antiquity. I have suggested that his own interest in the period first surfaced in his studies of the tradition of a Christian Seneca, but it also reflects the Italian scholarship of his youth. He was always a master of the opening sentence; but to the English reader, brought up on Robert Browning, Walter Pater, and Bernard Berenson, there can be few more arresting beginnings than that of his British Academy Italian Lecture of 1955, 'Cassiodorus and Italian Culture of His Time':

> When I want to understand Italian history I catch a train and go to Ravenna. There, between the tomb of Theodoric and that of Dante, in the reassuring neighbourhood of the best manuscript of Aristophanes and in the less reassuring one of the best portrait of the Empress Theodora, I can begin to feel what Italian history has really been.[12]

The cultural history of late antiquity in the English-speaking world begins from this essay, from that on the *Historia Augusta* (1954),[13] and from *The Conflict between Paganism and Christianity*.[14] Before these were written, there were only the *Byzantine Studies* of Norman Baynes, themselves edited by Momigliano and another, and some minor works on the conversion of Constantine – translations of a couple of books by Andreas Alföldi, and an essay of A.H.M. Jones. The tradition of J.B. Bury and Sir Samuel Dill was effectively dead. Momigliano's most important influence undoubtedly lies in the example he gave to his younger English colleagues, notably Peter Brown and Alan and Averil Cameron.[15] Of course, English scholarship would have rediscovered late antiquity without him: Syme's interest in the subject became evident a decade later, from 1964, and had a profound influence on John Matthews, Timothy Barnes, and others; Jones's magisterial work on the administrative history of *The Later Roman Empire* was also published in 1964, and others of his studies were written earlier in the 1950s. Jones can indeed be seen as Bury's most obvious successor, and his influence can be traced in the work of his pupil at University College London, G.E.M. de Sainte Croix, who combined an English philological and legal approach with an *odium theologicum* attributed to Karl Marx. It is indeed clear that University College has had a significant influence on the history of late antiquity, through the succession of professors Baynes, Jones, and Momigliano. But the specific contribution of Momigliano was to insist in a crucial period on the importance of that un-English activity of the history of ideas, rather than prosopography and administrative history.

The second important area of scholarship which we owe to Momigliano is that which he had declared his own in the 1940s – the history of historiography. English readers have always felt most at home with his essays on ancient historians, for traditionally the study of the ancient world in England begins with reading Herodotus, Thucydides, Polybius, and Tacitus in their entirety. The great series of essays on these and other ancient historians has therefore been Momigliano's most valued contribution to classical studies in the Anglo-Saxon world. But the real evidence for Momigliano's understanding of English culture, and his greatest contribution to it, lies in another area of historiography, the study of the eighteenth and nineteenth centuries. The two English masters of ancient history were largely unrecognized until his essays of the 1950s. Gibbon was a great stylist, read, alongside Macaulay, by every young student of modern (not ancient) history; but almost the only aspect of Gibbon's historical method that had attracted attention was his notorious anti-clericalism. In two related papers, 'Ancient History and the Antiquarian' (1950) and 'Gibbon's Contribution to Historical Method' (1954),[16] Momigliano succeeded in establishing him as our greatest and most relevant master of historical method. Those articles remain today the fundamental texts for an understanding of Gibbon; and it is one of my private sadnesses that I never found the opportunity to discuss with Arnaldo the important new discoveries of P.R. Ghosh on the manuscripts and working methods of Gibbon, published in the *Journal of Roman Studies*[17] or the masterly recreation of the first edition of Gibbon by David Womersley.[18]

In the 1890s when my grandfather studied Greek history at Oxford, George Grote's *History of Greece* was still a standard work, for I inherited his prize copy of it; as late as the 1930s a one-volume abridgement remained in use as a textbook. But few of my contemporaries at university read Grote, and our teachers betrayed no knowledge of him. In contrast, Momigliano had gained deep respect for him by the time of completing *Filippo il Macedone* in 1932. His inaugural lecture at University College London in 1952, 'George Grote and the Study of Greek History',[19] revealed the origins of the English liberal obsession with Athenian democracy, and of our distaste for the fourth century with its descent into absolute monarchy. Since then, the elective affinity between two naval imperial democracies has become an accepted presupposition for all interpretations of the nineteenth-century cultural scene; but it was Momigliano with his 'admittedly rather imperfect map of a mythical London' who demonstrated the importance of history in the programme of the greatest English heresy after Pelagianism and Protestantism – Utilitarianism.[20]

In two other concerns Momigliano was less successful. The study of the origins of Rome has never taken root in England, despite his example; but perhaps that is not surprising. For all the acuteness of his work in this area, as exemplified in the 'Interim Report on the Origins of Rome' of 1963,[21] and continued in a series of articles down to the chapter for the new *Cambridge Ancient History*, volume VII,[22] the fundamental force affecting the new picture of early Rome in the last generation has been the work of practising archaeologists; this history therefore has its natural home in Italy.

A second area of difficulty is revealed through the programmatic element in Momigliano's inaugural lecture of 1952, concerning the critical situation of Greek history. I was not the only young scholar to be turned towards the study of the Greeks by the proposals he there put forward. Yet seventy years later it may be doubted whether we have yet achieved the results that he expected. Perhaps it was reflection on these two areas that lay behind the last remarks which Momigliano made to me, when Tim Cornell and I visited him in hospital a fortnight before his death. As we were leaving he turned to Tim, and with a characteristically mischievous smile said, 'Why is it that Greek history has become more interesting than Roman history? The Roman historians must look out.' True or false, it seemed like a challenge thrown down to two of his closest disciples, each of us identified with an area that he found problematic to the end.

In 1965 there began a series of seminars at the Warburg Institute, which Momigliano ran in collaboration with Sally Humphreys almost every year, and often throughout the year, until 1982–83, eight years after his retirement. For seventeen years these seminars were the focal point of ancient history in London, and a meeting place for historians from many other universities and other countries. It was a modest and informal context, with a regular audience of around thirty, but its impact was great.[23] Each set of seminars was normally devoted to a particular theme, often methodological; papers on all periods of history and from other disciplines (especially anthropology) were welcome. Momigliano himself would often be seen on the afternoon of the seminar in the library, reading in preparation for the evening. He always dominated the discussion, and the discussion usually dominated the paper. He was capable of great generosity, especially toward younger scholars, whose ideas he would develop towards conclusions that they had not themselves envisaged; he could be terrifying in his dismissal of pretentious contributions by senior scholars. The seminar itself was a relatively recent introduction into British university life: Eduard Fraenkel had made a great stir when he introduced this German method of teaching to Oxford. By the 1960s some of us had attended graduate seminars; the difference in those of Momigliano was that they were essentially meetings of younger colleagues around a man whose leadership and status as a master were freely acknowledged, in a climate where equality was the norm. We belonged to independent institutions and often different disciplines, and were meeting on neutral ground. There was therefore no place for hierarchies or displays of self-importance. I believe that this absence of artificial constraints on the activities of scholarship was something which Momigliano especially valued, and which he had come to expect from his years in Oxford, outside any formal academic structure.

In retrospect two themes seem dominant in this period of the Warburg seminars. The first and most obvious was the relationship between ancient history and anthropology. This was the time when the two subjects developed as a joint degree at University College, a process in which both Momigliano and Sally Humphreys were deeply involved. They collaborated in research projects, notably that to offer 'a new *Cité antique*'. Links were forged with Greek historians in Paris and with a wide range of European intellectuals: in 1973–74 the seminar programme on 'the History of Ideas' included Momigliano himself, Peter Brown, Jonathan Miller the intellectual polymath, Franco Venturi, and Jean-Pierre Vernant. Momigliano's delight in new ideas and new methodologies was especially evident in this period, but in his own work he always kept his distance. I do not think the methods of anthropology had a great effect on his writing of history, and the difficulties of collaboration with an anthropologist are well exemplified in the different approaches shown in the respective sections of the 'Report to the Social Science Research Council' by Momigliano and Humphreys, published in her book *Anthropology and the Greeks* (1978).[24] Momigliano's contribution to this project was related firmly to earlier work, in the history of historiography, and in the study of freedom of speech, heresy, and religious dissent, according to methods he had already worked out.

I think in fact that the most significant consequence of this collaboration was to reawaken Momigliano's interest in the relationships between classical culture and other ancient cultures in a post-colonial age: it was the range of problems rather than the methods of anthropology that attracted him. This is shown in his two most important publications of the 1970s, both appearing in 1975: the seminal paper

'The Fault of the Greeks', and the slim but dense volume *Alien Wisdom*.[25] In this work the problem of Judaism begins to emerge again; but also very striking is the almost aggressively positivist and empirical method of argument.

The other important theme of these years is only distantly related to anthropology. The attempt to write a history of Greek biography occupied a great deal of Momigliano's time, and left many of his English friends puzzled. It seemed intrinsically probable that no such tradition had ever existed; at least the evidence scarcely permitted a full historiographical study. Nor were the consequences of success obvious: it was not easy to find any significant influence of such a biographical genre in extant Greek literature. While admiring the skill with which Momigliano explored the theme, I for one was left with the impression he had ultimately demonstrated that the problematic evidence reflected the problematic status of biography before the Roman period. It seems to me now that such criticisms miss the importance of these studies in his development. Interest in biography was the expression in historiographical terms of his earlier interest in the history of freedom, especially the freedom of the individual. The essay by Benjamin Constant on the difference between ancient and modern conceptions of liberty had posed a basic question for him as early as 1931.[26] The problem of the freedom of the individual in the ancient world required us to demonstrate the existence of the individual apart from the community; the study of biography was a way of studying the history of the concept of the person. It was characteristic of Momigliano to return again and again to certain fundamental problems, whose significance he had perhaps recognized earlier, but which could now be reconsidered in the light of ideas about the concept of personality developed in sociology and anthropology. This he finally explained in an essay on 'Marcel Mauss and the Quest for the Person in Greek Biography and Autobiography', which appeared in a variety of forms as late as 1985.[27] We may feel that ultimately Greek biography portrays types, not individuals, and therefore exemplifies the views of Constant; but Momigliano at least forces us to recognize that biography is not merely a literary genre, but that form of historiography most concerned with the freedom of the individual.

It is worth making two further points. The first concerns his literary style. Rereading the *Contributi* has reminded me what a distinctive style he had. Unlike some of the émigrés of his generation, Momigliano was not a great lecturer; his accent made his words difficult to follow, and he seldom departed from the written text, which was often too long, and therefore read too fast. Audiences respected his understanding of the problems and his learning, but were not often inspired by him. On the written page, however, he is one of the masters of modern English; wit and elegance combine with clarity and informality to recall vividly his personality. The diversity, the range of subjects, and the lack of academic stiffness in the *Contributi* reflect perfectly his preferred mode of communication, the conversation and the scarcely more formal discussion. Secondly, I have become ever more conscious of the continuities in his approach to history. His underlying methodology perhaps never changed; it rested on the traditional Italian scholarship of his youth, and combined a positivist philological respect for the evidence, derived ultimately from German *Altertumswissenschaft*, with the philosophical tradition from Croce; or, to place it in a longer historical perspective and in terms of his own research on the eighteenth century, he united the traditions of the *érudit* and the *philosophe*. The same continuity can perhaps be seen in the problems that engaged him: it is as if he had a programme in mind from the start, and what changed was the focus of attention. Themes that became important at a later stage can usually be found prefigured in the writings of the Italian period, and I may well have exaggerated the extent to which his research was influenced by external forces.

This impression has been confirmed for the later part of his life by the astonishing facts revealed in the posthumous publication of the 1962 Sather lectures, *The Classical Foundations of Modern Historiography* (Berkeley 1990). Most of us had I think imagined that this text remained unpublished because it represented the culmination of a phase in Momigliano's thought, and was perhaps laid aside because its views no longer satisfied him or because the ideas that it contained required further research. But thanks to the generosity of Anne Marie Meyer, I was able in the summer of 1991 to compare the final revised text as published with the original typescripts of 1961–62, now in the Momigliano archive of the *Scuola Normale* at Pisa. It is true that Momigliano continued to revise and add to the lectures over the last thirty years of his life; and two chapters, as Riccardo Di Donato says in his preface, those on national historiography and on Tacitism, received substantial additions in 1975 and 1978 respectively. But the surprising fact is that the changes in the other four chapters are so slight – mere corrections of errors and minor modifications of opinion; and even in the two revised chapters the changes consist in additions to an existing text that do not alter in any significant way the original argument. The implication of this for the development of Momigliano's thought is enormous. The crucial period in his intellectual formation was indeed that between 1939 and 1961. By 1962 he already possessed a clear map of the entire history of Western historiography, and had well-formed views on its significance; his knowledge deepened, but his methodology and his approach scarcely changed over the subsequent thirty years. *The Classical Foundations* should be read not as an independent work, but as an introduction to the ten volumes of the *Contributi*, as the text to which the essays of some forty years are the footnotes. Momigliano's intellectual pilgrimage was already complete when my generation came to know him, which helps indeed to explain the sureness of touch and the generosity with which he could discuss any problem. What is truly amazing is the distance that separated Momigliano from his contemporaries in 1962; and if the message of the Sather lectures seems to us now to offer few surprises, that is because of all he had taught us since the 1960s.

The problem of Judaism is an example of an even longer continuity; it lay at the basis of Momigliano's concern with history, and in the earliest period took equal prominence with the classical world, of which it was indeed a part. But it was not until the 1970s that it returned to the centre of his interests; it was only then that Jewish themes began to be discussed regularly with us. At the same time we noted a return to a more philological and antiquarian approach, which gave a new density to some of his later work. The signs of impatience with theoreticians became more prominent: in later life he admired Foucault and Marshall Sahlins perhaps, but was visibly distressed by the view of his American colleague Hayden White that history was a form of rhetoric. The best expression of this last phase is however the series of seminars that Momigliano gave at Pisa on the founding fathers of nineteenth-century German philological positivism. He seemed to be calling us back to an older tradition, warning us of the dangers of trivializing history by subordinating it to theory. The attitude is one that reflects his own youthful training as much as the English milieu in which he chose to live. The trouble was that his investigations seemed to reveal that our forefathers had been a good deal less philological and more philosophical, more emotional even, and certainly more romantic, in their approach to classical scholarship than we had ever imagined. That is the message of *Tra storia e storicismo*,[28] and his legacy to those of us who find empiricism as problematic as historicism in an age of ideologies.

After his retirement from the professorship at University College London in 1975, Momigliano continued to give seminars in London; but he was able to spend more time elsewhere, especially at the universities of Chicago and Pisa. Peter Fraser arranged a position for him at All Souls College, Oxford, for seven years, and we held seminars together for a time in Oxford; they were not as successful as those at the Warburg. Momigliano never talked of his earlier Oxford days: perhaps he did not wish to notice the contrast between the discomfort and the intellectual excitement of wartime Oxford and the self-absorption and evident prosperity of the contemporary scene; perhaps also Oxford held too many ghosts. He made little impact on the younger classical Fellows of All Souls, and often seemed relieved to be on his travels to Pisa or Chicago, or returning to London. When his post came to an end, he was offered first a Visiting and then an Honorary Fellowship at Peterhouse, one of the most conventional of Cambridge colleges; once again he seemed the detached observer on the edge of the playing field.[29] Yet his own words about Croce in 1966 describe far better the impression he left on his English friends: 'But Croce was well aware that his contemporaries had not his Goethean temperament, and he treated them with that mixture of severity and sympathy, sheer amusement and curiosity, condescension and wholehearted solidarity, which was his fascination and his personal mystery.'[30]

The School of Paris

Fernand Braudel (1902–1985)

17
Fernand Braudel and the Mediterranean

Fernand Braudel (1902–1985) was the greatest historian of the twentieth century. So universal has his influence been on the study of history since the publication of his first major work sixty years ago that it is almost impossible for us to remember what history was like before Braudel; and for that reason we often tend to forget how important was this revolution in historical method.[1]

Braudel liked to think of himself as a typical Frenchman from the provinces: in his memory he belonged to a peasant family from Lorraine on the borders of France and Germany, where because of poor health he had indeed spent his early years in the village of Luméville-en-Ornois at his paternal grandmother's smallholding, with its chickens, stone walls, and espalier fruit trees, in a world that (as he described it) was still centred on the blacksmith, the wheelwright, the itinerant woodcutters, and an ancient mill. The contemporary realities of industrial Lorraine and the ever-present threat from Germany were subsumed into this idyll, as was the fact that his later childhood and adolescence were spent in Paris and its suburbs, where his father was a teacher of mathematics. On leaving school, Braudel did not compete for entry to the elite institution of the École Normale Supérieure, but went to the Sorbonne, where he found himself attracted by the lectures of professors of history outside the mainstream, in economic and social history or the study of ancient Greece, which attracted audiences of between four and seven. In 1923, at the age of twenty-one, he travelled to his first post as a teacher of history at the grammar school of Constantine in Algeria, and here he saw the Mediterranean for the first time. He had chosen resolutely to identify himself with the margins of French society and to escape from his Parisian bourgeois background to a career in the provinces.

His true intellectual formation began in Algeria, a world where a young man could take himself seriously. He turned from the study of Lorraine (which he came to think too full of national problems) to Spain, and began to contemplate a historical thesis on the Mediterranean policy of Philip II between 1559 and 1574; by 1927 he was publishing reviews of books on Spanish history. But he was also fascinated by the new history of Lucien Febvre, based on the science of human geography and exemplified in a book written in 1913 but not published until 1922, *La Terre et l'évolution humaine*, translated as *A Geographical Introduction to History* (London 1932). Braudel read the book in 1924; but as usual his approach was cautious: it was three years before he began to write to Febvre, and their close personal friendship did not begin for another ten years. Meanwhile, in his first reply to Braudel, Febvre had planted a serious doubt about his subject of research:

> Philip II and the Mediterranean, a good subject. But why not the Mediterranean and Philip II? A much larger subject. For between these two protagonists, Philip and the middle sea, the division is not equal.

Braudel was a successful schoolteacher and was becoming known as an expert in his chosen area: in 1932 he returned to Paris, and was nominated to a series of more and more prestigious *lycées*; in 1933 he married one of his earliest pupils in Algiers. Then he made a decision that was to change his life: in 1935 he took the offer of a five-year secondment to the new university being established with French help at São Paulo in Brazil. This project marked the opening up of French culture in South America, where it remains still important, and it was a golden chance for him and for others of his generation who had not followed the easy road to break into French academic life; at least one of his contemporaries and friends in that enterprise became equally famous – the anthropologist Claude Lévi-Strauss.

'It was in Brazil that I became intelligent.' Braudel was always an eminently practical man. He managed to rent a large mansion complete with a Chevrolet and an Italian chauffeur from someone who conveniently spent the period of the university terms in Europe. Each winter Braudel would return to Europe and work in the archives of the great Mediterranean trading cities, such as Venice and Dubrovnik (Ragusa). In his research he was an innovator in two respects, conceptual and practical. He made the move from government archives to commercial archives; and by chance he invented the microfilm, which he used in order to copy two or three thousand documents a day, to be read during the university year in Brazil:

> I bought this machine in Algiers: it belonged to an American cameraman and was used to make rough images of scenes for films. On it you had a button that allowed you to take one photo at a time, or you held it down and took the whole shoot at once. When I was offered it, I said to the cameraman, 'Photograph me that: if I can read it, I'll buy it.' He made me a magnificent photo. And that's how I made kilometres of microfilms. It worked so well that when I was in Brazil I could spend whole days reading documents.

In 1936, on the long voyage back to Brazil in a cargo boat, he told his wife that he had decided to make the Mediterranean the focus of his research. A year later he was offered and accepted a post with a much lower salary at the main research centre in Paris, the École Pratique des Hautes Études, in one of the two non-scientific sections, the *IV*^e^ *Section* (historical and philological sciences). By chance the boat on which he and his wife travelled home from Brazil in 1937 was carrying Lucien Febvre back from a lecture tour in Buenos Aires: in the two weeks of the voyage they became close friends. Febvre, now aged sixty and a professor at the Collège de France, had been one of the two young professors at Strasbourg who founded in 1929 the polemical journal *Annales*, which sought to create in a provocatively colloquial style a new and more open approach to history, defined mostly by its search for 'a larger and a more human history' (Marc Bloch), by its denial of all historical barriers and by its rejection of the traditional history of politics and government in favour of a deeper analysis of social and economic forces. From this time on Febvre became Braudel's friend, intellectual adviser, and confidant.

Shortly after Braudel began planning his new book in the summer residence of Febvre, war was declared, and Braudel was mobilized in the artillery and stationed on the frontier in Alsace; he saw no fighting, but was caught in the encirclement of the French army by the Germans. Despite formal German and Vichy guarantees of liberty on his surrender, he was imprisoned at Mainz in 1940, where he remained until 1942; then he was denounced by fellow officers as being a supporter of de Gaulle rather than Pétain, and was sent to a special 'discipline camp' for 'enemies of Germany' at Lübeck, where he remained until 1945. There he was reasonably happy, protected by the strict adherence of the Wehrmacht to the protocols of the Geneva Convention governing prisoners of war, amid all sorts of 'dissidents' – partisans of de Gaulle, French Jewish officers, sixty-seven French priests of all descriptions, escapers, 'all the best types in the French army', together with English airmen and Dutch, Swedish, and Polish officers, and the sons of Joseph Stalin and the socialist Prime Minister of France, Léon Blum.

It was during these five years of captivity that Braudel wrote the drafts of his monumental work *The Mediterranean and the Mediterranean World in the Age of Philip II*. Assisted by a few books, but mainly using his prodigious memory and the long period of his pre-war researches, he constructed a work that combined a vast chronological and historical sweep with a huge mass of minute details, covering the entire Mediterranean world from the Renaissance to the sixteenth century. This immense intellectual achievement was written in school exercise books on a small plank in a room shared with twenty prisoners. At intervals parcels of the manuscript would arrive through the Swiss Red Cross in Paris for criticism by Febvre; by the end of the war the work had been finished in two or three successive versions (some 3,000–4,000 pages: the first version of 1,600 pages was already finished by the end of 1941), only to be rewritten with the help of Braudel's pre-war notes, retrieved from their hiding place in a Paris cellar, at the rate of thirty to fifty pages a day until it was finally presented in 1947 as a thesis of 1,160 pages; by then he had reached the age of forty-five.

The transformation of Braudel's thought in captivity seems to have been fundamental, although he destroyed the wartime versions of his book (with the exception of one section that survived by chance), and the correspondence between him and Febvre remains unpublished in the Archives Nationales. The condition of French officers was relatively easy: they still received their monthly salaries, and could order some books through the Red Cross; while at Mainz he obtained the privilege of borrowing German books from the civic library. Nevertheless, it was a time of limited communication with the outside world, a time when the *histoire événementielle* might lose importance and the *longue durée* might acquire more significance. In one sense Braudel's retreat into the past was, as he said, 'a work of contemplation',[2] an escape into a world that he could control and whose detailed realities he could believe in with greater ease than the artificial world of prison life. In 1941 he wrote a rare letter from Mainz to his wife (who was living in Algeria), 'as always I am reading, writing, working. I have decided to expand my work to the period from 1450 to 1650: one must think big, otherwise what is the point of history?' And at Lübeck he wrote to her, 'My imagination never leaves me alone. All the stories that I shall not tell my daughters, I tell them as I walk along the barbed wire.'

In the two camps he gave miniature university lectures to his fellow prisoners. A book containing a version of these was published in 1997: it combines notes made by his auditors from two periods of his confinement, one from 1941 and the other from 1943–44. It is clear from this text that the reflective experience of prison camp was the turning point in his historical thought, for in these lectures he sets out virtually all the great themes which he presented after the war.[3] In these he had declared his opposition to *l'histoire événementielle* and the importance of a historical geography acting as a cause in human events. His lectures began from the traditional history of events, the actions of kings and conquerors, victories, political decisions, and showed how transitory and trivial these were and how they were predetermined by deeper forces. Beyond the events lay social history, the group activities that governed the course of events. And underlying these was '*l'histoire profonde*', what he later called the '*longue durée*', the deep forces of society, geography, climate, and the economy as an expression of human activity with its perpetual rhythms. The impact of these lectures was immediate: already in 1941, after each victory of the Wehrmacht that summer, the prisoners were to be heard shouting in the corridors of the citadel, 'But it's just an event, nothing but an event' (*Mais c'est de l'événement, rien que de l'événement!*). This interpretation of the different levels of historical research came to be identified with Braudel as his main contribution to historical method; but at this time it was still conceived of in terms of different levels of causation, and therefore ultimately was tied to the historical explanation of events.

Shortly before the presentation of his thesis, Braudel had been passed over as Professor of History at the Sorbonne in favour of a more conventional historian. At his viva voce examination, his rival (who was on the jury of examiners) sought '*suavement*' to justify the choice: 'Monsieur, you are a geographer, allow me to be the historian.'[4] In retrospect it is clear that this moment marked a turning point in the intellectual history of France: over the next thirty years the Sorbonne remained a largely conventional institution.

Meanwhile in 1947 a project agreed before the First World War was finally implemented with the help of money from the Rockefeller Foundation, to establish a centre for research in *sciences sociales*, economics, social studies, and anthropology as an autonomous 'sixth section' of the École Pratique des Hautes Études: Febvre, as a social historian independent of the other disciplines, was asked to establish it, but agreed only to be president, with Braudel as his director: so Braudel came back from a holiday in South America to find himself the head of a new institution for which he had to recruit a staff and establish a structure.[5] Thus almost fortuitously, outside the traditional history of events and the university system, a new type of history, identified as one of the social sciences, was established, and Braudel proceeded to construct his great empire of 'the human sciences', and to open a series of vistas that could never have found their place within a more conventional university atmosphere, where orthodoxy in teaching was valued above originality of ideas.

Braudel made his reputation with *La Méditerranée*, which was published in 1949; a second revised and reorganized edition was published in 1966, in preparation for the English edition of 1973, in the magnificent translation of Siân Reynolds; with the translation of this new edition Braudel became the best-known historian in the world. My generation was brought up to believe in the words of its preface: the old history of events was indeed dead, 'the action of a few princes and rich men, the trivia of the past, bearing little relation to the slow and powerful march of history . . . these statesmen were, despite their illusions, more acted upon than actors'. In their place Braudel offered, not 'the traditional geographical introduction to history that often figures to so little purpose at the beginning of so many books, with its description of the mineral deposits, types of agriculture and typical flora, briefly listed and never mentioned again, as if the flowers did not come back every spring, the flocks of sheep migrate every year, or the ships sail on a real sea that changes with the seasons', but a whole new way of looking at the past, in which the historian recreated a lost reality through a feat of historical imagination based on detailed knowledge of the habits and techniques of the ploughman, the shepherd, the ironworker, the potter and the weaver, the skills of the vintage and the olive press, the milling of corn, the keeping of records of bills of lading, tides and winds. It began to seem as important for a historian to be able to ride a horse or sail a ship as to sit in a library or an archive. Only the third section of Braudel's book returned to the history of events, 'surface disturbances, crests of foam that the tides of history carry on their strong backs'; Philip II became only a chronological peg, to be mentioned as an individual briefly in the last few pages of the book.[6] Braudel taught us to see that historical time was divided into three forms of movement, the *longue durée* or geographical time, social time, and individual time, but that beyond this the past was a unity and a reality – all these movements belonged together: 'history can do more than study walled gardens'.[7]

This was the ultimate expression of the intellectual ambitions of the *Annales* school, which was reborn after the war and the execution by the Nazis of Marc Bloch, one of its two founders and a hero of the resistance.[8] Braudel became a member of its editorial board. In 1949 he was elected to the Collège de France, and in the same year he was given the immensely powerful position of president of the *agrégation* in history, the general qualifying examination for teaching in secondary schools. The record of what he sought to achieve is contained in a little textbook that he wrote for teachers in this period called *A Grammar of Civilizations* (written in 1962–63 and republished in 1987),[9] which was designed to introduce contemporary history and world history into the school curriculum: history was divided geographically into six 'civilizations' – Islam, black Africa, the Far East (China, India, Oceania, and Japan), Europe, the Americas, Muscovy or Soviet Russia, all relevant to a France still at least in memory committed to its status as a colonial power. Braudel's reforms were resisted by the teaching profession, then (as now) concerned with the teaching of a national history in chronological order;[10] but it took them six years before they could dislodge him in 1955: his attempts at reform were destroyed by an unholy alliance of right and left; for he was one of the few French intellectuals who belonged to neither camp. His views were therefore unpopular with the teachers of conventional history and in the France of Georges Pompidou, who held proto-Thatcherite views on the unimportance of all history apart from the history of one's own country, and who was later to regard Braudel as responsible for the events of 1968; at the same time he was denounced by orthodox communists as 'a willing slave of American imperialism'.

Lucien Febvre died in 1956, and Braudel inherited control both of the new sixth section of the École Pratique and of the journal *Annales*. In the first institution, through his appointments, he created and fostered one of the most extraordinary collections of talent in the twentieth century: to mention only the most famous of his colleagues, they included the historians Georges Duby, Jacques Le Goff, and Emmanuel Le Roy Ladurie, the philosopher and semiotician Roland Barthes, the psychologists Jacques Lacan and Georges Devereux, the sociologist Pierre Bourdieu, the anthropologist Claude Lévi-Strauss; and the classical scholars Jean-Pierre Vernant and Pierre Vidal-Naquet. Braudel tried hard to create a separate institution or building, where all his colleagues could work together, and where a succession of foreign visitors could be invited as associate professors; this idea, begun about 1958, did not achieve physical shape until the opening of the Maison des Sciences de l'Homme in 1970. And it was only after he retired in 1972 that the *VIe Section* finally metamorphosed into its present status as a new and independent teaching institution, the École des Hautes Études en Sciences Sociales.[11]

In and through *Annales*, Braudel sought to promote and defend his conception of history. For thirty years the great debates on the nature of history took place in its pages. In retrospect one can see four successive but overlapping issues with which he engaged.

The first debate was provoked by the claims of the anthropologist Claude Lévi-Strauss that the theory of structuralism offered an explanation of human social organization. Braudel had been possibly the first historian to use the word 'structure' in his original thesis; but he saw that the structuralism of Lévi-Strauss was fundamentally anti-historical, 'From the moment I knew him – and I have known him since he was twenty-five years old, that is forty years ago – Claude Lévi-Strauss was entirely closed to history. He does not know what it is and does not want to know.'[12] Lévi-Strauss sought to explain all human societies in terms of a single theory of structures: the notions of difference and of change that are basic to all historical thought were simply dismissed as irrelevant to the search for a universal underlying structure, which existed in the human mind if not in the physical universe itself. Against this, in an article in *Annales* 1958 on his conception of the *longue durée*,[13] Braudel sought to explain his own historical conception of the varieties of underlying forces influencing human society, which he had already formulated during the writing of his thesis in relation to the static forces and the slow movements behind the ephemeral history of events. Braudel's conception of the *longue durée* (usually translated rather misleadingly as the 'long perspective') is complex and not easy to express in non-historical terms as a theoretical concept; for it is the recognition that human society develops and changes at different rates in relation to different underlying forces, and that all the elements within any human situation interact with each other. There are underlying geographical constraints, there are natural regularities of behaviour related to every activity, whether climatic or seasonal or conventional, there are social customs, there are economic pressures, and there are short-term events in history with their resulting consequences – battles, conquests, powerful rulers, reforms, earthquakes, famines, diseases, tribal loves and hatreds. To translate this messy complication which constitutes the essence of history into a general theory is impossible, and this fact represents the ultimate problem of trying to subsume history within any abstract theory, from whatever philosophical or sociological or anthropological source it is derived.

During this period Braudel developed further his idea of the *longue durée* into a conception of *l'histoire globale*, not a total history of the world in the sense of a compilation of independent individual histories (such as UNESCO was busy promoting), but the idea of a history without frontiers, inclusive of all possible interrelations and methodologies, and composed of problems related to *conjunctures* or structures: 'There is no problem in history, in my view, that is surrounded by walls, that is independent.'[14]

The second debate concerned quantitative history: after *The Mediterranean*, Braudel became more and more attracted to the idea of quantification in economic history, the notion that history could become scientifically respectable through the use of graphs and tables and the collection of hard quantifiable data. It took the example of his disciple Pierre Chaunu, who sought to surpass Braudel with his immense work of 7,800 pages on Seville and the Atlantic trade (finally published in 1963), to convince Braudel that something was missing from this type of statistical history:[15] history was something more than the effect of the fluctuations in the Spanish American trade on the economic cycle of boom and decline in the sixteenth and seventeenth centuries. It was in response to this debate that Braudel wrote his second great work, translated as *Civilization and Capitalism, 15th–18th Century* (1982). The first volume of this work had originally been published in 1967, and was translated into English in 1973 as *Capitalism and Material Life 1400–1800*. It presented a vivid picture of social life and its structures before the Industrial Revolution, in terms of population, bread, food and drink, fashion, housing, energy sources, technology, money, cities and towns. This was revised and incorporated into a three-volume work published in 1979 with a one-word addition to the title: *Material Civilization, Economy and Capitalism*; the work now approached the whole question of the origins of modern-world capitalism: the second volume dealt with the organization of commerce, manufacture, and capitalism, the third with the growth of a world economy and world trade. His conclusion was both historical and practical: it is small-scale business and freedom of trade that both produce and sustain capitalism, not state enterprise or large-scale capitalism; without the independent small artisan and the merchant-shopkeeper no economic system can survive, and these smaller entities are embedded in the social fabric, so that society and economy can never be separated from each other. His work stands therefore as a refutation through the study of history of both communism and capitalism.

The third issue with which Braudel was involved was a consequence of his growing distance from the most talented of the historians whom he had called to join him in the management of *Annales*. The new history of the 1960s was turning away from the factual certainties of economic and descriptive social history, and exploring the 'history of mentalities'.[16] The historical world was created out of perceptions, not out of events, and we needed to recognize that the whole of history was a construct of human impressions. The crucial question for a history which still sought a degree of certainty and an escape from arbitrariness or fiction was to analyse the mental world that had created the record of an age or a civilization. The medieval historians Duby, Le Goff, and Le Roy Ladurie pioneered this approach from 1961 onwards; it meant a wholescale return to the Burckhardtian conception of cultural history, and to the use of literary and artistic sources alongside archival material. This was perhaps one of Braudel's blind spots: to him it was the realities of peasant or merchant existence that mattered, not the way in which they might be expressed in artistic or literary form. He was also more and more interested in the global sweep, and saw the detailed studies of the mental world of small communities undertaken by his colleagues as a betrayal of this grand vision. As he said to Le Roy Ladurie in relation to his famous book *Montaillou* (1975), 'We brought history into the dining-room, you are taking it into the bedroom.' His disapproval of these trends and his tendency towards authoritarian control cost him the direction of his journal, and by 1969 he had abandoned *Annales*, sidelined by a collective of those whose careers he had started and whom he had originally invited to join him.

Braudel's reply to this development was long in coming and remained incomplete: it was his last great projected work, 'The Identity of France'. Two volumes were published after his death in November 1985, comprising the first two parts on geography and demography and economy: these were for him traditional territory.[17] With the third he would be entering new territory, by writing about the state, culture, and society, and in the fourth about 'France outside France'. Fragments of the third volume were published in 1997. They suggest that what he was really aiming at in this last work was to confound his critics by demonstrating that the 'mentality' of France was contained within its physical, social and economic history. The peasant was the key to the history of France, and a true history of mentalities could only be written in the *longue durée* and from a long perspective. History must do more than study walled gardens.

The difficulty of translating *longue durée* as the phrase the 'long perspective' reveals another problem, which was perhaps to emerge in the later debates with Michel Foucault, whose importance Braudel had recognized early: in a letter to Foucault he explained that he was unable to appoint him to the *VIe Section*, because that would damage his chances of election to the Collège de France, which took place with Braudel's support in 1969–70. Braudel never claimed that his categories were absolute: they were only a means of organizing the explanatory factors in any situation. But equally he was not prepared to see them simply as constructs fashioned by the observer for his immediate purposes: however indeterminate and changeable, they did possess a real existence as forces in the field of history. This was challenged by the theories and methods of Foucault, who published *Words and Things* in 1966, and *The Archaeology of Knowledge* in 1969. The idea of historical relativity introduced in these works and adopted by postmodern history took one step beyond the history of mentalities. Not only did the uncertainty contained in the study of history rest on its derivation from a set of human impressions rather than events: the crucial role in this process belonged to the historian as interpreter. Indeed, the whole organization of knowledge could be seen as a construction designed to control the world: history, like all the social sciences, was an aspect of power; so that history was both the history of forms of control and itself a form of control, not an innocent activity. All this remains highly contested today, but for Braudel it was one step worse than the history of mentalities. The historian was no longer the innocent observer but himself complicit in society's attempt to marginalize categories such as the woman, the primitive, the mad, the criminal, the homosexual, and through its control of the psychology of humanity to construct mechanisms of social power – or ultimately (in Foucault's latest work) a more beneficent form of the control of the self.[18] Moreover, Foucault singled out the Braudelian conception of history for special attack: it was ideas and the sudden rupture created by them (exemplified in his own books), not the long perspective, which mattered in a history dominated by random change, by discontinuities not structures.

This theoretical debate had just begun in 1968. Braudel was giving a lecture series in Chicago when he was recalled to face at the age of sixty-two the revolutionary student movement. Like many radical professors he was sympathetic to but uncomprehending of the anarchic streak in youthful protest; 'make no mistake: we became the orthodox'.[19] His interventions were paternalistic and not well received, and later he condemned the revolution because it made people less rather than more happy. He could not understand the desire to destroy everything that he had personally tried to build outside the university system, of which both he and the students disapproved, or their contempt for facts and research in the face of neo-communist and anarchist ideas.

More dangerous still for Braudel was the reaction, which brought the moderate conservatives under Pompidou to power, and which placed the blame, not on their own resistance to change, but on those who had tried to encourage change. Had not the 'events' of 1968 proved the importance of the history of events? Where now was the long perspective? 'Has structuralism been killed by May 68?', as a headline in *Le Monde* put it in November of that year. Either the new history (whatever it was) was responsible for the 'events', or it was disproved by them: as a conservative you could have it both ways, and both implicated Braudel along with all his intellectual opponents. This was to accuse the Enlightenment of causing the French Revolution; but the claim was successful in weakening Braudel's access to government circles for almost the first time in his career. The university conservatives had indeed lost, and the former Sorbonne was ultimately swept away: in 1978 it split along political grounds between the conservatives at the old Sorbonne (Paris IV), the moderate left at Paris I, and the extreme left at Paris VII and Vincennes-Saint-Denis. But the conservatives had their revenge on the man who had been most responsible for establishing their irrelevance to modern life.

Braudel ended his life as he began it, as an outsider, but not unhappy with his fate. He had always believed in the importance of accepting reality and the relative powerlessness of the individual in the face of his circumstances, even though he had himself ruled French intellectual life 'as a prince' for a generation. Above all, despite his recognition of the importance of the grand vision and the power of the *longue durée* and of structures, he had always upheld that crucial historical value, the centrality of the individual as the subject of history: not the individual great man but the anonymous yet real peasant, the ordinary unknown man. In this sense he remains more truly revolutionary than any of his intellectual opponents on the left or on the right.

How powerful the legacy of Braudel, and especially of his *Mediterranean*, still is and how modern its conception still appears, can be seen by considering its impact on later research. Barry Cunliffe's *Facing the Ocean: The Atlantic and its Peoples* (2001), sought to do for the Atlantic what Braudel had done for the Mediterranean, and the title of his last chapter makes explicit reference to Braudel's *longue durée*. For the ancient world the first response was Peregrine Horden and Nicholas Purcell's *The Corrupting Sea: A Study of Mediterranean History* (Oxford 2000). For all its immense bibliographical learning and resolute up-to-dateness, this work too is inconceivable without the example of Braudel.[20] It is an attempt to answer the same questions as Braudel for the centuries before the age of Philip II; when we were young we all of us indeed dreamed of writing a book on the Mediterranean which should replace in its title Philip II of Spain with that earlier Philip II of Macedon. But we forgot that this book had already been written a generation earlier by Michael Rostovtzeff in his monumental *Social and Economic History of the Hellenistic World*.[21] Subsequently, the *Mediterranean Historical Review* has continued the study of ancient maritime history, as has the work of its founder Irad Malkin.[22] Books centred on the Mediterranean now proliferate.[23]

Finally, Braudel's little book on the early history of the Mediterranean,[24] published posthumously in 1998, and originally written thirty years earlier before carbon dating revolutionized the chronology of prehistory, has proved the foundation of the new interpretation of the early Mediterranean in the Bronze Age. The most important development of recent years has been the realization that the first high culture of the Western world was the tiny Minoan palace civilization, the only world culture ever to exist without any military basis. It was a manufacturing and trading offshoot of the Bronze Age luxury trade route between the palace economies of Mesopotamia and Egypt, at the point where they touched the inner sea. The early advance of Mediterranean culture depended on this trade route, linking Afghanistan with Mesopotamia, Iraq and Egypt. Italian excavations at the Syrian site of Ebla, with its complex royal archive, have shown how this trade route created satellite centres, whose organizational structures and bureaucratic practices mirrored the great civilizations that they served.[25] Minoan culture is a small palace-based economy on the fringes of this trade route, dependent on it for its religious and institutional structures. The work of Cyprian Broodbank has revealed in details as fascinating as those of Braudel's *Mediterranean* how this culture spanning east and west began to transform the Mediterranean world, long before either Phoenicians or Greeks arrived in the area. Once again archaeology has saved history, showing that European civilization derives from Eurasian trade routes.[26] Compared with this legacy the sterile debate on the pseudo concept of 'Mediterraneanism' reveals itself as irrelevant presentism.

Braudel's legacy invites us to consider the Mediterranean not in terms of culture wars but in its broadest geographical context, inclusive of the great civilizations of Iraq and Egypt, the steppes of Russia, the forests of Germany, and the deserts of the Sahara. For him, Mediterranean history was always an aspect of world history. Within the context of human history he emphasized two themes. The first is what I would call the reality principle. Human history is a history of technological mastery and the development of the skills basic to ancient civilization: fire and water technology, pottery, weaving, smelting and metalworking, seafaring, and finally writing. This emphasis on the physical realities of early civilizations brought out the actual quality of life with a vividness that no amount of library study and reading in other books can achieve. The second theme is the importance of exchange, especially long-distance exchange: 'Our sea was from the very dawn of its protohistory a witness to those imbalances productive of change which would set the rhythm of its entire life.'[27] It is imbalance that creates exchange and therefore leads to progress. These two ideas were first formulated in the *Mediterranean* and subsequently explored in depth for the pre-industrial world in *Civilization and Capitalism*.

Ignace Meyerson and J.-P. Vernant at the liberation of Toulouse, 1944

18
The 'École de Paris'

THE PERSONALITIES

Towards the end of his long life Jean-Pierre Vernant (1914–2007)[1] was asked whether he saw any connection between his wartime exploits and his work as a scholar. Surprised by the question, he reflected briefly, and replied that perhaps his later obsession with the figure of Achilles and the concept of the youthful heroic death (*la belle mort*) did indeed reflect the experiences of himself and his friends in the Resistance.

He was born in 1914, the son of a father who was killed in the First World War; his mother died shortly afterwards. In 1937 he passed out top in the *agrégation* in philosophy for the whole of France, shortly after his brother had achieved the same distinction. Discharged from the army after the fall of France in the summer of 1940, the two found themselves in Narbonne in August of that year at the height of the anti-British feeling caused by the British destruction of the French fleet at Mers-el-Kebir, resulting in the deaths of 1,300 French sailors; their first known act of defiance was to paste the walls of the city with the slogan, *Vive l'Angleterre pour que vive la France!* (Long live England that France may live!).

In 1940, at the age of twenty-six, Vernant was appointed teacher of philosophy at the main boys' school in Toulouse; his pupils did not guess the other life of their young professor. He helped form the Armée Secrète in 1942, and by the end of the war, as Colonel Berthier of the Forces Françaises de l'Intérieur, was commander of the entire Resistance movement in Haute-Garonne, organizing the liberation of Toulouse on 19–20 August 1944. His ability to unify the many independent groups made Toulouse a centre of the Resistance and one of the most active theatres of clandestine warfare in France. Assisted by sympathizers in the railways, the police, the factories, and local government, from among the refugees from Fascist Italy and the Spanish Civil War and French Jewish refugees from the north, with the help of military supplies spirited away from the army after the fall of France or dropped by the British Special Operations Executive (whose office in London was organized by my father), their operations included disrupting railway and road supplies, sabotaging factory production, executing collaborators, and organizing the main escape route to Spain for Allied pilots who had escaped or were shot down. A potentially disastrous police raid on their headquarters in October 1943 led to the capture of five members and the movement's records. A message was sent to the prefect of police, that if any of these records were transmitted to the Germans he would personally be executed on the orders of London: the records disappeared. Three agents were sprung with the help of a technique subsequently often used again, involving the fabrication of orders for their immediate release written on genuine official paper, and sent by official courier precisely at the last moment on Saturday before the closure of all offices for the weekend, when no telephone message could be sent to query the order. A forged official confirmation arrived on Monday; and the operation was repeated for the other two people arrested. So successful was this method that after the war the French government refused the title of member of the Resistance to one of Vernant's team, because his record showed that he had been officially declared to be a collaborator of the Germans.

Vernant himself escaped arrest partly because (as he later discovered) his government dossier had become inextricably confused with that of his brother: when finally in spring 1944 he was about to be 'dismissed' by the Vichy education authorities and handed over to the French fascist organization known as the Milice, he received two anonymous letters (both misspelling his name in different ways) warning him not to trust the headmaster or the school inspector, and went into hiding. After the war he was surprised to find that there was no record of any decision to dismiss (or reinstate) him in the archives, and finally concluded that, though a decision had indeed been taken, it had not been recorded because the authorities had postponed action over the holidays, being unwilling to commit themselves to anything at this stage of the war. Instead, when the war was over, Vernant received a promotion and a letter of commendation for his 'professional qualities and civic courage' signed by the very same inspector whom he suspected of denouncing him. Otherwise he was given little recognition, since in their efforts to re-establish conservative control of France, the Allies, Charles de Gaulle, and the French establishment united in refusing to recognize the popular Resistance movements, which were dominated by the left. Vernant himself was a member of the Communist Party from 1932 intermittently until 1970; but his independence from the party line dates from the Hitler–Stalin pact of 1939, and he was often publicly critical of the party, regarding himself as a Marxist rather than a party loyalist.

His experiences in Vichy France taught Vernant that official history and official records were a worthless farrago of falsehoods; and the memory of his fellow fighters in the hour of victory was scarcely more reliable. The success of the Resistance had been due to the fact that it had created an alternative structure of 'reality' that ran alongside the structures of the Vichy regime; the only truth was the psychological experience of the group, as Tolstoy had understood it – *mes copains*, Vernant called them. Returning to academic life he began a thesis on the notion of work in Plato, and pursued a form of research into Greek civilization inspired by the social psychology of his colleague in the Resistance, Ignace Meyerson: Vernant sought to understand the specifically Greek conceptions of those general ideas common to all human experience, such as labour, value, time, space, memory, the will and the person, imagination and sacrifice, or the difference between us and them, Greeks and barbarians (*altérité*). Between 1948 and 1962 he followed the seminars of Louis Gernet, veteran sociologist and pupil of Emile Durkheim. From these two influences Vernant developed one of the first and most successful approaches in the *histoire de l'imaginaire*. He was always open to new ideas, being editorial secretary for the *Journal de Psychologie* in the 1950s, and later embracing anthropology and structuralism without becoming imprisoned by them.

Never a man to waste words, Vernant's first book of 130 pages, *Les Origines de la pensée grecque* (1962), changed the history of Greek studies: in the wake of the decipherment of Linear B it asked the simple questions. What is the relationship between the newly discovered Mycenean world of palace bureaucracies and the invention of rationality by the Greeks? And how does Greek rationality relate to modern ideas? To him the answers lay in the democratic political experience of archaic Greece, and the forms of verbal exchange developed in relation to civic duties. In this book he posed the fundamental questions that have been the starting point for all studies of ancient Greece for the last sixty years. His later work concentrated on the place of religion in Greek society and the evidence of literature and art for Greek social forms.

In 1948, Vernant entered the CNRS and in 1958 he joined Fernand Braudel in the *VIe Section* of the École Pratique des Hautes Études (later the École des Hautes Études en Sciences Sociales) in Paris, as assistant director to Ignace Meyerson in a section called the Centre de recherches de psychologie comparative; in 1964 he established his own research centre, the Centre de recherches comparées sur les sociétés anciennes, which was given the former house of Auguste Comte, and was devoted to 'comparative research on ancient societies': initially, the group included experts not only on ancient Greece and Rome but also on Assyria, Egypt, India, China, and Africa, and a number of anthropologists. Religion was treated as a central aspect of all societies, which must be studied for their unifying principles. This cramped huddle of five rooms with its library doubling up as a seminar room in Rue Monsieur-le-Prince, near Odeón, became the focus of intellectual activity in comparative history of the ancient world throughout Europe and the United States: everyone would make the pilgrimage to the Centre; the revolutionary approach to ancient history of the 'École de Paris' changed the face of modern scholarship.

Slowly, and to the regret of Vernant himself, the pressures of academic life and the interests of enthusiastic young researchers pushed the focus of the Centre towards the classical world, until by the time he handed over its direction to his friend and collaborator Pierre Vidal-Naquet, it had emerged as the centre for a new type of Greek and Roman history. Once again, as during the war, Vernant had created an alternative structure of subversion alongside the official academic cursus: when the events of 1968 arrived, it was members of the recently founded Centre who led the revolution in the universities, and under Vidal-Naquet the Centre Louis Gernet became the most significant international institution for the study of Greek civilization. Vernant was proud of having established what an outsider called the 'École de Paris': 'neither my work nor my life nor my personality can be separated from the team: . . . may the Centre continue. A living research team is an institution and a sort of family, with all its tensions.' Although he always remained closely connected to the Centre, from 1975 to 1984 Vernant was Professor of the Comparative History of Ancient Religions at the

Collège de France, where his lectures were famous for the clarity and elegance of their French style.

The charisma of Jipé (as he was called by all his friends) rested on the warmth of his personality: he always used the '*tu*' form and recognized you as a fellow worker whatever your age; in seminars he had an uncanny ability to understand what the speaker really meant, and to formulate it afterwards to the speaker privately. As an orphan he had built his life on friendship: it was easy to understand how people could have risked their lives for him. Once he told me the story of how he came to acquire a holiday house on the exclusive island of Belle-Île. For many years he and his adored wife Lida (the daughter of Russian émigrés, whom he had met in 1932 when she was fourteen, and married in 1939) had rented the house for holidays; one day the owner came to him to say that he had to sell. Regretfully Jipé said that he could not possibly afford to buy it. 'You don't understand,' the owner said, 'I want to sell it to you. Tell me the price.'

Jipé was a very private person, who only revealed aspects of his past life in extreme old age, and accepted the honours heaped on him simply as the gifts of friends. He retained his mental and physical powers until the end,

Jean-Pierre Vernant (1914–2007)

and was a champion swimmer able to outpace all rivals even in his late eighties. He nursed his wife until her death from Alzheimer's in their idyllic Russian-style house at Sèvres outside Paris; their only daughter died soon after. But he continued to retain his positive attitude to life, looked after by his son-in-law and surrounded by disciples and friends, the most loved and revered classical scholar of his age.

Pierre Vidal-Naquet[2] had a double life as a fearless public campaigner against modern lies and as one of the founders of the new French scholarship on the ancient Greek world. In the first role he came to prominence as the chief exposer of the systematic use of torture by the French government in Algeria. Approached by the widow of a young university teacher of mathematics who had 'disappeared' in 1957 in Algiers while in the custody of a paratroop regiment, he launched an investigation that resulted in a famous book, *L'Affaire Audin* (1958), which concluded that Maurice Audin had been tortured to death, and that the military authorities had concocted an elaborate charade of an alleged escape from custody.[3] The murderers were named, but what was important to Vidal-Naquet was the complicity of the authorities up to the highest level: in the year 2000 new evidence revealed the truth of his claims. The subsequent public campaign against systematic torture in Indochina and other French colonial territories led to books on *La Raison d'état* (1962), *Torture: Cancer of Democracy* (Penguin 1963, only later published in France as *La Torture dans la république*, 1972), and *Les Crimes de l'armée française* (1975). He took part in the *événements* of 1968, and with Alain Schnapp, one of the student leaders (subsequently a professor at the Sorbonne), compiled the essential dossier of student documents, *Journal de la commune étudiante* (1969).

In 1971 he joined with Michel Foucault in founding the *Groupe d'information sur les prisons*, which took up the rights of prisoners judged victims of injustice. He mounted a systematic attack on the infamous claims of Robert Faurisson denying the existence of the Nazi concentration camps (*Les Assassins de la mémoire – Un Eichmann de papier et autres textes sur le révisionnisme*, 1987). His many campaigns for the truth in modern Jewish history are preserved in three volumes of *Les Juifs, la mémoire et le présent* (1981–95); but (despite disillusionment with the continuation of torture in independent Algeria) he was deeply critical of 'Israeli arrogance', and supported the rights of the Palestinians: his last public act was to sign a manifesto against the war in Lebanon. To the end he was active in denouncing publicly the lies to be found in the memoirs of retired generals, and challenging them to sue him for libel. He wrote to one general asking for a copy of his book on the 'truth' of the North African war: the general replied, 'It is free to the general public, 80 francs to traitors. For you it costs 40 francs.' Vidal-Naquet sent him a personal cheque for 80 francs.

'Vaccinated against orthodoxy', Vidal-Naquet never joined the Communist or (except very briefly) any other party: 'I am not a man for party politics: in a party one practises the conditional as soon as something does not fit its logic; one shows a sort of mistrust of the indicative truth . . . There is always a point where you must choose between party and truth.' It was his inheritance that explained his passion: he belonged to an extended clan of Jewish intellectual French patriots who included Dreyfus; he was taught by his father that the Dreyfus Affair was part of his birthright. He believed in his campaigns for justice as the highest form of patriotism; and the success of the Audin campaign, which was one of the ten cases that began Amnesty International, was based on explicit comparison with the Dreyfus Affair.

His father was a prominent constitutional lawyer, and an early member of the Resistance; the family fled to Vichy Marseilles. On 15 May 1944 the thirteen-year-old boy was returning from school when he was dragged off the tram by a teacher and some of his schoolmates: 'The Germans have arrested your parents: you can't go home.' By various means all the children of the family escaped to be protected by Protestant communities in the mountains, but they never saw their parents again: Vidal-Naquet's father was tortured by the Gestapo and both his parents were murdered in Auschwitz. The detailed story is recorded in his *Mémoires* (1995–58), which demonstrate an amazing memory for events and people, both friends and betrayers, whom he never forgot or forgave.

In 1950, Vidal-Naquet declared to his future wife, 'as an atheist, history is for me the only possible substitute for religion'. 'Strongly engaged in the present, and yet having already secretly renounced it' (in the words of Pierre Pachet), he describes in *Le Choix de l'histoire* (2004) how he drifted into ancient rather than modern history almost by chance. A pupil of the Catholic historian and musicologist Henri-Irénée Marrou, who taught him to reject positivism, after a brief career in the provinces Vidal-Naquet joined J.-P. Vernant in 1966 in the newly created Centre de recherches comparées; when Vernant was elected to the Collège de

France, Vidal-Naquet became director of the renamed Centre Louis Gernet.

Marrou had set him the task of understanding why Plato hated history and historians so much. This began a lifelong interest in the relation between reality, the imagination, and utopianism, both of which he regarded as mirrors reflecting society. Vidal-Naquet wrote extensively on Plato, Greek tragedy, and the myth of Atlantis from antiquity to the present. He also studied the modern use of the myth of ancient democracy from the French Revolution to the present; he was fascinated by the relation between truth, memory, and history. He claimed his most personal work was that on Flavius Josephus (provocatively entitled *Du bon usage de la trahison*, 1977), a man 'who refused to accept Jewish history as tragic and wished to make an entirely positive history of Judaism'. It demonstrated 'the role of the historian as eternal traitor'. Josephus had actually of course changed sides: of himself Vidal-Naquet said, 'I hope to be a more subtle traitor'; he certainly never changed sides.

Fierce but fair, honest with himself and others, he became more impatient in later life and was not always an easy colleague; but he was intensely loyal, not least to his many English friends. A botched medical operation in his mid-forties led to lifelong problems that he bore with ill-concealed irritation, helped by his devoted wife Geneviève; he died

Pierre Vidal-Naquet (1930–2006)

suddenly from a brain haemorrhage while on holiday at his beloved country retreat at Fayence.

THE 'ÉCOLE DE PARIS' AND THE ANGLOPHONE WORLD

When I was young the traditions of French scholarship seemed as well fixed as those of British empiricism; and although then we saw only the differences, today it is the similarities that are far more striking. British classical scholars studied at Oxford and Cambridge; they passed a year or so at the British Schools of Athens or Rome. They wrote commentaries, they despised aesthetics and were interested only in textual criticism, geography and topography, or philosophically speaking in the eternal validity of the arguments of Plato and Aristotle, as set out in the *Republic* and *Nicomachean Ethics*, and no other work – let alone any other philosopher. They tended to publish *nel mezzo del cammin* – neither earlier nor later, and normally only once; thereafter they became professors and withdrew, pipe in mouth, to cultivate their gardens.

The French were much the same: they studied at the Sorbonne or the École Normale Supérieure; they progressed to the Écoles françaises of Rome or Athens. They too published only once and *nel mezzo del cammin*, a *grande thèse* of such monumentality that it silenced both the author and his critics; thereafter they withdrew, to examine other *thèses*, and to supervise the *baccalauréat* or their own universities. Their books were slightly different from English books: though they too usually studied authors, they wrote from a more literary point of view, with an interest in the generic forms, rather than the textual tradition or the information that the text contained; in contrast to English writers (who believed that everything they read in a dead language was or ought to be true), the French appeared to believe that all statements in literary texts were or ought to be strictly false, being more conditioned by tradition than by observation; they therefore allowed themselves greater scope for invention (or at least interpretation). Their history was likely to be more diplomatic than topographical, but the results were regarded as equally certain. Occasionally the elders of these two cultures would visit each other's universities and deliver formal addresses of stupefying pomposity in their respective languages to audiences who were mostly asleep or monoglot. This ensured that each side could respect the wisdom and traditions of the other, without any danger of comprehension; and it instilled respect for their elders in the young.

The antediluvian state of classical studies in these two worlds of the early 1960s was then not so different. In Britain scholarship was dominated by the absolute separation of classical literature, history, and philosophy into three unconnected disciplines. 'Literature' concerned itself with prose and verse composition between the ancient and modern languages and with textual criticism in the traditional sense – the discovery of the original *ipsissima verba* of a text assumed to have been written down by the author himself and corrupted over the centuries by careless copyists. The practice of literary criticism had been abandoned in the early twentieth century as a sentimental late Victorian aberration; there remained only the notion of a literary tradition, based on the idea of a written text that had evolved in the private study of the writer without contact with any external world, but simply through consideration of his predecessors. 'Ancient history' was confined to the study of classical Greece and Rome of the late Republic and early Empire. History itself was deemed to consist of facts and dates, and to be concerned primarily with battles, political events, and institutions, together with a form of practical agrarian economic history originally designed to assist future British administrators in governing the Indian Empire. There was always one and only one truth: the only uncertainties permitted were caused by the paucity of sources, and the generally agreed unreliability of our surviving historical texts, which it was the duty of the ancient historian to correct according to the demands of a modernizing rational historical consensus. The influence of German Jewish refugees from 1933 onwards had merely reinforced those various forms of philological positivism that were already endemic, and derived from nineteenth-century admiration of German *Altertumswissenschaft*. The situation in France was little better, since the ancient world was (and still is) rigidly divided into three separate university faculties, under *Philosophie*, *Histoire*, and *Études classiques*; so it scarcely mattered that we were completely ignorant of French scholarship (though unlike the modern generation we could still speak and read the French language).[4]

Fifty years ago I wrote an article on the career of André Aymard, the teacher of Pierre Vidal-Naquet:[5] it seemed easy to characterize his life with gentle irony and total unawareness that I was describing a common culture; perhaps it was simpler to see the oddities of this world *vu d'ailleurs* than to recognize that it was my world too. Many years later Vidal-Naquet was generous enough to say to me that my essay was the best appreciation of Aymard that he knew. Of course, the *ancien régime* still survives in places, perhaps we may fear that it is even once again on the increase (at least in Britain). But in so far as the historical world has changed for the better, this is due not to the English, but to the generation of historians of ancient Greece whom irreverent and sometimes hostile outsiders designated as *l'école de Paris*: even if there is no such entity, as Pierre has taught us, the categories of *l'imaginaire* are usually more powerful than the illusions of reality.

It is difficult to separate the influence of Jipé Vernant from that of his colleague Pierre Vidal-Naquet, because they collaborated so often and so closely in their published work; nevertheless I shall try to explain their separate contributions. Initially it seemed to the English that Vernant and Vidal-Naquet were structuralists. In the preface to their first joint programmatic collection of articles *Mythe et Tragédie* (1973), they admitted that 'most of the studies in this book reflect what it is usual to call a structural analysis' (*la plupart des études réunies dans ce livre relèvent de ce qu'il est convenu d'appeler l'analyse structurale*), but what mattered to them was not a form of decoding – a decipherment of the myths to reveal an underlying binary structure – but what they called 'the sociology of literature and what one might call historical anthropology' (*la sociologie de la littérature et ce qu'on pourrait appeler une anthropologie historique*). What tragedy presents is not a myth, but the reflection of a myth in a social context – at the same time a reflection on myth and a communication through myth.

For us younger English scholars, who were the first generation to engage in organized doctoral research, three figures of the older generation stood out, all of them in one sense or another outsiders. In Oxford the Irishman E.R. Dodds in his revolutionary book *The Greeks and the Irrational* (1951), and in his earlier commentary on Euripides' *Bacchae* (first edition 1944), had suggested the relevance of psychology and anthropology to the study of ancient literature. In London the Italian refugee Arnaldo Momigliano showed us how we could liberate ourselves from the straitjacket of positivism by studying the classical and continental tradition of the history of ideas. And in Cambridge the former Marxist Moses Finley, exiled from the United States in the McCarthy era, revealed how economic history lay at the basis of any true understanding of the ancient world.

It was Finley (and later Momigliano) who first introduced us to the ideas and personalities of the École de Paris; although neither of our mentors was particularly close in historical method to the preoccupations of Vernant and Vidal-Naquet. Finley may perhaps have been initially attracted to them by the fact that both of them had been and still were active in the left-wing politics that he missed in contemporary Britain. But the author of *The World of Odysseus* (1954) also saw that the first book of Vernant, *Les Origines de la pensée grecque* (1962), was inspired by the same need that he had seen, to rethink the history of early Greece as a result of Michael Ventris's decipherment of Linear B. Both Vernant and Finley saw immediately the problem that the decipherment posed for the historian: how could this centralized Mycenaean palace economy, now proved to be Greek, relate to the archaic and classical world of the *polis*? Finley had sought a positivist economic solution in an interpretation of Homeric society as a product of the Dark Age, which was at this time only beginning to be studied by archaeologists. With this insight he inspired a generation of British archaeologists to move on from 'Homeric archaeology' as a form of antiquarian commentary on literary texts to the great achievements of the excavating age from Vincent Desborough to Mervyn Popham, John Boardman, Nicholas Coldstream, Anthony Snodgrass, and most recently Irene Lemos.

Vernant's answer was couched in terms of a change of mentality or *l'imaginaire*, and has in fact dominated the study of the ancient Greek world ever since. The problem as he saw it was not so much a question of the different economies of the two systems, their land tenure or their social structures. It was rather the development from a hierarchic and perhaps theocratic world to the rationality inherent in the principles of Greek thought; and the answer to the problem in his opinion lay in the creation of the public institutions of the Greek city-state, and in the development of a style of rational political argument. Almost everything that has been written since on the political history and the intellectual development of Greek thought still starts consciously or unconsciously from the questions that Vernant posed in 1962. This aspect of the influence of Vernant in the English-speaking world was well understood from the start, although its inherent contradiction with his emphasis on *altérité*, the difference between antiquity and the present, has never been fully recognized.

The name of Vernant was already well known in Britain by 1965, when (surely at the suggestion of Moses Finley) he and the Swiss scholar Walter Burkert were invited as the first European scholars ever to address the triennial conference of the classical societies of Britain at Oxford: the occasion was engraved on his memory as on mine. I was a young research student, and I was given the task of guiding Vernant in the pronunciation of English. He had chosen to speak on a newly discovered fragment of Alcman, which made reference to the image of the 'seiche'. The word 'seiche' was completely new to me; I searched in the dictionary and offered him the translation 'cuttlefish'. But the word 'cuttlefish' was then equally unknown in English (except among fishmongers selling exotic fish); and in the delivery of his lecture the combination of this unfamiliar word, completely out of context as far as philologists were concerned, uttered in a heavy French accent, created in the lecture room (which was circular) an echo which ran continuously round the room – 'ze cootlefeesh, cootlefeesh, cootlefeesh' – until the point that the audience themselves began to resemble a net full of cuttlefish, staring at the lecturer with open mouths. To begin with Vernant thought that they were transfixed by his argument, but after a few minutes he realized that their amazement was due to the fact that they could not understand a word of what he was saying, and he was nevertheless forced to continue with his paper for another forty minutes. It is a moment in his professional career that he often recalled to me, and because of which he remained resolutely francophone for thirty years, until a visit to the monoglot United States with young French colleagues who were able to offer him better protection than I was. In 1999, Vernant's second visit to Oxford took place when the University presented him with an honorary doctorate at the annual feast of Encaenia: in reply to my speech of welcome before the Faculty, he spoke long and eloquently, but in French.

Pierre Vidal-Naquet's relation to England was very different from that of Vernant. His connection went back to his childhood: in his *Mémoires* he writes of his young governess, Miss Mac, who introduced him to the famously chauvinist children's book on the history of England, *Our Island Story*, which begins with Queen Boadicea, courageous rebel against the Romans (prototype of Astérix), and King Alfred who burned the cakes, and continues with William the Conqueror, who managed to correct the fault of his French birth by his conquest of England, and finishes with Queen Victoria, empress of an empire on which the sun never sets. It seems that Pierre was so enamoured of England as a child that there was talk of sending him to the famous English public school of Eton. One wonders how his natural radicalism might have been affected by such early contacts with the English elite – although Eton was also the school of the most famous of our left-wing writers, George Orwell.

At any rate, since his wartime childhood Pierre was a passionate Anglophile who spoke English fluently and who knew the works of Shakespeare almost by heart. He was particularly proud of the honorary doctorate given to him by the University of Bristol in 1998 at the instigation of his English admirer, Richard Buxton. Pierre always felt at home in England; but in fact from an English perspective, like Vernant he remained more French than he realized: the reception of his ideas in the Anglo-Saxon world always moved slowly and encountered fierce resistance.

'A century of Greek studies has resulted largely in distancing rather than connecting ourselves with Greece' (*Un siècle d'hellénisme moderne a abouti, dans une large mesure, à éloigner plus qu'à rapprocher la Grèce de nous*).[6] If there is one general shift in the contemporary image of the ancient world, which deserves the title of a decisive change in the history of mentalities, it is the idea of *altérité* (otherness). This change in the conception of our relationship to the past derives from that group of historians and scholars who have most influenced our generation: in France these include the disciples of Durkheim, notably Louis Gernet, and the school of *études comparées* founded by Vernant; in Britain they include the acknowledged masters of Vidal-Naquet, Moses Finley and Arnaldo Momigliano, but also E.R. Dodds (whom Pierre met for the first and only time in my house one evening in 1976).[7] Such attitudes can be traced further back to the relation between classics and anthropology in Oxford and Cambridge at the start of the century, and in France to Fustel de Coulanges two generations earlier. They were again reinforced by the dominating influence of anthropology in the 1960s, from Claude Lévi-Strauss and structuralism in France, and from studies on literacy by Jack Goody, Edmund Leach, and others in Britain. This common meeting ground between French and British scholarship was the starting point for the liberation of classical studies from the purely positivist and philological tradition of German scholarship, which had previously dominated the European scene. Italy, while sharing many characteristics with France, seems to have been more influenced by the Marxist analysis of ancient societies as socio-economic entities that was transmitted through the new archaeology of *Dialoghi di archeologia*. America in contrast has never ceased to believe in the modernity of the past, holding that every modern problem from democracy to slavery, colour prejudice, feminism, and the New Right has its analogue in the ancient world. To this extent it seems to me that Greek studies in France and England have in our generation shared a common set of presuppositions about the difference between the past and the present, and about the need to maintain a distance from the past, precisely because both cultures have felt themselves so close to the ancient world.

The first aspect of the thought of the 'École de Paris' that was important for the English was therefore their conception of *altérité*. But the alterities of Vernant and Vidal-Naquet were different from each other, and also a good deal more subtle than the English realized. For Vernant alterity seemed to be something internal: it consisted in the necessity of recognizing the difference between ourselves and the Greeks, the need to '*regarder la lune avec les yeux des Grecs*'. For Vidal-Naquet it was not an alterity that separated us from the Greeks: according to him it was necessary to see our problem as one that existed for the Greeks themselves. One might say that, whereas Vernant saw ancient society as a unity opposed to the view from the exterior, Vidal-Naquet saw it as a world in internal conflict.

For this reason Vidal-Naquet was always fascinated in his historical work by *les marginaux*, those excluded from the full status of citizen. His studies therefore concentrated on the mental worlds of groups such as artisans, adolescents, women, and slaves. But unlike Finley or G.E.M. de Sainte Croix he was not, I think, concerned with them as oppressed groups, who suffer at the hands of the dominant culture: to him the primary question was not moral but heuristic. For it is these marginal figures whose view most approximates to the view from outside which we possess, and who can therefore reveal to us the secrets of the society to which in some sense they still belong: they can mediate between the dominant culture and ourselves. The result was a series of studies of such groups that are marked less by indignation than by empathy, and which therefore possess a depth of historical understanding lacking in more committed work. And Vidal-Naquet was concerned with the range of possible responses within a particular situation, rather than with creating a positivistic set of conclusions; for the mental world is composed of possibilities not certainties.

It is evident to me that most of the questions asked by Vidal-Naquet relate to problems inherent in his concept of *altérité*. This difference was defined first as a rejection of the interwar idealization of 'the glory that was Greece' or '*le miracle grec*': the aim was now to understand *les grecs sans miracle*, in the phrase invented in 1983 by Riccardo Di Donato as the title for the collection of unpublished papers of Louis Gernet. It is surely this shared set of assumptions that enabled two scholars from such very different traditions as Moses Finley and Vidal-Naquet to find a common ground when they first met in 1968. And this common desire to deconstruct the idealized Greece led both historians to interest themselves in the oppressed groups within the dominant culture – the woman, the slave, the artisan.

But we also felt the Greeks to be 'desperately foreign', in the words of Finley recalled nearly thirty years later by Vidal-Naquet.[8] This was another sort of difference between us and them, and the effort to understand that foreignness led us all to anthropology. Our Greeks were foreign because they were primitive; and our aim was to analyse the ways in which they were primitive. The concept of *altérité* in the sense of a polarity between the external observer and the phenomenon observed has consequently been fundamental to all classical studies since the 1960s: we see ourselves now as anthropologists standing outside classical culture rather than natives viewing it from within.

What distinguished the work of Vidal-Naquet in this common enterprise is his deeper understanding of the potential uses of anthropology. Starting from earlier studies, most notably the comparisons of Henri Jeanmaire between African and ancient Greek customs, Vidal-Naquet was led to emphasize the importance of the rite of passage from adolescence to manhood in Greek religious ritual and social practices. In 'The Black Hunter Revisited'[9] he described the thrill in 1968 of discovering that, whereas in Paris his original paper on the 'Black Hunter' had been delivered to stony and uncomprehending silence at the *Association pour l'encouragement des études grecques*, a year later in the Cambridge Philological Society it excited animated discussion, especially among professional anthropologists. And there is no doubt that the Black Hunter is here to stay; even in parody it stands up to criticism: Vidal-Naquet demonstrated the importance of the particular rite of passage from adolescence to adulthood as a source of tensions within Greek society. He also showed in a number of studies how this moment of transition resulted in a period of liminality or marginality, in which the protagonist comes to represent an internal *altérité*, and so to expose the tensions within the social system: transition and marginalization are interconnected, and the new adult member of the community must pass through a period of exclusion.

His conception of an internal *altérité* is therefore more subtle and more significant for our understanding of Greek culture than the common practice today of contrasting identity and alterity. It is neither interesting nor perhaps true that the Greeks defined themselves in terms of the Other, that they learned to be Greeks by recognizing barbarians, or that the male defined his masculinity in terms of opposition with the female. That form of constructing a mental universe through the invention of mechanical polarities is something that Vidal-Naquet never accepted, with good reason, any more than that he subscribed explicitly to any structuralist system of binary oppositions. It is indeed difficult to understand those critics who refer to the structuralism of Vidal-Naquet; for in that sense we are all structuralists – the word is used too loosely. For Vidal-Naquet, as indeed for Lévi-Strauss, polarities are never simple, they are always embedded in a cultural matrix. So within Greek society the role of oppositions is not to define the opposites, but to reveal the tensions between them at the interface – the adolescent, the Amazon, the outcast hero Philoctetes.

When Vernant and Vidal-Naquet accepted in the preface to *Mythe et tragédie* that their approach was in some sense indebted to structuralism, they were not interested in *le décodage* in the sense of 'the decipherment of myths' (*le déchiffrement des mythes* in terms of an underlying binary structure), but in what they called the sociology of literature or historical anthropology. The approach that they pioneered was indeed new, for tragedy was not itself myth, but the reflection of myth in a social context: today one would I think with less hesitation describe them as engaged in what the English persist in calling 'the history of mentalities'.[10] The narratives of tragedy were the unique responses of individuals to inherited myth within a social context and as a form of public communication with other members of their society. These texts were therefore both reflexions of myth and communication through myth, and demanded analysis beyond literature at the intersection between three distinct disciplines – anthropology, sociology, and psychology. Not surprisingly there was opposition from both orthodox philology and the doctrinaire sociology of the left; but by the time of the preface to *Mythe et tragédie deux* (1986) the authors could also point to a growing body of disciples in France, England, and the United States. The truth is that in the last generation literary criticism in the classics has in the anglophone world become heavily historicized: literature is no longer seen as an independent entity in terms of a literary tradition, but as the product of a specific social context and an initial occasion of performance; we are all disciples of Vernant and Vidal-Naquet, even if in terms of their analyses some modern views seem extreme in their insistence on historicizing the myth and regarding the text as solely expressive of internal social conflicts.[11] One suspects that the *Mythe et tragédie* volumes, which are now seen as precursors of the dominant school, will in fact outlast that school because of their greater subtlety and tentativeness: certainly it cannot be true that the meanings of Greek tragedies are exhausted in their historical context, however useful they may be for the reconstruction of the historical *imaginaire*. Already in the preface to the second volume, the two authors were insisting on the element of ambiguity endemic in Greek tragedies and in their interpretation. And from the start the *Sic et Non* of Peter Abelard's earlier (twelfth-century) *école de Paris* was excluded:[12]

> We do not seek to unveil a mystery in these analyses. Was Sophocles thinking about ostracism or the *ephebeia* when he wrote his plays? We do not know, and will never know, we are not even sure if the question makes sense. What we wish to show is that, in the form of communication established between the poet and his audience, ostracism or the *ephebeia* constituted a common point of reference, a background that rendered intelligible the basic structures of the play.

Soixante-huit (1968) may also be an imaginary entity, but it symbolizes the difference between the English and the French traditions. We English never had our *soixante-huit*, because (like the Swiss) we like to pretend we did not need it, and unlike the French and the Americans we never had our Algeria or our Vietnam. But in France the date is surely symbolic of a revolution that dislodged the *ancien régime*, and gave freedom, power, and influence to a younger generation long before their allotted time of entry to the gerontocracy of the academic *gerousia*. For that my generation, condemned to wait in the corridors of power for another thirty years, always envied the French, and recognized their right to intellectual leadership on the grounds of youth and renewal.

The importance of Pierre Vidal-Naquet in this historical *événement* is evident. He was one of the leaders of the process of change in historical studies. But because Vidal-Naquet had always himself felt close to the Anglo-Saxon tradition he also served as an index of the essential polarity between the two cultures. His first book (written with his colleague Pierre Lévêque) occasioned a stern rebuke from its Oxford reviewer in the leading English classical journal:

> This is a curious book, meandering through the Greek world to the amazement of the student of Cleisthenes. The main theme is that Cleisthenes did what he did in the way he did because, perhaps, he was not just the electoral geographer drawing boundaries to suit himself but also the constitutional geometrician who gave political form to current theories of proportion, of *isonomia*. No doubt the authors are well prepared for sceptical reviews, and will not be surprised to learn that one reviewer considers that the book has practically nothing of historical importance to tell about Cleisthenes.[13]

The same journal did not deign to review the English translation of this work, which was belatedly published in 1996.[14] If it had, the reviewer might perhaps have noticed two ironical facts. One leading British historian has now opined that the most daring of all the hypotheses of the two Frenchmen, that there may have been precisely 100 Attic demes in Cleisthenes' reforms, a view which Vidal-Naquet himself abandoned, might after all be right.[15] And (far more significantly) it can now be seen that the basic hypothesis of the book, that Cleisthenes was creating a rational system based on theoretical principles, has been vindicated by the discovery of a complete and rational 'Cleisthenic system' of the mid-fifth century BC at Camarina in Sicily.[16]

Thirty years after this first book the young Oxford-trained historian John Ma illustrated the continuing gap in comprehension by a brilliant parody of the two styles of history as applied to the same ancient text, in a study entitled 'Black Hunter Variations';[17] but even in this sympathetic juxtaposition the failure of understanding is still revealed in Ma's plaintive search for an answer to the non-existent question: which style of interpretation is correct? 'Did Damon really become a Black Hunter? Certitude is impossible, for want of evidence. But the answer to the question can only be yes or no.'[18] On the contrary, one might wish to reply; Vidal-Naquet has taught us that the answer to any interesting question in history is seldom either yes or no, 'as if historical reality always obeyed the laws of logical exclusion'.[19]

The image of the Black Hunter which Vidal-Naquet used on the cover of his collection of essays with that name recalls his period eight years after the publication of his famous article as Nellie Wallace visiting lecturer at Oxford in 1976, and his encounter with that most numinous of all the paintings in the Ashmolean Museum, Paolo Uccello's *The Night Hunt in the Forest*. Vidal-Naquet's seminars during that autumn idyll were on Plato and history, a topic that he had made his own since his first dissertation for H.-I. Marrou, written under the influence of Victor Goldschmidt. To his younger English contemporaries the crucial question remained a factual one: why had Plato so deliberately sought in almost all his dialogues to present contradictory indications of the dramatic date? Did this necessarily invalidate any other conclusion that one might draw concerning the reality of his presentation of the Socratic circle? And was this connected with Plato's sublime disregard for 'the facts' in his presentation of the past, in the myth of Atlantis for instance and in the equally mythic description of the cycle of constitutions with their causes in *Republic*, Book viii? Did Plato despise history, and was his parody of Thucydides' funeral oration in the *Menexenus* part of a systematic programme to devalue the world of 'real' appearances in favour of the world of the philosophic Forms?

Vidal-Naquet recognized our problems, but sought to show us that the questions which we should be asking were different ones. They were concerned first with our understanding of the historical process, and our own relentless devaluation of the importance of ideas:[20]

> Is thought, however abstract, alien to historical reality? is there anything alien to historical reality? Of course there are *levels* of reality, degrees of reality, if you like, but I do not see how an idea, even a reactionary one, can be unrelated to historical reality.

The result of our failure to incorporate Plato completely into our conception of history was an impoverishment of our understanding of both Plato and history:[21]

> We might be tempted to say that the poverty of what historians write about philosophy is only equalled by the insignificance of what philosophers write about the historical context of the works that they study.

If there seemed to us something paradoxical in the historian who had read the whole of Plato for historical rather than philosophical purposes (much as the eccentric Henry Fynes Clinton read the whole of Plato's *Republic* in May 1819 *in five days* for the purpose of extracting chronological information),[22] nevertheless we were forced to recognize that it was wrong to accept the opposition that Plato perhaps himself believed in, between philosophy and history: 'I can never repeat enough that for the most part [the Platonic texts] do not describe the universe of the Platonic Forms but our world.'[23] And this is the first strand that seems to me to distinguish Vidal-Naquet, the *historien-philosophe*, who insists on the relationship between history and the universe of ideas.

Vidal-Naquet's *The Black Hunter* is at first sight a curiously modest collection of essays; yet it has changed the course of historical studies, and both in France and in the Anglo-Saxon world has become the most important book in Greek history of its generation, a work whose insights have continued to stimulate and to renew not just an *école* but Greek studies throughout the world. It is not so easy to explain why this should be so. It is composed of dreams in which reality is reorganized in order to improve it and to clarify the problems that it contains: the Greek imaginary is replete with social dreams from Homer's account of Phaeacia onwards. Vidal-Naquet showed how such utopias comment on the lines of exclusion in historical societies by causing them to disappear or at least to be drawn differently, how for instance women and slaves might be permitted in the imagination to rule in Sparta, but only women could rule in Athens.[24] In particular he showed how Plato's rejection or reconstitution of history used utopianism as part of a project to solve the problems of the present by appeal to the imaginary:[25]

> The process is one that Plato uses all the time. In the *Phaedrus*, in praise of a young Isocrates, when he was in fact an old man and his opponent, Plato appealed from the real Isocrates to a possible Isocrates, to the philosophical orator that he never was.

This reading of Plato takes him seriously as text seeking to act on the present, and therefore as an element in the history of the Athenian *imaginaire*:[26]

> At the crossroads of these crises of the fourth century, so eloquently reflected in the subversion of the Cynics, Platonic philosophy emerges as at the same time a document about the crisis and an attempt to resolve it, at least on the theoretical level. It is the extent to which the golden age was effectively at the centre of contemporary debate, and through this debate, that we must study what this theme meant for Plato.

This is the resolution of the problem that confronted us in the 1970s: Plato's view of history is subordinate to his view of how the world should be, and that view is itself an attempt to influence the contemporary scene. Plato therefore operates on two levels as a historical text: to speak of utopia is to speak of reality – *de te loquitur*; but it is also to seek to influence reality. The Platonic city is a form of *theatrokratia*, but one doomed to failure:[27]

> The true Platonic tragedy is in fact elsewhere. It is in the situation that Platonism found itself, in the ambiguity of history.

The same element of utopianism influenced Vidal-Naquet's discussion of the classical tradition, which is an intrinsic part of his conception of the significance of *les études classiques*. One of the crucial consequences of the distancing of the Greeks from us is to open up the possibility of their irrelevance to the modern world: if the Greeks are so different, why should we bother to study them? The more we emphasize alterity the more we reduce the importance of our study of the past. This fatal flaw in the modern conception of the classical tradition has gone largely unnoticed in the general crisis of confidence in Western culture. Vidal-Naquet sought to face the problem in his studies of the influence of the ancient world on the political traditions of post-revolutionary France, collected in *La Démocratie grecque vue d'ailleurs*.[28] In this he looked back to his eighteenth-century predecessor, Cornelius de Pauw.

Vidal-Naquet's studies of the classical tradition are therefore unlike those of the modern founder of the discipline, Arnaldo Momigliano, whose influence Vidal-Naquet recognized explicitly. If part of Momigliano's post-war enterprise involved an attempt to rebuild the foundations of a European culture shattered by totalitarianism, his focus was on the development of historical method, and on the foundations of what still to him appeared a viable positivist tradition. In contrast, the post-68 *marxisante* generation politicized the study of historiography, as of all the human disciplines, and regarded it as an exercise in demonstrating the manipulations by a dominant ideology. Vidal-Naquet, it seems to me, accepted neither of these approaches. He saw the influence of Greece in terms of the creation and use of historical utopias, a Sparta to which the revolutionary generation could appeal, and finally a bourgeois vision of an Athens that could not threaten the present. The history of Athens and Sparta in the eighteenth and nineteenth centuries thus ran parallel with the history of France, as a series of models for use in the present; some would see this as a perversion of the task of scholarship, but Vidal-Naquet seemed rather to accept it in a positive spirit, as the need to accept the function of history as a process of commentary on the present.

So in all the apparent disparity and diversity of the studies in Vidal-Naquet's two collections of essays there is a unifying thread: Greek history came to perform for him the same function as utopias did for Plato. Vidal-Naquet shared with the young Moses Finley[29] (though to a far higher degree) the desire for action; and for all his emphasis on *altérité*, Vidal-Naquet's conception of history acted as model and critique of the modern age, and justified the attempts of the historian to influence the events of his own day. For him, the *bios theoretikos* and the *bios politikos* belonged together.

One of the earliest English disciples of the French school, Richard Gordon, tried to capture the essence of what he saw as this structuralist approach in a selection of translated essays by Marcel Detienne, Louis Gernet, Vernant, and Vidal-Naquet, entitled *Myth, Religion and Society: Structuralist Essays* (Cambridge 1981). These were some of the earliest translations from the French of the 'École de Paris' to appear; but they had little impact in comparison with the far more radical structuralist approach that was being presented in the discipline of anthropology by translators of Claude Lévi-Strauss.

In what follows I shall concentrate on the more diffuse influence of Vernant and Vidal-Naquet, and confine myself to those younger contemporaries who had close contact with them, and formally acknowledged their influence. In Britain these include Geoffrey Lloyd, who was the centre of this influence in Cambridge and introduced Simon Goldhill to him, myself at Oxford, Simon Pembroke in London, Richard Buxton in Bristol, and in the USA James Redfield (Chicago), Charles Segal (Harvard), Froma Zeitlin (Princeton), and Page duBois (San Diego).[30]

For Britain it was individuals in the Cambridge Faculty of Classics who were the most important in the reception of French ideas; they perhaps saw the connection between an earlier Cambridge 'school' of ritualists, with Jane Harrison, Sir James Frazer, and F.M. Cornford; certainly they were much encouraged by the leading Cambridge anthropologist, Edmund Leach. Moses Finley sent a number of his pupils to study in Paris, notably Richard Gordon, Richard Winton, and Richard Buxton – 'les trois Richards' as Vidal-Naquet christened them; although Finley himself did not always approve of the results. The influence on Buxton especially of his contact with the 'École de Paris' has dominated his choice of research themes ever since.

Geoffrey Lloyd had already pursued a philosophical form of structuralism influenced by Durkheim and Lévi-Strauss in his first book, *Polarity and Analogy*, which was completed in 1957 but only published nine years later in 1966; at that time he was ignorant of the work of Vernant and Vidal-Naquet. He met both of them first in the house of Moses Finley during their visit to Cambridge in 1966; after that he was influential in introducing young Cambridge scholars to the ideas and to the institution of the Centre Gernet. His wife Janet (Ji) has been in herself one of the most important sources of their Anglo-Saxon influence; for she was responsible for a series of outstanding translations of works by Detienne, Vernant, and Vidal-Naquet, from *The Gardens of Adonis* (1977), *Cunning Intelligence* (1978), to *Myth and Society* (1980), *Myth and Tragedy* (1981), and *Politics Ancient and Modern* (1985). But although Lloyd was perhaps inspired by Vernant's comparative approach (as by Joseph Needham) in his later work on wider traditions such as India and especially China, he has been led to offer radical criticisms of the classical French tradition of *mentalité* from Lucien Lévy-Bruhl to Marcel Granet and Jacques Le Goff, in his polemical work *Demystifying Mentalities*. Although in two chapters (chs 2 and 4) he seeks to distinguish Vernant's insistence on the causal relationship between political institutions, science, and tragedy in the Greek world from this approach, it is hard not to see Vernant as influenced by the unifying tendency in French social anthropology, in the terms that Lloyd (following Peter Burke) cites: '(1) the focus on the ideas or beliefs of collectivities rather than on those of individuals, (2) the inclusion, as important data, of unconscious as well as conscious assumptions, and (3) the focus on the structure of beliefs and their interrelations, as opposed to individual beliefs taken in isolation'.[31] This was surely a major part of the tradition of Durkheim and Louis Gernet that Vernant inherited.

In a later Cambridge generation, Simon Goldhill, who was introduced as an undergraduate to both Vernant's and Vidal-Naquet's work by Geoffrey Lloyd, regards Vernant's most important contribution as his:

> . . . work on tragic language first and foremost; the work on *le moment traqique* secondly; then the whole apparatus of myth and *pensée*. Their openness and intellectual verve were of crucial importance, of course, but mostly what had an instant and lasting impact was a linguistics that went beyond the Victorian philology still dominating the field (I was reading lots of linguistics in those days), and, secondly, a politics of theatre that went to the heart of tragedy as a civic event.

Vernant's general contribution is to be seen:

> . . . partly in tragedy: everyone is post-Vernant now except for a few self-appointed hyper-conservative loons: we will never go back to naïve positive linguistics or the belief that tragedy has no contact with a world of politics and city life (I hope). There are now dozens of close readings of tragedies based on Vernant's insights. But his 'structuralist' analyses of myth are just as important in the general field of classics: the tri-partite systematization of man-beast-god; sacrifice as a system; food as signifying system; divinity as a network not as multiple monotheisms – these are all crucial and still being worked out – and taken for granted by everyone who works on ancient religion.

My own debt to Vernant and Pierre Vidal-Naquet, and more generally to the *équipe* of the Centre Gernet, is difficult to disentangle. My closest academic friends were the members of the Centre, Alain Schnapp, Pauline Schmitt Pantel, and François Lissarrague; and I spent three long periods in Paris as *professeur attaché*, two in rue Monsieur-le-Prince and the last in rue Vivienne; my website of the Bibliotheca Academica Translationum (bat.ehess.fr) continues to be hosted by the Centre ANHIMA, the successor to the Centre. As Vidal-Naquet retired, at a time when the Centre Gernet seemed to be threatened with closure, I was asked in June 1996 to write an official assessment for the EHESS of its international importance; my conclusion was:[32]

> The *Centre* may not compare in terms of facilities with the Institute of Advanced Study at Princeton, the Center for Hellenic Studies at Washington, All Souls College Oxford or the Wissenschaftskolleg in Berlin, but in terms of productivity and intellectual excitement it is superior to all of these. I have enjoyed my duties enormously, and I know where I would rather work, despite all the frustrations of French academic life.

Certainly I was deeply influenced by reading *Les Origines*, as can be seen from the argument of my article 'Cities of Reason' (1987, 1990), which seeks to explain the problem of the difference and identity of Greek political thought in relation to the modern world.[33] Beyond that I responded to the combination of history and philosophy that I recognized in both Vernant and Vidal-Naquet. My approach to the Greek *symposion* not only reflected a close collaboration with Pauline Schmitt Pantel and François Lissarrague; it also rested on the belief (learned at least in part from Vernant) that social rituals have a significance in the investigation of mental attitudes or *l'imaginaire*, and that the Greek experience should be viewed as a whole in art, philosophy, literature, and history. The only aspect of Vernant's thought that I found difficult to assimilate is the idea that religion has an especially privileged position as an explanatory tool for understanding the Greeks; but in that I recognize I am very much in a minority. If I were to try to characterize my personal approach to history, I would see it as learned almost equally from Arnaldo Momigliano and from Vernant and Vidal-Naquet.

The move across the Atlantic was some ten years later than the start of the influence of Vernant on British culture, and was largely due to two individuals in the United States. Froma Zeitlin described the importance of the influence of Vernant in her introduction to the translation of Vernant's *Collected Essays*, two-thirds of which were brilliantly translated by herself for the first time.[34] More personally she says:

> Vernant was instrumental in my intellectual development from the moment that I discovered his work. My own involvement with Greek tragedy profited enormously from his structuralist approach: tragedy, more than any other genre, because of its tight organization and closed circuit, as it were, of language and event, lent itself to the construction of binaries and oppositions as a key to understanding the workings of drama. Jipé's further insistence on the relations between tragedy and the society from which it arose and in which it remained embedded remained again a continuing source of enlightenment. A second strand of influence for me was his work on the image, a topic that engaged him for many years, and was the subject of a number of his inquiries at the *Collège* and after. Starting already with Homer and focusing on the changes from the archaic to the classical period and the decisive intervention of Plato regarding the issues of mimesis, the mirror, the question of copy and model, and the gradual secularization of the image, he produced seminal work, whether on the *kolossos* or the eye of the Gorgon, and so much more. A final word on his engagement with matters of religion (his chair was in Comparative Religion), whether the nature of the gods (his piece on the body of the gods, for example, remains exemplary), the uses of ritual and cult, and his treatment of sacrifice in particular all contributed to the development of my own ideas. At the same time, the work he did with Detienne on *métis* in their collaborative volume on the nature of cunning intelligence stands for me as one of the finest pieces of scholarship I know, the source of endless ramification beyond the limits of that study.

Page duBois has offered a different perspective from that of Froma Zeitlin:

> For people in literary studies, I think Jipé was more influential than Pierre, who always seemed more of a historian than someone interested in what we call literary questions, although for Jipé they were not literary but cultural questions.

> I see Jipé more within the context of Marxism than perhaps others do. His early work on Marx on the Greeks, on class struggle, was very important to me in reconciling '60s radicalism and anti-war activism with academic study of ancient Greece. He was always very engaged politically, although Pierre was better-known perhaps for contemporary interventions on questions of Algeria, torture, holocaust denial, etc. I think Jipé retained some elements of Marxist historicism in his approach, although he became estranged from official Stalinist politics. In the essays on Oedipus, I see the traces of a struggle between a rigorous historicism, in which the ideas of a particular historical moment are specific to that time, that place, and a desire to comment on the human condition in a more general sense. I actually found his collaboration with Marcel Detienne, the early encounter with Lévi-Straussian structuralism, to be fascinating, but problematic. The brilliance of Detienne's Adonis book seemed revelatory but shocking. Jipé's earlier work was so historically specific, and the book on *métis* left behind that specificity to range very far, from Homer into late sources. I found that disappointing at the time, and I think he continued to struggle with a sense of a strongly rooted historical psychology, so influenced by Meyerson, and the temptations of a wider-ranging description of antiquity as an epoch.
>
> I do agree that he created the scholarly world of many progressive classicists – undoing boundaries between sub-fields for many of us. But there were and continue to be real obstacles between those working on ancient culture in a broader sense, and those who do 'literary studies', philosophy, epigraphy. I think for some classicists the Parisian school seemed very radical at first; then it was domesticated and defanged in the US, to some degree. Like the work of Derrida and others, Jipé's work on a few literary texts became exemplary, read in isolation from the rest of his work, and much of the radical purchase of his method, which was much more broadly cultural, was lost.[35]

Vernant and Vidal-Naquet introduced the English-speaking world to two forms of *l'imaginaire*. Behind the different responses lies a general recognition of the importance of their methodology, as much as of the positive results from their researches: it is their methods and style of approach that have had more importance than any particular theories or discoveries. One of the most important aspects of Vernant's approach is that expressed in the title of his last work, *La Traversée des frontières*

(Paris 2004). For whether or not the present generation realizes it, classical studies in the anglophone world live in a post-Vernant age, in the sense that we cannot escape from his influence – just as in other respects we are all post-Freudian, post-Marxist, and post-structuralist, so we now inhabit a world that Vernant and Vidal-Naquet created, which results from their work on Greek myth and its use for reconstructing the history of the Greek mentality. It was their insistence that myth was *pensée*, that ideas were history, that texts were expressions of the mental world of a real and contemporary society which was in no way identical with our own, that the sphere of *'imaginaire* is the reality of history, that created the scholarly world we now all inhabit – a world where performance is a historical event, where tragedy is a public art, where poetry is created for an occasion, and where there are no longer any barriers between Greek literature, Greek philosophy, and Greek history. Their achievement, not just in France, but throughout the world of classical scholarship, is indeed this unification of classical studies. And in that sense their gift to us is not so much in the conclusions of the articles and books that they wrote, but in presenting us with a new and unified method of research. So internalized, problematized, with all its uncertainties, the history of mentalities finally taught the English-speaking world that positivism must be abandoned.

But more widely the old traditions die hard, and the present generation seems to be turning its back on the achievements of the École de Paris. It seems that the Anglo-Saxon classical world is once more fragmenting into a series of technical disciplines and only perhaps in one respect is the approach of Vernant still being actively pursued: as Froma Zeitlin observed, in his later work he became interested in the problem of perception and the image. In collaboration with Françoise Frontisi-Ducroux, and in parallel with the interest in iconography of other members of the Centre Gernet, he explored the changing modes of vision. He saw that in the archaic world the image was not representation but a double, with independent power to act; it was Plato who created the conception of imitation. In modern Anglo-Saxon scholarship, whether consciously or not, this has found expression in a proliferation of studies on the body and the gaze.[36]

This leads me to reflect that we have not yet taken seriously enough the ideas that underlie the central insight of Vernant. The unifying theory beneath all the work of Vernant on comparatism, *mentalité*, *l'imaginaire*, was his belief in the importance of the ideas of his old comrade in the Resistance, Ignace Meyerson. As conceived by Meyerson, human psychology was both universal and historically determined: it embodied the changing response to basic human functions, perceptions and activities, such as space, time, work, the gaze. This theory, as Vernant saw, validated the comparative approach and the search for distinctive *mentalités* in different periods; it allowed for the historical development of psychological processes, while maintaining a materialistic, indeed Marxist framework. It made possible the continued search for *l'imaginaire*. And it especially established the importance of Greek literature and Greek myth in reconstructing how to 'see the moon with the eyes of the Greeks'.

Few who have written on Vernant have paid much attention to the decade of the 1950s, in which he formulated these ideas as assistant to Meyerson, and as editorial secretary of the *Journal de Psychologie*. Towards the end of his life, Vernant allowed Riccardo Di Donato to publish two volumes entitled *Passé et Présent*,[37] which record in detail his activities in this period. They show how his original impulse towards the *histoire de l'imaginaire* was derived from a belief in the changing nature of human psychology in relation to the fundamental forces in society as formulated in Marxist social theory. He accepted Meyerson's conception of 'historical psychology', and its claim that there is no universal science of psychology, that we are all conditioned by the society in which we live, and so that there can be no permanent unchanging concept of the individual persona outside the forces of history: 'There is no eternal and unchanging human nature, but people engaged in social realities and transforming themselves along with these'; and again, 'there exists a history of psychology just as there exists a social history of humanity':[38]

> For what differentiates the human being from other animal species is that his activity physical and spiritual is oriented towards the creation of a structured universe which presents itself at the same time as material objects, capable of being conserved and transmitted, and as systems of signification expressing mental forms.

The history of mentalities is the most important aspect of historical consciousness; without it all study of human psychology is meaningless. A generation dominated by the claims of neuroscience, in which epigraphists can study ancient Greek emotions while ignoring philosophy and literature, reveals both how little the influence of Vernant has penetrated into the Anglo-Saxon consciousness, and how essential it is that we return to his insights. For epigraphy is concerned with words carved on stone, whereas Vernant saw that what was important was their changing meanings: 'In this sense the psychologist can make his own the famous remark of Marx, that the whole of history is nothing more than the continuous transformation of human nature.'[39]

Unfinished Business

Salomo Luria (1891–1964)

19
Dark Times: The Cold War and the Triumph of Capitalism

Venio in campos et lata praetoria memoriae

Saint Augustine, *Confessions* 10, 8

And somewhere from the dim ages of history the truth dawned upon Europe that the morrow would obliterate the plans of today. Preparations for the slaughter of mankind have always been made in the name of God or some supposed higher being which men have devised and created in their own imagination.

Jaroslav Hašek, *The Good Soldier Schweik* (1921–23)

Quid nos, dura aetas, perpessi non sumus? Unde
hostilis nobis non metuenda manus?
Vidimus horrifero concussum turbine mundum
vix bene cardinibus sedere mole sua,
Vidimus heu foede civilia iura perempta –
absint a verbis omina dira meis.

(What have we not suffered in this harsh age? From where did we not have to fear the force of our enemies? We have seen the world shaken by a terrifying whirlwind, with its mass hardly settling back on its roots, we have seen, alas, civil rights foully destroyed – may these awful events never happen again)

Jakov M. Borovskij, professor of Latin in the Soviet Union, funerary epigraph (*c.* 1977)[1]

After the collapse of confidence in bourgeois liberalism in the trenches of the First World War, the terrors unleashed by Communism, Fascism, Nazism, and the threat of nuclear destruction devastated the European intelligentsia more effectively than any wars of religion. The twentieth century was the bloodiest century since the seventeenth for the persecution of intellectuals, and the end of the Second World War did not lead to the reunification of the Republic of Letters. Instead, the victorious Allies began a new 'cold' war between themselves, which created an 'iron curtain' between the scholars of the 'free world' and those of the Soviet bloc. In the West, Marxism became a contested word; and all contact with scholars in the Eastern bloc was discouraged on the one side, and prohibited on the other under the totalitarian Soviet regimes; this division was yet more absolute than the religious fanaticism of the period of the Reformation. The two worlds grew apart, and even today, a generation after the effective end of the Soviet Empire in 1989 with the fall of the Berlin Wall, the so-called democratic capitalist societies of the West continue to act as if the Cold War still exists, and will continue to exist to the end of time. Meanwhile we ignore some of the most important modern aspects of the classical tradition.

The Soviet Empire proclaimed its adherence to a Marxist theory of history, in which history was subordinated to the dialectic of a predetermined theory of historical progress through a series of revolutionary stages to the final triumph of the revolution, and the achievement of a golden age in the dictatorship of the proletariat. Now discredited as a theory of the inevitability of revolutionary change, the Marxist view retains much of its power as an analysis of the forces underlying the development of human society. For few would deny the central Marxist conception that it is the economy which determines the basic types of human society. The organization of labour creates the surplus upon which the complexity of cultural structures is raised, from the primitive centralized palace economies of the Bronze Age to the more sophisticated and complex structures of the early city-state in the Middle East and Mediterranean, with the development of craft manufacture and trade. The organization of labour in order to extract a surplus is determined by the ability of religious or power elites to create and exploit organizational forms suited to the economic and productive capacities of their societies. All labour can therefore be viewed as a form of exploitation by the rulers for their benefit of the surplus production of the working classes, through their ownership of landed assets and the social control of labour. After the primitive stage of family and tribal economies came the various forms of indentured labour from debt bondage to helotry and chattel slavery, to be replaced in turn by feudalism, and modern wage labour and capitalism, and now by the exploitation of the underdeveloped world for the benefit of the 'advanced' Western societies:

> With slavery, which reached its fullest development in civilization, came the first great cleavage of society into an exploiting and an exploited class. This cleavage has continued at each stage of civilization. Slavery was the first form of exploitation, peculiar to the world of antiquity; it was followed by serfdom in the Middle Ages, and by wage labour in modern times. These are the three great epochs of Western civilization; open, and latterly, disguised slavery, are its steady companions.
>
> F. Engels, *Origin of the Family*[2]

> Slavery had been invented. It soon became the dominant form of production among all peoples who were developing beyond the old community, but in the end was also one of the chief causes of their decay. It was slavery that first made possible the division of labour between agriculture and industry on a larger scale, and thereby also Hellenism, the flowering of the ancient world. Without slavery, no Greek state, no Greek art and science; without slavery, no Roman Empire. But without the basis laid by Greek culture, and the Roman Empire, also no modern Europe. We should never forget that our whole economic, political and intellectual development presupposes a state of things in which slavery was as necessary as it was universally recognized. In this sense we are entitled to say: without the slavery of antiquity no modern socialism.
>
> It is very easy to inveigh against slavery and similar things in general terms, and to give vent to high moral indignation at such infamies. Unfortunately all this conveys is only what everyone knows, namely, that these institutions of antiquity are no longer in accord with our present conditions and our sentiments, which these conditions determined. But it does not tell us one word as to how these institutions arose, why they existed, and what role they played in history. And when we examine these questions, we are compelled to say, however contradictory and heretical it

> may sound, that the introduction of slavery under the conditions prevailing at that time, was a great step forward.
>
> F. Engels, *Anti-Duhring*[3]

The study of ancient Greece was therefore an intrinsic part of the Marxist world picture; and it was moreover well entrenched in the surviving remnants of the post-Nazi educational structures of all Eastern European countries, especially Germany and (more intermittently) Russia. The study of the ancient world continued, and was even strengthened by the universalist claim that all societies, Eastern and Western, had been part of the same historical process, so that Egyptian, Near Eastern, Indian and Chinese cultures were subsumed in the search for a general theoretical approach. Neither Marx nor Engels had said much in detail about ancient societies, other than that they were characterized by the slave mode of production. Initially there was tension between the traditionalists, educated before the Russian Revolution, and the new professoriate appointed by the party. The various attempts to create a coherent Marxist theory of ancient world history were successively sabotaged by the paranoia of Stalin and the KGB intent on waging the class war. An early definition of the 'Asiatic mode of production' was abandoned.[4] A coherent definition of a Marxist theory of ancient history was pursued by the State Academy for the History of Material Culture (GAIMK) in Leningrad in the early 1930s, but in 1935 its leaders were liquidated, as the party intensified its control over academic life. The official line was established by A.V. Mishulin, editor of the Journal of Ancient History (*Vestnik Drevnej Istorii*), who wrote an editorial in the first number in 1937 'Against the servility towards foreignness in the field of ancient history' and sought to create university textbooks and a collaborative 'World History' around the slave mode of production and a theory of 'slave revolutions', which was taken to be a favourite idea of Stalin. After Stalin's death in 1953, from that decade onwards ancient historians sought to evolve a more eclectic Marxist approach based on the acceptance of an economic interpretation of historical forces. The most interesting of these approaches argued that alongside the slave-owning society there existed a peasant economy of at least equal importance.[5] This interpretation is of course not simply Marxist, but fundamentally rooted in the Russian experience, which had already been explored by Mikhail Rostovtzeff both before the Revolution, and in his later two great works in exile, *The Social and Economic History of the Roman Empire* and *The Social and Economic History of the Hellenistic World*;[6] they represent a revival of a truly Russian scholarship that leads back through its greatest historian to the vision of the age of Tolstoy.

One aspect of the study of antiquity progressively evolved under Soviet Marxism. Unlike other areas of study more obviously relevant to Marxist revolutionary aims, and unlike the 'democratic' ideology of the West, the study of ancient history lacked any immediate political relevance, and the scholars of the ancient regime were well entrenched in the educational system. As a consequence perhaps it was less closely and less effectively patrolled, so that, as the totalitarian control of Marxist-Leninist orthodoxy by the secret police intensified, those who wished their lives to escape notice found refuge in subjects that were of little interest to the political authorities. Eventually it can be argued that an alternative historiography based on a form of internal migration emerged, and paradoxically Greek scholars in the Soviet Empire became less Marxist than their corresponding ideologues of the West. Many indeed found the Classics an effective form of secret resistance to Marxism: as A.K. Gavrilov said in a report of 1995, under Soviet control:[7]

> The Classics were perceived as a panorama of political and personal individual diversity in the history of mankind. Thus the historically-based idea of human continuity and constancy became a source of inspiration.
>
> Not only can the good shelter something bad; luckily the opposite is also possible. Russian society filled the void created by ideological oppression and its erosion of knowledge about alternative possibilities and realizations of the human mind. It compensated with a strong urge to attain an inner fulfilment and freedom in spite of all obstacles. The antagonistic ways of the Russian intelligentsia proved again to be a strong and effective force, this time, luckily, the intelligentsia came out for rather than against classical learning. It was probably a form of escapism – an escape from such things as listening for hours at a stretch to the words of a Marx or a Lenin! But it was more than that. Knowledge about the remote past made it possible to think about other, more advanced, civilizations, about the Classics. Moreover the study of classical civilization, with its old traditions and its internationalism, provided a model, both modern and universal, for scientific study of the humanities. Here was a truly humanistic impetus, a source of inspiration obviously

> superior to Marxist laws and Leninist frameworks . . . With the hindsight of history, can we not say that the study of the Classics speaks decisively about human unity in diversity, that is, about the basic continuity of human nature?

In Russia and elsewhere translation of ancient works was a safe alternative to academic research and therefore flourished: books were 'available to everyone at least with regard to price . . . Another reason for the pursuit of translation projects was a strong artistic impetus and longing to escape reality, to reject the patronizing new ideology for the sake of aesthetic and historical, that is, eternal values.'

The career of one Russian scholar exemplifies the problems of this period. Salomo Luria (1891–1964) had studied at St Petersburg before the Revolution under Rostovtzeff and the Polish scholar Th. Zielinski (who died in 1944). After the Revolution, Luria taught at Petrograd and Samara, until 1929 when ancient history was excluded from universities, but was reinstated in 1934; in 1940 he published the first part of his *History of Greece*, but later fell out of favour as a Jew; he was accused in 1949 of 'cosmopolitanism' (a normal cover for anti-Semitism) and 'unprincipled grovelling before West European science'; he had already been criticized because his book on Herodotus cited Jacoby, Meyer, Cary, and Ehrenberg, but no Russians: 'The teaching of Marx – Engels – Lenin – Stalin is omnipotent, because it is true.'[8] Luria was dismissed and became a junior researcher at the Academy of Sciences, until at last in 1953 he returned to Leningrad as Professor of Classical Philology. A papyrologist and epigraphist, a distinguished Egyptologist and an outstanding historian of ancient Greek science and Democritus, Luria had corresponded in his youth with Wilamowitz; in 1939 he had suggested that the Mycenaean Linear B script was Greek, and after Ventris's decipherment corresponded with him.[9] In 1930, Luria wrote for his son a children's story inspired by a papyrus letter from a child to his father (P.Oxy.119r); it went through eleven editions, and spawned a whole genre of children's stories about the classical world, which helped to keep alive classical knowledge in the Soviet Union. After his death a secret diary written in the Cypriot syllabic script was discovered:[10]

> The typical features of the Soviet system are its special 'two realities'. The citizens of the Soviet Union not only suffer a hard and dull life but also

> must play their roles through all of it – as the actors in a joyful, spectacular show of an earthly paradise not corresponding with everyday reality . . . From the point of view of the Marxist methodology of history the Soviet regime is a slave-owning system.

In other areas of the Soviet Empire political and social history was pursued on firmly Marxist principles, with varying success.[11] Poland with its strong classical tradition was perhaps least affected: 'The link to tradition was very important for those who wanted to oppose a reality they found unacceptable . . . Classical scholarship became a refuge, a field where the rules of logic were observed, where the desire for truth was satisfied.'[12] The problem of establishing a coherent approach was intensified by the conflict between the bourgeois and independently wealthy Latinist K. Kumaniecki (1905–1977)[13] and his Marxist rival B. Biliński (1913–1996); eventually the former prevailed, and created such solidarity within the classical community that no informers or communists are recorded, and Biliński was neutralized by being appointed director of the Polish Academy in Rome, where he spent twenty-seven years as a respected and innocent scholar. Classical studies were also protected by the fact that Josef Cyrankiewicz, the Polish prime minister from 1947 to 1970 (and president until 1972), was proud of being a pupil of the Roman jurist Rafael Taubenschlag.[14]

East Germany was less fortunate. The ruthless Werner Hartke (1907–1993), dean of the Faculty of Philosophy at Rostock University and later President of the Berlin Academy and Rektor of the Humboldt University in Berlin, had been an intelligence officer in the Nazi-Abwehr, but joined the SED Communist Party after the war: he was responsible for the persecution of individual scholars, sending some of his colleagues to execution or life imprisonment with hard labour.[15] Equally sinister were the activities of the distinguished Byzantinist Johannes Irmscher (1920–2000), who described himself as 'a communist without a party', and used his international scholarly reputation to further his own career by volunteering to act as an agent of the Stasi from 1947 to 1989: his writing was so illegible he had to report verbally to his controller, who knew him as 'the Social Informant, a typical bourgeois intellectual'; he was a personal friend of the ambassadors of Greece, Albania, and China, on whom he reported regularly to the Stasi, and even directly to the Soviet KGB. Yet apart from denouncing his rival, the great theologian Kurt Aland (1915–1994), who was dismissed from his university and escaped to the West in 1958, and warning of other impending defections, Irmscher seems to have avoided compromising his immediate colleagues, reserving his activities for undermining the national and international organizations to which he belonged.[16] Still:

> Even in the iciest period of the Cold War, the contact with classicists the world over could not be completely interrupted by the communist governments. Over all these years we were grateful for books, for offprints, for invitations to conferences. To be sure, both parties knew pretty well that such invitations could not be accepted, but the mere existence of these invitations made regime-conforming university authorities hesitate to wipe out totally the scattered remnants of classical studies.[17]

One East German scholar belonged to a true Marxist tradition. As a young woman Elisabeth Charlotte Welskopf, née Henrich (1901–1979), had hidden Jewish and political dissidents in her flat, one of whom (Rudolf Welskopf) she married after the war; in 1944 she had been interrogated by the Gestapo, but was released. She later wrote a semi-autobiographical novel about her exploits.[18] She worked as a government statistician, and in 1946 joined the SED party. She developed a parallel career as a writer of hugely popular novels about the American Indians, with whom she had been fascinated since childhood.[19] In 1949 she enrolled to study ancient history at Humboldt University, and (despite her career being consistently opposed by Hartke for obvious reasons, which created a personal enmity) eventually became Professor of Greek History in 1960, and was the first woman to be elected a member of the Deutsche Akademie der Wissenschaften, as well as an honorary member of the Sioux tribe. Her work was coherently Marxist; her *Habilitation* was published as *Probleme der Musse im alten Hellas* (Berlin 1962), and contained a final chapter on 'the discovery and development of Aristotelian ideas on leisure by Marx and Engels' – '*mais il est prodigieusement intéressant*', a contemporary Western reviewer said.[20] In 1974 she published perhaps the most coherent Marxist interpretation of Greek history in a collective four-volume work, *Hellenische Poleis: Krise, Wandlung, Wirkung* (Berlin 1974), with contributions from sixty Eastern and Western scholars. This was a remarkable work: it abandoned the conventional interest in politics and personalities, periodization and even the contrast between Athens and Sparta, to establish a conceptual framework not dissimilar to Burckhardt's view of *Kulturgeschichte*. It centred on *Soziale Typenbegriffe*, social concepts conceived as a fusion of ancient and modern ideas; the first volume discussed economic and political structures, the second Hellenization in the eastern and western Mediterranean even as far as India. The third volume was devoted to the reflection of the 'crisis of the classical Greek city' in religion, theatre, literature, and art, the fourth discussed science, medicine, and philosophy. This was the most impressive and original attempt on either side of the 'Iron Curtain' to understand the significance of Greek culture in the twentieth century.[21]

The opposition of Hartke in the *Akademie* caused Charlotte Welskopf in her last years to use her own wealth (derived from her royalties as a novelist) to organize and publish a remarkable posthumous seven-volume work *Soziale Typenbegriffe im alten Griechenland und ihr Fortleben in den Sprachen der Welt* (Social Concepts in Ancient Greece and their Survival in the Languages of the World, Berlin 1981–5). Again, the last five volumes offered a collection of essays by eighty-six Eastern and Western scholars on the relation between Greek and modern political vocabulary among not just European and Russian languages but also Chinese, Arabic, and other world languages, including Swahili and Thai. It was preceded by a selective concordance of ancient Greek socio-political terms. Despite unevenness in the individual essays (due partly to Charlotte's death) it was a remarkable enterprise in search of a theory. The idea of exploring *Typenbegriffe* across languages replaced orthodox philology with the study of conceptual groupings, similar to the socio-psychological categories of J.-P. Vernant,[22] and offered a genuine Marxist approach to the history of mentalities. In her teaching Welskopf encouraged freedom of thought, and long after her retirement she held informal seminars in her villa at Treptow Park outside Berlin for a devoted group of disciples. Because of the record of her past career she was untouchable. As she said to an American journalist:[23]

> You are dangerous because you are a journalist, even though you probably have endearing and valuable qualities as a private individual. And I know very well that your [Western] newspaper prefers to write about opposition figures when you write about East German writers. I am not an opposition figure. Of course I'm not a member of the 'East German National Council' – an utterly fictitious rumour – any more than I'm a

> member of the Oglala tribe. I have always been politically engaged, but I am no kind of 'organization woman'. I'm a comrade. And I'm tough. I'm unbelievably tough. Like a cat.

After her death in 2002 a conference in her memory was organized by her disciple, Isolde Stark. In her two compilations Welskopf had built on the East German tradition of collective enterprises and her own idiosyncratic vision of *Typenbegriffe* to create a bridge between Marxism and Western scholarship, and to offer a coherent interpretation of the ancient world that transcends the faults in its execution.

Elisabeth Charlotte Welskopf (1901–1979)

East German scholarship was indeed productive in exploring socio-economic aspects of ancient history susceptible to a Marxist interpretation, but themes inherited from German pre-war projects like the prosopography of the Roman imperial upper classes languished,[24] in favour of projects such as the study of slave names and the exploration of land tenure in the archaeologically rich peninsula of the Crimea. The choice of subjects and the interpretation of political and social history reflected the theoretical stance imposed by Marxism. But both Eastern and Western post-war German studies of ancient history were contaminated by the extraordinary efficiency of the Nazi regime in infiltrating and perverting the proud tradition of *Altertumswissenschaft*, and since virtually no Jewish scholars were prepared to return to a divided Germany, and most prominent scholars had collaborated with the regime, but were nevertheless retained in their post-war academic positions, it has taken more than a generation for German scholarship to recover a semblance of its former authority.[25]

The scholars of other countries suffered exile, continuity, resistance, and other fates almost randomly in accordance with their individual traditions and leadership, since there was little attempt to create central control, although there were of course certain general similarities, especially in the interference in classical scholarship by the secret police. The isolation between East and West caused serious problems for the East in access to bibliographical resources, due in part to censorship controls, but mainly to the lack of Western currency experienced by Eastern institutions and individual scholars. This was occasionally mitigated by personal friendships that resulted in gifts from West to East, as for instance the connections between Moses Finley in Cambridge and Jan Peçirka in Prague, or of Vernant and Vidal-Naquet with Benedetto Bravo and Eva Wipszycka in Warsaw, or of myself and Manuela Tecuşan in Bucharest. But these were tiny drops in the ocean of publications.

The Western study of Greek history was dominated by the attempt of the Anglo-Saxon world to take over and continue the pre-war 'empirical' German tradition of detailed antiquarian studies, with little interest in theoretical questions of interpretation. This has borne great fruit in studies of Greek religion, where the constraints of monotheistic interpretations have slowly been abandoned, although there has been little comparative study of other polytheistic belief systems such as Hinduism.[26] This apparently anodyne form of positivism is well suited to the triumph of capitalism and disguises the essentially neo-liberal and conservative ideology of most modern scholarship on the ancient world. The absence of an overarching interpretative framework favours a form of detailed research that has only been encouraged by the acceptance of new discoveries in archaeology. Only in Italy were these combined with a Marxist approach that transformed traditional archaeology by turning attention away from grand and easily identifiable structures such as civic centres, temple complexes, and display buildings, and brought a new interest in rural settlements and the practical contextualization of social history.[27]

The most influential historian of the Western post-war Anglo-Saxon world had indeed experienced an initial contact with Marxist ideas, and was one of the few Western scholars to maintain connections with Eastern scholars throughout his life. Moses Finley (1912–1986) had started his academic career as a researcher at the Institute for Social Research, founded in 1929 by Jewish Marxist intellectuals and known as the Frankfurt School, which relocated to New York during the Nazi period and the Second World War, splitting and partly returning to Frankfurt during the McCarthy persecutions of the 1950s. For a time in youth he was an active communist,[28] during the war he was national campaign director of the Russian Jewish War Relief charity (1942–46), and even in later life he retained a number of friendships across the Iron Curtain. In 1952 he was dismissed from Rutgers University, after he pleaded the

Sir Moses Finley (1912–1986)

Fifth Amendment and refused to answer questions from the Un-American Activities Committee, run by Senator McCarthy.[29] Finley was invited to Oxford and Cambridge while attempts were made to find him a post, and in 1955 he was appointed as a university lecturer and later elected a Fellow of Jesus College, Cambridge. During his subsequent career in England he was the most important influence on the liberal reform of the school and university curricula in Classics and Ancient History, along with John Sharwood Smith of the London Institute of Education, which successfully substituted the study of the ancient texts (often in translation) for the rote learning of modern views and linguistic exercises. Finley ended as a pillar of the English establishment, Professor of Ancient History (1970–79), knighted (1979), and Master of Darwin College, Cambridge (1976–82).

Finley's early experiences in the Institute for Social Research gave him a continuing openness to theoretical ideas that he never lost. In his first book after migrating to England, *The World of Odysseus* (1954), he focused on the same problem as J.-P. Vernant of the difference between the centralized palace economy, revealed as Greek in the decipherment of Linear B by Michael Ventris, and the later early Greek world: he asserted the separate historical existence of the Homeric world in economic terms, as a post-Mycenaean late Dark Age society, based on gift exchange and a hierarchical conception of reciprocity, honour, and patronage, from which both the centralized palace economy and economic rationality were absent. This book is the foundation of all subsequent historical and archaeological studies on late Dark Age Greece. The chief influence on his interpretation came from the New York seminars of Karl Polanyi on 'non-market economies', which were embedded in an anthropological and social framework.[30]

Finley's view was generalized across the ancient world in *The Ancient Economy* (1973). This primitivist approach based on the ideas of Max Weber and Karl Polanyi has perhaps come to seem less plausible as the archaeological evidence increases; and the relation between agriculture, manufacture, and trade remains problematic. The chief weakness in Finley's interpretation of the ancient economy was indeed his refusal to recognize the importance of trade and exchange in the Mediterranean city-states, which for him were primitive agrarian economies; and he consistently downplayed the importance of archaeological evidence for the distribution of goods around the Mediterranean.[31]

More successful was his increasingly relevant attempt to interpret *Democracy Ancient and Modern* (1973), in which he argued that the modern idea that democracy rests on the apathy of an electorate is disproved by the ancient example of direct democracy.

In *Ancient Slavery and Modern Ideology* (1980, new edition 1998) he tackled modern approaches to ancient slavery, dismissing both the Marxist interpretation of it as a primitive form of economic exploitation, and the anti-Marxist response of the West German research project run by the Mainz Akademie der Wissenschaften under the former Nazi Joseph Vogt, which attempted to sanitize ancient slavery in terms of an emphasis on human relationships. Instead, Finley argued for a view which replaced the idea of ancient slavery as a general stage in the economic development of class in the Marxist sense with a Weberian definition of it as a social and legal status encompassing a diversity of forms, such as chattel slavery, debt bondage, and helotage, and tried to relate the experience of ancient slavery to modern American plantation slavery. This last comparison was once again controversial, given the absence of colour prejudice in antiquity and the fact that the evidence for any form of plantation agriculture in the Greek world at least is problematic. Finley's interpretation was bitterly opposed by Marxists, but has proved perhaps the most important attempt to understand the complexity of the problem of forced labour in antiquity: it was especially influential in France.[32] In this book Finley was however more successful in demolishing the ideas of others than in creating a firm position of his own. Indeed, although he always accepted the need for models in history, his general approach in all his later writing was polemical rather than theoretical, as if he were more interested in disproving other modern views than establishing a coherent position of his own; and his use of a variety of theoretical approaches perhaps ultimately lacked unity, as subsequent critics have pointed out. But his most important contribution in his study of slavery was in creating a dialogue between East and West. He was openly opposed to any demonization of the East, particularly on the part of West German historians, and, apart from his openness and friendships with Eastern colleagues, after the death of Stalin in 1953 his approaches had considerable influence on the reformulation of Marxist theory in relation to ancient history by writers such as his friend Jan Peçirka. Finley's books circulated unofficially in the East, and his ideas about the complexity of slave systems in different societies were even quoted in Eastern publications.[33]

A great deal of modern Western scholarship has been concerned with analysing the relation between ancient and modern ideas of democracy, encouraged by the fetish for Western democratic values and the alleged 2,500th anniversary of 'the invention of democracy' in 1993.[34] Much of this work remains problematic because it ignores the fundamental difference between the structures of direct and representative democracies, and the importance of ritual and tradition in the formation of viable political systems; little of it progresses beyond the views of George Grote.

The most systematic and interesting analysis is that of Mogens Herman Hansen. He began his approach on empirical principles, and argued from two positions. The first was purely practical, in terms of physical constraints: how many male citizens could be accommodated on the Pnyx in its different configurations, how long did Athenian assemblies last, how long were speeches, how did the assembly actually vote, how often did they meet, how did the leaders assert their authority and establish any continuity of policy, what social class did they come from? Hansen established the practices of the assembly, the nature of the leadership exercised by the distinct classes of orators and generals (*rhetores* and *strategoi*) in the absence of any form of partisan political structures, the importance of

Mogens Herman Hansen (born 1940)

mood and rhetoric on the opinions of the mass assembly. Many of these questions were answered through analogy with the only surviving modern institutional forms of direct democracy, the Swiss *Landsgemeinde*.[35]

His second and most crucial argument was based on the fact that all previous interpretations of Athenian democracy had ignored the fundamental change in the nature of Athenian democracy as a result of its defeat in the Peloponnesian War and the reforms of 403/2 BC. Basically, the democracy had moved from a system in which the assembly was sovereign to one that was ruled by the distinction between laws (*nomoi*) that were permanent and decisions (*psephismata*) that had to be made in conformity with the laws, and could be challenged in the courts if they were not. Hansen's interpretation of Athenian democracy was therefore based on the evidence of the existing fourth-century assembly speeches, and the resulting book was entitled *The Athenian Democracy in the Age of Demosthenes* (1991), which was explicitly contrasted with the fifth-century Periclean democracy, about which little could be known. This is perhaps the most effective modern long-term study of Greek history conducted without any theoretical presuppositions. Hansen has gone on to analyse in similar fashion the traditions and similarities of ancient and modern democracy.[36]

The paradoxical contrast between Eastern and Western historiography was brought to a head in the book of François Furet, *Le Passé d'une illusion* (1995). Analysing the collapse of communism in relation to the intellectual tradition of Europe, he asked why did all the intellectuals of Western Europe (apart from the Catholic right) believe in communism for two generations? Furet himself had been a member of the party; he showed us the inevitability of believing in Marxism against the background of contemporary history, the means by which that illusion was sustained, and the stages of disillusionment. The experience of the First World War convinced the peoples of Europe that the bourgeois liberalism that had sent them to be massacred in the name of nationalism was a rotten system designed to perpetuate the wealth and power of the bourgeoisie; and both workers and bourgeoisie were subsequently converted to right-wing populism by the loss of their wealth in the great recession. As a result of the discrediting of democratic liberalism, two popular movements arose: nationalist parties like those in Italy, Germany, Spain (and to a lesser extent in France) and the great international movement of Marxism. That was the choice on offer for those who wished to ensure that the mistakes of the nineteenth century were not repeated; and the experience of the terrors of Nazism in the East merely reinforced the argument. It was obvious which choice an intellectual would make. Only the rarity of thinkers in the English-speaking world prevented the anglophone West from joining this mass intellectual movement – and one still has a right to be proud of the fact that the most important English area where a true Marxist tradition was established in the 1930s was in the study of history, with Christopher Hill, E.P. Thompson, E.A. Thomson, George Rudé, Eric Hobsbawm, Frank Walbank, and Geoffrey de Sainte Croix (who throughout his life upheld a Western and purely theoretical form of Marxism).

For two generations the study of Greek history has resembled a hall of mirrors, in which both Eastern and Western scholars have stared at their own reflections: few have managed to step through the looking glass into the opposing world behind their present. And under the conflict between the interpretations of both sides lies the fundamental question that is posed by Greek history: are the ideas of democracy and civilization possible without ancient slavery and its modern form, the exploitation of the underprivileged?

MEMORIES OF THE COLD WAR[37]

With the opening of the secret state files of the Eastern bloc and the emergence of the unpublished memoirs of their victims the complexity and randomness of the history of the relation of Eastern and Western attitudes to Greek history can begin to be written.[38] It is important that Western survivors should also record their memories of this great schism before they die; here are my personal memories. At a certain point one wakes up to discover that one has become truly an 'ancient historian' (as I declared my profession to be on my first passport: no one understood, except an Italian frontier official – '*Ah, la storia antica*'). That is, one has become not a historian, but a part of history itself.

I was born in 1937;[39] my generation came of age in the 1950s, and was dominated by the propaganda of the Cold War. In 1956 I was conscripted into the British army to fight Communism, but instead was assigned to the invasion of the Suez Canal; fortunately the Americans ordered the British to withdraw before we went out as the second wave of the occupying force. I had already decided to become a deserter, because we, who were busy painting our vehicles sand-coloured with a big white H on top (since it was intended that the Israelis should destroy the Egyptian air force before the invasion), already believed that the expedition was the result of a corrupt and secret plot between Britain, France, and Israel; this fact has been definitively revealed by the memoir of Patrick Dean, the junior British official who took part in the negotiations. The British Prime Minister burned his copy of the agreement in the fireplace of No. 10 Downing Street, the French copy is 'lost'; but the Israeli copy survives at least in photocopies.[40]

That taught me the essential lesson that foreign policy is normally based on lies and misconceptions, and that politicians and generals are fools who do not understand the nature of the historical tragedies that they unleash. The aborted invasion of Egypt resulted only in the destruction of yet another of the greatest and most civilized cities of the modern world – Alexandria, which rots in decay after the expulsion of all Italians, Greeks, and Jews: the city of Cavafy, Ungaretti, and Lawrence Durrell was destroyed by the stupidity of politicians along with Smyrna and Salonica, and perhaps now London.[41] The same year the Soviets invaded Hungary, but because of the moral corruption of the West we were unable to intervene.

Instead, I spent the rest of my military service defending the non-existent frontier between Northern Ireland and the Republic, until I was demobbed with a resoundingly ambiguous testimonial to two years as a private soldier: 'Somewhat lacking in initiative and drive. But this (*what?*) should be more apparent in his civilian life.' I had clearly joined the honourable ranks of the Good Soldier Schweik.

So I went to Oxford University and entered the ancient Republic of Letters, where I vowed to devote myself to ignoring the Iron Curtain that we were not supposed to penetrate. Friendship was my only weapon. Most of my teachers were second-rate historians, whose careers had been stunted by seven years of war work. The intellectual life of the academic world was sustained by the Jewish refugees who had fled Nazi persecution in the 1930s. I was saved by two great figures of this diaspora, both of them connected to the Warburg Institute. The first was the art historian Ernst Gombrich (1909–2001), Director of the Warburg from 1959 to 1972, who opened my eyes to the visual element in history. The second was my doctoral supervisor Arnaldo Momigliano (1908–1987), the most learned historian of his age, a refugee from Fascist Italy. It was from him that I learned the importance of the classical tradition for the defence of European culture.

As a penniless graduate student, I earned money by teaching Latin to less than enthusiastic young women. I recall a traumatic moment on 27 October 1962, the day of the Cuban Missile Crisis. We were translating Ovid's *Ars amatoria* (which I had selected as a suitable text to interest a bored young girl), when I became aware of an immense throbbing noise in the air: in order not to be caught on the ground, all the B52 bombers from the American airbases were circling above Oxford, fully armed with nuclear warheads. I continued my lesson, reflecting that if this was to be the last day of Western civilization, there could be no better way to die 'waiting for the barbarian' than reading Ovid on the art of love. Nevertheless, it caused me to join the Aldermaston March of the Campaign for Nuclear Disarmament in 1963.[42]

My first Eastern friend was the Polish archaeologist and papyrologist Zbigniew Borkowski (1936–1991). In 1970 the Fondation Hardt in Switzerland was the only place where Western and Eastern scholars could meet;[43] we bonded late at night over the Baron's last bottle of whisky. We agreed that we had both been fools deluded by propaganda: we searched vainly for the Red Star in the night sky. Zbigniew told me that he had once been a member of the Communist Youth: 'I am so convinced I even denounce my grandmother because she is reactionary.' 'But I thought all grandmothers were by definition reactionary.' 'Yes,' he replied with Polish Catholic logic, 'but she is MY grandmother.'

Zbigniew taught me to understand the holes that allowed transit through the Iron Curtain.[44] In 1946 the great papyrologist Rafael Taubenschlag had returned to Warsaw from exile in the USA, and founded the very specialized *Journal of Juristic Papyrology*. In the Communist era, because of the protection of his former pupil Josef Cyrankiewicz, it was thought essential to maintain its publication; so Polish papyrologists were permitted to travel abroad to Western institutions to consult other collections. While on a mission in Syria (to Palmyra?) Zbigniew and his group were ordered to go to Alexandria and transform themselves into archaeologists (where he published the inscriptions from the late Roman hippodrome). They sent a telegram, '*Arrivons jeudi complètement ivres*' ('We arrive on Thursday completely drunk').

The reason for this sudden change of career was hidden deep in the economic arcana of the Cold War. After Suez the Soviets were secretly rearming the Egyptians with weapons made mainly in Czechoslovakia. But the Egyptians had no foreign currency to pay for these weapons. So the Soviets ordered the Poles to undertake major excavations and restoration work in Egypt, in order to supply the necessary Soviet bloc currency.[45] Thus archaeology was turned into armaments.

Later Zbigniew visited Oxford to work on the Oxyrhynchus archive, and lived with me. In the summer evenings after work we would depart with a bottle of whisky in my camping van to the woods nearby, and spend the night singing Russian folksongs – the most haunting one I remember was 'The Girl on the High Trapeze'. He would talk of the trackless forests of Eastern Poland that we would one day visit together. Alas, twenty years later he died on just such an expedition, unwilling to go to hospital for a minor complaint.

In the late 1970s I met Gert Audring from the East German Academy of Sciences when he was on an official visit to England: he invited me to visit East Berlin. I well remember the fear with which I passed through Checkpoint Charlie, famous from so many spy stories: Gert was waiting for me discreetly hidden about a hundred yards into the Soviet Zone, and showed me round the remnants of former German culture, the Altes Museum, the Pergamon Museum, the opera house, Unter den Linden, and the other side of the Berlin Wall. He was very brave to offer friendship to a Western colleague. It was then that I formed the opinion that one day Germany might perhaps be reunited; but no, all my young West German colleagues said it was impossible. I have not seen Audring since the reunification of 1992, but know that he has devoted himself to publishing the papers of the ancient historian Eduard Meyer.[46]

Gert told me that if I ever went to Prague I must visit the great epigraphist and archaeologist, Jan Peçirka (1926–1993), who possessed the best collection of Western books in the East, thanks to his friend in Cambridge, Moses Finley, who would send them to him: every Eastern scholar, he said, would visit Peçirka in his private flat for study, despite the fact that he had been expelled from the university for political reasons. Later I did indeed visit him, towards the end of his life: his seminal work in the Crimea had been suspended and he was a very bitter man.

My visit to Prague was for the 16th Eirene conference in 1982, at the invitation of Pavel Oliva (1923–2021). The previous year I had invited him to come to Oxford to give a set of lectures on ancient Sparta as the visiting 'Nellie Wallace Lecturer'. We took great care with the invitation, since we knew that Oliva was in trouble with the authorities: before issuing the formal invitation we had sent a private letter through a friend in the Netherlands to ask him whether he would like to be invited: he replied in the affirmative. And to our surprise he was allowed to visit together with his wife Vera Olivova. This was perhaps the first sign of that *perestroika* of 1986, when Gorbachev admitted he had been inspired by the 'Socialism with a human face' of Alexander Dubcek of Czechoslovakia. Something was moving in the Soviet bloc.

The reason for Oliva's difficulties was that, despite being a senior member of the Czech Academy and well known in the West, he had been involved in the Prague Spring of 1968, and his wife had signed the famous Charter; unfortunately shortly afterwards in 1972 her book on Tomas Masaryk had (without her knowledge) been translated into English under the inflammatory title *The Doomed Democracy*. Before the secret police could arrest her, medical friends certified her insane, and she spent the next five years in a mental hospital, where as long as she was a patient she could not be dismissed from her university post; finally she was declared 'cured' and returned to the university, but was not allowed to write on modern history: instead she became an expert on ancient sport (in her youth she had been an international athlete). The problems of the Olivas were further compounded by the fact that both their children had recently fled to the West.

Nevertheless, they came to Oxford and were made members of Balliol College Senior Common Room. I recall a moment during a guest night in Balliol, where the college silver is laid out and good food and vintage wine are served. As we sat talking in the common room after dinner, suddenly with her characteristic honesty and directness Vera said, 'How strange it is that here we are sitting in all this luxury, and thirty-five years ago Pavel was a starving boy walking barefoot across Europe with the SS guards from one concentration camp to another.' 'Yes,' added Pavel, with a melancholy smile of regret, 'and now perhaps you understand why I joined the Communist Party. I wanted a better world.' In that moment, which I have never forgotten, I first fully understood the reality of the history that we had all experienced and the futility of the Cold War; that was reinforced later the next year, when I was one of the few Western scholars to attend the Eirene conference in

Prague, and met so many colleagues from Eastern Europe; then too I visited the exhibition of art by my exact contemporaries, the Jewish children of the concentration camps who had not survived the war, and reflected on the suffering that everyone in our generation had known, directly or indirectly.

That visit was memorable in so many other ways. Oliva took me round the university; every so often we would meet an elderly man with a brush wearing worker's overalls, and Pavel would formally introduce me to the Professor of Medieval History or Philosophy: they were all victims of the purge after 1968, but their colleagues still treated them as if they were in post. I began to respect the wit and ingenuity whereby the Czechs were circumventing the Communist system, worthy indeed of the Good Soldier Schweik.

The level of dissidence among Eastern classical scholars at the conference was obvious. The Russians had been ordered to give their communications in Russian; the majority insisted on speaking French. The conference was very friendly and everyone was keen to speak to the few Western scholars who had come; only when a member of the East German delegation entered the room would they all suddenly fall silent.

We went on an expedition to Konopiště, the hunting lodge of the Archduke Franz Ferdinand, assassinated at Sarajevo in 1914. It was the most effective piece of propaganda against the former ruling classes of Europe that I have ever seen: every inch of the walls was decorated with stuffed birds and animals, all meticulously listed in books recording their massacre by the crowned heads of Europe in great hunting expeditions across India, Africa, the Far East, and Europe. I began to understand how the First World War was an extension of this royal pre-war shooting party, in which they were using machine guns to exterminate the peasants and the working classes for their pleasure.

We took our lunch at Konopiště, and I sat with Professor Irena Svencickaya (1929–2006) and her husband. The meat was surprisingly good: 'Do you have meat like this in Moscow?' I asked; 'In Moscow we have no meat,' she replied, and pointed across the room to a handsome young man with a broken arm in plaster (much younger than any of the rest of the Russian contingent – where had he got that broken arm? I thought). 'That is the KGB man,' she said in a conversational tone. My English philosophy colleague said brightly 'Oh, I thought he was a poet.' I lost all faith in the intelligence of philosophers.

Later I told this story to a young Romanian scholar, Manuela Tecuşan; the Romanians were housed apart from all the other delegates in a hostel far from the centre of Prague. 'We have a KGB man,' she said mournfully, 'but we do not know who he is.'

We kept in touch with Pavel and Vera, and I contributed to his Festschrift in 1999, and to the celebration of the centenary of his birth in 2023;[47] I was delighted to meet him again on a second visit to Prague in 2014. His wife was already ill, and died in 2015.

Manuela Tecuşan was a Romanian rebel, who had been inspired by her uncle Petru Creţia (1927–1997), professor of Greek, poet and literary critic, the great expert on Eminescu, in ideals of classical education that went back to the 1930s. She was fluent in French and English, and was determined to escape from Communism. She was helping her uncle prepare the first translation of Plato into Romanian; at great personal risk she contributed an article on Plato's sympotic writings to my book *Sympotica* (1990), and I would send her classical texts and lexica to Romania: sometimes these would be returned as subversive literature, but they usually got through on the second attempt.

Finally, Manuela escaped to England. Because she had not been a party member she had been prevented from studying for a doctorate; so I persuaded the students at Balliol to appoint her as a refugee scholar, paid for by their personal contributions; and she studied for a doctorate with me, which eventually won the Conington Prize as the best classical thesis of the year.[48] She now lives in Cambridge.

Through Manuela my wife and I became friends with Petru Creţia, who visited us in Oxford in 1989. On 20 December, Petru was due to return to Bucharest. He decided to compose an open 'birthday letter' of denunciation of Ceausescu, and we helped him translate it into English: he declared his intention of leaving it to be broadcast on the BBC Romanian service as he returned. I knew that he was signing his own death warrant, but could not dissuade him. The day of his departure it was raining torrentially; and I wandered for hours through the streets of Oxford, distraught and wondering what I could do to save him. Finally I decided that the only chance was to publish his text in English in the *Times* newspaper, in the hope that the resulting publicity in the West might protect him from summary execution. Through friends on the newspaper the essay was published next day, on 21 December, the same day on which Ceausescu fell from power. Later I discovered that Petru had not gone home on arrival, but had hidden for several days underneath the railway arches until it was safe to emerge. Petru subsequently became the editor of a literary journal and a leading politician in the chaotic new party system. He visited us once again, but died in 1997.

With the arrival of *perestroika* and *glasnost*, personal relations between Eastern and Western scholars became easier. But Western governments did not respond; they were still imprisoned (as they are today) in a Cold War mentality, and simply tried to capitalize on the economic and political difficulties in the Soviet bloc. So I established a research programme that would offer bursaries for young scholars throughout Europe, but especially from the East. This was called Bibliotheca Academica Translationum, and aimed to create a bibliographical database of all translations of works of classical scholarship between all European languages. The idea was to offer travel awards to young scholars across Europe, so that they could work on the project in their own and foreign libraries. It was moderately successful and still continues, funded first by Oxford University and the British Arts and Humanities Research Council, then by the European Union, Google Books, and the Onassis Foundation, and based first in Oxford, then in Paris and now in Athens. We established links with young scholars in France, Germany, Spain, Italy, Greece, Russia, Hungary, and the USA.

One of my earliest contacts was with a remarkable man, Grigory Bongard-Levin (1933–2008) of the Russian Academy of Sciences, who did more than any other individual to protect and promote Classical Studies in the difficult days of the collapse of the Russian economy. He was a wise and good friend who is sadly missed. He had devised a similar scheme that created funds for young Russian scholars, by using his contacts to obtain for them short study trips to Western libraries: these travel bursaries, small enough by Western standards, provided Western currency sufficient to enable them to live for three or four years in Russia. So the leaders of the next generation were preserved for Russian scholarship. Sergei Karpiuk, an editor of *Vestnik Drevnej Istorii*, was one of Bongard-Levin's beneficiaries, who has become a close friend, and has stayed with us twice on his visits to Britain. It was through this connection that I first travelled to Moscow and to the excavations at Anapa (Gorgippia) on the Black Sea, where I met Professor Gennadiy Andreevich Koshelenko (1935–2015), the teacher of another beneficiary of such East-West contacts, who later came on a Soros Scholarship to Oxford, my former pupil, the Georgian scholar Gocha Tsetskhladze (1963–2022). The BAT contacts also provided me with another friend in Hungary, Attila Ferenczi of Budapest, with whom we now have reciprocal ties of hospitality.

In September 1996 I was invited to tour the sites of the Crimea by my former pupil Raymond Asquith, British envoy at the Ukrainian Embassy (and himself a major protagonist in the Cold War, whose ancestor had taken part in the 'charge of the Light Brigade' during the Crimean War, and returned with a captured Russian musket, which is still in the family). Together we visited the classical sites of the Crimea at a time when the archaeological service was deprived of virtually all funds: I was amazed at the dedication of archaeologists who were working without regular pay to preserve one of the greatest collections of classical sites in the world: in particular I think of one young woman who was spending the winter in a pair of metal shipping containers at the site of Kalos Limen, supplied only with food from a friend at the local collective farm, in an attempt to prevent the peasantry from removing the foundation stones for use as hard core in the entrances to their fields: she said it was better than being an out-of-work secretary. We also met the staff of the museum and site at Chersonesos (Sevastopol), surviving in their historic monastery only because of an ownership dispute between the Ukrainian and Russian Orthodox Churches. A second visit with Raymond in 2013 occurred just before the Russian annexation of the Crimea, which has once again put in jeopardy the future of this World Heritage Site.[49]

In 1995, in preparation for the attempt to wrest the Olympic Games from the stranglehold of the West, contacts with China began to open up. One of the first visitors to Oxford was the doyen of Chinese Western ancient historians, Professor Wang Dunshu (born 1934), who has established at Nankai University (where my great-uncle started a missionary university around 1910) a graduate school of Western classical historiography which is now the largest in the world. Initially it was intended to produce experts in every ancient language from Sumerian to Egyptian, Greek and Latin; now it seems to specialize especially in Silk Road studies. I presume that this enterprise is part of a programme of world domination: since the first principle in understanding Chinese civilization is the study of the teachings of Confucius, it was assumed that successful diplomacy with the West must begin with training diplomats in the origins of Western civilization, despite the fact that these have long been forgotten in our cultures.

We invited Wang Dunshu to dinner to meet some Oxford colleagues. Halfway through the meal he said 'this wine is not strong enough, have you anything stronger?'[50] After some thought I produced a bottle of vintage *grappa*, of which he proceeded to drink about half. When the meal was over we began to discuss the differences between Western and Chinese political systems. Wang Dunshu emphasized the importance of calligraphy, poetry and dancing in the training of the traditional Chinese elite (he himself was a survival from the mandarin class, whose uncle had passed out top in the Imperial Chinese Civil Service examinations in these three skills, and had immediately been appointed in his twenties as ambassador to the whole of South America). He told us that the current rulers of China were still experts in ballroom dancing, which they had learned as impoverished refugees in the dance-halls of Paris in the Twenties: Chou En Lai was especially famed for his skill at the foxtrot and the quickstep – all that is except Chairman Mao, who had no sense of rhythm (although of course he married a dancer). This seemed a damning criticism of the Great Leader. Wang Dunshu ended with a display of the forgotten art of performing ancient Chinese drinking songs accompanied by dancing that reminded me of the chorus of old men in Plato's *Laws*.

As a consequence of this friendship I was asked to partake in the First International Congress of Ancient World Historians at Nankai University (Tianjin), and subsequently visited by primitive coach and train the ancient capitals from Xian onwards, and crossed the Gobi Desert to the Buddhist caves of Dunhuang and the cities of Turfan, Urumchi and Kashgar along the Silk Road. We returned on a decrepit plane borrowed from Uzbeki Airlines, which had the unfortunate reputation of a mere sixty per cent of successful flights. Twenty years later I was invited to another conference at Nankai, and participated in another Silk Road trip, this time in brand-new aeroplanes and through brand-new airports, as if several centuries had intervened.

One comment from our first proceedings stays in my mind. Professor Lin Zhi-chun in his nineties asked why Western scholars had been invited to the conference: after all, he said, the West kept forgetting its past, and was always needing to have Renaissances, whereas China had been a continuous civilization for five thousand years.[51] This reminded me of the rebuke of the Egyptian priests in Plato: 'you Greeks are but children compared to us Egyptians.'[52] The poverty of the Western tradition was exposed.

These memories are tiny footnotes in the dark history of a century of intellectual persecution; but when I look back in my eighties I feel that I have tried to uphold the traditions of the ancient Republic of Letters that were defended in 1914 by my great-grandfather, Sir James Murray, editor of the *Oxford English Dictionary*.[53] But will the Republic of Letters survive the triumph of ruthless capitalism and nationalism that is the curse of the twenty-first century? Only the next generation can answer that question: 'through suffering we learn wisdom: *pathei mathos*'.

The lesson of the Greeks for the twentieth century is indeed their importance in the history of suffering: generations of scholars have learned the truth first discovered by the scribes of the Dark Ages, that against the sufferings of the present, there might once have been a civilization that valued the freedom of the intellect above the dogmas of religion. And we have more to learn from the experiences of the Eastern bloc than simple Marxism. For them, as for the earlier victims of nationalism and racism, the Greeks embodied the despairing hope expressed by Walter Benjamin in the image of the Angelus Novus, for the survival of the freedom of the human spirit and a refuge from the evils of the contemporary world.

20
The Crisis of Theory in History

A scientist who thinks he must invent all his tools anew may well enter the research situation with an empty mind – but he will also leave it with an empty mind.

Karl Wittfogel, *Oriental Despotism* (1957)

L'idée d'avoir soif ne crée pas une molécule d'eau.

Jean-Pierre Dequeker, *Poteries Dequeker* (2023)

The collapse of the Soviet Empire and its satellite totalitarian communist regimes does not imply necessarily the collapse of Marxism as a historical theory – and I would argue that we are all post-Marxists and can only impoverish our understanding of history if we try to avoid Marxist ideas. Nevertheless, I do think that, whether or not the relation between theory and practice can be separated, it was inevitable that the collapse of the value system sustaining the most vibrant and most interesting schools of history in France and Italy has produced a crisis of theory in history. This collapse was slow, and began with the mass exodus of intellectuals from the party in 1956 over the Soviet invasion of Hungary. But in the 1970s and early 1980s much of the theoretical ground had been won back by the new history in France and the new archaeology in Italy: it really looked as if Marxist ideas, divorced from membership of the Soviet Empire, did illuminate whole areas of history far more effectively than any other general theory of history: once rigid orthodoxy was discarded Marxism took on a new lease of life. It would be an interesting study to seek to understand how that buoyant marriage of theory and empirical research was eroded in the age of Brezhnev, who was able for the first time to make communism boring, and of the

Yeltsin era, which allowed us to see that it had been also as corrupt as all the other government systems of modern Europe.

It is not just Marxism then, but all belief systems that have been eroded. Where are the grand theories of history now? We can see how barren the landscape is by noting how it has become populated with massive books of historical entertainment which purport to present grand themes, all of them distinguished by their lack of any theoretical underpinning and their grasshopper methodology. Grand history has become a sort of performing flea circus, compared with the days of Fernand Braudel, who knew how to connect detailed facts with valid generalizations.

To talk of the collapse of grand theories or of ideologies alone is to look at the question in too positive a light – for it is probably a good idea to get rid of or at least reduce the power of global perspectives on the past, although it is equally true that we need to mend the black holes that have appeared in the theoretical structure of our historical universe before we are all sucked into them. What worries me far more, and has worried many commentators on the writing of history, is the rise of relativism. Relativism, like scepticism in the seventeenth century, has become to my mind the crucial problem for the student of history: its aim is to neutralize the power of history, to subordinate it to the prevailing ideology of the present. So far in the present age it has appeared in two forms.

The first is the idea that history is rhetoric, that it is an art form which should be analysed in terms of whatever literary theories are currently in vogue. On this view the aim of history is persuasion or the telling of a story. The concept of truth, and the development of a method for the finding of that truth, are irrelevant to the genre of history: they rest on a confusion between history and science. So Hayden White saw history as a set of tropes or modes of thought, and analysed the great age of historical writing in terms of romance, comedy, tragedy, satire – with the ultimate historical perception being irony rather than commitment to truth.[1] I remember the fury with which this was greeted by Arnaldo Momigliano in the seventies, who tried to persuade us sleepy British positivists that here was the greatest threat to history writing of the present age. I think he was right in the long term, though Hayden White himself has not had much influence on the writing of history itself: historians inoculated themselves against his ideas by claiming that they are only relevant to the study of historiography, not to history, oblivious to the fact that historians write history books as well as doing research – and that they will one day suffer the indignities of misrepresentation that have been imposed on Gibbon, Ranke, Hegel, Burckhardt, Marx, Nietzsche, and Croce. Maybe modern historians do not need to have much fear of being analysed for their literary style; but they should surely be afraid of a theory which says that their facts and methods are irrelevant to their ability as historians. And the threat is not over, for modern literary theory has taken up the task of imposing on historians who regarded themselves as truthful (but authors' intentions are irrelevant) or scientific the rules of narratology. The analysis of closure in Thucydides is now a major industry, and a good thing too that Thucydides should be treated as a narrator of considerable art, even if he spectacularly failed to close his own narrative. But we should beware of coming to believe that this is the meaning of Thucydides' enterprise, that history is its tropes. Momigliano of course had his own agenda, for he believed that the study of historiography would uncover the slow development of historical method, and so enable us to understand what it is to be a historian, to practise more perfectly that skill or *techne* which Thucydides began but understood only imperfectly. History for him was a science with a method, but it differed from modern science in being more like philosophy – a discourse in which the individual thinker or historian had the benefit over the research group. Perhaps it would clarify matters if I say that fundamentally I agree with him.

The second form of relativism is a sort of universalization of scientific relativism. Here history is dependent on the view of the observer, who distorts the reality in a way that makes it impossible ever to discover the underlying truth. All history serves an ideology, and we had better recognize this. This theory is related to the late nineteenth-century principles of source criticism, in which each historical source was traced back through a series of lost forerunners, each with its own detectable bias of presentation, until one arrived by a process of divination at 'the facts' undistorted by any observer's prejudices. The modern version of this similarly often seems to presuppose that there is again at least hypothetically 'a set of facts' behind the distortion presented by the observer, but it is interested in identifying that distortion – the ideology of our sources, rather than the facts. Here I believe we are on traditional historical ground. This late nineteenth-century type of analysis is still one of the most powerful methodological devices in our box of tools, and it has very far-ranging uses. It will enable us for instance to free women's studies from their dependence on male-oriented sources, or to recognize the class prejudices of historians, ancient or modern. It will enable us to write histories of cultures which have completely different value sets from our own, whether by understanding our own prejudices and writing in their mode or vice versa. It is often criticized as destructive of historical research, when for instance Marxist influenced historians allege that all our sources are biased by being created from the point of view of the property-owning elite, or claim that the voice of slaves has been systematically muted. But these statements, though they inspire scepticism in particular cases, if true represent valid criticisms from the historical point of view. Our sources are not ideologically neutral, and it must be better to recognize this, even if it leads to greater uncertainty in conclusions. It is only seriously disastrous for historical truth in one of two situations. The controversy about *Black Athena* showed that a theory based on the claim of ideological prejudice on the part of historians (in this case that nineteenth-century White Male Hellenists had systematically rewritten the relationship between Egypt and Greece) is capable of engendering a global interpretation of Greek culture as 'Afroasiatic' – but only if the evidence of archaeology were systematically ignored, the evidence of Near Eastern influences played down, and a conspiracy theory alleged on the part of European historians. Anyone who followed Martin Bernal through to his conclusions had to believe far too many impossible things before breakfast. By this point it becomes just as possible that ancient civilizations were created by beings from outer space, and belief and suspension of belief are equally irrelevant.[2]

A second point of self-destruction is reached when scepticism about the truth value of individual accounts is generalized to imply the relativism of all historical accounts. But that is simply the old mistake of the seventeenth-century sceptics that the uncertainty of one sense perception implied the logical impossibility of any form of certainty; and this is to confuse inductive modes of reasoning with deductive logic. So however many narratives are ideologically biased, even if all known narratives suffer from observer distortion, this does not imply that there is no reality to be observed; and even if we cannot be certain of the facts in such a situation it is still reasonable to keep on searching.

This is why I find that Michel Foucault in all his varied attempts to emphasize the primacy of the discourse over the event, and his assertions that perceptions are relative to the needs of the perceiver, to be the most interesting of all modern writers on the theory of history, but not (as some have seen him) as representing a serious threat to history as a discipline. It seems to me that Paul Veyne for instance has misunderstood his message, which merely tells us to be wary of generalizations but does not declare them to be impossible or unknowable. Veyne's theory of history is indeed the most extreme version of nihilistic scepticism that I know. According to him theories are irrelevant to the task of history, which is simply to narrate the events of a 'sublunary world' where all generalization is falsification. This has led him to long attacks on the claims not just of Marxism, but of psychology, literary theory, economics, and sociology: a brief flirtation with Max Weber as a possible model has ended with the reading of Nietzsche and the discovery of Foucault. But Veyne is not just an English-style positivist, for it is not merely theories that he wants to abolish: it is also any form of generalization. We are not allowed to talk of empires, democracies, institutions, structures of any sort, of religion, freedom, or any other intellectual idea. History is simply the realm of unconnected facts discovered by the historian who decides for himself what is 'interesting' and what is not. This total scepticism is nihilist in its implications: it can be liberating in its attempt to study the evidence without any prejudices; but because there is no way of justifying how what is interesting to one historian can be interesting to his audience, it makes history into a game of solitaire suitable only for very grand French professors who have no pupils, and who believe that their position validates their pronouncements.[3]

To judge from the fact that historians still continue to write and to generalize, others have believed that the activity justifies itself. I think it is true that this process of research, of the collection of evidence and its evaluation by methods designed to attribute truth values to it, is a basic and crucial element in what we mean by history. That is why some of the theories I have been discussing look so implausible. Ultimately history must include the antiquarian collection of data, and it must be justified by empirical research. Empiricism is a historical virtue. But empiricism in itself is not history, which demands also interpretation (and not simply narration) of the results; otherwise we are condemned to follow the evidence wherever it may lead. The example of Paul Veyne shows in the modern world how the empirical facts are not sufficient to explain history, any more than antiquarianism in the Enlightenment was a satisfactory answer either to scepticism or to the *philosophes*.

There is surely a distinction to be made between the historical virtue of empiricism and something that is often confused with it – positivism. Positivism is the belief that the facts exist, and can be found and make sense when found, without the need for anything other than the application of common sense. When we stop thinking we are most of us positivists most of the time. But we must continue to stop thinking, or we will be set about by doubts. For how do we justify the common-sense assumptions we make? Is human nature always the same? Can we construct the political life of fifth-century Athens or republican Rome as if it were modern America? Is there such an entity as constitutional law? To all these questions we modern sophisticated historians would reply, NO; and we would decry projects such as the *Cambridge Ancient History* for their bland assumption that there is a form of history which is the same for all periods and places. But in fact we often continue to be positivists at the deepest level. We assume that sexual behaviour is biologically rather than culturally determined, that homosexuality is the same in all periods, that domination and penetration are universal aspects of sexuality, rather than acceptance and communion. We assume that food is food, that tastes remain constant, that wine is the same in all societies and leads to something called drunkenness, which is a physical state, that we can talk about pleasure or happiness as constant entities that all human beings desire, that religions satisfy similar identifiable human needs, that nudity and clothing are constant entities. Empiricism is the spirit of enquiry, without which history cannot exist; positivism is the refusal to think. Its result is a study of history that is necessarily conservative: the reason why we study certain aspects is because it is traditional to study them. The great edifices of political and military history, of the constitution, religion and the economy, of Art with a capital A, were built up by our ancestors; and it is our duty to continue servicing them. So the theses thud out and the graduate students lie like so many sleepers under the railway track, for the heavy engines of their professors to roll over. The most that we can allow is the freedom to reject what has been said by some previous historian: revisionism allows us to reverse over the same track.[4] In positivism presuppositions and prejudices take the place of theories: it is not that there is no theoretical base, but simply that what it is has been forgotten long ago.

There are indeed more sophisticated versions of positivism, which have created an order out of prejudice. The modern American school of historical ideology, as practised by Josh Ober, Barry Strauss, Paul Rahe and others in Greek history seems to me to attribute an almost metaphysical status to modern perceptions. Greek democracy is interpreted as a forerunner of modern democracy, and the analysis follows the sort of framework that a Senate report on democratic forces in Afghanistan or Iraq might take; freedom (in the interpretation of Orlando Patterson) is an identical construct in the ancient world and in modern post-slavery America.[5] There is a great excitement in such studies, because they make the ancient world relevant to the modern through a form of presentism, believing that the only function of the past is to serve the present.[6] But they rest on an assertion of continuity or structural similarity which seems to me unjustified.

Perhaps the most prevalent assumption behind positivist history is what two generations ago Herbert Butterfield identified as 'the Whig interpretation of history' – a view of history that sees it as progress towards some slightly unclear liberal endpoint, in which everything is for the best in the best of all possible worlds because it is interpreted as another step on the goal towards parliamentary government, freedom of speech, modern economic pluralism, the welfare state, the liberation of the proletariat, or whatever is the ultimate goal of the writer. This theoretical backing is particularly common, not just because it is optimistic or can accommodate most forms of historical prejudice about the future, but also because it expresses a fundamental flaw in the logic of positivist history.[7] It seems inevitable that the history of events is the story of the victor: failed politicians, generals, armies, cultures, epochs get lost in the march of history which is only concerned with what leads on to something else. And yet at any one point in time there are more events that do not happen than the actual event that does – more dreamers of a different future than creators of the winning one, more unsuccessful politicians than dictators: and the feel of living in a period is the feel of the complexity of these hopes and dreams, not the hard reality of what is yet to come. The great historian of the imagination Frances Yates once wrote:

> History as it actually occurs is not quite the whole of history, for it leaves out of account the hopes that never materialised, the attempts to prevent the outbreak of wars, the futile efforts to solve differences by conciliatory methods. Hopes such as these are as much a part of history as the terrible events which falsify them, and in trying to assess the influence of their times upon idealists and lovers of peaceful activities such as our poets and academicians the hopes are perhaps as important as the events.[8]

This version of positivism presents an interpretation of history as progress; but here the progress is conceived of as that of a crude Darwinian selection. At one level the survival of the fittest is an obvious lesson to learn from history: what wins is best, or at least strongest. So we can avoid the idea that history has a moral goal in the present world without changing our system of ordering events. But Darwinian thought is not exhausted by the idea of mechanical selection through the survival of the fittest. It offers a far more sophisticated analogy to human history in its formulation of the processes of biological history, in which the emergence and survival or disappearance of species are subject to a process of random change affected by two great forces, consilience and contingency: the multiplicity of factors in the biological world creates a form of chance through the confluence of unpredictable causes, and their successful survival or disappearance is equally random. Such a model closely resembles the march of human history, in which the theories of the historian can explain the past by invoking a series of complex interactions, but are unable to predict the future precisely because of the complexity of these factors. The structures of Darwinian thought do indeed bear a close relationship to the ways that historical processes seem to work; and I have found a lot of illumination in trying to relate historical causation to the randomness of natural selection as described by the modern interpreter of Darwinian thought Stephen Jay Gould, who argues that the essential teaching of modern Darwinism is the consilience and contingency of biological (and historical) mutation over time.[9]

But Darwinian theory has been responsible for one major mistake in historical thought. In the nineteenth century the idea of origins came to dominate history; and we still assume that if we can find the original form of an institution, if we can discover how it began, we are thereby revealing its essence or its logical structure.[10] Almost every history book and almost every thesis begins with the origins of the phenomenon under discussion, as if these were relevant in some especially privileged way to its fundamental nature and to the way it operated at a later stage. Thus Greek democracy expresses the essence of modern democracy, despite the fact that it belongs to a fundamentally different society.

I have argued that positivism is not history without theory, but simply history in which the theory has been forgotten or suppressed. If so, it seems to me that we cannot write history without theory, and the new scepticism or relativism about theory is even more dangerous than the old scepticism about facts. What can we do about it? I think we should go back to the fundamental question: why do we write history? Why did the Chinese, the Jews, the Greeks and the Arabs invent it? In essence it involves both critical interpretation and theorizing about the past, and I suggest it has at least four separate aims.

The first is the desire for truth: there is an irreducible element of antiquarianism in all true historians, a natural love of the empirical and a curiosity about the facts and events of the past. This is what distinguishes history from fiction or poetry or other literary genres, and what gives it *its* connections with the biological sciences. The development of historical method as a system for the discovery of truth is, as Momigliano saw, the crucial element in understanding historiography, the science of history.

Secondly, we write history in order to understand the present. This relationship between past and present is reciprocal. We may wish to understand or even defend the present by appeal to the past. In this sense history is a deeply conservative force. So Jewish history preserves the community by holding it to its religious traditions. Chinese history, ancient and modern, is still an elaborate defence of the traditions of Confucianism, even if its first and most critical exponent, Sima Qian, was concerned to expose the truth about the past in order to record the deviations from the True Path. The historians of medieval Islam were obsessed with the decline of the caliphate and the corruption of the present, leading to the end of the world.[11] More positively, Greek history I would argue derives from the importance of the charter myth, and exemplifies especially the use of the past to explain and justify the present. In that sense history is both the forerunner and the explanation of the present state. In another and more sophisticated later version, history is the re-enactment of past events: only that which is living for the present can truly be regarded as history. This is the theory of Croce and Collingwood, which is still I think one of the most persuasive ways of looking at the relationship between past and present. For it recognizes that there is a relationship between the two which is essential and not pernicious, and it explains how each generation must write its own history and discover new aspects and areas of the past to write about.

The experience of the twentieth century has shown that a further use of history is to enable the individual to escape from the intolerableness of the present: the generation of the Holocaust took refuge from their fate in contemplating and idealizing the past. The historians of Soviet Russia were not so different from their contemporaries, the poets and authors such as Vassily Grossman and Aleksandr Solzhenitsyn, who sought to record present suffering in great historical novels in the tradition of Tolstoy and Dostoyevsky. This use of history is as old as the classical tradition; the vision of classical history as a refuge from medieval Christianity can be traced through the successive Renaissances of the Western world.[12]

Finally, we may write history in order to influence the present. To understand the past is to liberate ourselves from it, and to enable ourselves to plan a rational future unencumbered by the dead beliefs and charter myths of an earlier generation. This is the reason why Marx and Engels had to write history (though they too were caught in the old Darwinian trap of believing that the historical process was a one-way development towards a determinate future). And this is also the attitude that lies behind the early attempts to understand history of Michel Foucault, for whom the exposition of a historical process would inevitably liberate society and bring about change – as when his work on the history of madness presented it as a phenomenon continually reinvented by society to constrain the behaviour of its members, and caused the great movement across Europe to regard society, not the mad, as responsible for their condition, and to teach society how to live with its own outsiders.[13] The result has been to empty the lunatic asylums of countries like Italy and Britain onto the streets, with varied success according to the willingness of governments to provide the money for care within the community.

What is interesting is that all these reasons for writing history, with the exception of the first, treat history as a sort of myth – by which I mean a story with a serious purpose. Historians are serious people who write about the past but inhabit their contemporary world. And it is the need to have a serious purpose that explains why history needs theory. But that is not to say it needs a single grand theory. So my final question is, what sort of theories does history need?

Certainly not solipsistic theories invented in the bath for the purpose of illuminating particular arbitrarily chosen events. No, it needs theories that help the mythic purposes of history. For instance, Marxism as transpositional equation: as Einstein was able to relate mass to energy, so one of the chief uses of Marxist theory is to relate wealth to labour through the medium of exploitation. It enables us to understand how society needs to organize its productive capacities, how essential the development of private property is in the process of political control in both ancient and modern states, and how destructive is the accumulation of wealth. Ultimately Gibbon was right when he wrote in his juvenile work, *Essai sur l'étude de la littérature*, that history required both the researches of the *érudits* and the vision of the *philosophes* if it was to encompass the story of the rise and the decline and fall of a civilization.[14]

'To write history is so difficult that most historians are forced to make concessions to the technique of legend.'[15] Neither Eastern nor Western experiences in the twentieth century have resulted in a viable and practicable theory of history; it may be that Welskopf and the renewal of the Rostovtzeff tradition in post-Marxist Russian historical studies offer a more promising future for the study of the Greeks than anything evolved in the West. Yet in the words of my friend the potter Jean-Pierre Dequeker, '*choisir, c'est mourir un peu*'. At present the best that can be said of both Marxism and Western capitalism is that they can produce statements about methodology, but not about the meaning of history: both communism and liberalism are equally barren, and therefore useless as exemplars for the present and guides to the future of humanity. Yet for three centuries Greek history has tried to serve all these purposes, as all true history must. Each generation has created and will continue to create its own myth of the Greeks; our own is no exception, because the Greeks are an essential part of our mental image of history.

Every interpretation is an intervention that brings the past into contact with the interests of the present. Thus in the developing theory of Foucault's *History of Sexuality* the past interprets the present and reflects the control of the present over the past: no interpretation is neutral and all belong to the desire to master the historical discourse in order to confirm the arbitrary rules of modern society.[16] But in the course of investigating the problematization of the rules of homosexuality in antiquity, Foucault came to emphasize the importance they give to self-control, the care of the self. This is the theme of his last three lecture courses at the Collège de France (1981–84), as he was dying of AIDS.[17] Beginning from the question that Socrates offers Alcibiades, 'what is it to know yourself, what is self and what is knowledge?', *The Hermeneutics of the Subject* leads to a meditation on the meaning of the relation between self-control and self-knowledge as profound as anything Foucault wrote: the search for the meaning of history becomes in the subsequent lectures a spiritual exercise based on his interpretation of later classical writers such as Lucian, Plutarch, Marcus Aurelius, Fronto, and Pliny. The last course breaks off almost in mid-argument: 'There, listen: I had some things to say to you about the general structure of these analyses. But finally it is too late. So thank you.' In a note he added, 'But what I wanted to insist on in conclusion is this: there is no establishment of the truth without an essential position of otherness: truth is never the same, you cannot have truth except through the shape of another world and another life.'[18] With these words Foucault leaves it ambiguous as to whether he is talking about the Greeks or about the Afterlife.

These are the limited experiences of one Western scholar, a late survivor of the Republic of Letters. As Burckhardt showed, theory is only the organizing principle that holds the events of the past together and gives history its meaning. But the truth is hard to come by. Saint Augustine records his encounter with a beggar in the streets of Milan in AD 385, while he was struggling to compose a panegyric in praise of the emperor 'wherein I was to deliver many a lie, and to be applauded for my lies, even by those who knew I was lying'.[19] He realized that his own lust for wealth and fame was worthless, compared with the temporary drunken happiness of the beggar. Like Augustine, I once encountered an ancient alcoholic. Mine was on a bus in Santa Fe. 'What's wrong?' the driver said as his passenger got on, 'Why so gloomy? It's a lovely day; you better enjoy it, it'll only get worse.' 'What's your evidence?' asked the drunk. 'That's History. It always does,' replied the driver. And the true historical study will give proper attention to the varieties of theory and their functions for understanding the past and enabling history to fulfil its role as true myth, to inform rather than conform to the present.

Ibn Khaldun

You who have known the ravages of the nomads,
who have seen the desert
creeping slowly over the centuries of man,
who have tried to understand
the forces of desolation,
to reduce to order the wild movements
of alien desires, from your tower
on the edges of that point in time
when the world broke in two,
spanning the distances
from Cordova to Baghdad,

what movement led your soul,
what love of god or woman
gave you to understand
the dust of time?

(*Poems*, 1972)[20]

Acknowledgements

This book represents a lifetime of research into the study of Greek history over the last six decades. I thank first the Leverhulme Trust, which in 2021–22 awarded me an Emeritus Fellowship in my eighty-sixth year, without which the work could never have progressed towards publication. This grant enabled me to employ my devoted amanuensis and friend Vanessa Casato, whose researches in the Bodleian Library over six months supplemented and illuminated so many aspects of the subject, and who has helped me with all the subsequent stages of the preparation of the book. I also thank my old college Balliol and John-Paul Ghobrial, Praefectus of Holywell Manor, for providing Vanessa with accommodation during her period in Oxford.

For thirty-five years my favourite publisher has been Stuart Proffitt, whose care for his authors, scholarly judgement, and passion for history have been a constant inspiration. I am deeply grateful to him for his confidence in me, and for accepting this book, which was not at all the book that I was originally contracted to produce. I also thank the team at Penguin Press, together with my copy-editor Richard Mason, for their work during production.

The final draft was read and checked by Nino Luraghi, to whom I owe especial thanks, and in the sections relevant to their expertise by a number of friends: Carmine Ampolo, Olivier Contensou, Carlotta Dionisotti, Kinch Hoekstra, Alain and Annie Schnapp, Marek Węcowski.

Many colleagues in historical disciplines across the world have helped me in my travels and researches, from North America, China, Japan, Russia, Australia, New Zealand, and the EU (France, Ireland, Italy, UK, Germany, Belgium, Netherlands). I thank especially:

Australia: Jaynie Anderson

Belgium: Athena Tsingarida

Canada: Olivier Contensou, †Raymond Klibansky

China: Wang Dunshu

Czech Republic: †Pavel Oliva

Denmark: Mogens Herman Hansen

France: Jean-Pierre and Michelle Dequeker, François Hartog, †François Lissarrague, Pauline and Jean-Claude Schmitt, Alain and Annie Schnapp

Germany: H.-J. Gehrke, Susannah Stark

Greece: Chryssanthi Avlami, Michael Konaris, Alexandra Lianeri

Ireland: David Dickson, Muriel McCarthy

Italy: Carmine Ampolo, Gianbiagio Conte, Paolo Desideri, Riccardo Di Donato, Luca Iori, †Leandro Polverini

Netherlands: Josine Blok

Poland: †Zbigniew Borkowski, Marek Węcowski

Russia: †Grigory Bongard-Levin, Sergei Karpiuk, Ivan Ladynin

Switzerland: Barbara von Reibnitz, Thomas Späth, Jürgen von Ungern-Sternberg

United Kingdom: Toby Barnard, Ewen Bowie, Richard Buxton, Hannah Collins, Tim Cornell, Carlotta Dionisotti, Sibylla Jane Flower, Peter Ghosh, Simon Goldhill, Martin Goodman, Tom Harrison Georgy Kantor, Geoffrey Lloyd, Colin Lucas, Nino Luraghi, Henry Lytton-Cobbold, Grant McIntyre, David McClay, Nicoletta Momigliano, Alfonso Moreno, Tony More, Mick Morris, Penelope Murray, Ros Murray, Olga Ivannikova Murray, Ruth Padel, Sanja Perovic, Frank Prochaska, Mohan Rao, Nigel Richie, Tim Rood, †Sheila Stern, Christopher Stray, John S. Taylor, Dorothy Thompson, Fiona Wailes-Fairbairn, Claudia Wedepohl

USA: Victor Behr, Peter Brown, Robert Darnton, Page duBois, Tony

Grafton, Kinch Hoekstra, Ken Lapatin, Suzanne Marchand, †Bruce Mazlish, Albert Pionke, Froma Zeitlin

Three of these chapters are modified versions of prefaces to books that I edited: I am grateful to the publishers for permission to include them:

Edward Bulwer-Lytton, *Athens: Its Rise and Fall*, Bicentenary edition edited by Oswyn Murray (Routledge 2004), 1–34 (ch. 6)

Jacob Burckhardt, *The Greeks and Greek Civilization*, translated by Sheila Stern, edited with an introduction by Oswyn Murray (HarperCollins 1998), xi–xliv (ch. 9)

Fernand Braudel, *The Mediterranean in the Ancient World*, translated by Siân Reynolds, with an introduction by Oswyn Murray (Penguin 2001), ix–xxii (ch. 17)

Other chapters were first presented as ideas in lectures and seminars across the world, in Belgium, the Czech Republic, Denmark, France, Germany, Greece, Hungary, Italy, the Netherlands, Slovenia, Russia, Canada, the USA, Pakistan, China, and New Zealand. Preliminary versions have appeared over the years in journals or collections of essays, as follows:

'The Western Futures of Ancient History', in *Knowing Future Time in and through Greek Historiography*, ed. A. Lianeri (De Gruyter 2016), 385–99 (ch. 1)

'British Sparta in the Age of Philhellenism', in *The Contribution of Ancient Sparta to Political Thought and Practice*, ed. N. Birgalias, K. Buraselis, and P. Cartledge (Alexandria Publications 2007), 345–89 (ch. 2)

'Ireland Invents Greek History: The Lost Historian John Gast', *Hermathena* 185 (2008), 22–106 (ch. 3)

'Marathon and the Philhellenes', in *Marathon: The Day After*, ed. K. Buraselis and E. Koulakiotis (European Cultural Centre of Delphi 2013), 217–28 (ch. 4)

'Niebuhr in Britain', in *Historiographie de l'antiquité et transferts culturels: Les histoires anciennes dans l'Europe des XVIIIe et XIXe siècles*, ed. Chryssanthi Avlami, Jaime Alvar, and Mirello Romero Recio (Rodopi 2010), 239–54 (ch. 8)

'Burckhardt and the Archaic Age', in *Jacob Burckhardt und die Griechen*, ed. L. Burckhardt and H.-J. Gehrke (Schwabe 2006), 247–61 (ch. 10)

'Burckhardt, Nietzsche and Socrates', in *Jacob Burckhardt: Storia della cultura, storia dell'arte*, ed. M. Ghelardi and M. Seidel (Marsilio 2002), 55–61 (ch. 11)

'In Search of the Key to All Mythologies', in *Translating Antiquity*, ed. Stefan Rebenich, Barbara von Reibnitz, and Thomas Späth (Schwabe 2010), 119–29 (ch. 12)

'Le Repentir de Gilbert Murray', in *La République des Lettres dans la Tourmente (1919–1939)*, ed. A. Compagnon (CNRS 2011), 125–34 (ch. 13)

'Edgar Wind and the Saving of the Warburg Institute' in *Edgar Wind, Art and Embodiment*, ed. Jaynie Anderson, Bernardino Branca and Fabio Tononi (Peter Lang 2024) 275–97 (ch.14)

'Momigliano on Peace and Liberty (1940)', *Acta Universitatis Carolinae – Philologica I Graecolatina Pragensia XXIII* (2010), 81–96 (ch. 15)

'Arnaldo Momigliano in England', in *The Presence of the Historian: Essays in Memory of Arnaldo Momigliano*, ed. M. P. Steinberg (*History and Theory* Beiheft 30)(Wesleyan University 1991), 49–64 (ch. 16)

'Pierre Vidal-Naquet', obituary, *The Independent*, Friday 4 August 2006 (ch. 18)

'Jean-Pierre Vernant', obituary, *The Independent*, 11 January 2007 (ch. 18)

'Pierre Vidal-Naquet et le métier d'historien de la Grèce: l'"école de Paris"', in *Pierre Vidal-Naquet, un historien dans la cité*, ed. François Hartog, Pauline Schmitt, and Alain Schnapp (La Découverte 1998), 154–66 (ch. 18)

'The Reception of Vernant in the English-Speaking World', in *Annales in Perspective*, vol. 1, ed. D. Roksandić, F. Šimetin Šegvić, and N. Šimetin

Šegvić (CKHIS, FF Press 2019), 97–108 = *History of Classical Scholarship* (online) 2 (2020), 131–57 (ch. 18)

'Between East and West: Memories of the Cold War', *History of Classical Scholarship* (online) 1 (2019), 252–64 (ch. 19)

Finally, since this book is addressed to all those who belong to the Republic of Letters, I would like to thank those friends and colleagues who have sought to promote translations in their respective countries, successfully or not: Miguel Palmeira (Brazil), Yang Juping (China), Alain Schnapp, Vinciane Pirenne-Delforge (France), Kai Brodersen, Achim Gehrke (Germany), Antonios Rengakis (Greece), Bruno D'Agostino, Maurizio Giangiulio (Italy), Yasunori Kasai (Japan), Ivan Ladynin (Russia), Jaime Alvar (Spain). May their efforts bear fruit.

Notes

INTRODUCTION

1. A revised version of this poem was later published as 'The Wild One' in *The Mara Crossing*, Chatto & Windus (London 2012), 128–9.
2. The title is indeed that recorded in the inventory of the effects of Vermeer's widow. But Vermeer's picture contains none of the images prescribed by Ripa under the heading 'Pittura'; and there is no such thing in antiquity as a Muse of Painting. Whatever the interpretation given to it by Vermeer's family, the programmatic subject of the painting is clearly the Muse of History: see for details the entry in the catalogue *Vermeer* (Amsterdam 2023), 266–9, by Sabine Pérot. Among the variations on the basic iconography, commentators have noted: the crease on the map of the Netherlands, dividing the Spanish and rebel provinces; the careful rendering of the underside of a Turkish carpet; the plaster mask on the table (perhaps Hercules signifying the fame of a great man); and the mysterious book with its ribbons towards us. The whole scene shows clear use of a camera obscura; see P. Steadman, *Vermeer's Camera* (Oxford 2002), and more generally David Hockney's revolutionary *Secret Knowledge* (London 2006). Note also the fact that the image of Vermeer is out of proportion with the rest of the painting, suggesting a double use of the camera obscura: two minute focus points have in fact been noted, on the edge of the map and on one leg of the artist's stool.
3. Cesare Ripa, *Iconologia* (Rome, 1603 edn), 347.
4. Ibid. (Venice, 1645 edn), II, 269.
5. T. S. Eliot, 'What is a Classic? An address delivered before the Virgil Society on the 16th of October 1944' (London 1944), 30; the passage is quoted by Ryszard Kapuściński in his *Travels with Herodotus* (London 2007), 271.
6. *Tractatus Logico-Philosophicus* 1.1.
7. For the curious history of the rise of Oxford to become a leading centre of the teaching of Ancient History in the world, see my chapter 13 'Ancient History, 1872–1914', in *The History of the University of Oxford*, vol. VII, part 2, ed. M.C. Brock and M.C. Curthoys (Oxford 2000), 330–60.

CHAPTER 1

1. B. Constant, 'De la liberté des Anciens comparée à celle des Modernes', in *Écrits politiques*, ed. M. Gauchet (Paris 1997), 580–619.
2. For the Jewish tradition of Josephus, which is complicated by the existence of the medieval Josippon, see M. Goodman, *Josephus's* The Jewish War*: A Biography* (Princeton 2019); for the hostile verdict see esp. P. Vidal-Naquet, *Flavius Josèphe, ou du bon usage de la trahison, préface à 'La guerre des Juifs'* (Paris 1977).
3. *The Famous and Memorable Workes of Josephus, A Man of much Honour and Learning Among the Jews. Faithfully translated out of the Latin, and French, by Tho. Lodge, Doctor in Physicke* (Humfrey Lownes 1602).
4. *The Works of Flavius Josephus. Translated into English by Sir Roger L'Estrange, Knight* (London 1702).
5. Published by Henry Galbraith, Dundee.
6. *The Genuine Works of Flavius Josephus the Jewish Historian* (London 1737). The standard bibliography of Josephus by L.H. Feldman claims but does not list some 217 editions of this translation.
7. J. E. Force, *William Whiston: Honest Newtonian* (Cambridge 1985); W. Whiston, *Memoirs of the life and writings of Mr. William Whiston: Containing, memoirs of several of his friends also* (London 1749–50).
8. *L'histoire et la religion des Juifs depuis Jesus-Christ jusqu'à present. Pour servir de suplément et de continuation à l'Histoire de Josèphe*, 5 vols (Rotterdam 1706–7, 1711, 1716). For Basnage see A. Sutcliffe, *Judaism and Enlightenment* (Cambridge 2003), 79–89.
9. *The Whole Genuine and Complete Works of Flavius Josephus, the learned and authentic Jewish Historian and celebrated Warrior.* 'Translated from the Original in the Greek Language To which is added Various Useful Indexes also a Continuation of the History of the Jews from Josephus down to the present Time Including a Period of more than One thousand seven hundred Years, by George Henry Maynard, Ll.D.' The date of this work is 1785 according to the Harvard University catalogue.
10. The date of this work is given as [1792?] in the Harvard University catalogue.
11. *The Whole Genuine and Complete Works of Flavius Josephus . . .*, trans. Thomas Bradshaw, p. iv.
12. There is an excellent account of the Jewish Question from 1833 to 1858 in G. Himmelfarb, *The People of the Book: Philosemitism in England from Cromwell to Churchill* (New York 2011), ch. III.
13. M. Goodman, 'The Disraeli Family and the History of the Jews', *Journal of Jewish Studies* 71(1) (2020), 141–60.

14. I have used primarily the second edition, of 1830, which seems to differ in only minor details from the first. Milman revised his text for the 1863 edition shortly before his death in 1868; this is most easily available in the Everyman's Library.
15. *Geschichte der Isräeliten seit der Zeit der Maccabäer*. For the verdict see Milman, vol. III, 158–9: 'We differ from Jost, who is a pupil of Eichhorn, on many points, particularly the composition of the older Scriptures, but we gladly bear testimony to the high value of his work, which, both in depth of research and arrangement, is far superior to the desultory, and by no means trustworthy, volumes of Basnage.'
16. On these see ch. 8.
17. A.P. Stanley, *Essays chiefly on questions of Church and State* (London 1870), 576. In 1863 the work was republished in a revised edition with some concessions to orthodoxy and an excellent preface by the author defending his approach. Milman's subsequent histories of Christianity (1840) and of Latin Christianity (1854–5) did not improve matters, for they continued to pursue a historical rather than a theological approach to the history of religions. For this movement see D. Forbes, *The Liberal Anglican Idea of History* (Cambridge 1952).
18. A. Dickson Wright, A *History of the Warfare of Science with Theology in Christendom* (New York 1896).
19. H.H. Milman, *The History of the Jews* (London 1909), vol. I, 4, 7–8.
20. Ibid., vol. III, 424.
21. Ibid., vol. II, 122.
22. Ibid., vol. I, 20.
23. Translated with an important editorial introduction and other material in H. Graetz, *The Structure of Jewish History and Other Essays*, ed. I. Schorsch (New York 1975), from which I take my quotations.
24. Ibid., 49.
25. Ibid., 93.
26. Ibid., 126.
27. Ibid., 136.
28. Ibid., 175.
29. Ibid., 187.
30. On Treitschke's reaction to Graetz see M.A. Meyer, 'Heinrich Graetz and Heinrich Von Treitschke: A Comparison of their Historical Images of the Modern Jew', *Modern Judaism* 6 (1986), 1–11. Graetz's emphasis on the centrality of the Diaspora is perhaps no longer in fashion. In the modern post-Holocaust world, Jewish history may be turning back from this cultural interpretation of the Jewish tradition to a form of nationalist historiography reflecting that evolved by its persecutors in the second half of the nineteenth century, in a search for a political myth based on the Promised Land.

CHAPTER 2

1. There was an earlier translation of Thucydides by Thomas Nicolls (1550), made from the French translation of Valla's Latin version by Claude de Seyssel (1527).
2. *The Peloponnesian War: The Thomas Hobbes Translation*. Edited by D. Grene, with an Introduction by B. De Jouvenel (Ann Arbor 1959), vol. II, 572–3. For the history of the reception of Thucydides in Britain see L. Iori, *Thucydides Anglicus: gli 8 bookes di Thomas Hobbes e la ricezione inglese delle storie di Tucidide (1450–1642)* (Rome 2015); and the studies of Kinch Hoekstra listed there.
3. See in general J. Moore, I. Macgregor Morris, and A.J. Bayliss (eds), *Reinventing History: The Enlightenment Origins of Ancient History* (London 2008); G. Ceserani, 'Modern Histories of Ancient Greece: Genealogies, Contexts and Eighteenth-Century Narrative Historiography', in A. Lianeri (ed.), *The Western Time of Ancient History* (Cambridge 2011), 138–55.
4. See esp. G.F. Schömann, *Die Verfassungsgeschichte Athens nach G. Grote's History of Greece kritisch geprüft* (Leipzig 1854), trans. Bosanquet: *Athenian Constitutional History, as represented in George Grote's History of Greece, critically examined* (Oxford 1878). For the history of the long conflict between the constitutions of Sparta and Athens see the excellent account of J.T. Roberts, *Athens on Trial: The Anti-Democratic Tradition in Western Thought* (Princeton 1994).
5. Temple was the younger brother of Abraham Stanyan; he entered Christ Church, Oxford, in 1695, and died in 1752; he is discussed in his brother's notice by T. Seccombe, *Old DNB* 54 (1898), 975.
6. T. Stanyan, *The Grecian History* (London 1774), vol. I, 85.
7. Ibid., 88–9.
8. Ibid., 180–81.
9. I have used the following edition: *Mr. Rollin, The Ancient History translated from the French* (Edinburgh 1820). For Sparta see vol. II, Bk. V, Articles VI and VII.
10. Article VIII, p. 204.
11. See E. Rawson, *The Spartan Tradition in European Thought* (Oxford 1969), chs 15–17; C. Avlami, 'L'Antiquité grecque à la française: Modes d'appropriation de la Grèce au XIXe siècle' (Thèse EHESS, Paris 1998).
12. A. Ferguson, *An Essay on the History of Civil Society*, ed. F. Oz-Salzberger (Cambridge 1995), 142 and 178–9.
13. There was a second edition, Edinburgh, 1778; his Life is attached to the third edition of 1803. See also T. Seccombe, *DNB* 48 (1896), 430–31.
14. G. Ceserani, 'Narrative, Interpretation, and Plagiarism in Mr. Robertson's 1778 *History of Ancient Greece*', *Journal of the History of Ideas* 66 (2005), 413–36. According to the *DNB*, the book referred to is Pons-Augustin

Alletz, *Abrégé de l'histoire grecque à l'usage des collèges et de tous les lieux où l'on instruit la jeunesse tant de l'un que de l'autre sexe* (Paris 1763). This title is remarkable: it seems to be the first suggestion that girls as well as boys might profit from the study of Greek history. I have not seen the work and cannot comment in detail on its relation to Robertson; but it too was popular in France. Alletz (1703–1785) was a lawyer born in Montpellier, author of many works of theology and elementary instruction.

15. W. Robertson, *The History of Ancient Greece* (2nd edn, Edinburgh 1778), 45
16. The book was republished in 1820 and 1825.
17. L.C. Sanders, *Old DNB* 16 (1888), 153.
18. G. Dunbar, 'A Concise General History of the Early Grecian States', in J. Potter, *Archaeologia Graeca* (Edinburgh 1813), vol. II, 17–18.
19. Ibid., 19.
20. Ibid., 22.
21. Ibid., 27.
22. A. Ferguson, *Essay on the history of civil society* (1767), 155.
23. Dunbar, *o.c.*, 47–8.
24. Ibid., 52.
25. R. Koselleck, *Futures Past* (1979, Eng. trans. Columbia 2004).
26. For Tom Paine see *Rights of Man*, Part II (1792), 177 and 180: 'We see more to admire and less to condemn, in that great, extraordinary people, than in anything which history affords', and 'What Athens was in miniature, America will be in magnitude', in *Political Writings*, ed. B. Kuklik (Cambridge 2000); for Voltaire see Roberts, *Athens on Trial*.
27. Roberts, Rawson and Avlani (see notes 4 and 11, above).
28. In English, *Travels of Anacharsis the Younger in Greece* (1793), from which I quote. For his influence on the philhellenes, cf. M. Mazower, *The Greek Revolution* (London 2021), 220.
29. *Mémoires sur la vie et sur quelques-uns des ouvrages de J.-J. Barthélémy, écrits par lui-même en 1792 et 1793* (Paris, Didot jeune, l'an VII). His patroness 'Citoyenne Choiseul' was a paragon of virtue in a dissolute age, described by Horace Walpole as 'The most perfect being of either sex. Nothing that I ever saw anywhere was like the Duchess of Choiseul, who has more parts, reason and agreeableness than I ever met in such a delicate little creature. You would take her for the Queen of an Allegory ... in whom industrious malice could not find an imperfection.'
30. Gibbon's work was written in the 1750s and published in 1761: see A. Momigliano, 'Gibbon's Contribution to Historical Method (1954)', in *Studies in Historiography* (London 1966), ch. 2; K. Jackson Williams, 'Antiquarianism: A Reinterpretation', *Erudition and the Republic of Letters*, vol. 2 (2017), 56–96.
31. The most recent account is the curiously unsympathetic and misleading chapter by Carlo Ginzburg, 'Anacharsis Interrogates the Natives: A New

Reading of an Old Best Seller', in *Threads and Traces: True False and Fictive*, trans. A. and J. Tedeschi (Berkeley 2012), 115–25. See rather Chantal Grell, *Le dix-huitième siècle et l'antiquité en France 1680–1789* (Oxford 1995), 342–50, 716–18.

32. Around 1739–40 a group of young Whig aristocratic friends at Cambridge led by Charles and Philip Yorke amused themselves by producing a collection of letters allegedly written by a Persian agent in Athens during the Peloponnesian War: *Athenian Letters: or the Epistolary Correspondence of an agent of the King of Persia*, originally published privately and anonymously in 1741 and 1743, and reprinted several times; but only formally published in 1781 and 1798. These rather pedestrian letters cover the first ten years of the Peloponnesian War, and the authors subsequently claimed that they had inspired Barthélemy; but he showed that he was not aware of the book until after he had published his *Anacharsis*.
33. On Barbie du Bocage see G. Tolias, 'Antiquarianism, Patriotism and Empire: Transfers of the Cartography of the *Travels of Anacharsis the Younger in Greece* (1788–1811)', *Historical Review, Institute for Neohellenic Research* 2 (2005), 67–91.
34. English trans., 180, 184.
35. Revived by P. Schmitt Pantel, *Hommes illustres: moeurs et politique à Athènes au Ve siècle* (Paris 2009).
36. 'On a dit qu'en faisant parler des Grecs, il leur donne souvent un air Français et des moeurs à peu près Françaises' (Baron de Sainte-Croix, quoted by Tolias, *o.c.*, 68 n. 4).
37. G. Beyerhaus, 'Abbé de Pauw und Friedrich der Grosse, Eine Abrechnung mit Voltaire', *Historische Zeitschrift* 134 (1926), 465–93.
38. 'Le savant Auteur des *Recherches sur les Américains, les Egyptiens & les Chinois*, M. de Pauw, nous a donné des articles d'*Antiquités, d'Histoire* & de *Critique* dignes de la réputation qu'il s'est acquise' (Avertissement au Supplément).
39. Apart from de Pauw and his nephew, others included Beethoven, Jeremy Bentham, Robert Burns, Alexander Hamilton, James Madison, Tom Paine, Heinrich Schiller, George Washington, and William Wilberforce.
40. Jean-Baptiste, Baron de Cloots, changed his name to 'Anacharsis' under the influence of Barthélemy's novel; see G. Avenel, *Anacharsis Cloots, l'orateur du genre humain* (Paris 1865).
41. G. Keynes, *The Library of Edward Gibbon* (London 1940), 215. Although Magdalen College, Oxford, refused to buy the library of their famous alumnus because of the insults he had inflicted on them in his posthumous *Memoirs*, by 1935 they had relented sufficiently to purchase a small number of his books from the final auction of his library at Sotheby's London; among these was Gibbon's copy of the first Berlin edition (1788) of the *Recherches philosophiques sur les Grecs*; there are no markings

and some of the pages are uncut (information from Dr Alfonso Moreno, Magdalen College).

42. T. Carlyle, *The French Revolution*, ch. 2.1.III: *The Muster*.

43. The first serious modern discussion of his ideas will be published by the young French-Canadian scholar, Olivier Contensou of the Université Laval (Quebec), who is preparing a thesis on him. With great generosity M. Contensou has given me access to an early version of his thesis.

44. See A. Gerbi and J. Moyle, *The Dispute of the New World: The History of a Polemic* (Pittsburgh 1973).

45. A. Cloots, 'À mon oncle Corneille Pauw', in *La république universelle ou addresse aux tyrannicides* (Paris 1792), 124–63:

> Je vous félicite du succès prodigieux de vos Grecs. Cet ouvrage profond et lumineux fera époque dans la république des lettres. Nonobstant le grand nombre de vos admirateurs, la voix glapissante de trois ou quatre critiques s'est fait entendre. Mais si le plus célèbre des Grecs a trouvé un Zoïle, n'est-il pas naturel que l'auteur des Recherches sur les Grecs ait rencontré un Fréron? C'est le sort inévitable des plus illustres écrivains, d'être loués par les uns et blâmés par les autres (p. 124).
>
> Un philosophe dont les écrits ont contribués à la destruction de toutes les aristocraties sacrées et profanes. Les Français placent votre nom sur la liste des grands ouvriers de la liberté civile et religieuse. Voltaire, Rousseau, Pauw, etc., sont nos véritables libérateurs (p. 128).

Zoilus was a Cynic and grammarian in the Hellenistic age, allegedly killed for slandering Homer. It is not clear which Fréron Cloots is referring to. Louis-Marie Stanislas Fréron (1754–1802) inherited the editorship of *L'Année Littéraire* in 1776 after his father Elie-Catherine Fréron's death. An anonymous hostile review did appear in *L'Année Littéraire* on 16 September 1788 (vol. 6, no. 37, 289–325); but Cloots may be alluding to the anti-*philosophe* reputation of the father. The son was a revolutionary journalist and member of the National Convention (1792–5), and was later an unsuccessful suitor for the hand of Pauline Bonaparte.

46. The name of the translator is revealed in the article by G.E. Bentley Jr, 'Copyright Documents in the George Robinson Archives: William Godwin and Others 1713–1820', *Studies in Bibliography* 35 (1982), 67–110 at p. 88 (under Des Carrières). For Smollett's review see *The Critical Review or Annals of Literature*, London, 11 May 1794, 77–84. I thank Sanja Perovic and Nigel Ritchie of the *Radical Translations* project for identifying de Pauw's translator.

47. J. G. Alder, *Glimpses of the French Revolution* (London 1894), in his account of Cloots, 90–96.

48. For the renewal of interest see P. Vidal-Naquet, *La Démocratie grecque vue d'ailleurs* (Paris 1990), 172–4, and *Politics Ancient and Modern* (Oxford 1995), 91; C. Mossé, 'Un éloge inattendu de la démocratie

athénienne au XVIIIe siècle: les *Recherches philosophiques sur la Grèce* de Cornelius de Pauw', in C. Avlami, J. Alvar, and M. Romero Recio (eds), *Historiographie de l'antiquité et transferts culturels* (Amsterdam 2010), 99–104; 'Une Image négative de Sparte à la fin du XVIIIe siècle. La quatrième partie des *Recherches philosophiques sur les Grecs* de Cornelius de Pauw', in D. Foucault and P. Payen (eds), *Les Autorités: dynamiques et mutations d'une figure de référence à l'Antiquité* (Grenoble 2007), 51–8; *Regards sur la démocratie Athénienne* (Paris 2014) 104–16; 'Cornelius de Pauw et la justice athénienne', in *Métis, Dossier Émotions* (EHESS Paris 2017), 365–73. De Pauw is also briefly discussed by Roberts, *Athens on Trial*, 171–3; K. Vlassopoulos, 'Constructing Antiquity and Modernity in the Eighteenth Century: Distantiation, Alterity, Proximity, Immanency', in L. Foxhall, H.-J. Gehrke, and N. Luraghi (eds), *Intentional History* (Stuttgart 2010), 341–60.

49. C. de Pauw, *Philosophical Dissertations on the Greeks* (London 1793), vol. I, Preliminary Discourse, 1.
50. L.G. Michaud, *Biographie Universelle*, 2nd edn, vol. 32 (Paris 1861), 321–2.
51. Pauw, *o.c.*, vol. I, Preliminary Discourse, 2.
52. Ibid., 8.
53. Ibid., vol. II, 205.
54. Ibid., vol. I, 1.
55. John Gillies, Scottish Historiographer Royal and author of a *History of Ancient Greece* (1786): see ch. 5.
56. Pauw, *o.c.*, vol. II, 136.
57. Ibid., 117–18 (French original, vol. II, 115: 'le raisonneur le plus inconséquent qui ait jamais paru, qui prétendait que les Dieux seuls peuvent vivre dans une démocratie; mais quand ensuite on lui demandoit quels étoient ces êtres qu'on nommoit les Dieux, il ne savoit plus que répondre').
58. Ibid., vol. I, 210 (French original, vol. I, 278. 'le plus grand des compilateurs et le plus petit des critiques'). Ibid., vol. II, 185.
59. G.B. de Mably (1709–1785), although he was an admirer of Sparta, was in fact a fellow radical, and an important influence on revolutionary thought both before and after the Revolution: see S. Roza, 'L'abbé de Mably, entre modérantisme et radicalité', *Tangence* 106 (2014), 29–50.
60. Pierre Augustin Guys, *Voyage Littéraire de la Grèce, ou Lettres sur les Grecs anciens et modernes, avec un parallèle de leurs moeurs* (Paris 1771), translated as *A Sentimental Journey through Greece in a series of letters written from Constantinople* (London 1772).
61. Pauw, *o.c.*, vol. I, 90.
62. Ibid., 105.
63. Ibid., 109.
64. Ibid., 141

65. Ibid., 254–5.
66. 'It is a circumstance equally remarkable and surprising, that while the territory of Athens abounded with men whose corporeal faculties discovered the highest degree of perfection, no age or situation ever produced women there who were celebrated for beauty' (ibid., 78)! The 'causes of homosexuality' were discussed in a special section entitled 'Corruption of Instinct in the Greeks' (ibid., 82–9) ('De la corruption de l'instinct dans les Grecs', French original, vol. I, 109–20). See also on Sparta, ibid., vol. II, 254: 'that unfortunate passion, which shocks all the designs of nature'.
67. Ibid., vol. I,195.
68. See S. Schama, *The Embarrassment of Riches* (Berkeley, Los Angeles, and London 1987); J. Brewer and R. Porter (eds), *Consumption and the World of Goods in the Seventeenth and Eighteenth Centuries* (London 1993); M. Berg and E. Eger (eds), *Luxury in the Eighteenth Century: Debates, Desires and Delectable Goods* (Basingstoke 2002); O. Murray, 'Greek Luxuries', *Histos* 11 (2017), civ–cx.
69. Pauw, *o.c.*, vol. I, 196.
70. Ibid., 200.
71. Ibid., 205.
72. Ibid., 218.
73. Ibid., 231.
74. Ibid., 234.
75. Ibid., 242.
76. Ibid., 245.
77. Ibid., 245–6.
78. Ibid., 253–6.
79. Ibid., 263. Jacques Necker, banker and chief minister of Louis XVI (1777–81 and 1788–9), struggled to save France from bankruptcy, until he was driven into exile in 1791 during the Revolution; he retired to Coppet near Lausanne on Lake Geneva. He was married to Suzanne Courchod, Edward Gibbon's first and only flame; their daughter was Mme de Staël. In 1781 he had published the *Compte rendu au Roi*, the first public account of the revenues of the French or any other monarchy. For Necker's importance in the Revolution see R. Darnton, *The Revolutionary Temper: Paris, 1748–1789* (Allen Lane 2023)
80. Pauw, *o.c.*, vol. II, 1.
81. Ibid., 8–11.
82. Ibid., 7–8.
83. Ibid., 2.
84. Ibid., 5.
85. Ibid., 19.
86. Ibid., 23. The importance of the Nicomachean reforms is usually thought to have been established by M.H. Hansen: see ch. 19.

87. Pauw, *o.c.*, vol. II, 27ff.
88. Ibid., 33.
89. Ibid., 37.
90. Ibid., 110–11.
91. Ibid., 116–18.
92. Ibid., 120.
93. Ibid., 120.
94. Ibid., 121–2.
95. Ibid., 137.
96. Ibid., 140.
97. Ibid., 140.
98. See E.A. Beeny and F. Whitlum-Cooper, *Poussin and the Dance* (London 2021). Pauw, *o.c.*, vol. II, p. 157.
99. Ibid., 148–9.
100. Ibid., 153–5.
101. Ibid., 162.
102. Ibid., 163. It is clear that de Gourcy was in fact the chief target of de Pauw's polemic; for François-Antoine-Étienne de Gourcy's (1719–1805) *Histoire philosophique et politique des Loix de Lycurgue* (Paris 1768), see M.E. Winston, *From Perfectibility to Perversion: Meliorism in Eighteenth-Century France* (New York, 2005)
103. Pauw, *o.c.*, vol. II, 165–6.
104. Ibid., 221–2.
105. Ibid., 234–41.
106. Ibid., 289.
107. Ibid., 243–6.
108. Ibid., 253–4.
109. Ibid., 261.
110. Ibid., 284.
111. Ibid., 285.
112. The phrase is derived from the fundamental work of Montesquieu, *Considerations sur la Grandeur des Romains et de leur Décadence* (1734), which echoes through the historical works of the eighteenth century until its ultimate use by Gibbon.
113. Pauw, *o.c.*, vol. II, 285–6.
114. Ibid., 280.
115. Ibid., 285.
116. Ibid., 287. According to de Pauw, Greek colonies were of four different kinds, military, commercial, agricultural, and political, and 'in general were composed of foreign vagabonds' (ibid., 292). It is not clear how he reconciled these views of colonials with the departure of his son for the United States in the cause of freedom (see n. 119).
117. Ibid., 298.

118. The book reached the United States, and its tone was mentioned by the reviewer in *The Monthly Review* 79 (1788), 626–34: 'there is, in the whole of his work, a supercilious, dogmatical manner, which disgusts the reader: and he treats those with whom he differs with a contempt which is the less excusable, because, from the nature of the subject, he, as well as the authors who fall under his censure, is often obliged to have recourse to conjecture, in order to supply the want of historical evidence' (p. 626).
119. Unlike his works, de Pauw's descendants seem to have prospered. An article at the time of the endowment and renaming of Depauw University, Indiana, reveals that Washington Depauw was the great-grandson of the son (!) of the 'abbé' Cornelius de Pauw, who had emigrated to America with Lafayette to fight in the War of Independence. The aptly named Washington, by now a Methodist, was a banker who became very wealthy on the proceeds of the first plate-glass manufactory in the USA, and endowed the university towards the end of his life in 1885: J.C. Redpath, 'Washington Charles Depauw, founder of Depauw University', *The Methodist Review* 72 (May–June 1890), 383–98. H.W. Church, 'Corneille de Pauw, and the Controversy over his *Recherches philosophiques sur les Américains*', *Publications of the Modern Language Association of America* 51(1) (1936), 178–206, is sceptical about this relationship.

CHAPTER 3

1. See P.J. Raftery, 'The Brocas Family, Notable Dublin Artists', *Dublin Historical Record* 17(1) (December 1961), 25–34; Patricia Butler, 'Introducing Mr. Brocas: A Family of Dublin Artists', *Irish Arts Review Yearbook* 15 (1999), 80–86.
2. J.C. Beckett, 'Eighteenth-Century Ireland', Introduction to T.W. Moody and W.E. Vaughan (eds), *A New History of Ireland, IV, Eighteenth-Century Ireland* 1691–1800 (Oxford 1986), lx.
3. Horace Walpole, letter to Horace Mann, 28 January 1754 (*Walpole's Correspondence*, vol. 20, 407–11).
4. See I. Hilton, *The Chastleton Diaries: Change and Continuity in the Nineteenth Century* (National Trust 2011).
5. This account was originally published in the Trinity College Dublin classics journal, *Hermathena* 185 (2008; published 2011), 23–106. The documents on which it rests are printed there: Appendix 1: Materials for a Biography of John Gast, 60–73; Appendix 2: Correspondence and other material related to the publication of John Gast's History of Greece (1782) by John Murray, 74–106.

6. See M. Kennedy, 'John Exshaw: Champion of Dublin's Merchants', in R. McManus and L.-M. Griffith, *Leaders of the City: Dublin's First Citizens 1500–1950* (Dublin 2013), 74–84. From the 1730s Exshaw had published a literary journal, *Exshaw's Magazine*, which focused significantly on European and especially French literature: see G. Sheridan, 'Irish Literary Review Magazines and Enlightenment France 1730–1790', in G. Gargett and G. Sheridan, *Ireland and the French Enlightenment 1700–1800* (Dublin 1999), 21–46. Joseph Stock (1740–1813) later became Bishop of Killala; in 1778 he was captured during the French invasion, and played an important part in liaison with the invaders; see his anonymous *Narrative of what passed at Killala in the summer of 1778 by an Eyewitness*. He ended as Bishop of Waterford.
7. Printed by S. Powell for the author.
8. It also contains the autograph of J. Freer; there are a number of marginal notes and underlinings in the early pages as far as p. 53; but it is not clear which of the two owners is responsible for which of these. The bookseller, Dr Christian White of Ilkley, could only tell me that it had come ultimately from a private collection in Lincoln, and that, interestingly, the boards are covered with marbled paper that resembles that used in a volume of medical notes owned by Erasmus Darwin in the 1750s, and now in the Library of St John's College, Cambridge.
9. See J. Gilbert, *History of the City of Dublin* (Dublin 1854–9), i, 90.
10. See ch. 5.
11. I am grateful to my friend Grant McIntyre, former editor at John Murray, for drawing my attention to the archive, and to Dr Toby Barnard of Hertford College, Oxford, for confirming to me its importance for Gast.
12. I therefore decided with the permission of the National Library to publish all the relevant documents as appendixes to my original article on Gast: see *Hermathena* (n. 5, above). Compare *The Letters of David Hume to William Strachan*, ed. G. Birkbeck Hill (Oxford 1888). The best general account known to me of the publishing industry in this period is W. St Clair, *The Reading Nation in the Romantic Period* (Cambridge 2004).
13. *Hermathena* (n. 5, above), Appendix 2, p. 98. Malone was also one of the subscribers to the Dublin edition of 1793, *The History of Greece, properly so called*, vol. I: *To the Accession of Alexander of Macedon*; vol. II: *From the Accession of Alexander of Macedon, to the Present Time.*
14. *European Magazine*, May 1782, 354–5; June 1782, 429–30.
15. *The Monthly Review* (1st Series, London, 1749–89). For William Enfield see the entry in the *Old DNB* lxvii (1882), 424–32. The *Review* was edited by the well-known literary figure and publisher Ralph Griffiths, whose set of volumes I have used: it is in the Bodleian Library, and is marked with the names of his reviewers; see B.C. Nangle, *The Monthly review, first series 1749–1789: indexes of contributors and articles* (Oxford 1934).
16. *Critical Review* 63 (1782), 433–9; 64 (1782), 125–32.

17. See W. Zachs, *The First John Murray and the Late Eighteenth-Century London Book Trade* (London 1998), 72–4; 209, n. 306: on Murray's death in 1793, 56 copies were unsold, and in 1807 the book could still be bought in a London remainder shop.
18. L.T. Kosegarten (1758–1818), poet and translator, also translated Adam Smith, Goldsmith's *History of Rome*, and John Gillies' *History of Greece*; these references are drawn from the digital archive of the *Bibliotheca Academica Translationum*.
19. *Histoire de la Grèce, traduite de plusieurs auteurs anglois [O. Goldsmith et J. Gast, par la Desse de Villeroy], revue et corrigée par J.-J. Leuliette, suivie d'un tableau de la littérature et des arts chez les Grecs jusqu'au règne de Julien, par l'éditeur* (Paris, Cerioux jeune 1812).
20. There are brief references to Gast in later German handbooks by Arnold Heeren, son-in-law and successor of Christian Gottlob Heyne as a professor at Göttingen University, and August Boeckh.
21. *Pinnock's Improved Edition of Dr. Goldsmith's History of Greece, abridged for the use of schools, 12th edition by W.C. Taylor, A.B. of Trinity College Dublin* (London 1837), iii: perhaps Taylor's use of Leland and Gast is due to his Dublin connection.
22. This is repeated at the start of the 1782 (pp. viii–xiii) and 1793 (pp. xxviii–xxxii) volumes, and already prefigured in *Rudiments*, p. 7 note *h*. It seems original to Gast: the division offered by Tourreil (see below, n. 83) is quite different, involving four ages 'till at last she sunk under the power of the Romans' (Eng. trans. p. 4).
23. The dialogue form was used more appropriately for philosophical argument by Lord Shaftesbury in *The Moralists* (1709) and Bishop Berkeley in his *Three Dialogues* (1713) and *Alciphron* (1732), as later by David Hume in his *Dialogues concerning Natural Religion* (1779). In antiquarian studies it had been used by Joseph Addison in his *Dialogues upon the Usefulness of Ancient Medals* (written *c.* 1703, published 1721); but none of these had the didactic purpose of Gast.
24. Gast, *Rudiments*, Dialogue IV, p. 132. But even Gast sometimes nods: in the 1753 edition in a moment of pure hallucination he calls the girl Iphigenia; this is silently corrected in 1793 (vol. I, p. 119) to Polyxena. Who on earth persuaded Wolfgang Petersen, the director of *Troy* (2004), 'the greatest sword and sandal epic of all time', to revive this forgotten ancient fantasy? I fear someone must have been reading Robert Graves.
25. See the memories of Gast's method of teaching given by Joseph Stock in his final, 1793 edition of the revised work, xxii–xxiv.
26. This explanation is largely derived from Banier. For comparison in most cases I give references to Gast's works in both the original volumes, Gast, 1753 (*Rudiments*) and Gast, 1782 (*History of Greece*), and the later combined edition, Gast, 1793. Gast, 1753, I, 26–8; 1793, 29–33.

27. *Explication historique des Fables* (2nd edn., Paris 1715). Banier was the standard euhemerist interpretation of ancient mythology, first published in 1711, and popular deep into the nineteenth century. By 1738 the third edition extended to three volumes under the title *La Mythologie et les Fables expliquées par l'histoire*. An English translation of this edition was published as *The Mythology and Fables of the Ancients, explain'd from history* (London 1739–40).
28. 'Au reste, pour rendre moins ennuieuse la lecture d'un Livre qui traite d'une matière assez séche, on a préféré le style de Dialogue à celui des Dissertations. La maison de campagne d'Eliante est le lieu où se passent les scènes; l'Abbé Théophile est comme le Docteur de la pièce, qui parle presque toujours; Alcidon son ami joint ses conjectures à celles de l'Abbé, et Eliante y mêle quelques reflexions, telles qu'une femme d'esprit peut fournir.'
29. Gast, 1753, 11.
30. Ibid., 33.
31. Ibid., 143–53. This fascinating account is best studied in the expanded version that appears as a long appendix in the 1793 edition (vol. I, 539–85), called 'a Dissertation *on the love of the marvellous so prevalent among the ancient Greeks*'; the editor had relegated it to this position as 'too prolix' for its intended place in the first book.
32. Here he cites Thomas Blackwell's *Enquiry into the Life and Writings of Homer* (London 1735), 169.
33. Gast, 1753, 66; 1793, I, 59–60.
33. Gast, 1793, I, Book III, [misnumbered as II], Section 1.
35. Ibid., Book IV, Section I.
36. See ch. 10.
37. Gast, 1753, 230.
38. Ibid., 233–4.
39. Gast, 1753, 255; 1793, I, 195.
40. Gast, 1793, I, Book IV, Section 2.
41. A. Grafton, *Joseph Scaliger: A Study in the History of Classical Scholarship, Vol. II: Historical Chronology* (Oxford 1993); F.E. Manuel, *Isaac Newton Historian* (Cambridge 1963).
42. Gast, 1793, I, Book IV, Section 3.
43. Gast, 1753, 332; 1793, I, 253.
44. Gast, 1793, I, Book V, Section 1.
45. Gast, 1753, 355; 1793, I, 271. By the 1793 edition this praise of Athens had become what 'cannot surely be esteemed an uninteresting digression' (pp. 272–81).
46. Gast, 1753, 359; 1793, I, 274.
47. Gast, 1753, 363; 1793, I, 277.
48. Gast, 1753, 365; 1793, I, 279.

49. Gast, 1793, I, Book V, Section 2.
50. Ibid., Book VI, Section 1.
51. Gast, 1753, 448; 1793, I, 345.
52. Gast, 1753, 471; 1793, I, 365.
53. Gast, 1753, 492; 1793, I, 385.
54. Gast, 1793, I, Book VII, Section 2, and Book VIII.
55. Gast, 1753, 623; cf. 1793, I, 513.
56. Gast, 1753, 569–92; 1793, I, 460–83.
57. Gast, 1753, 575; 1793, I, 466.
58. Gast, 1753, 588; 1793, I, 480.
59. Gast, 1753, 647; 1793, I, 537.
60. Gast, 1753, 647; 1793, I, 537–8.
61. The best contextual analysis of this imperialist strand is by the young Turkish scholar C. Akça Ataç, 'Imperial Lessons from Athens and Sparta', *History of Political Thought* 27 (2006), 642–60, who discusses Gast in passing.
62. *Journal britannique* (July–August 1754), Article IV, 286–305.
63. For Rollin see above, p. 33.
64. Gast, 1782, 505; 1793, II, 451.
65. Gast, 1782, 580; 1793, II, 517.
66. Gast, 1782, 584; 1793, II, 520–21.
67. Gast, 1782, 618; 1793, II, 552.
68. Gast, 1782, 628; 1793, II, 560.
69. Gast, 1782, 636–45; 1793, II, 567–76. See p. 90 for the origin of these (at first sight) curious views.
70. *Anthologia Hibernica*, vol. 2 (Dublin, August 1793), p. 128.
71. Momigliano does indeed give a reference to the work of 1782 in a footnote to his inaugural lecture ('George Grote and the Study of Greek History', in *Studies in Historiography* [London 1966], 72 n. 7), but without any comment; he is not mentioned in his 1977 essay 'Eighteenth-Century Prelude to Mr. Gibbon', *Sesto contributo* (Rome 1980), I, 249–63 (see esp. the list on p. 254). In his own country Gast was not entirely forgotten: his 1753 dialogue is briefly mentioned in W.B. Stanford, *Ireland and the Classical Tradition* (Dublin 1976), 148–9, as 'now more of a curiosity than a work to be consulted seriously'; although when Stanford claims that the 1793 edition was 'widely read in [Irish] schools until Goldsmith's history supplanted it', it is not clear how long the alleged period of its use as a school textbook can have been, given that Goldsmith's educationally far more useful narrative compendium *The Grecian History* was published in 1774, and specifically 'abridged for the use of schools' at least as early as 1787. Recent work on the eighteenth century has begun to recognize the existence of Gast; there are passing references in Akça Ataç, 'Imperial Lessons from Athens and Sparta', n. 61 above; G. Ceserani, (Ch. 2, n. 14), mentions Gast's

1753 volume in a footnote (n. 15). A.J. Bayliss uses Gast more extensively in his survey of eighteenth-century perceptions of Macedonia: 'Greek but not Grecian? Macedonians in Enlightenment Histories', in J. Moore, I. Macgregor Morris, and A.J. Bayliss (eds), *Reinventing History: The Enlightenment Origins of Ancient History* (London 2008; published 2009), 219–46.

72. According to Stock, Gast had indeed originally intended to discuss Syria and Egypt, but he was persuaded to postpone them to a third volume.
73. See ch. 2.
74. *New Letters of David Hume* (Oxford 1954), ed. R. Klibansky and E.C. Mossner, nos 27 and 28, 47–8. I owe this reference to Ceserani. But neither Hume nor Ceserani mentions Gast.
75. Letter 28, 7 April 1759, p. 48 (*o.c.* n. 12 above).
76. Gast, 1782, 672; 1793, II, 600.
77. For this section, which constitutes the original plan of Gibbon's work, see P.R. Ghosh, 'Gibbon Observed', *Journal of Roman Studies* 81 (1991), 132–56; and 'The Conception of Gibbon's *History*', in R. McKitterick and R. Quinault (eds), *Gibbon and Empire* (1997), 271–316. Gibbon took great care in planning the conclusion of each section of his *History* as they were separately published, as can be seen from the first scholarly edition of Gibbon by David Womersley (London 1994).
78. R. Whelan, 'The Huguenots and the Imaginative Geography of Ireland: A Planned Immigration in the 1680s', *Irish Historical Studies* 35 (2007), 477–95.
79. R. Hylton, 'The Huguenot Settlement at Portarlington', in C.E.J. Caldicott, H. Gough, and J.-P. Pittion (eds), *The Huguenots and Ireland: Anatomy of an Emigration* (Dublin 1987), 297–320.
80. Edward Gibbon, *Memoirs of My Life* (1769).
81. See ch. 5.
82. M. Espagne, *Les Transferts culturels franco-allemands* (Paris 1999).
83. Tourreil's work was translated into English in *The Orations of Demosthenes, to which is prefix'd the Historical Preface of Monsieur Tourreil* (London 1702). See Ceserani, 'Narrative . . .' (*o.c.* n. 71 above).
84. Leland is mentioned as a forerunner of Gillies by Momigliano, and he notes that the interest in Greek history was 'stimulated by a discussion on the decline of Greece in the fourth century BC which started in France and continued in Ireland before passing to England – or Scotland' (*o.c.* n. 71, p. 58); these remarks show what a pity it was that he failed to comment on John Gast, whose life as an exile so closely reflected his own experience.
85. See S. Deane, 'Montesquieu and Burke', in G. Gargett and G. Sheridan (eds), *Ireland and the French Enlightenment 1700–1800* (Dublin 1999), 47–66.

86. Gibbon himself owned a copy of the Paris edition of 1755: G. Keynes, *The Library of Edward Gibbon* (London 1950), 201.
87. *Esprit de lois* (1748) 3.3; quoted by Gast, 1793, II, p. 571.
88. Gast, 1753, 218–19; 1793, I, 167.
89. See the chapters by L.M. Cullen ('Economic Development 1750–1800', 159–95) and J.H. Andrews ('Land and People, *c.*1780', 236–64) in T.W. Mood and W.E. Vaughan (eds), *A New History of Ireland, IV, Eighteenth-Century Ireland 1691–1800* (Oxford 1986).
90. It was hard not to recall this in the Dublin of 2009, when the National Gallery of Ireland mounted the magnificent exhibition *Thomas Roberts 1748–1777*; see William Laffan and Brendan Rooney, *Thomas Roberts: Landscape and Patronage in Eighteenth-Century Ireland* (Dublin 2009).
91. The imagined village of Auburn that Goldsmith described became a symbol of exile and loss for generations of Irish migrants to the New World and Australia: three townships of Auburn are listed in Australia, two in Canada, and no fewer than twenty-three in the United States.
92. Gast, 1782, 710–12; 1793, II, 635–6.
93. A. Momigliano, 'Ancient History and the Antiquarian' and 'Gibbon's Contribution to Historical Method', in *Studies in Historiography* (*o.c.* n. 71), chs 1–2.
94. See above all the studies of Anthony Grafton in *Defenders of the Text* (Harvard 1991) and *Worlds Made by Words* (Harvard 2009).

CHAPTER 4

1. *Edinburgh Review*, October 1846, reprinted in Mill's *Dissertations and Discussions* 2, part 2, 283.
2. *Westminster Review* 17 (1832), 158.
3. S. Johnson, *A Journey to the Western Islands of Scotland* (Dublin 1775), 242.
4. *Childe Harold's Pilgrimage*, Canto 2, stanzas 88–90.
5. Morris (below n. 11) 235 cites a passage from E.D. Clarke (*Travels in Various Countries*, 1812), who visited Marathon in 1801, and experienced on the plain of Marathon a similar 'sense of that Eternity'.
6. He probably first read the statement in a school textbook derived from Oliver Goldsmith's *Grecian History* (Goldsmith 1774, 109–10); on the many school versions of Goldsmith see above ch. 2.
7. See above ch. 3. Both Stanyan and Rollin had given a full account of the battle (book vi, ch. 1), but they lack the forthright connection between democracy and martial victory that Gast asserted. Goldsmith's account is however more explicit: was he aware of his fellow Irishman's work?
8. Gast, *The Rudiments of the Grecian History* (Dublin 1753), 355.
9. Ibid., 385–6.

10. See ch. 2.
11. On Thermopylae see I. Macgregor Morris, '"Shrines of the Mighty": Rediscovering the Battlefields of the Persian Wars', in E. Bridges, E. Hall, and P.J. Rhodes (eds), *Cultural Responses to the Persian Wars* (Oxford 2007), 233–63; P. Cartledge, *Thermopylae: The Battle that Changed the World* (London 2006), ch. 9.
12. Herodotus, *Histories*, §78.
13. O. Murray, 'Ancient History, 1872–1914', in *History of the University of Oxford*, VII.2 (2000), 346–9; R. Symonds, *Oxford and Empire* (Oxford 1986); P. Vasunia, *The Classics and Colonial India* (Oxford 2013).
14. Bulwer-Lytton, *Athens: Its Rise and Fall* (London [1837] 2004), 254; see below ch. 6.
15. T.J. Rood, 'From Marathon to Waterloo: Byron, Battle Monuments, and the Persian Wars', in *Cultural Responses to the Persian Wars* (above n. 11), 268–98.
16. Plut. *De glor. Ath.* 3 [*Mor.* 347C]; Lucian *Laps.* 3.
17. Tim Rood tells me that the original idea in fact came from the philologist Michel Bréal.
18. Rollin 1730–38, vol. 2, book 6, ch. 1.
19. Goldsmith 1774, 105, 112–13.
20. See the full discussion in Rood (*o.c.* n. 15), 269.
21. I owe this information to François Lissarrague; Tim Rood tells me that Louis-Philippe also commissioned a painting on the subject from Auguste Couder, 'La victoire de Marathon annoncée dans Athènes', of which a lithograph was published in 1830.
22. Unfortunately the standard work on the Prix de Rome concludes with the prize of 1863, so the details of the competition are not available: P. Grunchec, *Les Concours des Prix de Rome, 1797–1863* (Paris 1986).
23. R. Jenkins, *The Dilessi Murders* (London 1961).
24. Hansard, 20 May 1870, vol. 201, cols 1123–60; Jenkins, *The Dilessi Murders*.
25. J.P. Mahaffy, *Rambles and Studies in Greece* (London 1876), 191–4.

CHAPTER 5

1. Reprinted in *Studies in Historiography* (London 1966), 56–74. Momigliano went on to modify this statement a little by discussing the reasons why the predecessors of Mitford and Gillies could not be regarded as true historians of Greece, and by considering their backgrounds in the antiquarian tradition.
2. My pupil Patrick Commons of Christ's College, Cambridge, found fifty letters of Gillies in the Hope family archive in Edinburgh in 1981, concerning the Grand Tour, but of little interest.

3. From Gillies' entry in the *DNB* (W.W. Wroth, revised by I.C. Cunningham), which quotes T.J. Mathias, *The pursuits of literature, second dialogue* (1796), 118, 120. On Gillies see de Pauw's scathing remarks above, p. 51.
4. My *Bibliotheca Academica Translationum* project, listing translations of academic works between the various European languages (1701–1919), published on the web, records French editions of 1787–8 and 1841 (abridged), German editions of 1781 and 1787–97.
5. He quotes Christoph Meiners' *Geschichte der Luxus der Athenienser* (Lemgo 1782). Meiners was professor of 'Weltweisheit' at Göttingen, the protagonist of a theory of 'scientific racism', and an opponent of Kant and the Enlightenment.
6. My information on Mitford is drawn from the online *DNB* (W. Wroth, revised J.S. Taylor 2004), and the biographical introduction dated 1829 by his younger brother Lord Redesdale, ancestor of the Mitford sisters, which I read first in Balliol College Library in Benjamin Jowett's copy of the New Edition of 1835. See also the unpublished thesis by my pupil J.S. Taylor, 'William Mitford and Greek History' (D.Phil. Oxford 1984). Mitford's *History of Greece* was published in many different formats, and continually revised during his lifetime; but the chapters are ordered numerically across ultimately ten volumes, and divided into sections. In referring to it I have therefore used chapter and section numbers, rather than page references.
7. Quoted in the *Old DNB* article from Bowring's *Life of Bentham*. See my account of the state of Oxford studies in ancient history during this period in *The History of the University of Oxford*, vol. VI, part 1, ed. M.C. Brock and M.C. Curthoys (Oxford 1997): 'The Old Learning', 520–25.
8. See M.S. Montecalvo, *Guillaume-Emmanuel-Joseph Guilhem de Clermont-Lodève, Baron de Sainte-Croix, 1746–1809* (Firenze 2014). The Baron de Sainte-Croix was the founder of modern views on the sources for Alexander the Great, and clearly influenced that part of Mitford's *History*, which mentions him explicitly: see P. Briant, *The First European: A History of Alexander in the Age of Empire* (Harvard 2017), ch. 2.
9. W. Mitford, *The History of Greece*, 10 vols (1784–1810), footnote to ch. XLIV, sec. I.
10. His brother's comment in his short account of the author (above, n. 6), p. xiii.
11. *Don Juan*, canto xii, stanza xix, note.
12. 1.76; this was derived from Leland's *History of Ireland* and Giraldus of Wales.
13. Mitford, *o.c.*, ch. II, sec. III.
14. Ibid., ch II, sec. IV.
15. Ibid., ch. X, sec. II.
16. Ibid., ch. IV, sec. I; ch. V, sec. IV and see the index under 'Slavery', and below n. 37.
17. Ibid., ch. XXI, sec. I.

18. Ibid., ch. VII, sec. V.
19. Ibid., ch. XI, sec. I.
20. Ibid., ch. XI, sec. I.
21. Ibid., ch. XII, sec. I.
22. Ibid., ch. XII, sec. II.
23. Ibid., ch. XIII, sec. I.
24. Ibid., ch. XX, sec. V.
25. Ibid., ch. XIV, sec. III.
26. Ibid., ch. XIV, sec. I.
27. Ibid., ch. XXI.
28. Ibid., sec. II.
29. Ibid., ch. III, sec. II.
30. Ibid., ch. IV, sec III.
31. These numbers are derived from 'Ktesikles' (Stesikleides, *FGH* 245 F 1) in Athenaeus 6.272; for the early controversy see also R. Wallace, *A Dissertation on the Numbers of Mankind in Ancient and Modern Times* (Edinburgh 1753); J. Millar, *Observations Concerning the Distinctions of Ranks in Society* (London 1771). For the wider context of the controversy in the Scottish Enlightenment see G. Cambiano, *Polis: un modello per la cultura europea*, (Bari, 2000), ch. VII, 312-69. For the importance of this controversy down to the modern age see the discussion in J.T. Roberts, *Athens on Trial*, 263–74. Recent assessments suggest a relationship in Athens between the slave and free population of 4 to 1 (adult males), see M.H. Hansen, *Demography and Democracy: The Number of Athenian Citizens in the Fourth Century B.C.* (Herning 1985); *Three Studies in Athenian Demography* (Copenhagen 1988). For a negative view of Hansen's calculations (but with no new evidence) see B. Akrigg, 'Demography and Classical Athens', ch. 2, in C. Holleran and A. Pudsey (eds), *Demography and the Graeco-Roman World: New Insights and Approaches* (Cambridge 2011).
32. Mitford, *o.c.*, ch. V, sec. IV.
33. 'Of the Populousness of Ancient Nations', in *Essays Moral Political and Literary* (1777), Essay XI.
34. Mitford, *o.c.*, ch. IV, sec. I. At the end of this section, in a footnote, Mitford has a fascinating account of the nomenclatures of the various constitutions in French, English, and among Greek authors.
35. Mitford, *o.c.*, ch. XX, sec. III.
36. Ibid., ch. XXVII, sec. II.
37 'Mitford's sensitivity to the evil of ancient slavery set him far ahead of the nineteenth-century liberal historians of Greece who turned their eyes from slavery in Greece, as they did from the plight of the contemporary poor' (F.M. Turner, *The Greek Heritage in Victorian Britain* [New Haven 1981], p. 196).
38. Mitford's entry in the *Old DNB* (W.W. Wroth), p. 534.

39. See the excellent discussion in Taylor, 'William Mitford' (*o.c.*, n. 6, above), ch. 3.1: 'Contemporary reviews', 172–225. Nevertheless, Bentham had a high opinion of the work and maintained a friendly correspondence with his fellow college student Mitford throughout their lives.
40. 'On Mitford's History of Greece', in *Macaulay's Complete Works, vol. XI, Speeches, Poems and Miscellaneous Writings* I (1898), 365–93 (originally in *Knight's Quarterly* for November 1824). See also Macaulay's passing favourable description of the Athenian popular assembly in his review of a new edition of Boswell's *Johnson* in 1831, *Critical and Historical Essays* 1 (1854), 401.
41. *Westminster Review* 5 (April 1826), 269–331 (280–85). This review is mentioned but not reprinted in Grote's *Miscellaneous Works*.
42. This assertion is quite unfair: Mitford mentions 'the learned Archbishop Potter', but not as his sole source.
43. This is the general view of the contributors to *Brill's Companion to George Grote and the Classical Tradition*, ed. K.N. Demetriou (Leiden 2014). See also the essays in the bicentenary volume *George Grote Reconsidered*, ed. W.M. Calder III and S. Trzaskoma (Hildesheim 1996).
44. See Jeffrey A. Winters, *Oligarchy* (Cambridge 2011), who classifies Athens as an oligarchy on the same grounds as Mitford, for its exclusion of women and slaves. Yet the Athenian *demos* exercised far more control over the wealthy through its law courts and system of liturgies, or taxation for war and festivals, than any modern society has managed to achieve. There was no equivalent of the Income Defence Industry in Athens.

CHAPTER 6

1. Carlyle, 'On History Again' (1833), in *Critical and Miscellaneous Essays* IV (London 1869), 225.
2. Macaulay, 'History' (1828), in *Complete Works, vol. VII, Essays and Biographies*, vol. I (London 1913), 217.
3. The fundamental study is that of G. Lukacs, *The Historical Novel* (London 1962), ch. 1: 'The influence which he exercised over the whole of European literature is immeasurable' (69–70); see also J.W. Burrow, *A History of Histories* (London 2008).
4. J. Mitchell, *The Walter Scott Operas* (Tuscaloosa 1977).
5. T. Carlyle, 'Sir Walter Scott' (1838), in *Critical and Miscellaneous Essays* VI (London 1869), 275. For Carlyle and history, see J.D. Rosenberg, *Carlyle and the Burden of History* (Oxford 1985).
6. For Scott's influence in France, note especially Thierry's praise of Scott written in 1834, reprinted in *Philosophie des sciences historiques. Le moment romantique.* Textes réunis et présentés par Marcel Gauchet (Paris 2002), 53.

7. On Niebuhr and Müller see ch. 9; Mommsen's *Römische Geschichte* 1854–6 (Eng. trans., *History of Rome* [new edition, London 1867]) was written as a result of his experiences of the revolutionary movements of 1848: S. Rebenich, *Theodor Mommsen, eine Biographie* (Munich 2002).
8. The radical political economist J.C.L. Sismondi's influential *History of the Italian Republics* (16 vols) was written between 1807 and 1818.
9. T. Carlyle, *History of the French Revolution* (London 1837); T. Macaulay, *The History of England from the Accession of James the Second* (London 1848).
10. Balzac, *Comédie humaine introduction*: 'D'abord, presque toujours ces personnages, dont l'existence devient plus longue, plus authentique que celle des générations au milieu desquelles on les fait naître, ne vivent qu'à la condition d'être une grande image du présent. Conçus dans les entrailles de leur siècle, tout le cœur humain se remue sous leur enveloppe, il s'y cache souvent toute une philosophie. Walter Scott élevait donc à la valeur philosophique de l'histoire le roman, cette littérature qui, de siècle en siècle, incruste d'immortels diamants la couronne poétique des pays où se cultivent les lettres. Il y mettait l'esprit des anciens temps, il y réunissait à la fois le drame, le dialogue, le portrait, le paysage, la description; il y faisait entrer le merveilleux et le vrai, ces éléments de l'épopée, il y faisait coudoyer la poésie par la familiarité des plus humbles langages ... Quoique, pour ainsi dire, ébloui par la fécondité surprenante de Walter Scott, toujours semblable à lui-même et toujours original, je ne fus pas désespéré, car je trouvai la raison de ce talent dans l'infinie variété de la nature humaine. Le hasard est le plus grand romancier du monde: pour être fécond, il n'y a qu'à l'étudier. La Société française allait être l'historien, je ne devais être que le secrétaire. En dressant l'inventaire des vices et des vertus, en rassemblant les principaux faits des passions, en peignant les caractères, en choisissant les événements principaux de la Société, en composant des types par la réunion des traits de plusieurs caractères homogènes, peut-être pouvais-je arriver à écrire l'histoire oubliée par tant d'historiens, celle des mœurs.'
11. Bulwer-Lytton, *Paul Clifford* (1830), ch. I.
12. Thus my interest having been first aroused by the chance reading of a Dutch bookseller's catalogue on the web, when I wanted a cheap copy of the book in order to scan it onto disk, I was able to purchase on the web a first American edition (Harper Brothers 1837), for a total of $32 – volume I once belonged to Eugene H. Lynch and was located in Beaverton, Oregon, costing $24, volume II without an owner's inscription was found in Houston, Texas, at $8. Were these two separate broken sets, or the same far-flung set which had suffered separate journeys over 160 years to Oregon and Houston in wagons or railway trains, individually left on seats, forgotten at the houses of distant relatives, inherited and reinherited – only to be reunited by a mad English professor? It certainly says something for the American reverence for books that neither of them, useless as they separately were, had been thrown away.

13. See, p. 135.
14. Bulwer-Lytton, *Pelham* (1828), ch. XLIII.
15. For this episode see W. St Clair, *That Greece Might Still Be Free* (Oxford 1972), ch. 22; M. Mazower, *The Greek Revolution* (London 2021), ch. 11.
16. T.H.S. Escott, *Edward Bulwer, First Baron Lytton of Knebworth* (London 1910), p. 67. This work remains the best account of Bulwer-Lytton's literary career; the family biographies are rather stiff and formal. See also L. Mitchell, *Bulwer Lytton: The Rise and Fall of a Victorian Man of Letters* (London 2003).
17. '*Pelham* caused the black swallow-tail coat to become compulsory for evening wear' (Escott, *o.c.*, n. 16).
18. Bulwer-Lytton, *Pelham*, preface to the London 1848 edition, p. iv.
19. Today Knebworth (or Knobworth as Mick Jagger insists on calling it) is still in the family: it is now a banqueting centre famous as 'the stately home of Rock', where since 1974 the Rolling Stones, Queen, Led Zeppelin, Pink Floyd, Oasis and all the rock stars from Freddy Mercury to Eric Clapton have performed.
20. There are inevitably many stories about this episode and its consequences; see Escott, *o.c*, 297, and Mitchell, *o.c.*, ch. 3.
21. Her voluminous letters to her husband were preserved at Knebworth as evidence against her, and were finally published as *The Collected Letters of Rosina Bulwer Lytton*, ed. by M. Mulvey Roberts and S. Carpenter (London 2008); see the review of Jonathan Keates, 'A Very Serpent', *TLS*, 31 October 2008, p. 9.
22. Escott, *o.c.*, 239.
23. And as Snoopy's favourite author: for it is Snoopy's continual attempt to rewrite that first sentence, 'It was a dark and stormy night', which lies behind the creation of the annual Bulwer-Lytton Fiction Contest for the worst first sentence in any unpublished novel of the year, and so of a flourishing cult in America with its own website (which I thoroughly recommend).
24. *The Victorians and Ancient Greece* (Oxford 1980) and *The Greek Heritage in Victorian Britain* (New Haven and London 1981). Jenkyns mentions the title (p. 74); Turner briefly misrepresents the book (pp. 210–11). Elizabeth Rawson dismisses it in a footnote: 'Lytton also wrote a history of Athens, pre-Thirlwall, and wisely left it unfinished' (*The Spartan Tradition in European Thought*, 360); doubtless she did not like its denunciation of Sparta. K.N. Demetriou in his excellent and learned monograph on George Grote devoted four pages to Bulwer-Lytton (*George Grote on Plato and Athenian Democracy* [Frankfurt 1999], 47–50). But I am puzzled by his claim that Bulwer-Lytton's work is 'divided into two parts, one historical and the other dealing with the arts and literature of the Athenians. The plan of a literary section already forms a glaring innovation.' Such a division was in fact commonplace; the originality of Bulwer-Lytton lies in the fact that there is no such division in his book, but rather an integration of the two aspects.

25. M. Bernal, *Black Athena: The Afro-Asiatic Roots of Classical Civilization*, vol. I (London 1987).
26. See M. Mazower, *The Greek Revolution*, ch. 17.
27. 'Thus the largest portion of that history which we commonly call ancient is practically modern, as it describes society in a stage analogous to that in which it now is; while on the other hand, much of what is called modern history is practically ancient, as it relates to a state of things which has passed away.' Appendix I, Arnold's Thucydides. vol. I. p. 630.
28. Escott, *o.c.*, 225.
29. Bulwer-Lytton, *Pelham*, ch. XLIII.
30. Escott, *o.c.*, 7–8.
31. 1. *Athen, seine Erhebung und sein Fall, nebst Ueberblicken ueber die Literatur, die Philosophie und das buergerliche und gesellige Leben des athenischen Volks* (im Verlage der J.B. Metzler'schen Buchhandlung, 1837–8), trans. Dr Gustav Pfizer. 2. *Athens Grösse und Verfall, nebst Untersuchungen über die Literatur, die Philosophie und das gesellige Leben des Atheniensischen Volkes* Aachen 1837, Mayer (*Sämmtliche Werke* Bd. 23/24 & 25/26), 4 pts in 2 vols, trans. O. v. Czarnowski. 3. (no translator specified) *Athens Aufschwung und Fall, mit Hinblick auf die Literatur, die Philosophie und das gesellige Leben des Atheniensischen Volkes*, 5 parts; parts 1–4: Zwickau 1837, Gebrüder Schumann in Leipzig (E.L. Bulwer, *Werke* Teil 40–43); Part 5 in: Edward Bulwer-Lytton, *Athens Aufschwung und Fall, mit Hinblick auf die Literatur, die Philosophie und das gesellige Leben des Atheniensischen Volkes*, Teil 5 – Ernst Maltravers, Zwickau: Gebrüder Schumann in Leipzig (E.L. Bulwer, *Werke* Teil 44–48) (1837).
32. *Athens, its rise and fall* (English text) Leipzig 1837, Fleischer (*The Complete Works of E.L. Bulwer*, vol. XII/XIII), 2 vols. *Athens, its rise and fall* (English text) (extracts from text) Leipzig 1884 (Siegismund & Volkening).
33. *Atene, il suo innalzamento e sua caduta*, prima versione italiana di Francesco Ambrosoli, Milano: Vedova di Andrea Stella e figlio, 1838 (information from Carmine Ampolo).
34. *Athenen, dets Opkomst og Fald: med Udsigt over det atheniensiske Folks Litteratur, Philosophie og sociale Liv*, trans. Joachim Chr. Møller, *Bulwers Skrifter*, 33–6, Copenhagen, Chr. Steen & Søns Forlag (information from Mogens Herman Hansen).
35. Giovanni Antonio Galignani, an Italian who had married the daughter of an English publisher during a period of refuge in London from the French Revolution, returned to Paris to run a publishing house, a coffee shop and reading room, and a series of journals for British tourists; his dynasty survives today, and the bookshop Galignani in the Rue de Rivoli now proudly boasts of being the oldest English-language bookshop on the continent. See the magnificent article by Giles Barber, 'Galignani's and the Publication of English Books in France from 1800 to 1852', *The Library* 16 (1961),

267–86; also the bicentenary volume published by the firm – Diana Cooper-Richet and Emily Bourgeaud, *Galignani* (Paris 1999). Bulwer-Lytton himself mentions Galignani's 'reading room' in his novel *Pelham* (ch. XXII).

36. Princeton Special Collections: Morris Parrish Collection, Box 18, folder 3, AM 86–120.
37. My friend Grant Mcintyre, who knows the Byron correspondence well, tells me that he has never heard of such an agreement; but it may have been more common than literary historians recognize: there are a suspicious number of apparently simultaneous pirated publications in this period; in the absence of any copyright agreements and with widespread pirating in France, America, and Ireland, it did offer some means of retaining control and earning money from these pirated editions. For the practice see W. St Clair, *The Reading Nation in the Romantic Period* (Cambridge 2004), ch. 15.
38. See Bernal, *o.c.*, n. 25.
39. *Edinburgh Review*, July 1837, p. 164.
40. *The History of the Manners and Customs of Ancient Greece*, 3 vols (London 1842), p. vi.
41. Bulwer-Lytton, *The Caxtons* (Edinburgh and London 1849), vol. I, 160. For the melancholy Clinton, see my sketch in ch. 15 of *The History of the University of Oxford vol. VI, Nineteenth-Century Oxford, Part 1*, ed. M.G. Brock and M.C. Curthoys (Oxford 1997), 523–5.
42. See Bulwer-Lytton, *Athens: Its Rise and Fall*, Advertisement. This finishing point is found for instance in William Robertson; it was also Mitford's original intention, although he never reached beyond Alexander. The death of Philip (Stanyan) or of Alexander (Gillies, Grote) is more usual; Thirlwall ostensibly carried his narrative down to the modern age, though in a very perfunctory fashion.
43. Bulwer-Lytton, *Athens*, book I, ch. VI, sec. I.
44. Ibid., sec. IV.
45. Here note the reference to 'Müller's Dorians': see ch. 8.
46. Bulwer-Lytton, *Athens*, book I, ch. VI, sec. VII.
47. Ibid., sec. IX.
48. Ibid., sec. XI.
49. Ibid., sec XV.
50. Ibid., ch. VIII, sec. XVI.
51. Ibid., book II, ch. I, sec. XVI.
52. *Edinburgh Review*, July 1837, p. 155.
53. As Chryssanthi Avlami has said to me, if Greece had been freed in the eighteenth century, Sparta would now be the capital of Greece; in the nineteenth century it could only be Athens. Sparta is now (with Navarino-Pylos) the handsomest and best-preserved of the Neohellenic towns of Greece, and there is a lively debate around its conservation: see the dossier of town

plans and photographs on sale in the city, entitled *Sparta: The Foundation and the Urban Planning Development of the Town From 1834 To This Day*, and the conference proceedings of 1994, *New Cities for Old: The Example of Sparta* (in Greek).

54. *Edinburgh Review*, July 1837, 151–77 (by Sir D.K. Sandford, 1798–1838, Professor of Greek at Glasgow); *British and Foreign Review* vii (1838), 36–85 (by W.B. Donne, Cambridge Apostle and descendant of the poet).
55. *Fraser's Magazine*, September 1837, 347–56. The editor and main contributor to *Fraser's Magazine* was the Irish wit and drunkard William Maginn, one of whose infuriated victims resorted to horse-whipping and a duel.
56. [Sir Archibald Allison], review of E.L. Bulwer, *Athens, its Rise and Fall*, *Blackwood's Edinburgh Magazine* 42 (1837), 44–60; reprinted in his *Essays, Political, Historical and Miscellaneous* II (Edinburgh 1850).
57. Tom Harrison first drew my attention to this letter, which is now displayed at Knebworth. I thank especially Sibylla Jane Flower for identifying the recipient, and providing me with information about him. The new novel referred to is *Ernest Maltravers*.

CHAPTER 7

1. J.S. Mill, 'Childhood and Early Education', *Autobiography*, ed. H.J. Laski (London 1924), 10. The central importance of democratic Athens for the development of Mill's conception of liberty and political obligation is recognized in the detailed study by Nadia Urbinati, *Mill on Democracy: From the Athenian Polis to Representative Government* (Chicago 2002). But her tendency to pair the names of Mill and Grote overestimates the importance of the publication of Grote's *History of Greece* in the formation of Mill's ideas: his own education and works such as Bulwer-Lytton's *Athens* combined to establish the direction of the principles of his political philosophy long before Grote, despite his later lavish praise of the book.
2. B. Mazlish, *James and John Stuart Mill* (New York 1975), 249–51.
3. *The Early Draft of John Stuart Mill's Autobiography*, ed. J. Stillinger (Urbana 1961), 155. This was amended in the version revised under the influence of Harriet Taylor or her daughter, and appears only as a general remark in the later *Autobiography* (ed. Laski), 166.
4. 'A mild and philosophical man, possessing the highest order of moral and intellectual endowments; but wanting something which for need of a better phrase I shall call *devil.* He is too abstract in his tone of reasoning and does not aim to influence others by any proof excepting that of

ratiocination' (John Morley, *The Life of Richard Cobden* [London 1906], 136–7).

5. On Harriet Grote ('I never understood the meaning of the word grotesque until I met Mrs Grote,' one enemy said) see Sarah Richardson, 'A Regular Politician in Breeches', ch. 5 in *Brill's Companion to George Grote and the Classical Tradition* (Leiden 2014), 134–60. After Grote's death she presented to his fellow Radical MP Sir William Clay his set of John Henning's miniature plaster casts of the Elgin Marbles, which were given to me by a descendant, and remain in my family.
6. *The Early Draft of John Stuart Mill's Autobiography*, 94, contrasted with Harriet Grote, *The Personal Life of George Grote* (1873), 49, already suspected in 1952 by A. Momigliano, 'George Grote and the Study of Greek History (1952)', in *Studies in Historiography* (London 1966), 60, and M.L. Clarke, *George Grote* (London 1962), 33–5.
7. The essay was first published as an appendix to W.M. Calder and S. Trzaskoma, *George Grote Reconsidered: A 200th Birthday Celebration with a First Edition of his Essay 'Of the Athenian Government'* (Hildesheim 1996), 75–94.
8. *Autobiography* (ed. Laski), ch. IV.
9. This is the theme of Mazlish, *o.c.*, n. 2.
10. The distinction between dandy and fribble is crucial: Pelham 'though a dandy is never a fribble, but always a remarkably shrewd and intellectual man of the world' (Escott, *o.c.*, ch. 6, n. 16).
11. *The Earlier Letters of John Stuart Mill 1812–1848*, ed. F.E. Mineka (Toronto 1963), no. 147 (17 October 1835).
12. Ibid., no. 182 (29 November 1836); see also no. 186 (January 1837). In 1836 Bulwer-Lytton commiserated with Mill on the death of his father (no. 181).
13. Ibid., no. 206 (May or June 1837).
14. Hansard, 3rd series, 40 (1838), 399.
15. Edward Lytton Bulwer, *England and the English* (Paris 1833), Bk. IV, ch. X. Compare Ruskin's verdict on Grote, p. 162.
16. See my comments on the manuscript of Bulwer-Lytton's 'Vol. III', ch. 6 above.
17. The writing was apparently begun in 1842; vols 1–2 were published in 1846, vols 3–4 in 1847, and vols 5–6 were reviewed in the *Edinburgh Review* for 1849.
18. Quoted in K.R. Popper, *The Open Society and its Enemies*, vol. 1 (2nd edn, London 1952), 297 n. 15.
19. G. Grote, *A History of Greece* (New Edition, London 1888), vol. III, pp. 358–9.
20. Review of Grote's *History of Greece* (*Spectator*, 5 June 1847) in J.S. Mill, *Newspaper Writings*, ed. A.P. and J. Roloson, *Collected Works*, vol. 24 (Toronto 1986), 1087.

21. K.N. Demetriou, *George Grote* (*o.c.* ch. 6 n. 24 above) devotes seven pages (pp. 100–106) to explaining the originality of Grote's treatment of Cleon and Nicias. On the other hand he is correct in asserting the originality of Grote's treatment of the sophists and of Plato: Bulwer-Lytton's history never reached this point, but it is unlikely that he would have been able to match the depth of Grote's philosophical interests.
22. Grote, *History of Greece* (1888 edn), vol. II, 298–9, on Lycurgus.
23. Ibid., vol. 1, 366 note (a long footnote defending his views against reviewers). For a brief summary of his views see 401–5.
24. Ibid. 396; Grote's text and footnotes show a careful study of the theories of Vico, Müller, Creuzer, Lobeck and the brothers Grimm among others; see Turner, *o.c.* (ch. 6 n. 24 above), 85–94.
25. See ch. 11.
26. *Edinburgh Review*, 1846, reprinted in *Dissertations and Discussions* (1867), vol. II, 283–334; but it was already being dismissed by Max Müller in his essay 'Comparative Mythology', *Oxford Essays* (Oxford 1856), 1–87, reprinted in *Chips from a German Workshop*, vol. 2 (London 1868), 1–146. For the method compare F. Buffière, *Les Mythes d'Homère et la Pensée Grecque* (Paris 1956).
27. See p. 354.
28. The young Austrian radical Theodor Gomperz, Mill's translator, was one of the few to approve of this interpretation: see his *Greek Thinkers* (London 1901), book III, ch. V.
29. Grote, *History of Greece*, vol. III, ch. XXXI. I owe this insight to a former pupil, Mohan Rao of Magdalen College, whom I assisted with an undergraduate thesis for his degree finals in 2007 on 'Grote and Kleisthenes', which he has kindly allowed me to consult.
30. See M.H. Hansen, 'Solonian Democracy in Fourth-Century Athens', *Classica et Mediterranea* 40 (1989), 71–99; 'The 2500th Anniversary of Cleisthenes' Reforms and the Tradition of Athenian Democracy', in *Ritual, Finance, Politics: Athenian Democratic Accounts presented to David Lewis*, ed. R. Osborne and S. Hornblower (Oxford 1994), 25–37.
31. Sir William Young MP (1749–1815) wrote a pamphlet in 1777 entitled *The Spirit of Athens*, which thirty years later he expanded into a book *The History of Athens; Including a Commentary on the Principles, Policy, and Practice, of Republican Government; and of the Causes of Elevation and Decline, which operate in every free and commercial state* (1804). An enthusiast for the civil liberty of Montesquieu, in his somewhat confused account he regarded Kleisthenes as a self-serving aristocrat, praised him as a reformer and approved of the institution of ostracism, but decried the fifth-century radical democracy as a perversion of the moderate earlier democracy. See also de Pauw in ch. 3.
32. Grote, *Westminster Review* 5 (1826), p. 293.

33. G.F. Schömann, *De Comitiis Atheniensium libri tres* (1819); *A Dissertation on the Assemblies of the Athenians*, trans F.A.P. (Cambridge 1838), Bk. III. Schömann protested against this use of his research: see *Athenian Constitutional History, as represented in Grote's History of Greece, critically examined by G.F. Schömann*, trans. B. Bosanquet (Oxford 1878).
34. Grote, *History of Greece* (1888 edn), vol. III, p. 373.
35. A. Bain, 'The Intellectual Character and Writings of George Grote', in *The Minor Works of George Grote* (London 1873), p. [84].
36. Wilamowitz's *Aristoteles und Athen* (Berlin 1893) was the first work to realize the importance of this text; in England only W.L. Newman had any inkling of its significance: see my chapter 'Ancient History 1872–1914', in *The History of the University of Oxford*, vol. VII, part 2, 352.
37. G. Gilbert, *The Constitutional Antiquities of Sparta and Athens* (London 1895); C. Hignett, *A History of the Athenian Constitution to the End of the Fifth Century B.C.* (Oxford 1952).
38. See ch. 19.
39. F.G. Kenyon, *Aristotle on the Constitution of Athens* (London 1891); D.M. Lewis, 'Cleisthenes and Attica', *Historia* 12 (1963), 22–40; J.S. Traill, *The Political Organization of Attica*, Hesperia Supplement XIV (Princeton 1975); J.S. Traille, *Demos and Trittys* (Toronto 1986).
40. *Dēmokratia: A Conversation on Democracies, Ancient and Modern*, J. Ober and C. Hedrick, eds (Princeton 1996). The point at which the word 'democracy' replaced 'liberty' or 'freedom' is discussed by me in 'Modern Perceptions of Ancient Realities from Montesquieu to Mill', in M.H. Hansen et al. (eds), *Démocratie athénienne – démocratie moderne: tradition et influences*, Fondation Hardt LVI (Vandoeuvres 2010), 137–60.
41. Bain, *o.c.* (n. 35 above) [100–101]; Mill, *Dissertations* 333; though he defended his 'best style of ethical narrative', 513.
42. F. Darwin, *The Life and Letters of Charles Darwin*, vol. 1 (Cambridge 1887), 77.
43. J. Ruskin, 'Arrows of the Chace' (1886), in *The Works of John Ruskin*, ed. E.T. Cook and A. Wedderburn (London 1903–12), vol. xxxiv, 586.
44. *Edinburgh Review* (1853), reprinted in *Dissertations and Discussions* II (1867), 510–54.
45. Turner, *o.c.* (ch. 6 n. 24 above), 196.
46. Mill, *o.c.* in n. 44 above, 518–19. For Mill's view of de Tocqueville see his review, and F.K. Prochaska, *Eminent Victorians on American Democracy: The View from Albion* (Oxford 2012), ch. 2. Yet Bain, *o.c.* (n. 35 above) [162–70], records Grote's great speech in 1862 to the senate of University College London in favour of his proposal to admit women to degrees.
47. Vols 3–4, 5 June 1847 (*CW*, 24:1084–88); vols 5–6, 3 March 1849 (*CW*, 25:1121–28), and 10 March 1849 (*CW*, 25:1128–34); vols 7–8, 16 March

1850 (*CW*, 25:1157–64). Vols 9–11 were reviewed in the *Edinburgh Review* in October 1853 (*Dissertations and Discussions* II [1867], 510–54; *CW*, 11:307–37); vol. 12 (1854).

48. [H. Reed], 'Autobiography. By John Stuart Mill. London 1873', *The Edinburgh Review*, vol. 139, issue 283 (1 January 1874), 91–129.
49. Clarke, *o.c.* (n. 6 above), 86–7.
50. A. Pionke, 'Reconstructing an Ancient Monument to Mid-Victorian Liberalism, One Annotation at a Time: John Stuart Mill's Marginalia in George Grote's *History*', *Victorian Institute Journal* 48 (2021), 130–60; A. Pionke, 'Dating Mill's Marginalia', *Mill Marginalia Blog*, 20 March 2022.
51. Grote, *History of Greece* (1888 edn), vol. II, 25 (ch. XX).
52. J.S. Mill, *The Later Letters of John Stuart Mill, 1849–1873*, ed D.N. Lindley and F.E. Mineka (Toronto 1972), Letter no. 538.
53. Ibid., Letters nos 232–7. Pionke, 'Reconstructing an Ancient Monument', p. 146, suggests that verbal similarities between Mill's geographical descriptions and changes in later editions of Grote suggest that he may have given Grote sight of his journal after Harriet's death.
54. A. Bain, *John Stuart Mill. A Criticism: with Personal Recollections* (London 1882), p. 133.

CHAPTER 8

1. A. Schopenhauer, *The World as Will and Representation* (1819), trans. David Carus and R.E. Aquila (Abingdon 2011), vol. II, 139. Cf. F. Waquet, *Le Latin, ou l'empire d'un signe, XVIe–XXe siècle* (Paris 1998).
2. For female translators see below, n. 40; for data on the translation of classical scholarship between European languages in the 17th–19th centuries see my online project *Bibliotheca Academica Translationum*.
3. See esp. A.D. Momigliano, 'New Paths of Classicism', in *Studies on Modern Scholarship* (Berkeley 1994), 223–85.
4. The best translation is G.W.F. Hegel, *The Philosophy of History*, trans. J. Sibree (1857); on its alleged inadequacies see Duncan Forbes' introduction to H.B. Nisbet's 'new translation' of the *Introduction to the Lectures on the Philosophy of World History* (Cambridge 1975). Despite Nisbet's dismissive claim, his translation is virtually identical with that of Sibree.
5. F. Nietzsche, *Unfashionable Observations*, trans. R.T. Gray (Stanford 1995), 143.
6. Hegel, *o.c.*, 16.
7. Hegel, *o.c.*, 17–19.
8. This is the only reference in Hegel to the young Leopold von Ranke, author of the famous definition of history as 'wie es eigentlich gewesen'.
9. Hegel, *o.c.*, 23.

10. He entered Christ Church in 1824 and was elected to a studentship (research post) in 1828.
11. *History of the Doric Race*, Bk. III, ch. 1, § 10.
12. *Life and Letters* II, 99; cf. 256.
13. See C. Moorhead, *Iris Origo, Marchesa of Val d'Orcia* (London 2006). In 2012 the Palazzo Orsini atop the Theatre of Marcellus was on sale for £26 million.
14. *The Life and Letters of Berthold George Niebuhr* (ed. Susanna Winkworth, London, 1852), 118–19.
15. Scott's first major publication was precisely in 1799, a translation of Goethe's play *Goetz von Berlichingen*. For this period of his life see J.G. Lockhart, *Memoirs of the Life of Sir Walter Scott* (Paris 1838), vol. I, ch. ix.
16. F. Baroness Bunsen, *A Memoir of Baron Bunsen* (London 1868), vol. I, 374–5.
17. I have used the second edition (Berlin 1848), p. vii, published by Niebuhr's son for the benefit of the German navy.
18. I quote from the preface to the first English edition (Cambridge 1828), p. x.
19. See A. Momigliano, *Secondo contributo alla storia degli studi classici* (Rome 1960), 74–7.
20. On its publication it was attacked (in a review of *Dr. Granville's Travels* by John Barrow) in the *Quarterly Review* on the grounds of Niebuhr's alleged political opinions and religious unorthodoxy, to which Hare replied in a pamphlet entitled *A Vindication of Niebuhr's History of Rome from the Charges of the Quarterly Review* (Cambridge 1829).
21. *On the Credibility of Early Roman History* (London 1855). See on this work Momigliano, *Contributo alla storia degli studi classici* (Rome 1955), 256–62.
22. *Life and Letters*, II, 451–2.
23. *Quarterly Review* 32 (1825), 67–92; the quotation is at 84–5.
24. A.P. Stanley, *The Life and Correspondence of Thomas Arnold*, 2nd edn (London 1890), 497.
25. Reprinted in *The Miscellaneous Works of Thomas Arnold D.D.* (London 1845), 79–112.
26. On Thirlwall, see the article by K.N. Demetriou, 'Bishop Connop Thirlwall, Historian of Ancient Greece', *Quaderni di Storia* 56 (2002), 49–90, and Peter Liddel, *Bishop Thirlwall's History of Greece: A Selection* (Bristol 2007).
27. D.A. Winstanley, *Early Victorian Cambridge* (Cambridge 1955), 73–8.
28. The most distinguished Cambridge ancient historian in this period was the Irish-educated J.B. Bury, who was officially professor of modern history (1902–27). The subsequent long reign of F.E. Adcock (1925–51) produced little apart from the monumental and old-fashioned twelve volumes of the first *Cambridge Ancient History* (1923–39); the Oxford-trained A.H.M. Jones was the first professor of distinction at Cambridge (1951–70). For Moses Finley see ch. 19.

29. See my chapter in *The History of the University of Oxford, vol. VI, Part I*, 520–42.
30. On Twiss see the frank account of his life in the *Old DNB*, 1320–24, he was forced out of public life when he tried to defend his wife's honour in a libel case, which collapsed when she was revealed not to be a Polish aristocrat but an adventuress with a lurid past.
31. M. Pattison, *Memoirs* (London 1885), 84–5.
32. Scriblerus Redivivus [E. Caswall], *The Art of Pluck* (Oxford 1835).
33. Quoted in G.P. Gooch, *History and Historians in the Nineteenth Century*, 2nd edn (London 1952), 22.
34. B. Jowett and A.P. Stanley, *Suggestions for an Improvement of the Examination Statute* (Oxford 1848), 27.
35. M. Burrows, *Pass and Class* (Oxford 1861), 112–13.
36. London, 1849. This book had a third edition in 1869, rearranged to provide a standard textbook of which I possess a cheap one-volume edition published in 1903 which calls itself the ninth edition. Being more extensive and more readable than the *History of Rome*, it seems to have been used as a standard textbook at least until the publication of H.F. Pelham's *Encyclopedia Britannica* article appeared as *Outlines of Roman History* (London 1893).
37. See the *Old DNB*, 562. The reference works are still useful, and have indeed recently been reprinted under the editorship of C.A. Stray.
38. His biography (above n. 16) makes reference to Heyne, Niebuhr, A. von Humboldt, Boeckh, Schleiermacher, Lachmann, Bernays, Schopenhauer, Savigny, Mendelssohn, Platner, Thorwaldsen, Leopardi, Champollion, Chateaubriand, Renan, Sir Walter Scott, Arnold, Stanley, Thirlwall, the Hares, Carlyle, Florence Nightingale, Layard, Max Müller, Wellington, Gladstone, Macaulay, Peel, and Palmerston. In 1839 he received an honorary degree from Oxford alongside Wordsworth.
39. See L. and J. Hamburger, *Contemplating Adultery* (London 1991), for a fascinating sidelight on Austin and his wife, the translator Sarah Austin.
40. See S. Stark, *'Behind Inverted Commas': Translation and Anglo-German Relations in the Nineteenth Century* (Clevedon 1999), esp. ch. 2. For the biographies of these two women see the full accounts in the new *DNB*.
41. As Paolo Desideri reminds me, Leopardi also knew Niebuhr personally and his work well, and was asked to review the English translation of the *History of Rome* on its appearance in 1828. In his *Zibaldone*, 4450–4458, Leopardi copied out some ten pages of Niebuhr's theory of the *carmina convivalia*. For their relationship see P. Treves, *Lo Studio dell'antichità classica nell'ottocento* (Milan 1962), 480–9; L. Polverini, 'Lettere di Giacomo Leopardi a B.G. Niebuhr', *Rivista storica italiana* 100 (1988), 220–33; P. Desideri, 'Leopardi e la storia romana del Niebuhr', in L. Melosi (ed.), *Leopardi a Firenze* (Florence 2002), 321–38.

42. *Gentl. Mag.*, XCV. I. 348.
43. T. Arnold, *History of Rome* (London 1840), vol. I, 257 n. 6.
44. This discovery is my personal contribution to the online edition of my great-grandfather's *Oxford English Dictionary*.
45. Coleridge, prefatory note to *The Wanderings of Cain*, 1829.
46. T. De Quincey, *Works* (1890), XIII. 346.
47. Thomas De Quincey, 'The Palimpsest', *Suspiria de Profundis*, 1845.
48. *Aurora Leigh*, I, 826.
49. For his influence in Germany see S. Rytkönen, *Barthold Georg Niebuhr als Politiker und Historiker* (Helsinki 1968) and G. Walther, *Niebuhrs Forschung*, (Stuttgart 1993), neither of which has anything to say about Britain.
50. Since it is not easy to find a list of the works of Niebuhr published in English, I append one here:

    The History of Rome by B.G. Niebuhr, trans. Julius Charles Hare, M.A., and Connop Thirlwall, M.A., 2 vols (Cambridge 1828).

    The History of Rome by B.G. Niebuhr, trans. Julius Charles Hare, M.A., and Connop Thirlwall, M.A., new edition, 3 vols (London 1851). (The third volume was in fact translated by Leonhard Schmitz and William Smith.)

    Lectures on the History of Rome, ed. Dr. Leonhard Schmitz, 2nd edn, 3 vols (London 1849; 1st edn 1844); many subsequent editions.

    Lectures on Ancient History, trans. Dr Leonhard Schmitz, 3 vols (London 1852).

    Lectures on Ancient Ethnography and Geography, trans. Dr Leonhard Schmitz, 2 vols (London 1853).

    The Life and Letters of Barthold George Niebuhr with Essays on his character and influence by the Chevalier Bunsen and professors Brandis and Loebell, 2 vols, with *The Life and Letters of Barthold George Niebuhr, and selections from his minor writings*, vol. III supplementary, ed. and trans. Susanna Winkworth (London 1852).

CHAPTER 9

1. See the excellent account of Lionel Gossman, *Basel in the Age of Burckhardt* (Chicago 2000).
2. See the claim of W. Dilthey, 'diese Manier . . . nicht . . . der Anfang einer neuen geschichtlichen Behandlung (ist), sondern die Auflösung aller Geschichte', cited in K. Christ, *Griechische Geschichte und Wissenschaftsgeschichte*, Historia Einzelschriften 106 (Stuttgart 1996), 139.
3. The standard biography of Burckhardt is that of W. Kaegi, *Jacob Burckhardt, Eine Biographie* (Basel 1947–82), in seven volumes. Burckhardt's letters are cited from Max Burckhardt, *Jacob Burckhardt, Briefe* (Basel

1949–94), in eleven volumes; there is a good selection in *The Letters of Jacob Burckhardt*, trans. Alexander Dru (London 1955); where possible I have used Dru's translation, which also contains an excellent brief discussion of his life in the introduction. The *Weltgeschichtliche Betrachtungen* are cited in the edition of the Wissenschaftliche Gesellschaft (Darmstadt 1962) as *WB*, and in the translation of M.D.H., *Reflections on History* (London 1943).

4. J. Burckhardt, *The Greeks and Greek Civilization*, trans. S. Stern (London 1998), 9; also 'we should maintain an attitude of reserve towards the present-day devastation of the mind by newspapers and novels': *WB*, 13; *Reflections*, 26.
5. Letter to H. Schauenburg, 28 February–5 March 1846: no. 174 (*Briefe* II, p. 208); *Letters*, pp. 96–7.
6. Remarks quoted from Heinrich Wölfflin's diaries, cited in *Letters*, p. 32; the original is not available to me, but see also on his personal relations with Burckhardt, H. Wölfflin, *Gedanken zur Kunstgeschichte* (2nd edn, 1941), 135–63.
7. Letter to H. Schreiber, 2 October 1842: no. 69 (*Briefe* I, p. 217); the letters of this period are full of plans for a new history: see also esp. nos 59 and 61 (to G. Kinkel), 62 (to W. Beyschlag), and 63 (to K. Fresenius).
8. G.P. Gooch, *History and Historians in the Nineteenth Century* (2nd edn, 1952), 529; I have not been able to trace the source of this quotation.
9. *The Age of Constantine the Great*, trans. M. Hadas (London 1949).
10. Ibid., 229.
11. Ibid., 242.
12. Ibid., 214.
13. Quoted in Gooch, *o.c.*, 532. The English translation of the *Civilization of the Renaissance* by S.G. Middlemore was first published in 1878; henceforth I quote from the Phaidon edition (London 1950).
14. Ibid., 81.
15. Ibid., 104.
16. The idea of cultural history can be traced back to de Pauw (above, ch. 2) and to Voltaire's *Essai sur les Moeurs*: see O. Murray, 'Renewing *l'histoire des moeurs*', in *The Symposion: Drinking Greek Style* (Oxford 2018), 399–405. On the development of *Kulturgeschichte* and its relations to *Geistesgeschichte*, the best introduction in English is E.H. Gombrich, 'In Search of Cultural History', in *Ideas and Idols* (Oxford 1979), 24–59.
17. *Letters*, p. 28.
18. Letter to Bernhard Kugler, 5 October 1874: no. 653 (*Briefe* V, p. 252); *Letters*, p. 161.
19. A repeated phrase: e.g. to F. von Preen, 31 December 1870: no. 560 (*Briefe* V, p. 120; *Letters*, p. 46).
20. *Historische Zeitschrift*, vol. I (1859), III–IV.

21. *Letters*, p. 32.
22. For the details of the development of the text of these lectures, and the role of Jacob Oeri, see the introduction of Peter Ganz to Jacob Burckhardt, *Über das Studium der Geschichte* (Munich 1982). Since Ganz's edition does not offer a readable text, I have continued to refer to the traditional German text of Oeri (see above, n. 3).
23. He promises to study it in the summer of 1842: letter to K. Fresenius, 10 June 1842: no. 631 (*Briefe* I, p. 207).
24. Ganz, *o.c.*, 35–6; cf. 18–19; on the general question see the lecture of E. Heftrich, *Hegel und Jacob Burckhardt* (Frankfurt 1967).
25. *WB*, 2; *Reflections*, 15: derived from A. Schopenhauer. *The World as Will and Representation*, trans. E.F.J. Payne (New York 1966), vol. II, ch. xxxviii, 439.
26. *WB*, 3; *Reflections*, 17.
27. *WB*, 20; *Reflections*, 33.
28. See Ganz, *o.c.*, 23.
29. *WB*, 180; *Reflections*, 203. The final chapter of the traditional *WB* as published, on fortune and misfortune (or happiness and unhappiness) in history, in fact belongs originally to a separate lecture, which was later incorporated into the introduction of the series: see Ganz, *o.c.*, 231–46.
30. *WB*, 19; *Reflections*, 32.
31. *WB*, 20; *Reflections*, 33.
32. The best account of the intellectual relations between Burckhardt and Nietzsche known to me is K. Löwith, *Jacob Burckhardt, Der Mensch inmitten der Geschichte* (Lucerne 1936; Stuttgart 1984), ch. I; see also the polemical anti-Nazi book first published in 1940, A. von Martin, *Nietzsche und Burckhardt* (4th edition, Munich 1947); and the essay of Erich Heller, 'Burckhardt and Nietzsche', in *The Disinherited Mind* (Cambridge 1952).
33. Letter to C. von Geersdorff, 7 November 1870; no. 107 in *Nietzsche Briefwechsel*, ed. G. Colli, M. Montinari II.1 (Berlin 1977), p. 155; also quoted in *Letters* of Burckhardt, p. 23.
34. Letter to A. von Salis, 21 April 1872: no. 585 (*Briefe* V, p. 158); *Letters*, p. 150.
35. Letter to F. von Preen, 27 September 1870: no. 334 (*Briefe* V, p. 112); *Letters*, p. 144.
36. The letters, which are printed in the respective collections of their authors, are conveniently gathered together in E. Salin, *Jacob Burckhardt und Nietzsche* (Basel 1938), 207–29.
37. F. Nietzsche, *Twilight of the Idols* (Harmondsworth 1968), 63–4.
38. Letter to L. von Pastor, 13 January 1896: no. 1598 (*Briefe* X, p. 263); *Letters*, p. 235.
39. Nietzsche, *Twilight of the Idols*, 108.
40. There is however a clear reference to *The Birth of Tragedy* in a later version of the lectures on the study of history, where Burckhardt mentions 'the

mysterious development of tragedy from the spirit of music', and the importance of Dionysus in this process. This must have been written not before the publication of the book in January 1872: see Ganz, *o.c.*, 289; Kaegi, *o.c.*, n. 3, 6.1.119f.; *WB*, 55; *Reflections*, 69. See also Salin, *o.c.*, 96–106. I have not seen K. Joel, *Jacob Burckhardt als Geschichtsphilosoph* (Basel 1918).

41. I use the translation of R.T. Gray, *Unfashionable Observations* (Stanford 1995); the reference to Burckhardt is on p. 103.
42. Ibid., 116–18.
43. Ibid., 124.
44. Letter to Nietzsche, 25 February 1874: no. 627 (*Briefe* V, p. 222); *Letters*, p.158. Compare 'our aim is not to train historians, let alone universal historians': *WB*, 12; *Reflections*, 26.
45. The German word is *Dilettantismus*: *WB*, 16; *Reflections*, 30.
46. *Unfashionable Observations*, 145.
47. Letter to F. von Preen, 31 December 1870: no. 560 (*Briefe* V, p. 119); *Letters* p. 145.
48. Letter to Bernhard Kugler, 30 March 1870: no. 535 (*Briefe* V, p. 76); *Letters*, p. 136.
49. *Griechische Kulturgeschichte* I, 5.
50. *WB*, 3; *Reflections*, 17.
51. The exact relation between the views of Burckhardt and Nietzsche on the *agon* is obscure: see ch. 10.
52. See most strongly A.W.H. Adkins, *Merit and Responsibility* (Oxford 1962).
53. For an excellent general account of the genesis of the lectures on cultural history, see Kaegi, *Burckhardt* VII, ch. 1.
54. Letter to Otto Ribbeck, 10 July 1864: no. 406 (*Briefe* IV, p. 155).
55. So described in a letter to Ribbeck, 16 October 1865: no. 431 (*Briefe* IV, p. 197).
56. Letter to F. von Preen, 3 July 1870: no. 546 (*Briefe* V, p. 99; *Letters*, p. 142). 'Zwischen aller Bewunderung gerathe ich da auf die respectlosesten Gedanken und sehe zeitweise in ein feierliches Philisterium hinein, welchem Pindar mit dem grössten Pathos nachlaufen muss. Offenbar hat er bisweilen mit wahren Rüpeln sich abgeben müssen.'
57. Letter to F. von Preen, 23 December 1871: no. 581 (*Briefe* V, p. 150; *Letters*, p. 49): 'Was mich tröstet, ist die Gewissheit das ich allgemach eine schöne Portion unabhängiger Wahrnehmungen über das Alterthum rein aus den Quellen gewonnen habe, und das ich weit das Meiste, was ich zu geben habe, als mein Eigenes werde geben können.'
58. Letter to the publisher, E.A. Seemann, 29 November 1889: no. 1283 (*Briefe* IX, p. 224); these two sentences constitute the entire letter.
59. H. Gelzer, 'Jacob Burckhardt als Mensch und Lehrer', *Ausgewählte kleine Schriften* (Leipzig 1907), 297.

60. The will is quoted by Ganz, *o.c.*, 13.
61. Wilamowitz, *Griechische Tragödie* (Berlin 1899), vol. II, *Vorwort*, 7.
62. *The Complete Letters of Sigmund Freud to Wilhelm Fliess 1887–1904*, ed. and trans. J.M. Masson (Harvard 1985), 342.
63. Albert Oeri quoted by Kaegi, *o.c.*, 102; Albert was the son of Jacob Oeri, and compiled a plea to be used in a legal case arising from one of these attacks on his father as editor of Burckhardt.
64. *WB*, 70; cf. 25; *Reflections*, 86; cf. 38 (a quotation from Schlosser).
65. *WB*, 64; *Reflections*, 78. This passage about Greece occurs under the heading 'Culture determined by the State'; it reflects views expressed by Benjamin Constant in his famous lecture 'On the Liberty of the Ancient Greeks Compared with that of the Moderns' (1819): see ch. 1 n. 1.
66. See the polemical work of W. Gawantka, *Die sogennante Polis* (Stuttgart 1985), ch. 1, arguing that Burckhardt was responsible for the invention of an illegitimate entity.
67. *WB*, 82; cf. 100; *Reflections*, 97; cf. 118.
68. *WB*, 29; *Reflections*, 42.
69. R. Klibansky, E. Panofsky, and F. Saxl, *Saturn and Melancholy* (New Edition, Quebec 2019).
70. A. Schopenhauer, *The World as Will and Representation*, trans. E.F.J. Payne (New York 1966), vol. II, chs XLVIII–IX; consistently Schopenhauer believed that modern tragedy was greatly superior to Greek tragedy: vol. I, 252–5; II, 433–8.
71. See M.S. Silk and J.P. Stern, *Nietzsche on Tragedy* (Cambridge 1981).
72. *WB*, 33; *Reflections*, 46.
73. Letter to Nietzsche, quoted above, n. 44.
74. *WB*, 171; *Reflections*, 193.
75. See my essay 'Cities of Reason', in O. Murray and S. Price (eds), *The Greek City from Homer to Alexander* (Oxford 1990), 1–25.
76. Note on the text of the *History of Greek Culture*: An earlier version of this chapter was published as the introduction to a selection from Burckhardt's *GK* entitled *The Greeks and Greek Civilization*, translated by Sheila Stern (London 1998), responsibility for which I inherited from Moses Finley on his death in 1986, which in turn goes back to one of my first reviews of a previous translation in *Classical Review* 15 (1965), 209–12, on which Moses had congratulated me. The text that we used was that established by Burckhardt's nephew Jacob Oeri in his edition a hundred years earlier (1898–1902). In the first two volumes it had the authority of a revised manuscript by Burckhardt himself; thereafter it was based on his notes for various courses, and the notes of his auditors; this is especially true of the fourth volume, where Oeri was almost entirely dependent on the audience of the lectures, in the absence of an author's manuscript. Oeri was a highly conscientious classical scholar and a schoolmaster, who is described as

rising daily about seven o'clock to retire to his summerhouse in the garden and work on his uncle's manuscripts until eleven in the morning, when he left for the town. Nevertheless, as Burckhardt said, lecture notes are like the underside of a carpet, 'where the threads and the general patterns are visible, but the liveliness and the details of the original design are lost'.

A new scholarly edition of the lectures on Greek culture was in preparation for many years in Basel at the *Burckhardtarchiv*, supported by Basel University and by the Swiss Science Council; it was finally completed in 2012. The principles on which the editorial team worked were the same as those followed by Peter Ganz for the lectures on the study of history – that is, to give exact transcripts of the variant versions in Burckhardt's notes and those of his listeners, rather than offering a composite and readable text. The end of the process is to place us once again at the table in the summerhouse where Jacob Oeri worked, in possession of all the material that he had before him (and perhaps a little more), but faced with his same problem – how to reconstruct the actual set of lectures which his uncle gave on a series of occasions, with all their variety. And we lack that one essential ingredient, the insight into Burckhardt's mind that was possessed by his favourite nephew and literary executor, who had himself attended his uncle's lectures. For this reason I believe that the text of Jacob Oeri will never be replaced, however much our understanding of the lectures and of the development of Burckhardt's thought has been enriched.

CHAPTER 10

1. The first person clearly to distinguish a Hellenistic age was Christian Gottlob Heyne in his *prolusio* 'De Genio Saeculi Ptolemaeorum' (1763): see *Opuscula Academica Collecta* (Göttingen 1789), vol. I, 76–134.
2. G.W. Most, 'Zur Archäologie der Archaik', *Antike und Abendland* 35 (1989), 1–23.
3. *OED sv* citing H. Ellis, *Elgin Marbles* i. v.1 11 (1933); E.A.T.W. Budge *Hist. Egypt* II. i. 1: 'With the ending of the IIIrd Dynasty we close our chapter on the archaic period of Egyptian civilization' (1902) etc.
4. I quote from the fifth edition, p. 604: 'Die Periode, die sich vom Beginn der geschichtlichen Zeit Griechenlands an bis zu dem gewaltigen Einschnitt im Leben des Volkes, den Perserkriegen, und der darauf folgenden Hochblüte der griechischen Kultur erstreckt, wird oft die archaische Zeit genannt; mitunter spricht man von dem Mittelalter oder der Ritterzeit Griechenlands.'
5. *Vorwort*, p. 7: 'das archaische Griechentum, die Zeit also, in der die Kräfte Griechenlands mächtig aufblühen und auf allen Gebieten die Grundlagen des europäischen Lebens gelegt werden. Heute, wo der Weiterbestand dieses

Europas so sehr in frage gestellt ist, schien es besonders am Platz, dorthin den Blick zurückzuwenden.'

6. See also his *Ancient Sicily* (London 1979), where there is a chapter on 'Archaic Society and Politics'. I am not sure whether the use of 'l'époque archäique' in Michel Austin's and Pierre Vidal-Naquet's *Économies et sociétés en Grèce ancienne* (Paris 1972) counts as French or English usage. It is perhaps symptomatic that John Boardman entitled his book in the Penguin series Style and Civilization, *Pre-Classical: From Crete to Archaic Greece* (Harmondsworth 1967).
7. It is interesting that the first Italian translation of my book in 1983 was given the title *La Grecia arcaica*; this was almost immediately changed to *La Grecia delle origini*. In contrast, I am aware that I was the first to borrow the phrase 'orientalizing period' from art history and to apply it to a historical period, in conscious reference to Burckhardt's double periodization discussed here. But both these words and ideas were in the air, and were given their classic formulation in Walter Burkert's essay of 1984 (Eng. trans. *The Orientalizing Revolution: Near Eastern Influence on Greek Culture in the Early Archaic Age* [Harvard 1992]). Now the concept can be simply assumed: see all the chapters in *Archaic Greece: New Approaches and New Evidence*, ed. N. Fisher and Hans van Wees (London 1998).
8. Later in his book *La fine del mondo antico*, Mazzarino's admiration for Burckhardt's 'genialissima *Età di Costantino*' is evident: 'Polibio sta alla crisi della repubblica romana come Burckhardt e Nietzsche stanno alla crisi del nostro tempo' (p. 25). For the beginning of his interest in *habrosyne* the crucial article is 'Per la storia di Lesbo nel VI° Secolo a.c.', *Athenaeum* 21 (1943), 38–78, from which derives the central emphasis on the theme in *Fra Oriente e Occidente*.
9. For Curtius the excavator of Olympia see S.L. Marchand, *Down from Olympus* (Princeton 1996), 77–91; for the reaction to his Greek History see E. Meyer, *Geschichte des Altertums* (6th edition, Stuttgart 1953), iv.1 273, cf. iii 227; in England, where it was soon translated (1868–73), he earned the reputation of being 'as untrustworthy as he is brilliant' (J. Wells in A.A.M. Stedman, *Oxford: Its Life and Schools*, London 1887, 257).
10. For the relation between Curtius and Burckhardt see esp. K. Christ, *Griechische Geschichte und Wissenschaftsgeschichte*, Historia Einzelschriften 106 (Stuttgart 1996), 123–43.
11. Burckhardt once described Curtius' oracular style in allusive biblical language: 'Curtius ist ein Priester der Wissenschaft; wenn der spricht, so ist es allemal ein Lied aus dem höhern Chor' (H. Gelzer, *Ausgewählte Kleine Schriften*, 346, cited in Christ, *o.c.*, 138).
12. Diese Sprache ist, wie Curtius sagt, 'die erstliche geschichtliche Tat der Hellenen, und diese erste Tat ist eine künstlerische' (their language is, as Curtius

says, 'the first historical achievement of the Greeks, and this first achievement is a work of art'), *Griechische Culturgeschichte* (*GC*) iv 12.

13. *GC* i 285.
14. *Göttinger Festreden* (1864): 'Die ganze Poesie der Hellenen ist im Wettkampfe gross gezogen. In den Palästen der Fürsten, an den Grabhügeln der Helden, vor den Tempeln der Götter, auf die vollen Märkten der Städte wetteiferten die Rhapsoden' (p. 9); 'Sollte ich Ihnen mit einem Worte ein Kennzeichen des hellenischen Lebens angeben, durch das es sich von dem aller anderen Völker unterscheidet – ich würde sagen, es sei der Kranz' (p. 3). K. Christ, *Von Gibbon zu Rostovtzeff* (Darmstadt 1989), 74–5, notes this passage in his chapter on Curtius, and regards it as '*in nuce*' the agonal principle of Burckhardt. For a post-war version of the naïve idealism of Curtius see H. Berve, 'Vom agonalen Geist der Griechen' (lecture first delivered in 1965), *Gestaltende Kräfte der Antike* (2nd edn, 1966), 1–20.
15. See 'Der Weltgang der griechischen Cultur', a *Festrede* delivered in 1858.
16. See the excellent summary of this section in Christ, *o.c.* n. 14 above, 147.
17. *GC* iv 65: he refers to Seneca *ad Helviam* 7 and Plato *Laws* IV 708b; I now deeply regret having excluded from my 1998 English translation the section on colonial man, as 'really only of antiquarian interest, since the picture has been radically transformed by archaeology in this century' (p. xliii).
18. 'Es herrscht eine grosse, wesentlich von Grundrenten lebende städtische Aristokratie, deren Lebenszweck und Ideal wiederum der Kampf, aber weniger der Krieg als der Wettkampf unter Gleichen ist' (*GC* iv 118).
19. 'Dabei hat man es hier weder mit einem isolierten Landjunkertum noch mit einem Reichsrittertum zu tun, sondern dieser Adel ist eher dem Patriziat mittelalterlicher, zumal italienischer Städte vergleichbar: die Kaste wohnt in der Stadt beisammen und übt gemeinsam und mit Eifer die Herrschaft; zugleich bildet sie die Gesellschaft; schon das Agonale würde genügt haben, um sie zusammen zu treiben' (*GC* iv 82).
20. Burckhardt quotes this poem which he attributes to Lorenzo the Magnificent at the end of his chapter. I am not therefore inclined to see the origin of Burckhardt's agonal age as a reflection of the *Hellenismus* of Droysen (in Most's dramatic statement: 'Die Archaik ein Kind des Hellenismus war', *o.c.* n. 2 above, 13).
21. See the final chapters of A.M. Snodgrass, *The Dark Age of Greece* (Edinburgh 1971); N. Coldstream, *Geometric Greece* (London 1977); also *The Greek Renaissance of the Eighth Century B.C.: Tradition and Innovation*, ed. R. Hagg (Stockholm 1983).
22. See O. Murray, *The Symposion: Drinking Greek Style* (Oxford 2018), ch. 26 on 'Histories of Pleasure'.
23. S. Bauer, *Polisbild und Demokratieverständnis in Jacob Burckhardts 'Griechischer Kulturgeschichte'* (Basel 2001), Anhang I, 213–21; ch. 9, xxx.

24. See also 'Die letzte Redaction der Theognidea' – his first paper presented in Leipzig to Ritschl's seminar in 1866 – 'es ist die Zeit, wo ich zum Philologen geboren wurde'.
25. 'Es lautet sehr gross, wenn die Griechen als dasjenige Volk gepriesen werden, in welchem, wer irgend konnte, für das Ganze sich ausbildete und lebte und nicht für ein Besonderes; allein wir als Nachwelt fühlen uns doch einigen von jenen Einseitigen mehr verpflichtet als denen, die sich vor lauter harmonischer Kalokagathie gar nicht mehr zulassen wussten' (*GC* iv 129).
26. 'Auch heute haben ja diejenigen Tätigkeiten gewisse Schranken, die sich ein sogenannter "Gebildeter", ja einer, der auch nur in einer Sekundarschule gewesen ist, gefallen lässt: Steinklopfer und dergleichen will ein solcher nie warden. Allein diese Schranken sind unendlich weiter gezogen; Manipulationen selbst sehr derber Art schliessen nicht von der "Bildung" aus, welche gewissermassen die damalige Kalokagathie vertritt, und künstlerische Tätigkeit adelt in der neuern Zeit vollends die leibliche Aktion, die damit verbunden ist' (*GC* iv 137–8).
27. L. Gossman, *Basel in the Age of Burckhardt* (Chicago 2000).
28. Compare the modern work of M.H. Hansen on 'The Athenian *ecclesia* and the Swiss Landsgemeinde' (ch. 19); this I think is also the deeper significance of Gibbon's abortive intention to write a *History of the Liberty of the Swiss* (*Memoirs*, ed. G.B. Hill, London 1900, 147, 171).
29. *WB*, 5; *Reflections*, 19.
30. Letter to Heinrich von Geymüller, 6 April 1897: no. 1643 (*Briefe* X, 316); *Letters* 236.

CHAPTER 11

1. G. Vlastos, *Socrates* (Cambridge 1991), p. 30.
2. S. Kierkegaard, *The Concept of Irony with Continual Reference to Socrates*, ed. and trans. H.V. and E.H. Hong (Princeton 1989), 18–21. As this is the most available translation, I refer to its pagination, and have normally used it; but I have occasionally borrowed phrases from the earlier more literate but less literal translation of L.M. Capel (London 1966).
3. G.W.F. Hegel, *Lectures on the History of Philosophy*, trans. E.S. Haldane (London 1892), I, 389–96.
4. Ibid., p. 448.
5. S. Kofman, *Socrates: Fictions of a Philosopher* (London 1998), 40.
6. Hegel, *o.c.* n. 3 above, 409.
7. Ibid., 398–402.
8. Kierkegaard, *o.c.* n. 2 above, 9.
9. Ibid., 12.
10. Ibid., 259.

11. Ibid., 36.
12. Ibid., 45.
13. Ibid., 49.
14. Ibid., 55.
15. Ibid., 37.
16. Ibid., 193.
17. References are to E. Zeller, *Die Philosophie der Griechen* IV.1 (4th edn, Leipzig 1889); I have added references to the English translation of the shorter first edition: *Socrates and the Socratic Schools*, trans. O.J. Reichel (London 1868).
18. Zeller, *o.c.*, 36, Eng. trans. 37
19. Ibid., 141, Eng. trans. 117.
20. Ibid., 120–23; Eng. trans. 103–6.
21. Ibid., 90–91, Eng. trans. 80–81.
22. Ibid., 'Das Schicksal des Sokrates', I A III 191–232 = Eng. trans. ch. x.
23. Ibid., 181, Eng. trans. ch. ix.
24. J. Burckhardt, *Griechische Kulturgeschichte* (Darmstadt 1957), vol. III, 352.
25. Burckhardt's intense dislike of Attic comedy is to modern scholars one of the less attractive aspects of his rejection of the values of Athenian democracy.
26. See L. Gossman, *Basel in the Age of Burckhardt* (Chicago 2000).
27. F. Nietzsche, *Socrates und die griechische Tragödie. Ursprüngliche Fassung der Geburt der Tragödie aus dem Geist der Musik*, ed. H.J. Mette (Munich 1933).
28. The sections that appear as 13–15 in the printed version are virtually unchanged from the original ms.
29. Sections 12–14.
30. Section 15.
31. For instance, by M.S. Silk and J.P. Stern, *Nietzsche on Tragedy* (Cambridge 1981), 193–6.
32. A. Nehamas, *The Art of Living* (Berkeley 1998), 155.

CHAPTER 12

1. The story of Mark Pattison and his wife later inspired the plots of two other novels, Rhoda Broughton's *Belinda* (1883), and the more sympathetic *Robert Elsmere* (1888) by Mrs Humphry Ward, Pattison's former protégée.
2. George Eliot, *Middlemarch*, ch. 20.
3. S. Stark, 'Marian Evans, the Translator', in S. Bassnett (ed.), *Translating Literature* (Cambridge 1997), 119–40. For this period of Marian Evans's (George Eliot's) life see Rosemary Ashton, *142 Strand: A Radical Address in Victorian London* (London 2006).

4. A. Baltrusaitis, *La Quête d'Isis: Introduction à l'Égyptomanie* (Paris 1967).
5. 'The Life of Heyne', in *Critical and Miscellaneous Essays* (London 1907), vol. 2, 54–84, from the *Foreign Review* 4 (1828).
6. For the importance of Heyne see esp. the excellent account of Fritz Graf, *Greek Mythology: An Introduction* (Eng. trans. Baltimore 1993), ch. I, with bibliography p. 204; for the relation between Creuzer and Müller see J.H. Blok, 'Quests for a Scientific Mythology: F. Creuzer and K.O. Müller on History and Myth', *History and Theory* 33 (1994), 26–52; S. Marchand, 'Herodotus and the Embarrassments of Universal History in Ninettenth-century Germany', *Journal of Modern History* 95 (2023) 308–48.
7. Above, ch. 1.
8. See A. Momigliano, 'K.O. Müller's *Prolegomena zu einer wissenschaftlichen Mythologie* and the Meaning of "Myth"', in *Settimo contributo* (Rome 1984), 271–86. On the English translation by John Leitch see A. Kennedy, 'John Leitch, John Kenrick, History and Myth: The Textbook as a Signpost of Intellectual Change', *Paradigm, Journal of the Textbook Colloquium* 2 (4), December 2001 (on the web). My copy of the book has the bookplate of Darwin's friend, Sir John Lubbock (Lord Avebury), 1834–1913, banker, politician, naturalist, anthropologist and archaeologist, who coined the words 'palaeolithic' and 'neolithic'.
9. K.O. Müller, *Introduction to a Scientific System of Mythology* (London 1844), 166, 169, 185–7.
10. E. Will, *Doriens et Ioniens* (Paris 1956); J. Hall, *Ethnic Identity in Greek Antiquity* (Cambridge 1997).
11. Above, ch. 7.
12. M. Müller, in *Oxford Essays Contributed by Members of the University* (Oxford 1856), 69 = Müller, *Chips from a German Workshop* 2 (London 1868), 117. On Müller see the unsympathetic essay by H. Lloyd-Jones, *Blood for the Ghosts* (London 1982), ch. 13.
13. G.B. Grundy, *Fifty-Five Years at Oxford* (London 1946), 66.
14. H. Butterfield, *The Whig Interpretation of History* (London 1931).
15. E.B. Tylor, *Primitive Culture* (3rd edn, London 1891), 452.
16. A. Lang, *Myth, Ritual and Religion* (London 1887).
17. R.M. Dorson, *The British Folklorists: A History* (London 1968); *Peasant Customs and Savage Myths: Selections from the British Folklorists*, 2 vols (London 1968).
18. Their collections of tales were often retold or translated, but the only systematic work to be translated was Jacob Grimm's *Deutsche Mythologie* (first published 1835), which finally appeared towards the end of the century, translated by James S. Stallybrass from the fourth edition of 1875 as *Teutonic Mythology*, 4 vols (London 1880–88).
19. M. Espagne, *Les Transferts culturels franco-allemands* (Paris 1999), ch. 4.
20. Momigliano, *o.c.* n. 8 above, 284.

21. I would especially like to thank my former pupil Michael Konaris for discussing some of the ideas in this chapter with me, while he was preparing his book, *The Greek Gods in Modern Scholarship* (Oxford 2016).

CHAPTER 13

1. For the history of this image, which belonged successively to Walter Benjamin, Georges Bataille, Theodor Adorno, Gershom Scholem, and now resides in the Israel Museum Jerusalem, see A. Danchev, 'The Angel of History', *International Affairs* 90 (2014), 367–77.
2. A. Grafton, *Worlds Made by Words: Scholarship and Community in the Modern West* (Harvard 2009), ch. 1; M. Fumaroli (ed.), *La République des Lettres dans la tourmente (1919–39)* (Paris 2011).
3. V.H.H. Green, *Oxford Common Room: A Study of Lincoln College and Mark Pattison* (London 1957); M.G. Brock, 'A "Plastic Structure"', in M.G. Brock and M.C. Curthoys (eds), *The History of the University of Oxford, VII, Nineteenth-Century Oxford, Part 2* (Oxford 2000), 14–16; R.M. Ogilvie, *Latin and Greek* (London 1964); M.L. Clarke, *Classical Education in Britain 1500–1900* (Cambridge 1959); C. Stray, *Classics Transformed* (Oxford 1998).
4. The fundamental biography is that of Duncan Wilson, *Gilbert Murray O.M.* (Oxford 1987); see also C. Stray (ed.), *Gilbert Murray Reassessed* (Oxford 2007); B. Blanchet, *La Toge et la Tribune* (Paris 2004), ch. II.
5. E.R. Dodds, *Missing Persons* (Oxford 1977), ch. XIII.
6. See S.P. Albert, 'From "Murray's Mother-in-Law" to "Major Barbara" the Outside Story', *Shaw* 22 (2002), 19–65.
7. *Major Barbara*, Act 1, Penguin edition (1945), p. 62. Bernard Shaw received the Nobel Prize for Literature in 1925; the prize was founded by Alfred Nobel, inventor of dynamite.
8. 'La lutte engagée contre l'Allemagne est la lutte même de la civilisation contre la barbarie. Tout le monde le sent, mais notre Académie a peut-être une autorité particulière pour le dire. Vouée en grand partie à l'étude des questions psychologiques, morales et sociales, elle accomplit un simple devoir scientifique en signalant dans la brutalité et le cynisme de l'Allemagne, dans son mépris de toute justice et de toute vérité, une régression à l'état sauvage.'
9. See the excellent study of Jürgen and Wolfgang von Ungern-Sternberg, *Der Aufruf 'An die Kulturwelt!'*, Historische Mitteilungen der Ranke-Gesellschaft Beiheft 18 (Stuttgart 1996); less perceptive, R.E. Norton, 'Wilamowitz at War', *International Journal of the Classical Tradition* 15 (2008), 74–97, and J. Horne and A. Kramer, *German Atrocities 1914: A History of Denial* (New Haven 2001), both of which fail to mention that it was the British who began the war of the intellectuals, although the destruction of the historic library of the University of Louvain may stand as an excuse: Richard

Ovenden, 'The Twice-Burned Library', *Burning the Books* (London 2020), 107–17.

10. Samuel Harden Church, *The American Verdict on the War: A Reply to the Appeal to the Civilized World of 93 German Professors* (Columbus 1915).
11. None are known to Marc Fumaroli and the Collège de France.
12. Harold J.R. Murray, Sir James Murray, editor of the *OED*, typescript ms. p. 276 (copies in the *OED* archives and the Bodleian Library). At this point I should say that the name Murray is very common in the British Isles, and there is no connection between the family of Gilbert Murray (Irish, aristocratic, and Catholic) and my own (Scottish, peasant, and Calvinist).
13. 'Aus seine Rede klang Tatkraft und Ausdauer, aber auch Wohlwollen. Gleich Furnivall war er immer bereit, deutsche Mitforschung anzuerkennen. Wie viele ihrer Träger haben in seinem "Scriptorium" und seinem gastfreundlichen Hause in Oxford angeregte Stunden verbracht!' (K. Luick, 'Sir James A.H. Murray. Gestorben am 26. Juli 1915', *Almanach der kaiserlichen Akademie der Wissenschaften*, 1916, 426–30).
14. *The Autobiography of Bertrand Russell*, vol. II (London 1968). Russell includes letters to Gilbert Murray thanking him for his support and friendship.
15. D. Birn, *The League of Nations Union 1918–1945* (Oxford 1981).
16. Quoted in Wilson (*o.c.* n. 4), 78
17. M. Morris, '"That Living Voice": Gilbert Murray at the BBC', in C. Stray (ed.), *Gilbert Murray Reassessed* (Oxford 2007), 293–317.

CHAPTER 14

1. R. Chernow, *The Warburgs* (New York 1993), 30.
2. Bodleian archive Ms Wind 3 Folder 4/6.
3. K.W. Forster, introduction to Aby Warburg, *The Renewal of Pagan Antiquity* (Getty Research Institute 1999), 31.
4. F. Saxl, 'Ernst Cassirer,' in *The Philosophy of Ernst Cassirer*, ed. Paul A. Schilpp (New York 1958), 47.
5. Thus 'festivals and feasting' combines books from all periods; and 'Cicero' for instance is to be found on three of the four separate floors of the modern library, creating an instant liberating effect on any user.
6. E. Panofsky, *Studies in Iconology* (Oxford 1939), 3–17. To give an example, when I wanted to research the iconography of 'Europa and the Bull', I was directed to a series of filing cabinets entitled 'Zeus, Loves of'. There in the appropriate file I found all the relevant material in the form of engravings, old postcards, pictures removed from books, etc, and was rapidly able to discover that there were two basic representations in Western art of the Rape of Europa.

7. E. Sears, 'Keepers of the Flame: Bing, Solmitz, Klibansky, and the Continuity of the Warburg Tradition', in P. Despoix and J. Tomm, *Raymond Klibansky and the Warburg Library Network* (Montreal 2018), 36–7.
8. Bernhard Buschendorf, 'Auf dem Weg nach England– Edgar Wind und die Emigration der Bibliothek Warburg', in *Porträt aus Büchern. Bibliothek Warburg & Warburg Institute Hamburg – 1933 – London*, ed. Michael Diers (Hamburg, 1993), 85–128; Ben Thomas, *Edgar Wind: A Short Biography* (2015). Because of this break between Wind and Saxl, official accounts ignore or play down the role of Wind in the transfer; they are mostly collected in 'Warburg Bibliothek', *Engramma* 198 (January 2023; online); see Eric Warburg, 'The Transfer of the Warburg Institute to England in 1933', *The Warburg Institute Annual Report* (1952–3), 13–16; G. Bing, 'Fritz Saxl (1890–1948): A Memoir', in *Fritz Saxl 1890–1948: A volume of memorial essays from his friends in England*, ed. D.J. Gordon (1957); F. Saxl, 'The History of Warburg's Library', in E.H. Gombrich, *Aby Warburg: An Intellectual Biography* (London 1970), 325–38; Nicholas Barker 'The Warburg Institute', *The Book Collector* 39(2) (1990), 153–73. See also Elizabeth Sears, 'The Warburg Institute, 1933–1944: A Precious Experiment in International Collaboration', *Art Libraries Journal* 38 (2013), 7–15.
9. See E. Wind, *Hume and the Heroic Portrait*, ed. J. Anderson (Oxford 1986).
10. Agnes de Mille, *Speak to Me, Dance with Me* (Boston 1973), 65–6, 357–62: 'Edgar Wind did not marry me. He married someone else, and they lived, I presume, with reasonable happiness' (384). According to Margot Wittkower, in this period he broke the hearts of at least seven women: see the interview, *Partnership and Discovery: Margot and Rudolf Wittkower*, Getty Center for the History of Art: Art History Oral Project, 198–214.
11. There are various versions of this memorandum: that in the Warburg Institute archive has been redacted to serve as a founding document for the Warburg (omitting the last two heads). The original version is preserved in the University of London's vice-chancellor's archive (UPI/10/1). Wind returned to Hamburg on 17 June to obtain Max Warburg's approval.
12. See the section in the Warburg catalogue, FHO M258: 'Magic and Science: Divination and Prophecy: Prophecy and World War'. The section now contains only a small number of books from before the exile (information from Philip Young, assistant librarian).
13. L. Labowsky, *Bessarion's Library and the Biblioteca Marciana* (Rome, 1979). Lotte Labowsky was herself one of the Warburg refugees, who collaborated with Klibansky on his Plato project, and ended as a much-loved Fellow of Somerville College, Oxford.
14. Lord Beveridge, *A Defence of Free Learning* (Oxford 1959); J. Seabrook, *The Refuge and the Fortress: Britain and the Flight from Tyranny* (London 2009).
15. *In Defence of Learning*, Proceedings of the British Academy 167 (2011), ed. S. Marks, P. Weindling, and L. Wintour.

16. For Tess Simpson, who was of Jewish Russian extraction and became a Quaker in her youth, secretary of the Society from 1933 to 1978: see *Refugee Scholars: Conversations with Tess Simpson*, ed. R.M. Cooper (Leeds 1992); J. Eidinow, *Esther Simpson* (London 2023). See also for the contribution of Oxford, S. Crawford, K. Ulmschneider, and J. Elsner (eds), *Ark of Civilization: Refugee Scholars and Oxford University, 1930–1945* (Oxford 2017).
17. Paul Jacobsthal's vivid memoir of internment is printed in Cooper, *o.c.*, 198–228. See also Beveridge, *o.c.*, ch. 4, for other accounts, and S. Parkin, *The Island of Extraordinary Captives* (London 2022).
18. Stefan Weinstock was a Catholic who had the misfortune to have been born of Hungarian parents in Romania; he could not therefore prove 'Aryan descent' and was deprived of his citizenship. He was helped by Jesuits in Rome and by Campion Hall in Oxford, and eventually became Lecturer in Roman Religion and a Fellow of Exeter College.
19. For the complex history of *Saturn and Melancholy* see *Raymond Klibansky and the Warburg Library*, ed. P. Despoix and J. Tomm (Montreal 2018), part 3. The Warwick conference was later published as *Genius: The History of an Idea* (Oxford 1989).
20. Bodleian MS. S.P.S.L. 316.
21. R. Klibansky, *Le philosophe et la mémoire du siècle, Entretiens avec Georges Leroux* (Paris 1998); see also Despoix and Tomm, *o.c.*
22. 'Über die Entwicklung der griechischen Historiographie und den Plan einer neuen Sammlung der griechischen Historikerfragmente', *Klio* 9 (1909), 80–123 = *Abhandlungen zur griechischen Geschichtsschreibung* (Leiden 1956), 16–64; Eng. trans. *On the Development of Greek Historiography*, *Histos* suppl. 3 (2015). Jacoby went on to collect systematically all the fragments of lost Greek historians preserved in later authors, and so laid the foundations for a systematic study of the ancient Greek historical tradition; he was a member of Christ Church from 1939, and was given an Honorary D. Litt. Oxon., aged 79.
23. Cf. *Griechischer Roman und hellenistischer Geschichtsschreibung* (Frankfurter Studien zur Religion und Kultur der Antike) vi (1934).
24. Bodleian MS. S.P.S.L. 292/4.
25. 'The final move was the result of one of Eva's wonderful letters which through her old friend Irene Charnley and her husband, a Methodist minister, living opposite Rydal School and Colwyn Bay, reached Mr. Costain, the headmaster, who was greatly impressed by that letter. He at once agreed to take Ludwig, and then Gottfried too, on nominal fees' (Ehrenberg's privately published memoir; copy at the Institute for Classical Studies London).
26. Bodleian MS. S.P.S.L. 252/1–2, 37.
27. 'Thus, in 1938 was published "Alexander and the Greeks". With it began my long connection with Basil (now Sir Basil) Blackwell; he was a real

English gentleman, aloof and yet warmhearted, a good businessman and at the same time a pleasant publisher, with a genuine interest in the Classics. I might almost call him a friend.' I knew Sir Basil at the end of his life (1889–1984), when he was still visiting our neighbour, the elderly widow of a Professor of German – a most courteous and faithful man.

28. Sir Maurice Bowra was one of the few Oxford figures who responded to Ehrenberg's predicament, writing a moving review of this book which recognized the circumstances of its creation (*The New Statesman and Nation*, 10 April 1943, 243).
29. See H. Lloyd-Jones, *Journal of Hellenic Studies* 76 (1956), 112–13; Lloyd-Jones wrote to me as late as 1975, when I reviewed one of Ehrenberg's books favourably, 'no need to gush over the second-rate, even if he is 85 and has always meant well'.

CHAPTER 15

1. After his exile Arnaldo Momigliano wrote no books, except for short published lecture series. Instead, his many writings are collected in the ten volumes of his *Contributi alla storia degli studi classici* (sometimes divided into two, continuously paginated volumes), published by Edizioni di Storia e Letteratura, Rome, from 1960 to 2012; I refer to them by their volume numbers.
2. Benedetto Croce, *History as the Story of Liberty*, English translation (London 1941), p. 22.
3. M.A. Levi, *Storia della Storiografia* 16 (1989), 5–14 on p. 10: 'Queste contrapposizioni politiche non avevano eco nella vita universitaria del secondo decennio del secolo, anche se De Sanctis e tutti i suoi allievi, a eccezione di chi scrive, avevano assunte posizioni ostili al fascismo in maniera generalmente non attiva, mentre L. Pareti aveva aderito al fascismo sin dall'inizio.' After Momigliano's death his personal enemies tried to assert that he had been a Fascist on the basis of his compulsory membership of the party, a deliberate misrepresentation.
4. See A. Magnetto (ed.), *Piero Treves: Tra storia ellenistica e storia della cultura* (Pisa 2021).
5. There is an excellent account of the role of the *Enciclopedia* in classical studies during the Fascist period by M. Cagnetta, *Antichità classiche nell'Enciclopedia Italiana* (Bari 1990).
6. See e.g. Giovanni Gentile, *Che cosa è il fascismo* (Florence 1925); and the justification of his death by Carlo Dionisotti in 1944: *Scritti sul fascismo e sulla Resistenza* (Turin 2008), 41–60.
7. D.M. Pippidi (1905–93; see the obituary by I. Fischer, *Studii Clasice* 28–30 (1997), 211–16: Momigliano contributed to the number of this journal in

honour of Pippidi (*Ottavo contributo* [Rome 1987], 121–34). For their close relations as young men see D.M. Pippidi, 'L'epistolario con D.M. Pippidi. A. Momigliano a D.M. Pippidi', *Storia della storiografia* 16 (1989), 15–33.

8. When I met Mason Hammond in Rome in the early sixties, he recalled walking with a distraught Momigliano around the city for the last time before he went into exile.
9. A. Momigliano, *Claudius: The Emperor and his Achievement*, trans. W.D. Hogarth (Oxford 1934).
10. MS Bodleian S.P.S.L. 316/3. He also wrote on 17 October to M.I. Rostovtzeff, whom he had met in Rome in the thirties (*Contributo* [Rome 1955], 342), as a fellow exile likely to be sympathetic, about the possibility of finding a position in the USA: see the correspondence published by G. Bongard-Levin, A. Marcone, *Athenaeum* 83 (1995), 510–12.
11. See the reference to Klibansky in Momigliano's SPSL file.
12. Giglioli, who from 1910 was a committed member of what later became the Fascist Party and a close associate of Mussolini, nevertheless in 1938 spoke in Parliament against the racial decree and sought to protect his Jewish pupils: R.T. Ridley, 'Augusti manes volitant per auras: The Archaeology of Rome under the Fascists', *Xenia* 11 (1986), 19–46, esp. 43; P.G. Guzzo, *Antico e archeologia. Scienza e politica delle diverse antichità* (Bologna 1993), 102–7; U. Quatember, 'Archäologie und Faschismus', *Forum Archaeologiae* 43/VI (2007).
13. For Momigliano's complex personal and intellectual relationship with Croce, see Carlo Dionisotti's masterly exposition, 'Arnaldo Momigliano e Croce', *Belfagor* 43 (1988), 617–41, reprinted in *Ricordo di Arnaldo Momigliano* (Bologna 1989), 27–64.
14. *Terzo contributo* (Rome 1966), 832–3.
15. Minio-Paluello was working in London with the BBC for most of the war.
16. *Sesto contributo* (Rome 1980), 767–8.
17. The letter of 17 March 1940 is printed in Dionisotti, *Ricordo*, 103.
18. *Decimo contributo* (Rome 2012), 37. Was Herbert Butterfield (1900–1979) present? He was a Fellow (and subsequently Master) of Peterhouse, the college to which Momigliano also belonged towards the end of his life; he had already published *The Whig Interpretation of History* (1931). Of all Momigliano's contemporaries in Britain he was the one who shared most of his interests, in Lord Acton and the history of liberty, in his belief in the importance of Christianity in history, together with a mutual distaste for Lewis Namier; yet his presence seems unlikely. Despite Momigliano's later occasional complimentary references to Butterfield (esp. *Terzo contributo*, 273) and one review (*Quinto contributo* [Rome 1975], 891–3), there is no sign of a personal relationship.
19. P. Brown, *Proceedings of the British Academy* 74 (1988), 413. Jocelyn Toynbee (1897–1985), sister of Arnold Toynbee, had been Fellow of

Newnham and Lecturer in Classics at Cambridge since 1931; she was Laurence Professor of Archaeology from 1951 to 1962. The economist Piero Sraffa, who was later a fellow inmate with Momigliano of the internment camp on the Isle of Man, was in Cambridge at this time, and may have been one of the 'thin row of refugee professors'.

20. She was a student at Oxford from 1938 to 1942, and his pupil and close friend; although, when I asked her, she denied that Momigliano had contributed to her portrait of the Roman historian Mischa Fox in her novel *The Flight from the Enchanter* (1956).

21. The complete MS of these lectures was discovered in a notebook in Momigliano's flat in Hammersmith after his death. They were first published by Riccardo Di Donato in an Italian translation (*Pace e Libertà nel mondo antico, Lezioni a Cambridge gennaio-marzo 1940* [Florence 1996]), and finally in English ('Peace and Liberty in the Ancient World') in Di Donato (ed.), *Decimo contributo*, 3–105. Thanks to Momigliano's literary executor Anne Marie Meyer I had the privilege of working on the manuscript itself before it was transferred to the Momigliano Archive in Pisa where it now resides.

22. *From Alexander to Constantine* (Oxford 1956); *Social and Political Thought in Byzantium* (Oxford 1957). In the first of these he refers indeed to the inspiration he derived from Momigliano's inaugural lecture at University College London of 1952 (p. vii). These books of Barker were the only English books that encouraged me in the sixties in my research under Arnaldo Momigliano into ancient ideas of monarchy.

23. See above, ch. 14, n. 17.

24. Letter to Carlo Dionisotti of 22 October 1944, printed in Dionisotti, *Ricordo*, 104.

25. It is of course the same antithesis that I explore in ch. 2.

26. See Momigliano's lecture of 1985, 'Classical Scholarship for a Classical Country: The Case of Italy in the Nineteenth and Twentieth Centuries', in *Ottavo contributo*, 73–89.

27. 'Anch'io dunque una vittima del Bimillenario,' he wrote ironically to Pippidi on 27 July 1937 (Pippidi, 'Epistolario', *o.c.*, 24).

28. Guido De Ruggiero (1888–1948): his *History of European Liberalism* was translated into English by R.G. Collingwood (Oxford 1927); he signed Croce's Manifesto of Anti-Fascist Intellectuals in 1925, was dismissed from his post at Rome University and arrested in 1942, and liberated in 1943 to be appointed Rector of Rome University. Adolfo Omodeo (1889–1946) was originally a pupil of Gentile but broke with him over Fascism; he was a catholic liberal, Rector of Naples University, and was persecuted for his ideas under Fascism. On the collapse of Fascism both men were founder-members of the resistance Partito d'Azione, and (like Croce) served briefly as ministers in the post-liberation Badoglio and Bonomi governments. For

the complex history of the liberation of Italy see R. Luraghi and D. Puncuh, *Per dignità non per odio* (Rome 1966).

29. Croce, *History as the Story of Liberty*, 19.
30. In his 1981 attack on his Chicago colleague Hayden White (*Settimo contributo* [Rome 1984], 49–59), Momigliano distinguishes the views of Croce from those of White (p. 55).
31. From 1916 to 1923 as a German citizen Beloch was prevented from teaching and suffered internment.
32. On the importance of Beloch for Italian scholarship see esp. *Terzo contributo*, 239–65.
33. Lecture 1, in *Decimo contributo*, 4.
34. *Contributo*, 296 (my translation). On the concept of liberty in the school of De Sanctis see esp. C. Ampolo, 'Discutere di storia greca e libertà negli anni Trenta alla scuola di Gaetano De Sanctis: Ferrabino, Momigliano, Treves tra Croce e Gentile', in Magnetto, *o.c.* (n. 4), 23–52.
35. See for instance the essay of M.P. Charlesworth, 'The Virtues of a Roman Emperor: Propaganda and the Creation of Belief', *PBA* 23 (1937), 105–33.
36. J. Carcopino, *Histoire Romaine*, vol. II, *César* (Paris 1936).
37. M.A. Levi, *Ottaviano capoparte*, 2 vols (Florence 1933).
38. A. von Premerstein, *Vom Werden und Wesen des Prinzipats*, Abh. der bayer. Akad. der Wiss., Phil.-hist. Abt., n. s., XV, 1937.
39. R. Syme, *The Roman Revolution* (Oxford 1939). Lecture 1, in *Decimo contributo*, 14–15.
40. For Wilhelm Weber (1882–1948, Professor at Berlin from 1931) and his influence see K. Christ, *Römische Geschichte und Deutsche Geschichtswissenschaft* (Munich 1982), 210–44; Weber contributed some very strange chapters to the *Cambridge Ancient History*, XI–XII, full of racial stereotyping. Mario Attilio Levi (1902–98) was an active political journalist and a *sindaco* (mayor) when he competed with Momigliano for the chair at Turin, and Momigliano wrote to Pippidi that he was certain to be preferred. Nevertheless, as a Jew he was dismissed from his post at Milan University in 1938 in the same list as Momigliano; after the war he was reinstated as Professor at Milan: see 'Commemorazione in memoria di Mario Attilio Levi', *Acme* 51 (1998), 219–47. Jérôme Carcopino (1881–1970) was Professor of Roman History at the Sorbonne (1920–37), when he became Director of the French School in Rome; Director of the École Normale Supérieure at Paris (1940–42); as Minister of Education (1941–2) he was responsible for the dismissal of Jews from the educational services. In 1944 he was imprisoned and deprived of all his functions and honours as a collaborator, being finally restored to his duties in 1951, and inexplicably elected a member of the Académie Française in 1955.

41. See his post-war review of the Italian translation of Berve's *Griechische Geschichte* in *Terzo contributo*, 700–708, and my review of his reprinted and falsified essays, *Gestaltende Kräfte der Antike*, in *CR* 17 (1967), 102–4.
42. See Momigliano's review of *The Roman Revolution* in *Journal of Roman Studies* 30 (1940), 75–80 (*Settimo contributo*, 407–16), and his 1962 introduction to the Italian translation of *The Roman Revolution* (*Terzo contributo*, 729–37, esp. 730–31); what is suggested there is insisted on even more definitely in his review of Syme's *Tacitus* (1961) in 1966, reprinted in *Terzo contributo*, 729.
43. Hugh Last (who would have been on the appointment committee) certainly wanted Momigliano to put his name forward for the Professorship (unpublished letter of Isobel Henderson 9 June 1953): see *Archivio Momigliano Inventario Analitico* a cura di G. Granata (Rome 2006), 226.
44. Letter of Isobel Henderson, 19 March 1958, *Archivio Momigliano*.
45. Groag (Austrian) and Stein (Hungarian) had reached volume III before they were dismissed from their posts as Jews: Groag survived in hiding in Vienna, and died in 1945; Stein survived three years in a concentration camp, and returned after the war to edit *PIR* under the auspices of the (East German) Berlin Academy of Sciences until his death in 1950; the ill-starred enterprise has been continued with an increasingly international body of helpers, surviving the war and the reunification of Germany, and being finally completed in 2015 under the editorship of Werner Eck.
46. See esp. 'La Formazione della moderna storiografia sull'impero romano' (1936), in *Contributo*, 107–64.
47. Anton von Premerstein (1869–1935), Austrian historian, epigraphist and papyrologist, travelled with Josef Keil in Asia Minor and taught at Vienna and Prague before becoming professor at Marburg; he is now chiefly remembered for the publication in 1927 with Sir William Ramsay of the Antioch text of Augustus' *Res Gestae*, which vindicated the reading *auctoritate omnibus praestiti* instead of Mommsen's *dignitate*. See V. Losemann, *Neue Deutsche Biographie* 20 (2000), 692–3.
48. Lecture I, in *Decimo contributo*, 15.
49. Lecture II, in ibid., 19–20.
50. Lecture II, in ibid., 25.
51. Lecture II, in ibid., 26.
52. Lecture III, in ibid., 31.
53. *Terzo contributo*, 457. The articles on *koine eirene* are reprinted in *Terzo contributo*: 'La *koine eirene* dal 386 al 338 a.C.' (1934), 393–419; 'Un momento di storia greca: la pace del 375 a.C e il Plataico di Isocrate' (1936), 421–55; 'Per la storia della pubblicistica sulla *koine eirene* nel IV secolo a.C. (1936), 457–87; 'L'Europa come concetto politico presso Isocrate e gli Isocratei' (1933), 489–97.

54. *Contributo*, 192.
55. Lecture III, in *Decimo contributo*, 40. Virgil, *Aeneid* VI, 853.
56. *Quinto contributo*, 906–7.
57. See 'Genesi storica e funzione attuale del concetto di ellenismo' (1935), in *Contributo*, 165–93; 'Per il centenario dell' Alessandro Magno di J.G. Droysen; un contributo' (1933), in ibid., 263–73.
58. *Contributo*, 273.
59. L. Polverini, 'Momigliano e De Sanctis', in L. Polverini (ed.), *Arnaldo Momigliano nella storiografia del novecento* (Rome 2006), 11–35; the letter is on pp. 18–19.
60. See R. Di Donato, *Athenaeum* 83 (1995), 213–44.
61. L. Cracco Ruggini, 'Gli anni d'insegnamento a Torino', in Polverini (ed.) (above n. 59), 77–123, quoted on 121–2. Momigliano insisted that his daughter be brought up without a religious education.
62. *Ottavo contributo*, 88–9 (a lecture given in Chicago, November 1985).
63. Luke 2.14.
64. 4. 7.
65. 'E'n sua voluntade è nostra pace', *Paradiso*, III, 85.
66. I. 20.
67. Lecture IV, in *Decimo contributo*, 49–52.
68. Lecture V, in ibid., 54.
69. Lecture V, in ibid., 53–4.
70. I. Berlin, *Two Concepts of Liberty* (inaugural lecture, Oxford 1958); reprinted many times, most recently in *Liberty: Incorporating Four Essays on Liberty*, ed. H. Hardy (Oxford 2002). The relation between Momigliano and Berlin was always tense: Momigliano mistrusted the depth of Berlin's knowledge on topics as diverse as liberty and Vico, while Berlin was unduly ready to accept the accusations made against Momigliano after his death (personal letter to me).
71. The essential connection between the Cynic/Stoic tradition and Christianity is discussed in the remarkable book by D. Dawson, *Cities of the Gods: Communist Utopias in Greek Thought* (New York 1992).
72. Lecture I, in *Decimo contributo*, 15.
73. B. Croce, 'Un avversario del "regime totalitario nell' antichità', *Quaderni della Critica II* (1946), 25–35.
74. See M. Mazower, *Dark Continent: Europe's Twentieth Century* (London 1998), esp. chs 1 and 2 above, and O. Murray, 'Modern Perceptions of Ancient Realities from Montesquieu to Mill', in M. Hansen et al. (eds), *Démocratie athénienne–démocratie moderne: tradition et influences* (Vandœuvres, 2010), 137–60.
75. Dionisotti, *Ricordo*, *o.c.* (n. 13), 104.
76. At the end of the war he was also proposing a book on 'Aspects of Political Thought: From Seneca to Tacitus': see R. Di Donato, 'Da Seneca a Tacito:

aspetti del pensiero politico romano in un inedito di Arnaldo Momigliano', *Archivio di storia della cultura* 20 (2007), 217–45. But he was still talking of publishing the lectures in 1950 (letter to D.M. Pippidi, 25 January 1950; above n. 7).

77. Lecture VII, in *Decimo contributo*, 8.
78. F. Meinecke, *Die Deutsche Katastrophe* (Wiesbaden 1946), Eng. trans. *The German Catastrophe* (Harvard 1950).
79. *Ottavo contributo*, 430.

CHAPTER 16

1. At the zoo itself Frank Walbank recalled one confrontation between Arnaldo and a large chimpanzee, which sat in his cage eyeing cynically the assembled professors, 'controlling his emotions (if emotions he had) completely. This sight led Arnaldo to remark, "Isn't he exactly like a librarian!" and then to embark on a typical Momiglianesque disquisition on the libraries of Moscow, where stage one in the reader's progress was to obtain admission, and stage two – far more difficult – to get access to the catalogue.' In the modern world this event has metamorphosed into yet another boring conference open to all, held in a university residence or a motel, and complete with learned papers.
2. Of the others, during his lifetime Jones also always came, Finley often, and Syme seldom.
3. For the wartime origins of the study of Seneca see Carlotta Dionisotti, 'Momigliano and the Medieval Boundary', in T.J. Cornell and O. Murray (eds), *The Legacy of Arnaldo Momigliano* (London 2014), 1–11.
4. A. Momigliano, 'Friedrich Creuzer and Greek Historiography', *Journal of the Warburg and Courtauld Institutes* 9 (1946), 152–63 = *Contributo alla storia degli studi classici* (Rome 1955), 233–48 (see ch. 15 above, n. 1, on references herein to the volumes of his *Contributi*).
5. C. Dionisotti, *Ricordo di Arnaldo Momigliano* (Bologna 1989).
6. *Sesto contributo* (Rome 1980), 329.
7. *Contributo*, 67–106; also in *Studies in Historiography* (London 1966), 1–39.
8. *Secondo contributo* (Rome 1960), 105–44; also in *Studies in Historiography*, 143–80.
9. *Quarto contributo* (Rome 1969), 13–41; also in *Essays in Ancient and Modern Historiography* (Oxford 1977), 179–204.
10. *Terzo contributo* (Rome 1966), 153–77; also in *Essays in Ancient and Modern Historiography*, 253–76.
11. Arnaldo Momigliano, *The Classical Foundations of Modern Historiography* (Berkeley 1990).
12. *Secondo contributo*, 191; also in *Studies in Historiography*, 181.

13. *Secondo contributo*, 105–43; also in *Studies in Historiography*, 143–80.
14. Edited by Momigliano (Oxford 1963).
15. See my entry on Alan Cameron in the online *Dictionary of National Biography* (14 January 2021).
16. *Contributo*, 67–106 and 195–211; also in *Studies in Historiography*, 1–55.
17. P.R. Ghosh, 'Gibbon's Dark Ages: Some Remarks on the Genesis of the *Decline and Fall*', *Journal of Roman Studies* 73 (1983), 1–23; 'Gibbon Observed', *Journal of Roman Studies* 81 (1991), 132–56.
18. *The History of the Decline and Fall of the Roman Empire*, ed. David Womersley (Penguin 1996).
19. *Contributo*, 213–31; also in *Studies in Historiography*, 56–74.
20. See ch. 7 above. Compare his interest in the views of Sir George Cornewall Lewis on early Rome, *Contributo*, 249–62.
21. Published first in *Settimo contributo* (Rome 1984), 379–436.
22. *Terzo contributo*, 545–98.
23. In 2008 on the centenary of Momigliano's birth, Tim Cornell and I attempted to reproduce the impact of these seminars by inviting former participants to a seminar series at the Warburg to reflect on their debt to his work; the results were published as *The Legacy of Arnaldo Momigliano* (London 2014).
24. S. Humphreys, *Anthropology and the Greeks* (London 1978), first published in *Annali della Scuola Normale di Pisa* 4 (1974).
25. *Alien Wisdom: The Limits of Hellenization* (Cambridge 1975); 'The Fault of the Greeks' was reprinted in *Sesto contributo*, 509–23, and in *Essays in Ancient and Modern Historiography*, 9–24.
26. See *Quinto contributo* (Rome 1975), 906–7.
27. See esp. *Ottavo contributo* (Rome 1987), 179–90.
28. Pisa 1985. This is a selection of his later essays from the *Settimo* and *Ottavo contributo*.
29. Frank Walbank reported rather differently: 'I was surprised at the extent to which he identified himself with the college. He gave several open lectures there and he once volunteered to me the unexpected but emphatic remark: "I love the place."'
30. *Quarto contributo*, 115. Apart from personal memories, I have in addition consulted the archives of Oxford University Press and (for the Sather lectures) the Momigliano papers now in Pisa.

CHAPTER 17

1. In writing this chapter I have been helped by Braudel's own brief description of his historical development, 'Ma formation d'historien', in *Écrits sur l'histoire*, vol. II (Paris 1990), 9–29, and *L'Histoire au quotidien* (Paris 2001), 11–31 (first published in English in the *Journal of Modern History*

44 [1972], 448–67); for an American perspective see the long essay by J.H. Hexter, ibid., 480–539 = *On Historians* (Harvard 1979). See also the account of his wife Paule, *Annales* 47 (1992), 237–44; and the magnificent biography by Pierre Daix, *Braudel* (Paris 1995).

2. Braudel records a remark of a young Italian philosopher after the war: 'So you wrote the book in prison: that is why it has always given me the impression of a work of contemplation.' *Écrits sur l'histoire* II, 15; *L'Histoire au quotidien*, 17.
3. The lectures from the period of the Second World War, and the fragments related to the third volume of Braudel's *L'Identité de la France*, are published in *Les Ambitions de l'Histoire* (Paris 1997). For the conditions under which he wrote see the vivid account of Paule Braudel, 'Braudel en captivité', in *Autour de F. Braudel*, ed. P. Carmignani (Perpignan 2002), 13–23; P. Schöttler, 'Fernand Braudel, prisonnier en Allemagne', *Soziale.Geschichte Online* 10(2013), 7–25.
4. *L'Histoire au quotidien*, 232.
5. Outside the formal documents, the best account of this extraordinary episode is in Paule Braudel, 'A propos de l'histoire globale: Réflexions et digressions', in *Autour de F. Braudel*, 121–42.
6. The missing 'biography' of Philip II is to be found in an Italian essay of 1969, translated in *Écrits sur l'histoire* II, 209–53.
7. These remarks were already present in the original preface of 1949, which is reprinted in *Les Ambitions de l'Histoire*, 343–51.
8. For Braudel's long relationship with the journal *Annales*, see A. Bourguière, *L'École des Annales: une histoire intellectuelle* (Paris 2006).
9. *Grammaire des civilisations* (Paris 1987) = *A History of Civilizations* (London 1994).
10. 'Il faut que l'histoire soit ce qu'elle était hier, cette petite science de la contingence, du récit particularisé, du temps reconstruit et, pour toutes ces raisons et quelques autres, une "science" plus que demi absurde' (1960), in *Écrits sur l'histoire* (Paris 1969), 88.
11. For Braudel as an administrator see esp. G. Gemelli, *Fernand Braudel* (Paris 1995), and M. Aymard's preface to F. Braudel, *L'Histoire au quotidien*, i–viii.
12. *L'Histoire au quotidien*, 240.
13. *Annales* (1958), 725–53 = *Écrits sur l'histoire*, 41–83; *Les Ambitions de l'histoire*, 191–230.
14. *L'Histoire au quotidien*, 237.
15. *Annales* (1963), 541–53 = *L'Histoire au quotidien*, 462–75 ; *Écrits sur l'histoire*, 134–53.
16. It is significant that Braudel, though mentioned in specific articles (under *Annales*, 27–32; *Braudel*, 83–6) in the past tense, was not a contributor to the manifesto of the 'new history', *La nouvelle histoire*, 1st edn, ed. J. Le Goff, R. Chartier, and J. Revel (Paris 1974).

17. F. Braudel, *L'Identité de la France* (Paris 1986), vols I–II. For the fragments of the third volume of *L'Identité de la France* see *Les Ambitions de l'Histoire*, 493–636.
18. M. Foucault, *Histoire de la sexualité 3: Le Souci de soi* (Paris 1984); *L'Herméneutique du sujet: Cours au Collège de France 1981–2* (Paris 2001); *Le Gouvernement de soi et des autres* (2008); *Le Courage de la vérité* (2009).
19. *L'Histoire au quotidien*, 233.
20. For a defence of their Braudelian conception against the sterile criticism of 'Mediterraneanism' see P. Hordern, 'Mediterranean Excuses: Historical Writing on the Mediterranean since Braudel', *History and Anthropology* 16 (2005), 25–30.
21. See ch. 19 n. 6.
22. I. Malkin, *A Small Greek World* (Oxford 2011).
23. David Abulafia's *The Great Sea* (London 2011) is an attempt to re-establish *histoire événementielle* against the vision of Braudel, attacking and misunderstanding him in equal measure; John Julius Norwich's *The Middle Sea* (London 2007) is a compilation of events.
24. *Les Mémoires de la Méditerranée* (Paris 1998) = *The Mediterranean in the Ancient World* (London 2001).
25. M. Liverani, *The Ancient Near East: History, Society and Economy* (Abingdon 2014); P. Matthiae, *Ebla, un impero ritrovato* (Turin 1995).
26. C. Broodbank, *The Making of the Middle Sea* (London 2013); compare Braudel's remark: '. . . grâce à l'archéologie à qui il faut de vastes espaces chronologiques, le rôle d'avant-garde des études consacrées à l'antiquité classique. Hier elles ont sauvé notre métier' (*Les ambitions de l'Histoire*, 197).
27. *Les Mémoires*, 67 = *The Mediterranean in the Ancient World*, 58.

CHAPTER 18

1. Jean-Pierre Vernant, Resistance leader and classical scholar: born Provins, 4 January 1914, died Sèvres 9 January 2007; Directeur d'Études, École Pratique des Hautes Études, 1958–75; Directeur, Centre de recherches comparées sur les sociétés anciennes, 1964–75; Professeur, Collège de France, 1975–84; married Lida Nahimovitch/Josefson in 1939 (died 1992); one daughter. Compagnon de la Libération; Commandeur de la Légion d'Honneur; honorary doctor of the Universities of Chicago, Bristol, Brno, Naples, Oxford, and Crete. For his wartime exploits see M. Goubet and P. Debauges, *Histoire de la Résistance en Haute-Garonne* (Milan 1986), and Vernant's own memories in *La Traversée des frontières* (Paris 2004), 17–59.

2. Pierre Vidal-Naquet, historian and intellectual: born Paris, 23 July 1930; assistant professor, University of Caen, 1956–60, Lille, 1961–2; attached to CNRS, 1962–4, maître de conférences, University of Lyons 1964–6, directeur d'études, École des Hautes Études, 1966–1998, director of the Centre Gernet, 1984–1998; married in 1952 Geneviève Railhac (three sons, five grandchildren); died Nice, 29 July 2006. See the full biography by François Dosse, *Pierre Vidal-Naquet, une vie* (Paris 2020).
3. See P. Schmitt Pantel, 'Pierre Vidal-Naquet, historien engagé. Autour de l'affaire Audin', *Anabases* 15 (2012), 11–25.
4. There were naturally certain exceptions to my negative picture already beginning to emerge, notably R.P. Winnington-Ingram, Bernard Knox, John Sullivan, John Gould, and Peter Green; but these had hardly yet had time to produce much impact.
5. 'A. Aymard', *Rivista storica italiana* 85 (1973), 217–21. On Vidal-Naquet in France see F. Hartog, *Vidal-Naquet, historien en personne* (Paris 2007).
6. P. Vidal-Naquet, *Le Chasseur noir* (2nd edn, Paris 1983), 322.
7. P. Vidal-Naquet, *Mémoires*, vol. 2 (Paris 1998), 308.
8. M.I. Finley, *Aspects of Antiquity* (London 1968), Introduction, quoted by Vidal-Naquet, *Politics Ancient and Modern* (Cambridge 1995), 67.
9. *Proceedings of the Cambridge Philological Society* 32 (1986), 126.
10. The difference between *l'histoire des mentalités* and *l'imaginaire* in French discourse is scarcely understood by the English: it is unrecognized in G.E.R. Lloyd, *Demystifying Mentalities* (Cambridge 1990).
11. Cf. the criticisms of J. Griffin, 'The Social Function of Attic Tragedy', *Classical Quarterly* 48 (1998), 39–61.
12. 'Nous ne tentons pas par ces analyses de dévoiler un mystère. Sophocle a-t-il ou non pensé à l'ostracisme ou à l'éphébie en écrivant ses pièces? Nous ne le savons pas, nous ne le saurons jamais; nous ne sommes pas même sûrs que la question ait un sens. Ce que nous voudrions montrer, c'est que, dans la communication que s'établissait entre le poète et son public, l'ostracisme ou l'éphébie constituait un cadre de référence commun, l'arrière-plan qui rendait intelligibles les structures même de la pièce' (*Mythe et tragédie en Grèce ancienne* [Paris 1973] 10).
13. G.L. Cawkwell, *Classical Review* 15 (1965), 202. Cawkwell, who died just before his centenary, was the most conservative of historians and the most revolutionary of academic reformers.
14. *Cleisthenes the Athenian*, trans. David Ames Curtis (New Jersey 1996).
15. R.G. Osborne, *Greece in the Making* (2nd edn, London 2009), 286, though I believe his arguments to be fallacious; Vidal-Naquet's recantation can be found in the preface to the new translation, p. xxxv.
16. F. Cordano, *Le tessere pubbliche dal tempio di Atena a Camarina* (Rome 1992); cf. O. Murray, 'Rationality and the Greek City: The Evidence from

Kamarina', in M.H. Hansen (ed.), *The Polis as an Urban Centre and as a Political Community* (Copenhagen 1997), 493–504.

17. *Proceedings of the Cambridge Philological Society* 40 (1994), 49–80.
18. Ibid., p. 73.
19. 'comme si la réalité historique obéissait toujours aux lois d'une logique d'exclusion' (*Le Chasseur noir*, 235).
20. 'La pensée, fût-elle abstraite, est-elle étrangère à la réalité historique? Y a-t-il quelque chose d'étranger à la réalité historique? Il y a certes des *niveaux* de réalité, des degrés de réalité, si l'on veut, mais on ne voit pas comment une pensée, même réactionnaire, peut être étrangère à la réalité historique': 'Platon, l'histoire et les historiens', in *La Démocratie grecque vue d'ailleurs* (Paris 1990), 134.
21. 'On serait tenté de dire que la pauvreté de ce qu'écrivent les historiens sur la philosophie n'a d'égale que l'insignifiance de ce qu'écrivent les philosophes sur le milieu historique qui est celui des oeuvres qu'ils étudient' (ibid., 135).
22. See *The History of the University of Oxford, vol. VI, Nineteenth-Century Oxford, Part 1*, 524.
23. 'On ne répétera jamais assez que, dans leur immense majorité [les textes platoniciennes] décrivent non l'univers des formes mais le nôtre' (*Le Chasseur noir*, 295).
24. See the section 'Les femmes, les esclaves, les artisans' in *Le Chasseur noir*, 209–316.
25. 'Le procédé est de ceux dont Platon use à tout moment. Dans le *Phèdre*, faisant l'éloge du jeune Isocrate, alors que celui-ci était un vieillard et son adversaire, Platon fait appel de l'Isocrate réel à un Isocrate possible, le rhéteur-philosophe qu'il n'a pas été' (*Le Chasseur noir*, 359).
26. 'Au carrefour de ces crises du IVe siècle, dont la subversion cynique témoigne si éloquemment, la philosophie platonicienne se présente à la fois comme un document sur la crise et comme un effort pour la résoudre, au moins sur le plan théorique. C'est dans la mesure où l'âge d'or était effectivement au cœur des débats contemporains et c'est à travers ce débat qu'il nous faut étudier ce que devient ce thème chez Platon' (*Le Chasseur noir*, 368–9).
27. 'La véritable tragédie platonicienne est effectivement ailleurs. Elle est dans la situation même du platonisme, dans l'ambiguïté de l'histoire' (*Le Chasseur noir*, 380).
28. Paris, 1990; Eng. trans by Janet Lloyd, *Politics Ancient and Modern* (Cambridge 1995).
29. On Finley see ch. 19, pp. 402–404.
30. The following comments are based on the responses of the individuals to my requests for their views.
31. *Demystifying Mentalities*, p. 4.

32. 'The External Rapport on the Centre Gernet, 1996', in *Qu'est-ce que faire école? Regards sur 'l'école de Paris', Cahiers 'Mondes anciens'* 13 (online). I am told that my intervention on this occasion was indeed significant.
33. 'Cities of Reason', in *The Greek City from Homer to Alexander*, ed. O. Murray and S. Price (Oxford 1990), 1–25.
34. J.-P. Vernant, *Mortals and Immortals: Collected Essays*, ed. F. Zeitlin (Princeton 1991), 3–24.
35. See also P. duBois, 'Inscription, the Law and the Comic Body', *Mètis* 3 (1988), 69–84.
36. For the English reader this is well highlighted by the selection of essays translated by Zeitlin and entitled 'Image' in part 3 of *Mortals and Immortals*.
37. J.-P. Vernant, *Passé et Présent: Contributions à une psychologie historique, réunies par Riccardo De Donato*, 2 vols (Rome 1995).
38. 'Il n'y a pas une nature humaine éternelle et immuable, mais des hommes engagés dans les réalités sociales et se transformant en même temps qu'elles'; 'il y a une histoire psychologique comme il y a une histoire sociale de l'homme'; 'Or ce qui différencie l'homme des autres espèces animales, c'est que son activité, physique et spirituelle, est orientée vers l'édification d'un monde d'oeuvres, qui se présentent à la fois comme des objets matériels, susceptibles d'être conservés et transmis, et comme des systèmes significatifs exprimant des contenus mentaux': Vernant, *Passé et Présent*, I, 47–8, 59–60, and 81–95 (articles of 1951 and 1960).
39. 'En ce sens, le psychologue peut faire sienne la formule célèbre de Marx selon laquelle l'histoire tout entière n'est qu'une transformation continue de la nature humaine': 'Histoire et psychologie', in *Religions, histoires, raisons* (Paris 1979), 73, trans. as ch. 15 in Zeitlin (ed.), *Mortals and Immortals*, 261–8. See also the section 'Psychologie et anthropologie historiques' in Vernant, *Entre mythe et politique* (Paris 1996).

CHAPTER 19

1. See A.K. Gavrilov, 'Jakov M. Borovskij, Poet of Latin in the Soviet Union', in G. Karsai, G. Klaniczay, D. Movrin, and E. Olechowska (eds), *Classics and Communism: Greek and Latin behind the Iron Curtain* (Lujbljana, Budapest, Warsaw 2013), 19–36.
2. *Selected Works of Marx and Engels*, vol. 3 (Moscow 1970), 331–2.
3. Marx and Engels, *Pre-Capitalist Socio-Economic Formations* (Moscow 1979), 240–41.
4. It survived only in the version of K.A. Wittfogel, *Oriental Despotism: A Comparative Study of Total Power* (New Haven 1957); for the contested history of the theory in the East see esp. the discussion in V.V. Dementieva, 'Welskopfs "Produktionsverhältnisse im Alten Orient und in der

griechisch-römischen Antike" als Gegenstand der Historiographie: der Einfluss ikrer sowjetischen Vorgänger', in I. Stark (ed.), *Elisabeth Charlotte Welskopf und die Alte Geschichte in der DDR* (Wiesbaden 2005), 157–69.

5. I.A. Ladynin, 'Osobennosti landshafta (Naskol'ko marksistskoy byla "sovetskaya drevnost' "?') ['Peculiarities of the landscape (How Marxist was the "Soviet Antiquity"?)'], *Vestnik Universiteta Dmitriya Pozharskogo [Journal of Dmitriy Pozharskiy University]* 2(4) (2016), 9–32; English version: *'Soviet Antiquity': Looking for a Cohesive Theory* (National Research University Higher School of Economics, Moscow 2017).
6. M.I. Rostovtzeff, *The Social and Economic History of the Roman Empire* (Oxford 1926; 2nd edn, 1957); *The Social and Economic History of the Hellenistic World* (Oxford 1941).
7. See the report of 1995 made at a meeting of the American Philological Association, ed. V. Bers and G. Nagy, *The Classics in Eastern Europe: From the End of World War II to the Present* (American Philological Association Pamphlet Series, 1996). From this I take the comments of A.K. Gavrilov (Russia), H. Geremek (Poland), and W. Krenkel (Rostock, Germany).
8. Unsigned but presumably by the editor Mishulin.
9. See B. Vitz-Margulis, 'Solomon Luria and his Contribution to the Study of Antiquity', *Scripta Classica Israelitica* 22 (2003), 273–6. Luria indeed published his own (well-received) work on Mycenaean Greek, *Yazyk i kul'tura Mikenskoj Gretsii* (Moscow and Leningrad 1957, 'Language and Culture of Mycenaean Greece').
10. Quoted in E. Ermolaeva, 'Classical Antiquity in Children's Literature in the Soviet Union', ch. 16 of *Our Mythical Childhood . . . The Classics and Literature for Children and Young Adults*, ed. K. Marciniak (Leiden 2016), 254. I owe knowledge of this to my former pupil Dr Georgy Kantor of St John's College, Oxford.
11. See the collection of essays in Karsai et al. (above, n. 1).
12. H. Geremek in Bers and Nagy (above, n. 7), 46.
13. For an early descriptive resumé of Polish scholarship see K. Kumaniecki, 'Twenty Years of Classical Philology in Poland (1945–1965)', *Greece & Rome*, vol. 14, no. 1 (1967), 61–75. Kumaniecki organized classical studies in a clandestine university in 1945: 'we are not going into the forest, we are building a university'. He was a signatory of 'the letter of 34' in 1964, protesting to the Prime Minister at the restrictions on publication in Poland. His hero was Cicero, whom he defended against the slanders of J. Carcopino, the collaborator and member of the Vichy government in France. For a balanced account of his career see J. Axer, 'Kazimierz Kumaniecki and the Evolution of Classical Studies in Poland', in Karsai et al. (above, n. 1), 187–211. For Biliński see E. Olochowska, 'B. Biliński, a Bolshevik without a Party Card', in ibid., 213–35.

14. For Taubenschlag (1881–1958) see W. Wolodkiewicz, 'Rafael Taubenschlag and Roman Law in Poland during Real Socialism', in Karsai et al. (above, n. 1), 237–56.
15. For Hartke: see W. Krenkel in Bers and Nagy (above, n. 7); and I. Stark, 'Die Alte Geschichte im Berlin (DDR): zur Bedeutung von Elisabeth Charlotte Welskopf', in Stark (above, n. 4), 201–5. Hartke was the author of a curious work, *Römische Kinderkaiser: eine Strukturanalyse römischen Denkens und Dase*ins (Berlin 1951), which advocated a 'querschnittliche Methode' in history; his own life was certainly devious: he was also editor of the most prestigious German journal *Klio* and president of the *DAW*, an extremely powerful man.
16. Irmscher was exposed by I. Stark, 'Johannes Irmscher's Unofficial Activity for the State Security of the German Democratic Republic', in Karsai et al. (above, n. 1), 46–71 (Eng. trans. of *Hallische Beiträge zur Zeitgeschichte* 5 [1998]).
17. W. Krenkel in Bers and Nagy (above, n. 7), 58–9.
18. *Jan und Jutta* (1953), actually first written in 1943.
19. For Welskopf on American Indians see T. Kramer '"Die Söhne der Grossen Bärin" und "Das Blut des Adlers": Liselotte Welskopf-Henrichs Indianerbücher 1951–1980', in Stark (above, n. 4), 206–28, and *LWH Projekt* (online).
20. R. Thouvenet, *Revue des études anciennes* (1968), 472.
21. The only serious discussion of its contents known to me is that by the English Marxist Robert Browning, 'The Crisis of the Greek City – a New Collective Study', *Philologus* 120 (1976), 258–66.
22. No serious account of the genius of Rostovtzeff, whose achievement is lost in the turmoil of the Russian Revolution, yet exists; see A.D. Momigliano *Studies in Historiography* (London 1966), 91–104, and my review of J.G. Manning, *History in Time of War*, in *Gnomon* 91 (2019), 760–61.
23. Cited in the excellent Wikipedia article on her, without a source reference.
24. See the fate of the *Prosopographia Imperii Romani* above, ch. 15 n. 45.
25. This is the devastating verdict of S. Rebenich, 'Nationalsozialismus und Alte Geschichte. Kontinuität und Diskontinuität in Forschung und Lehre', in Stark (above, n. 4), 42–64. See also S. Marchand, *Down from Olympus* (Princeton 1996), ch. 10.
26. The most productive work on Greek religion belongs to the anthropological approach of Walter Burkert, and the eclectic studies of Robert Parker.
27. See the work of R. Bianchi Bandinelli and his disciples, notably A. Carandini, F. Coarelli, M. Torelli, and the group around the journal *Dialoghi di Archeologia* founded by him in 1967: F. Iacono, 'A Pioneering Experiment: *Dialoghi di Archeologia* between Marxism and Political Activism', *Bulletin of the History of Archaeology* 24(5) (2014), 1–10.

28. Now confirmed by the report of his youthful friend and fellow student Emily Kazakovich (née Grace), 'M.I. Finley: A Note on his Life and Work', prepared for the Soviet delegates to the 11th Congress of Historical Studies in Stockholm 1960, and published by S.I. Karpiuk, *Vestnik Drevnei Istorii* 76 (2013), 780–84.
29. See W.V. Harris (ed.), *Moses Finley and Politics* (Leiden 2013), esp. the chapters by D.P. Tompkins and E. Schrecker. He was named before the Committee as a former communist by his colleague K. Wittfogel, author of *Oriental Despotism* (above n. 4).
30. Karl Polanyi (with C.M. Arensberg and H.W. Pearson), *Trade and Market in the Early Empires* (1957); *Primitive, Archaic and Modern Economies: Essays of Karl Polanyi*, ed. G. Dalton (New York 1968); cf. S.C. Humphreys, 'History, Economics and Anthropology: The Work of Karl Polanyi', in Humphreys, *Anthropology and the Greeks* (London 1978), 31–75.
31. *The Ancient Economy*, ed. W. Scheidel and S. von Reden (New York 2002).
32. C. Mossé, Regards sur la démocratie Athénienne (Paris, 2013), pp. 165–84. P. Ismard, 'Classes, ordres, statuts: la réception française de la sociologie finleyenne et le cas Pierre Vidal-Naquet', *Anabases* 19 (2014), 39–53. A whole section of this journal number is devoted to the influence of Finley in France.
33. See D.P. Tompkins, 'What happened in Stockholm? Moses Finley, the Mainz Akademie and East Bloc Historians', *Hyperboreus* 20 (2014), 1–2, 436–53.
34. See ch. 7 n. 40.
35. M.H. Hansen, *The Athenian Ecclesia: A Collection of Articles 1976–83* (Copenhagen 1983); *The Athenian Ecclesia II: A Collection of Articles 1983–89* (Copenhagen 1989).
36. See also his work on the Greek city-state in his major project supported by the Carlsberg Foundation and known as the Copenhagen Polis Centre.
37. These memories were first shared with colleagues and students of the ELTE University Budapest in June 2019, in the presence of Professor Zsigmond Ritoók, whose career was stalled by his signing a protest at the sentencing to death of one of his colleagues in 1956. They were also presented to a meeting of the European Network for the Study of Ancient Greek History at Utrecht in October 2019, where they received a standing ovation.
38. The horror of these potential sources is slowly being revealed: see the special number of the Slovenian journal *Keria: Studia Latina et Graeca* 15 (2013), with English abstracts, 219–26. J. Sarkady (1927–2006) in Hungary was beaten and physically forced by the secret police to report on his colleagues, and his life was ruined.
39. If I had been born five years earlier, I would have been killed in the Korean War; for my battery in the Royal Artillery (170 Imjin Battery) fought at the battle of the Imjin River in 1951 alongside the 'Glorious Glosters', and like them was wiped out.

40. Full text and translation in S. Ilan Troen, 'The Protocol of Sèvres: British/French/Israeli Collusion against Egypt, 1956', *Israel Studies* 1 (1996), 122–39; see also A. Shlaim, 'The Protocol of Sèvres, 1956: Anatomy of a War Plot', *International Affairs* 73 (1997), 509–30.
41. M. Mazower, *Salonica, City of Ghosts* (London 2004); M. Haag, *Alexandria, City of Memory* (New Haven 2004). I finally visited Alexandria in November 2014.
42. The Aldermaston Marches from the Nuclear Weapons Research Establishment, Aldermaston, to Central London (52 miles) were a mass protest against nuclear weapons that began in 1958; organized by the Campaign for Nuclear Disarmament, they took place at Easter each year, and had a considerable effect on public opinion and ultimately government policy.
43. A. Hurst, 'The Fondation Hardt and Classical Philology in the Socialist Countries', in Karsai et al. (above, n. 1), 375–84.
44. Years later I read the wonderful book of Ryszard Kapuściński, *Travels with Herodotus* (London 2007), and understood the great gulf that separated Poland from the West in the fifties.
45. See Z. Borkowski, *Inscriptions des factions à Alexandrie* (Warsaw 1981); *Queen Hatshepsut and her Temple 3,500 Years Later*, ed. Z.E. Szafrański (Warsaw University Polish Centre of Mediterranean Archaeology in Cairo 2001).
46. In 2022 I made contact with Audring, and discovered that he too remembered our earlier meetings.
47. *Eirene* 35 (1999), *Studia Graeca et Latina in honorem Pavel Oliva*.
48. 'Symposion and Philosophy' (D. Phil. Oxford 1993), alas still unpublished.
49. For the earlier story of archaeology at this historic site, see the excellent anonymous account on the web, entitled *Chersonesos Taurica and all that is related – About Chersonesos – competent but not officially* (http://www.chersonesos.org/?p = accessed 16.07.2022).
50. Subsequently I learned that in Chinese the same word is used to denote all forms of alcohol.
51. This same observation is the basis of the argument in S. Settis, *The Future of the Classical* (Cambridge 2006), esp. chs 15–16.
52. Plato, *Timaeus* 22b.
53. See above, p. 267.

CHAPTER 20

1. H. White, *Metahistory* (Baltimore 1973).
2. M. Bernal, *Black Athena*, 3 vols (London 1987–2006); M. Lefkowitz, *Not Out of Africa*, revised edition (New York 1997); M. Lefkowitz, *History Lesson, a Race Odyssey* (New Haven 2008).

3. P. Veyne, *Comment on écrit l'histoire, suivi de Foucault révolutionne l'histoire* (Paris 1978). Veyne's theory is of course at odds with his earlier work, notably *Le Pain et le cirque* (Paris 1976).
4. J.M. Banner, *The Ever-Changing Past: Why All History is Revisionist History* (New Haven 2021).
5. O. Patterson, *Freedom in the Making of Western Culture* (Harvard 1992).
6. D. Lowenthal, *The Past is a Foreign Country* (Cambridge 1985).
7. H. Butterfield, *The Whig Interpretation of History* (London 1931).
8. F.A. Yates, *The French Academies of the Sixteenth Century* (London 1988), 199.
9. S.J. Gould, *Wonderful Life: The Burgess Shale and the Nature of History* (London 1990), 282–3.
10. M. Bloch, *The Historian's Craft* (New York 1953); M. Montanari, *Il mito delle origini: Breve storia degli spaghetti al pomodoro* (Turin 2021).
11. A. Cheddadi, *Ibn Khaldûn, l'homme et le théoricien de la civilisation* (Paris 2006); R. Irwin, *Ibn Khaldun* (Princeton 2018); N. Rabbat, *Writing Egypt: Al-Maqrizi and his Historical Project* (Edinburgh 2023).
12. O. Murray, 'Gnosis and Tradition', in J.P. Arnason and P. Murphy (eds), *Agon, Logos, Polis: The Greek Achievement and its Aftermath* (Stuttgart 2001), 15–28.
13. M. Foucault, *Madness and Civilization: A History of Insanity in the Age of Reason* (London 1965).
14. See A. Momigliano, 'Gibbon's Contribution to Historical Method (1954)', in *Studies in Historiography* (London 1966).
15. E. Auerbach, *Mimesis: The Representation of Reality in Western Literature* (Princeton 1953), 17.
16. The turning point in Foucault's thought comes between vol. 1 *of Histoire de la sexualité, La volonté de savoir* (1976), and vols 2–3, *L'usage des plaisirs* and *Le souci de soi* (1984). See also E.R. Dodds, *Pagan and Christian in an Age of Anxiety* (Cambridge 1965); Pierre Hadot, *Qu'est-ce que la philosophie antique?* (Paris 1995).
17. *L'herméneutique du sujet* (Paris 2001); *Le gouvernement de soi et des autres* (2008); *Le courage de la vérité* (2009). *The Hermeneutics of the Subject* (New York 2005) *The Government of Self and Others* (2010), *The Courage of Truth* (2011).
18. *Le courage de la vérité*, 309–11; 'Il n'y a pas d'instauration de la vérité sans une position essentielle de l'altérité. La vérité, ce n'est jamais le même. Il ne peut y avoir de vérité que dans la forme de l'autre monde et de la vie autre' (328). The English translation of G. Burchell (p. 356) interprets this in a transcendental sense: 'there can be truth only in the form of the other world and the other life'.
19. Augustine, *Confessions* VI, 6.
20. Michael Whitby, P. Hardie, and Mary Whitby (eds), *Homo Viator: Classical Essays for John Bramble* (Bristol 1987), 331.

List of Illustrations

PLATES

1. Jan Vermeer, *The Art of Painting, or the Muse of History* (1665–8). Vienna Kunsthistorisches Museum (Bridgeman Images)
2. Nicholas Poussin, *The Triumph of Pan* (1638). Painted for the Cabinet du Roi in the Chateau of Cardinal de Richelieu: London, National Gallery (Bridgeman Images)
3. Jacques Wilbaut, the antiquary J.-J. Barthélemy with the Duc de Choiseul and the famous beauty Mme de Brionne, royal favourite, examining a medal from the Cabinet des Médailles (c. 1775): J. P. Getty Museum, California, formerly collection of the Duc de Choiseul (J. P. Getty Museum / Wikimedia Commons)
4. Napoleon's memorial to Cornelius de Pauw, Xanten (Wikimedia Commons)
5. Luc-Olivier Merson, *Le soldat de Marathon*. Grand prix de Rome de peinture d'histoire 1869): (Ècole Nationale Supérieure des Beaux-arts, Paris).
6. Hablot Knight Browne ('Phiz'). A caricature of Edward Bulwer Lytton, Yale Center for British Art, Paul Mellon Fund.
7. Paolo Uccello, *The Night Hunt in the Forest* (*c.*1465–70), Ashmolean Museum, Oxford (Bridgeman Images)
8. Paul Klee, *Angelus Novus*. Monoprint 1920: Jerusalem, Israel Museum (Bridgeman Images)

INTEGRATED ILLUSTRATIONS

p. 28 *Eight books of the Peloponnesian warre. Interpreted by T. Hobbes.* 1629, London for H. Seile: Titlepage (photo: Bodleian Library, Oxford)

p. 62 John Gast, *History of Greece*: Dublin, T. Exshaw 1793, frontispiece; engraving by Henry Brocas (1766–1837) (photo: Oswyn Murray)

p. 94 William Page (1794–1872) *View of the Plain of Marathon*, 1818 (brown wash on paper: Oswyn Murray; formerly in the collection of Sir Henry Mortimer Durand 1850–1924)

Index